Lecture Notes in Computer Science   14703

Founding Editors

Gerhard Goos
Juris Hartmanis

The series Lecture Notes in Computer Science (LNCS), including its subseries Lecture Notes in Artificial Intelligence (LNAI) and Lecture Notes in Bioinformatics (LNBI), has established itself as a medium for the publication of new developments in computer science and information technology research, teaching, and education.

LNCS enjoys close cooperation with the computer science R & D community, the series counts many renowned academics among its volume editors and paper authors, and collaborates with prestigious societies. Its mission is to serve this international community by providing an invaluable service, mainly focused on the publication of conference and workshop proceedings and postproceedings. LNCS commenced publication in 1973.

Adela Coman · Simona Vasilache
Editors

Social Computing and Social Media

16th International Conference, SCSM 2024
Held as Part of the 26th HCI International Conference, HCII 2024
Washington, DC, USA, June 29 – July 4, 2024
Proceedings, Part I

 Springer

Editors
Adela Coman
University of Bucharest
Bucharest, Romania

Simona Vasilache
University of Tsukuba
Tsukuba, Japan

ISSN 0302-9743 ISSN 1611-3349 (electronic)
Lecture Notes in Computer Science
ISBN 978-3-031-61280-0 ISBN 978-3-031-61281-7 (eBook)
https://doi.org/10.1007/978-3-031-61281-7

This Springer imprint is published by the registered company Springer Nature Switzerland AG
The registered company address is: Gewerbestrasse 11, 6330 Cham, Switzerland

If disposing of this product, please recycle the paper.

Foreword

This year we celebrate 40 years since the establishment of the HCI International (HCII) Conference, which has been a hub for presenting groundbreaking research and novel ideas and collaboration for people from all over the world.

The HCII conference was founded in 1984 by Prof. Gavriel Salvendy (Purdue University, USA, Tsinghua University, P.R. China, and University of Central Florida, USA) and the first event of the series, "1st USA-Japan Conference on Human-Computer Interaction", was held in Honolulu, Hawaii, USA, 18–20 August. Since then, HCI International is held jointly with several Thematic Areas and Affiliated Conferences, with each one under the auspices of a distinguished international Program Board and under one management and one registration. Twenty-six HCI International Conferences have been organized so far (every two years until 2013, and annually thereafter).

Over the years, this conference has served as a platform for scholars, researchers, industry experts and students to exchange ideas, connect, and address challenges in the ever-evolving HCI field. Throughout these 40 years, the conference has evolved itself, adapting to new technologies and emerging trends, while staying committed to its core mission of advancing knowledge and driving change.

As we celebrate this milestone anniversary, we reflect on the contributions of its founding members and appreciate the commitment of its current and past Affiliated Conference Program Board Chairs and members. We are also thankful to all past conference attendees who have shaped this community into what it is today.

The 26th International Conference on Human-Computer Interaction, HCI International 2024 (HCII 2024), was held as a 'hybrid' event at the Washington Hilton Hotel, Washington, DC, USA, during 29 June – 4 July 2024. It incorporated the 21 thematic areas and affiliated conferences listed below.

A total of 5108 individuals from academia, research institutes, industry, and government agencies from 85 countries submitted contributions, and 1271 papers and 309 posters were included in the volumes of the proceedings that were published just before the start of the conference, these are listed below. The contributions thoroughly cover the entire field of human-computer interaction, addressing major advances in knowledge and effective use of computers in a variety of application areas. These papers provide academics, researchers, engineers, scientists, practitioners and students with state-of-the-art information on the most recent advances in HCI.

The HCI International (HCII) conference also offers the option of presenting 'Late Breaking Work', and this applies both for papers and posters, with corresponding volumes of proceedings that will be published after the conference. Full papers will be included in the 'HCII 2024 - Late Breaking Papers' volumes of the proceedings to be published in the Springer LNCS series, while 'Poster Extended Abstracts' will be included as short research papers in the 'HCII 2024 - Late Breaking Posters' volumes to be published in the Springer CCIS series.

I would like to thank the Program Board Chairs and the members of the Program Boards of all thematic areas and affiliated conferences for their contribution towards the high scientific quality and overall success of the HCI International 2024 conference. Their manifold support in terms of paper reviewing (single-blind review process, with a minimum of two reviews per submission), session organization and their willingness to act as goodwill ambassadors for the conference is most highly appreciated.

This conference would not have been possible without the continuous and unwavering support and advice of Gavriel Salvendy, founder, General Chair Emeritus, and Scientific Advisor. For his outstanding efforts, I would like to express my sincere appreciation to Abbas Moallem, Communications Chair and Editor of HCI International News.

July 2024   Constantine Stephanidis

HCI International 2024 Thematic Areas and Affiliated Conferences

- HCI: Human-Computer Interaction Thematic Area
- HIMI: Human Interface and the Management of Information Thematic Area
- EPCE: 21st International Conference on Engineering Psychology and Cognitive Ergonomics
- AC: 18th International Conference on Augmented Cognition
- UAHCI: 18th International Conference on Universal Access in Human-Computer Interaction
- CCD: 16th International Conference on Cross-Cultural Design
- SCSM: 16th International Conference on Social Computing and Social Media
- VAMR: 16th International Conference on Virtual, Augmented and Mixed Reality
- DHM: 15th International Conference on Digital Human Modeling & Applications in Health, Safety, Ergonomics & Risk Management
- DUXU: 13th International Conference on Design, User Experience and Usability
- C&C: 12th International Conference on Culture and Computing
- DAPI: 12th International Conference on Distributed, Ambient and Pervasive Interactions
- HCIBGO: 11th International Conference on HCI in Business, Government and Organizations
- LCT: 11th International Conference on Learning and Collaboration Technologies
- ITAP: 10th International Conference on Human Aspects of IT for the Aged Population
- AIS: 6th International Conference on Adaptive Instructional Systems
- HCI-CPT: 6th International Conference on HCI for Cybersecurity, Privacy and Trust
- HCI-Games: 6th International Conference on HCI in Games
- MobiTAS: 6th International Conference on HCI in Mobility, Transport and Automotive Systems
- AI-HCI: 5th International Conference on Artificial Intelligence in HCI
- MOBILE: 5th International Conference on Human-Centered Design, Operation and Evaluation of Mobile Communications

List of Conference Proceedings Volumes Appearing Before the Conference

23. LNCS 14706, Virtual, Augmented and Mixed Reality: Part I, edited by Jessie Y. C. Chen and Gino Fragomeni
24. LNCS 14707, Virtual, Augmented and Mixed Reality: Part II, edited by Jessie Y. C. Chen and Gino Fragomeni
25. LNCS 14708, Virtual, Augmented and Mixed Reality: Part III, edited by Jessie Y. C. Chen and Gino Fragomeni
26. LNCS 14709, Digital Human Modeling and Applications in Health, Safety, Ergonomics and Risk Management: Part I, edited by Vincent G. Duffy
27. LNCS 14710, Digital Human Modeling and Applications in Health, Safety, Ergonomics and Risk Management: Part II, edited by Vincent G. Duffy
28. LNCS 14711, Digital Human Modeling and Applications in Health, Safety, Ergonomics and Risk Management: Part III, edited by Vincent G. Duffy
29. LNCS 14712, Design, User Experience, and Usability: Part I, edited by Aaron Marcus, Elizabeth Rosenzweig and Marcelo M. Soares
30. LNCS 14713, Design, User Experience, and Usability: Part II, edited by Aaron Marcus, Elizabeth Rosenzweig and Marcelo M. Soares
31. LNCS 14714, Design, User Experience, and Usability: Part III, edited by Aaron Marcus, Elizabeth Rosenzweig and Marcelo M. Soares
32. LNCS 14715, Design, User Experience, and Usability: Part IV, edited by Aaron Marcus, Elizabeth Rosenzweig and Marcelo M. Soares
33. LNCS 14716, Design, User Experience, and Usability: Part V, edited by Aaron Marcus, Elizabeth Rosenzweig and Marcelo M. Soares
34. LNCS 14717, Culture and Computing, edited by Matthias Rauterberg
35. LNCS 14718, Distributed, Ambient and Pervasive Interactions: Part I, edited by Norbert A. Streitz and Shin'ichi Konomi
36. LNCS 14719, Distributed, Ambient and Pervasive Interactions: Part II, edited by Norbert A. Streitz and Shin'ichi Konomi
37. LNCS 14720, HCI in Business, Government and Organizations: Part I, edited by Fiona Fui-Hoon Nah and Keng Leng Siau
38. LNCS 14721, HCI in Business, Government and Organizations: Part II, edited by Fiona Fui-Hoon Nah and Keng Leng Siau
39. LNCS 14722, Learning and Collaboration Technologies: Part I, edited by Panayiotis Zaphiris and Andri Ioannou
40. LNCS 14723, Learning and Collaboration Technologies: Part II, edited by Panayiotis Zaphiris and Andri Ioannou
41. LNCS 14724, Learning and Collaboration Technologies: Part III, edited by Panayiotis Zaphiris and Andri Ioannou
42. LNCS 14725, Human Aspects of IT for the Aged Population: Part I, edited by Qin Gao and Jia Zhou
43. LNCS 14726, Human Aspects of IT for the Aged Population: Part II, edited by Qin Gao and Jia Zhou
44. LNCS 14727, Adaptive Instructional System, edited by Robert A. Sottilare and Jessica Schwarz
45. LNCS 14728, HCI for Cybersecurity, Privacy and Trust: Part I, edited by Abbas Moallem
46. LNCS 14729, HCI for Cybersecurity, Privacy and Trust: Part II, edited by Abbas Moallem

47. LNCS 14730, HCI in Games: Part I, edited by Xiaowen Fang
48. LNCS 14731, HCI in Games: Part II, edited by Xiaowen Fang
49. LNCS 14732, HCI in Mobility, Transport and Automotive Systems: Part I, edited by Heidi Krömker
50. LNCS 14733, HCI in Mobility, Transport and Automotive Systems: Part II, edited by Heidi Krömker
51. LNAI 14734, Artificial Intelligence in HCI: Part I, edited by Helmut Degen and Stavroula Ntoa
52. LNAI 14735, Artificial Intelligence in HCI: Part II, edited by Helmut Degen and Stavroula Ntoa
53. LNAI 14736, Artificial Intelligence in HCI: Part III, edited by Helmut Degen and Stavroula Ntoa
54. LNCS 14737, Design, Operation and Evaluation of Mobile Communications: Part I, edited by June Wei and George Margetis
55. LNCS 14738, Design, Operation and Evaluation of Mobile Communications: Part II, edited by June Wei and George Margetis
56. CCIS 2114, HCI International 2024 Posters - Part I, edited by Constantine Stephanidis, Margherita Antona, Stavroula Ntoa and Gavriel Salvendy
57. CCIS 2115, HCI International 2024 Posters - Part II, edited by Constantine Stephanidis, Margherita Antona, Stavroula Ntoa and Gavriel Salvendy
58. CCIS 2116, HCI International 2024 Posters - Part III, edited by Constantine Stephanidis, Margherita Antona, Stavroula Ntoa and Gavriel Salvendy
59. CCIS 2117, HCI International 2024 Posters - Part IV, edited by Constantine Stephanidis, Margherita Antona, Stavroula Ntoa and Gavriel Salvendy
60. CCIS 2118, HCI International 2024 Posters - Part V, edited by Constantine Stephanidis, Margherita Antona, Stavroula Ntoa and Gavriel Salvendy
61. CCIS 2119, HCI International 2024 Posters - Part VI, edited by Constantine Stephanidis, Margherita Antona, Stavroula Ntoa and Gavriel Salvendy
62. CCIS 2120, HCI International 2024 Posters - Part VII, edited by Constantine Stephanidis, Margherita Antona, Stavroula Ntoa and Gavriel Salvendy

https://2024.hci.international/proceedings

Preface

The 16th International Conference on Social Computing and Social Media (SCSM 2024) was an affiliated conference of the HCI International (HCII) conference. The conference provided an established international forum for the exchange and dissemination of scientific information related to social computing and social media, addressing a broad spectrum of issues expanding our understanding of current and future issues in these areas. The conference welcomed qualitative and quantitative research papers on a diverse range of topics related to the design, development, assessment, use, and impact of social media.

A considerable number of papers this year focused on research on the design, development, and evaluation of social media, exploring topics such as opinion data crawling, crowdsourcing, and recommendation systems, and delving into aspects related to user experience and user behavior. The undeniable influence of Artificial Intelligence on the technological landscape has prompted numerous works focused on the use of AI and Language Models in social media, investigating their multifaceted impact in the field, such as for the identification of malicious accounts and deepfakes, the improvement of search capabilities, the recognition of emotions and detection of human values, as well as the development of improved recommendation systems. The power of social media and its positive impact across various application domains inspired contributions regarding education and learning, culture, business, eCommerce, as well as computer-mediated communication. In the context of learning, the topics explored include academic writing, learning experience, ethics in education, specialized social networks for researchers, platforms for students with disabilities, and the impact of AI in education-related social media and platforms. In business and eCommerce, papers delve into aspects related to branding, consumer behavior, as well as customer experience and engagement. Finally, appraising the role of social media in fostering communication, strengthening social ties, and supporting democracy, contributions explored novel interpersonal communication approaches, hybrid working environments, opinion analysis, media memory shaping, disaster management, social learning, and online citizen interaction. As editors of these SCSM proceedings volumes, we are pleased to present this unique and diverse compilation of topics offering valuable insights and advancing our understanding of the current and future issues in the field.

Three volumes of the HCII 2024 proceedings are dedicated to this year's edition of the SCSM conference. The first focuses on topics related to Designing, Developing and Evaluating Social Media, User Experience and User Behavior in Social Media, and AI and Language Models in Social Media. The second focuses on topics related to Social Media in Learning, Education and Culture, and Social Media in Business and eCommerce. Finally, the third focuses on topics related to Computer-Mediated Communication, and Social Media for Community, Society and Democracy.

The papers in these volumes were accepted for publication after a minimum of two single-blind reviews from the members of the SCSM Program Board or, in some cases, from members of the Program Boards of other affiliated conferences. We would like to thank all of them for their invaluable contribution, support, and efforts.

July 2024   Adela Coman
                                                                  Simona Vasilache

16th International Conference on Social Computing and Social Media (SCSM 2024)

Program Board Chairs: **Adela Coman**, University of Bucharest, Romania, and **Simona Vasilache**, University of Tsukuba, Japan

- Francisco Javier Alvarez-Rodriguez, *Universidad Autónoma de Aguascalientes, Mexico*
- Andria Andriuzzi, *Université Jean Monnet Saint-Etienne, Coactis, France*
- Karine Berthelot-Guiet, *Sorbonne University, France*
- James Braman, *Community College of Baltimore County, USA*
- Magdalena Brzezinska, *WSB Merito University, Poland*
- Adheesh Budree, *University of Cape Town, South Africa*
- Hung-Hsuan Huang, *University of Fukuchiyama, Japan*
- Ajrina Hysaj, *University of Wollongong in Dubai, UAE*
- Ayaka Ito, *Reitaku University, Japan*
- Carsten Kleiner, *University of Applied Sciences & Arts Hannover, Germany*
- Jeannie S. Lee, *Singapore Institute of Technology (SIT), Singapore*
- Kun Chang Lee, *Sungkyunkwan University (SKKU), Korea*
- Margarida Romero, *Université Côte d'Azur, France*
- Gabriele Meiselwitz, *Towson University, USA*
- Ana Isabel Molina Diaz, *University of Castilla-La Mancha, Spain*
- Takashi Namatame, *Chuo University, Japan*
- Hoang D. Nguyen, *UCC, Ireland*
- Kohei Otake, *Sophia University, Japan*
- Daniela Quinones, *Pontificia Universidad Católica de Valparaíso, Chile*
- Virginica Rusu, *Universidad de Playa Ancha, Chile*
- Cristian Rusu, *Pontificia Universidad Católica de Valparaíso, Chile*
- Tomislav Stipancic, *University of Zagreb, Croatia*
- Yuanqiong Wang, *Towson University, USA*

The full list with the Program Board Chairs and the members of the Program Boards of all thematic areas and affiliated conferences of HCII 2024 is available online at:

http://www.hci.international/board-members-2024.php

HCI International 2025 Conference

The 27th International Conference on Human-Computer Interaction, HCI International 2025, will be held jointly with the affiliated conferences at the Swedish Exhibition & Congress Centre and Gothia Towers Hotel, Gothenburg, Sweden, June 22–27, 2025. It will cover a broad spectrum of themes related to Human-Computer Interaction, including theoretical issues, methods, tools, processes, and case studies in HCI design, as well as novel interaction techniques, interfaces, and applications. The proceedings will be published by Springer. More information will become available on the conference website: https://2025.hci.international/.

General Chair
Prof. Constantine Stephanidis
University of Crete and ICS-FORTH
Heraklion, Crete, Greece
Email: general_chair@2025.hci.international

https://2025.hci.international/

Contents – Part I

AI and Language Models in Social Media

Contents – Part II

Social Media in Business and eCommerce

Contents – Part III

Designing, Developing and Evaluating Social Media

A Crowdsourcing Approach for Identifying Potential Stereotypes in the Collected Data

Evgenia Christoforou[1]([✉]), Kalia Orphanou[2,3], Marios Kyriacou[1], and Jahna Otterbacher[1,3]

[1] CYENS - Centre of Excellence, Nicosia, Cyprus
`evgenia.christoforou@gmail.com`
[2] The Cyprus Institute of Neurology and Genetics, Nicosia, Cyprus
[3] Open University of Cyprus, Latsia, Cyprus

Abstract. Data generation through crowdsourcing has become a common practice for building or augmenting an Artificial Intelligence (AI) system. These systems often reflect the stereotypical behaviors expressed by humans through the reported data, which can be problematic, especially when dealing with sensitive tasks. One such task is the interpretation of images depicting people. In this work, we evaluate a crowdsourcing approach aimed at identifying the stereotypes conveyed in the collected annotations on people images. By including closed-ended, categorical responses as well as open-ended tags during the data collection phase, we can detect potentially harmful crowd behaviors. Our results suggest a means to assess descriptive tags, as to their alignment with stereotypical beliefs related to gender, age, and body weight. This study concludes with a discussion on how our analytical approach can be applied to pre-existing datasets with similar characteristics or to future knowledge being crowdsourced such as to audit for stereotypes.

Keywords: crowdsourcing · image tagging · stereotypes · bias · fairness

1 Introduction

The goal of the European Commission (EC), as stated in the 2020 White Paper on AI is to promote the use of AI systems and the widespread sharing of AI systems, processes and resources (e.g., datasets, algorithms)[1]. To this end, the EC has put forth a vision of trustworthy and fair AI systems, which must conform to human values[2]. Multiple approaches have been proposed for detecting and mitigating discrimination and fairness issues in AI systems such as auditing image search engines [12,17,20], detecting bias and stereotypical behaviors in

---

[1] https://commission.europa.eu/publications/white-paper-artificial-intelligence-european-approach-excellence-and-trust_en.

[2] https://ec.europa.eu/futurium/en/ai-alliance-consultation.1.html.

image tagging services [1, 18] or auditing input data using datasheets for datasets developed by the system stakeholders during the system development [8].

Stereotypical behaviors are inevitable when the AI system judges or interacts with people or artifacts (e.g., images, audio, texts) that depict or represent people; therefore, the issue is whether or not such behaviors constitute unfair social bias. It is even more challenging when the training and input data of an AI system are generated by humans, who judge or interact with people or artifacts (e.g., images, audio, texts) that depict or represent people. Social stereotypes are transmitted and learned between people [10,13,25,26] and they can easily be propagated when someone is asked to judge/describe another person, without having enough information concerning that person [27]. Over time, social stereotypes detected in a dataset used to train an AI system may lead to a discriminatory decision or outcome. An example is the study of Matsangidou and Otterbacher [18] who audit the output of four image tagging services that generate tags to describe portrait images from the Chigago Face Database (CFD) [16], by compiling a dictionary of tags that are related to attractiveness (e.g., attractive, pretty, beautiful, cute, handsome). Among other results, they found that images of women were systematically more likely to receive "attractiveness" tags by the algorithms, as compared to images of men. They identified that these image tagging algorithms tend to perpetuate stereotypes related to gender.

Crowdsourcing, the process of recruiting humans to generate/augment data, is one means by which social stereotypes can easily be propagated to an AI system, through biased data. Crowdworkers, like most humans, have their own biases and express stereotypical behaviors that many times accompany the generated data, thus possibly biasing the final outcome of the AI system trained on those data. To handle these issues, several approaches have been proposed for mitigating bias in the collected data through the design of a crowdsourcing task. For instance, Draws et al. [5] composed a list of cognitive bias arising through crowdsourcing tasks, which they accompanied with insights on how to improve the task design for the generation of more reliable and trustworthy data sets. Hube et al. [9] proposed and reviewed three mitigation methods for a text annotation crowdsourcing task: i) Social projection, where the workers are asked to label a text according to what they believe the majority of workers would choose; ii) Awareness reminder, trying to make workers aware of the controversial and subjective nature of the task to influence their judgment when completing the task; iii) Personalized Nudges, giving personalized instructions to the workers according to the tendencies they exhibit in forming a judgment. The authors note that all three mitigation approaches reduce the total bias and average bias of workers with extreme opinions. Leung et al. [14] proposed another task design that reduces the number of choices that the crowdworkers have for their responses, which can reduce potential discrimination on the data generated by the responses. In a similar way, Kamar et al. [11] propose a method for automatically recognizing and correcting task-specific biases using probabilistic graphical models.

1.1 Our Approach

Most recent approaches emphasize the design of the crowdsourcing task for the generation of a less-biased dataset. In contrast, our approach aims at providing a way to evaluate the generated data through the structure of the crowdsourcing task for stereotypical behaviors, rather than "indiscriminately" mitigating potential biases arising from crowdsourcing, without first understanding the biases that arise and the reason for their existence. Our work presents a way for receiving indirect feedback on the data generated by crowdworkers, which allows us to explore the reasons for the generation of systematic stereotypical beliefs in a dataset. In a sense, the crowdworkers act both as the "producer" of the data and the "evaluator" at the same time.

To better explore our approach, we consider the case of image recognition, via "tagging." Various forms of image analysis and recognition (e.g., object recognition, captioning) have become popular in recent years, and have become an asset to researchers and developers, who need to add vision capabilities to a project, product or service. In most of the large datasets available for training such models (e.g., ImageNet, MS-COCO), crowdsourcing has played a key role in their creation and evaluation.

Inspired by this, we consider the example of image tagging via crowdsourcing and we ask the crowdworkers to provide tags for a set of highly standardized people images from the Chicago Face Database (CFD) [16]. These are passport-style images, with a neutral background, which allows us to capture tags directly relevant to the depicted person, thus avoiding background noise for this study. The crowdsourcing task, i.e., Human Intelligence Task (HIT) provided to the crowd is a collection of open and closed-form questions regarding the image. By collecting both categorical data on certain traits of the depicted person and a set of tags matching the depicted person, we aspire to both create a dataset useful for image tagging algorithms and audit the stereotypical beliefs of the crowdworkers collectively. Thus, we address the following research questions:

RQ1: Can the inclusion of categorical values on certain person's traits help in identifying potentially harmful stereotypes in an image tagging dataset?
RQ2: Is it advantageous to include complementary open and closed-form questions in the same HIT for the identification of stereotypical behaviors?

To explore the above research questions, we examine the generated data set for any correlation between abstract i.e. attractiveness, trustworthiness, and concrete concepts i.e. weight, age, and gender that may propagate stereotypes such as: *Are younger people perceived as more attractive*, or *Are overweight people perceived as less attractive?*

The remainder of the paper is organized as follows. In Sect. 2, we present our methodology for collecting and processing the crowdsourced dataset. In Sect. 3, we present the analysis of the crowdworkers' responses to both closed-form and open-form questions and the identified stereotypes from the dataset. In Sect. 4, we discuss our main findings with regard to the two research questions, we provide a discussion on how we could generalize our approach to other types of data and we discuss the limitations of this work. Finally, we provide some general remarks on this work and we discuss the possible future directions in Sect. 5.

2 Methodology

Data Collection. We recruited US-based crowdworkers through the Clickworker platform[3] and asked them to provide us with their observations (a.k.a., a description of the depicted person) on each of the 597 images of the Chicago Face Database (CFD) [16] data set. Images of CFD[4] are highly standardized, with individuals depicted in the image self-reporting their gender and race. Out of the 597 images of the CFD, 109 depict Asian, 197 Black, 108 Latino/a and 183 White people. Additionally, gender is balanced per group.

After providing our crowdworkers a description of the task, we obtained their informed consent for participation; they were also explicitly informed of their right to leave the task at any time. We then asked them a series of questions regarding an image from the CFD data set.[5] In particular, we asked them a control question concerning if they were able to see a person in the depicted image. After this question, we posed the following open-form question: "Fill in the 3 text fields below, providing a description of the depicted person with a maximum of 2 words." This question was followed by a set of closed-form questions. Crowdworkers were asked to respond, via a 1–7 Likert item (1 being the lowest, 7 the highest), as to how attractive they find the depicted person and how trustworthy they find them. Additionally, they were asked to gauge the weight of the person ([Underweight, Normal Weight, Overweight]), the person's race ([Asian, Black, Latino/a, White]), skin color ([Light, Medium, Dark]) and gender([Male, Female, Other]). Moreover, they were asked to report on the age of the person with an open-form question. Finally, workers were asked to complete a brief demographics questionnaire.

The crowdsourcing campaign sought out US-based participants, 18 years old or above to participate in the task. We asked for the participation of male and female crowdworkers in separate instances of the task, asking both genders to provide us with their opinion on all 597 images. Thus, we collected in total 1.194 responses from crowdworkers, each image receiving an annotation from both a male and a female crowdworker. Participants were rewarded with 0.6 euro per task and they took a median time of 4 min to complete the task.

Data Set Pre-processing. Crowdsourced data cannot be blindly trusted [7]. Thus we have pre-processed our dataset removing the answers received from crowdworkers who: 1) did not see a person in the depicted image, 2) reported that they

---

[3] https://www.clickworker.com/.

[4] Sample images can be found at: https://www.chicagofaces.org/.

[5] Our research protocol has undergone ethical review and received approval by the Cyprus National Bioethics Committee.

were below 18 years of age, 3) reported that their gender was not the one specified during the task announcement, 4) provided us with gibberish tags. Hence, from the 1.194 responses we considered only 1.119.

Characteristics of the Dataset. For the purpose of repeatability of our results and methodology, we provide here the main characteristics of our data set. Regarding the images depicting a person included in the dataset they are originally from the CFD data set showing individuals in a passport-like image, forward-facing the camera, wearing a grey t-shirt and having a neutral facial expression. This characteristic of the CFD has allowed us to observe the annotations of the crowdworkers as freely as possible from "attention biases" introduced to the tags due to the environment where the individual is portrayed. Open-form questions in the crowdsourcing task are pre-seeding the closed-form questions. This was done in an attempt to reduce the anchoring effect [5] that crowdworkers might have from introducing closed-form questions regarding the traits of the depicted person upfront.

3   Analysis and Results

We provide an analysis of the collected data looking into the responses of the crowdworkers to the open and closed-form questions. First, in Sect. 3.1, we consider the way crowdworkers reported on the more concrete characteristics that describe a person (i.e., gender, age and weight) and we compared them against the responses they provided for the abstract characteristics of a person (i.e., attractiveness and trustworthiness). Section 3.2 analyzes the frequencies with which certain tags were mentioned by the crowdworkers when a specific value was selected for the closed-form characteristics (both abstract and concrete).

Crowdworkers reported their perceived attractiveness and the trustworthiness of the depicted person using 7-point Likert items. For the purposes of this analysis, we collapsed the answers from the crowdworkers into three groups: (a) non-attractive/non-trustworthy (responses 1–3), (b) neutral (4), and (c) attractive/trustworthy (5–7).

The crowdworkers' reported values for age have also been divided into four groups: a) 15–24 years old, b) 25–34 years old, c) 35–44 years old, and d) 45+ years old.

3.1   General Results of Closed-Form Questions

Responses on Each Characteristic. We first present the total number of crowdworkers' responses on each abstract and concrete characteristic for female and male images. In Table 1, we present the number of responses of the crowdworkers on each of the three attractiveness groups and on each of the three trustworthiness groups for female and male images respectively. We can observe that more females have been perceived as attractive, in contrast to males who have mostly been perceived as neutral or non-attractive. Regarding the trustworthiness of

Table 1. Table with the responses for Attractiveness and Trustworthiness

	Attractive	Neutral	Non-Attractive
Female Images	260	157	149
Male Images	168	191	194
	Trustworthy	Neutral	Non-Trustworthy
Female Images	230	260	76
Male Images	190	257	106

the people depicted in the images, most of the females and males have been perceived as neutral.

In addition, as shown in Table 2, most of the people depicted in the images have been described to be of normal weight. Regarding age, we can observe that the majority of the people depicted in the images have been described to be in the age group 25–34.

Table 2. Table with the responses for Weight and Age

	Underweight	Normal Weight	Overweight
Female Images	18	454	94
Male Images	22	470	61
	15-24	25-34	35-44	45+
Female Images	110	329	100	27
Male Images	119	273	135	26

Attractiveness v. Weight and Gender. To detect any association between the responses of crowdworkers on the abstract concept of attractiveness and the concrete concept of weight, we examine the way crowdworkers perceive a person's attractiveness, considering the description they provide of a person's weight for both images depicting a male (see Fig. 1b) and images depicting a female (see Fig. 1a).

From an initial inspection of the results, it appears that crowdworkers who characterize a person as *overweight*, also tend to perceive the person as *non-attractive*, in both images depicting male and female subjects. Looking at the crowdworkers responses for female images, subjects depicted as having a *normal weight* also tend to be perceived as *attractive* or *neutral* rather than *non-attractive*. However, for male images, there is a very small difference between the number of responses provided to characterize a person as both *attractive* and of *normal weight*, and the number of responses provided to characterize a person as both as *non-attractive* and of *normal weight*. In other words, while we observe a uniform distribution over the value *normal weight* for the different values of *attractive* for the images depicting male subjects, this is not the case for the images depicting female subjects. On the contrary, more images depicting females marked as *attractive* receive also the *normal weight* value. Another observation we can make from Fig. 1b and Fig. 1a is that the *overweight* value is more frequently used for people marked as *non-attractive*, and it drops for *neutral* and *attractive* for both male and female subjects.

Attractiveness v. Age and Gender. We looked for an association between crowdworkers' perceptions of the attractiveness of a person and the age of the person depicted in an image. As observed from Fig. 1c, crowdworkers tend to perceive young females (around 15–24 or 25–34 years old) as being *attractive* more often than *non-attractive*, while they tend to perceive older females (over 45 years old) as *non-attractive*, and the females in the age group, 35–44 years old, as *neutral*. Based on these results, we observe that there is an association between the crowdworkers' responses regarding the age of a female person and their perceived attractiveness. However, observing the results shown in Fig. 1d, the stereotype that "younger people are more attractive than older people" has not been detected in responses concerning the male images. For males, we observe little difference between the number of responses that characterize a person as being *attractive* and in the younger (or older) age groups, and the number of responses that characterize a person as being *non-attractive* and in the younger (or older) age groups.

Trustworthiness v. Weight and Gender. We repeat the same analysis, this time looking into a possible relationship between the crowdworkers' perceptions of a person's trustworthiness, and their description of the person's weight, for images depicting a male (see Fig. 2b) and for images depicting a female (see Fig. 2a). As shown in both figures, the majority of crowdworkers perceive people depicted in both male and female images as *trustworthy* or *neutral* independently of their weight.

Trustworthiness v. Age and Gender. Figure 2c and Fig. 2d depict the analysis considering possible associations between crowdworkers' perceptions of a person's trustworthiness and his or her age, for female and male images, respectively. For both female and male images, the largest percentage of responses describe a person, in any of the age groups, as *trustworthy* or *neutral* rather than *non-trustworthy*.

Trustworthiness v. Attractiveness and Gender. In considering the relationship between perceived trustworthiness, perceived attractiveness and gender, we detect that there is an association between attractiveness and trustworthiness. As shown both in figures, Fig. 3a and Fig. 3b, the majority of depicted people who have been perceived as being *attractive*, are also perceived as being *trustworthy*, while the majority of people who have been perceived as being *non-attractive* (or *neutral*) have also been perceived as being *non-trustworthy* or *neutral*.

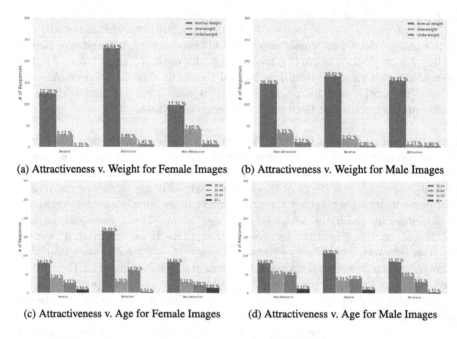

(a) Attractiveness v. Weight for Female Images   (b) Attractiveness v. Weight for Male Images

(c) Attractiveness v. Age for Female Images   (d) Attractiveness v. Age for Male Images

Fig. 1. Perceived Attractiveness v. Age and Weight, by Gender.

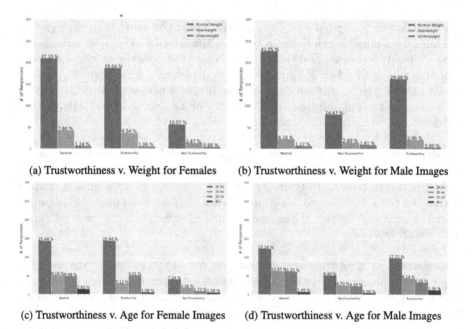

(a) Trustworthiness v. Weight for Females   (b) Trustworthiness v. Weight for Male Images

(c) Trustworthiness v. Age for Female Images   (d) Trustworthiness v. Age for Male Images

Fig. 2. Perceived Trustworthiness v. Age and Weight, by Gender.

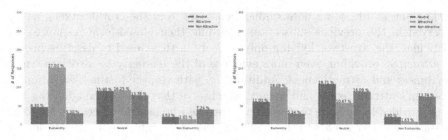

(a) Trustworthiness v. Attractiveness for Female Images

(b) Trustworthiness v. Attractiveness for Male Images

Fig. 3. Perceived Trustworthiness v. Perceived Attractiveness, by Gender.

3.2   Results from Open-Form Questions

We now compare the open and closed-form responses provided by the crowdworkers. We consider the tags that were used by the crowdworkers when a certain value of the closed-form questions was selected for both abstract and concrete characteristics of a person. In particular, we look at the percentage of the number of occurrences of a specific tag over the total number of tags provided for a specific value of the attractiveness, trustworthiness, age, gender, and weight characteristics (i.e., closed-form questions). Generated plots in this section depict tags with more than five occurrences, to remove the effects of any outliers.

Attractiveness Tags. Figure 4a shows the percentage of tag occurrences over the total number of tags given when the workers' closed-ended response indicates that the depicted person is *attractive*. In contrast, Fig. 4b shows the percentage of tag occurrences over the total number of tags given when the *non-attractive* value was selected by the crowdworkers.

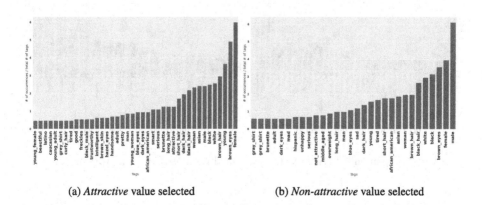

(a) *Attractive* value selected

(b) *Non-attractive* value selected

Fig. 4. Open-ended (tags) v. Closed-ended responses on Attractiveness.

Looking at Fig. 4, we note similar behaviors from the crowdworkers, as we observed in the previous subsection regarding their closed-form responses. In particular, the "trustworthy" tag only appears in those used to describe people as *attractive*, providing even more evidence of the tendency to associate trustworthiness and attractiveness. Additionally, with respect to the association of a person's attractiveness and weight, we observe that the "overweight" tag has been provided by workers to characterize people who have also been perceived as *non-attractive*. This adds to the evidence that overweight people are considered less attractive by the crowdworkers.

Another interesting finding is that crowdworkers use negative emotions such as "sad", "mad" and "unhappy" more often when they perceive a person as *non-attractive*, while positive traits and characteristics i.e., "smart", "intelligent", "good" are used to describe people perceived as *attractive*.

Trustworthiness Tags. Figure 5a shows the percentage of occurrences of the tags given to describe a person perceived as being trustworthy, while Fig. 5b shows the percentage of occurrences of the tags used to describe a person perceived as non-trustworthy. As shown in both figures, more concrete tags, such as demographic characteristics or those describing physical appearance, appeared more often to characterize people who have been perceived as *non-trustworthy*. In contrast, for people perceived as *trustworthy*, crowdworkers also provide more abstract characteristics i.e., "attractive", "serious", "smart", and "calm". Adding evidence to the conclusion that "people perceived as attractive are also perceived as trustworthy", as shown in Fig. 5a, attractiveness-related tags have been given to people who have been perceived as *trustworthy* i.e., "handsome", "attractive", "pretty" and "beautiful".

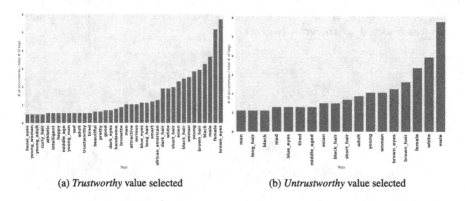

(a) *Trustworthy* value selected   (b) *Untrustworthy* value selected

Fig. 5. Open-ended (tags) v. Closed-ended responses on Trustworthiness.

We notice that tags like "young", "adult", and "middle-aged" described both people who have been perceived as *trustworthy* and as *untrustworthy*. This observation supports the one extracted above from the closed-form questions, that crowdworkers perceive the depicted subjects as trustworthy or not, independently of their age. Finally, another interesting finding is that the tag "female" has been given more often to people who have been perceived as *trustworthy*, whereas "male" has been given more often to people who have been perceived as *non-trustworthy*.

4   Discussion and Limitations

4.1   Crowdworkers as Data "Evaluators"

Considering the responses to both the open and closed-form questions, we observed that crowdworkers' answers tend to reflect "established" stereotypical beliefs and opinions, which are prevalent in society. In summary, we found evidence that the following stereotypes are reflected in the collected data: overweight people are unattractive [22,23], women are (or should be) attractive [3], and beautiful people are also "good" [4] or, more specifically, more trustworthy [24].

In particular, the crowdworkers in our study perceived people that they judged as *overweight* more often as *non-attractive* compared to *neutral* and *attractive*. Additionally, female subjects have been considered more *attractive* than male subjects. These observations concur with stereotypical beliefs related to weight and attractiveness [22] as well as to gender and attractiveness [3]. On the other hand, we didn't observe any definitive connection between age and attractiveness in the crowdworkers answers. Finally, comparing the responses received from the crowdworkers on the closed-form questions regarding the abstract traits of a person (i.e., attractiveness and trustworthiness), we have seen that independently of the gender of the depicted person, depicted subjects being marked as *non-trustworthy* were more frequently marked as being *non-attractive* and vice-versa. A similar conclusion was observed in the open-form questions with tags describing the attractiveness of a subject matching the value of trustworthiness in the closed-form question. This behavior of the crowdworkers adheres with the stereotype that more attractive people are regarded as more good [4] and in extension more trustworthy. Thus, it is evident that crowdworkers have stereotypical opinions which are expressed in the generated data.

Hence, the above observations provide us with an *affirmative answer to RQ1*. Using closed-form questions that require the workers to directly express an opinion on certain traits of a person (i.e., trustworthy and attractive) in combination with questions that regard the general perception of a person in a concrete manner (i.e., gender, age, weight), can provide useful insights on the stereotypical beliefs that influence their work.

We have observed that the majority of the stereotypical beliefs expressed by the crowdworkers are reflected through the closed-form questions and confirmed from the open-form questions which are analyzed considering the responses of the crowdworkers regarding the closed-form questions. Thus, *in response to RQ2, it is advantageous to include complementary open and closed-form questions in the same HIT*. First of all, in image tagging HITs, open-form questions are desirable many times; thus, closed-form questions are desirable for recognizing stereotypical beliefs. Secondly, we have noticed that certain behaviors – such as attributing tags of "smart", "serious" and "calm" to subjects marked as *trustworthy*, and tags like "smart", "intelligent" and "good" to subjects marked as *attractive*, while subjects marked as *non-attractive* received tags as "sad", "mad", and "unhappy"– could only be noticed through the use of both types of questions. It is important to note that training data reflecting an association between a depicted subject's emotional state and how attractive that person is, could lead to undesirable behaviors for a machine learning algorithm, e.g., systematically labeling humans that showed negative emotions as being non-attractive. Thus, it appears that this approach could potentially aid in "identifying" such behaviors in the dataset that are not easy to capture otherwise.

4.2 Generalizing the Approach

Having received a positive answer to both research questions, for the example of crowdsourced image tag generation for people images, we would like to highlight the main characteristics of our approach that allowed us to identify these stereotypical behaviors. This will allow us to provide some insides into how this approach could be generalized to other types of images and crowdsourced data.

Crowdsourced Data. Our approach focused on crowdsourced data for image tag generation. We accompanied the HIT by asking crowdworkers to provide tags for a person depicted in images, with closed-form questions with the goal to identify the following main elements of the crowdworker's perception of the depicted person: (a) demographic characteristics (i.e., more concrete characteristics), (b) personality traits (i.e., more abstract characteristics). Demographic characteristics are necessary to establish the cworker's perception when annotating an image beyond the ground truth. In other words, when studying worker behavior, it is more helpful to know what gender/age the worker perceives the depicted person as having, rather than the ground truth. On the other hand, personality traits are valuable as we saw in identifying more "subtle" stereotypical behaviors. Pre-existing datasets with similar characteristics to the ones we describe above could be audited for systematic stereotypical beliefs. Moreover, when generating new data that describe an image content with the aid of the crowd, an approach of using both open and closed-form questions can be applied. It is important though that the open questions precede the closed-form questions to avoid confirmation bias [5].

Furthermore, although we have looked into the paradigm of image tagging, this approach could be applicable to other types of crowdsourcing tasks that could benefit from an audit of the stereotypical beliefs of crowdworkers in a measurable way (i.e., through closed-form questions). A prime example is that of subjective tasks where the crowdworkers are asked to perform content moderation or sentiment analysis [6] and have a way to capture their perception in a measurable way.

Stereotype Identification. To draw relevant conclusions on the existence of systematic stereotypical behaviors from the crowdworkers, the open and closed-form questions must be complementary. In other words, closed-form questions must establish in a countable manner, certain beliefs of the crowdworkers, so as to be compared against more qualitative responses. Identification of the stereotypes could be in a similar manner as in our analysis.

4.3 Limitations

Although we collected the crowdworkers' responses on the race and skin color of the depicted person, we decided not to use these "concrete" characteristics in the analysis we have performed. Results on these two answers need a more thorough investigation, since many of the CFD images appear to depict multiracial subject, despite that the dataset provides a discrete race label. Thus, it is not easy to appropriately capture the perception of crowdworkers into meaningful results.

The analysis regarding the relationship of the tags with the concrete and abstract characteristics of the depicted person could be even more elaborated with the use of an appropriate dictionary that would categorize the tags, as in [2]. The dictionary presented in [2] could potentially be applied to this work, but to our understanding the categorization of the tags would need to be updated to better capture how crowdworkers judge a person. For example, the abstract characteristic categories should expand to include the education of a person, socioeconomic status and other social attributes, while the emotions category should expand to include both positive and negative emotions.

4.4 Stakeholder Upskilling

The latest developments in Generative AI have shown the clear potential of the technology, and AI in general, in the efficient creation of content. However, what is less clear is the creation of appropriate and trustworthy datasets for developing and evaluating these AI models [15]. Bias detection and mitigation are crucial components when developing fair and explainable algorithmic systems, particularly in applications that involve social aspects, such as healthcare and education. A survey by Orphanou et al. [19] underscores the need to look into the system's components as well as the perspective of the stakeholders when auditing and mitigating bias. In this work, we focused on the evaluation of the produced datasets via crowdsourcing, providing an approach for identifying stereotypical beliefs of the crowdworkers. To this respect, as mentioned in Sect. 4.2 requesters of the crowdsourcing task must adapt their task in such a way as to be able to compare the more quantitative responses to the qualitative ones. Additionally, we have briefly discussed the characteristics that an existing crowdsourced dataset must have in order to be audited under the approach we have described.

The major stakeholders in the case of generating and using datasets for the creation and evaluation of AI models are usually software developers, researchers and industry practitioners. It is crucial to educate stakeholders on both the ramifications of training AI models with biased datasets, and the consequences of relying on datasets generated exclusively by a specific demographic group of crowdworkers. This education is essential for helping requesters comprehend the importance of evaluating the generated dataset and for establishing appropriate mechanisms to conduct such evaluations. Perikleous et al. [21] presented a tool for raising the stakeholders' awareness showing the behavior of four biometric tasks trained on crowdsourced image annotations.

On the other hand, another stakeholder in this equation are the users of an AI model, thus, crowdworkers also fall under this category. Raising awareness on the crowdworkers' side can be also beneficial. Although tools like the one mentioned above [21] can be of great help in educating crowdworkers a-priori, it is usually the case that they will significantly impact the cost of the crowdsourcing task. Given the current operational structure of commercial crowdsourcing platforms, it would be more advantageous if awareness on such issues were disseminated directly through the platform environment, integrated into a qualification scheme for crowdworkers.

5   Conclusions

This work presents a crowdsourcing approach for identifying stereotypical beliefs of the crowdworkers through the use of open and closed-form questions in the crowdsourcing task. Considering the paradigm of image recognition via tagging, a crowdsourcing task is designed for collecting tags from the crowdworkers on the CFD images together with the crowdworkers' perception on certain closed-form questions. Closed-form questions capture the perception of the crowdworkers both on concrete (i.e., gender, age, weight) as well as abstract features (i.e., attractiveness and trustworthiness). Analysis of the collected responses found evidence that crowdworkers considered women to be attractive, overweight people to be unattractive and attractive people to be more trustworthy and these beliefs were reflected on the tags provided by the crowdworkers. This work showed that not only crowdworkers' beliefs aligned with known social stereotypes but also that the use of both open and closed-form questions in combination can expose systematic behaviors of the crowdworkers that can be missed otherwise.

In the future, we aim at constructing a dictionary that would aid the identification of stereotypes in tags in line with our approach. Additionally, we aspire to apply this approach to other types of crowdsourcing tasks, such as text annotation and sentiment analysis. Finally, we would like to extend our current experiments to understand the degree to which the crowdworkers' demographics (e.g., their reported gender, race and/or nationality) correlate to the stereotypical beliefs observed in the generated data.

Acknowledgments. This project has received funding from the Cyprus Research and Innovation Foundation under grant EXCELLENCE/0421/0360 (KeepA(n)I), the European Union's Horizon 2020 Research and Innovation Programme under Grant Agreement No. 739578 (RISE), and the Government of the Republic of Cyprus through the Deputy Ministry of Research, Innovation and Digital Policy.

References

1. Barlas, P., Kyriakou, K., Guest, O., Kleanthous, S., Otterbacher, J.: To "See" is to Stereotype: image tagging algorithms, gender recognition, and the accuracy-fairness trade-off. Proc. ACM Hum.-Comput. Interact. **4**(CSCW3), 232:1–232:31 (2021). https://doi.org/10.1145/3432931
2. Barlas, P., Kyriakou, K., Kleanthous, S., Otterbacher, J.: Social b (eye) as: human and machine descriptions of people images. In: Proceedings of the International AAAI Conference on Web and Social Media, vol. 13, pp. 583–591 (2019)
3. Chrisler, J.C.: "Why can't you control yourself?" Fat should be a feminist issue. Sex Roles **66**(9–10), 608–616 (2012)
4. Dion, K., Berscheid, E., Walster, E.: What is beautiful is good. J. Pers. Soc. Psychol. **24**(3), 285 (1972)
5. Draws, T., Rieger, A., Inel, O., Gadiraju, U., Tintarev, N.: A checklist to combat cognitive biases in crowdsourcing. In: Proceedings of the AAAI Conference on Human Computation and Crowdsourcing, vol. 9, pp. 48–59 (2021)
6. Gadiraju, U., Kawase, R., Dietze, S.: A taxonomy of microtasks on the web. In: Proceedings of the 25th ACM Conference on Hypertext and Social Media, pp. 218–223 (2014)
7. Gadiraju, U., Kawase, R., Dietze, S., Demartini, G.: Understanding malicious behavior in crowdsourcing platforms: The case of online surveys. In: Proceedings of the 33rd Annual ACM Conference on Human Factors in Computing Systems, pp. 1631–1640 (2015)
8. Gebru, T., et al.: Datasheets for datasets. Commun. ACM **64**(12), 86–92 (2021). https://doi.org/10.1145/3458723, https://dl.acm.org/doi/10.1145/3458723
9. Hube, C., Fetahu, B., Gadiraju, U.: Understanding and mitigating worker biases in the crowdsourced collection of subjective judgments. In: Proceedings of the 2019 CHI Conference on Human Factors in Computing Systems. CHI '19, pp. 1–12. Association for Computing Machinery, New York, NY, USA (2019). https://doi.org/10.1145/3290605.3300637
10. Hussain, M., Naz, A., Khan, W., Daraz, U., Khan, Q.: Gender stereotyping in family: an institutionalized and normative mechanism in Pakhtun society of Pakistan. SAGE Open **5**(3), 2158244015595258 (2015)
11. Kamar, E., Kapoor, A., Horvitz, E.: Identifying and accounting for task-dependent bias in crowdsourcing. In: Proceedings of the AAAI Conference on Human Computation and Crowdsourcing, vol. 3 (2015)
12. Kay, M., Matuszek, C., Munson, S.A.: Unequal representation and gender stereotypes in image search results for occupations. In: Proceedings of the 33rd Annual ACM Conference on Human Factors in Computing Systems. CHI '15, pp. 3819–3828. Association for Computing Machinery, New York, NY, USA (2015). https://doi.org/10.1145/2702123.2702520
13. Lay, J.C., Holman, M.R., Bos, A.L., Greenlee, J.S., Oxley, Z.M., Buffett, A.: Time for kids to learn gender stereotypes: analysis of gender and political leadership in a common social studies resource for children. Polit. Gender **17**(1), 1–22 (2021)
14. Leung, W., et al.: Race, gender and beauty: the effect of information provision on online hiring biases. CHI '20, pp. 1–11. Association for Computing Machinery, New York, NY, USA (2020). https://doi.org/10.1145/3313831.3376874
15. Liang, W., et al.: Advances, challenges and opportunities in creating data for trustworthy AI. Nat. Mach. Intell. **4**(8), 669–677 (2022)

16. Ma, D.S., Correll, J., Wittenbrink, B.: The Chicago face database: a free stimulus set of faces and norming data. Behav. Res. Methods **47**(4), 1122–1135 (2015)
17. Magno, G., Araújo, C.S., Meira Jr., W., Almeida, V.: Stereotypes in search engine results: understanding the role of local and global factors. arXiv preprint arXiv:1609.05413 (2016)
18. Matsangidou, M., Otterbacher, J.: What is beautiful continues to be good: people images and algorithmic inferences on physical attractiveness. In: Lamas, D., Loizides, F., Nacke, L., Petrie, H., Winckler, M., Zaphiris, P. (eds.) INTERACT 2019. LNCS, vol. 11749, pp. 243–264. Springer, Cham (2019). https://doi.org/10.1007/978-3-030-29390-1_14
19. Orphanou, K., et al.: Mitigating bias in algorithmic systems-a fish-eye view. ACM Comput. Surv. **55**(5) (2022). https://doi.org/10.1145/3527152
20. Otterbacher, J., Bates, J., Clough, P.: Competent men and warm women: gender stereotypes and backlash in image search results. In: Proceedings of the 2017 CHI Conference on Human Factors in Computing Systems, pp. 6620–6631. ACM, Denver Colorado USA (2017). https://doi.org/10.1145/3025453.3025727, https://dl.acm.org/doi/10.1145/3025453.3025727
21. Perikleous, P., et al.: How does the crowd impact the model? A tool for raising awareness of social bias in crowdsourced training data. In: Proceedings of the 31st ACM International Conference on Information and Knowledge Management, pp. 4951–4954 (2022)
22. Puhl, R.M., Heuer, C.A.: The stigma of obesity: a review and update. Obesity **17**(5), 941–964 (2009). https://doi.org/10.1038/oby.2008.636
23. Seacat, J.D., Mickelson, K.D.: Stereotype threat and the exercise/dietary health intentions of overweight women. J. Health Psychol. **14**(4), 556–567 (2009)
24. Shinners, E.: Effects of the "what is beautiful is good" stereotype on perceived trustworthiness. UW-L J. Undergraduate Res. **12**, 1–5 (2009)
25. Tan, A.S., Li, S., Simpson, C.: American tv and social stereotypes of Americans in Taiwan and Mexico. Journal. Q. **63**(4), 809–814 (1986)
26. Tortajada-Giménez, I., Araüna-Baró, N., Martínez-Martínez, I.J.: Advertising stereotypes and gender representation in social networking sites. Comunicar **21**(41), 177–186 (2013)
27. Veletsianos, G.: Contextually relevant pedagogical agents: visual appearance, stereotypes, and first impressions and their impact on learning. Comput. Educ. **55**(2), 576–585 (2010)

Understanding Multi-platform Social Media Aggregators: A Design and Development Case Study with BTS-DASH

Alexandra Hinton and Tania Roy[✉] [iD]

New College of Florida, Sarasota, FL 34243, USA
{alexandra.hinton18,troy}@ncf.edu

Abstract. In the current digital landscape, individuals are challenged by the proliferation of social media platforms, making it arduous to aggregate and comprehend information on critical topics efficiently. This fragmentation necessitates a tool that can consolidate and exhibit information succinctly for user consumption. We address this issue by conceptualizing and creating a user-centric dashboard, utilizing the K-pop group BTS as a model for our case study. We used an iterative design methodology to develop the features. The primary focus areas for the dashboard were accessibility, functionality, data integrity, and visual appeal. These features were modified to ensure an intuitive and trustworthy user experience. The final version was built with AngularJS and hosted on Firebase. The dashboard displays data aggregated from multiple reliable social media sources. We subsequently ran a preliminary pilot usability study to illustrate the efficacy of our approach in simplifying the user's interaction with diverse data sets. Our re-search contributes to the field by proposing guidelines for constructing dashboards that distill multiple social media inputs into an accessible format. We demonstrate how such a tool can significantly aid users in staying informed without being overwhelmed, paving the way for better information management in an era of information overload and empowering users through effective information design.

Keywords: Dashboard Design · Usability Study · Social Media aggregation

1 Introduction

In the digital age, where the deluge of data grows incessantly, the ability to efficiently monitor, analyze, and interpret this information becomes paramount. Dashboards, as defined by Few [1], are visual displays that consolidate critical information needed to achieve objectives, presented in a manner conducive to quick comprehension. This paper introduces BTS-Dash, a dashboard designed to aggregate and visually represent data about the K-pop band BTS from disparate social media sources, which has garnered a massive and active online following. The purpose of BTS-Dash is to streamline the vast and multifaceted information landscape into a cohesive and user-friendly interface. The ubiquity of social media has transformed fan engagement, creating communities that

A. Coman and S. Vasilache (Eds.): HCII 2024, LNCS 14703, pp. 19–43, 2024.
https://doi.org/10.1007/978-3-031-61281-7_2

are not only highly active but also geographically and culturally diverse. As a result, the challenge lies in data collection and the accurate representation and accessibility of that information to the fans who seek it. With their significant digital footprint, BTS presents an ideal case study for this research. The dashboard development underwent iterative design phases, incorporating user feedback to enhance usability and effectiveness.

2   Background

2.1   Social Media and Information

Social media encompasses a variety of networked information and communication technologies that emphasize user engagement, interaction, and content creation. It represents a shift from traditional one-to-many communication models to a more dynamic structure that includes one-to-one and many-to-many interactions [2]. The primary characteristics of these platforms are the reliance on us-er engagement and crowd-sourcing of information where the users can actively interact with the con-tent [3]. Tools such as Twitter, Facebook, Flickr, and Blogs facilitate the swift creation and exchange of ideas and offer summarized information, providing time-saving benefits for individuals. Addition-ally, with benefits such as ease of access and information diversity, an increasing amount of news in-formation is generated and spread on social media at an increasingly fast speed, attracting a growing number of online news users [4, 5]. From recent topics of national and international importance, such as COVID-19, immigration, and international conflicts, to sports, weather, and health-related news, the consumers of information on these social media platforms [6, 7] have increased tremendously. Based on a 2020 survey conducted by the PEW research center, over half of the U.S. adults (53%) reported receiving news from social media "often" or "sometimes." Research from PEW in 2023 also noted that the percentage of U.S adults who consume news from social media use Facebook (30%), YouTube (26%), Instagram (16%), TikTok (12%) and Twitter (12%). In 2020–2021, for social media site users, Twitter was used 59% as a news source; however, it has decreased significantly over the three years.

This paper discusses the evolution of BTS-Dash through its design iterations, culminating in a final usability study to validate the efficacy of the design decisions. The study's goal was twofold: to test the dashboard's ability to convey information clearly to users and to examine the dashboard's functionality in addressing the problem of infor-mation overload and misinformation. The dashboard's effectiveness was measured by its capacity to present data in an accessible, accurate, and aesthetically pleasing manner tailored to the target audience—BTS fans. The iterative design process of BTS-Dash highlights the importance of user-centered design in creating digital tools that cater to specific communities. By focusing on the unique characteristics of fan culture and engagement on social media, this paper aims to contribute to the broader discourse on dashboard design and its implications for fan-based communities in social media spaces.

2.2   Social Media Aggregators in HCI

Social media aggregators have emerged as crucial tools in managing the vast amounts of data generated across platforms, providing users with a cohesive view of content relevant to their interests [8]. In HCI, the design of such aggregators involves a deep understanding of user needs, preferences, and interaction patterns [9]. The effective aggregation of social media content requires addressing challenges in data variability, user interface design, and information overload to ensure accessibility and usability [10].

2.3 Principles of Dashboard Design

Dashboards are an online tool used in the business world since the 1990s to assist business executives in tracking their company logistics and overhead. They have enjoyed a steady increase in popularity since then and an expansion outside the bounds of the business world. Today, dashboards are used not only by companies but also by online influencers and content creators to track their engagement and following. For a formal definition of a dashboard, Stephen Few [1] states that "a dashboard is a visual display of the most important information needed to achieve one or more objectives; consolidated and arranged on a single screen so the information can be monitored at a glance." Few further breaks down the critical parts of a dashboard in terms of content, concise display, medium, and audience. Content in this context is defined as all information required to achieve the objective should be displayed; straightforward display refers to the information is displayed on a single computer, not on multiple pages, and should use the available space fully; medium states dashboard should be viewable on an appropriate medium, whether that is a projector screen, a computer screen, or a phone screen and audience focus suggests that the design of the dashboard should be tailored to the specific audience, in terms of usability, content and aesthetics.

2.4 Use-Cases of Existing Applications

Social media aggregators functioning as a cohesive platform for a particular topic or dashboard have been prevalent in sports, such as F1Dash monitoring race car-related social media topics, and Can-COVID monitors Misinformation related to COVID-19 [11]. Clemson University's social media Listening Center observed using multiple social media platforms to understand the role of the NCAA in minor league baseball [12]. These applications focus on a singular topic and provide a multi-dimensional perspective. The choice of BTS as a case study for dashboard design is mainly motivated by fan culture and a high number of social media interactions.

2.5 Fan Cultures, Social Media Engagement, and Integrating HCI Principles in Fan-Centric Design.

The engagement of fan communities on social media is marked by active participation, content creation, and social interaction [13]. For K-pop fandoms, platforms like Twitter, Instagram, and dedicated forums play a vital role in fan activities, including information sharing, community building, and fan-driven projects [14]. The unique characteristics of fan culture, such as emotional investment, collective identity, and the pursuit of an immersive experience, necessitate tailored approaches in designing digital tools that cater to these communities [15]. Applying HCI principles to develop fan community tools involves creating intuitive, engaging, and aesthetically pleasing interfaces that resonate with the users' cultural and emotional contexts [16]. For BTS-Dash, this entails a user-centered design process that prioritizes ease of use, visual appeal, and the facilitation of fan engagement through curated content and interactive features.

Additionally, ensuring the trustworthiness and timeliness of aggregated content is crucial in maintaining user satisfaction and loyalty [17]. User Experience (UX) design plays a pivotal role in HCI, optimizing the usability, accessibility, and pleasure provided in the interaction between the user and the product [18, 19]. Research in this area emphasizes the importance of understanding user needs, behaviors, and contexts to design effective digital interfaces. This is particularly relevant for social media aggregators like BTS-Dash, whose design must cater to BTS fans' interests and interaction preferences. The strategies for engaging fan communities on digital platforms involve more than just con-tent aggregation; they include fostering a sense of community, interaction, and participation [20]. Studies have explored various aspects of online community engagement, including the role of content personalization, interactive features, and social networking tools in enhancing user engagement [21]. Incorporating features that enable personalization, community interaction, and content sharing for BTS-Dash could significantly improve the user experience.

2.6 Our Contributions

It isn't easy to find information about a specific topic when the authorities and experts are spread across different platforms and parts of the internet. Between that and the abundance of misinformation, it can be extremely difficult and time-consuming for an individual to find the information they are searching for [10, 22]. A dashboard that collects information on a particular topic from a set number of known and trusted sources on various platforms could be an incredibly useful tool for mitigating this problem [23]. To do this, the dashboard must be laid out effectively, allowing users to find and understand the information presented by the dashboard easily. This paper aims to create a dash-board that gathers information on a single topic from multiple sources and to test the efficacy of the dashboard in how well it displays the information collected to users. The topic of interest chosen for this dashboard is BTS, a Grammy award-nominated K-pop band called Bangtan Sonyeondan, or Bangtan Boys, frequently shortened to just "BTS." They are a seven-member band that debuted in 2013 and have since become one of the most popular bands in the world [24]. As one of the most popular bands today, BTS has an extensive, active online community built around them. It generates enormous amounts of data daily through discussions, fan works, and sharing official content [25]. The band members are also active on various social media platforms, with the band even having multiple official accounts on the same platform in some cases. Their followers across Twitter, Instagram, TikTok, and the proprietary fan platform Weverse are cumulatively over 200 million [26].

With a large volume of daily online activity and widespread activity across various parts of the inter-net, BTS is an ideal topic for a case study to test the efficacy of the dashboard design created for this paper. The primary goal of this paper is to develop whether the paradigm of trust, usability, and accessibility impacts the overall usage of such a dashboard [27, 28].

3   System Architecture and Technology

We used an iterative design model to develop BTS-Dash [29, 30], each designed to incrementally refine and enhance the application's features and user experience. Central to the BTS-Dash architecture is the division into client and server components (see Fig. 1). The server, implemented in Python, is engineered to manage a WebSocket server. This choice was dictated by the need for a robust, full-duplex communication channel capable of sustaining a persistent connection between the server and the client—a static Angular.js application [31]. This continuous connectivity is paramount for providing a seamless, dynamic user experience as it facilitates real-time updates and interactions. The client interface is developed using Angular.js, with Material Design for Bootstrap [32], enhancing the visual aspects and ensuring a consistent, user-friendly interface. Iteration 2 of BTS-Dash introduced Firebase [33] to the technology stack. It serves a dual purpose: to authenticate users, manage their sessions effectively, and deploy the application in a scalable cloud environment.

The application's data richness is sourced from various APIs, including Twitter [34], YouTube [35], and Spotify [36], allowing BTS-Dash to curate a comprehensive multimedia dashboard experience. The server-side architecture employs a feature-centric handler system, with each handler tasked with interpreting, processing, and responding to client-sent JSON messages. For instance, the Tasks Handler exclusively manages task-oriented communications, processing the logic and issuing appropriate responses. This modular approach aids in maintaining clarity of purpose within the server's operations, enabling a scalable and maintainable codebase. The client employs a subscription model to handle server-sent messages. Components within the client application register callback function with the Socket service, predicated on specific message channels. Upon receiving a message, the Socket service invokes the relevant callback, which then delegates the message to the appropriate component for further handling. These design and development philosophies ensure that BTS-Dash is usable, accessible, and scalable for future purposes. Note that this dashboard was developed between 2020 and 2022, so we continue to refer to X as Twitter in this paper.

4   Software Artifact Design: Iteration 1

4.1   Banner

The header consists of a banner image at the top, followed by the name of the website and a sticky hamburger menu [37] that has a link back to the website's home page and a link that will allow the user to log in (see Fig. 1b).

4.2   Youtube and Spotify Player

A two-card layout displayed the latest YouTube videos and the top ten BTS songs on Spotify (see Fig. 2a and 2b). As the topic of the dashboard is a music group and one that frequently posts choreographed music videos, the two platforms that host their music and music videos were deemed the most relevant and, therefore, were placed first on the

(a)   **(b)**

Fig. 1. a. Illustrates the system architecture of BTS-Dash that was followed across all iterations. **b.** Header for the Dashboard

(a)   **(b)**

Fig. 2. a. YouTube and Spotify section. **b.** Twitter Feed

page. Both cards had a button that linked back to the YouTube channel and the Spotify profile, each in the pink-purple gradient to add color to the otherwise white cards, and it's the relevant social media logo.

4.3   Twitter Scroller

As the band actively engaged with fans on Twitter, having a feed was prioritized. The feed displayed the ten most recent tweets from BTS's two official Twitter accounts. The description text was added to clarify and encourage user interaction with the dashboard. Each tweet had a container around it to create a visual separation between tweets. Along with the tweet timestamps, usernames and a link to the tweet were included to ensure the dashboard user has a sense that they are accessing reliable information.

4.4   Twitter Engagement Graphs

The second part of this dashboard contained information behind a verification screen. The first card on this page displayed #BTS-related statistics from Twitter, such as likes and retweets, to categorize the data. The x and y axis showed the amount of activity and time respectively. A short description below the visualization provided context and clarity. Below are two additional visualizations with the likes and retweets shown separately (see Figs. 3a and 3b). These two are vertically oriented to provide some visual difference from the combined graph above, and the colors of each are kept consistent with the combined graph.

(a)   (b)

Fig. 3. a. Twitter Activity Graphs showing individual likes and retweets. **b.** Twitter likes and retweets combined.

In social media, metrics such as likes and retweets hold substantial importance, serving multiple critical functions to users and the platforms. They act as essential gauges of engagement, capturing user interaction and helping to assess a post's impact or potential virality. Retweets extend a post's reach beyond its original audience, serving as a vital tool for information dissemination and awareness campaigns. Likes are a form of immediate feedback, offering content creators a quick nod of approval or appreciation from their audience without the commitment required by a comment or retweet. Together, these metrics serve as social proof, bolstering the perceived value of content and influencing further user engagement and following. The algorithmic implications of likes and retweets play a pivotal role in shaping the visibility of content within feeds, with highly engaged content often prioritized by platform recommendation systems. Moreover, likes and retweets are leveraged for sentiment analysis, providing insights into public opinion on various topics, which can inform and refine marketing strategies and public relations efforts. This multifaceted importance of engagement metrics underscores their relevance in the digital communication landscape, offering a nuanced understanding of public interaction and sentiment [7, 38, 39].

4.5 Spotify Metrics

In addition to being the top platform for streaming BTS's music, Spotify provides a substantial body of metrics about each song produced by an artist to help artists identify what makes a particular song popular. The graph of audio features is a vertically oriented bar chart that shows the audio features, according to Spotify, of the most popular BTS song at the time of the website's development [40–43]. Audio features are followed by the top 10 most popular BTS songs categorized by geographical region. These countries were chosen based on a third-party platform. This feature has a description to clarify the dataset's source to avoid misconceptions. The evidence-based metrics from Twitter and Spotify indicate whether the product (BTS) can convert Twitter Likes and Retweets into music streams (see Fig. 4).

Iteration 1 was completed, and a comprehensive review was conducted after doing usability evaluations with undergraduate students in Computer Science. These students

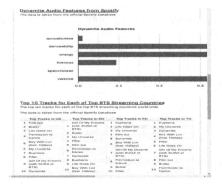

Fig. 4. Spotify metrics and preference selection

were part of a Software Engineering cohort, and although they were not domain experts or fans, they provided some crucial initial insight. The important conclusion was that the two-page dashboard needed to be a usable option, and the login system for a dashboard like this needs to be more intuitive. It best allows a social aggregator dashboard to be consolidated and streamlined. As all the information we display falls under the public domain, a login system is an over-engineered approach.

5 Software Artifact Design: Iteration 2

Iteration 2 was developed on a refactored Iteration 1 framework, and features were streamlined and consolidated for a uniform experience. This section only highlights significant changes that the dashboard underwent during this phase.

5.1 Header Section

(a)   (b)

Fig. 5. a. Header of BTS-Dash. **b.** Expanded About BTS section

The header image and pink-purple gradient were kept the same, but we removed the hamburger menu from the bar. We need the website title, BTS-Dash, and iconography associated with BTS and their fanbase to increase visibility. These two logos are commonly used in fan spaces, which is conversely the purpose of this website. A compact layout of the Spotify player was used and moved into the *About section* to tie the description with the product - music. A small sidebar was placed in the middle of the page (see Fig. 5b) to allow the user to navigate to primary features on the main page. The two-page version was merged into a one-page dashboard to improve accessibility and avoid infinite scrolling (see Fig. 5a and 5b).

5.2 Twitter Feed

Fig. 6. a. Twitter feeds, with official tweets and trending tweets (Right). b. YouTube feeds for BTS and Hybe Labels (Left)

This iteration combined the two Twitter feeds into one row (see Fig. 6a). Additionally, they were placed at the top of the webpage since Twitter is the social media platform that BTS is the most active [44]. It was carefully designed to enhance user experience. Each card is labeled with a clear and concise title and features an underlined subtitle [45]. This subtitle provides users with valuable information, indicating the last time the feed content was updated and the frequency of these updates. It ensures users have the most current data and understand the regularity of content refreshes.

5.3 YouTube Feeds

This iteration has two YouTube feeds instead of one (see Fig. 6b). Both feeds are displayed together in a new row and are the second main feature on the page. As a K-pop band, a significant part of their image is heavily choreographed dancing in music videos, so having the ability to watch the most recent music videos released is essential. On the left side, we have preferred the band's personal YouTube channel. On the right, we have also included the YouTube feed of their record label. Both cards have links to the respective YouTube channels.

5.4 Metrics Dropdowns (New Feature)

A metrics section was added, as metrics are a common and essential component of dashboards and provide a way for dashboard users to quantify how well the dashboard's topic is doing online (see Fig. 7a). The four subcategories under Metrics are Engagement, Likes & Shares, Followers, and Impressions. These were chosen based on research into other existing dashboards to determine precisely how online performance is quantified [46].

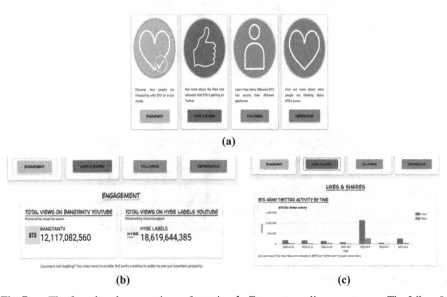

Fig. 7. a. The four dropdown sections of metrics. b. Engagement live counters. c. The Likes & Shares section shows the graph of BTS Twitter activity

The Engagement section (see Fig. 7b) has two live counters, updated every ten seconds by *Mixerno.space* [47] and show the total number of views both YouTube channels show above. The total views are significant to ascertain how many people engage *passively* with BTS content online. The band's channel is on the left to mirror the layout of the YouTube feed higher on the page. Both counters are labeled appropriately and have subtitles with hyperlinks to the website the counters are pulling from. As with all sections with these live counters, the bottom contains a message about enabling cookies to ensure the counters are visible.

5.5 Likes & Shares

Contrasting with the passive interactions of the Engagement section, the Likes & Shares section (see Fig. 7c) is meant to show how many people are *actively* interacting with BTS content, primarily by leaving likes on their posts on Twitter or by sharing their posts directly via retweeting them. It contains a bar graph comparing the total number of likes and retweets that the top posts in the band's hashtag on Twitter. The likes are in dark pink, and the retweets are in blue. These two colors are picked from the secondary palette set out by this data section since yellow was already used in the above Twitter feed. The pink was explicitly chosen to show how many likes there were to keep with the convention of likes being displayed frequently as pink or red hearts on social media platforms. The graph has the appropriate title, a subtitle clarifying which hashtag is displayed, and a time-period snapshot.

5.6 Followers

The Followers section allows the users to compare the size of the following BTS across each significant social media platform since choosing to follow BTS on any of these platforms is another form of active interaction that fans can do. Twitter and Instagram are the two most frequently used platforms, and both have a text and image-based posting method; the counters for the band's Twitter and Instagram accounts have been put together in one card at the top of the section. Next, since both are video-based posts, we have put together the counters for the band's YouTube and TikTok accounts. We have put the Spotify player by itself last because it has the fewest followers. All cards link to the site the counters are from and specify the names of each account (Fig. 8a).

5.7 Impressions

(a)   (b)   (c)

Fig. 8. a. The contents of the Followers section show live follower counters (Right). **b.** The Impressions section shows the Audio Features graph and the Top Tracks charts (Left). **c.** Contents of the Impressions section, with the Views/Likes/Dislikes counters

Impressions represent the final sub-category meant to give users a way to see how the band is perceived online, good, or bad, and how strong that perception is. The Impressions section contains two columns. In the left column, we have a bar graph of the audio features of one of their songs, shown in Fig. 8b. At the time of development for this iteration, the song chosen was their most popular one. The data is taken from Spotify, and Spotify chose the metrics displayed in that graph. Following the Spotify graph, live counters track the total views, likes, and dislikes for the same track as in the audio features graph. These are shown in Fig. 8c and were chosen so that the users could compare how many people liked the music video with how many people disliked the music video, in addition to how many times the video had been watched in total.

Though Spotify is the most popular platform for streaming BTS's music, YouTube is where fans go to watch their music videos. Their music videos are heavily choreographed, and the dancing is integral to BTS's reputation. Since we included the metrics from Spotify for their song, Butter, the likes, dislikes, and views counters for YouTube were included in this section to include impressions for both audio and visual content.

5.8   Limitations of Iteration 2

After the completion of Iteration 2, an internal review with the research team was conducted for code, layout, and design consistency. Several issues were identified with content display across different devices, such as spacing and cramped space with excessive information from API calls. As the live counters depended on third-party developers, limited customization was available, along with considerable downtime. These also relied on third-party cookies, making displaying on specific web browsers difficult. Google Charts [48] was used for graphs and charts in the data dropdowns and limits customizations. In the Impressions section, the audio features metrics from Spotify were difficult to comprehend due to a lack of explanation of what each feature on the graph meant.

6   Chapter Three: Iteration 3

This iteration primarily refined the features added in iterations 1 & 2 with only minor tweaks and improvements. In this iteration, Google Charts was replaced by Chart.js [49] as the library used for data visualization. Chart.js is JavaScript-based and has existing libraries to streamline its use with Angular apps. Additionally, it makes the graph more reactive, providing a seamless experience.

6.1   Back-End Changes

Our system's backend operations used task scheduling scripts for Firebase, which autonomously manage vital tasks. These include aggregating new data from external APIs such as Twitter and Spotify, updating our storage with this data, purging outdated records, and disseminating the latest data to user devices for seamless access. Central to this operation are two primary scripts that activate daily at 12:00 EST. This once-daily data retrieval strategy effectively curtails API calls, preserving our quota within the limits of our API key and averting potential service interruptions on our platform during high-traffic periods.

The database architecture of our website is optimized for speed and efficiency, particularly when loading data for user interaction. Upon the website's initiation by a user, internal scripts activate, instructing the database to dispatch stored Twitter and Spotify data to the website and to format it appropriately for display. This internal data transfer is significantly faster than direct API calls to Twitter or Spotify for each user session due to the inherent latency of external calls, which must navigate outside the website's system. Uniform storage of tweet data in JSON files ensures consistency, enabling straightforward code development for reliable data retrieval. This data organization allows for constructing analytical visuals like the weekly Twitter activity graph for the #BTS hashtag, utilizing a 12-day tweet record. Separately storing each day's data facilitates streamlined data management, avoiding the computational burden of parsing through a single, cumulative file. This approach simplifies backend file management and maintains a lean database by systematically replacing older files with new data, making the database compact and up-to-date.

6.2   Individual Feature Changes: Twitter Feeds, Metrics, and Impressions

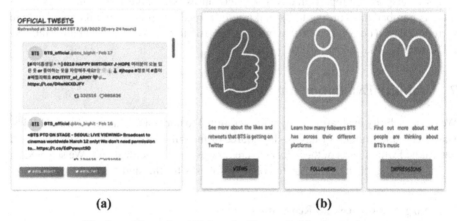

(a)   (b)

Fig. 9. a. The updated Twitter feed layout. b. Metrics section

The Twitter feed layout was updated to add a moused-over-dark effect along with the Like, and Retweet counts for each tweet displayed at the bottom. Additionally, the tweets now show the individual who retweeted them to clarify that all the tweets in the official BTS Twitter feed are actually from the official BTS Twitter accounts. The timestamps on the tweets were condensed to date and month. All these changes provide consistency with the appearance of Twitter feeds on the Twitter website itself (see Fig. 9a).

The Engagement section was eliminated in the Metrics section (see Fig. 9b) as the information was vague and minor. The Likes & Shares section was retitled to Views to match user expectations and label clarity.

The primary front-end design change was made to the YouTube section, as YouTube updated its API and web interface and removed the ability to see dislikes on videos. We removed the Impressions feature to view likes and dislikes from all platforms to minimize dependence on third-party counters, as they were unreliable. The Spotify

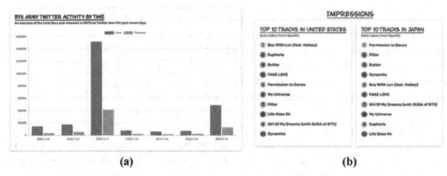

Fig. 10. a. Graph in the Views section. **b.** The new layout of the Top 10 Tracks by country charts in the Impressions section

audio analysis graph was also removed due to the metrics needing to be more readily understandable. We also removed Spotify's custom visualization cards and used a custom layout to display the top 10 tracks from 5 countries with large BTS followings. Each track is numbered according to its ranking for a specific country, and the numbers are surrounded by a colorful circle that matches the palette followed by the album Butter by BTS (see Fig. 10a and Fig. 10b).

7 Usability Evaluation for Iteration 3

We ran a usability evaluation study with Iteration 3 to understand the feasibility of BTS-Dash being the primary or day-to-day source of information about BTS. Specifically, I determined which parts of the website were intuitive and which weren't. We selected an online survey as the best method to collect responses for the study.

7.1 Target Audience and Recruitment

Our target audience was BTS fans, as someone who isn't a BTS fan would be unable to provide domain-specific information related to aesthetics, content comprehension, and choice of engagement metrics. The anonymous survey was given an Exempt status by the New College of Florida's IRB and administered via Qualtrics. Participants were above 18 years old and had reading and writing proficiency in English. Participants were recruited using snowball sampling through social media and student boards from the home institutions.

7.2 Study Goals

We identified four categories of information we wanted from the study, which were *1) Usability, 2) Trust, 3) Aesthetics, and 4) Miscellaneous.* Under the usability category, we were interested in understanding whether a) buttons, menus, and other interactive features behave as expected, b) titles and subtitles are clear and informative, and c) the website design encourages users to explore independently. For Trust, we were interested in learning a) Do users believe data presented in graphs, charts, and live counters? b) Do users believe we have the latest tweets? c) Do users understand the source of data displayed on the website? For the category Aesthetics, we wanted to learn whether a) users find the site attractive. b) Does the color scheme remind them of BTS? c) Do the chosen fonts remind them of BTS? d) Do the Twitter feeds remind users of Twitter? Additionally, we wanted feedback on the FAQ page and provided space for additional open-ended feedback.

7.3 Survey Design

We added a domain knowledge test to determine users' engagement level with BTS, along with the standard demographic questionnaire. Questions included information readily available on the news and information only long-term fans would know. The primary survey had nine task-based questions. An example of one of these questions can be seen above in Fig. 11. The task-based for each section of the website follows the same format and is focused on determining usability and data trust. This was done to determine if any sections of the site were less effective than the rest.

After the task-based questions, a block of questions asked the user about their overall satisfaction and likelihood of using the site again. A user's willingness to continue using a site can tell us a lot about their experience on the site since it is very well known that a person will not continue to use websites that they had a poor experience on [50]. This block also asks questions that fall into the category of Trust, asking them how much they believe the data presented and whether they feel that enough information is being provided.

The final block of questions for the users taking the survey asks them the Aesthetics questions to determine if the design choices adequately remind them of the topic of BTS and if the website is something they would want to use on their own. It also asks the users if they can think of other uses for websites like BTS-Dash. This aims to determine if users feel that this type of dashboard layout could be helpful for any topics other than BTS since the underlying goal is to assess the efficacy of this layout for displaying information. There is also a free response box for users to provide other comments.

7.4 Results

Six participants completed all the responses; they were in the 18–25 age range, resided in the United States, and self-reported English as their primary language. Additionally, 2 participants completed part of the survey. Depending on the task, the number of participants is mentioned in the results to ensure data consistency. Most participants used Twitter as their primary source of information on BTS (62.5%), with YouTube as the next largest primary source. YouTube was the most popular secondary choice given. These results support our decision to have Twitter and YouTube feeds at the top of the dashboard. A quarter of our participants used a mobile device; the rest accessed it on a computer. This was a critical distinction yet a reassuring statistic to ensure the application worked on both devices. As the number of participants is low, we are not inferring statistical significance but instead identifying similar patterns from the responses.

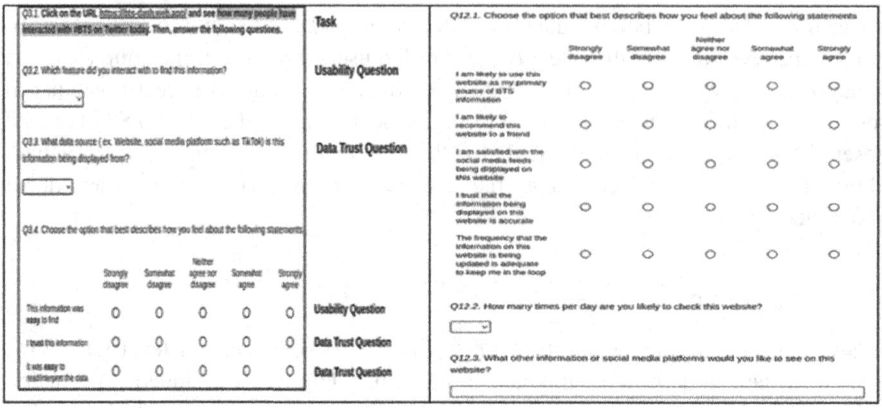

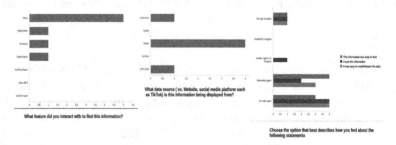

Fig. 11. An example of one of the task-based questions on the survey, with categories labeled.

Task 1 (Fig. 12) shows the responses to the question asked about the activity graph for #BTS, which 5 of 8 participants could locate successfully. One participant thought the question asked them to find the #BTS Twitter feed and located that feature instead. Another participant found the follower counter for Twitter instead of the graph. One participant went to the Impressions section, which does not have any Twitter information. Overall, while 5 of 8 participants found what the question asked them to, 2 additional participants located a similar feature, suggesting that they needed clarification on the wording of the survey question rather than the website. This can be seen in Fig. 12. 4 participants correctly identified Twitter as the data source.

In comparison, 7 of 8 participants reported that the data was easy to find and interpret. 6 of 8 participants said that they trusted the data, and 1 participant was neutral on trusting the data. One participant reported that the data was difficult to find or interpret and that they needed to trust it. This participant was likely the one who needed help locating any Twitter-related features.

Fig. 12. Graphs of the responses to Task 1

Task 2 asked users to locate the follower counter for TikTok. As seen in Fig. 13, 7 of 8 participants could locate the counter in the Followers section, and one could not. 6 of 7 participants reported the data source correctly for this question, with one person

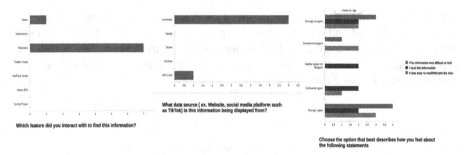

Fig. 13. Graphs of the responses to Task 2

incorrectly identifying BTS-Dash as the data source. This participant is likely the same participant who answered BTS-Dash in the first task and needs clarification about the survey question. One participant did not answer this question, most likely the participant who was unable to locate the counter in the first place. Despite more participants correctly locating the counter, half responded that the counters were challenging, and half responded that the counters were easy to find. Half responded that the counters were easy to read, and half answered that they were difficult to read. Half reported that they trusted the counters, a quarter reported that they were neutral on trusting them, and a quarter reported that they did not trust the counters. The increase in perceived difficulty in locating this feature could be because the specific counter participants were asked to find was at the bottom of the Followers section, meaning users had to scroll down instead of seeing it immediately after clicking on the Followers section. The increase in perceived difficulty in interpreting the data could be because the counters are labeled with the account's profile picture. BTS uses the same image for most of their profile pictures, making many of the counters look very similar. The decrease in trust is likely due to the fact that one of the live counters was unavailable during the survey period, meaning users saw an error message instead of a counter for one part of the Follower section.

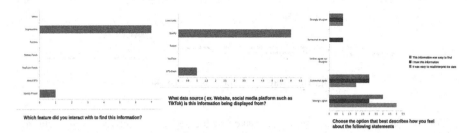

Fig. 14. Graphs of the responses to Task 3

Task 3 asked users to locate the Spotify charts. 7 of 8 users could identify the chart successfully, and the one user who did not find the chart instead located the Spotify player, suggesting confusion with the survey question rather than the website. This is shown in Fig. 14. One user again reported BTS-Dash as the data source, which is likely the same user. All other participants correctly identified the data source: 7 of 8 reported that the data was easy to find and interpret. 6 of 8 reported that they trusted the information. One participant reported difficulty finding, analyzing, and trusting the data. Given that all participants could locate the data and identify the data source, it is hard to determine what challenges this user encountered.

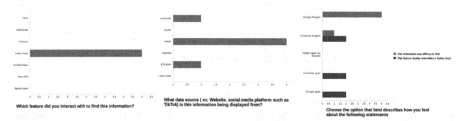

Fig. 15. Graph of the responses to Task 4

Task 4 asked the participants to locate the official Twitter feed. As shown in Fig. 15, all participants could do this successfully. This was likely the most straightforward feature because it was close to the top of the page. Two participants should have identified the data source. One participant, likely the same as before, again reported BTS-Dash as the data source. Another participant reported Livecounts as the data source. It needs to be clarified where the confusion happened for this participant since all participants were seemingly able to locate the Twitter feed. All participants reported that the feed was easy to find.4 of 6 participants felt that the Twitter feed on BTS-Dash resembled an actual Twitter feed, while 2 participants felt that it did not.

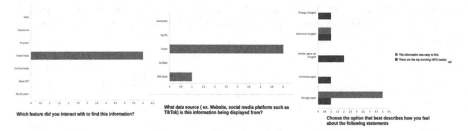

Fig. 16. Graph of responses to Task 4a

For this part of Task 4a, users were asked to locate the Twitter feed with trending tweets. Again, all participants were able to locate the feed successfully. This can be seen in Fig. 16. Except for the one participant who consistently answered BTS-Dash as the data source, all participants correctly identified the data source as Twitter. 5 of 6 participants reported that this feature was very easy to find. One participant reported that it was somewhat difficult to find. The challenges this participant experienced need to be clarified, given that they could locate the feed successfully. The participants reported a wide range of levels of trust for this feature. This is most likely due to the highly subjective nature of this feature. Since this feature is meant to show the top trending tweet from Twitter, it will display tweets from any user who ends up trending in the BTS hashtag, which may be something other than users that our participants follow or have even heard of.

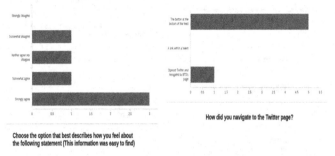

Choose the option that best describes how you feel about
the following statement (This information was easy to find)

Fig. 17. Graph of responses to Task 4b

For Task 4b, users were asked to locate the button that linked them to BTS's Twitter page directly; 5 of 6 participants were able to use the button to open Twitter. 4 of 6 participants reported that the button was easy to find, one person reported that it was neither easy nor difficult, and one person reported that it was somewhat difficult to find. The participant who reported that the button was difficult to find was most likely also the participant who could not find the button. It is possible that this user did not realize that the buttons at the bottom of the Twitter feeds were clickable (see Fig. 17).

Task 6 asked participants to play a song with the Spotify player. All participants could locate the Spotify player and reported that it was easy to find. As with the Twitter feeds, users likely found this feature easily because it was at the top of the webpage.

Task 7 asked users to read about BTS in the About section. All participants were able to locate the information in the About section. Participants needed help with determining the data source of the About section. Half of the participants incorrectly answered that BTS-Dash was the source of this information. 5 of 6 participants reported that the About section was straightforward to find, and one reported having difficulty finding it. This may be the same participant who was also unable to find the button linked to Twitter and YouTube, indicating some general difficulty in finding our buttons.

Task 8 asked users to use the navigation bar on the side of the website. 4 of 6 participants correctly located the navigation bar, which can be seen in Fig. 18. 4 participants reported that the navigation bar was easy to find, which were most likely the same 4 participants who could locate it. The other two participants who could not locate the bar reported that it was difficult to find or that it was neither easy nor difficult.

7.5 Perception and Aesthetics

Overall, all 6 participants reported that they trusted the information displayed on the website. This indicates that our participants see the website as trustworthy. 4 of 6 participants felt that the information was updated frequently enough. One participant felt

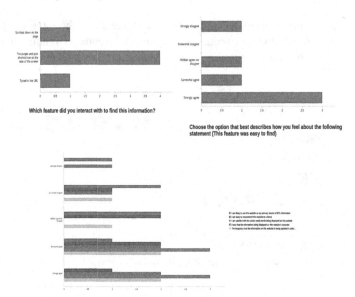

Fig. 18. Graphs of the responses Task 8. Figure 18 Graph of the responses to the intent of use questions

neutral about it, and one felt that it wasn't quite frequent enough. 4 of 6 participants felt that the social media feeds present were sufficient, while 2 of 6 felt that there were not enough. 3 of 6 participants reported that they were likely to recommend the website to a friend, 1 participant felt neutral, and one reported that they were unlikely to recommend it to a friend. 3 of 6 participants reported that they were unlikely to use this website as a primary source of BTS information, 2 reported that they were neither likely nor unlikely, and only one reported that they were likely to use this as a primary source of information about BTS. All of these can be seen in Fig. 18. Given that the majority of the participants use Twitter as their primary source, participants would not consider BTS-Dash as an adequate replacement for Twitter, given that BTS-Dash does not have a way to allow for interacting with other fans.

Additionally, the users who reported they were unlikely to consider BTS-Dash as a primary source were also likely the same ones who were not satisfied with the amount of information and the frequency of updating and were unlikely to suggest it to a friend. All participants responded that they would check BTS-Dash once per day. This makes sense, given that the website updates once a day. This answer could indicate that all participants clearly understood the update frequency of the website.

All participants agreed that the images and icons reminded them of BTS, and 5 of 6 agreed that the color scheme reminded them of BTS. The one participant who disagreed felt neutral about it. However, only 2 of 6 felt that the fonts reminded them of BTS, with 1 being neutral and 3 6 feeling that the fonts did not remind them of BTS. When asked about other uses for a website like BTS, only one participant responded and suggested a forum-like site with more options for users to interact with each other. While this makes sense in context with the other feedback received in this section, it needs to determine if users see this layout as effective for this dashboard style.

Though no definitive statements can be made due to the study's small sample size, initial data indicates that most layout choices were adequate.

Participants had the least difficulty locating features that were higher up on the webpage, meaning that the choice to place the most relevant features first was an effective one. Overall, the majority of participants were able to locate every feature. Participants needed help locating features requiring them to click buttons with minimal text, such as the links to the external Twitter and YouTube pages and the navigation sidebar.

Although most participants could locate every feature, many still reported that they would not use BTS-Dash as a new primary source of BTS information. This results from the need for more options for users to interact directly with other users. This desire is particular to the target audience of the topic chosen since BTS fans are used to a large and interactive online community. Given that the goal with BTS-Dash is to develop guidelines for more general dashboard design, features that involved direct user interaction were not included since that is not a generalizable feature in the same way that social media feeds are. In a future study, participants should instead be asked if they would consider BTS-Dash a source of information at all rather than precisely the primary source.

Future work on this would address the areas where the dashboard's design was less effective and where the study was less effective. With the dashboard, the areas that could use improvement seem to be subtitles and buttons. To make their intended use more self-evident to users, they changed the text, increasing contrast or font size and changing the font itself since the font seemed less effective in reminding users of the topic. The survey, as mentioned, was small, so a larger sample size would be useful for future work to make more conclusive statements. Additionally, at least one participant was confused by the wording of some questions on the survey, such as the participant who did not understand what the data source questions asked. Therefore, future work should include reworking some survey questions to clarify them for prospective participants.

8 Limitations and Conclusion

Though no definitive statements can be made due to the study's small sample size, initial data indicates that most layout choices were adequate. Participants had the least difficulty locating features that were higher up on the webpage, meaning that the choice to place the most relevant features first was an effective one. Overall, the majority of participants were able to locate every feature. Participants needed help locating features requiring them to click buttons with minimal text, such as the links to the external Twitter and YouTube pages and the navigation sidebar. Even though most participants could locate every feature, many still reported not using BTS-Dash as a new primary source of BTS information. This seems to result from the lack of options for users to interact directly with other users. This desire is particular to the target audience of the topic chosen since BTS fans are used to a large and interactive online community. As this work was conducted from 2020 to 2022, the Twitter API has evolved drastically, eliminating open-source access to the tweets; not having a paid subscription would limit data aggregation on this level.

9   Design Guidelines, Future Work, and Extending Beyond BTS-Dash

Given that the goal with BTS-Dash is to develop guidelines for more general dashboard design, features that involved direct user interaction were not included since that is not a generalizable feature in the same way that social media feeds are. In a future study, participants should instead be asked if they would consider BTS-Dash a source of information at all rather than precisely the primary source. In conclusion, the development of BTS-Dash aimed to establish guidelines that could be applied to the broader scope of dashboard design. Notably, features requiring direct user interaction were intentionally omitted from this iteration. This design choice was predicated on the understanding that such features possess a different level of generalizability than, for instance, the integration of social media feeds. During the study, it became evident that enhancements in the dashboard's subtitles and buttons could significantly augment user comprehension and interaction. In response, modifications were made to the text, contrast, font size, and font selection to render the dashboard's thematic elements more intuitive and accessible to users.

The pilot survey, albeit limited in scope, provided invaluable insights. However, future studies will require a larger cohort of participants to derive more substantial and statistically significant conclusions. Additionally, a refinement of the survey's phrasing is warranted, as evidenced by participant confusion over specific questions, particularly those about data sources.

Future investigations will also explore the potential of BTS-Dash as a foundational model for single-topic dashboards. The modular design of BTS-Dash, facilitated by Angular's component-based architecture, allows for effortless customization and scalability. Adaptations to color themes and data sources will be pivotal in tailoring the dashboard to various topics.

Efforts are underway to leverage the insights garnered from this study to craft a preliminary framework for a regional environmental issues tracker. This application will amalgamate Twitter feeds with daily guidelines from relevant ecological and local governmental entities, aiming for a cohesive and accessible user experience [51].

During the critical COVID-19 pandemic, the need for such an aggregator became acutely apparent. The disparate and evolving guidelines from numerous agencies highlighted the challenges associated with data organization and accessibility, particularly aggregating data from multiple sources cohesively. Consequently, this paper aspires to offer preliminary guidelines and a versatile framework that integrates many data inputs.

The overarching takeaway from BTS-Dash is that, while the allure of interactivity was universally noted among participants, a dashboard devoid of such features remains practical for specific domains. Specifically, topics that prioritize the dissemination of information—like environmental statistics or health guidelines—may not necessitate an interactive component. The principles of usability, trust, and accessibility remain paramount, as they do across all facets of dashboard development. The lessons learned here will be a cornerstone for future endeavors in creating informative and user-friendly dashboards.

Acknowledgments. We acknowledge the support of NCF undergraduate students Karl Dinang, Vlad Tsimoshchanka and Connar Williams for their review and feedback for Iteration 1 and Iteration 2. This work is part of Alex Hinton's undergraduate honor's thesis [29] we acknowledge the support of committee members.

References

1. Few, S.: Information Dashboard Design: The Effective Visual Communication of Data. O'Reilly Media, Inc. (2006)
2. McFarland, L.A., Ployhart, R.E.: Social media: a contextual framework to guide research and practice. J. Appl. Psychol. **100**, 1653–1677 (2015). https://doi.org/10.1037/a0039244
3. Howard, P.N., Parks, M.R.: Social media and political change: capacity, constraint, and consequence. J. Commun. **62**, 359–362 (2012). https://doi.org/10.1111/j.1460-2466.2012.01626.x
4. Wang, Y.D., Emurian, H.H.: An overview of online trust: concepts, elements, and implications. Comput. Hum. Behav. **21**, 105–125 (2005)
5. Wang, P., Hu, Y., Li, Q.: The trust-building process in the social media environment of rumour spreading. In: Companion of the 2020 ACM International Conference on Supporting Group Work, Sanibel Island Florida USA, pp. 95–98. ACM (2020). https://doi.org/10.1145/3323994.3369882
6. Li, A., Farzan, R., Lin, Y.-R., Zhou, Y., Teng, X., Yan, M.: Identifying and understanding social media gatekeepers: a case study of gatekeepers for immigration related news on Twitter. Proc. ACM Hum.-Comput. Interact. **6**, 1–25 (2022). https://doi.org/10.1145/3555195
7. Liu, I.L., Cheung, C.M., Lee, M.K.: Understanding Twitter usage: What drive people continue to tweet (2010)
8. Bruns, A., Stieglitz, S.: Towards more systematic *Twitter* analysis: metrics for tweeting activities. Int. J. Soc. Res. Methodol. **16**, 91–108 (2013). https://doi.org/10.1080/13645579.2012.756095
9. Nielsen, J.: Usability inspection methods. Presented at the Conference Companion on Human Factors in Computing Systems (1994)
10. Lin, C.-Y., Li, T.-Y., Chen, P.: An information visualization system to assist news topics exploration with social media. In: Proceedings of the 7th 2016 International Conference on Social Media & Society, pp. 1–9. Association for Computing Machinery, New York (2016). https://doi.org/10.1145/2930971.2930995
11. Ryerson Misinformation Dashboard. https://cancovid.ca/resources/ryerson-misinformation-dashboard/. Accessed 03 Mar 2024
12. Research at the Clemson University Social Media Listening Center. www.clemson.edu/centers-institutes/smlc/research.html. Accessed 03 Mar 2024
13. Jenkins, H.: Fans, Bloggers, and Gamers: Exploring Participatory Culture. NYU Press (2006)
14. More than K-pop fans: BTS fandom and activism amid COVID-19 outbreak: Media Asia: Vol 48, No 4 - Get Access. https://www.tandfonline.com/doi/full/https://doi.org/10.1080/01296612.2021.1944542. Accessed 03 Mar 2024
15. Cooper, B.L.: Understanding Fandom: An Introduction to the Study of Media Fan Culture. Popular Music and Society (2015)
16. Norman, D.A.: Human-centered design considered harmful. Interactions **12**, 14–19 (2005)
17. Fogg, B.J.: Persuasive technology: using computers to change what we think and do. Ubiquity. **2002**, 2 (2002). https://doi.org/10.1145/764008.763957
18. Hassenzahl, M., Tractinsky, N.: User experience - a research agenda. Behav. Inf. Technol. **25**, 91–97 (2006). https://doi.org/10.1080/01449290500330331

19. Bergin, J.: Adapting Research Methods to Construct a Learning Design Research Agenda (2016)
20. Annamalai, B., Yoshida, M., Varshney, S., Pathak, A.A., Venugopal, P.: Social media content strategy for sport clubs to drive fan engagement. J. Retail. Consum. Serv. **62**, 102648 (2021). https://doi.org/10.1016/j.jretconser.2021.102648
21. Kang, M., Shin, D., Gong, T.: The role of personalization, engagement, and trust in online communities. Inf. Technol. People **29**, 580–596 (2016). https://doi.org/10.1108/ITP-01-2015-0023
22. Diakopoulos, N., De Choudhury, M., Naaman, M.: Finding and assessing social media information sources in the context of journalism. In: Proceedings of the SIGCHI Conference on Human Factors in Computing Systems, pp. 2451–2460. Association for Computing Machinery, New York (2012). https://doi.org/10.1145/2207676.2208409
23. Tsou, M.-H., et al.: Social media analytics and research test-bed (SMART dashboard). In: Proceedings of the 2015 International Conference on Social Media & Society, pp. 1–7. Association for Computing Machinery, New York (2015). https://doi.org/10.1145/2789187.2789196
24. Courtney, M., Jin, D.Y.: "You can't help but love them": BTS, transcultural fandom, and affective identities. Korea J. **60**, 100–127 (2020). https://doi.org/10.25024/KJ.2020.60.1.100
25. #KpopTwitter achieves new record of 6.7 billion Tweets globally in 2020. https://blog.x.com/en_us/topics/insights/2021/kpoptwitter-achieves-new-record-of-6-billion-tweets-globally-in-2020. Accessed 03 Mar 2024
26. BTS smash followers record on Instagram, Twitter and TikTok. https://www.guinnessworldrecords.com/news/2022/3/bts-smash-followers-record-on-instagram-twitter-and-tiktok-694194. Accessed 04 Mar 2024
27. Petrie, H., Hamilton, F., King, N.: Tension, what tension? Website accessibility and visual design. In: Proceedings of the 2004 International Cross-Disciplinary Workshop on Web Accessibility (W4A), pp. 13–18. Association for Computing Machinery, New York (2004). https://doi.org/10.1145/990657.990660
28. Nielsen, J.: Trust or bust: Communicating trustworthiness in web design. Jacob Nielsen's Alertbox (1999)
29. Hinton, A.: BTS-Dash: A Multi-Platform Social Media Aggregator (2022). https://ncf.sobek.ufl.edu/AA00027447/00001?search=alex
30. Hinton, A.: hintona/bts-dash (2022). https://github.com/hintona/bts-dash
31. Angular. https://angular.io/. Accessed 03 Mar 2024
32. Material Design for Bootstrap 5 & 4. https://mdbootstrap.com/. Accessed 03 Mar 2024
33. Firebase | Google's Mobile and Web App Development Platform. https://firebase.google.com/. Accessed 03 Mar 2024
34. Twitter API Documentation. https://developer.twitter.com/en/docs/twitter-api. Accessed 03 Mar 2024
35. YouTube Data API. https://developers.google.com/youtube/v3. Accessed 03 Mar 2024
36. Web API | Spotify for Developers. https://developer.spotify.com/documentation/web-api. Accessed 03 Mar 2024
37. kps3admin: The 3 Golden Rules of Sticky Menu Navigation. https://contentsquare.com/blog/the-3-golden-rules-of-sticky-menu-navigation/. Accessed 03 Mar 2024
38. Aisyah, A.: Korean-English language translational action of k-pop social media content: a case study on bangtan sonyeondan's (BTS) official twitter. 3L Southeast Asian J. English Lang. Stud. **23**, 67–80 (2017). https://doi.org/10.17576/3L-2017-2303-05
39. Pancer, E., Poole, M.: The popularity and virality of political social media: hashtags, mentions, and links predict likes and retweets of 2016 U.S. presidential nominees' tweets. Soc. Influence **11**, 259–270 (2016). https://doi.org/10.1080/15534510.2016.1265582

40. Sharma, N., Pareek, P., Pathak, P., Sakariya, N.: Predicting music popularity using machine learning algorithm and music metrics available in spotify. JDMS **09**, 10–19 (2022). https://doi.org/10.53422/JDMS.2022.91102
41. Nijkamp, R.: Prediction of product success: explaining song popularity by audio features from Spotify data. https://essay.utwente.nl/75422/. Accessed 01 Mar 2024
42. Essential Spotify Metrics Gitnux. https://gitnux.org/spotify-metrics/. Accessed 01 Mar 2024
43. Voigt, K.-I., Buliga, O., Michl, K.: Passion for music: the case of spotify. In: Voigt, K.-I., Buliga, O., Michl, K. (eds.) Business Model Pioneers: How Innovators Successfully Implement New Business Models, pp. 143–155. Springer, Cham (2017). https://doi.org/10.1007/978-3-319-38845-8_12
44. Ngo, D.C.L.: Measuring the aesthetic elements of screen designs. Displays **22**, 73–78 (2001). https://doi.org/10.1016/S0141-9382(01)00053-1
45. Dashboard Design Best Practices - 4 Key Principles. https://www.sisense.com/4-design-principles-creating-better-dashboards/. Accessed 03 Mar 2024
46. Technologies, B.: How to Design a Powerful Social Media Dashboard: 5 Tips. https://basis.com/blog/social-media-dashboard. Accessed 03 Mar 2024
47. Mixerno.Space - The advanced way of checking statistics for Youtube, Twitter and more! https://mixerno.space. Accessed 03 Mar 2024
48. Charts. https://developers.google.com/chart. Accessed 03 Mar 2024
49. Chart.js. https://www.chartjs.org/. Accessed 03 Mar 2024
50. Altaboli, A., Lin, Y.: Investigating effects of screen layout elements on interface and screen design aesthetics. Adv. Hum.-Comput. Interact. **2011**, 1–10 (2011)
51. Skripnikov, A., Wagner, N., Shafer, J., Beck, M., Sherwood, E., Burke, M.: Using localized Twitter activity to assess harmful algal bloom impacts of Karenia brevis in Florida, USA. Harmful Algae **110**, 102118 (2021)

Improving Usability in Open Source Projects Through State Transition Diagrams: A Case Study on Sports Tactics Board

Lucrecia Llerena[1]([⊠]) [iD], Paola Benitez[1] [iD], John W. Castro[2] [iD], and Ericka Bravo[1] [iD]

[1] Faculty of Engineering Sciences, Quevedo State Technical University, Quevedo, Ecuador
{lllerena,pbenitez,ericka.bravo2018}@uteq.edu.ec
[2] Departamento de Ingeniería Informática y Ciencias de la Computación,
Universidad de Atacama, Copiapó, Chile
john.castro@uda.cl

Abstract. Open Source Software (OSS) is software whose source code is accessible to the public, allowing its modification and distribution at no cost. This feature encourages the active collaboration of the community of developers, who come together to learn and contribute to the project. The objective of this research work has been to validate the incorporation of the adapted State Transition Diagrams technique in the Open Source Software project "Sports Tactics Board" to improve its usability. The research results reveal that implementing this technique facilitated the understanding of the requirements and functionalities of the software, as well as the identification and efficient resolution of errors. In addition, using the State Transition Diagrams technique increased user satisfaction and adoption of the software. Despite the challenges and difficulties encountered in applying this technique, such as the need for closer collaboration between developers and usability experts, the findings indicate that implementing techniques during the OSS development process can significantly improve its usability.

Keywords: Open-Source Software · Usability Techniques; Evaluation · State Transition Diagram

1 Introduction

Open Source Software (OSS) is a term that refers to software whose source code is accessible and can be modified and distributed by anyone. This means that, rather than being controlled by a single company or individual, the software is collaboratively developed by a worldwide community of programmers [1]. The term "open source" or "free software" dates back to the GNU projects. This type of software aims to prioritize freedom over price, allowing many users to use it free of charge to run, distribute, study, and improve it [2]. Rather than providing unrestricted access to the source code, the concept of free software is broader.

OSS has unusual features compared to commercial systems. These features include: (i) Global collaboration: OSS allows programmers worldwide to collaborate in developing and improving the software, which brings a wide variety of perspectives and skills.

A. Coman and S. Vasilache (Eds.): HCII 2024, LNCS 14703, pp. 44–59, 2024.
https://doi.org/10.1007/978-3-031-61281-7_3

(ii) Free distribution: OSS can be distributed free to anyone anywhere in the world, meaning anyone can use it without paying expensive licensing fees. This means any-one can use them without paying expensive licensing fees. (iii) Lack of usability teams or experts: working with open-source projects can be more difficult due to the lack of teams or experts dedicated to software usability [3]. These features make OSS an attrac-tive alternative to commercial software and can significantly impact how people and organizations use and develop software.

According to Nielsen, usability is not limited to a single user interface feature but comprises several components such as learning, efficiency, productivity, numberability, errors, and satisfaction [2]. Considering this definition, usability evaluates software and achieves a quality standard in computer systems. Lack of usability in a project can result in sloppy interaction with the system and is often underestimated in commercial and non-commercial projects [2]. Therefore, it is essential to evaluate the usability of OSS projects by applying usability techniques.

There are several design techniques to improve software usability, such as parallel design, integrative design, interface content modeling, and state transition diagrams, among others. Thus, for example, the parallel design technique involves developing the functionality and usability of the software at the same time instead of focusing first on functionality and then on usability. This allows continuous feedback between design and development, resulting in more usable software [4]. The integrative design technique focuses on integrating different aspects of software, such as functionality, usability, and accessibility, from the beginning of development. These techniques aim to create software that is easy to use, accessible to all and meets the users' needs [4]. The interface content modeling technique focuses on the content and organization of the user interface, including elements such as buttons, labels, and navigation [5]. Its goal is to create a straightforward and efficient interface that is easy for users.

The Human-Computer Interaction (HCI) area studies all the factors related to the interaction between humans and interactive systems and applies techniques to improve their usefulness, efficiency, and usability [6]. However, these methods are particular to HCI and are governed by different principles than those of Software Engineering (this includes the OSS development process, which is source code-centric and does not allow many of the HCI usability techniques to be directly incorporated) [7].

The HCI technique of state transition diagrams has been selected for this research work. This technique is used to model the behavior of a system over time [5]. It is represented by a diagram that specifies the different states of the system and the transi-tions between them, indicating the conditions or events that cause these transitions. This technique helps represent and document the behavior of finite systems in software devel-opment, allowing developers to understand and plan the software project's development more effectively [5].

The choice of the state transition diagram technique for this research is justified for several reasons. First, this technique provides a concise, visual representation of software functionalities, which helps to understand its operation and the performance of specific tasks. In addition, developers can identify potential usability problems and troubleshoot them more efficiently by clearly visualizing the flow of tasks and transitions between states. This leads to more efficient software development and a final product with improved usability.

For this research, the OSS Sports Tactics Board (STB) project, a software designed for coaches and sports teams to create and visualize sports tactics and strategies, has been selected. This software allows users to create detailed and customized game plans for sports such as soccer, volleyball, field hockey, and rugby. Users can draw diagrams, add notes, and represent offensive and defensive plays. In addition, they can save and share their tactics with other team members. The software also includes animation and simulation tools that make it easy for coaches to visualize the development of plays in real time. The sports field generally lacks comprehensive tools that allow coaches to work efficiently and access all the possibilities offered by data digitization. Therefore, the OSS STB project is an ideal candidate for usability testing, given that its design has lagged behind current trends of minimalist designs and presents complexity in the presentation of information.

The present research aims to address the low usability of the STS project, using the state transition diagramming technique to identify and solve usability problems. The study examines how this technique can improve the software development process in an OSS project, adapting it specifically to the case of STS. This research aims to contribute to the OSS community by providing a deeper understanding of how the State Transition Diagramming technique can improve software development, promoting innovation and strengthening the STS community.

This document is organized as follows. Section 2 describes the related work. Section 3 describes the proposed solution. Section 4 discusses the results. Finally, Sect. 5 describes the conclusions and future research.

2 Related Work

Some research papers have reported on the use of usability techniques in OSS development [1, 3, 8–14].

The study presented by Dawood et al. [1] focuses on the importance of OSS usability to ensure its adoption and long-term success. To achieve this goal, they used mapping and analysis techniques to identify and evaluate the usability of various OSS projects. The mapping involved identifying and collecting relevant information about the selected OSS projects, including features, functionality, documentation, and support. The analysis involved evaluating the usability of these projects based on established criteria, such as accessibility, usability efficiency, and user satisfaction.

In their investigation, Yu et al. [3] present an OSS platform for computational histopathology with a user-friendly interface and image analysis tools to study biological tissues. It is suggested that this platform improves the efficiency and accuracy of disease diagnosis. The advantages of using an OSS platform, such as customization and extension of functionalities and the involvement of a broader community in its development, are discussed. However, although a usability evaluation is reported, the name of the usability technique used to perform the interface design is not specified.

Lamberti et al. [8] present a virtual character animation system based on motion capture and reconfigurable tangible interfaces. The system uses a technique to collect motion data from the user and a reconfigurable tangible interface to control and manipulate the virtual character animation intuitively. It has been tested in various applications, such as video games and education. It is a low-cost, easy-to-use system accessible to developers and end users. User testing and heuristic evaluation were used to assess ease of understanding and to detect usability issues in the interface design.

The work of Xiang et al. [9] focuses on the problem of uneven latency in data center networks using error-corrected encrypted files. The author proposes a traffic engineering approach to adjust latency for different file types and applications. In this study, usability evaluation is performed on designing and developing the interfaces and mechanisms used to implement and manage the system. However, no specific mention of which usability technique has been applied to perform this evaluation.

The study reported by Kafadar et al. [10] introduces RaspMI, a Raspberry Pi-based system for monitoring and recording seismic ambient noise. RaspMI consists of a Raspberry Pi and a connected accelerometer used to collect and store seismic noise data. Test results show that RaspMI efficiently collects and stores this data and is a cost-effective and scalable solution for ambient seismic noise monitoring. User testing and heuristic evaluation were performed to assess the comprehensibility and usability of the interface, identifying potential usability issues in the design.

In their investigation, Park and Lee [11] present an approach to compress photo-plethysmogram (PPG) signals efficiently and estimate heart and respiratory rates at the same time. The approach uses a machine learning-based signal compression algorithm to reduce the required data. Usability techniques, such as user testing and heuristic evaluation, are employed to evaluate the interface and detect potential usability-related design issues.

The study of Asame et al. [12] focuses on the design of a platform for quick-response quizzes or exams. The SUS survey was used to ensure the quality of the software and evaluate the user experience. In addition, the usability heuristic evaluation technique was used to evaluate the electronic assessment tool's effectiveness and ease of use.

The study by Dawood et al. [13] elaborates a unified criteria model for evaluating OSS usability. This is achieved using a fuzzy Delphi method, which is based on the agreement between usability and OSS experts to identify and define relevant criteria for usability evaluation in this context.

Finally, the study by Llerena et al. [14] investigates adopting of the visual brainstorming technique in open-source software (OSS) development, with HistoryCal OSS as a case study. It explores adapting this technique to OSS development features, such as voluntary participation and geographic distribution of collaborators. Despite challenges like low user participation and unfamiliarity with usability techniques, the study finds that adaptations benefit for OSS projects.

In conclusion, research papers report the use of usability techniques in OSS developments. However, none report the use of the State Transition Diagram technique. Although not all studies have detailed the usability techniques used, they have all demonstrated the importance of evaluating usability in OSS software design and development to ensure user satisfaction and the final product's success.

3 Proposed Solution

In this section, we describe the characteristics of the selected STS OSS project, followed by the state transition diagram technique as prescribed by Hix and Hartson [5], and finally, the results of applying the state transition diagrams technique in the STB project.

3.1 Design of the Case Study

The description of the case study followed the guidelines of Runeson et al. [15], focusing on understanding what was happening and then describing how we applied the adapted technique to improve the usability of the OSS project. A case study was conducted to incorporate the adapted technique state transition diagrams in the OSS project. This study seeks to determine whether it is feasible to integrate the adapted technique in an OSS project and to evaluate the usability of the selected OSS project. In this research, we detail the steps implemented to integrate the technique and report how the usability evaluation was carried out with the participation of the OSS community. The case study was based on the research question: How do we integrate the state transition diagramming technique into the design activities of the OSS development process?

As discussed earlier in this study, the state transition diagrams technique was used in an OSS project called STB. This digital tool is used in various sports to plan and visualize game tactics and strategies. The software allows coaches and players to create graphical representations of the playing field and players' movements to facilitate communication and understanding of the tactics to be implemented. We used the SourceForge web platform, specialized in the OSS community, to find the project object of this research. The SourceForge platform allows filtering options by operating system, category, license, language, programming language, or status. STB was chosen as the software to apply the usability technique in our case.

The graphical interface of STB is very unintuitive. Generally, it consists of a main window showing the playing field, where different elements can be drawn, such as players, balls, and passing lines. It also usually has a toolbar, where the drawing, selection, and editing tools are located, as well as different configuration and customization options. Figure 1 shows the main interface of the OSS STB project.

3.2 Description of the State Transition Diagrams Technique

The state transition diagram technique is widely used in software engineering to represent the evolution of a system over time. It consists of nodes representing system states and links representing possible transitions between them, labeled with user actions and system responses [13]. This technique helps to understand how software can change from one state to another through the actions of a particular user. Its application is crucial in developing software products since it allows for anticipating possible changes that may occur during the user's interaction with the system, avoiding usability problems in the long term, and facilitating the implementation of modifications. In addition, it is essential to consider the complexity of the software and make sure that the diagram is clear and easy to understand for other developers [16].

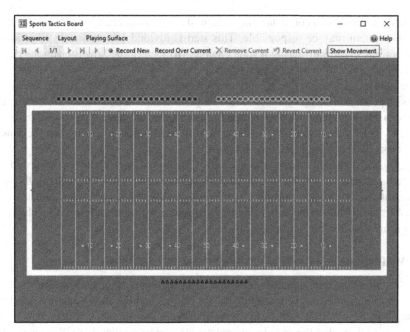

Fig. 1. Main interface of the Sports Tactics Board project.

The number of users needed to apply this technique is not explicitly defined by authors Hix and Hartson [5]. However, according to Nielsen and Faber [2], most usability problems can be discovered with at least five users, although additional problems can be identified with more users. As the number of users and states in the system increases, understanding and maintaining the diagram may become more challenging. It is, therefore, essential to consider the software's complexity to be developed and ensure that the diagram is sufficiently clear and understandable to the developers involved. This technique is valued by experts in the field, such as Hix and Hartson [5], who emphasize its importance for understanding system behavior in different situations and designing systems that are easy to use and maintain. According to Hix and Hartson [5], the State Transition Diagrams technique consists of 5 steps, which are detailed as follows:

- The first step consists of identifying the system states, for which it is necessary to perform the following tasks: (i) Identify the "key" or most important states to be modeled in the system through an exploratory investigation; (ii) Once these states have been identified, determine how the states can be classified, either by priority, function, events, among others; (iii) Identify the most critical states to be modeled in the system, through an exploratory investigation; (iv) Identify the most critical states to be modeled in the system, through an exploratory investigation; and (v) Identify the most critical states to be modeled in the system, through an exploratory investigation.
- In the second step, the events that can cause a change in the system states must be identified. This step requires two critical tasks to be executed: (i) Identify all events and determine which ones can cause a change of state; (ii) Once identified, these events are classified either by input type or by user action.

- The third step consists of identifying actions during a state change for which the users or the system may be responsible. This step is divided into two tasks: (i) Identify the actions that occur during a state change; (ii) Determine how the actions can be classified either by function or by event.
- The state transition diagram must be created or designed in the fourth step. To execute this step, the following two tasks must be performed: (i) Use the states, events, and actions that were previously identified to create the state transition diagram; (ii) Make sure to include all states, events, and actions in the diagram to ensure that the flow of the tasks does not produce new problems.
- Finally, the fifth step ensures that the state transition diagram must be reviewed and tested, and can be carried out by performing the tasks of: (i) Reviewing the state transition diagram to ensure that it adequately reflects the behavior that has been established for the system; (ii) Testing the project with different testing techniques, to ensure that it works appropriately.

3.3 Adaptations to the State Transition Diagrams Technique

After presenting the steps and tasks of the technique as prescribed by Hix and Hartson [6], the integration framework proposed by Castro [5] to adapt the state transition diagrams technique to be incorporated in this type of project and to know which may be the adverse conditions that the pure technique presents to be applied in OSS projects. The unfavorable conditions that were found were the following.

1. The state transition diagrams technique requires a usability expert for its application. Instead, it is recommended to replace it with an HCI student (under the supervision of a mentor).
2. User participation is required to apply the technique, so remote participation via videoconferencing tools is recommended.
3. Several users must be physically together, so it is proposed that the meetings be held virtually through videoconferencing tools.

Table 1 presents the proposed adaptations for application in OSS projects to facilitate their incorporation.

The 11 steps of the technique adapted for incorporation into OSS projects are presented below:

- Step 1. Run the usability pilot test: Nielsen and Faber [2] recommend using at least five users to perform usability tests on a system to obtain meaningful results. Pilot tests are conducted with the selected users, who must be supervised and evaluated by a moderator who records their comments and observations. An e-mail invitation is sent to the users to perform the pilot test and learn about the current status of the OSS project.
- Step 2: Identify system states. The usability experts identify the system states and report through the document "System States."
- Step 3: Identify system events. The usability experts prioritized the events found and documented them in the "System Events" template.
- Step 4: Identify the actions users take to trigger changes. Usability experts have to monitor each action the user performs to identify the respective changes in state.

Table 1. Adverse conditions and proposed adaptations to the state transition diagram technique.

Steps of the Technique		Adverse Conditions	Adaptations Proposed
1	Identify the states of the system	• It is essential to have a usability expert to apply the technique	• The usability expert is replaced by an HCI student or group of students (under the supervision of a mentor)
2	Identify the events that can cause a state change		
3	Identify the actions that occur during a state change		
4	Create the state transition diagram	• User participation is necessary to apply the technique • It is necessary for several users to be physically together	• They participate remotely through (i) forums or e-mails, (ii) feedback through bug reporting tools, and (iii) comments on a wiki • Meetings are (i) virtual (e.g., via chat), and (ii) replaced by a wiki, where anyone involved in the project can contribute their ideas
5	Review and test the state transition diagram	• User participation is necessary to apply the technique • It is necessary for several users to be physically together • A usability expert must be available to apply the technique	• They participate remotely through (i) forums or e-mails, (ii) feedback through bug reporting tools, and (iii) comments on a wiki • Meetings are (i) virtual (e.g., via chat), and (ii) replaced by a wiki, where anyone involved in the project can contribute their ideas • The usability expert is replaced by a student or group of students from the HCI (under the supervision of a mentor)

- Step 5: Redesign the interface. After conducting the pilot test, the usability experts list favorable design ideas for the interface. In addition, a detailed user interface design is developed for selected interaction contexts.
- Step 6: Final usability testing and prototype inspection. To select a final design, the prototype is inspected by the users of the OSS community, who will also contribute ideas, and finally, the prototype preferred by this community can be obtained.

- Step 7: Identify all components and actions to be contained in the diagram. The usability experts will review step by step the feedback provided by the users to identify the components and actions that the state transition diagram should contain.
- Step 8: Create the state transition diagram. Once the states, events, and actions identified previously in the document "Software components and final actions" have been obtained, we will create the state transition diagram. This state transition diagram has been created using the Lucid Chart tool.
- Step 9: Review and test the state transition diagram. Once the state transition diagram is established, usability experts analyze the entire diagram to verify its completeness and that there are no errors. To do this, they use automation tools to review the diagram.
- Step 10: Improvements or corrections in the diagram. Once the diagram has been tested, if any errors are found, the improvements and corrections that the diagram needs will be made.
- Step 11. Construction of the interface. The project interface is designed with the improvement proposals. This final interface is presented in the blog https://n9.cl/7rvpm. In addition, the usability expert is the one who makes the prototype.

A summary of the steps of the state transition diagram technique adapted for OSS projects is presented in Table 2.

Table 2. Steps and tasks of the adapted state transition diagram technique.

Steps of the technique		Tasks
1	Execute a pilot test	• Invite users to participate in the pilot tests via email • The tasks to be carried out in the pilot test are sent to
2	Identify system states	• Identify only the most critical system states
3	Identify system events	• Identify the necessary events that can lead to a change of state
4	Identify actions taken by users to trigger changes	• Identify the actions that occur during a change of state • Determine how the actions can be classified (e.g., by function, by event)
5	Prototyping	• Develop a list of favorable design ideas for the interface • Develop detailed user interface design for selected interaction contexts
6	Final usability test - prototype inspection	• Invite users from the OSS community to inspect the prototype • Take note of the users' ideas to improve the prototype and obtain the prototype most chosen among them

(continued)

Table 2. (*continued*)

Steps of the technique		Tasks
7	Identify all components and actions to be contained in the diagram	• Analyze all feedback provided by users before diagram creation • Verify that the statuses match the operation of the system
8	Create the state transition diagram	• Create the state transition diagram by using the identified states, events, and actionsam • Be sure to include all the states, events, and actions identified in the diagram. Therefore, only the most necessary ones are recommended
9	Review and test the state transition diagram	• Review the state transition diagram to reflect the system's behavior adequately • Allocate the time for team members to review and perform the necessary tests • Test the diagram using different test cases to ensure it works properly • Use automated tools to review and test the diagram
10	Improvements or corrections to the diagram	• Apply improvements to the diagram design based on the final results and the review of the usability expert • Apply logic corrections to states and transitions
11	Build the interface	• Design the end user interface with the proposed improvements • Present the final built interface

3.4 Results of the Case Study

The state transition diagrams technique used in an actual OSS project is a technique that corresponds to the design activities in the Software Engineering phases. However, in the first instance, the STB project was evaluated to detect existing usability problems and obtain the necessary information to create an interface to solve these problems. First, a letter requesting authorization to participate in the STB project was sent to the lead developer's e-mail address. Although the developers' contact information was not on the SourceForge platform, a link to the STB project website where this information was obtained to request authorization to participate in the project was found. Figure 2 illustrates an excerpt of this request.

After two days, we obtained a positive response from one of the leading developers of the STB project to participate in the usability study implementing the adapted state transition diagrams technique. Once permission was obtained, a pilot test was conducted to evaluate the usability of the STB project with the participation of Software Engineering

Fig. 2. Request for authorization to the STB project developer.

students from the State Technical University of Quevedo (UTEQ). The project was reviewed in this pilot test, and the tasks to be performed in the tests were designed. An e-mail invitation was sent to three users (friends and/or acquaintances of the researchers who are students at UTEQ), including the date and time to perform the pilot test; two links were attached. The first was to enter the WhatsApp group, and the second was to download the project to evaluate STB, as shown in Fig. 3.

Fig. 3. Invitation to users for the pilot test – STB.

A second e-mail was sent to the pilot test users with the meeting link and two attachments containing the tasks to be performed in the test and the consent to use the images. The virtual meeting began with a gratefulness to the participants for their collaboration. A brief introduction of the project to be evaluated was presented so that users would have a clear idea of its scope before performing the usability test. In the link https://n9.cl/x2xon, it is possible to consult the consent signed by each user for taking images both in the recorded video and for the use of the image in the research.

Once the pilot test was completed, users reported the inconveniences they faced while performing the assigned tasks due to their lack of familiarity with the project in question. To obtain more accurate feedback, users were asked to detail the inconveniences encountered during each task, errors in the project, and desired improvements. For the usability pilot test of the STB project, two tasks were posed to users, with a time limit of 20 min per user. The details of the tasks performed by each user can be found in the link: https://n9.cl/ytwe1x. The results of the pilot tests are presented in three tables: the first contains the inconveniences reported when performing the tasks; the second one contains the errors detected in the project; and the third one contains the suggestions for improvement proposed by the users. The formats of these tables and the results of executing the tasks are presented in the following link: https://n9.cl/j45h7.

In the next step, "Identify system states," the current state of the STB project system is identified. To carry out this analysis, we have relied on the experience and knowledge of usability experts, who have examined the project in-depth and have identified the points where the system has deficiencies or areas for improvement; the usability experts are a group of students under the supervision of a usability expert mentor. The results of this analysis are available at https://n9.cl/6ujbgx.

In this step, "Identify system events," it is indicated that after identifying the different system states of the STB project, the errors found by the usability experts during their review are documented. These errors are essential since they allow us to know the specific aspects of the project that present deficiencies or problems that affect its usability and efficiency. The complete results are available at: https://n9.cl/puz3x.

In the "identify actions" step, pilot tests are carried out in the STB project to identify the actions that cause changes in the system when performing the tasks provided to users by the usability experts. These tests are a fundamental part of improving and optimizing the system since they allow us to know how it behaves in natural use conditions. From these data, it was possible to identify the actions that caused system changes, which may affect its usability and efficiency. The results of the actions found through the pilot tests are available at the following link: https://n9.cl/8ci47.

In the next step, "Prototyping," the prototypes designed by the usability experts are presented in a blog. Three prototypes were made so that users could inspect, evaluate, and choose the best among the proposals presented (see https://n9.cl/uxtq7). The proposal was chosen by voting in the blog comments, and the most voted was proposal 2.

The selection process of participants for the final usability test (inspection of the prototypes) is described below. To carry out this selection, a formal invitation was made through the SourceForge platform, where the project is stored. In the invitation, two links are provided: one to access the blog about the project and another to access a form where users interested in participating in the final usability test can provide their contact information. This participant selection process is essential to carry out the final usability test, as it allows the participation of real users who use the project regularly, as shown in the link below: https://n9.cl/6r4q7. Actual users are those who are registered in the STB project forum.

Having actual users participate in the final usability test allows us to obtain valuable information about the use of the project under natural conditions. This information can be used to identify errors and deficiencies that affect the system's usability and efficiency and correct them before its launching to the general public. Once the information was obtained from the users interested in the project, a formal invitation was sent by e-mail, where two links were joined. The first link directs the participating users to the blog created by the researchers, where the prototypes to be evaluated can be found. The second link is to the WhatsApp group where the user can solve their doubts about the final usability test by inspecting prototypes, as shown in https://n9.cl/gkmen8.

The final usability test was carried out with the participation of actual users of the STB project. In the link: https://n9.cl/uxtq7, the evaluated prototypes, and real users' comments are presented on the STB project blog. Based on the comments obtained in the blog, it was decided to combine Proposal 1 with Proposal 3 and add a new functionality: the basketball court.

In this step, "Identify all the components and actions that the diagram will contain," we identify the components and actions of our OSS project; once the final usability test (prototype inspection) was performed, the results reported in the following link were obtained: https://n9.cl/0khf2.

In the step "create the state transition diagram," the diagram is created with the components and actions identified in the previous step. For this step, we use the Lucid chart tool where our STB project state transition diagram will be hosted. This diagram can be viewed at the following link: https://n9.cl/e4bh5.

In the next step, "Review and test the state transition diagram," once the state transition diagram was made, it was reviewed and tested to see if it adequately reflects the project's behavior. It is corrected or improved if the diagram does not comply with the request.

In the step "Improvements or corrections in the diagram," corrections or improvements were made to the diagram because it did not comply with the behavior reflected in the project and was sent for a new revision. The improved state transition diagram can be viewed at the following link: https://n9.cl/ln2mn. Based on this new diagram, we proceed to construct the final interface.

In the "Interface construction" step, the new interface of the STB project was designed, with the improvements or observations provided by the users in the final usability test and the new functionality requested. Figure 4 shows the final interface built.

4   Discussion of the Results

The communication process with the STB community was somewhat complicated since only one project developer responded to our request to work on improving the project. In addition, it has been considered that the project is licensed under SourceForge to work with free access. Initially, a pilot test was carried out with users/friends of the usability experts (UTEQ students), where it was determined that they had a medium level of experience in using the SBT project and other similar projects. The pilot test was essential to identify opportunities for improvement and address any errors that

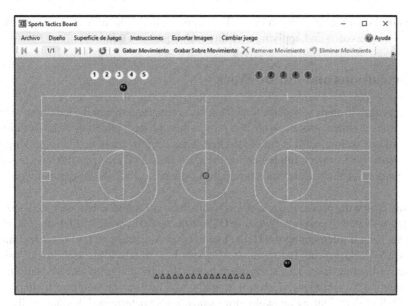

Fig. 4. New interface of the OSS project "Sports Tactics Board".

could affect the final usability evaluation of the SBT project. Both tests considered the characteristics of the OSS community, which often presents unique challenges, such as a lack of usability experts and low participation of the OSS community.

During the pilot test, real expert users and active contributors from the OSS community were invited to participate. Their valuable comments provided a critical perspective on the usability of the STB project, highlighting functionalities that required enhancements. This feedback was instrumental in ranking new enhancements to be incorporated into the project. Each enhancement proposal identified during the pilot test was assigned to a member of the usability expert team (in their role as developers) responsible for its implementation in the STB project. This ensured that the proposed adaptations were effectively addressed and carried out following OSS community standards.

Based on the pilot test results, the final usability test was performed on the selected OSS project. This phase involved three users specifically selected for their experience in OSS projects of this category (i.e., gaming strategies). The final test focused on prototype inspection, where users could choose between three proposals presented on the OSS project blog. The choice was made by voting, and prototype two was selected as the best proposal.

Summarizing, this research emphasized the adaptation of the State Transition Diagram's usability technique to the OSS community's particularities, such as the lack of usability experts. In addition, a detailed and practical process for integrating the selected technique into the OSS development process was formalized. The validation of the State Transition Diagram technique performed in an actual OSS project, such as STS, demonstrated the usefulness of our adaptations and improvements in an environment where unfavorable conditions, often related to low user involvement and lack of experts, are common. In summary, our focus was on optimizing the usability of the STB project in the context of the OSS community. This stands out as a significant achievement in open-source research and applying usability techniques in OSS.

5 Conclusions and Future Work

This study aims to analyze how the State Transition Diagrams technique has improved the software development process in an OSS project through its application. After examining the use of this technique, it is concluded that it has been instrumental in improving the quality of the OSS project. Implementing the State Transition Diagram has led to a better understanding of the maintenance process and greater clarity in the requirements and tasks.

After reviewing previous work, it was found that very few studies have used usability techniques related to design activities in OSS projects. In the work of Llerena et al. [17], the focus is on implementing the Help Organization According to Use Case Technique in the OSS Sleek project. The research addresses how to adapt this usability technique to improve the interface. This study identifies challenges and proposes adaptations for implementing the technique, demonstrating that usability can be significantly improved in the OSS project. During an exploratory study, it was determined that, generally, one of the causes of low usability in the interface of OSS projects is the lack of operability. Therefore, the resulting model for integrating the state transition diagramming technique into the OSS project is based on the researchers' suggestions and previous experiences. The feedback from users has made it possible to identify areas for improvement and ensure that the implemented changes meet their expectations, resulting in a more satisfactory experience for users and, therefore, improving the project's usability. Usability in non-commercial tools is usually very neglected and often underestimated. This study has positively validated the feasibility of incorporating adapted usability techniques related to design activities in the OSS development process.

Despite the progress made, there is still work to be done in the STB project. The state transition diagramming technique will be a valuable resource for developing new functionalities. In future work, it is proposed to continue to explore new strategies and techniques to ensure the long-term sustainable success of the project. Over time, the STB project is expected to continue to improve and meet the expectations of users and the developer community.

References

1. Dawood, K.A., Sharif, K.Y., Zaidan, A.A., Abd Ghani, A.A., Zulzalil, H.B., Zaidan, B.B.: Mapping and analysis of open source software (OSS) usability for sustainable OSS product. IEEE Access **7**, 65913–65933 (2019). https://doi.org/10.1109/ACCESS.2019.2914368
2. Nielsen, J., Faber, J.M.: Improving system usability through parallel design. Computer **29**(2), 29–37 (1996). https://doi.org/10.1109/2.485844
3. Yu, X., et al.: An open source platform for computational histopathology. IEEE Access **9**, 73651–73661 (2021). https://doi.org/10.1109/ACCESS.2021.3080429
4. Castro, J.W.: Incorporación de la usabilidad en el proceso de desarrollo open source software. Tesis PhD, Universidad Autónoma de Madrid, Madrid, España (2014)

5. Hix, D., Hartson, H.R.: Developing User Interfaces: Ensuring Usability Through Product & Process, 1st edn. Wiley (1993)
6. Granollers, T., Lorés, V., Sendin, M., Perdrix, F.: Integración de la IPO y la ingeniería del software: MPIu+a. III Taller en Sistemas Hipermedia Colaborativos y Adaptativos (2005)
7. Llerena, L., Rodriguez, N., Castro, J.W., Acuña, S.T.: Adapting usability techniques for application in open source software: a multiple case study. Inf. Softw. Technol. **107**, 48–64 (2019). https://doi.org/10.1016/j.infsof.2018.10.011
8. Lamberti, F., Paravati, G., Gatteschi, V., Cannavò, A., Montuschi, P.: Virtual character animation based on affordable motion capture and reconfigurable tangible interfaces. IEEE Trans. Visual Comput. Graphics **24**(5), 1742–1755 (2018). https://doi.org/10.1109/TVCG.2017.2690433
9. Xiang, Y., Aggarwal, V., Chen, Y.F.R., Lan, T.: Differentiated latency in data center networks with erasure coded files through traffic engineering. IEEE Trans. Cloud Comput. **7**(2), 495–508 (2019). https://doi.org/10.1109/TCC.2017.2648785
10. Kafadar, O.: RaspMI: raspberry pi assisted embedded system for monitoring and recording of seismic ambient noise. IEEE Sens. J. **21**(5), 6306–6313 (2021). https://doi.org/10.1109/JSEN.2020.3043753
11. Park, C., Lee, B.: Energy-efficient photoplethysmogram compression to estimate heart and respiratory rates simultaneously. IEEE Access **7**, 71072–71078 (2019). https://doi.org/10.1109/ACCESS.2019.2919745
12. El Asame, M., Wakrim, M., Battou, A.: Designing e-assessment activities appropriate to learner's competency levels: hybrid pedagogical framework and authoring tool. Educ. Inf. Technol. **27**(2), 2543–2567 (2021). https://doi.org/10.1007/s10639-021-10607-y
13. Dawood, K.A., Sharif, K.Y., Ghani, A.A., Zulzalil, H., Zaidan, A.A., Zaidan, B.B.: Towards a unified criteria model for usability evaluation in the context of open source software based on a fuzzy delphi method. Inf. Softw. Technol. **130**, article 106453 (2021). https://doi.org/10.1016/j.infsof.2020.106453
14. Llerena, L., Rodriguez, N., Gomez-Abajo, P., Castro, J.W., Acuña, S.T.: Adoption of the visual brainstorming in the open source software development process. In: Proceedings of the 2018 IEEE/ACM 40th International Conference on Soft-ware Engineering: Companion (ICSE'18-Companion), Gothenburg, Sweden, pp. 232–233 (2018)
15. Runeson, P., Höst, M., Rainer, A., Regnell, B.: Case Study Research in Software Engineering: Guidelines and Examples, 1st edn. Wiley (2012)
16. Shneiderman, B.: Designing the User Interface: Strategies for Effective Human-Computer Interaction. Addison-Wesley Longman Publishing Co., Inc., Boston (1997)
17. Llerena, L., Rodriguez, N., Angelita, B., Castro, J.W., Mera, L.: Adoption of the organization of help according to the use case technique in the open-source software development process. In: Arai, K. (eds.) Intelligent Computing. SAI 2023. Lecture Notes in Networks and Systems, vol. 739, pp. 1039–1059. Springer, Cham (2023). https://doi.org/10.1007/978-3-031-37963-5_72

Evaluation of Location Detecting Accuracy Using Smart Watch BLE Connection

Takaaki Mimura[1]($\boxtimes$), Kohei Otake[2], and Takashi Namatame[3]

[1] Graduate School of Science and Engineering, Chuo University, 1-13-27, Kasuga, Bunkyo-ku, Tokyo 112-8551, Japan
a19.7yx6@g.chuo-u.ac.jp
[2] School of Information and Telecommunication Engineering, Tokai University, 2-3-23, Takanawa Shinagawa-ku, Tokyo 108-8619, Japan
otake@tsc.u-tokai.ac.jp
[3] Faculty of Science and Engineering, Chuo University, 1-13-27, Kasuga, Bunkyo-ku, Tokyo 112-8551, Japan
nama@kc.chuo-u.ac.jp

Abstract. In this study, we evaluated the location detection accuracy using smartwatch with BLE connectivity. Our experiments were conducted at an electronics store to measure radio wave strength in an environment that reproduced the actual marketing measures being implemented. Based on the radio wave strength obtained in the experiment, the attenuation coefficient was calculated, and the distance was calculated using it. As a result, the error was small for the area near the center of the store, while the error was large for the area in the corner of the store.

Keywords: Bluetooth connection · Smartwatch · RSSI · three-point positioning

1 Introduction

Location information is an extremely valuable source of information in the analysis of consumer behavior. This information is used to trace how people move and where and how long they stay. From a marketing perspective, this information can be used for a variety of purposes, such as sending push notifications and distributing location-based lottery games.

There are various methods for measuring location information, including GPS, beacons, and Bluetooth. While each method has its merits, each has significant disadvantages when it comes to measuring location information for use as a daily marketing measure. Specifically, GPS is excellent for outdoor positioning detection because it uses satellites, but it is difficult for signals to reach indoor locations and cannot provide accurate positioning inside a store. Moreover, it is difficult to measure altitude using GPS. Beacons require the installation of many transmitters that emit ultrasonic waves [1–5].

A. Coman and S. Vasilache (Eds.): HCII 2024, LNCS 14703, pp. 60–71, 2024.
https://doi.org/10.1007/978-3-031-61281-7_4

In this study, we focus on Bluetooth and use a BLE (Bluetooth Low Energy) connection to measure location. There are three reasons for using BLE.

First, the receiver can be a commercially available device such as a smartwatch, making it reasonably to measure radio wave strength. Second, Bluetooth is generally low power consumption, which is advantageous in situations where battery life is a consideration. Third, the signal can be used in many indoor environments. In this research, a Bluetooth transmitter is installed because it is necessary to know the correct answer to distance and other calculations, but in the future, it will be possible to estimate location using radio waves that are already flying.

On the other hand, since the BLE connection has issues in guaranteeing accuracy, so, it is valuable to try in how to evaluate its accuracy and measure location with high accuracy.

To obtain radio wave strength from BLE units, we used smartwatches in this study. Smartwatches are currently the most popular wearable devices and can be obtained reasonably. In addition, Smartwatches are also used as a means of receiving notifications and communicating; from an HCI (Human-Computer Interaction) perspective, information should be presented to the user based on the appropriate timing and context. This allows users to effectively receive information and communicate with the device.

2   Our Objectives

While smartwatches' BLE connectivity offers advantages, ensuring accuracy in location measurements poses challenges. This research aims to address these challenges and proposes an evaluation methodology for assessing the precision of location data obtained through BLE connections.

Our key challenges include:

1. Precision Assurance: BLE connections may face limitations in maintaining high accuracy. The study will explore strategies to enhance precision, considering factors such as signal strength, interference, and device variability.
2. Real-World Applicability: The proposed methodology will be tested in diverse real-world scenarios, including indoor environments with varying levels of interference. This confirms that the research findings are applicable to conditions in a marketing environment, rather than an environment created specifically for experiments.

The image of data collection is as follows (Fig. 1).

3   Experiment

In this study, location was measured by obtaining RSSI (Received Signal Strength Indicator) values using a BLE connection with a smartwatch in a physical store. Summary of our experiment is as follows:

- Experiment Environment: a floor of an electrical store
- Transmitter Device: SwitchBot thermo-hygrometer
- Number of Transmitter Device: 8 devices

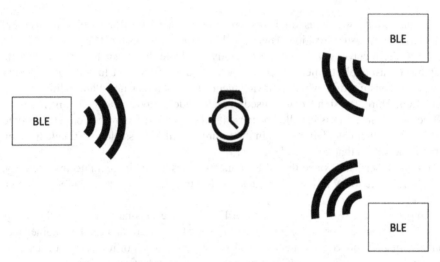

Fig. 1. The Image of Data Collection

- Number of Measurement Point: 5 points
- Number of Measurements People: 7
- Number of Data: 121

The relationship between distance and RSSI is as follows (Fig. 2).

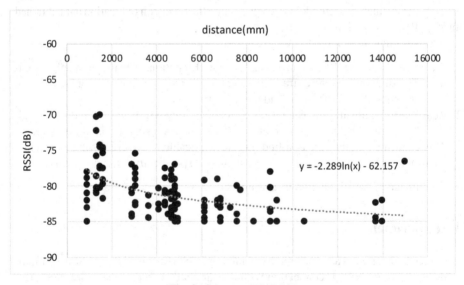

Fig. 2. Distance VS. RSSI

It is known that RSSI follows a logarithmic relationship with distance.

4   Analysis Methods

4.1   Calculation of Attenuation Coefficient

The relationship between the radio signal strength (RSSI) value and distance is given by the following equation.

$$RSSI = RSSI_0 - Nlog_{10}(D)$$

D: Distance(m)
$RSSI$: Measured RSSI value
$RSSI_0$: Unit RSSI value (RSSI value at 1 m)
N: Attenuation coefficient (theoretical value: 20)

The attenuation coefficient is a theoretical value of 20 but varies depending on the environment in which the experiment is conducted.

In this study, attenuation coefficients were calculated based on distance and RSSI values. To determine the attenuation coefficient for the experimental environment, the average of the calculated attenuation coefficients was calculated, and the likelihood was estimated when the attenuation coefficient was used as a random variable.

4.2   Three-Point Positioning

In general, by knowing the RSSI values from three points, the point at which the radio wave was received can be estimated to be a single point.

In this study, three-point positioning was performed with ranges and coordinates. For positioning by range, it is estimated that the point is at the point where the range of the radio acquisition point estimated from the three radio transmission points overlaps. For positioning by coordinates, the least-squares method was used to estimate the inverse of the distance with a penalty, the exponential function of the distance with a penalty, and the exponential function of the distance without a penalty.

5   Result

5.1   Calculation of Attenuation Coefficient

The table below shows the results of obtaining Unit RSSI value for the radio transmitters used in this study (Table 1).

The Unit RSSI value (RSSI value at 1 m) of the radio transmitter used in this study was obtained, with an average value of -67.125.

Using these values, the attenuation coefficient (theoretical value: 20) was calculated. The average value of all attenuation coefficients was 23.8. Using this attenuation coefficient to determine the distance, the mean squared error between the actual and estimated distance was 11.5.

Table 1. Unit RSSI Value of 8 Radio Transmitters

$RSSI_0$:
−69
−71
−59
−68
−62
−67
−69
−72

Next, the calculated attenuation coefficients were taken as random variables and likelihood calculations were performed. After fitting several distributions, the results were as follows (Fig. 3).

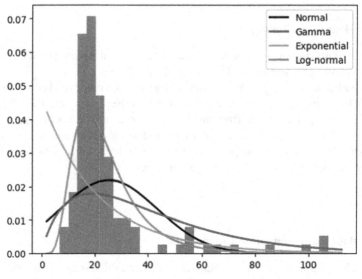

Fig. 3. Result of Fitting Distributions

It can be said that the lognormal distribution is the best fit. The likelihood estimation revealed the parameters: $\mu = 3.08$ and $\sigma = 0.49$. The maximum value of this likelihood function was 17.13.

Using this value, the mean squared error of the distance between the actual and estimated distance was 9.20.

Since the error was smaller than the mean squared error (11.5) when the distance was measured using the average calculated attenuation coefficient, the subsequent analysis was performed assuming an attenuation coefficient of 17.13.

5.2 Three-Point Positioning

The distances estimated from the radio wave strength for points 1 to 5 were calculated and illustrated on the floor map to confirm the overlap (Figs. 4, 5, 6, 7 and 8).

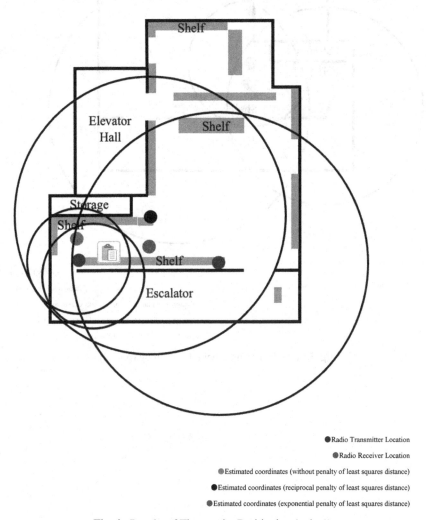

●Radio Transmitter Location

●Radio Receiver Location

●Estimated coordinates (without penalty of least squares distance)

●Estimated coordinates (reciprocal penalty of least squares distance)

●Estimated coordinates (exponential penalty of least squares distance)

Fig. 4. Results of Three-point Positioning (point1)

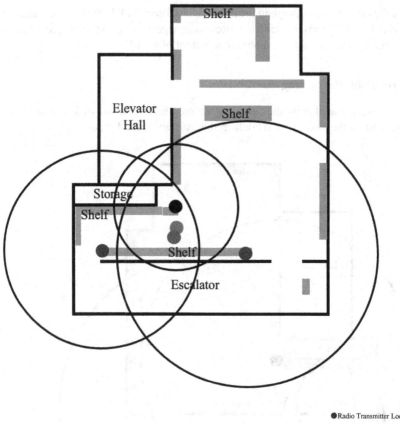

Radio Transmitter Location
Radio Receiver Location
Estimated coordinates (without penalty of least squares distance)
Estimated coordinates (reciprocal penalty of least squares distance)
Estimated coordinates (exponential penalty of least squares distance)

Fig. 5. Results of Three-point Positioning (point2)

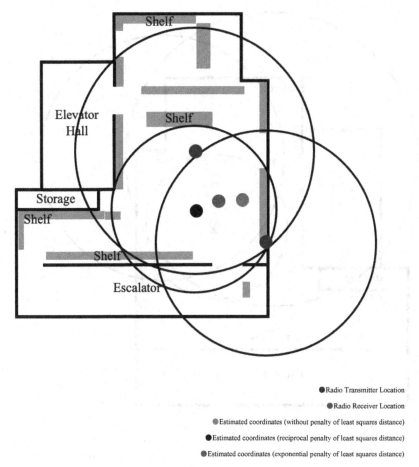

●Radio Transmitter Location

●Radio Receiver Location

●Estimated coordinates (without penalty of least squares distance)

●Estimated coordinates (reciprocal penalty of least squares distance)

●Estimated coordinates (exponential penalty of least squares distance)

Fig. 6. Results of Three-point Positioning (point3)

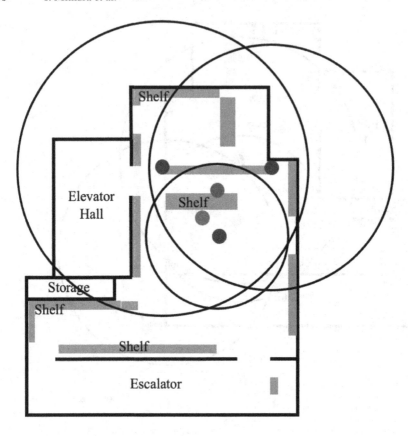

Shelf

Elevator
Hall

Shelf

Storage
Shelf

Shelf

Escalator

● Radio Transmitter Location
● Radio Receiver Location
● Estimated coordinates (without penalty of least squares distance)
● Estimated coordinates (reciprocal penalty of least squares distance)
● Estimated coordinates (exponential penalty of least squares distance)

Fig. 7. Results of Three-point Positioning (point4)

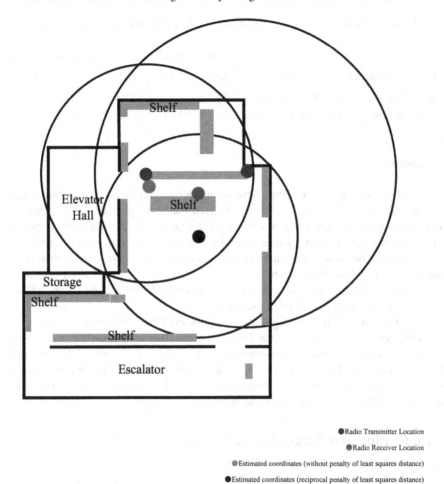

●Radio Transmitter Location

●Radio Receiver Location

●Estimated coordinates (without penalty of least squares distance)

●Estimated coordinates (reciprocal penalty of least squares distance)

●Estimated coordinates (exponential penalty of least squares distance)

Fig. 8. Results of Three-point Positioning (point5)

Ideally, the concentric circles of distances from the three transmitters intersect at one point. However, this situation did not apply in all cases.

The error between the calculation results and the correct coordinates using the respective least squares method was determined as shown in the following table (Table 2).

Table 2. The error between the calculation results and the correct coordinates[m]

	Point 1	Point 2	Point 3	Point 4	Point 5
without penalty of least squares distance	**4.58**	**0.61**	**1.49**	1.59	**3.05**
reciprocal penalty of least squares distance	4.81	1.21	2.99	**1.43**	4.33
exponential penalty of least squares distance	4.59	**0.61**	1.50	1.59	3.06

6 Discussion

As a result of the range positioning, there are no results that include other observation points except for point 5, and it can be considered that if the points to be observed are not too close to each other, it can be correctly determined which observation point was used to see. In addition, as in the result of point 3, it is considered possible to determine which corner the brand is staying at for brands that have corners spread out over a certain wide area. And by knowing the size of the store in advance, it is considered possible to assume with a higher degree of accuracy because the backyard and escalators will not be presumed to be the backyard and escalators.

As for the results of positioning at the four corners of the store (point 1 and point 5), the distance error was large, and it can be said that measurement at the four corners has limitations in terms of position measurement, or it is necessary to devise a better way to place the transmitter. On the other hand, for the points surrounded by three points near the center of the store, the error is smaller, but further study is needed to determine how much error can be tolerated in marketing measures.

7 Conclusion and Future Issues

7.1 Conclusion

In this study, we evaluate location detecting accuracy using smart watch BLE connection.

When positioning in a range, the measured points were included, but some other observation points were also included. When coordinates were obtained, both results had a larger error in the results of positioning at the edge of the store (point1 and point5).

7.2 Future Issues

Currently, without knowing the MAC address of BLE devices, it is difficult to recognize the device. This makes it difficult to know exactly which device is where. A solution to this problem is needed to develop an identification method for devices and a method that takes privacy into consideration. Reliable identification of devices is essential for automatically sending push notifications to specific devices, and it is important to resolve issues related to this.

In addition, smartwatches can collect biometric information such as heart rate. Therefore, by integrating this with location information, it will be possible in the future to estimate emotions based on heart rate and send push notifications.

Acknowledgments. This study was supported by JSPS KAKENHI Grant Numbers 21K13385, 21H04600.

References

1. Wakana, N., Yu, K., Ryo, K.: Improvement of Positionings Accuracy by Estimationg Unit RSSI, Information Processing Society of Japan, Kansai Branch Chapter Convention (2017)
2. Sakai, M., Morita, H.: Indoor Location Estimation using Bluetooth Devices, the Japan Society for Management Information, Fall National Research and Presentation Conference (2016)
3. Ito, S.: Indoor Global Localization using Wi-Fi and Depth Camera, Multimedia, Distributed, Collaborative and Mobile Symposium (2014)
4. Kudou, D., Horikawa, M., Furutachi, T., Okamoto, A.: The Proposal of Indoor Positioning System by Area Estimation Using BLE Beacon, Information Processing Society of Japan (2016)
5. Yuki, M., Akira, U., Hirozumi, Y., Teruo, H.: A Method of Supporting Passengers' Trips Using Public Transportation Systems, Information Processing Society of Japan (2014)

Methods of User Opinion Data Crawling in Web 2.0 Social Network Discussions

Dmitry Nepiyushchikh[(✉)] , Ivan S. Blekanov , Nikita Tarasov ,
and Aleksei Maksimov

St Petersburg State University, Universitetskaya Embankment. 7-9,
199034 St Petersburg, Russia
d.nepiyushchikh@gmail.com, i.blekanov@spbu.ru
https://spbu.ru/

Abstract. It is widely accepted that nowadays a significant part of the content on the internet is generated by users of social media platforms which form the basis of Web 2.0. That is why modern media researchers use user-generated content to test their scientific hypotheses using automated data analysis methods and data mining tools. In this study we examine the main approaches to user opinion data crawling in modern social media platforms for subsequent analysis for scientific and research purposes. We propose a data collection approach based on reverse engineering of APK applications, which allows for data extraction from social networks that will not differ in completeness from data from mobile applications. A comparative analysis of the proposed methods in terms of completeness and execution speed is also carried out. According to our findings, implementing a custom REST API is the best approach as it is both reliable and computationally efficient.

Keywords: Web Crawler · Data Crawling · Data Collection · API · SSL Pinning · gRPC · User Opinion

1 Introduction

Analysis of user opinions on the Web 2.0 platforms has become an increasingly important task. In particular, collecting large amounts of user opinion data is crucial for research purposes in social, economic, medical and various other fields of scientific research. For example, social studies often use AI technologies to solve various tasks, including: analysis of user opinions [1–3], bot detection [4], fake news detection [5], detection of malicious use of AI [6], etc. To effectively solve these problems and improve the reliability of the obtained experimental results, it is necessary to be able to crawl the data at scale, since the quality of the analysis directly depends on the size and expert evaluation (data labels) of the collected data.

In the study [1] authors say that a web page can be defined as a response to a successful HTTP request. Also, an HTTP response may prompt the browser to

A. Coman and S. Vasilache (Eds.): HCII 2024, LNCS 14703, pp. 72–81, 2024.
https://doi.org/10.1007/978-3-031-61281-7_5

make other requests to get CSS, JavaScript, or any media data. Unlike archiving, web scraping selectively saves data, ignoring, for example, images, multimedia content and style sheets when working with text data. It should be noted that resource owners most often oppose automated data collection. This is due to the fact that automated data acquisition increases the load on the server, which can interfere with performing the tasks for ordinary users [1].

Also in the study [2] the authors discuss that it is necessary to get the more important URLs of the resource at the beginning. Additionally, this study lists important attributes for identifying key indicators, as well as an address ordering scheme. According to [4], scalability, manageability, page refresh policy, and the web crawler's etiquette are extremely important. The crawling etiquette in this case relates to the aggressive data collection and the behavior of the data collector mimicking the behavior of a real user. It is difficult to imagine user behavior aimed only at receiving posts, but not comments under them or any attached media content, such as videos or images. It is also unlikely that the user is able to scroll through hundreds of posts per second.

Web 2.0 data can be useful for independent researchers to test theories on unbiased data, which is a key characteristic necessary for research on fake news, opinions on medical issues (which has become one of the more pressing issues during the COVID-19 pandemic) and many other social issues. However, despite the usefulness of user opinion data for research purposes, there are significant barriers commonly encountered in the process. Developers are increasingly utilizing neural networks to detect and prevent unauthorized access to data, which undoubtedly adds complexity to the process of obtaining data. And while important, this harms the data collection for ethical, independent research purposes. Thus, in this study we ask the following questions.

- Is it possible to use alternative methods of crawling user opinions from social media platforms other than methods based on existing APIs?
- Can methods of crawling user opinions from social media platforms based on REST API and reverse engineering APK applications be more effective than methods based on the API?
- Is it possible to organize data crawling from a social media platform application without using its web version?

2   Approaches to Data Crawling

In this study we consider four main approaches to data collection [7,9,11,13] of user opinions in modern social media platforms for subsequent analysis for scientific and research purposes. In the following subsections we describe various approaches to user opinion data crawling.

2.1   Resource API-Based Approach

This approach allows researchers to get data from a resource using methods provided by the developers themselves. This approach is quite simple in terms of implementation. But it also has a number of disadvantages, namely:

- Resource limit on the number of concurrent requests. In this case, the speed of data acquisition decreases [12]
- Incomplete data - APIs often limit search results based on various, sometimes unclear criteria, for example the number of posts returned by APIs is often limited [12]
- Sometimes it is difficult to access the API (for example, Twitter API, Facebook API). Here, the complexity may be due to both the time spent on obtaining API keys and the cost of access
- Not all data can be accessed using the API - some APIs limit the types of metadata returned - information present on the web version or the app might not be returned by API

2.2   User Emulation-Based Approach

An approach based on emulating user actions in a browser or application This approach is generally even simpler to implement, but requires significantly more computing resources. A large amount of computing resources is due to the fact that it is required to store in memory all the content from HTML pages on which media content is most often present. Also, sometimes a server hardware with a graphical shell installed on it is required to collect data. When collecting data using a mobile application, it is now increasingly necessary to have a real mobile device and most often with the Android operating system. In this scenario, a stable connection between the device and the computer is required to control the mobile device. But this approach is even slower, since it takes time to transfer commands to a mobile device, receive them to a computer for subsequent processing. The disadvantages of this approach include:

- High computational costs
- Potentially incomplete data

2.3   REST API Based Approach

A REST API request/response approach [8,10] to a web service or application This approach is more complex than the ones described previously. It is necessary to filter the traffic of the web application or mobile application. Next, get all the necessary request headers and only then make requests to the application server. In general, getting the relevant headers is not a trivial task, due to the presence of dynamic JavaScript elements. The disadvantages of this approach include:

- The complexity of the implementation
- Constant support and adaptation to resource changes are required

2.4   Reverse Engineering-Based Approach

An approach based on reverse engineering of APK applications. Nowadays, the usage of SSL Pinning is more and more common in applications (for example in

Snapchat or Instagram). There may also be situations where the web version of the application has limitations (for example, Snapchat). In the above situations, it is not possible to use the approach mentioned previously. For this approach, a method of obtaining Protobuf for gRPC [17] was proposed. This approach is the most difficult to implement, but it allows for obtaining large collections of data for subsequent analysis. This approach also solves the problem of data completeness, obtaining the data which may not be present in the web version. The disadvantages of this approach are:

– Extremely difficult implementation
– The need for constant support

GRPC and PROTOCOL BUFFER. gRPC is an open source Remote Procedure Call (RPC) system that was developed at Google in 2015. It uses HTTP/2 as the transport protocol and Protocol Buffers as the interface description language and data format.

GPS allows to define and implement four types of service methods: unary, server streaming, client streaming and bidirectional streaming. gRPC also supports various functions such as authentication, compression, cancellation, timeouts, and metadata.

In gRPC, a client application can directly call a method of a server application on another computer, as if it were a local object, which simplifies the creation of distributed applications and services [16]. As with many RPC systems, gRPC is based on the idea of defining a service, specifying methods that can be called remotely, with their parameters and return types [14]. On the server side, the server implements this interface and starts the gRPC server to handle client calls. On the client side, the client has a stub (called simply the client in some languages) that provides the same methods as the server. gRPC clients and servers can work and interact with each other in a variety of environments - from servers inside Google to their own desktop - and can be written in any of the languages supported by gRPC. For example, gRPC can easily be created in Java, with clients in Go, Python or Ruby. In addition, the latest Google APIs will have versions of gRPC interfaces, which will make it easy to integrate Google features into personal applications (Fig. 1).

One of the common features used by RPC implementations to ensure interoperability is the use of data description languages (DDL), which are languages that define data structures which allows for interaction between remote modules, regardless of the platform and language used in the implementation of the procedure.

The data description language commonly used by cloud applications today is Protocol Buffer. According to [18], Protocol Buffer is a neutral function that allows to structure the data for multi-level transmission over the network. Protocol Buffer is an alternative to JSON (Javascript Object Notation), a widely used notation for representing data in web applications [19]. Although JSON has advantages such as good human readability, it also has a number of limitations. Data transmitted using JSON is not encoded by browsers and is transmitted in

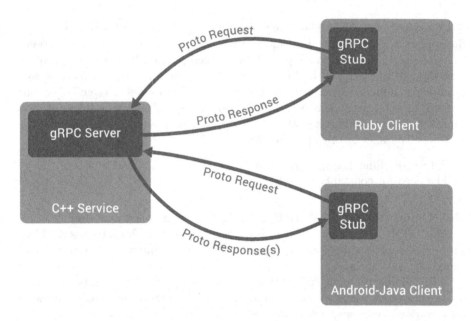

Fig. 1. gRPC architecture overview from the official documentation [15]

plain text, which creates important performance and power consumption limitations in embedded systems.

On the other hand, Protocol Buffer is designed to take up less memory space (unlike JSON), which makes messaging between cross-platform and embedded applications more efficient [18]. Using protocol buffers as DDL to ensure interoperability, gRPC presents itself as a general purpose framework that allows HTTP/2-based RPC communication as a transport to bypass proxy servers and firewalls. There are a number of advantages to using the GRPC platform on various devices such as desktops and mobile devices. The key advantage of this approach is low resource demand - mainly low RAM usage. Applications using Protocol Buffer serialize data in a structure called proto file, regardless of the language used. Protocol Buffer has its own data types, which can be represented through the data types of programming languages [19]. An example of using Protocol Buffer for the Python programming language is provided in the documentation [20].

The main reasons gRPC is commonly used in applications are:

– Minimization of network load by optimizing the data exchange protocol. Due to the growing number of users of social networks and messengers, the number of requests to the application server increases accordingly. With the standard approach of data exchange, namely REST JSON/XML API, the speed of data exchange decreases [15]. To reduce the cost of server hardware and increase the speed of applications in large systems, a gRPC-based approach is commonly used.

– Increased processing and data exchange speed, which allows users to generate and upload more content to the application server.

That is, with frequent transmission of big data over the network, gRPC is often used.

3 Experimental Analysis

The evaluated approaches to collecting user opinions were tested in the following social networks:

– VKontakte
– Instagram

3.1 Experiment Description

During the experiment, operating times (in seconds) were estimated for each approach with the same amount of data collected for each one. The data was collected during the same time frame and only once. This approach allows for baseline testing of different approaches and while it has major limitations (namely the lack of testing for various latent variables) it still highlights the speed and efficiency characteristics of each approach.

Described approaches were implemented using the Python 3 programming language. A series of experiments were conducted to evaluate each approach.

In each series of experiments, the results obtained were parsed and stored in a relational database managed by the PostgreSQL database management system. For each type of experiments the resulting times were averaged across multiple tests.

3.2 Experimental Results

Comparison of the API and Emulation. To emulate the action in the browser, the Playwright library was selected [21], and the requests library was used to work with the VK API [22]. The Playwright library allows to generate code in the python 3 programming language for working with a web application, which significantly reduces the development time for the research purposes.

In this experiment, the first 100 000 posts were collected to compare API and emulation of actions in the browser using the example of the VK API (Table 1).

Table 1. Emulation and API tests for VK

	VK API	VK emulation
Number of posts	100 000	100 000
Time is seconds	1158	2436

In the next experiment, comments on previously collected posts were collected. To do this, we must either pass it to the API method, or click on the link to this post in the browser (Table 2).

Table 2. Comments collection for VK

	VK API	VK emulation
Number of comments	100 000	100 000
Time is seconds	3191	9157

Comparison of REST API and Emulation. Comparative analysis between the native REST API and emulation of actions in the browser was performed using the example of Instagram. The complexity of collecting data from Instagram is due to the need to mimic a real user. Alternatively this problem can be solved by using a large number of accounts. As part of this experiment, a second way to solve the problem was chosen.

When developing a custom REST API, full request emulation to the application server is required. For this purpose, the developer console in the browser was used and requests were sniffered. Next, all requests were executed using the Requests library of the Python 3. The Playwright library was used to emulate actions in the browser (Table 3).

Table 3. Comments collection for VK

	Instagram REST API	Instagram emulation
Number of users	1 000 000	1 000 000
Time is seconds	12691	49870

Comparison of REST API and gRPC API. REST API based approach was additionally compared with gRPC API based approach. In this experiment, a solution developed using the REST API. To implement the gRPC API, the Requests library was used to make requests from the mobile application (Table 4).

Table 4. Comments collection for VK

	Instagram REST API	gRPC API
Number of users	1 000 000	1 000 000
Time is seconds	12691	9658

4   Conclusions and Discussion

4.1   Key Findings

Currently, obtaining data from Web 2.0 for research purposes is becoming an increasingly urgent problem. Four key approaches to data acquisition were identified. As a result of experiments, it was shown that emulating actions both in the browser and in the application is the least productive, while also requiring significant computing resources.

In this study we find that approaches that don't rely on existing APIs can result in more complete datasets.

According to our findings, implementing a custom REST API is the best approach if data is available in the web version of the application. This approach is significantly easier to implement compared to the gRPC and Protocol buffer recovery approach. This approach is also easier to maintain.

If it is necessary to collect a large amount of data, a distributed data collection system can be implemented, which will generally increase the collection performance. According to our findings, an approach based on gRPC and Protocol buffer should be used only if the necessary data is missing in the web version or the SSL Pinning mobile version of the application is used. The use of API services is a low priority, since it is impossible to guarantee the completeness and reliability of data in the general case.

4.2   Methodology Limitations

For subsequent studies, we plan to expand the experiment and introduce modifications to the methodology and implementation. In this paper, momentary data collection was carried out in each of the experiments. In general, this approach can slightly distort the conclusions based on the results of the experiment. In future studies, the methodology of the experiment can be summarized as follows: conduct several experiments and take the average results. This will allow the results to be processed more correctly, and external influences such as network load during peak hours, load on server equipment, and other factors to ensure that these latent variables do not have a significant impact on the obtained results.

References

1. Gheorghe, M., Mihai, F.-C., Dârdală, M.: Modern techniques of web scraping for data scientists. Int. J. User-Syst. Interact. **11**(1), 63–75 (2018). https://doi.org/10.1080/10691898.2020.1787116
2. Bahana, R., Adinugroho, R., Gaol, F.L., Trisetyarso, A., Abbas, B.S., Suparta, W.: Web crawler and back-end for news aggregator system (Noox project). In: 2017 IEEE International Conference on Cybernetics and Computational Intelligence (CyberneticsCom), pp. 56–61. IEEE (2017). https://doi.org/10.1109/CYBERNETICSCOM.2017.8311684

3. Cho, J., Garcia-Molina, H., Page, L: Efficient crawling through URL ordering. Comput. Netw. ISDN Syst. **30**(1–7), 161–172 (1998). https://doi.org/10.1016/S0169-7552(98)00108-1

4. Sharma, S., Gupta, P.: The anatomy of web crawlers. In: International Conference on Computing, Communication and Automation, pp. 849–853. IEEE (2015). https://doi.org/10.1109/CCAA.2015.7148493

5. Blekanov, I.S., Tarasov, N., Bodrunova, S.S.: Transformer-based abstractive summarization for Reddit and Twitter: single posts vs. comment pools in three languages. Future Internet **14**(3), 69 (2022). https://doi.org/10.3390/fi14030069

6. Blekanov, I.S., Tarasov, N., Bodrunova, S.S., Sergeev, S.L.: Mapping opinion cumulation: topic modeling-based dynamic summarization of user discussions on social networks. In: Coman, A., Vasilache, S. (eds.) HCII 2023. LNCS, vol. 14025, pp. 25–40. Springer, Cham (2023). https://doi.org/10.1007/978-3-031-35915-6_3

7. Bodrunova, S.S., Blekanov, I., Smoliarova, A., Litvinenko, A.: Beyond left and right: real-world political polarization in Twitter discussions on inter-ethnic conflicts. Media Commun. **7**, pp. 119–132 (2019). https://doi.org/10.17645/mac.v7i3.1934

8. Nguyen, H.-D., et al.: Supervised learning models for social bot detection: literature review and benchmark. Expert Syst. Appl. (2023). https://doi.org/10.1016/j.eswa.2023.122217

9. Das, S.D., Basak, A., Dutta, S.: A heuristic-driven uncertainty based ensemble framework for fake news detection in tweets and news articles. Neurocomputing **491**, 607–620 (2022). https://doi.org/10.1016/j.neucom.2021.12.037

10. Pashentsev, E., Blekanov, I., Chernobrivchenko, A.: Personal data protection in russia and the risks of malicious use of artificial intelligence technologies: new challenges to psychological security. Sociološki pregled **57**(2), 471–490 (2023). https://doi.org/10.5937/socpreg57-42986

11. Dhenakaran, S.S., Thirugnana Sambanthan, K.: Web crawler-an overview. Int. J. Comput. Sci. Commun. **2**(1), 265–267 (2011)

12. Nepiyushchikh, D., Blekanov, I.: Data crawling approaches for user discussion analysis on web 2.0 platforms. In: Smirnov, N., Golovkina, A. (eds.) SCP 2020. LNCISP, pp. 793–800. Springer, Cham (2022). https://doi.org/10.1007/978-3-030-87966-2_91

13. Wu, H., Liu, F., Zhao, L., Shao, Y.: Data analysis and crawler application implementation based on python. In: 2020 International Conference on Computer Network, Electronic and Automation (ICCNEA), pp. 389–393. IEEE (2020)

14. Fang, T., Han, T., Zhang, C., Yao, Y.J.: Research and construction of the online pesticide information center and discovery platform based on web crawler. Procedia Comput. Sci. **166**, 9–14 (2020). https://doi.org/10.1016/j.procs.2020.02.004

15. gRPC framework https://grpc.io/docs/. Accessed 1 Feb 2024

16. Wang, X., Zhao, H., Zhu, J.: GRPC: a communication cooperation mechanism in distributed systems. ACM SIGOPS Oper. Syst. Rev. **27**(3), 75–86 (1993). https://doi.org/10.1145/155870.155881

17. Araújo, Mateus, Marcio EF Maia, Paulo AL Rego, and Jose N. De Souza.: Performance analysis of computational offloading on embedded platforms using the gRPC framework. In 8th International Workshop on ADVANCEs in ICT Infrastructures and Services (ADVANCE 2020), pp. 1–8 (2020)

18. Kaur, G., Fuad, M.M.: An evaluation of protocol buffer. In: Proceedings of the IEEE Southeastcon 2010 (southeastcon), pp. 459–462. IEEE (2010)

19. Ye, Q., Delaware, B.: A verified protocol buffer compiler. In: Proceedings of the 8th ACM SIGPLAN International Conference on Certified Programs and Proofs, pp. 222–233 (2019)
20. Protocol Buffers Documentation. https://protobuf.dev/getting-started/pythontutorial/. Accessed 1 Feb 2024
21. Playwright library. https://playwright.dev/python/. Accessed 1 Feb 2024
22. Requests library. https://requests.readthedocs.io/. Accessed 1 Feb 2024

Adapting the Interface Content Modeling Technique in an Open Source Software Project: The Case of Koodo Reader

Nancy Rodríguez[1]([✉]) [iD], Kenya Guerrero[1] [iD], John W. Castro[2] [iD],
and Iván Manzaba[1] [iD]

[1] Faculty of Engineering Sciences, Quevedo State Technical University, Quevedo, Ecuador
{nrodriguez,kguerrero,imanzabag}@uteq.edu.ec
[2] Departamento de Ingeniería Informática y Ciencias de la Computación, Universidad de
Atacama, Copiapó, Chile
john.castro@uda.cl

Abstract. Open Source Software (OSS) refers to software whose source code is publicly available, allowing its modification and distribution at no cost. However, due to these OSS projects' collaborative and community-based nature, they often lack resources to focus on quality aspects, such as efficiency and usability. This research aims to apply the adapted Interface Content Model usability technique in the open-source software Koodo Reader project. We participated as volunteers in this project, although we did not have the authorization of the leading developer. To validate the effectiveness of the adapted technique, tests were conducted with representative users, covering a variety of interactions with the Koodo Reader interface. The results of these tests were used for prototyping, which was evaluated and validated by the user community of the Koodo Reader project. In conclusion, the successful application of the Interface Content Modeling technique has proven to be a tool that helps improve the quality of projects. It makes it easier for the developer community to collaborate to improve the end-user experience and make the project more appealing to users. This case exemplifies how collaboration and teamwork in the OSS context can generate innovative and effective solutions.

Keywords: Open Source · Design · Usability · User Interface · Interface Content Model Technique

1 Introduction

Open Source Software (OSS) is a form of software development in which the source code is freely published and can be used, modified, and distributed by anyone [1]. In 1998, the Open Source Initiative (OSI) was created, and the term OSS was adopted as a brand name to introduce open-source software into the commercial world [2]. OSI defines OSS as "That the user has the freedom to run, copy, distribute, study, modify and improve the software." The objective of OSS is to promote the development of free and quality software, improving efficiency, innovation capacity, and continuous improvement [3].

OSS differs from closed-source software because of its collaborative and transparent nature [4]. In OSS, anyone can access the source code and contribute improvements, leading to diverse perspectives and approaches to design and functionality.

OSS and usability are closely related, as both seek to improve software quality and make it more accessible to users [5]. Therefore, usability is considered one of the most critical factors in the quality of a software product. Because of this, it is interesting to have methodologies to measure the usability of applications [6]. Nielsen, one of the leaders in usability research, states that people have a low tolerance for difficulties in website design. Most users do not want to wait to learn how to use a website, as they expect to understand how it works immediately after reviewing the home page. This is because usability applies mainly to computer products and services, web interfaces, and interactive multimedia [6].

In the context of OSS, usability can be a critical factor in the success or failure of these projects, as people with different levels of technical skill often use them. Some of these unusual features of OSS that can affect usability include [7]: (i) OSSs are developed by a community of volunteers and professionals, which means that the quality and performance of the software may vary depending on the contribution of this community. (ii) OSSs are usually developed with a focus on accessibility, meaning that they are designed for use by different types of people. (iii) Users can customize OSS, meaning they can modify the system to suit their specific needs.

Currently, many specific techniques are used to ensure that a product or service is easy to use and be understood by users; among these techniques, we have: (i) Prototyping used to create a basic, functional version of a product or service for testing and to obtain feedback from users. (ii) Heuristic analysis is a process for evaluating the usability of a product based on a set of principles known as usability heuristics. (iii) User-centered design based on understanding users' needs, motivations, and constraints.

This research focuses on adapting the Interface Content Modeling technique for OSS projects. Thus, this work can be beneficial for several reasons. Although Hu-man-Computer Interaction (HCI) is a valuable approach to interface design, its integration into open-source projects can pose challenges. One important reason is that the HCI process can be complex and require specialized skills, which could make it difficult for the OSS community to participate in its implementation. In addition, the process may lack scalability in large OSS projects, where the diversity of contributors and development dynamics can make the application of a precise technique about HCI more cumbersome. Adapting the Interface Content Model technique to an OSS project may involve simplifications or more modular approaches that allow for a more significant and simplified contribution, thus addressing the inherent limitations of the HCI approach in this specific context.

This research work aims to apply the Interface Content Modeling technique with adaptations focused on OSS projects and to evaluate the usability of the selected project. For this study, the Koodo Reader project was selected as a suitable candidate for implementing the adapted Interface Content Model technique for several reasons. Among the reasons is that being an OSS project, Koodo Reader aligns with the collaborative and transparent nature that the adaptation of this technique requires. In addition, being a digital document reader software, Koodo Reader benefits from a representative user interface, in which the Interface Content Modeling technique could substantially improve its usability. Being a project with an active and diverse community, there is a real potential for the contribution and validation of the adapted technique by different developers and users, which could enrich and speed up the implementation process.

This document is organized as follows. Section 2 describes the related work. Section 3 describes the proposed solution. Section 4 discusses the results. Finally, Sect. 5 describes the conclusions and future research.

2 Related Work

There are research papers that have reported the use of some usability techniques in OSS developments [8–16].

In the area of usability of OSS projects, several research studies have been conducted that explore approaches and tools to improve the user experience. Dawod et al. [8] undertook a systematic mapping that spans multiple databases, focusing on incorporating usability into the projects identified in their review. Their approach involves evaluation methods such as user testing, heuristic evaluations, and expert reviews. Through surveys, they determined the level of effort devoted by developers to ensure usability in their creations.

An interesting case is that of Yu et al. [9], who presented the SlicerScope platform, an OSS computational histopathology tool. This platform stands out for its user-friendly interface and its range of image analysis tools applied to the study of biological tissues. After extensive testing and prototyping, the authors support its effectiveness in improving the diagnostic accuracy of diseases. The advantage of the OSS platform lies in its potential for customization and expansion and fostering collaboration in its development.

Another innovation comes from Lamberti et al. [10], who introduced a virtual character animation system that uses motion capture and tangible interfaces. User testing demonstrated its ease of use and low cost, making it suitable for developers and end users. A particular focus in the medical domain is the work of Étienne et al. [11], who designed NousNav, an affordable neuronavigation solution for neurosurgeons in resource-constrained environments. Its intuitive user interface and simplified workflow were subjected to successful user testing. These tests recorded execution times and errors, demonstrating that the system fulfills its purpose of being user-friendly and practical.

In digital health, Brotherton et al. [12] detail the design of HCE Hikma Health, an electronic health record system adapted for settings with limited Internet access. Evaluation of its usability involved interviews in a variety of healthcare settings. Using prototypes generated through design tools, they identified crucial features for an effective system in the healthcare setting.

Hoskere et al. [13] contribute InstaDam, software that allows the analysis of infrastructure images for damage detection. The platform, enriched with annotation functions, was subjected to usability tests that pointed out its ease of use. Although some problems were identified, most users agreed on the platform's accessibility.

Dawood et al. [14] propose a unified criteria model for evaluating usability in OSS projects. Based on expert consensus, their approach includes heuristic inspection evaluations, user testing, and satisfaction surveys. The model highlights criteria such as effectiveness, efficiency, user satisfaction, accessibility, and security.

Llerena et al. [15] investigate the adoption of the visual brainstorming technique in OSS development, using HistoryCal OSS as a case study. They explore adapting this technique to OSS development features, such as voluntary participation and geographic distribution of collaborators. Despite challenges like low user participation and unfamiliarity with usability techniques, the study finds that adaptations benefit OSS projects.

Finally, in the study by Llerena et al. [16], the usability technique 'Help organization according to use cases' was implemented in the context of the OSS 'Sleek' project during the design phase. As a result of this implementation, adverse conditions were identified, and specific adjustments were proposed to adapt the technique to OSS projects. The findings of this study were positive, demonstrating that the applied modifications resulted in significant improvements in the usability of the OSS 'Sleek' project.

The works discussed above use techniques to identify usability defects and apply different processes to resolve them. These works are valuable as a guide for the detection of usability problems. However, none of them specifically report the use of the Interface Content Modeling technique.

3 Proposed Solution

This section presents the characteristics of the selected OSS Koodo Reader project, followed by the adaptation of the Interface Content Model technique for implementation in OSS projects, and finally, the results of applying this technique in the selected OSS project.

3.1 Case Study Design

In this section, we describe the case study, which we investigated, following the guidelines of Runeson and Host [17]. An adaptation of the Interface Content Model technique by authors Constantine and Lockwood [18] was performed to design and evaluate the usability of user interfaces. The goal of this technique is to provide a structured representation of the interface content to understand how elements are related and how they are accessed. We adapt the Interface Content Modeling technique for application in OSS projects and describe the steps to implement and evaluate usability with real users. The research presented in this case study focuses on answering the question: How do we incorporate the Interface Content Modeling technique into design activities in the OSS development process?

The adapted technique was applied to the OSS Koodo Reader project on the Source-Forge platform. This tool allows users to read documents and manage their library. With this application, users can access a wide variety of titles in digital format and organize and search their books efficiently. In addition, it also offers additional features, such as the ability to add notes and bookmarks. It has format support for epub, pdf, mobi, txt, md, and docx, among others. Also, it allows text-to-speech conversion, translation, progress slider, and batch import. Figure 1 shows the main interface of the OSS Koodo Reader project.

Fig. 1. The main interface of the OSS Koodo Reader project.

3.2 Description of the Interface Content Modeling Technique

Constantine and Lockwood [18] propose a user-centered design methodology based on three abstract models: role model, task model, and content model. The content model focuses on representing the user interface content and its components. It is applicable in GUI design and facilitates interaction design tasks. Its primary purpose is to serve as a communication tool between the interaction designers and the user interface development team, showing how the user will interact with the application and how the application will respond [19]. The interface content model abstractly represents the contents of the different interaction spaces of a system. It can be modeled using paper (with a sheet for each interaction space) and sticky notes representing the tools and materials offered to the user [20]. It aims to provide a logical and coherent content structure to facilitate user navigation and understanding. This is achieved by identifying main topics, hierarchizing the information, and organizing the content into logical sections. According to the authors Constantine and Lockwood [18], the technique consists of the following steps described below:

- Step 1. Conduct user research: To understand the needs and desires of these users for the creation of the interface, you can use information-gathering techniques such as interviews and surveys to get a clear idea of what you want to achieve with the design of this user interface.

- Step 2. Analyze the content: A content analysis should be performed to create a map of the content and better visualize how it is related, how it can be accessed, and the most essential elements for users.
- Step 3. Create a content map: Once the content is organized and prioritized, a visual map is created to show the key elements using different levels of detail.
- Step 4. Design the user interface: The user interface was designed using the content map as a guide. For this, it is essential to consider the usability and accessibility of the user when using this interface.
- Step 5. Testing and validating the design: In this step, the usability is verified to ensure that the user interface is easy to use and provides a satisfactory experience. This step checks usability to ensure the user interface is easy to use and provides a satisfactory experience.

Table 1 reports the unfavorable conditions and adaptations proposed for each Interface Content Modeling technique step.

Table 1. Technique steps, adverse conditions and proposed adaptations.

Technique Steps		Adverse Conditions	Proposed Adaptations
1	Conduct user research	• It is necessary for several users to be physically together • User participation is necessary to apply the technique	• Meetings are virtual (e.g., via chat or videoconference) • Users participate remotely through: forums or e-mails, or by commenting on a blog
2	Analyze the content	• It is essential to have a usability expert to apply the technique	• The usability expert is replaced by a student or group of HCI students (under a mentor's supervision)
3	Create a content map		
4	Design the user interface		
5	Test and validate the design	• It is necessary for several users to be physically together • User participation is necessary to apply the technique	• Meetings are virtual (e.g., via chat or videoconference) • Users participate remotely through: forums or e-mails, or by commenting on a blog

3.3 Adaptations to the Interface Content Modelling Technique

According to Constantine and Lockwood [18], the Interface Content Model technique seeks to improve usability by designing a user-centric interface based on the user's needs and expectations [18]. However, there may be some difficulties in this technique when applying it in an OSS project. To adapt this technique, 13 steps have been performed, which are described below:

- Step 1. Define the preconception and essential purpose of the software design: Goals are set for improving GUI features and content. A usability expert does this (this expert is replaced by a student or group of HCI students under the supervision of a mentor).
- Step 2. Conduct a pilot test: Usability tests are conducted to learn about the usability of the current graphical user interface. To perform this step, users of the OSS community can be called to participate in meetings; the meetings are virtual, e.g., via chat or videoconference. Tools such as Google Meet can set up a virtual meeting with the pilot users.
- Step 3. Perform content modeling: All graphical user interfaces are examined, content modeling is performed, and a content map is created to find inconsistencies in the content modeling of the current graphical user interface. The realization of the content map and modeling has to be done by the usability expert (replaced by a student or group of HCI students under the supervision of a mentor). To create a content map, a document is created, where each page corresponds to each page or section of the website or software to which the graphical user interfaces are to be created. The content modeling describes the content elements the page or section will contain. Finally, the content map is obtained by relating the pages of the website or software section.
- Step 4. Perform the user role inventory: Considering the inconsistencies found, an inventory of user roles is performed to determine the system activities related to each role. The inventory is performed by a usability expert (a student or group of HCI students under the supervision of a mentor).
- Step 5. Refine user roles: List the user roles obtained with the role inventory from step 4. These roles are described in detail, indicating the characteristics of each role. In case there are doubts or ambiguities related to each user role, they are solved through the participation of the OSS community members in forums or e-mails or by commenting on a blog. If they do not exist, it is suggested that a web artifact be created to establish communication among the OSS community.
- Step 6. Prioritize user roles. The usability experts order the roles by priority of fulfillment and determine the users' intentions and involvement with the system.
- Step 7. Conduct the task inventory: For each role, the usability expert assigns tasks to be fulfilled according to the role. In addition, users' doubts are solved through discussions. This task inventory is reported in the document "task inventory."
- Step 8. Describe the tasks: Each task's criticality, complexity, and interest is established.
- Step 9. Organize tasks: Tasks are assigned to users according to their role and are followed up by observations. In addition, if there were any iterations previously, the pending tasks are assigned before the others.
- Step 10. Perform abstract prototyping: This step involves creating a simplified system representation that focuses on information organization and navigation without including visual or graphical design details. The resulting model is a prototype used to evaluate the structure and navigation of the system, as well as the functionality and effectiveness of user interaction. The prototype is developed in an online tool for collaboration with other team members.

- Step 11. Perform user interface design: After prototyping, usability experts make a list of favorable design ideas for the interface. In addition, a detailed design of the user interface for the selected interaction contexts is performed.
- Step 12. Refine the prototype: To select a final design, the prototype will be inspected by users of the OSS community, who will also contribute with ideas and recognition of incompatibilities found. The final design of the OSS case study interface is at the following blog: https://n9.cl/blogkoodoreader
- Step 13. Building the user interface: The user interface is designed with proposals for improvement concerning the prototype. The contribution of the OSS community is critical, as the developers use the specifications and designs provided by the usability expert to create an attractive and user-friendly visual interface. The final interface built by the development team will be presented on the project blog.
- Table 2 shows the steps of the Interface Content Model technique adapted to be applied to the OSS Koodo Reader project.

Table 2. Steps of the technique Model of the adapted interface content.

Technique Steps		Tasks
1	Define the preconception and essential purpose of software design	• Clarify the organization's and the user's purposes user • Fantasize and let go of preconceived ideas about GUI features and content
2	Conduct a pilot test	• Conduct a pilot test with friends and acquaintances
3	Create a model of the content	• Conduct an exploratory analysis to determine inconsistencies in the modeling of GUI content
4	Perform inventory of user roles	• Request the community to carry out a project activity • Build an inventory of user roles related to the system
5	Refine user roles	• Describe the aspects of each user role • Follow-up on doubts and ambiguities about user roles
6	Prioritize user roles	• Order the roles by priority of fulfillment in the project • Determine user intentions and involvement with the system
7	Conduct task inventory	• Build a task inventory to support previously identified user roles • Realizar discusiones sobre dudas acerca de las tareas

(continued)

Table 2. (*continued*)

Technique Steps		Tasks
8	Describe the tasks	• Describe the level of criticality, complexity, and interest of each task
9	Organize tasks	• Assign tasks to users • Follow up on pending tasks to be performed • Relate the user role to the tasks to create an interaction context
10	Perform abstract prototyping	• Develop a content model for interaction contexts that support a selected subset of tasks • Prototyping in online user interface prototyping tools
11	Perform user interface design	• Develop a list of favorable design ideas for the interface • Develop detailed user interface design for selected interaction contexts
12	Refine prototype	• Invite users from the OSS community to inspect the prototype • Take note of ideas incompatibilities encountered by users
13	Build the user interface	• Design the user interface with proposals for improvement

3.4 Case Study Results

The Interface Content Modeling technique with adaptations was applied in the OSS Koodo Reader project selected from the SourceForge repository. Koodo Reader is an e-book reader. The essential purpose of designing this interface is to ensure that the information is organized and coherent with the content, allowing users to quickly understand and use the project OSS and improving the user experience when using the e-book manager and reader.

In the first instance, a letter was sent by e-mail requesting authorization for the application developer to participate in the OSS Koodo Reader project by incorporating the Interface Content Model technique. After ten days, we did not receive a reply. However, we have considered that the author has made the license type "GNU Affero General Public License v3.0" public in his GitHub repository. This license allows us to modify and distribute the software our way. However, the license comes with certain conditions: any modified project must have the same license, include information on the original authors, and make the source code public, among other things. More information on the Koodo Reader project license is available at https://n9.cl/lignu. Considering the above, we cloned the original project to the team's GitHub repository. We created the maintenance branch, which is the branch where we uploaded the changes made to the project.

As a next step, a pilot test was conducted with students of the Software Engineering course at the Quevedo State Technical University (UTEQ) to evaluate the usability of the OSS Koodo Reader project. These users tested the software, and for this purpose, they were provided with the document with the steps for the installation of the project and the respective tasks to be performed during the pilot test. These tasks were chosen to corroborate that the functionalities and interface of the OSS project worked correctly. However, at no time is it intended to bias the perception of the usability of the OSS project users. The tasks performed in this test were: (i) change the reading settings of a.docx file, (ii) perform a backup of the library, and (iii) restore a backup. The files with the tasks can be viewed at https://n9.cl/pruebapilot.

For the pilot test, three users were invited by e-mail, attaching a link to the virtual meeting via Google Meet, and another to join the WhatsApp group to maintain open communication with users in case they had any questions or problems during the test.

After finishing the pilot test, a problem was observed in task three, which consisted of restoring the library backup since no user could perform it because the OSS Koodo Reader project presented problems. To report the bugs encountered by the users, a Word document was sent for them to write down all the inconveniences, bugs, and suggestions for improvements for this project. The results of the pilot test can be viewed at https://n9.cl/resultadopp.

To conduct the pilot test, an e-mail was sent to users requesting their authorization using informed consent to use their image and data provided. It is critical to emphasize that informed consent is essential to ensure users' privacy and rights. By obtaining their consent, we ensure that users fully understand how their data and image will be used and the potential risks and benefits associated with its use.

In this case, sending this email complies with the ethical and legal obligation to obtain informed consent from users before using their information. This provides greater transparency and confidence in the process for users and any other parties involved. Informed consent completed by users can be viewed at https://n9.cl/consentimientoc alidad.

On the other hand, its graphical interface was modeled to obtain a clear and precise understanding of the OSS Koodo Reader project. Modeling is a process by which a complex system is broken down into simpler, easier-to-understand components. In this case, the user interface was broken down into essential elements to define each precisely. Thanks to this process, defining the elements that make up the graphical user interface in the Koodo Reader project was possible. These elements include the toolbar, the main menu, the book display area, the navigation buttons, and the customization options.

The user role inventory for the Koodo Reader project was performed through the following steps. First, user identification was performed to determine who the users performing the activities in the OSS project would be. For this purpose, an announcement was published in the SourceForge repository discussion forum, which can be viewed at https://n9.cl/sourceforgek, to encourage the community to participate in this study. Second, once the potential users were identified, we refined the roles by describing in detail the aspects each role should fulfill in the Koodo Reader project. This process allowed us to clearly define the tasks and responsibilities of each user role, thus avoiding any ambiguity or doubt about their functions.

Subsequently, users were categorized, and a profile was generated to prioritize user roles and order them according to their importance in the OSS project. Once this information was collected, specific roles were assigned to each profile, ensuring they were accurate and relevant to the project.

We used the template predefined by the development team to create the task inventory. This template allowed us to have a solid and coherent structure that facilitated the identification of the tasks assigned to each user role. The development team met virtually through the Google Meet tool to prepare the inventory. The process to be followed for this inventory was explained during the meeting.

The development team included all the tasks identified for each user role. The task inventory was then organized to make it easier to understand. In addition, discussions were held to clarify questions about the tasks and ensure that all tasks necessary to support the user roles were included. Each task's criticality, complexity, and interest level were also described to help the team prioritize appropriately and assign the corresponding roles.

After completing all steps in task prioritization, a comprehensive log of all tasks to be completed by each user was generated. This record includes detailed information about each task, description, and the responsible user. The purpose of this inventory is to plan, organize, and monitor the process of each user when performing the tasks. These tasks can be viewed at https://n9.cl/calidadtareas.

After organizing the tasks that each user would perform in the Koodo Reader project, the next meeting was held with the development team to create the first abstract prototype and thus obtain a more visual representation of the new user interface. Once we had a clear idea of what we wanted to achieve with this new interface, we identified the key elements that would compose it, such as new buttons, images, and icons. For this purpose, a sketch was created showing how the elements relate.

Once the abstract sketch of the new interface was obtained, it was refined and improved, adding more details and making sure it was easy to understand for the user and linked to the objectives defined at the beginning. We built two prototype proposals considering the abstract sketch that was defined to have a guide of the interface to be created. For a better visualization of the prototypes, go to https://n9.cl/prototipocalidad.

To obtain better feedback on the interface proposals created by the researchers in their role as developers, real users from the OSS community were invited to perform a usability evaluation of the prototypes. For this purpose, a formal email invitation with the steps to follow was sent to the users. These emails were obtained via an invitation through the SourceForge repository discussion forum. This announcement included a description of the test and a link for users to provide their data to contact them.

The final test with real users was precious since feedback was obtained by evaluating the usability of the proposals of the researchers in their role as developers and determining which of them was the best option. In these comments, most users prefer proposal number 2 because its options are more visible and the interface is more intuitive, although some prefer proposal number 1 aesthetically. In addition, there is a common suggestion among users to change the color tone used in proposal 2, as it seems opaque and may negatively affect the aesthetics of the interface. In the link: https://n9.cl/prototipokoodoreader, user comments can be displayed.

As a last step, the improved interface of the book manager and reader "Koodo Reader" was constructed. As a result, an easy-to-use and effective user interface for end users was implemented. The key content elements necessary for managing and displaying books to the reader during the construction process were identified. These elements were then organized into coherent and accessible sections to allow users to navigate and perform tasks intuitively. Figure 2 shows the final interface of the Koodo Reader project.

Fig. 2. The final interface of the OSS Koodo Reader project.

4   Discussion of Results

In this research work, the application of the Interface Content Modeling technique in the Koodo Reader project was detailed, resulting in the adaptation of the technique that initially consisted of a total of 5 steps. This is to ensure that the information in the interface is clear, consistent, and easy to use for users, thus improving usability when using the Koodo Reader book manager and reader. The adapted technique consists of 14 steps to make it feasible to apply in the selected OSS project—the steps of the adapted technique range from identifying the objectives of the interface to performing usability tests.

A pilot test was conducted to evaluate the usability of the OSS project selected for this research and to detect errors, bugs, and improvements. In this test, the users commented on their observations, which were used to classify the new improvements made in the Koodo Reader project. In a matrix, each proposal was classified according to its type: error (E), failure (F), and improvement (M). The degree of difficulty was also measured between low, medium, and high, the priority between 1 and 3, and each proposal was assigned to a team leader.

On the one hand, in terms of design, improvements were made to usability and accessibility. New functionalities were added, and existing ones were optimized, ensuring that users could complete their tasks more efficiently and quickly. To meet the objective of this research and modify the Koodo Reader project interface, the development team relied on the public license policy "GNU Affero General Public License v3.0" found in the GitHub repository of the creators of this project.

On the other hand, the usability of the developers' proposals was evaluated through the inspection of prototypes with real users. The results obtained from this evaluation showed that proposal number 2 was the most attractive option for most users due to its intuitive interface and more visible options. However, some preferred the aesthetics of proposal number 1. We considered these suggestions to improve the user experience and improve satisfaction with the tool. To this end, changes were made to the original interface considering the implementation of proposal 2 to improve its aesthetics.

Answering the research question "How to incorporate the Interface Content Model technique into the design activities in the OSS development process," it can be highlighted that for the application of the technique in the OSS Koodo Reader project, it was necessary to make adaptations to it, this helped to significantly improve the usability of the software and increase the efficiency of the development, as well as to encourage greater participation of the users in the development process. The adapted Interface Content Model technique can be used in OSS projects to design and evaluate the usability of user interfaces in a structured and transparent way. It is important to note that implementing this technique requires a careful approach and a solid understanding of user needs and expectations.

In line with the findings reported by Llerena et al. [16], the present research also provides results that mainly support the feasibility of adaptations made to the Interface Content Model technique during the design phase for its effective integration in developing OSS projects.

5   Conclusions and Future Work

The present research aims to evaluate the feasibility of using the Interface Content Modeling technique in the OSS Koodo Reader project. Based on the evaluation results, we can affirm that the Interface Content Modeling technique can be beneficial in OSS projects since it allows a better understanding of the interface structure, ease of use, and design quality. Quality improvement in OSS projects is possible thanks to applying usability techniques. In this case, the Interface Content Model technique was applied in the Koodo Reader project, improving the usability to be more attractive to end users. The development of the improvements in this project was carried out thanks to the support of the user community, who, through testing and validation, gave us the feedback to complete the steps in the adapted technique. The users identified the problems in the project and proposed new functionalities to make it more usable. With the help of the prototypes, users could see that the interest in improving the project was confirmed, resulting in a new interface that fits the preferences of this community.

Furthermore, this work represents a significant scientific contribution to the field of usability and HCI in the context of OSS projects. The proposal and adaptation of the Interface Content Model technique in the "Koodo Reader" project offer an innovative perspective to improve the user experience in this type of application. However, it is essential to note that although we have validated the adapted technique in this project, the decision as to whether it will be adopted rests with the original developer of "Koodo Reader" at their discretion. The adaptation has been designed based on the needs and features of the software. However, the final implementation will depend on several factors, such as the project's vision, the availability of resources, and the alignment with the objectives of the development team.

One of the future work is to continue to improve the efficiency and usability of the user interface and functionalities of the selected OSS project. This could be achieved through continuous user feedback and usability testing to identify areas for improvement. In addition, consideration could be given to incorporating new functionality and features to make the project even more valuable and attractive to users. It would also be essential to keep the source code up to date and ensure that the project is compatible with the latest technologies and industry standards to ensure its longevity and relevance.

References

1. Viñar, D.: Free software, free science: exploring some lessons that free software can bring to open science. Informatio **27**(1), 336–371 (2022). https://doi.org/10.35643/Info.27.1.9
2. González, J., Seoane, J., Robles, G.: Introducción al software libre. Primera edición. Fundació per a la Universitat Oberta de Catalunya (2003)
3. The Open source definition: Open source initiative (2006). https://opensource.org/osd. Accessed 19 Jan 2023
4. Timoftei, S., Brad, E., Sarb, A., Stan, O.: Open source software in robotics. Acta Technica Napocensis Ser. Appl. Math. Mech. Eng. **61**(3), 519–526 (2018)
5. DiBona, C., Ockman, S., Stone, M.: Open Sources: Voices from the Open Source Revolution, 1st edn. O'Reilly Media (1999)
6. Enriquez, J.G., Casas, S.I.: Usabilidad en aplicaciones móviles. Informe Científico Técnico UNPA **5**(2), 25–47 (2013). https://doi.org/10.22305/ICT-UNPA.V5I2.71
7. Nielsen, J.: Nielsen's 10 Usability Heuristics (2006). https://www.heurio.co/nielsens-10-usability-heuristics. Accessed 19 Jan 2023
8. Dawood, K.A., Sharif, K.Y., Zaidan, A.A., Abd Ghani, A.A., Zulzalil, H.B., Zaidan, B.B.: Mapping and analysis of open source software (OSS) usability for sustainable OSS product. IEEE Access **7**, 65913–65933 (2019). https://doi.org/10.1109/ACCESS.2019.2914368
9. Yu, X., et al.: An open source platform for computational histopathology. IEEE Access. **9**, 73651–73661 (2021). https://doi.org/10.1109/ACCESS.2021.3080429
10. Lamberti, F., Paravati, G., Gatteschi, V., Cannavo, A., Montuschi, P.: Virtual character animation based on affordable motion capture and reconfigurable tangible interfaces. IEEE Trans. Visual Comput. Graphics **24**(5), 1742–1755 (2018). https://doi.org/10.1109/TVCG.2017.2690433
11. Léger, E., et al.: NousNav: a low-cost neuronavigation system for deployment in lower-resource settings. Int. J. Comput. Assist. Radiol. Surg. **17**(9), 1745–1750 (2022). https://doi.org/10.1007/s11548-022-02644-w

12. Brotherton, T., Brotherton, S., Ashworth, H., Kadambi, A., Ebrahim, H., Ebrahim, S.: Development of an offline, open-source, electronic health record system for refugee care. Front Digit Health **4**, paper 847002 (2022). https://doi.org/10.3389/fdgth.2022.847002
13. Hoskere, V., et al.: InstaDam: open-source platform for rapid semantic segmentation of structural damage. Appl. Sci. **11**(2), paper 520 (2021). https://doi.org/10.3390/APP11020520
14. Dawood, K.A., Sharif, K.Y., Ghani, A.A., Zulzalil, H., Zaidan, A.A., Zai-dan, B.B.: Towards a unified criteria model for usability evaluation in the context of open source software based on a fuzzy Delphi method. Inf. Softw. Technol. **130**, 106453 (2021). https://doi.org/10.1016/J.INFSOF.2020.106453
15. Llerena, L., Rodriguez, N., Gomez-Abajo, P., Castro, J.W., Acuña, S.T.: Adoption of the visual brainstorming in the open source software development process. In: Proceedings of the 2018 IEEE/ACM 40th International Conference on Software Engineering: Companion (ICSE'18-Companion), Gothenburg, Sweden, pp. 232–233 (2018)
16. Llerena, L., Rodriguez, N., Angelita, B., Castro, J.W., Mera, L.: Adoption of the organization of help according to the use case technique in the open-source software development process. In: Arai, K. (eds.) Intelligent Computing. SAI 2023. Lecture Notes in Networks and Systems, vol. 739, pp. 1039–1059. Springer, Cham, (2023). https://doi.org/10.1007/978-3-031-37963-5_72
17. Runeson, P., Höst, M., Rainer, A., Regnell, B.: Case Study Research in Software Engineering: Guidelines and Examples, 1st edn. Wiley (2012)
18. Constantine, L.L., Lockwood, L.A.D.: Software for Use: A Practical Guide to the Models and Methods of Usage-Centered Design, 1st edn. Addison-Wesley Professional (1999)
19. Ferré, X.: Marco de integración de la usabilidad en el proceso de desarrollo software. Tesis PhD, Universidad Politécnica de Madrid, Madrid (España) (2005). https://doi.org/10.20868/UPM.THESIS.440
20. Castro, J.W.: Incorporación de la usabilidad en el proceso de desarrollo open source software. Tesis PhD, Universidad Autónoma de Madrid, Madrid, España (2014)

Developing Custom-Made Comment-Recommendation Prototypes with a Modular Design Framework

Jan Steimann$^{(\boxtimes)}$ (iD) and Martin Mauve

Heinrich Heine University, Universitätsstraße 1, 40225 Düsseldorf, Germany
`jan.steimann@hhu.de`

Abstract. Comment sections of news articles are a popular way to discuss the contents of these articles. But the number of comments posted every day has become so large that almost no one can get a solid overview about the discussion. To address this problem, there are many approaches for comment recommendation systems. However, they tend to focus mostly on the development of sophisticated models to combat this problem while evaluating their systems in limited and mostly artificial settings. In our paper, we introduce a modular open-source software framework for the development of comment recommendation prototypes that can be used to evaluate models in real-world environments. The modularity allows developing systems that are adapted exactly to the use-case or model one needs. This concept allows exchanging and adapting the different components of the concept to test e.g. different user-interfaces or recommendation models. To show the usability of our framework we present the implementations of two comment-recommendation applications.

Keywords: Information Retrieval · User-Interface · Software Development Framework · Recommendation System

1 Introduction

Comments are a popular tool for the exchange of views in online discussions of news media articles. They offer readers the opportunity to exchange opinions about the content of articles and to discuss different points of view. However, the number of comments posted every day has become so large that it is hard – if not impossible – to get a good overview of the discussion. Articles about controversial topics like booster shots for COVID-19 can have a few hundred comments like [7] or even a few thousand like articles about Russia's president Putin [13]. To aid users in navigating the flood of comments posted every day, there exist various approaches, which we will take a look at in Sect. 2.

Many of these approaches so far have focused primarily on developing sophisticated models and only present prototypes in mostly artificial settings. However,

© The Author(s), under exclusive license to Springer Nature Switzerland AG 2024
A. Coman and S. Vasilache (Eds.): HCII 2024, LNCS 14703, pp. 97–112, 2024.
https://doi.org/10.1007/978-3-031-61281-7_7

to realistically assess a model's effectiveness, it is equally important to test it in authentic scenarios. Therefore, it is crucial to evaluate these models under real-world conditions to obtain a genuine impression of their capabilities.

In this paper, we present a solution to this problem by introducing our open-source software framework for developing practical comment recommendation prototypes. These prototypes can be customized for various real-world applications while at the same time reduce the development effort for the evaluation of recommendation models. For this, we provide a complete infrastructure with several exchangeable components. This infrastructure consists among other things of a front-end user interface and backend server. Adjustments to the different components can be easily done without making major changes to the rest of the system. Our new framework reduces the development effort for testing e.g. a new user-interface or recommendation model.

In the following section, we take a look at previous work in the field of comment recommendation. In the third section, we elaborate on the concept for our comment recommendation system and in the fourth section, we explain the implementation of the framework based on the concept of section three. In the last section, we present two example implementations to demonstrate the usefulness of the framework to speed up the development of comment recommendation prototypes that can be used in real-world scenarios.

2   Related Work

Recommendation systems for comment sections of news article have been a popular research field for quite some time since this is an important field of the public debate. These systems can help the reader to get a well-informed opinion by suggesting articles and comments that cover topics which are of great interest for the user. For example, [14] uses the comments of the discussion in which the user currently participates to suggest articles that may interest them. The authors of [11] try a similar strategy by recommending news stories that the user probably will comment.

The recommendation of articles and news stories that the user finds especially interesting is only the first step in supporting the public debate. The actual participation in the public debate begins when the user takes an active part in the discussion and reads comments of other users and formulates their own contribution. Since the beginning of online discussions, various problems have emerged, which are partly induced by the medium itself.

One problem is the vast amount of comments which are posted under the articles. Some article may have few hundred or even a few thousand comments if they cover a current and very controversial topic. For this reason, there are different approaches to help the user navigate the flood of comments. For example, [15] uses a personalized comment recommendation system which sorts out low quality comments and classifies the rest in *insightful view* or *informal comment*. At the end, the system recommends comments to the user based on previous posts from the user. Another approach [5] tries to help the user navigate large discussions by using topic modeling. The system extracts an initial set of topics for the discussion and improves them with on-the-fly user feedback. The topics are then visualized in a user-interface that should help the user to get a better overview of the discussion and quickly identify insightful views in the debate.

Another major problem of online discussion in general is the creation of echo-chambers and filter bubbles. Here, users often find a very homogeneous set of opinions and thus are rarely confronted with ideas that are contrary to their worldview. As a result, these opinions become entrenched, and when users with different opinions clash on a controversial issue such as climate change or migration, a constructive debate is hardly possible.

To address this issue, there are various research approaches, which all have in common that they try to present the user a broader spectrum of opinions during the opinion forming process. In [2], the authors use various techniques like dimensionality reduction with PCA, collaborative filtering, etc. and then present the user an interface that automatically highlights comments that many other users found particularly insightful. The authors of [4] try to help the user to reflect on their own position on the topic by presenting comments which oppose their own stance for the topic and mark them as *recommended*. Comments that align with the view of the user are marked as *not-recommended*.

2.1   Ethical Considerations, Impact, and Intended Application

All these approaches have in common that they mainly focus on the development of algorithms for recommending comments and articles to the user. However, often the evaluation under real-world conditions is not emphasized as much and only demonstrations in a mostly artificial settings are presented. Some work even presents only a design idea how an application for the presented recommendation algorithm might look like. Nevertheless, we believe that the development of prototypes to test the algorithm in a real-world scenario is as important as the development of even more sophisticated algorithms. Therefore, we want to bridge the gap between theoretical research and real-world applications with this paper by presenting an open-source framework for the development of such prototypes.

This framework will help researchers to speed up the evaluation of recommendation models by offering a customizable ready-to-use prototype where only the algorithm that should be tested has to be injected. The researcher can use the prototype for the early development and first internal tests and afterwards customize the prototype, e.g. the user-interface, for further evaluation in larger user studies. Additionally, the framework offers a complete web scraper that only has to be configured for the website that should be included as a data source. Alternatively, the researcher can import any CSV dataset into the database with the provided script.

Our work shares the same ethical implications as all work on recommendation systems in general. It can be used, intentionally or unintentionally, to develop systems that shape certain user behavior in a mischievous way. For example to reinforce opinions about a topic by presenting only article and comments to the user that support a certain opinion. Preventing intentional mischievous behavior is out of scope for our work. However, we believe that our system can help researchers to rigorously test their recommendation algorithm as realistic as possible and by this identify potential negative implications.

3   Comment Recommendation Framework Concept

In this chapter we will explain the concept and structure of our comment recommendation framework and the individual components. We expound on the details of the components and how they interact with each other. In the following, we start from a high level design point of view and then outline the details.

3.1   High Level Design

In the following subsection, we take a look at the contribution of our concept from a high level.

Framework. The main contribution of our framework is the rapid prototyping of comment recommendation systems through our ready-to-use system. The researchers only have to implement the model they would like to test and populate the database either with the news agency scraper or importing a dataset via the CSV reader component which we will both explain in Sect. 3.3. Another advantage of our system is that it can be used in both, a controlled lab scenario as well a real-world scenario, thus providing the researcher with a vast variety of evaluation possibilities. This provides a huge advantage compared to the previous approaches, we have examined in Sect. 2, which often present demonstrations in mostly artificial settings. Furthermore some approaches only present ideas or concepts of how their system could be used in a real-world scenario because the development of a prototype is very time-consuming. Especially, these works would benefit of our framework.

Interchangeable Components. We developed the recommendation framework with a modular design concept in mind. Therefore, the framework consists of several components that can replaced or updated to a new use-case if needed. This allows researches to change or replace every component of the prototype to adapt it to their use-case or to test the effect of changes e.g. in the user-interface or model. This way, they can quickly test new ideas or models without developing a new prototype. Instead, they only replace or change a specific component.

Data Acquisition. A key point of a comment recommendation system is the data and how they are acquired. We provide two solutions for this problem with our framework. If the researches already have a dataset and would like to use it for the prototype, then we provide the CSV reader component to import the dataset into the database of the recommendation prototype. However, if the researchers would like to create a new data basis for their prototype, we offer a news agency scraper system that the researchers can use with little configuration to scrape different news agency sites.

3.2 System Overview

Next, we examine the system in its entirety. As explained in Sect. 3.1, the system consists of several components that were developed independently of each other and are intended to fulfill different roles in the framework. We developed the concept in a modular design web application approach so that every component can easily be replaced or extended. This way, the comment recommendation system should be adaptable for various purposes and we can use the prototype in a laboratory and also in a real-world setting.

If we take a look at the system in its overall form in Fig. 1 we see that the system can be divided into two main parts, front-end and backend.

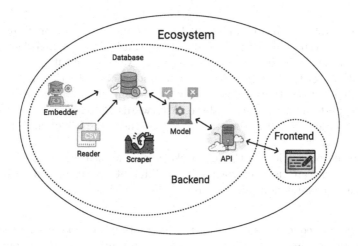

Fig. 1. Overview of the ecosystem concept and its different components. Icons by [6]

On the one hand, we have the front-end, which handles the direct interaction with the user and presents them with the results of the recommendation process.

When the user triggers the recommendation process, a request is sent to the backend server. The backend server receives and extracts all necessary information for the recommendation model from the request. Subsequently, the model is triggered with this information to start the retrieval process. For this purpose, the model makes several queries to the database to gradually extract the final result set, which is then transferred back to the front-end component to render the recommendations.

The database, from which the suggestions have been extracted, builds the foundation for the entire recommendation process. All suggestions that can be presented to the user are extracted here. Having a sufficient data basis is therefore of decisive importance for presenting suitable suggestions. For this purpose, the database is regularly populated with the help of a comment scrapper. The scraper can be configured to query different news agency websites and collect the comments of the current articles and save them in the database. Additionally, if the user possess a dataset they would like to use, our framework provides a CSV reader component to import the dataset into the database. Afterwards, we have to trigger the embedder which calculates the embedding vectors of the new comments and articles with a machine learning model and stores them in the database.

3.3   Components in Detail

In the following, we take a look at the individual components in detail and examine what function they fulfill within the framework.

Frontend. First, we take a look at the front-end component. Depending on the purpose of the system, different user-interfaces can be implemented here to help the reader to interact with comment sections on various websites.

When the user triggers the recommendation process, the UI sends a request with the informations that are needed by the recommendation model to extract suitable suggestions from the database. Afterwards the user-interface waits for the corresponding response from the server to render the list of suggested comments for the user.

Due to the separation of UI and backend communication, it is also easy to replace the complete user-interface with a different approach and to integrate the comment recommendation system in a larger web-system.

API. After the request has been sent by the front-end, the backend server takes over by processing and extracting all necessary information for the recommendation model from the request. The server then hands over the information to the model and afterwards receives the recommendations. Finally, the backend transmits the generated suggestions as a response back to the front-end. Therefore, the backend serves as the interface between the front-end and the recommendation engine.

We choose to use an interface structure so that the recommendation model can be replaced very easily by another model, depending on the purpose of the application prototype. To use another model, we only have to adapt the information extraction from the request.

Model. The model acts as the core of the system. It uses the informations the reader transmits to retrieve a selection of comments from the database.

For the framework, it is irrelevant which model we use. Depending on the use case of the system a different model can be injected into the system at any time if the model uses the same information as before. If the model needs a different set of information for the retrieval process, then these have to be part of the request from the front-end and the API needs to updated accordingly.

When the model is integrated in the code, it is only important that the model provides the correct interface method. How the model extracts the suggestions from the database is of no concern for the rest of the system. This way, it is easy to replace the model.

Database. For the database, we use a graph database which has the great advantage that the connections of the data are first level citizens. This means that we do not have to create the connections between our data by using joins, like relational databases, but the connections are already stored in the database like the nodes. Therefore, the retrieval process can run faster. This is essential for a system that is used in a real-time scenario like an online discussion. If the user has to wait several minutes for the recommendations they will most likely do not use the system.

News Agency Scraper. To present a suitable selection of comments to the user, the recommendation model needs a solid data basis and therefore, we need a system to populate the database. For this, we offer a comment scraper that allows the researcher to scrape arbitrary news agencies that use comment sections. It retrieves the comments from the articles and stores them in the database according to the database schema the recommendation model needs.

CSV Reader. If the researchers already have a dataset they would like to use instead or as an addition to the news agency scraper, we provide the CSV reader component that imports the given dataset into the database.

Embedder. In order for the recommendation model to work with the comments and articles in the database, the text must be in a format that can be processed by the model. For this reason, the last component needed for the framework is an embedder. Here, the researchers implement the embedding method that provides the embeddings that are needed for their recommendation model. We provide a script that fetches the new comments and articles that were just stored in the database by the scraper and calculates the embeddings for the texts. Afterwards, the nodes in the database are updated with the new embeddings.

4   Implementation of the Framework

In the following, we will examine the implementation[1] of the concept presented in Sect. 3. The system was developed in such a way that every component can

---

[1] https://github.com/hhucn/Comment-Recommendation-Framework.

be easily extended or replaced. By this, the implementation can be adapted to various use-cases. Here we take a look at how the concept has been implemented and how to utilize the framework to help researches with rapid prototype development. In Fig. 2, we see an overview of the framework with the concrete tools and libraries we use.

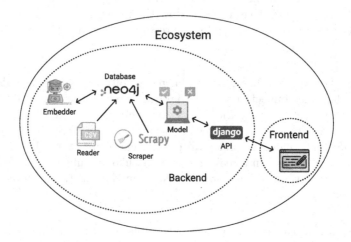

Fig. 2. Overview of the implementation of our framework. Icons by [6]

4.1 Components

In the following, we take a look at how the individual components have been implemented.

Front-End Component. For the user interface we decided to use a Chrome Extension with React [8]. A Chrome Extension is a very small application that can be installed in any Chrome Browser. This gives the researchers various possibilities for their experiment. On the one hand, they can provide a controlled laboratory scenario with pre-configured computers with the Chrome Extension already installed. Or on the other hand, the participants of their study can install the Chrome Extension on their personal computer at home. This opens more opportunities for the researcher to conduct their experiments.

The extension interacts with the website of the news agency and extracts the necessary information for the recommendation model. It then sends these information to the backend server and renders the response with the recommended comments to the user.

The advantage of a Chrome Extension is that it is build modular and we can replace the individual components of the extension at any time. Due to the modularity, we can update or replace different aspects of our user-interface with minimal changes on the rest of the components.

API Component. For the API, we use the Django framework [3] to process the requests from the front-end component. One advantage of Django is that we need very little configuration to process the requests. We only need one view where we instantiate our recommendation model and extract the information for the model from the request. Afterwards the model is called to retrieve the selection of comments from the database and finally the selection is packed in a JSON-response and send to the front-end component.

Database Component. For the implementation of the database explained in Sect. 3.3, we use a Neo4j graph database [9]. We choose a Neo4J graph database because it offers various advantages for our recommendation system prototype. As explained in Sect. 3.3, one advantage is that the connection between the nodes are already stored in the database and do not have to be queried. This speeds up the retrieval process if we need to connect a lot of nodes in the database.

The database schema for our implementation consists of two kinds of nodes. On the one hand, we have the comment nodes where we store the text of the comment and later the embedding vector for the comment text as fields in the node. On the other hand, we have the article nodes where we store the title, keywords, publication date, URL of the article, and the embedding for the article. Every comment that appeared in the comment section of an article is stored as a comment node and is connected to the corresponding article node as we can see in Fig. 3.

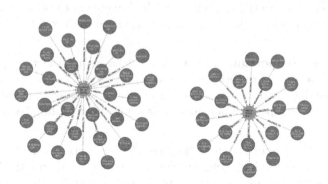

Fig. 3. Extract from the graph database. The blue nodes are the articles and the red ones are the corresponding comment nodes. (Color figure online)

This is the default configuration for the database nodes that is most likely sufficient for the majority of the prototypes. However, the system can be easily adapted with different attributes or even new node types as we will see in Sect. 5.2.

Recommendation Model Component. For the model component, we provide an abstract super class which specifies the interface method that all models have to implement. This method defines that it receives a dictionary with the data extracted from the request and returns a list of comments to be rendered by the user interface. Due to this, we can very easily replace the model with arbitrarily more complex models with only minimal changes to the system. Our new model just needs to extract the information needed from the dictionary and return a list of comments. It is completely irrelevant for the framework and the prototype how much complexity is behind the new model because of the interface method from the abstract super class.

News Agency Scraper Component. As explained in Sect. 3.3, our framework uses a comment scraper that can be configured to scrape arbitrary news sites to populate the database of Sect. 4.1.

For every news site that we want to scrape, we just need to create a new scraper component with functions specific to the HTML structure of the website.

For our implementation, we chose to use the Scrapy Framework [1] to scrape the websites. Our scraper component always works on the same principle. It uses the super class with the code for all news agency specific classes and makes a request to the website of the corresponding news agency for a list of articles. This list is then processed to extract all necessary information such as title, URL, keywords, and publication date. Normally, the comments are loaded in a second request for every article. This request is then also processed to get all comments belonging to the respective article. Finally, all these informations are stored accordingly to the database schema explained in Sect. 4.1.

CSV Reader Component. If the researchers have a dataset they want to use for their prototype and experiment, we also provide a CSV Reader component to import the data into the database. This can also be used as a supplement to the news agency scraper component to provide a sufficient data basis.

Embedder Component. After the News Agency Scraper or CSV reader is done with retrieving or importing articles and comments, we use the Embedder Component written as a Python script to compute the embeddings. The embedder calculates the representations the recommendation model from Sect. 4.1 needs to find the recommendations. For this, it queries all comments and articles from the database that do not have an embedding and computes a vector representation of the information the models needs with the embedding model the user implements.

4.2   Utilization of the Framework

In the following section, we examine how the framework can be utilized to develop custom-made comment recommendation systems.

Package. We implement the framework as a Python package[2] which allows the easy development of recommendation system prototypes. The user just needs to install the package and execute it. Afterwards, the package asks different questions with a dialog to determine which components of the package are needed for the prototype the user would like to develop and then creates a folder only containing the components needed. For example, if the user already has a dataset with articles and comments they would like to use for their experiment, the news agency scraper is obsolete and does not need to be part of the system. Instead, the CSV reader component is used.

Docker and Docker-Compose. To simplify the usage of the prototype in the development and experiments, we dockerized[3] the system and provide different docker-compose files[4] for the components of the system. This allows to run the recommendation system in an isolated environment and by this an easy portability and installation on different systems. Only Docker and Docker-Compose must be installed there. The necessary libraries and images will be downloaded and installed by Docker.

5   Example Implementations

In the following section, we demonstrate how easy two prototypes can be developed using our new open-source software framework. We present the implementations of two different recommendation models. We assume that we do not have a dataset we could use for our experiment and for the first implementation, we only want to test our new recommendation model. Therefore, for the first prototype we do not need to develop a new user interface, but can use the user-interface provided by the framework and we need to use the news agency scraper component to populate the database.

5.1   Example Implementation 1: Comment-Centric Comment Recommendation

In the first example implementation[5], we followed an approach from [12] that differs from previous comment recommendation systems. In contrast to comment recommendation systems so far, the suggestions are not based on previous interests and behavior of the user, but on the comments of the discussion. The user select a comment they would like to see different perspectives for and the model retrieves a selection of comments from the database that provide different points of view for the topic of this comment. According to [12], this approach is called comment-centric comment recommendation.

---

[2] https://pypi.org/project/Comment-Recommendation-Framework/.
[3] https://docs.docker.com/.
[4] https://docs.docker.com/compose/.
[5] https://github.com/hhucn/Example-Implementation-1.

Model. The model consists of a two-step approach. In the first step, it creates a candidate set of comments that it extracts from the database by using the keywords of the article. The candidates are determined using a k-nearest neighbor search using the vector representation of the keywords to find similar articles and taking all comments that appeared under these articles as a candidate set. By this, it reduces the number of possible comments to a manageable amount (Fig. 4 left).

In the next step, it sorts the candidate set based on semantic similarity to the comment the user is interested in (Fig. 4 right). It then takes the top-n comments and send them to the front-end component for rendering.

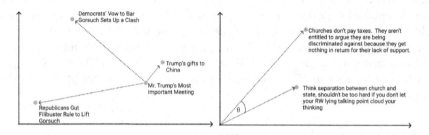

Fig. 4. Left Figure: Find the most similar articles with k-nearest neighbor search. Right figure: Calculate the semantic similarity θ between the comment vectors. Figure from [12]

User-Interface. For the user-interface, we use the ready-to-use built-in UI (Fig. 5) explained in Sect. 4.1. This user-interface renders the suggested comments as a list and provides meta information about the comment while hovering over it, like the article title and URL where the comment has been published.

Implementation Effort. Because we do not have a dataset we could use for our experiment, we have to scrape data from a news agency to test our new model. Therefore, we use the news agency scraper component provided by the package. Here, we only have to write the class that extracts the necessary information from the news agency HTML response. Every news agency has a different HTML structure, hence, we always have to write a class for every news agency we would like to scrape. The rest of the code e.g. to process the data and store them in the database is handled by the framework and has only to be changed if we would like to parse the data in a different way or store other data in the database.

After this, we need to implement the embedding model. Our recommendation model needs vector representations of the article keywords and comments. Therefore, we have to compute these embeddings and store them in the database. Fist, we have to implement the embedding method and then we have to update the script that manages the computation of the embeddings. The script queries

Fig. 5. The recommendations of the model are rendered as a list. If user hover over a certain comment, they are presented with meta information about the comment like the article where it has been posted.

all comments and articles from the database which do not have an embedding, computes the embedding, and then updates the node with it.

In the next step, we need to implement our model. For this, we use the model presented in [12].

At last, we have to consider the user-interface. However, since we use the built-in UI, we do not have any effort here.

5.2 Example Implementation 2: Most Popular Comment Recommendation

In the second example implementation[6], we follow an approach based on [10]. Here, the model recommends comments based on their popularity, and thus helping the user to get an overview which are the most popular opinions about the topic of the discussion.

Model. The model recommends comments by querying similar articles to the article the user is currently interested in and then creates a candidate set of comments from all these articles. Afterwards, the comments are sorted by the number of up-votes they received to find the most popular comments for the topic of the discussion.

User-Interface. For this example implementation, we replace the built-in user-interface the framework offers with a carousel view to demonstrate how easily the user-interface can be adapted to different circumstances. As we see in Fig. 6, this UI displays one comment at a time and rotates though the list of comments when clicking on the left or right arrow.

---

[6] https://github.com/hhucn/Example-Implementation-2.

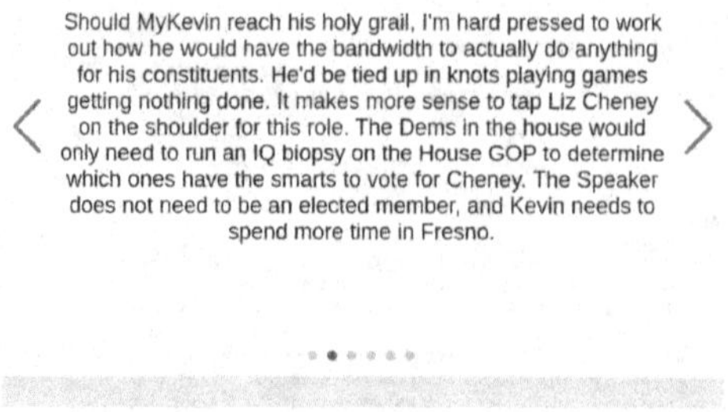

Should MyKevin reach his holy grail, I'm hard pressed to work out how he would have the bandwidth to actually do anything for his constituents. He'd be tied up in knots playing games getting nothing done. It makes more sense to tap Liz Cheney on the shoulder for this role. The Dems in the house would only need to run an IQ biopsy on the House GOP to determine which ones have the smarts to vote for Cheney. The Speaker does not need to be an elected member, and Kevin needs to spend more time in Fresno.

Fig. 6. The recommended comments are displayed one at a time in a carousel view. The user can rotate through the list of comments by clicking the left or right arrow.

Implementation Effort. The implementation effort for this example system is very similar to the example system in Subsect. 5.1. The only differences are that we need to scrape the number of up-votes a comment has received, the user-interface, and implement a different recommendation model.

To scrape the additional data, we need to update the database schema by adding an additional *up_votes* field to the *Comment* class and by this adding a new property to the comment node in the Neo4J database. Then, we need to update the *process_item* method in the *pipelines* file to store the new property in the database. The class with the news agency specific methods is nearly the same as in Sect. 5.1 with the exception that we also need to scrape the number of up votes a comment has received.

Next, we update the user-interface. For this, we only have to add a new *carousel component* to the *component* folder of the UI folder where we define how the list of comments should be rendered. Then we have to replace the build in *list* component with the new component in *App.js*.

At last, we need to implement the recommendation model from [10].

5.3 Saved Work

After we have developed the two example implementations and examined the implementation effort, we clearly see the amount of technical code that we did not have to write by using the comment recommendation framework. Let us take a look at the components we did not have to implement.

First, we did not need to implement the complete infrastructure provided by the framework like the user-interface, the API, and the database. Additionally, we use a system that scrapes, processes, and stores the data of news agency sites in the database. At last, all this is already containerized with docker and docker-compose and therefore, can be used on any device that has docker and docker-compose installed.

6 Conclusion

In our work, we introduced an open-source software framework for rapid proto-typing of comment recommendation systems to quickly evaluate new algorithms.

With this, we try to relieve researchers of the tedious work of developing prototypes from scratch. While at the same time offering the possibility to evaluate the recommendation model in a realistic setting.

The framework provides a complete modular infrastructure to run a recommendation system in a web application context. This allows to use the system in a laboratory as well as a real-world setting while also reducing the development effort because only prototype specific code has to be written.

Our approach for the development of custom made comment recommendation systems consists of several components which can easily be replaced or updated without major changes to the rest of the system. This allows the researcher to adapt the prototype to new use cases or test e.g. different user-interfaces.

Additionally, we offer a solution for a key point of a comment recommendation system, the data acquisition. A recommendation system can only provide solid suggestions if it has solid data basis. Therefore, we offer two approaches to populate the database for the system. On the one hand, we provide a script to import an existing dataset into the database. On the other hand, we offer a system to scrape arbitrary news agencies sites and store this data in the database.

In future work, we will continue the development of our comment recommendation framework by extending the framework for other kinds of recommendation systems and improving it in general. For this, we will provide more generalized user-interfaces and recommendation model interfaces. Additionally, we will continue to thoroughly test our system in larger field experiments with more sophisticated comment recommendation models and add more features.

References

1. Scrapy (2022). https://scrapy.org/
2. Faridani, S., Bitton, E., Ryokai, K., Goldberg, K.: Opinion space: a scalable tool for browsing online comments. In: Proceedings of the SIGCHI Conference on Human Factors in Computing Systems, pp. 1175–1184 (2010)
3. Foundation, D.S.: Django (2022). https://www.djangoproject.com
4. Gao, M., Do, H.J., Fu, W.T.: Burst your bubble! an intelligent system for improving awareness of diverse social opinions. In: 23rd International Conference on Intelligent User Interfaces, pp. 371–383 (2018)
5. Hoque, E., Carenini, G.: Convisit: interactive topic modeling for exploring asynchronous online conversations. In: Proceedings of the 20th International Conference on Intelligent User Interfaces, pp. 169–180 (2015)
6. Icons8: Interface, server, database, excavate icons by icons8 (2022). https://icons8.com
7. LaFraniere, S.: Biden administration plans to offer second booster shots to those 50 and up (2022). https://www.nytimes.com/2022/03/25/us/politics/biden-second-booster-shot-older-americans.html
8. Meta Platforms, I.: React framework (2022). https://reactjs.org/
9. Neo4j, I.: Neo4j graph database (2022). https://neo4j.com/
10. Reuver, M., Mattis, N.: Implementing evaluation metrics based on theories of democracy in news comment recommendation (hackathon report). In: Proceedings of the EACL Hackashop on News Media Content Analysis and Automated Report Generation, pp. 134–139 (2021)

11. Shmueli, E., Kagian, A., Koren, Y., Lempel, R.: Care to comment? Recommendations for commenting on news stories. In: Proceedings of the 21st International Conference on World Wide Web, pp. 429–438 (2012)
12. Steimann, J., Feger, M., Mauve, M.: Inspiring heterogeneous perspectives in news media comment sections. In: Yamamoto, S., Mori, H. (eds.) HCII 2022. LNCS, vol. 13305, pp. 118–131. Springer, Cham (2022). https://doi.org/10.1007/978-3-031-06424-1_10
13. Stephens, B.: What if putin didn't miscalculate? (2022). https://www.nytimes.com/2022/03/29/opinion/ukraine-war-putin.html
14. Wang, J., Li, Q., Chen, Y.P.: User comments for news recommendation in social media. In: Proceedings of the 33rd International ACM SIGIR Conference on Research and Development in Information Retrieval, pp. 881–882 (2010)
15. Zhou, M., Shi, R., Xu, Z., He, Y., Zhou, Y., Lan, L.: Design of personalized news comments recommendation system. In: Zhang, C., et al. (eds.) ICDS 2015. LNCS, vol. 9208, pp. 1–5. Springer, Cham (2015). https://doi.org/10.1007/978-3-319-24474-7_1

Spatial Design and Implementation
of an Agent System Leading to Bed

Xin Wan[1]([✉]) [iD] and Tomoko Yonezawa[2,3,4] [iD]

[1] Graduate School of Informatics, Kansai University, 2-1-1, Ryozenji-Cho, Takatsuki,
Osaka 569-1095, Japan
[2] Faculty of Informatics, Kansai University, 2-1-1, Ryozenji-Cho, Takatsuki,
Osaka 569-1095, Japan
[3] ATR Interaction Science Laboratories, 2-2-2, Hikaridai, Soraku-gun,
Kyoto 619-0288, Japan
[4] Keio University, 5322, Endo, Fujisawa, Kanagawa 252-0882, Japan
{k805631,yone}@kansai-u.ac.jp

Abstract. This research focuses on improving the sleep process for the
elderly, including those with dementia, and builds upon the works of
Wan et al. [20] and Zhang et al. [24]. Wan et al. introduced a wall
projection-type Humanitude agent system, employing multimodal interaction for the care of elderly individuals with dementia. This system uses
a naked eye stereoscopic agent for visual presentation and air currents
for tactile presentation, which has been confirmed effective in fostering an emotional connection. Zhang et al. proposed a blanket-type sleep
support agent addressing older adults' physical, cognitive, and psychological declines. This system uses visual presentation to lead the user
to bed and features tactile presentation with blanket-type arms for gestures like patting and hugging. Our study develops an innovative system
combining these approaches. It integrates visual presentation from the
Humanitude agent with tactile presentation from the blanket-type sleep
support agent. This system employs a projector for immersive visual
presentations and a physical contact device simulating actions like tapping and stroking. Leveraging Augmented Reality (AR) and multimodal
interaction, this study aims to provide a comforting sleep environment,
enhancing sleep quality for the elderly and the general population. We
evaluated the agent system's effectivity, and the experiments' results
confirmed the effectiveness of the proposed bed induction animation and
tactile feedback resembling touch. Yet, the progression towards achieving
deep sleep remains unverified.

Keywords: Elderly care system · Sleep support · Tactile
presentation · AR agent · User evaluation

1 Introduction

In recent decades, sleep issues like shorter duration, disturbances, and poor quality have escalated due to societal and economic factors [11]. These disturbances

are linked to increased suicide risk and may contribute to cognitive decline and dementia [6]. In dementia patients, inadequate sleep significantly raises health risks and mortality, burdening caregivers [2]. Approximately 40% of elderly individuals experience poor sleep. Besides, anxiety and sleep problems frequently occur together in this age group, and there is a significant relationship between them. Sleep problems impact physical function, affecting overall health and quality of life [12, 21].

Sensory stimulation, implemented in nursing homes, holds promise as an effective approach for enhancing conditions such as dementia, mood disorders, and behavioral issues. As a point in case, Humanitude is a caregiving approach specifically designed for the elderly, particularly those with dementia [7]. This method emphasizes non-violent communication, body language, and visual and tactile contact to build trust and intimacy.

Wright et al. [22] discuss the significance of physical contact (referred to as "skinship") in elderly care in Japan. It emphasizes the importance of touch in building trust and familial-like relationships between caregivers and residents, especially for those who cannot communicate verbally. Crucial for providing comfort and creating a sense of familial closeness, this tactile interaction, including hugging, patting, and massaging, is essential. In the Human-Robot Interaction (HRI) field, some robots equipped with tactile sensing capabilities have already been widely utilized in various fields, such as human-robot interaction, entertainment, and caregiving. Patients' health may be affected by companion bots. For instance, Paro [19], a robot designed to look like a seal, has been developed and utilized to aid the elderly at a day service center. Physical interaction with the seal robot has resulted in improved emotional well-being for the elderly. Furthermore, interacting with a mobile social robot named LOVOT through touch or hugs can evoke feelings of security. Additionally, professional caregivers have embraced LOVOT as a valuable tool in their work with dementia patients [5].

Touch communication is often considered the most primal method of interaction between parents and children [14], and touch is recognized as the most crucial and fundamental sense for humans [8]. It is known that both the one touching and the one being touched experience the secretion of neurotransmitters like oxytocin, essential for increasing attachment and emotional stability [18]. Thus, touch can be described as a fundamental and vital modality.

Also, Shibagaki et al. [13] found that a mother's rocking motion is the most effective inducing sleep in adults. There are specially designed rocking beds that offer vestibular stimulation, which may present a promising alternative to conventional pharmaceutical treatments for individuals with sleep problems. These beds can provide regenerative sleep without causing unwanted side effects [3, 15]. Therefore, we also consider simulating a mother's patting and stroking motions during sleep, which can alleviate anxiety and soothe emotions in adults, elderly individuals, or patients with dementia to induce sleep.

This study involves inducing users to the bed by visually presenting the agent projected on the wall screen as it approaches and enters the bed. Subsequently, tactile sensations such as patting and stroke touches are presented to the user using a robotic arm, helping to alleviate the user's mood until they fall asleep. It is expected that the trust established by elderly individuals in the agent through the sleep support system will lead to greater acceptance of care, stress reduction, emotional stability, and improved sleepiness promotion.

This paper reports the results of a verification experiment involving the proposed system, which investigates how an agent's comforting sleep environment through visual, tactile, and auditory cues affects the user's emotional state. The experiment involved analyzing variance (ANOVA); the findings are presented in this paper.

2   Related Research

2.1   Guide-Agent Systems

Research about interactive museum tour guidance [4] investigated the effectiveness of personalized guidance agents in museum tours. They found that employing anthropomorphic guidance agents can enhance visitors' experiences and engagement, increasing the museum's attendance rates. A study of nursing and daily-life guide agents [16] focused on utilizing personalized guidance agents in healthcare and daily life. They discovered that these agents can provide personalized support to patients, thereby improving the quality and efficiency of care. Besides, research about animation guide pups-pet [17] explored the impact of using animated guide puppets in the fields of education and entertainment. They found that these anthropomorphic characters can better guide users, enhancing the appeal of learning and entertainment experiences.

The aforementioned prior studies indicate that the effectiveness of anthropomorphic guidance systems lies in their ability to establish more natural and human-like interactions with users, thereby enhancing user engagement, communication, and overall user experience. This aligns with the purpose of our system. Our system aims to construct a personalized virtual agent to encourage users to go to bed and sleep.

2.2   Haptic Interactive Systems

Research in the field of haptics is gaining attention for its study of active haptic interactions, which aim to facilitate natural and effective communication and collaboration between humans and robots through tactile information.

Meng et al. [9] aimed to express emotions through various gripping styles on a user's hand using a robotic hand to present emotional, tactile information. They proposed a method of expressing emotions by utilizing various tactile actuators to modify the gripping force of the fingers and the duration of the robotic hand's grip. It was demonstrated that this robotic hand was perceived as more sensitive and exhibited higher affinity as the gripping force increased. Furthermore, an increase in affinity was observed with longer grip durations.

Nakagawa et al. [10] conducted an experiment where a robot's active touch boosted motivation. Participants performed tasks with the robot's active, passive, or no touch. Active touch increases actions and task time, enhancing motivation.

Touching by the robot itself can convey the robot's emotions and state to the user [1] and combining robot touch with speech can also influence the impression of the robot [23]. Thus, touching holds considerable potential, and it is considered beneficial to improve mood before sleep. In this study, we propose an agent that accompanies sleep by combining a naked-eye stereoscopic vision system to enhance the presence of the virtual agent and tactile feedback to simulate contact from the robot. The agent usually accompanies the user's daily life, visually indicating the invitation to bed. After the user gets into bed, it provides tactile feedback resembling comforting touches from a mother, aiming to improve the user's mood before and after sleep.

Physical touch, whether intentional or unintentional, is believed to be capable of expressing emotions. Intimate and emotional physical contact is expected to deepen relationships and evoke strong emotions in the recipient's heart. Additionally, such intimate and emotional communication is believed to impact individuals' daily quality of life, particularly the elderly and children.

3   System

3.1   System Overview

This system focuses on improving the process of falling asleep, specifically targeting general and elderly individuals, including those suffering from dementia, and aims to smoothly guide them to bed. Importantly, this system is not an isolated effort; it builds upon previous research [20,24] and seeks to develop a new system to assist sleep induction. The goal is to refine and expand these studies using Augmented Reality (AR).

This system's approach includes two key elements: 1) Integration of a visual presentation derived from the movements of the Humanitude agent, and 2) Combination of this with a tactile presentation from the tactile devices of a blanket-type sleep support agent. This system has created a new visual presentation component that effectively utilizes a projector to display these visual presentations on a wall, providing an immersive environment for the user. Configured to appeal to the senses of multimodal features (visual, auditory, and haptic features), the system operates as follows: 1) A room-accompanying agent, rendered in naked-eye stereoscopic vision, is projected onto a wall, speaking to the user to induce sleep. 2) When the user enters the bed, the agent approaches the bed. 3) The agent then cuddles next to the bed and, using a tactile generation device that simulates the human arm, repeatedly performs movements such as light tapping (patting) and stroking on the user, accompanied by voice commands to facilitate falling asleep.

The system consists of a PC, a projector, an Arduino[1], and a robotic arm controlled by a servomotor. The visual presentation is projected onto a white wall. The movement and strength of the tactile presentation are simply changed by a servomotor, which is controlled by the PC via the Arduino. The system's visual, auditory, and haptic presentation components are described as follows.

Fig. 1. The agent's appearance

3.2   Visual Presentation Part

The visual presentation of this system is based on the related research [20]. As shown in Fig. 1, an agent with a face, body, and limbs is projected onto a wall screen using a projector (EPSON EH-TW5200).

We designed a semi-transparent virtual agent using naked-eye stereoscopic technology and Processing[2] software. To enhance realism, augmented reality (AR) technology was utilized to integrate the 3D model of the agent into the real-world background. The agent uses voice and visual effects to guide the user to the bed. When the user lies down, an FSR406 pressure sensor attached to the pillow detects this action (refer to Fig. 2) and sends data to Processing via an Arduino (UNO R3 ATmega328P). In Processing, when the system detects that the user has lain down, it triggers the action of the agent approaching the user. The agent's walking animation (Fig. 3) is intricately designed to stimulate the process of gradually approaching the user, with the body simultaneously growing larger, enhancing the realism of the approach, and increasing presence. The agent walking up to the side of the bed is set to last for 3 s.

Then, the virtual agent collaborates with the tactile presentation, swinging its arms up and down to achieve the patting visual effect, as shown in Fig. 4, and moving its arms left and right to accomplish the stroking visual effect, as depicted in Fig. 5.

---

[1] https://www.arduino.cc/.
[2] https://processing.org/.

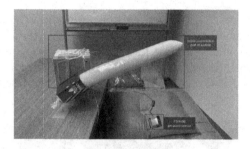

Fig. 2. Set of FSR406 pressure sensor and tactile device

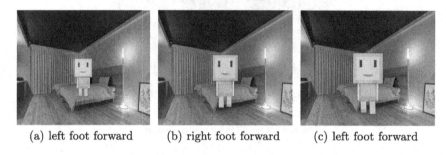

(a) left foot forward   (b) right foot forward   (c) left foot forward

Fig. 3. The agent's walk action

3.3 Tactile Presentation Part

The tactile presentation of this system is based on related research [24]. The blanket-type physical contact device is designed to simulate 'tapping' and 'stroking' actions (refer to Fig. 6). These tactile presentations are a crucial part of the sleep induction process, as they aim to replicate the soothing effects of human touch. By integrating these tactile cues, our system strives to create a comforting atmosphere conducive to sleep, encouraging the user to fall asleep more easily.

The tactile device of this system, as depicted in Fig. 2, consists of a servo motor (GWS S03N Standard) and a mechanical arm for simulating tactile sensations. The mechanical arm is a 50 cm cylindrical container made of plastic film filled with approximately 100 g of cotton. The servo motor is connected to the mechanical arm and is controlled by an Arduino to rotate it, thereby performing the patting and stroking actions.

Both the patting and stroking actions are accomplished using the same tactile device. During the patting, the servo motor is configured to rotate from 100 to 40° per second, with a pause of 1.5 s. The patting force is approximately 1 N. For the stroking action, the servo motor is configured to rotate from 90° to 0° per second, with a pause of 1 s.

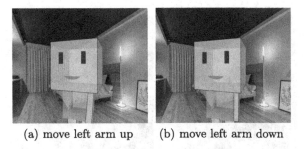

(a) move left arm up   (b) move left arm down

Fig. 4. The agent's patting action

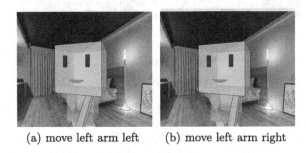

(a) move left arm left   (b) move left arm right

Fig. 5. The agent's stroke action

3.4 Auditory Presentation Part

The agent's speech is vocalized through a Text-To-Speech (TTS) Synthesis online application[3]. During the experimental preparation phase, a pilot experiment was conducted with 5 participants to select two different voices with pitch, volume, and speech rate variations. One voice was perceived as normal conversation, while the other was perceived as soft-spoken and gentle. The speech is played through external speakers.

The virtual agent's dialogue is set to fixed content. Initially, the dialogue content is: "Hey, hey, it's bedtime. Can't sleep? Let me help you fall asleep. Get into bed quickly, please."

Afterward, if the user lies in bed, the virtual agent will approach the user's bedside, triggering the voice prompt. At this point, the dialogue changes to: "Please relax."

The tactile feedback is activated after each "Please relax" voice prompt. This segment will last for 1 min and 30 s in the experiment.

4 Exploratory Evaluation

To investigate the effectiveness of this system, we administered the following within-subject design experimental research.

---

[3] https://voicespeaker.ai/.

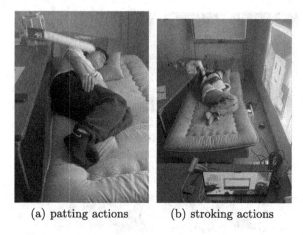

(a) patting actions   (b) stroking actions

Fig. 6. Tactile device

According to the mean opinion score (MOS) method, the participants provided scores using a five-point Likert scale (1 = strongly disagree, 2 = disagree, 3 = undecided, 4 = agree, 5 = strongly agree). The statements were as follows. Q1–Q4, Q7–Q8 were related to familiarity and kindness, Q5 was related to inner peace, Q6 was related to sleepiness, Q9–Q11 were related to favor, Q9 was related to presence, Q10–Q11 was related to discomfort.

4.1 Questionnaire Item

- Q1: When I was put to bed by the agent, I felt a sense of security.
- Q2: When I was put to bed by the agent, I felt a sense of trust.
- Q3: When I was put to bed by the agent, I felt loved.
- Q4: When I was put to bed by the agent, I felt happy.
- Q5: When I was put to bed by the agent, I felt calm.
- Q6: When I was put to bed by the agent, I felt sleepy.
- Q7: I feel a sense of goodwill towards the agent.
- Q8: I felt a sense of comfort from the agent.
- Q9: I felt like the agent was nearby.
- Q10: I felt fear towards the agent.
- Q11: When I was put to bed by the agent, I felt discomfort.

4.2 Hypotheses

- H1: When the agent puts the user to sleep, the user feels sleepier through visual and tactile cues, such as stroking motions, and audio cues, like murmurs.
- H2: When the agent puts the user to sleep, the user feels a sense of security, trust, and being loved through a visual and tactile presentation of caressing movements and audio presentation of a whisper-like voice.

– H3: When the agent puts the user to sleep, the agent's presence can be felt even more through the combination of the visual presentation of the stroking motion, the tactile sensation, and the audio presentation of the user's murmuring voice.

4.3 Participants

The experiment involved 16 participants from Kansai University aged 19 to 31 (8 males and eight females; average age: 24.00 years; standard deviation: 2.68). The participants were randomly selected and participated voluntarily.

In conducting this experiment, we have meticulously adhered to ethical standards to ensure the well-being of all participants and to align with legal requirements. Recognizing the potential risks associated with the behaviors of the agent system in our study, we incorporated comprehensive protocols for informed consent into our experimental design. This ensured that all participants were fully aware of the nature of the experiment and their right to withdraw at any time without consequence.

4.4 Procedure

Illustrate the image of the experimental setup in Fig. 7. The projector was positioned 30 cm away from the wall. The tactile feedback device was pre-adjusted to align with the participants' positions in the experiment. The room's lighting was dimmed by turning off the overhead lights to simulate a sleep environment.

Before commencing the experiment, participants were briefed about the nature of this study, a validation experiment for a sleep-inducing agent system. They were informed that the image projected onto the wall represented the agent, the device placed on the bed was a tactile feedback device, and they were requested to envision the experimental environment as if it were their bedroom.

Subsequently, participants were asked to lie on the bed before the experiment started. The position of the robot arm was adjusted to make contact with the participant's shoulder. Additionally, participants were instructed to orient their heads toward the screen to have a clear view of the visual cues. Participants were allowed to practice the session flow in preparation for the actual sessions (8 in total). Initially, participants would listen to the voice prompt, proceed to the bed, and lie down. Following this, tactile feedback was administered to confirm the positioning. During the actual sessions, after initiating the experiment with a signal, the agent played sleep-inducing voice prompts based on the experimental conditions. When participants lay down on the bed, the agent moved and provided approaching visual cues, concurrently driving the tactile feedback device in accordance with the specific tactile actions associated with the visual cues. After signaling the end of the experiment, the participants were asked to fill out the questionnaires in the presence of the data collector after signing written informed consent.

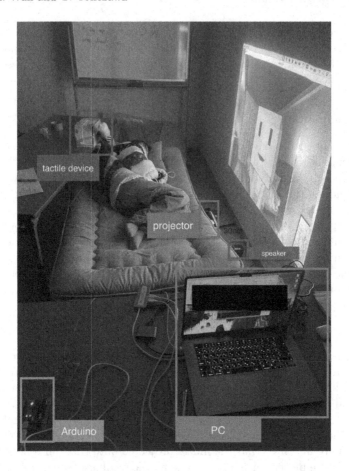

Fig. 7. Experiment environment

4.5 Experimental Conditions

There are three factors. Each factor has two conditions.

– Factor A: Visual Cues
  • A1: The agent guides the patient to the bed and displays a tapping or stroking action (action depended on the tactile cues).
  • A2: The agent remains next to the bed without movement.

– Factor B: Auditory Cues
  • B1: Speaks in a soothing whispering voice.
  • B2: Speaks in a normal tone.

– Factor C: Tactile Cues
  • C1: Tap
  • C2: Stroke

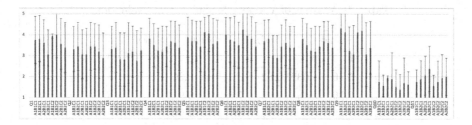

Fig. 8. Mean and SD

4.6   Experimental Result

This study evaluates the impact of three sensory modalities (visual, auditory, and tactile) on subjective assessments. Statistical analysis was conducted using ANOVA on the subjective scores for different sensory stimuli. The results of the ANOVA are shown in Table 1.

The experimental results under the visual modality showed significant differences for questions Q1, Q6, Q7, and Q9. This indicates that the visual sensory modality notably impacts scores related to feelings of security, sleepiness, goodwill towards the agent, and the agent's presence. The findings suggest that participants exhibited significant score differences in these areas under visual conditions, highlighting the importance of visual cues in influencing these perceptions.

As shown in Fig. 8, the mean scores and standard deviations (SD) for different questions in each sensory modality are represented in a bar graph. The range of score variations in the visual modality is large, with particularly high mean scores and relatively large standard deviations for question Q9, reflecting the high variability in scores. On the other hand, the variations in scores for the auditory and tactile modalities are smaller, with closely clustered standard deviations, indicating more consistency in scores.

The analysis of auditory presentation indicates that none of the questions exhibited a p-value lower than 0.05. As a result, it can be inferred that there were no noteworthy alterations in subjective scores during auditory conditions. Similarly, the analysis of tactile presentation reveals no significant statistical variances. However, the anticipated outcomes from the anticipated multimodal interaction effects encompassing visual, auditory, and tactile stimuli did not materialize.

Table 1. Analysis of Variance for Subjective Evaluation

	Visual		Auditory		Tactile		Significant Interaction
	F	p	F	p	F	p	
Q1	5.56	0.03*	0.82	0.38	1.34	0.26	–
Q2	2.56	0.13	0.10	0.76	0.01	0.91	–
Q3	2.52	0.13	0.81	0.38	0.00	1.00	–
Q4	1.91	0.19	0.42	0.52	0.40	0.54	–
Q5	3.72	0.07	0.36	0.56	1.63	0.22	–
Q6	5.09	0.04*	2.67	0.12	0.64	0.44	–
Q7	5.74	0.03*	0.12	0.74	1.00	0.33	–
Q8	1.91	0.19	0.42	0.53	0.40	0.54	–
Q9	11.29	0.00*	0.00	1.00	0.00	1.00	–
Q10	2.09	0.17	0.77	0.40	2.48	0.14	–
Q11	4.28	0.06	1.47	0.25	2.13	0.17	–

*$p < 0.05$

5 Discussion

Based on the experimental results, the study found that the visual modality plays a significant role in the effectiveness assessment of the sleep assistance system. In contrast, the auditory and tactile modalities have relatively minor effects. These results imply that visual stimuli are more effective in enhancing users' sense of security and sleepiness and their liking and presence with the agent. This discovery underscores the importance of visual elements in the design of sleep assistance systems. It may guide future research toward a greater emphasis on developing and utilizing visual stimuli to optimize the user experience. Furthermore, it suggests that the potential of auditory and tactile stimuli in enhancing sleep assistance systems has not been fully explored and requires further investigation.

In particular, regarding the result that visual cues had a soporific effect on the participants, we believe it may be attributed to the content of the visual stimuli, which simulated a relaxing and tranquil bedroom environment. This likely prompted a relaxation response from the participants, leading to a sensation of drowsiness. Furthermore, the visual stimuli predominantly featured an orange spectrum, akin to natural sunset lighting, which aided in preparing the body for sleep.

Besides, in a previous study [24], we found that tapping tactile feedback made it easier for participants to perceive affection, respect, and comfort from the agent system. Additionally, participants felt that the surrogate system was friendly, made them feel acknowledged, and treated them with respect, whether through visual or tactile means. Therefore, even if there were no apparent differences in the method of tactile feedback, we believe that this result indicates that the hugging-like and tapping tactile feedback used in this study has the same emotional transmission effect. In other words, they can provide a sense of presence, trust, and affection.

5.1 Limitation of This Study

After the experiment concluded, we conducted interviews with the participants. Regarding the auditory modality, some participants noted that the sound of the servo motor was too loud, overshadowing the system's audio. Thus, they did not notice the sensations brought about by the sound.

This suggests that the actual effectiveness of sound in the experiment was hindered by mechanical noise, which may explain why the auditory modality was not as pronounced as the visual modality in the experiment. Therefore, it is essential to consider the impact of environmental noise on experimental results in experimental design. Future research should consider exploring effective ways to utilize sound to enhance user experience or improve sound delivery systems to reduce background noise interference.

Besides, it's important to note that this experiment had a relatively small number of participants, which poses limitations on the data. Therefore, future research should involve more participants to validate the effectiveness of auditory and tactile stimuli further.

Additionally, before the experiment, participants were informed that it was related to a sleep-promotion system. Due to the expectancy effect, participants may have experienced drowsiness based on this information. Consequently, for future experiments, we consider incorporating objective data monitoring, such as heart and respiration rates, to assess whether the system induces drowsiness.

5.2 Safe and Secure Concerns and Countermeasure Guidelines

In this paper, we first emphasize the importance of delving into the improvement of robots in caregiving activities, specifically in terms of their verbal and behavioral expressions, to further enhance the accuracy and effectiveness of research. It is crucial to explore and understand the differences in comforting methods accustomed by individuals from various cultural and social backgrounds and appropriately translate these differences into the comforting actions of robots to avoid causing offense or discomfort. Moreover, we discuss the challenges that may arise in the technical implementation, particularly the potential discrepancy between the actual and apparent reliability of robots. We note that in real-world interactions, individuals often predict others' personalities and behavioral intentions based on their outward characteristics and actions. For instance, in caregiving scenarios for the elderly, caregiving actions based on respect can facilitate a smoother nursing process. However, the current system design has not fully considered this element, which could lead to inappropriate behavioral expressions by robots, thereby affecting their credibility.

To address these challenges, we propose several measures: firstly, to establish relevant laws and standards guiding the use and application of agents; secondly, to incorporate elements of the Humanitude caregiving method by researching practices in caregiving settings to optimize the language and behavioral expressions of the system in actual application scenarios.

We also express concern over the limitations of the agent system in simulating human-like behavior and language expressions, which may lead to user experience issues such as discomfort, psychological pressure, feelings of coercion, or harassment. To this end, we suggest allowing users to use the system with an understanding of the relevant disclaimers and providing customer service support to address feedback issues promptly and, if necessary, suspend user access and delete their data.

Lastly, we emphasize the importance of investigating the ethical and societal issues related to robots that express induced emotions, including the potential impact of such robots on human emotions and behaviors and the development of appropriate guidelines for their use. Although robots capable of inducing behaviors may play a role in managing and regulating user behavior and providing companionship, the potential risks of misuse and the resultant unease cannot be overlooked. Therefore, a more in-depth and long-term review of this research field is necessary to better understand the impact of robots exhibiting human behavioral characteristics on society.

6   Conclusion

In this study, we proposed a system aimed at gently guiding both dementia patients and the general population into sleep by combining visual cues using a wall-mounted projection agent to guide users to bed, auditory prompts inviting users to bed, and tactile feedback in the form of light tapping or stroking gestures directed towards the user.

The results of the experiments confirmed the effectiveness of the proposed bed induction animation and tactile feedback resembling touch, yet the progression toward achieving deep sleep remains unverified. Additionally, improvements are necessary to make the tactile feedback gestures feel more natural. Moving forward, evaluations of the sleep support effects using this system should be conducted, and future research should focus on further optimizing control objectives, such as minimizing noise emissions. This aspect is crucial for sleep-related applications.

Acknowledgments. This research was supported in part by JSPS KAKENHI 23K11202, 23K11278, 21K11968, 19K12090 and JST Moonshot R&D Program (Grant Number JPMJMS2215). JPMJMS2215 supported Investigating the proposed system's safety and security, and the others supported the system implementation and the experiment.

References

1. Biquand, S., Zittel, B.: Care giving and nursing, work conditions and humanitude®. Work **41**(Supplement 1), 1828–1831 (2012)
2. Bombois, S., Derambure, P., Pasquier, F., Monaca, C.: Sleep disorders in aging and dementia. J. Nutrition Health Aging **14**, 212–217 (2010)
3. Breuss, A., Suter, Z., Fujs, M., Riener, R.: Enhancing sleep quality with closed-loop autotuning of a robotic bed. In: 2023 International Conference on Rehabilitation Robotics (ICORR), pp. 1–6. IEEE (2023)
4. Burgard, W., et al.: Experiences with an interactive museum tour-guide robot. Artif. Intell. **114**(1–2), 3–55 (1999)
5. Dinesen, B., et al.: Use of a social robot (LOVOT) for persons with dementia: exploratory study. JMIR Rehabil. Assist. Technol. **9**(3), e36505 (2022)
6. Drapeau, C.W., Nadorff, M.R., McCall, W.V., Titus, C.E., Barclay, N., Payne, A.: Screening for suicide risk in adult sleep patients. Sleep Med. Rev. **46**, 17–26 (2019). https://doi.org/10.1016/j.smrv.2019.03.009, https://www.sciencedirect.com/science/article/pii/S1087079218301515
7. Fukuyasu, Y., et al.: The effect of humanitude care methodology on improving empathy: a six-year longitudinal study of medical students in Japan. BMC Med. Educ. **21**(1), 316 (2021)
8. McGlone, F., Wessberg, J., Olausson, H.: Discriminative and affective touch: sensing and feeling. Neuron **82**(4), 737–755 (2014)
9. Meng, X., Yoshida, N., Wan, X., Yonezawa, T.: Emotional gripping expression of a robotic hand as physical contact. In: Proceedings of the 7th International Conference on Human-Agent Interaction, pp. 37–42 (2019)
10. Nakagawa, K., Shiomi, M., Shinozawa, K., Matsumura, R., Ishiguro, H., Hagita, N.: Effect of robot's active touch on people's motivation. In: Proceedings of the 6th International Conference on Human-robot Interaction, pp. 465–472 (2011)
11. Patel, S.R.: Social and demographic factors related to sleep duration. Sleep **30**(9), 1077 (2007)
12. Reyes, S., Algarin, C., Bunout, D., Peirano, P.: Sleep/wake patterns and physical performance in older adults. Aging Clin. Exp. Res. **25**, 175–181 (2013)
13. Shibagaki, H., Ashida, K., Morita, Y., Ikeura, R., Yokoyama, K.: Verifying the sleep-inducing effect of a mother's rocking motion in adults. J. Robot. Netw. Artif. Life **4**(2), 129–133 (2017)
14. Shibata, M., et al.: Broad cortical activation in response to tactile stimulation in newborns. NeuroReport **23**(6), 373–377 (2012)
15. van Sluijs, R., et al.: Gentle rocking movements during sleep in the elderly. J. Sleep Res. **29**(6), e12989 (2020)
16. Taggart, W., Turkle, S., Kidd, C.D.: An interactive robot in a nursing home: preliminary remarks. Towards Soc. Mech. Android Sci. **2005**, 56–61 (2005)
17. Tochigi, H., Shinozawa, K., Hagita, N.: User impressions of a stuffed doll robot's facing direction in animation systems. In: Proceedings of the 9th International Conference on Multimodal Interfaces, pp. 279–284 (2007)
18. Tsuji, S., Yuhi, T., Furuhara, K., Ohta, S., Shimizu, Y., Higashida, H.: Salivary oxytocin concentrations in seven boys with autism spectrum disorder received massage from their mothers: a pilot study. Front. Psych. **6**, 58 (2015)
19. Wada, K., Shibata, T., Saito, T., Tanie, K.: Effects of robot-assisted activity for elderly people and nurses at a day service center. Proc. IEEE **92**(11), 1780–1788 (2004)

20. Wan, X., Yonezawa, T.: Basic study of wall-projected humanitude agent for pre-care multimodal interaction. In: Duffy, V.G. (ed.) HCII 2020. LNCS, vol. 12198, pp. 609–621. Springer, Cham (2020). https://doi.org/10.1007/978-3-030-49904-4_45

21. Wolitzky-Taylor, K.B., Castriotta, N., Lenze, E.J., Stanley, M.A., Craske, M.G.: Anxiety disorders in older adults: a comprehensive review. Depress. Anxiety **27**(2), 190–211 (2010)

22. Wright, J.: Tactile care, mechanical hugs: Japanese caregivers and robotic lifting devices. Asian Anthropol. **17**(1), 24–39 (2018)

23. Yoshida, N., Yonezawa, T.: Spatial communication and recognition in human-agent interaction using motion-parallax-based 3dcg virtual agent. In: Proceedings of the 3rd International Conference on Human-Agent Interaction, pp. 97–103 (2015)

24. Zhang, Y., Wan, X., Yonezawa, T.: Elderly sleep support agent using physical contact presence by visual and tactile presentation. In: Gao, Q., Zhou, J. (eds.) HCII 2021. LNCS, vol. 12787, pp. 348–362. Springer, Cham (2021). https://doi.org/10.1007/978-3-030-78111-8_24

User Experience and User Behavior in Social Media

Eye Tracking to Evaluate Usability with the Older Adults: A Secondary Study

John W. Castro[1,2]($\boxtimes$) (iD), Gianina Madrigal[1], and Luis A. Rojas[3]

[1] Departamento de Ingeniería Informática y Ciencias de la Computación, Universidad de Atacama, Copiapó, Chile
john.castro@uda.cl, gianina.madrigal.17@alumnos.uda.cl
[2] Centro Interuniversitario de Envejecimiento Saludable (CIES), Talca, Chile
[3] Facultad de Ingeniería, Arquitectura y Diseño, Universidad San Sebastián, Bellavista 7, 8420524 Santiago, Chile
lrojasp1@docente.uss.cl

Abstract. From 1980 to 2021, a significant increase in the global elderly population has been observed, a trend expected to persist until 2050. In this context, Information and Communication Technologies (ICTs) facilitate various aspects of daily life. Despite existing barriers to older adults using ICTs, studies report an increase in exposure and technology usage within this age group. Therefore, it is crucial to consider the usability of software systems used by older adults. One technique for evaluating usability is eye tracking. However, there is a lack of work compiling studies that report its use for usability evaluation involving the elderly. Our research aims to provide an overview of the use of eye tracking for usability evaluation involving older adults through a Systematic Mapping Study (SMS). We identified six primary studies reporting usability assessments using a mixed approach of qualitative and quantitative methods, combining eye tracking with other techniques such as questionnaires, interviews, and direct observation. These methods offer a comprehensive insight tailored to the specific needs of older adults. The consistency in the number of studies in recent years, except in 2020 and 2023, underscores the importance of incorporating usability considerations and the potential of eye tracking in designing technologies for older adults.

Keywords: Eye Tracking · Usability Evaluation · Older Adult · Exploratory Study

1 Introduction

For several decades, most highly developed nations have witnessed a growing population aging and are in the advanced stages of this demographic shift. In contrast, many developing countries are rapidly transitioning to become more aged societies. From 1980 to 2021, the number of older adults has grown significantly worldwide, and this trend is projected to continue until 2050 [1]. It is estimated that the regions of North Africa, Western Asia, and Sub-Saharan Africa will experience the highest growth rates in the population aged 65 and older, contributing to a 60% increase globally, reaching over

540 million people. At the same time, the population of individuals aged 80 and older is increasing even faster, and it is expected to reach 459 million by 2050, representing a 200% increase in all regions except Europe, North America, Australia, and New Zealand [1].

In the case of Chile, the population has been continuously aging over the last century, reflected in reduced fertility and mortality rates along with an increase in life expectancy. Currently, the 60 years and older age group constitutes 18.1% of the total population, and it is projected that this figure will double by 2050, reaching approximately one-third (32.1%) of the Chilean population [2]. In this global and national population aging scenario, the Internet and Information and Communication Technologies (ICT) play a fundamental role. These technologies facilitate various daily activities such as communication, participation, entertainment, and work [3].

With aging, individuals undergo significant changes in vision, cognition, motor skills, and literacy, which impact their interaction with technology. These changes make it essential to consider aging-related factors in interface design to enhance accessibility and usability for older adults. Doing so ensures they can make the most of technology in their daily lives [4]. Due to their diversity, characteristics, and specific needs arising from these changes, older adults represent a unique segment that can significantly benefit from technologies designed to address and adapt to these particularities [5, 6]. In recent years, applications have exploited the possibilities offered by new technologies, and older adults are increasingly benefiting from these advances [7]. Despite barriers limiting access and use of computer technologies for older adults, research shows that an increasing number are adopting these tools in their everyday lives [8].

Considering those above, the quality attributes of the software, specifically usability, must be considered as a critical aspect to determine its effectiveness [9–11]. Usability is defined as the ability of a group of users to achieve specific goals effectively, efficiently, and satisfactorily using a computer system [12]. To ensure adequate usability, tests are conducted to identify and rectify flaws in the initial designs that could confuse users or impose excessive mental burdens on them [12]. Usability evaluation is essential to prevent user dissatisfaction with the final product and ensure successful interaction with the technology [12]. Usability assessments are conducted through various techniques and methods to determine how effectively users interact with a system or product. Evaluating usability in software systems intended for older adults is crucial, given that, according to the United Nations, usability represents a significant challenge for technologies used by this demographic group [13].

For the usability evaluation, techniques are employed that focus on identifying and improving critical areas to make the interface, content, and functionality intuitive, efficient, and satisfying for the end user. An example of these techniques is eye tracking [14], which enables researchers to study users' visual attention, determining the exact location of gaze, duration of attention at specific points, and the visual path. This analysis provides a profound understanding of interface elements that capture user attention and those that may cause confusion or difficulty, essential aspects for an enhanced user experience. Eye tracking is divided into two main aspects: fixations, eye pauses in specific areas, and saccades, which are rapid eye movements connecting these fixations, allowing users to form a coherent and complete visual perception [15].

However, to best of our knowledge, no work compiles and reports on studies using eye tracking for usability evaluation involving older adults. Therefore, professionals and researchers seeking this information must invest time searching and locating relevant sources, carefully examining these resources following specific criteria, gathering information from various sources, and ultimately drawing conclusions based on the collected information. This difficulty is intensified by the scientific community's contribution to new bibliographic resources. The present research seeks to provide an overview of the use of eye tracking to evaluate the usability of software systems involving older adults.

Due to those above, in this research, we conducted a Systematic Mapping Study (SMS) to identify works reporting the use of eye tracking as a technique for usability evaluation involving older adults. From the conducted SMS, we identified six primary studies adopting a mixed approach of qualitative and quantitative methods. In other words, these studies employed eye tracking and other techniques to provide a detailed understanding of usability in controlled environments. While most studies combined eye tracking with other methodologies, one focused exclusively on eye tracking. We found that the most commonly used usability evaluation techniques alongside eye tracking include interviews, questionnaires, and direct observations simultaneously and sequentially. These techniques offer a comprehensive insight into how older adults interact with different interfaces and technologies, emphasizing the importance of designing for their needs. Differences in the application of eye tracking reflect the diversity in goals and target populations of the studies and the variety in application contexts. The results of these studies indicate that the number of research endeavors has been consistent in recent years, with a notable lack of studies for the years 2020 and 2023. These findings underscore the relevance of considering usability in designing technologies for older adults and how eye tracking can be a valuable tool.

This document is organized as follows. In Sect. 2, we present related works. Section 3 describes the research method (i.e., the SMS). In Sect. 4, we discuss the results of the SMS. Section 5 presents possible threats to validity, and finally, the conclusions are reported in Sect. 6.

2 Related Work

During the research, we identified two works [16, 17] related to our investigation. In the study by Wang et al. [16], the usability of mobile health applications for older adults is thoroughly examined, highlighting a wide range of critical usability metrics assessed in the incorporated studies, and the appropriateness of evaluation methods for this demographic group is discussed. The SMS search period was from 2010 to 2020. The literature review focused on identifying essential usability measures and evaluation methods employed explicitly in research on mobile health applications for older adults. The authors also analyze how these measures are distributed within the usability evaluation framework for mobile health applications for this demographic group. Additionally, the SMS sought to uncover emerging trends in research on mobile health applications for older adults and provide recommendations for future research in this field.

The second study by Jankowski et al. [17] conducted an exhaustive literature review from January 2000 to December 2020, spanning two decades of research in mobile health (mHealth) applications for older adults. The main objective of this study was to analyze in detail the usability evaluation of such applications, identifying how they have been adapted to the specific needs of this demographic group. Regarding the findings, a significant increase in research was observed from 2013, focusing on user satisfaction and ease of learning. The study employed various methodologies, including questionnaires and interviews, to explore the evolution of usability measures and tools. Additionally, various evaluation techniques were reported, such as the think-aloud method, performance metrics, behavior observations, screen recordings, eye tracking, and feedback. These techniques were specially tailored to older adults to enhance critical aspects such as satisfaction, ease of learning, and accessibility of mHealth applications. The study's results highlight the importance of selecting indicators that reflect aging characteristics and adjusting evaluation methods to the unique needs of the elderly, emphasizing the need to optimize mHealth applications for better health self-management in this population segment.

After analyzing the studies described above [16, 17], it is evident that the present work differs in three fundamental aspects. First, our focus is on using eye tracking to assess the usability of software systems in older adults, contrasting with the mentioned studies that concentrate on the usability evaluation of mobile health applications for this demographic group, using a variety of methodologies such as questionnaires and interviews. Second, while the study by Wang et al. [16] thoroughly analyzes metrics and usability evaluation methods suitable for older adults, and Jankowski et al. [17] identifies necessary adaptations for their needs, our work provides an overview of the state of the art of eye tracking in usability evaluation focused on the older adult. Finally, there is a difference in the study periods. Our analysis covers from 2018 to 2023, including the last three years not covered in the mentioned studies, whose research periods span from 2010 to 2020 and from 2000 to 2020, respectively.

3 Research Method

The reported secondary study has been conducted following the guidelines established by Kitchenham et al. [18] for performing a SMS. These guidelines include fundamental stages such as formulating research questions, defining search strategies, selecting primary studies, extracting data, and subsequently synthesizing it. Our purpose is to address the following Research Questions (RQ):

- (RQ1) What is the state of the art in using eye tracking to evaluate usability with the participation of older adults?
- (RQ2) What usability evaluation techniques are used in conjunction with eye tracking and involve older adults?
- (RQ3) How is eye tracking being utilized to assess usability with the participation of older adults?

3.1 Definition of the Search String

It is necessary to identify keywords to define different options for the search string. Tests were conducted with various alternatives before selecting the most suitable search string. We began by reading some initial studies on the research objective to gather the technical vocabulary commonly used in this field. After considering the opinions of two experts in the field of Human-Computer Interaction (HCI), we defined the following string: *(eye-tracking OR "eye tracking" OR "eye tracker") AND (system OR software OR "user interface" OR application) AND (study OR evaluation OR analysis OR test OR methods OR evaluate) AND ("older adults" OR "older people" OR aging OR "older users" OR elderly) AND usability.*

3.2 Databases and Search Protocol

The search was conducted sequentially in the Scopus, IEEE Xplore, and Web of Science databases. The options provided by each database determined the search fields used [19–21]. In Scopus and Web of Science, the search field used was Title-Abstract-Keywords, while in IEEE Xplore, we used the Abstract. Since eye tracking is an emerging technology in usability evaluation [14], the search range included publications from 2018 to October 2023. The criteria used to obtain primary studies are detailed below. The inclusion criteria are as follows:

- The study reports a topic related to the evaluation of usability in graphical user interfaces involving the use of eye tracking; AND
- The study reports usability evaluation involving older adults.

  Regarding the exclusion criteria, they are as follows:

- The study is not related to the evaluation of usability involving older adults; OR
- The study reports usability evaluation of devices that do not have a graphical user interface; OR
- The study does not use eye tracking for usability evaluation; OR
- The study is written in a language other than English.

3.3 Study Selection

Searches were conducted using the established search string. The search across the three databases yielded 60 studies. Subsequently, the entire set of studies was reviewed to identify duplicates by inspecting the title, authors, source, and publication year. In the case of duplicates, only the first occurrence of the study was counted and retained, eliminating the others. After removing duplicates, we obtained 42 studies; inclusion and exclusion criteria were applied to the title, abstract, and keywords for each of these studies. As a result of this analysis, we obtained 12 preselected studies. Two experts in HCI corroborated the results, and any discrepancies were discussed and resolved in meetings. Subsequently, we downloaded each of the preselected studies and applied the selection criteria to the full text. Figure 1 shows the entire filtering and analysis process with the inclusion and exclusion criteria used to select six primary studies (PS). The complete list of the primary studies can be found in Appendix A. Table 1 presents the results of applying different filters in each database during the selection process.

Table 1. Number of remaining studies after filtering the database results.

Database	Studies found	Duplicate-free	Pre-selected studies	Primary studies
Scopus	25	25	9	6
Web of Science	32	16	3	0
IEEE Xplore	3	1	0	0
Total	**60**	**42**	**12**	**6**

4 Results and Discussion

In this section, the results of the SMS are presented, and the research questions are addressed based on the identified primary studies.

4.1 State of the Art of Eye Tracking Usage for Usability Evaluation Involving Older Adults

In this section, the first research question is addressed: *What is the state of the art in using eye tracking to evaluate usability with the participation of older adults?* The six primary studies identified in the SMS were analyzed; all of them except one adopted a mixed approach, combining qualitative and quantitative methods. These studies were conducted in controlled environments, using eye tracking as the primary usability evaluation technique. Furthermore, it was observed that, for the most part, eye tracking is used in conjunction with other techniques to provide a richer and more detailed understanding of the user experience.

Figure 2 represents an overview of the identified primary studies. In this figure, the results are segmented into two areas. The first (left side) consists of two XY scatter plots (top and bottom) with bubbles at the intersections of category-type of publication-year (upper left side) and type of publication-usability evaluation techniques used in conjunction with eye tracking (lower left side). The types of publications are journals, book chapters, and conferences. The size of each bubble is determined by the number of primary studies classified as belonging to each category. In the second area (upper right side) of Fig. 2, the number of primary studies per publication year is presented.

On the upper left side, it is observed that publications are primarily in journals. Meanwhile, the lower left side shows that the most commonly used techniques in conjunction with eye tracking are questionnaires, video recording, and direct observation. The usability evaluation techniques used in conjunction with eye tracking include both qualitative and quantitative instruments. Furthermore, these techniques were applied both concurrently with eye tracking and sequentially. Finally, on the upper right side, it can be seen that between the years 2018 and 2022, the number of studies has been relatively constant, ranging from 1 to 2 per year. As shown in Fig. 2, no studies were found in 2020 and 2023. We believe that, in the case of 2020, the lack of publications was due to the impact of the COVID-19 pandemic. Regarding 2023, we consider that the absence of publications may be because the search was conducted in October (i.e., it

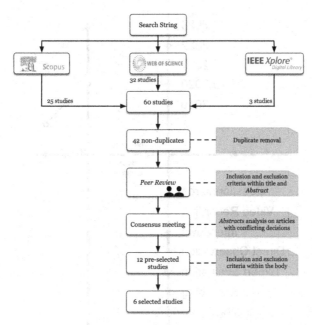

Fig. 1. Steps followed during the SMS.

does not include the entire year). Table 2 indicates the publication source of the primary studies and the publication type (J = Journal, C = Conference, B = Book Chapter).

4.2 Techniques Related to Usability Evaluation Used in Conjunction with Eye Tracking

In this section, the second research question is addressed: *What usability evaluation techniques are used in conjunction with eye tracking and involve older adults?* After analyzing the primary studies, seven usability evaluation techniques were identified: (i) questionnaires, (ii) interviews, (iii) expert evaluation, (iv) thinking aloud, (v) direct observation, (vi) video recording, and (vii) audio recording.

Table 3 details the primary studies that combined eye tracking with other usability evaluation techniques, except for the study conducted by Brady et al. [PS2], which focused exclusively on the use of eye tracking. In the other studies, the use of additional usability techniques is reported simultaneously or sequentially with eye tracking to evaluate usability. Additionally, Table 3 provides specific details about the device used in each study for conducting usability evaluation.

The most commonly used usability evaluation techniques in combination with eye tracking in the identified primary studies focus on a combination of quantitative and qualitative methods. Questionnaires are predominant, used in [PS1][PS4]-[PS6], to gather users' subjective perceptions of usability and satisfaction. Interviews complement this information with deeper insights into the user experience, present in [PS6]. Thinking Aloud [PS5] provides a real-time and reflective view of users' interactions. These techniques reflect a comprehensive approach to understanding and improving interface

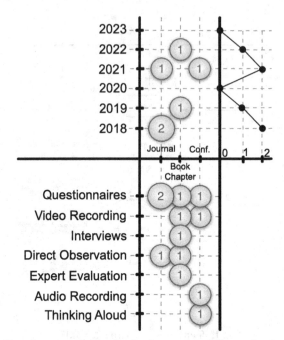

Fig. 2. Mapping for primary study distribution between usability evaluation techniques along with publication type.

Table 2. Publication source.

Primary Study	Publication Source	J	C	B
[PS1]	Assistive Technology	X		
[PS2]	The Australian Journal of Emergency Management	X		
[PS3]	RADIO--Robots in Assisted Living, Springer, Cham			X
[PS4]	Human Factors	X		
[PS5]	Proceedings of the XX Brazilian Symposium on Human Factors in Computing Systems (IHC'21)		X	
[PS6]	International Society of Transdisciplinary Engineering (ISTE TE'22),			X

usability. Some studies incorporate different techniques to complement eye tracking evaluation. Techniques such as questionnaires, expert evaluation, and interviews are often used after conducting the eye tracking evaluation [PS1] [PS3]-[PS6]. In contrast, other studies prefer a simultaneous approach, using eye tracking in parallel with techniques such as direct observation, audio recording, video recording, and thinking aloud [PS1] [PS3][PS4][PS6].

Table 3. Primary studies where eye tracking was reported in conjunction with other usability evaluation techniques.

Primary Study	Usability Evaluation Technique	Evaluated Device
[PS1]	Direct Observation, Questionnaires	Computer
[PS3]	Expert Evaluation, Video Recording	Tablet, smartphone, computer
[PS4]	Questionnaire (with likert-type questions)	Smartphone or computer
[PS5]	Audio Recording and Video Recording, Thinking Aloud and Questionnaires (SUS)	Computer (web site)
[PS6]	Direct Observation, Interviews (on user feedback) and Questionnaire (SUS modified)	Smartphone

For example, in the study conducted by Haesner et al. [PS1], after obtaining informed consent from participants, they conducted tests to assess various cognitive and motor skills, followed by an extensive battery of neuropsychological tests. Participants also completed questionnaires about their socio-demographic information and technological experience. In the laboratory, they underwent usability tests on a cognitive training platform, performing tasks of varying complexity on a PC. While performing these tasks, their eye movements were meticulously recorded using the FaceLAB 5.0 eye-tracking system. This tracking focused on the number and duration of fixations and areas of interest, providing precise data on visual interaction with the platform. After completing the tasks, participants evaluated the platform's usability through various questionnaires. Thus, the combination of eye tracking and questionnaires allowed for a detailed and multidimensional usability assessment focusing on effective interaction and user perception.

4.3 Eye Tracking as a Usability Evaluation Technique

This section addresses the third research question: *How is eye tracking being utilized to assess usability with the participation of older adults?* Each study employed eye tracking in specific contexts to assess usability, primarily in applications targeted at older adults or users with specific needs. The studies vary in focus and application, although all use eye tracking as the primary tool to understand and enhance user interaction with different interfaces and technologies.

The primary studies share several methodological similarities in using eye tracking to evaluate usability. All employ eye tracking devices to collect data on eye movements and fixations, using this information to understand how users visually interact with interfaces and where their attention is focused. This method enables the identification of problematic areas, comprehension of user navigation and attention flow, and provides a quantitative basis for usability optimization. Additionally, eye tracking gather's objective and detailed data in all studies, enabling researchers to make specific recommendations for improving the user experience. However, there are differences in how each primary study applies eye tracking, reflecting diversity in their goals, target populations, and application contexts. The studies vary in their specific objectives, ranging from evaluating interaction efficiency to understanding the readability of texts and icons in different demographic groups [PS1]-[PS6]. The target population also significantly differs among the studies, influencing the design and focus of eye tracking analysis.

Furthermore, the methodology and analysis tools vary, with some studies generating heatmaps or comparing gaze patterns between different interfaces [PS2][PS6]. These differences underscore how eye tracking adapts to meet specific needs in various usability research contexts. The following three examples illustrate how eye tracking has been employed in primary studies to understand user interaction with technology better, each with its specific context and objective.

The first study [PS1] on eye tracking in older adults describes the process and methodology used to evaluate web usability and differences in interaction between older adults with and without mild cognitive impairment (MCI). Due to common calibration issues in eye tracking studies with this population, data from 11 of the initial 50 participants could not be analyzed, reducing the sample to 39 participants. Researchers used Eye-Works Analyze Version 3.0 to extract valid eye movement data and conducted a quantitative descriptive analysis using IBM SPSS Statistics 22.0. In terms of the specific metrics analyzed, the study focused on gaze performance time or duration, the number of fixations, fixation duration, and the proportion of fixations in areas of interest (AOIs). Gaze duration is when participants focus on specific areas, indicating interest or comprehension difficulty. The number of fixations counts how often users stop their gaze at specific points, providing clues about areas that require more attention or are more complex. Fixation duration measures the time gaze is held at a point, with longer durations suggesting more incredible difficulty or interest in the content. Finally, the proportion of fixations in AOIs, calculated by dividing the number of fixations in these areas by the total fixations, indicates how focused the user's attention is on relevant interface areas. These data were calculated for each of the 39 participants and divided into two groups: 20 older adults and 19 older adults with MCI.

The analysis included calculating the proportion of fixations in AOIs adjusted for the different sizes of these areas across all tasks. Additionally, average performance time and average task success ratings were calculated for each group. Mann-Whitney U tests were used to compare the two demographic groups due to the non-normality of the data. These tests were applied to each measure of interest, including gaze duration, number of fixations, fixation duration, and the proportion of fixations in AOIs. Possible differentiating factors such as age, gender, and previous computer experience were also considered, using appropriate statistical methods to test their impact. Each task was examined separately due to different difficulty levels and requirements between tasks, using Pearson correlations to analyze the association between study measures. This methodological and analytical approach provides a detailed and nuanced understanding of how older adults, with or without MCI, interact with web interfaces, enabling researchers to identify specific areas for improving the usability and accessibility of these technologies for the elderly population.

In the second study [PS5], the authors established rigorous exclusion criteria, excluding participants who did not meet cognitive requirements or showed signs of depression, to ensure data quality and relevance. Data were collected through various sources, including eye tracking, screenshots, thinking aloud, and questionnaires, providing a comprehensive view of user behavior. The eye tracker recorded two primary eye behaviors: fixations and saccades, indicative of attention and visual transition. These data were processed in two ways: to assess the feasibility of classifying users with computer anxiety by analyzing features such as gaze distance and speed and to conduct a detailed analysis of fixations on AOIs in the interface. AOI analysis was enriched with the use of a Python script that annotated session videos with precise eye-tracking data, facilitating detailed visual and statistical analysis. AOIs were carefully defined based on relevant areas and groups of elements in the user interface, allowing researchers to examine how users interacted with specific interface components during defined tasks. Through statistical tests, significant differences in fixations between AOIs were sought better to understand the interface's impact on user behavior. This meticulous approach not only shed light on visual behavior patterns in users with computer anxiety but also provided valuable data to guide the design of more intuitive and less anxiety-inducing interfaces. In Table 4, specifications for usability tests in the primary studies found through the SMS are reported.

Table 4. Usability testing specification.

Primary Study	Eye Tracker Model	Evaluation Location	Sample Size	Age of the Elderly Adult
[PS1]	FaceLAB 5.0	Laboratory	50	61–93 years
[PS2]	Tobii T-120	Laboratory	8	>60 years
[PS3]	Tobii Glasses, Tobii T60 Eye tracker, Tobii X60/X120 Mobile Device Testing Solution	(unspecified)	(unspecified)	66–80 years
[PS4]	Tobii Pro Spectrum	Soundproof Laboratory	23	57–71 years
[PS5]	The Eye Tribe	(unspecified)	28	>60 years
[PS6]	Tobii Pro Glasses 2	Laboratory	16	45–59 years

It is important to note that the sample consists of participants who effectively completed the experiment. In particular, the primary studies [PS4][PS5] had larger samples than indicated in Table 4, with 48 and 31 participants, respectively. In the first study [PS4], the sample was reduced for two main reasons. First, twelve participants were excluded due to eye conditions such as cataracts and glaucoma or because they had undergone eye surgery. Second, thirteen additional participants were excluded due to the acquisition of invalid data resulting from eye-tracking failures. These exclusions ultimately left a total of 23 participants who completed the experiment. In the second study [PS5], the original sample was affected due to issues with gaze data capture in three participants: in two cases, eye tracking stopped during the experiment, and in the other case, the equipment calibration was not accurate enough to detect fixations. These technical and calibration issues resulted in only 28 initial participants being considered for gaze data analysis.

5 Validity Threats

In the SMS, we identified three threats to validity. Firstly, the validity of the SMS is jeopardized by including only studies written in English. Secondly, although the terms used in the search string were derived from the technical vocabulary used in the field and based on previous research experience, other terms used to describe relevant work may have been overlooked. Thirdly, authors may make judgment errors in selecting studies. To counteract this threat, we defined selection criteria directly related to the objective and research questions. Meetings were held among researchers to review the discarded preselected studies to verify agreement in the selection of studies.

Another aspect related to the study selection process is the stated scope of our research, as only articles published between 2018 and October 2023 were considered. Some studies directly related to the objective of our research may have been excluded by limiting the analysis to this period. Moreover, only the Scopus, WoS, and IEEE Xplore databases were considered. Despite obtaining results, there may have been more usability evaluations that could have been reported.

6 Conclusions and Future Work

In this research, we describe the SMS conducted to identify the state of the art in using eye tracking to assess the usability of software systems involving older adults. Our SMS identified six primary studies published from 2018 to October 2023, primarily in journals and conferences. Below, we present conclusions based on the research questions that were satisfactorily addressed.

RQ1: What is the state of the art in using eye tracking to evaluate usability with the participation of older adults? According to the SMS results, we gained insights into the overall landscape of using eye tracking to evaluate the usability of software systems involving older adults. Research on using eye tracking to assess usability in older adults reveals a mixed and detailed approach to implementation. Most of the six primary studies analyzed combine qualitative and quantitative methods in controlled environments, using eye tracking as the primary tool. This technique is used alongside other methodologies, such as interviews, questionnaires, and direct observation, for a deeper understanding of the user experience.

Furthermore, the research shows a consistent trend in the publication of studies related to this topic in recent years. However, no studies were found for 2020 and 2023, possibly due to the COVID-19 pandemic and search timing. This analysis underscores the importance of adapting technologies to meet the specific needs of older adults, using eye tracking as a crucial means to improve the usability and accessibility of digital interfaces.

RQ2: What usability evaluation techniques are used in conjunction with eye tracking and involve older adults? The SMS has revealed a diversity of usability evaluation techniques used with eye tracking, particularly in contexts involving older adults. These techniques, ranging from questionnaires to user testing [PS1]-[PS6], offer a multifaceted view of how older adults interact with different interfaces, contributing to a detailed understanding of their experiences and needs. The predominant use of questionnaires in various studies highlights the importance of collecting subjective user perceptions [PS1][PS4]-[PS6], while interviews [PS6] and expert evaluation [PS3] provide a deeper qualitative analysis of the user experience. User testing [PS3] allows for direct and comparative observation of user interaction with the interface, while Thinking Aloud [PS5] and recordings [PS5] offer an honest and reflective perspective on the interaction process. The techniques evaluated in these studies reflect a trend toward integrated approaches that combine quantitative and qualitative methods for a more comprehensive understanding of usability. Including older adults in these studies is particularly valuable, providing critical insights for designing accessible and user-friendly technologies for this demographic. As technology advances, these techniques and approaches will be crucial to ensure that interfaces are intuitive, efficient, and inclusive. Usability evaluation, especially when combined with eye tracking, is an indispensable tool for designers and researchers committed to creating products that meet users' functional needs and enrich their experience and quality of life.

RQ3: How is eye tracking being utilized to assess usability with the participation of older adults? Primary studies show a convergence in applying eye tracking devices to collect objective data on user visual behavior. This data provides crucial insights into where user attention is focused, which areas pose problems, and how navigation and interface design can be improved. Evaluation was reported in studies focused on web usability in older adults with and without mild cognitive impairment, detailed analyses of user interfaces on medical devices, and studies on the impact of design on users with computer anxiety. This demonstrates the applicability and flexibility of eye tracking in usability research. Through its specific approach and methodology, each of these studies contributes to a broader body of knowledge that enables researchers and designers to create more inclusive, intuitive, and compelling user experiences. The variability in the models of eye trackers used in the evaluation locations, the sample sizes, and the age of the participants reflected in Table 3 also emphasizes the customization and specificity with which these studies are approached. This customization responds to each study's technical and contextual needs and reflects a commitment to accuracy and relevance in data collection.

We are considering including other databases (e.g., SpringerLink and ScienceDirect) for future work. Additionally, due to the low number of primary studies found reporting the use of eye tracking to assess usability with the participation of older adults, we intend to conduct usability evaluations using an eye tracker in combination with other techniques.

Acknowledgment. This work was supported by the ANID FONDECYT-Iniciación project under Grant 11230496.

Appendix A: Primary Studies

In this appendix, the references of the primary studies used for the SMS described in this article are listed.

[PS1] Haesner, M., Chandra, J., Steinert, A., Steinhagen-Thiessen, E.: An eye movement analysis of web usability: Differences between older adults with and without mild cognitive impairment. Assistive Technology **30**(2), 66–73 (2018). https://doi.org/https://doi.org/10.1080/10400435.2016.1251994.

[PS2] Brady, D., Ferguson, N., Adams, M.: Usability of MyFireWatch for non-expert users measured by eye-tracking. The Australian Journal of Emergency Management **33**(4), 27–34 (2018).

[PS3] Rigou, M., Sirmakessis, S., Ventura, R., Fernández, A., Antonopoulos, C. P., Voros, N.: Designing user interfaces for the elderly. In: Karkaletsis, V., Konstantopoulos, S., Voros, N., Annicchiarico, R., Dagioglou, M., Antonopoulos, C. (eds) RADIO--Robots in Assisted Living (pp. 113–148). Springer, Cham (2019). -https://doi.org/https://doi.org/10.1007/978-3-319-92330-7_8.

[PS4]. Hou, G., Hu, Y.: Designing combinations of pictogram and text size for icons: Effects of text size, pictogram size, and familiarity on older adults' visual search performance. Human Factors **65**(8), 1577–1595, (2021). https://doi.org/https://doi.org/10.1177/00187208211061938.

[PS5]. Dos Santos, T.D., De Santana, V.F.: Gaze interaction and people with computer anxiety: Paving the way to user interface simplification. In Proceedings of the XX Brazilian Symposium on Human Factors in Computing Systems (IHC'21), pp. 1–12, article 27, Virtual Event Brazil, (2021). https://doi.org/https://doi.org/10.1145/3472301.3484319.

[PS6]. Xiang, Y., Chang, D., Yao, Y., Wang, L., Chen, A., Li, J.: Usability evaluation of elder-friendly design: Application to take alipay app. In: Moser, B.R. et al. (eds) Advances in Transdisciplinary Engineering 28. International Society of Transdisciplinary Engineering (ISTE TE'22), Global Conference (pp. 154–163), IOS Press (2022). https://doi.org/https://doi.org/10.3233/ATDE220642.

References

1. Wilmoth, J.R., Bas, D., Mukherjee, S., Hanif, N.: World social report 2023: leaving no one behind in an ageing world. United Nations (2023)
2. Hugo, F., Rodríguez, L., Rodríguez, J.: Envejecimiento en Chile: Evolución, características de las personas mayores y desafíos demográficos para la población. Documentos de trabajo. Instituto Nacional de Estadísticas (2022)
3. Observatorio del Envejecimiento: Uso de Internet y Tecnologías de la Información y Comunicación en las Personas Mayores. Centro de Estudios de Vejez y Envejecimiento de la Pontificia Universidad Católica de Chile y Compañía de Seguros Confuturo (2022)
4. Becker, S.A.: A study of web usability for older adults seeking online health resources. ACM Trans. Comput.-Hum. Interact. **11**(4), 387–406 (2004). https://doi.org/10.1145/1035575.1035578
5. Vines, J., Pritchard, G., Wright, P., Olivier, P. Brittain, K.: An age-old problem: examining the discourses of ageing in HCI and strategies for future research. ACM Trans. Comput.-Hum. Interact. (TOCHI), **22**(1), Article 2, 1–27 (2015)

6. Rogers, Y., Paay, J., Brereton, M., Vaisutis, K.L., Marsden, G., Vetere, F.: Never too old: engaging retired people inventing the future with makey makey. In: SIGCHI Conference on Human Factors in Computing Systems (CHI'14), Toronto, Ontario, Canada, pp. 3913–3922 (2014)

7. Casado-Muñoz, R., Lezcano, F., Rodríguez-Conde, M.-J.: Envejecimiento activo y acceso a las tecnologías: Un estudio empírico evolutivo. Comunicar: Revista Científica de Comunicación y Educación 22(45), 37–46 (2015). https://doi.org/10.3916/C45-2015-04

8. Wagner, N., Hassanein, K., Head, M.: Computer use by older adults: a multi-disciplinary review. Comput. Hum. Behav. 26(5), 870–882 (2010)

9. Castro, J.W., Garnica, I., Rojas, L.: Automated tools for usability evaluation: a systematic mapping study. In: Meiselwitz, G. (eds.) Social Computing and Social Media: Design, User Experience and Impact. HCII 2022. Lecture Notes in Computer Science, vol. 13315, pp. 28–46. Springer, Cham (2022). https://doi.org/10.1007/978-3-031-05061-9_3

10. Losana, P., Castro, J.W., Ferre, X., Villalba-Mora, E., Acuña, S.T.: A systematic mapping study on integration proposals of the Personas technique in agile methodologies. Sensors 21(18), article 6298, Special Issue Recent Advances in Human-Computer Interaction (2021)

11. Ren, R., Zapata, M., Castro, J.W., Dieste, O., Acuña, S.T.: Experimentation for chatbot usability evaluation: a secondary study. IEEE Access 10, 12430–12464 (2022)

12. Hertzum, M.: Usability testing: A practitioner's guide to evaluating the user experience. Synthesis Lectures on Human-Centered Informatics. Morgan & Claypool Publishers (2020)

13. World Health Organization: Progress report on the United Nations decade of healthy ageing, 2021–2023: Executive summary. Global Report, Decade of Healthy Ageing (2023). ISBN 978-92-4-008212-0

14. Conley, Q., Earnshaw, Y., McWatters, G.: Examining course layouts in blackboard: using eye-tracking to evaluate usability in a learning management system. Int. J. Hum.-Comput. Interact. 36(4), 373–385 (2020). https://doi.org/10.1080/10447318.2019.1644841

15. Rigou, M., Sirmakessis, S., Ventura, R., Fernández, A., Antonopoulos, C.P., Voros, N.: Designing user interfaces for the elderly. In: Karkaletsis, V., Konstantopoulos, S., Voros, N., Annicchiarico, R., Dagioglou, M., Antonopoulos, C. (eds.) RADIO–Robots in Assisted Living, pp. 113–148. Springer, Cham (2019). https://doi.org/10.1007/978-3-319-92330-7_8

16. Wang, Q., et al.: Usability evaluation of mHealth apps for elderly individuals: a scoping review. BMC Med. Informat. Decis. Mak. 22(1), article 317, 1–17 (2022)

17. Jankowski, J., Saganowski, S., Bródka, P.: Evaluation of TRANSFoRm mobile eHealth solution for remote patient monitoring during clinical trials. Mob. Inf. Syst. 2016, article 1029368 (2016). https://doi.org/10.1155/2016/1029368

18. Kitchenham, B.A., Budgen, D., Brereton, O.P.: Using mapping studies as the basis for further research – a participant-observer case study. Inf. Softw. Technol. 53(6), 638–651 (2011). https://doi.org/10.1016/j.infsof.2010.12.011

19. Castro, J.W., Acuña, S.T.: Comparativa de selección de estudios primarios en una revisión sistemática. In XVI Jornadas de Ingeniería del Software y Bases de Datos (JISBD'11), pp. 319–332, A Coruña, España (2011)

20. Magües, D., Castro, J.W., Acuña, S.T.: Usability in agile development: a systematic map- ping study. In: XLII Conferencia Latinoamericana de Informática (CLEI'16), Valparaiso, Chile, pp. 677–684 (2016). https://doi.org/10.1109/CLEI.2016.7833347

21. Ren, R., Castro, J.W., Acuña, S.T., De Lara, J.: Evaluation techniques for chatbot usability: a systematic mapping study. Int. J. Softw. Eng. Knowl. Eng. 29(11n12), 1673–1702 (2019). https://doi.org/10.1142/S0218194019400163

Analysing Coping Strategies of Teenage Girls Towards Instagram's Algorithmic Bias

Intisãr Constant, Pitso Tsibolane(✉) ⓘ, Adheesh Budree ⓘ, and Grant Oosterwyk ⓘ

University of Cape Town, Cape Town, South Africa
cnsint001@myuct.ac.za, {pitso.tsibolane,adheesh.budree,
grant.oosterwyk}@uct.ac.za

Abstract. Social media platforms encourage connection, community, and expression, but have also been associated with negative consequences like social comparison and anxiety. This study examines how algorithms on Instagram, a popular platform heavily used by teenage girls, exacerbate these negative experiences. While prior research explores social media's downsides, it often overlooks the specific impact on this crucial demographic. Employing a critical feminist lens with an intersectional approach, we explore how race, gender, location, and socioeconomic status shape online interactions for teenage girls. Qualitative, semistructured interviews with Instagram users reveal that algorithmic curation intensifies negative social comparison, impacting their platform usage and creativity. These findings align with existing literature highlighting the vulnerability of teenage girls on social media. This research informs policymakers by exposing the gendered inequities driven by algorithms. By understanding these complexities, we can advocate for policies that protect vulnerable users and promote healthier online experiences for teenage girls.

Keywords: Instagram · Social Media · Algorithm · Teenage Girls · Intersectionality

1 Introduction

Instagram, a popular social media platform, boasts a significant user base, with approximately 40% of its users being 22 years old or younger, and attracting over 500 million users daily (Omnicore, 2022).

Despite its widespread use, Instagram remains understudied, particularly about its algorithms and their impact on users. Recent revelations, stemming from the disclosure of internal Facebook documents by whistleblower Frances Hau-gen in late 2021, have shed light on the detrimental effects of Instagram's algorithms, especially on marginalized groups such as teenage girls (Wells et al., 2021).

These documents exposed Facebook's knowledge of the harmful effects of Instagram, revealing that the platform exacerbates body image issues for a significant part of its teenage girl users (Wells et al., 2021). So, there is a pressing need to delve deeper into the impact of Instagram's algorithms on the well-being of its users,particularly adolescent girls.

While social media platforms like Instagram offer many benefits, such as facilitating social connections, they also come with drawbacks, including social comparison, body image concerns, addictive usage, and mental health issues.Instagram's features, such as photo retouching and filters, can perpetuate unrealistic beauty standards and influence young users' self-perception. Despite growing concerns, research on Instagram's effects, especially on teenage girls, is still in its infancy.

Given this research gap and the increasing interest in the effects of Instagram on adolescent well-being, this study aims to contribute to the existing literature by examining how teenage girls cope with the negative effects of Instagram algorithms.This research will use a feminist intersectional framework to analyze the coping strategies employed by teenage girls in response to algorithmic biases on Instagram.

The paper will proceed as follows: Section 2 will provide a literature review on the impact of social media, particularly Instagram, on adolescent well-being. Section 3 will outline the research method employed in this study. Section 4 will discuss the findings of the research, focusing on teenage girls' coping strategies about Instagram algorithms. Finally, Section 5 will present the conclusion, summarizing the key findings and implications of the study.

2 Literature Review

2.1 Impact of Social Media on Mental Health

Over the past decade, research and investigations into the impact of social media on various groups of people have emerged, and there are comprehensive and clear sets of studies that outline the adverse effects for women, youth and children. Indeed, much of the existing literature emphasizes the negative consequences of using social media, the biggest consequence being social comparison anxiety (Cohen et al., 2017; Goldstraw et al., 2016; Mackson et al., 2019).

Vannucci et al. (2017) conducted research on the association between social media and anxiety, and discovered that among emerging adults, higher daily social media usage was associated with an increased likelihood for having an anxiety disorder. It has been further discovered that users who spend more than 2 h per day on social media are more prone to psychological distress disorders like anxiety and depression (Dobrean & Pasarelu, 2016).

Despite the resounding evidence of the negative psychological impact that social media has on users, it is still a highly pervasive technology where approximately 90% of young adults use social media (Vannucci et al., 2017). In fact, there exists a significant body of research that indicate positive associations as well. Social media allows users to stay connected with people around the world, socialize with loved ones daily, to meet new friends and to develop a sense of belonging and community (Mackson et al., 2019). Social media can be valuable for peer support, allowing users may or may not know (Dobrean & Pasarelu, 2016). According to Seabrook et al. (2016), the social support and connectedness that social media provides are consistently related to lower levels of depression and anxiety among users.

As this research will be exploring themes in the space of social media and mental health, the sharp rise in mental health disorders in the past 20 years (Lopez & Polletta, 2021), social media users may be at higher risk to psychological disorders, especially anxiety and depression (Vannucci et al., 2017) is important to note. Research in problematic teenage social media usage is scarce and very few studies have researched a connection between social media usage and mental health issues (Dobrean & Pasarelu, 2016). The following 3 areas will be discussed regarding the impact that social media has on mental health: social comparison anxiety, depression and guilt.

Social Comparison. Years of research show that exposure to ideal body images can be damaging to one's self-esteem, self-perception and performance (Bessenoff, 2016. Social comparison is "a cognitive process in which people compare themselves with presented information of others for self-evaluation" (Faelens et al., 2021, p. 7). Scholars have positioned social comparison as a way for individuals to confirm or deny aspects of their identity as they compare themselves to others (Lewallen, 2016). While comparison is most noticeable in younger children, appearance-based comparison only begins in late adolescence and preteens.

Generally, individuals partake in two forms of social comparison: upward comparison (self-enhancement) and downward comparison (self-evaluation) (Lewallen, 2016). Downward comparison is when individuals appraise their status in relation to their environment, whereas upward comparison occurs when individuals evaluate one status in comparison to others and are often done to protect one's self-esteem. Both forms of comparison can be healthy and result in positive outcomes, however, research has found that upward comparison may result in negative effects over time.

Women on social media tend to practice upward comparison when presented with imagery of body ideals, wealth and social ideals which almost always leads to dissatisfaction (Bessenoff, 2016). This phenomenon makes social comparison highly pertinent to social media networks (Tiggemann et al., 2018).

According to Festinger (1954) who developed the theory of social comparison, the need for self-evaluation encourages people to seek out others who are similar to them, rather than dissimilar. Therefore, rather than celebrities, peers are the primary target for social comparison. Social media users browse their feeds throughout the day, availing themselves to practice social comparison on a continual basis and allowing them to gain insights into the lives of their peers regularly.

2.2   Instagram

Female digital natives are familiar with technology from a young age and engage in culture of participation, sharing reviews, ratings, photos, experiences and more (Goldstraw et al., 2016). Instagram is at the forefront of the participation culture, where more than 80 million photos are shared every day. Of its 1.5 billion monthly users, it is most popular among women below the age of 24 (Statista, 2022).

The social networking service is one of the largest photo-sharing apps on the internet and has recently gained Senate attention in late 2021. Ex-Meta employee, Frances Haugen, leaked a series of internal documents that confirmed that Instagram had known about their harmful effects on many of its users, particularly teen girls, for years (Wells et al., 2021).

The leaked internal documents, composed by Meta researchers, exposed how the app contributes to a negative body image and comparison anxiety in teen girls. The effects of filtered and edited images of influencers or models have been found to normalize certain body ideals (Kleemans et al., 2018), as can be seen in the 'fitspiration' trend (Goldstraw et al., 2016). While what users see on their homepage is partially influenced by the accounts that they follow, ubiquitous curation algorithms decide the particulars.

2.3 Curation Algorithms of Instagram

Globally there are over 3.6 billion social media users (Statista, 2022) of which 1.5 billion are daily Instagram users (Omnicore, 2022). Even though the amount of data generated on the internet has increased exponentially, our ability to absorb and engage with the growing information has not increased (Bozdag, 2013). A way to balance the advent of this information overload was for users to be presented with newsfeeds that have been filtered, processed and personalised for the individual. This was the beginning of the algorithmically curated newsfeed.

Before 2016, Instagram's newsfeed was ordered from oldest to newest. When the algorithmically curated newsfeed was introduced, Instagram faced resistance to the algorithm from most of its users at the time. The algorithmically curated newsfeed was advertised as a way to bring posts to users that Instagram deems "you will care about the most". This curated newsfeed is filtered according to the data gathered and the consumer persona that Instagram has of the user (Cotter, 2019). The curated feed is carefully selected by Instagram to present users with posts that they are most likely to interact with in the form of a like, save or follow. Now, newsfeeds have no distinct endpoint and enable seemingly endless scrolling.

Six factors are currently being used by Instagram to determine the ranking and filtering of posts on newsfeeds. These include user interest, recency, relationship, frequency, following and usage. The exact nature of the algorithm and how the six factors are used remains a company secret with many users unaware of its presence (Eslami et al., 2015; Fouquaert & Mechant, 2021). Despite this, some insights have been gathered from user perceptions (Rader & Gray, 2015).

Existing studies on Instagram curation algorithms are limited to algorithm awareness (Fouquaert & Mechant, 2021; Rader & Gray, 2015), playing the 'visibility game' (Cotter, 2019), and perceived gender inequality (Ekström, 2021). Research into the Instagram curation algorithm is in its primary stages and a gap exists to study user experiences of the algorithm.

2.4 Algorithmic Bias

There exists a general misconception that due to the autonomous nature of algorithms, they are objective and impartial (Rader & Gray, 2015). However, there are many instances where algorithms have displayed biased outputs (Bozdag, 2013).

The first most notable example is Amazon's algorithmically driven recruitment tool that significantly favoured men over women for technical jobs (Dastin, 2018). A well-reported incident of gender bias includes a study that observed that an ad about STEM was shown to more men than women, despite their efforts to make the ad 'gender neutral' (Schroeder, 2020).

Social media algorithms have been studied for their effects on creating echo chambers (Cinelli et al., 2021) and polarization (Ramaciotti Morales & Cointet, 2021), which may lead to prolonged user screen time, which leads to increased profits for social media (Wells et al., 2021).

More notably, Instagram's algorithmically driven newsfeed that is tailored to each user's engagement patterns (Austin, 2021) has been proven to draw vulnerable groups into dangerous patterns of social comparison, which sometimes leads to unrealistic ideals of body shapes and sizes (Lopez & Polletta, 2021).

2.5   Algorithm Awareness of Social Media

Today, people are becoming increasingly reliant on online social-technical systems that make use of algorithmic curation: filtering, classifying and prioritising information for the user (Fouquaert & Mechant, 2021). An algorithm is a series of instructions that receive an input and produce an output (Kitchin, 2017), and systems like Instagram use algorithms as information intermediaries that decide what should be seen and what should be hidden (Rader & Gray, 2015).

As algorithms permeate our online lives, they have a direct influence on shaping user experiences and realities (Eslami et al., 2015), yet users are often unaware of their existence. However, a study on how digital influencers interact with Instagram algorithms has shown that users observe varying outcomes in the form of likes and views on their posts (Cotter, 2019). This leads to the phenomenon Bucher (2016) labels as the "threat of invisibility" or the potential for posts to go unnoticed on user feeds. Table 1 below is a summary of studies on user awareness of curation algorithms on various social media sites.

2.6   Intersectionality

The theoretical lens for this research is feminist intersectionality, a framework used to expose the marginalization of oppressed women under power structures. Intersectionality deepens our understanding of the ways in which different aspects of social identity converge to produce particular experiences of marginalization. It focuses on how a gender, race, class and more converge and interact on varying levels.

Table 1. Summary of existing literature on user awareness of social media algorithms

Social Media	Title of research	Notable Findings	Author
Facebook	"I always assumed that I wasn't really that close to [her]"	62% of sample were unaware of the algorithm	(Eslami et al., 2015),
Facebook	Understanding User Beliefs About Algorithmic Curation in the Facebook News Feed	22% of sample were unaware of algorithm	(Rader & Gray, 2015)
Facebook	The algorithmic imaginary: exploring the ordinary affects of Facebook algorithms	sample was largely aware	(Bucher, 2016)
Facebook and Google News	My News Feed is Filtered?	sample was largely unaware of algorithms	(Powers, 2017)
Instagram	Making curation algorithms apparent: a case study of 'Instawareness' as a means to heighten awareness and understanding of Instagram's algorithm	sample was largely unaware of algorithms	(Fouquaert & Mechant, 2021)

Zheng and Walsham (2021) have made a call for researchers to adopt intersectionality in the digital space as it sensitizes researchers to consider in their analysis the social standing of actors within multiple dominations, hierarchies, and systems of power.

This research will adopt an intersectional lens during analysis to highlight what is wrong with the current social reality of the Instagram algorithm and analyse:

- How teenage girls are marginalised on social media
- How teenage girls face constant scrutiny and pressures online

An intersectional framework can enable a nuanced understanding of the marginalisation of particular groups of adolescents across multiple identities (Baird et al., 2021).

In 1990, Lodon and Rosener developed a framework for thinking about the multiple dimensions of diversity within individuals and institutions which gives a proverbial view of the layers of identities that may intersect within intersectionality (NHS Scotland, 2022). This wheel will aid the research in analysing the findings withing the framework of intersectionality (Fig. 1).

Fig. 1. Diversity Wheel demonstrating how personal characteristics intersect with systems and structures to shape a person's experience (Loden & Rosener, 1990)

3 Research Methodology

3.1 Research Philosophy

A critical theory philosophy was be adopted in this research. (Ryan, 2018, p. 10) says that "critical theory (CT) seeks to critique world views and the underlying structures that create them". Critical research is particularly concerned with issues of power, class, gender, education and other social systems that contribute to a social system (Asghar & Marzban, 2013). This research critiques the experiences of teenage girls on Instagram and provides ways to alleviate their emancipation.

3.2 Research Approach

The approach adopted makes use of concepts that relate to statements which form an integrated framework used to describe, predict, explain, or prescribe a phenomenon. Inductive research focuses on the observations of a trend which allows for an analysis of patterns observed (Bhattacherjee, 2012). This research is largely inductive as it aimed to identify common themes and experiences of teenage girls using Instagram. This approach was chosen because the research attempts to account for an understudied phenomenon with few pre-existing ideas. During the analysis phase of the research, an intersectional feminist lens is adopted.

3.3 Research Strategy

The research strategy deemed appropriate for this study is qualitative semi-structured interviews where data from the interviews were analysed by the researcher (Bhattacherjee, 2012). This strategy enabled the researcher to engage with the participants and acquire their individual experiences while obtaining a broad view of the responses. Semi-structured interviews allowed all participants to be asked the same questions in a flexible framework (Corbin & Strauss, 2010). Participants were encouraged to talk about their experiences and the ordering of further questions was determined by their responses.

3.4 Time Horizon

The research was conducted over 9 months. Due to the brief period of research a cross-sectional time horizon was chosen as data will be collected and measured at the same time. Cross-sectional studies are relevant when the exposure and outcome are determined at the same time (Pandis, 2014).

3.5 Data Collection Methods and Research Instruments

The data was collected by means of semi-structured interviews; the interviews were conducted online through Microsoft Teams. Opting for remote interviews enabled a wider pool of participants and proved to be convenient for the respondents.

Semi-structured Interviews. Semi-structured interviews are a directed conversations between the participant and researcher, guided by themes and questions (Bhattacherjee, 2012). A critical paradigm was used by the researcher to derive questions and to identify areas to explore in the interview. The open nature of the questions aimed to encourage depth and vitality and to allow new concepts to emerge. The researcher was attentive, asked probing questions and aimed to ensure that the participant was comfortable answering the questions and giving valuable insight into the study.

Research Instrument. Data was collected using a research instrument structured out of literature reviewed. The interviews were between 30–65 min long. The interview questions were guided by background research collected in the literature review, intended contributions and the critical paradigm. The question categories were broken up into themes during the analysis phase. The themes are listed as follows:

- Section A: Demographic Information
- Section B: Usage Patterns
- Section C: Awareness of Algorithmic Distortion
- Section D: Effect of Algorithmic Distortion
- Section E: Reaction Towards Algorithmic Distortion
- Section F: Alleviation Strategies

Demographic Information. This section aimed to find the demographic information of the participants and how it plays a part in their perception of the Instagram algorithm.

Usage Behaviour. This section asked questions about how the participant uses Instagram. The focus was applied to the way they interact with the platform, their purpose for using it and when they began using it. The aim of this section is to gain a detailed account of the way the participant engages with the app and whether an increase in usage is linked to a higher rate of awareness and the effect of the algorithm.

Awareness of Algorithmic Distortion. This section asked questions about the level of awareness that the participant has of the Instagram algorithm. This was further broken down into their perceptions of the algorithm and whether it is a feature that they enjoy or not about the app.

Effect of Algorithmic Distortion. This section explored the way that the participants have been affected by the algorithm and the outcomes of those effects. Attention was drawn to how the participants felt after using Instagram and what the algorithmic distortion may have triggered in them.

Reaction Towards Algorithmic Distortion. This section explored the way the participants dealt with the previously identified effects of the algorithmic distortion. Attention was drawn to the way participants made sense of the algorithmic distortion.

Alleviation Strategies. This section focused on questions related to strategies that should be or have been applied by parents and Instagram as a platform to alleviate the effects of algorithmic distortion. It focused on questions in relation to how Instagram could improve the safety of minors on their platform, as well as the way parents or guardians can support and guide their children so that they can navigate the platform safely. These suggestions and responses can be collected as part of the research to improve the safety of teenage girls. Therefore, making social media safer for minors.

3.6 Research Sample

Target Population. The target population is defined as a set of people with the characteristics required for a specific study (Bhattacherjee, 2012). The target population used for this research was teenage girls between the age of 13 and 18 who use the social media app Instagram.

Sampling Procedure. The primary purpose of sampling is to choose a selection procedure for populations to be interviewed (Bhattacherjee, 2012). Qualitative researchers use non-probability sampling procedures which are made up of four key types. These types are namely convenience sampling, purposive sampling, snowball sampling and theoretical sampling.

The sampling technique chosen was a snowball sampling procedure. The snowball technique uses recommendations from the first participants since it is a multistage technique. This technique was appropriate as teenage girls are sample hesitant subjects and are more likely to participate in the study if they were referred by someone whom they know.

Sample Size. In qualitative research, there is no predetermined sample size that researchers need to find statistical differences (Lopez & Whitehead, 2013). Therefore, there is no guideline that has been determined to gauge the correct number of participants in this research. However, the sample size is still important as it is an indicator for the researcher to know when they have reached an adequate amount of data. In qualitative studies, the sample sizes range between 8 and 15 participants but will vary according to the topic of research (Cubit & Lopez, 2012).

The number of participants recommended by researchers for a study varies according to the topic of the study underway. Researchers recommend three to five participants for a case study, ten for a phenomenological study and fifteen to twenty for a grounded theory study.

This study was concerned with the experiences of teenage girls under the phenomenon of the Instagram algorithm, which is a phenomenological approach. As such, the 12 participants interviewed were teenage girls and used the Instagram app.

3.7 Data Analysis Methods

Data collection and analysis happened concurrently due to the short time horizon of the research. The analysis conducted in this research is thematic, where the researcher identified and explained themes and collected data (Braun and Clarke, 2006). Thematic analysis is the process of identifying themes within qualitative data (Kiger & Varpio, 2020).

Transcripts were uploaded to NVivo where it was used to find patterns and develop a conceptual framework for the research.

4   Discussion of Findings

4.1   Demographics of Respondents

All participants were situated in the Western Cape, South Africa when the interviews were conducted. The ages of the participants range from 13 to 18 years old, and the participants have varying backgrounds and races. Table 2 depicts the participant's demographics:

4.2   Algorithmic Distortion Insights

Effects of Algorithmic Distortion. The first theme to be discussed is the effects of algorithmic distortion. Findings related to the types of distortion shows that the effects experienced by participants occurs due to the concept of intersectionality. Intersectionality helps researchers to analyse the social positioning of the understudied in the context of the various hegemonies in which they inhabit (Zheng & Walsham, 2021). Teenage girls experience high levels of social comparison and body image issues because they are exposed to idealistic body images and lifestyles on their timelines.

These objects of comparison are both models and influencers (upward comparison) and their friends (downward comparison). Despite coming from various backgrounds, 75% of participants compared their lives to that presented by the accounts which they

Table 2. Demographic data of participants

ID No.	Age	Grade	Sex	Location	School Category	Followers	Following	Daily use
S01	16	10	Female	False Bay	Private	400	800	45 min
S02	17	11	Female	False Bay	Private	268	227	20 min
S03	16	10	Female	Cape Flats	Home-schooled	162	115	1 h
S04	18	12	Female	Cape Flats	Public	999	2626	1 h
S05	17	12	Female	Cape Flats	Public	~600	~1000	2 h
S06	16	11	Female	Northern Suburbs	Public	-	-	25 min
S07	17	11	Female	Southern Suburbs	Public	1326	1182	20 min
S08	17	11	Female	False Bay	Private	104	100	30 min
S09	17	11	Female	False Bay	Private	361	369	2 h
S10	13	8	Female	Southern Suburbs	Public	201	333	Twice a week
S11	15	10	Female	Vredenburg	Public	~500	~600	35 min
S12	17	11	Female	Cape Flats	Public	310	297	3 h

followed. This is echoed by the theoretical lens of intersectional feminism- as it exposes the marginalisation of girls in relation to their race, bodies, and their social standings (Crenshaw, 1992). Therefore, findings show that participants experienced a heightened level of social comparison because of the intersection of multiple layers of their identities.

Reactions Towards Algorithmic Distortion. The second theme to be discussed is the reactions towards the algorithmic distortion. The findings derived from this theme indicate that the race of participants impacted the way that they reacted toward the algorithm (Crenshaw, 1992). Participants categorised as White were inclined to reduce their usage, whereas participants categorised as Coloured were more likely to self-blame or have an apathetic reaction. Coloured people have a history of self-blaming due to cultural norms and historical oppression (Schoellkopf, 2012). This is echoed by the finding that some coloured participants claim that the reason for negative effects of the Instagram algorithm is due to the people who interact with the algorithm.

Most participants had an apathetic reaction to the outcomes of the algorithmic distortion. Participants who self-blamed claimed that the reason for negative effects of the Instagram algorithm is due to the people who interact with the algorithm. This reaction may be a result of having limited knowledge of the way the algorithm works.

While most participants claimed to be aware of an algorithm, it is clear that not many know the detailed behaviours of the way it works.

Usage Behaviour. The third theme to be discussed is usage behaviour which may directly influence the effect and reactions of the algorithmic distortion of news feeds. The finding derived from this theme showed that the time spent on Instagram contributes to the negative feelings experienced on the app, as the users who spent more than 2 h on Instagram have reported to feel the most negative from using the app.

This confirms the findings in literature. It also found that the less accounts that participants follow, the more likely they are aware of the way the algorithm works.

Awareness of Algorithmic Distortion. This theme also found that participants age contributes to how aware they are of the algorithm. Teenage girls who adopt Instagram at a young age tend to follow their friends profiles and popular accounts like celebrities and influencers. This is echoed by the findings where participants in their later teens claimed to have experienced a downward spiral in their early years of using Instagram characterised by prolonged usage and sever social comparison.

This lead to the teenage girls taking a break from social media to recount for their depleting mental health and on their return, they limited their usage habits on the app. This contrasts with the younger participants who are not aware of the algorithm.

Alleviation Strategies. The final theme to be discussed is the alleviation strategies which are required to emancipate the teenage girls and allow them to explore social media safely. The first subtheme to be discussed is parental intervention. Findings showed that most respondents feel that a strong parent child relationship is an important factor in alleviating the negative effects of using social media. Some participants believe that parents should join minors on the social media platforms so that they can monitor how they interact at a distance.

Additionally, when parents join minors on social media sites, the participants felt that it makes their parents more relatable. However, participants felt strongly against parents monitoring minors too closely. For this to be achieved, parents will need to develop a relationship of trust and communication with their teenage children.

Furthermore, findings showed that participants enjoyed that Instagram added the functionality to remove the like count from posts. The like count is sometimes seen as an indicator of affirmation by the followers of an account. Findings show that the number of likes on a post can determine whether it remains on a profile or is taken down. Since the removal of the like count, participants are less concerned over the number of likes attained on a post. In line with this, findings show that to further reduce the features used for comparison, Instagram should allow users to hide their following and follower count.

Finally, findings show that respondents would navigate Instagram safely if they were to be educated about the way it works and what they should be aware of. Some participants have experienced talks on the safety of social media at their schools, which they claimed has helped them reach a better space when navigating the app.

5 Conclusion

This study investigated the coping strategies of teenage girls towards Instagram's Algorithmic bias. The study was conducted qualitatively amongst teenage girls within the Western Cape in South Africa.

It was found that teenage girls tend to cope with the algorithmic distortion of their Instagram newsfeeds by reducing the manner and time in which they interact with the app. The research also investigated the social and cultural factors affecting how the respondents coped with the algorithmic distortion of their Instagram newsfeeds. It was found that teenage girls who have open communication channels with their parents are more likely to be less affected.

The findings have implications not only on how coping mechanisms need to be taught to young female users of social media, but also the need for platforms such as Instagram to introduce more parental controls so that parents can monitor and restrict the usage of their teenage children where necessary.

5.1 Research Limitations

A key limitation of this study were the time constraints. Due to the short time horizon of this research study, more in-depth research and analysis could have been done.

Another limiting factor of this research was that interview respondents did not always understand the depth of the questions, or the context of the study. The younger participants were less aware of important terms that were pertinent to the study.

5.2 Future Research Recommendations

Future recommendations of this research would be to interview a larger number of girls with similar backgrounds. There are trends that have been noticed in the sample of 12 participants. However, the number of participants with similar backgrounds was minimal and therefore an opportunity exists to explore the coping strategies of teenage girls within particular social groups.

References

Asghar, J., Marzban, A.: Critical paradigm: a preamble for novice researchers. Life Sci. J. **10**(4), 1097–8135 (2013). http://www.lifesciencesite.com
Austin, B.: Social media's toxic content can harm teens. Harvard T.H. Chan School of Public Health (2021). https://www.hsph.harvard.edu/news/features/how-social-medias-toxic-content-sends-teens-into-a-dangerous-spiral/

Baird, S., et al.: Intersectionality as a framework for understanding adolescent vulnerabilities in low and middle-income countries: expanding our commitment to leave no one behind. Eur. J. Dev. Res. **33**(5), 1143–1162 (2021)

Bessenoff, G.R.: Can the media affect us? Social comparison, self-discrepancy, and the thin ideal. Psychol. Women Q. **30**(3), 239–251 (2016). https://doi.org/10.1111/j.1471-6402.2006. tb00292.x

Bhattacherjee, A.: Social Science Research: Principles, Methods, and Practices. University of South Florida Scholar Commons (2012). http://scholarcommons.usf.edu/oa_textbooks/3

Bozdag, E.: Bias in algorithmic filtering and personalization. Ethics Inf. Technol. **15**(3), 209–227 (2013). https://doi.org/10.1007/s10676-013-9321-6

Braun, V., Clarke, V.: Using thematic analysis in psychology. Qual. Res. Psychol. **3**(2), 77–101 (2006)

Bucher, T.: The algorithmic imaginary: exploring the ordinary affects of Facebook algorithms. Inf. Commun. Soc. **20**(1), 30–44 (2016). https://doi.org/10.1080/1369118X.2016.1154086

Cinelli, M., de Francisci Morales, G., Galeazzi, A., Quattrociocchi, W., Starnini, M.: The echo chamber effect on social media. Proc. Natl. Acad. Sci. USA **118**(9) (2021). https://doi.org/10. 1073/pnas.2023301118/suppl_file/pnas.2023301118.sapp.pdf

Cohen, R., Newton-John, T., Slater, A.: The relationship between Facebook and Instagram appearance-focused activities and body image concerns in young women. Body Image **23**, 183–187 (2017). https://doi.org/10.1016/j.bodyim.2017.10.002

Cotter, K.: Playing the visibility game: how digital influencers and algorithms negotiate influence on Instagram. New Media Soc. **21**(4), 895–913 (2019). https://doi.org/10.1177/146144481881 5684

Corbin, J., Strauss, A.: Can. J. Univ. Continuing Educ. **36**(2) (2010). http://ejournals.library.ual berta.ca/index.php/cjuce-rcep

Cubit, K., Lopez, V.: Qualitative study of enrolled nurses transition to registered nurses. J. Adv. Nurs. **68**(1), 206–211 (2012). https://doi.org/10.1111/j.1365-2648.2011.05729.x

Dastin, J.: Amazon ditched AI recruiting tool that favored men for technical jobs. The Guardian (2018). https://www.theguardian.com/technology/2018/oct/10/amazon-hiring-ai-gender-bias-recruiting-engine

Dobrean, A., Pasarelu, C.-R.: Impact of social media on social anxiety: a systematic review. In: New Developments in Anxiety Disorders. InTech (2016)

Ekström, O.: The perceived role of the Instagram algorithm in gender inequality - analyzing the public discourse around the case of Nyome Nicholas-Williams (2021)

Eslami, M., et al.: I always assumed that I wasn't really that close to [her]. In: Proceedings of the 33rd Annual ACM Conference on Human Factors in Computing Systems, pp. 153–162 (2015). https://doi.org/10.1145/2702123.2702556

Festinger, L.: A theory of social comparison processes. Hum. Relat. **7**(2), 117–140 (1954). https:// doi.org/10.1177/001872675400700202

Faelens, L., et al.: The relationship between Instagram use and indicators of mental health: a systematic review. Comput. Hum. Behav. Rep. **4**, 100121 (2021). https://doi.org/10.1016/j. chbr.2021.100121

Fouquaert, T., Mechant, P.: Making curation algorithms apparent: a case study of 'Instawareness' as a means to heighten awareness and understanding of Instagram's algorithm. Inf. Commun. Soc. **25**, 1–21 (2021). https://doi.org/10.1080/1369118X.2021.1883707

Goldstraw, D., Keegan, J., James, B.: Instagram's 'Fitspiration' Trend and Its Effect on Young Women's Self-Esteem. BLED, pp. 190–198 (2016)

Kleemans, M., Daalmans, S., Carbaat, I., Anschütz, D.: Picture perfect: the direct effect of manipulated instagram photos on body image in adolescent girls. Media Psychol. **21**(1), 93–110 (2018). https://doi.org/10.1080/15213269.2016.1257392

Kiger, M.E., Varpio, L.: Thematic analysis of qualitative data: AMEE guide. Med. Teach. 131 (2020). https://doi.org/10.1080/0142159X.2020.1755030

Kitchin, R.: Thinking critically about and researching algorithms. Inf. Commun. Soc. **20**(1), 14–29 (2017)

Lewallen, J.: When image isn't everything: the effects of instagram frames on social comparison. J. Soc. Media Soc. **5**(2), 108–133 (2016). https://www.thejsms.org/index.php/JSMS/article/view/159/81

Loden, M., Rosener, J.B.: Workforce America ! Managing Employee Diversity as a Vital Resource. In McGraw-Hill Professional Publishing (Issue 3). McGraw-Hill Professional Publishing (1990)

Lopez, R.B., Polletta, I.: Regulating self-image on instagram: links between social anxiety, instagram contingent self-worth, and content control behaviors. Front. Psychol. **12**, 711447 (2021). https://doi.org/10.3389/fpsyg.2021.711447

Mackson, S.B., Brochu, P.M., Schneider, B.A.: Instagram: friend or foe? The application's association with psychological well-being. New Media Soc. **21**(10), 2160–2182 (2019)

NHS Scotland. What is meant by the concept of 'intersectionality'? (2022). http://www.gov.scot/publications/using-intersectionality-understand-structural-inequality-scotland-evidence-synthesis/pages/3/

Omnicore. Instagram by the Numbers (2022): Stats, Demographics & Fun Facts (2022). https://www.omnicoreagency.com/instagram-statistics/

Pandis, N.: Cross-sectional studies. Am. J. Orthod. Dentofac. Orthop. **146**(1), 127–129 (2014)

Powers, E.: My news feed is filtered? Digit. J. **5**(10), 1315–1335 (2017). https://doi.org/10.1080/21670811.2017.1286943

Ramaciotti Morales, P., Cointet, J.-P.: Auditing the effect of social network recommendations on polarization in geometrical ideological spaces. In: Proceedings of the Fifteenth ACM Conference on Recommender Systems, pp. 627–632 (2021). https://doi.org/10.1145/3460231.3478851

Rader, E., Gray, R.: Understanding user beliefs about algorithmic curation in the Facebook news feed. In: Proceedings of the 33rd Annual ACM Conference on Human Factors in Computing Systems, pp. 173–182 (2015). https://doi.org/10.1145/2702123.2702174

Seabrook, E.M., Kern, M.L., Rickard, N.S.: Social networking sites, depression, and anxiety: a systematic review. JMIR Mental Health **3**(4) (2016). https://doi.org/10.2196/mental.5842

Statista. Most used social media 2021 (2022). https://www.statista.com/statistics/272014/global-social-networks-ranked-by-number-of-users/

Schoellkopf, J.: Victim-Blaming: A New Term for an Old Trend. Lesbian Gay Bisexual Transgender Queer Center (2012)

Tiggemann, M., Hayden, S., Brown, Z., Veldhuis, J.: The effect of Instagram "likes" on women's social comparison and body dissatisfaction. Body Image **26**, 90–97 (2018). https://doi.org/10.1016/j.bodyim.2018.07.002

Vannucci, A., Flannery, K.M., Ohannessian, C.M.: Social media use and anxiety in emerging adults. J. Affect. Disord. **207**, 163–166 (2017). https://doi.org/10.1016/j.jad.2016.08.040

Wells, G., Horwitz, J., Seetharaman, D.: Facebook knows Instagram is toxic for teen girls, company documents show. Wall Street J. (2021). https://www.wsj.com/articles/facebook-knows-instagram-is-toxic-for-teen-girls-company-documents-show-11631620739

Zheng, Y., Walsham, G.: Inequality of what? An intersectional approach to digital inequality under Covid-19. Inf. Organ. **31**(1), 100341 (2021). https://doi.org/10.1016/j.infoandorg.2021.100341

Improving UX in Digital Transformation Projects Through Lean Principles

Héctor Cornide-Reyes[1]([envelope])[iD], Cristian Duran[1][iD], Sergio Baltierra[2][iD], Fabián Silva-Aravena[3][iD], and Jenny Morales[3][iD]

[1] Facultad de Ingeniería, Departamento de Ingeniería Informática y Ciencias de la Computación, Universidad de Atacama, Copiapó, Chile
{hector.cornide,cristian.duran}@uda.cl
[2] Facultad de Ciencias de la Ingeniería, Universidad Católica del Maule, Talca, Chile
[3] Facultad de Ciencias Sociales y Económicas, Departamento de Economía y Administración, Universidad Católica del Maule, Talca, Chile
{fasilva,jmoralesb}@ucm.cl

Abstract. Today, digital transformation remains a key strategic objective for most companies. Through these processes, they seek to stay ahead in a constantly changing industrial environment and improve their competitiveness in markets characterized by high uncertainty. In this context, Lean emerges as one of the most widely used business management methodologies because it seeks the maximum efficiency of the company by eliminating elements that represent an additional cost and do not add value to the product or service. However, despite various methodological proposals that guide digital transformation processes, challenges persist in implementing the necessary cultural changes. Therefore, it is essential to remember that the main focus of any digital transformation initiative must always be on people. In this context, user experience (UX) emerges as a critical element in the success of digital transformation initiatives, as it directly impacts customer satisfaction and the adoption of digital technologies. Driven by the need to explore the development of these processes, we have conducted a comprehensive review of the literature related to digital transformation, UX, and Lean. Our main goal is to understand the challenges inherent in improving UX in the context of digital transformation using Lean as a methodology. Following analyzing the selected primary studies, we have identified relevant Lean principles and practices to be considered in digital transformation processes. In addition, we identified the main challenges in their integration and the opportunities that this integration offers. The evidence gathered indicates that digital transformation will continue to be a priority for companies pursuing Industry 4.0. In future work, we plan to conduct a tertiary study to synthesize the knowledge captured in many existing systematic reviews.

Keywords: Digital Transformation · Project Management · Lean · User eXperience · Literature Review

A. Coman and S. Vasilache (Eds.): HCII 2024, LNCS 14703, pp. 161–178, 2024.
https://doi.org/10.1007/978-3-031-61281-7_11

1   Introduction

Digital transformation has been established as a crucial pillar for companies aspiring to thrive in the era of Industry 4.0. This metamorphosis goes beyond the mere adoption of technologies; it represents a reinvention of business processes and strategies to be at the forefront in an increasingly digitalized world [4,15,24]. The integration of advanced technologies such as artificial intelligence [23], big data analytics, and the Internet of Things (IoT) is redefining the way organizations operate and compete [17]. However, digital transformation is not without its challenges. One of the main obstacles is the alignment of digital technology with business objectives and organizational culture, which often leads to resistance and failures in implementation [10–12]. The focus of digital transformation processes must always be people: the users who belong to the company and the customers who receive the product or service they provide. Additionally, user experience (UX) has become a critical factor for the success of these processes. A well-designed UX can significantly improve the adoption and effectiveness of digital technologies, contributing to the success of digital transformation [13].

In this context, the Lean methodology is positioned as an effective approach to improving the odds of success in digital transformation. Originating in the manufacturing sector, Lean philosophy focuses on efficiency, waste elimination, and continuous improvement, emphasizing creating value for the customer [25]. Its application in digital transformation involves agile development, constant experimentation, and rapid learning, which allows companies to quickly adapt to new market demands and emerging technologies [6]. Integrating Lean into digital transformation processes boosts operational efficiency and enhances the user experience. By adopting a customer-centric approach, companies can develop digital solutions that are intuitive, accessible, and aligned with the end-user's needs [7]. This facilitates broader adoption of digital technologies and leads to greater customer satisfaction and loyalty, key factors for success in the digital age [22].

Lean UX is an evolution of user experience (UX) design inspired by Lean and Agile principles. It focuses on rapid prototyping, continuous feedback, and iteration to develop more effective user experiences in digital products. Its adoption has proven effective in improving both product quality and customer satisfaction while agilely adapting to the changing requirements and expectations of the market in the digital era. Unlike traditional UX approaches, Lean UX is less documented and more collaborative, emphasizing the importance of experimentation and rapid learning [9]. Therefore, the combination of Lean and digital transformation offers a powerful synergy, aligning operational agility with a deep focus on user experience, thus overcoming the challenges of digitalization and capitalizing on the opportunities of Industry 4.0.

Driven by the need to explore the development of these processes, we have conducted an exhaustive review of the literature related to digital transformation, UX, and Lean. Our main objective is to understand the challenges inherent in improving UX in the context of digital transformation using Lean as a methodology. To guide our research, we have defined the following research questions: What Lean principles/practices are most effective for developing digital transformation processes?; What are the challenges and opportunities of integrating Lean into digital transformation strategies for companies moving towards Industry 4.0? How can Lean approaches contribute to a better understanding of the user experience for Industry 4.0? To address these questions, we have developed a literature review that included the search for scientific evidence in academic databases such as Web of Science, Scopus, IEEE Xplore, and ACM Digital Library. These databases are chosen due to their great reputation in the scientific community and because we can download papers from our universities.

This paper is organized as follows: Sect. 2 describes the research method used. Section 3 shows the results obtained in the literature review and the evidence found to answer the research questions, and finally, in Sect. 4, the conclusions and future work.

2   Methodology

The main goal of this work is to understand the challenges inherent in improving UX in the context of digital transformation using Lean as a methodology. To achieve this objective, a literature review was conducted based on the guidelines proposed by [16,20]. The process was conducted through the following steps: 1) statement of research questions, 2) search process, 3) selection of studies, and 4) analysis of results. All these steps are described below.

2.1   Research Questions

We have defined three specific research questions for more detailed knowledge and a comprehensive view of the subject. The research questions to be answered in this study are as follows:

- RQ1. What Lean principles/practices are most effective for developing digital transformation processes?
- RQ2. What are the challenges and opportunities of integrating Lean into digital transformation strategies for companies moving towards Industry 4.0?
- RQ3. How can Lean approaches contribute to a better understanding of the user experience for Industry 4.0?

2.2   Search Process

The citation databases used were SCOPUS and Web of Science (WoS), while the scientific publication databases used were ACM Digital Library and IEEE Xplore. This selection is mainly due to the reputation of these databases in the discipline and the fact that we have full access to the published material. Table 1 details the method used to construct the search string. For this purpose, we use the method PICOC [8,16,19] whose acronyms represent the criteria that drive the process. The PICOC method is structured to formulate research questions and construct efficient search chains. PICOC is an acronym that stands for five key elements: **P** de Population; **I** de Intervention; **C** de Comparison; **O** de Outcomes y **C** de Context. The clarity in these elements facilitates systematic and comprehensive searches of databases and other information sources.The analysis criteria are

Table 1. Construction of the search string using the PICOC method

Population	Intervention	Comparison	Outcomes	Context
organizations and companies that have carried out digital transformation processes	Use of Lean to improve and digital transformation processes user experience	Not applicable	Guidelines Lean implementation methods Implementation success stories Implementation assessment	Industry 4.0
organization/company/Institution digital transformation/Industry 4.0/ Managment4.0	Lean User Experience	Not applicable		Industry 4.0
(organization or company or institution) AND (digital transformation OR Industry 4.0)	Lean OR Lean4.0 User eXperience OR UX	Not applicable	guidelines OR successful OR assessment OR evaluation OR implementation	Industry 4.0

Based on the PICOC method, the following search string was developed: *(organization OR company OR institution) AND ("digital transformation" OR "Industry 4.0" OR "management 4.0") AND (Lean OR Lean4.0 OR ux OR "use experience") AND (guidelines OR successful OR challenges OR implementation).* This search string was validated with a set of papers we identified and used as a control group. The investigation was initially carried out in November; its last update was mid-December 2023.

The inclusion/exclusion criteria were as follows:

- Published between 2018 and 2023.
- Contain information on Lean and digital transformation processes in companies.
- Only written in English.
- Only papers published in journals.

2.3   Selection of Primary Studies

The data extraction form was developed with the following fields: paper Title, Year, DOI; Published in (Journal, Conference); Study Type (Quantitative, Qualitative, Mixed); Research Method (Literature Review, Case Study, Interviews, Questionnaires, Observation); Objective; Main Findings; Main Conclusions; Future Work; Tributes to RQ1 (Yes/No); Evidence RQ1; Tributes to RQ2 (Yes/No); Evidence RQ2; Tributes to RQ3 (Yes/No); Evidence RQ3; Industry Sector; Number of people; Number of Women; Number of Men.

The methodology for searching and selecting papers was structured into three successive stages:

- **First Stage (1F):** We began by reviewing all titles and keywords of the papers obtained from each database. Subsequently, duplicates were removed to ensure the uniqueness of the documents.

- **Second Stage (2F):** Next, we conducted a detailed reading of the abstracts of those papers that passed the first filter. This step allowed a preliminary assessment of the relevance and pertinence of each paper.
- **Third Stage:** Finally, the papers selected after the second filter were downloaded, read in their entirety, and recorded in a form designed in Microsoft Excel, following the established protocol. This stage involved an exhaustive review to determine their final inclusion in the study.

After executing the search string in each consulted database, we obtained the following initial results: 127 papers from Web of Science (WoS), 139 from SCOPUS, 24 from IEEE Xplore, and 234 from ACM Digital Library. Subsequently, we applied the previously described filters (1F and 2F), which resulted in a more refined selection: 35 papers from WoS, 63 from SCOPUS, eight from IEEE Xplore, and 43 from ACM Digital Library. Finally, we selected 38 primary studies for detailed analysis and discussion.(see Table 2).

2.4   Analysis of Results

Figure 1 provides a clear and detailed chronological distribution of the selected primary studies over the years. This graph is particularly revealing, as it visually demonstrates the growing interest within the scientific community in digital transformation and Industry 4.0 topics. A notable increase in the number of studies conducted in recent years is highlighted, reflecting the growing recognition of the importance of these topics in the current context.

On the other hand, Table 3 offers an integrated and organized view of how the selected primary studies align with the previously defined research questions. This table shows the correspondence between the questions and the studies and facilitates a deeper understanding of the focus areas and specific aspects that each study addresses in relation to the posed questions. This provides a valuable tool for quickly identifying the key contributions of each study in the broader context of the research.

Furthermore, Table 4 establishes a relationship between the research questions and the research methods used in the selected primary studies. This table is crucial for understanding the methodologies adopted in the research and how they are applied to address the specific questions. The various methods used in the studies reflect the diversity and richness of approaches in the research of digital transformation and Industry 4.0, thus offering a broader view of the different perspectives and methodological approaches in this field of study.

2.5   Limitations

In conducting this research, we have adopted a selective and rigorous approach to data collection, focusing specifically on scientific contributions from the past five years. This time limitation is crucial as it allows us to concentrate on the most recent and relevant developments in the field, ensuring that our review reflects current trends and advancements in the subject matter.

Table 2. Selected primary studies (PS) and DOI

ID	Title	DOI
[PS_1]	A comparison on Industry 4.0 and Lean Production between manufacturers from emerging and developed economies [26]	10.1080/14783363.2019.1696184
[PS_2]	A Maturity Model to Become a Smart Organization Based on Lean and Industry 4.0 Synergy [27]	10.3390/su151713151
[PS_3]	A Socio-Technical Framework for Lean Project Management Implementation towards Sustainable Value in the Digital Transformation Context [28]	10.3390/su15031756
[PS_4]	A Sustainable Productive Method for Enhancing Operational Excellence in Shop Floor Management for Industry 4.0 Using Hybrid Integration of Lean and Smart Manufacturing: An Ingenious Case Study [29]	10.3390/su14127452
[PS_5]	Adaptation of the Lean 6S Methodology in an Industrial Environment under Sustainability and Industry 4.0 Criteria [30]	10.3390/su132212449
[PS_6]	Assessing the synergies between lean manufacturing and Industry 4.0 [31]	10.37610/dyo.v0i71.579
[PS_7]	Assessment by Lean Modified Manufacturing Maturity Model for Industry 4.0: A Case Study of Pakistan's Manufacturing Sector [32]	10.1109/TEM.2023.3259005
[PS_8]	Assessment of the Potential Impact of Industry 4.0 Technologies on the Levers of Lean Manufacturing in Manufacturing Industries in Morocco [33]	10.46338/ijetae0722_08
[PS_9]	Being lean: how to shape digital transformation in the manufacturing sector [34]	10.1108/JMTM-12-2020-0467
[PS_10]	Can Industry 4.0 Assist Lean Manufacturing in Attaining Sustainability over Time? Evidence from the US Organizations [35]	10.3390/su15031962
[PS_11]	Characterization of Industry 4.0 Lean Management Problem-Solving Behavioral Patterns Using EEG Sensors and Deep Learning [36]	10.3390/s19132841
[PS_12]	Compatibility, opportunities and challenges in the combination of Industry 4.0 and Lean Production [37]	10.23773/2022_09
[PS_13]	Development of a Data-Driven Decision-Making System Using Lean and Smart Manufacturing Concept in Industry 4.0: A Case Study [38]	10.1155/2022/3012215
[PS_14]	Development Trends of Production Systems through the Integration of Lean Management and Industry 4.0 [39]	10.3390/app12104885
[PS_15]	Digital Standardization of Lean Manufacturing Tools According to Industry 4.0 Concept [40]	10.3390/app13106259
[PS_16]	Enabling the Circular Economy transition: a sustainable lean manufacturing recipe for Industry 4.0 [41]	10.1002/bse.2801
[PS_17]	Enhancing the adaptability: Lean and green strategy towards the Industry Revolution 4.0 [42]	10.1016/j.jclepro.2020.122870
[PS_18]	How Industry 4.0 Can Enhance Lean Practice [43]	10.5937/fmet1904810P
[PS_19]	Identification of Key Brittleness Factors for the Lean-Green Manufacturing System in a Manufacturing Company in the Context of Industry 4.0 Based on the DEMATEL-ISM-MICMAC Method [44]	10.3390/pr11020499
[PS_20]	Impact of Industry 4.0 and Lean Manufacturing on the Sustainability Performance of Plastic and Petrochemical Organizations in Saudi Arabia [45]	10.3390/su132011252
[PS_21]	Impact of Industry 4.0 Concept on the Levers of Lean Manufacturing Approach in Manufacturing Industries [46]	10.15282/ijame.18.1.2021.11.0646
[PS_22]	Impacts of Industry 4.0 technologies on Lean principles [47]	10.1080/00207543.2019.1672902
[PS_23]	Implications of using Industry 4.0 base technologies for lean and agile supply chains and performance [48]	10.1016/j.ijpe.2023.108916
[PS_24]	Improving the Performance of a SME in the Cutlery Sector Using Lean Thinking and Digital Transformation [49]	10.3390/su15108302
[PS_25]	Industry 4.0 adoption as a moderator of the impact of lean production practices on operational performance improvement [50]	10.1108/IJOPM-01-2019-0005
[PS_26]	Industry 4.0, Lean Management and Organizational Support: A Case of Supply Chain Operations [51]	10.17512/pjms.2020.22.1.37
[PS_27]	Integrated Impact of Circular Economy, Industry 4.0, and Lean Manufacturing on Sustainability Performance of Manufacturing Firms [52]	10.3390/ijerph20065119
[PS_28]	Interpretive structural modelling of critical success factor for lean product lifecycle management in industry 4.0 [53]	10.4995/ijpme.2023.18840
[PS_29]	Lean 4.0 implementation framework: Proposition using a multi-method research approach [54]	10.1016/j.ijpe.2023.108988
[PS_30]	Lean and Industry 4.0: Mapping determinants and barriers from a social, environmental, and operational perspective [55]	10.1016/j.techfore.2021.121320
[PS_31]	Lean and Industry 4.0 mitigating common losses in Engineer-to-Order theory and practice: an exploratory study [56]	10.1007/s10696-023-09503-z
[PS_32]	Lean Manufacturing in Industry 4.0: A Smart and Sustainable Manufacturing System [57]	10.3390/machines11010072
[PS_33]	Lean Manufacturing Systems in the Area of Industry 4.0: A lean automation plan of AGVs/IoT integration into lean manufacturing [58]	10.1080/09537287.2021.1917720
[PS_34]	Synergies between Lean and Industry 4.0 for Enhanced Maintenance Management in Sustainable Operations: A Model Proposal [59]	10.3390/pr11092691
[PS_35]	The HyDAPI framework: a versatile tool integrating Lean Six Sigma and digitalisation for improved quality management in Industry 4.0 [60]	10.1108/IJLSS-12-2021-0214
[PS_36]	The implementation of the conjunction of lean six sigma and industry 4.0: a case study in the Czech Republic [61]	10.2478/mspe-2022-0028
[PS_37]	The Influence of Lean Practices and Leadership on Business Excellence: Malaysian E&E Manufacturing Companies [62]	10.25115/eea.v39i4.4562
[PS_38]	The interrelation between Industry 4.0 and lean production: an empirical study on European manufacturers [63]	10.1007/s00170-019-03441-7

Table 3. Matching research questions and primary studies

Research Questions	References to primary studies
RQ1. What Lean principles/practices are most effective for developing digital transformation processes?	[PS_1], [PS_2], [PS_5]. [PS_7], [PS_9], [PS_12], [PS_14], [PS_15], [PS_22], [PS_24], [PS_33], [PS_34], [PS_35]
RQ2. What are the challenges and opportunities of integrating Lean into digital transformation strategies for companies moving towards Industry 4.0?	[PS_6], [PS_9], [PS_12]. [PS_13], [PS_14], [PS_15], [PS_16], [PS_17], [PS_18], [PS_21], [PS_22], [PS_24], [PS_25], [PS_26], [PS_27], [PS_28], [PS_29], [PS_33]
RQ3. How can Lean approaches contribute to a better understanding of the user experience for Industry 4.0?	[PS_12], [PS_33], [PS_35]

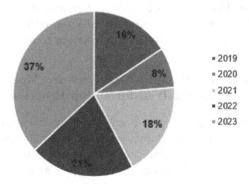

Fig. 1. Distribution of primary studies by year.

Table 4. Matching research questions with research method used in primary studies

Research Questions	Research method used		
	Literature review	Survey	Case study
RQ1. What Lean principles/practices are most effective for developing digital transformation processes?	[PS_12], [PS_14], [PS_22], [PS_35]	[PS_1]	[PS_2], [PS_5], [PS_7], [PS_9], [PS_15], [PS_24], [PS_33], [PS_34]
RQ2. What are the challenges and opportunities of integrating Lean into digital transformation strategies for companies moving towards Industry 4.0?	[PS_6], [PS_12], [PS_14], [PS_16], [PS_18], [PS_22]	[PS_25], [PS_26], [PS_27], [PS_28], [PS_29]	[PS_9], [PS_13], [PS_15], [PS_17], [PS_21], [PS_24], [PS_33]
RQ3. How can Lean approaches contribute to a better understanding of the user experience for Industry 4.0?	[PS_12], [PS_35]		[PS_33]

Moreover, given their recognized credibility and rigor in the peer-review process, we have restricted our search to studies published in academic journals. This decision is based on the premise that journals are often the preferred medium for publishing high-quality research with a significant impact on the scientific community. Therefore, this restriction ensures that the selected studies meet a high academic quality and relevance standard.

We have excluded other indexing forms such as SciELO or Latindex and conference proceedings. While these may contain valuable research, they often have different review processes and publication criteria, which could affect the consistency and comparability of the collected data. Additionally, conference proceedings, though important for the rapid dissemination of ideas and findings, often include works in more preliminary stages of research. By focusing exclusively on journal publications, we seek to ensure greater depth, methodological rigor, and maturity in the research that forms the basis of our study.

3 Discussion of Results

We implemented a meticulous process for analyzing the information to facilitate a detailed and meaningful discussion of the results. This process involved thoroughly analyzing and categorizing each of the selected primary studies. This categorization was based on their alignment with the specific research questions that led to our study. In doing so, we could understand not only how each study contributes individually to the overall body of knowledge but also collectively assess the progress and trends in the field in relation to our research questions.

3.1 RQ1. What Lean Principles/practices are Most Effective for Developing Digital Transformation Processes?

Following an exhaustive review of the selected primary studies, it is notably evident how Lean principles and practices have evolved from their origins in manufacturing to become an integral philosophy across various industries. They now play a crucial role in guiding organizations on their journey through digital transformation and Industry 4.0.

In the reviewed literature, the terms *principles* and *practices* are frequently used to denote the use or application of the Lean methodology. It is critical to note that these terms have significant conceptual differences. *Lean principles* refer to the fundamental concepts, philosophies, or beliefs that guide the Lean methodology as a whole. These principles are abstract in nature and form the ideological foundation upon which the entire Lean system is built. In contrast, *Lean practices* are specific techniques, tools, or methods used to implement Lean principles in concrete operations and processes. They represent tangible tactics or actions that can be taught, learned, and practically applied [2].

In [34], the approach of manufacturing companies to digital transformation and the impact of the Lean approach on this process are analyzed. The methodology includes multiple case studies with 19 manufacturing companies, assessing patterns of digital transformation and their relationship with the companies' Lean maturity. The results identify two patterns of digital transformation: a sustainable one, characterized by small and horizontal digital changes, and a disruptive one, marked by large and radical digital changes. Additionally, it was observed that Lean culture plays a significant role in guiding the digital transformation of companies.

In [40] examines the functionality and effectiveness of TPM (Total Productive Maintenance) software in digitizing Lean manufacturing tools. The TPM software was implemented and tested in a construction production company. The results indicated that using TPM improved efficiency by 15% compared to non-digital solutions, with a notable reduction in the control time of control points.

A particularly interesting study is presented in [49], demonstrating the efficacy of combining Lean principles with digitalization practices in improving business performance. This study focused on how implementing Lean Thinking and digital transformation can enhance performance in a small cutlery manufacturing company. Significant improvements such as reduced production time and increased productivity were achieved through a case study that included mapping and diagnosing production processes, followed by implementing Lean-based improvements and digitalization.

In reviewing primary studies whose methodology was a literature review, the main Lean practices related to digital transformation processes were identified and defined. The highlighted Lean practices include:

- **Lean Manufacturing:** This methodology focuses on efficient operation management, emphasizing process optimization, waste elimination, and maximizing production efficiency. Lean Manufacturing philosophy centers on creating value for the customer by promoting continuous improvement and eliminating any non-value-adding activities. The aim is to develop more agile and flexible processes that better respond to customer needs and enhance product quality while reducing operational costs. This methodology encourages an organizational culture based on teamwork and employee empowerment [31–33, 40, 41, 45, 46, 52, 57].
- **Lean 5S:** This term derives from five Japanese words that start with'S': Seiri (Sort), Seiton (Set in order), Seiso (Shine), Seiketsu (Standardize), and Shitsuke (Sustain). These principles work together to create an efficient, organized, and clean working environment. Seiri involves removing all unnecessary items from the work area. Seiton efficiently organizes the essential items. Seiso focuses on cleaning the workspace, while Seiketsu establishes standards to maintain this organization and cleanliness over the long term. Finally, Shitsuke refers to the discipline of maintaining and regularly reviewing these standards. Implementing 5S improves efficiency, reduces waste, increases safety, and fosters a culture of continuous improvement in the workplace [39].
- **Lean 6S:** An evolution of Lean 5S, adding a sixth element, "Safety" (Safety), to the traditional five principles of 5S: Seiri (Sort), Seiton (Set in order), Seiso (Shine), Seiketsu (Standardize), and Shitsuke (Sustain). While 5S focuses on creating an organized, efficient, and clean work environment, 6S incorporates safety as a crucial dimension, underscoring the importance of a safe working environment. "Safety" involves proactive identification and mitigation of workplace risks, which prevents accidents and injuries and enhances productivity and overall employee well-being. By integrating safety into the 5S system, Lean 6S becomes a more comprehensive tool for operational management, ensuring efficiency and organization are complemented by a firm commitment to workplace safety. This methodology is particularly valuable in industrial and manufacturing environments but is also applicable in various other work contexts [30].
- **Lean Six Sigma:** Combines the principles of Lean and Six Sigma to improve business performance by systematically eliminating waste and reducing vari-

ability in production and business processes. Lean, focusing on waste elimination and efficiency improvement, complements Six Sigma, which uses statistical tools to enhance quality and reduce variability. Integrating Lean and Six Sigma results in a powerful methodology that seeks both process efficiency and agility (Lean) and precision and error reduction (Six Sigma). Lean Six Sigma is characterized by its structured, data-driven approach, emphasizing decision-making driven by rigorous measurement and analysis [60,61].

– **Lean Thinking:** Emphasizes understanding and delivering what customers truly value while minimizing all non-value-adding activities (muda). It involves key principles such as identifying and mapping the value stream, creating more efficient and smooth processes, implementing a demand-based production system (pull), and constantly seeking perfection through continuous improvement (Kaizen). This philosophy is applied in production and manufacturing and has also extended to services, software development, and more, transforming how organizations approach quality, efficiency, and customer satisfaction. Adopting Lean Thinking, companies reduce costs and increase operational efficiency and foster a culture of employee empowerment and a customer-centric focus [49].

Similarly, the Lean principles that can be highlighted from the primary studies are:

– **Just in Time (JIT)**: A production strategy aimed at reducing inventory and increasing efficiency by producing only what is needed, when it is needed, and in the required amount [1].
– **Continuous Improvement**: A philosophy of ongoing improvement where all employees seek ways to enhance processes and work practices [3].
– **Pull System**: Contrary to the traditional "push" production system, the "pull" system is based on actual demand, minimizing inventory and lead times [14].
– **Jidoka**: The ability of a machine or process to stop itself when a problem occurs, allowing for immediate intervention and preventing the production of defects [5].
– **Poka-Yoke**: Process design or modifications that help prevent errors before they occur, improving quality and reducing defects [18].
– **Visual Management**: The use of visual tools, such as Kanban boards or indicators, to enhance communication, performance tracking, and process management [21].

3.2   RQ2. What are the Challenges and Opportunities of Integrating Lean into Digital Transformation Strategies for Companies Moving Towards Industry 4.0?

The incorporation of Lean in digital transformation processes represents a crucial strategic step for companies in the modern era. This approach, which focuses on achieving maximum business efficiency by eliminating non-value-adding elements, offers potentially transformative benefits in the digital realm. Through a review of the selected primary studies, we have identified key similarities in both the anticipated challenges and the opportunities arising from this integration (see Table 5).

On the one hand, adapting Lean principles to digital environments presents unique challenges. Companies must navigate the complexity of digitalizing processes that have traditionally been carried out manually or analogically, which requires not just an investment in technology but also a significant cultural shift. Moreover, the dynamic and ever-evolving nature of the digital environment demands continuous adaptation and updating of Lean practices to maintain their relevance and effectiveness.

On the other hand, the opportunities provided by merging Lean with digital transformation are extensive. This approach can lead to increased agility and responsiveness in business processes, crucial in a market characterized by rapid changes and constantly evolving customer demands. Implementing Lean principles in digital environments can also result in significant improvements in service or product quality, as it allows for quicker identification and correction of issues, as well as continuous optimization of processes.

Additionally, integrating Lean into digital transformation fosters a culture of efficiency and continuous improvement throughout the organization. This translates into greater employee engagement in innovation processes and decision-making, which can increase job satisfaction and productivity. Furthermore, the use of Lean tools and techniques in digital operations management facilitates the collection and analysis of data, leading to a better understanding of customer behavior and more informed and strategic decision-making.

Table 5. Lean Transformation Challenges and Opportunities

Primary Study	Challenges	Opportunities
[49]	Inventory management of raw materials and machinery configuration. Variability and lack of standardization in production processes	Implement actions to improve inventory management and reduce variability. Significant improvements in reducing WIP (Work In Progress) and total processing times
[58]	Integration of Industry 4.0 technologies with existing lean manufacturing systems. Managing interactions and power plays between social, technical, and operational factors	Developing an action plan for successfully integrating technologies like AGVs and IoT into lean operations. Improving operational efficiency and reducing waste through lean automation
[34]	Identification of suitable digital transformation patterns for companies with different maturity levels in Lean practices. Integration of Lean culture in the adoption of Industry 4.0 technologies	Development of models to guide digital transformation through a Lean approach. Empowering the role of operators in digitized processes to improve decision-making and problem-solving

In summary, we can summarise the challenges and opportunities of integrating Lean into digital transformation processes as follows:

1. **Challenges**:
   - **Complex Integration**: The complex integration of technology into Lean production tools and employees' resistance to accepting new forms of technology.
   - **Managing Volatility and Product Diversity**: Difficulty handling volatile demand volumes and the wide diversity of variants with classical Lean production concepts.
   - **Need for Standards and Coordination**: Challenges related to the standardization of processes and effective coordination between different stakeholders in the supply chain.
   - **Technology Adoption and Cultural Change**: Overcoming employee reluctance to adopt new technologies and managing the necessary cultural change.
2. **Opportunities**:
   - **Improved Operational Efficiency**: Potential to improve operational efficiency and production quality by integrating I4.0 into Lean processes.
   - **Process Optimisation**: Use of big data and optimized decision-making for more flexible response to disruptions and increased productivity.
   - **Continuous Improvement and Transparency**: Possibility to realize a superior continuous improvement process in the sense of Kaizen, thanks to the increased transparency and efficiency provided by I4.0 technologies.
   - **Lean Process Basis for Successful Integration**: The importance of having lean and efficient processes as a basis for successfully integrating I4.0 technologies.

3.3 RQ3. How Can Lean Approaches Contribute to a Better Understanding of the User Experience for Industry 4.0?

Lean play a crucial role in enhancing the understanding and optimization of the user experience (UX) within the context of Industry 4.0. When integrated with the advanced technologies of Industry 4.0, these practices enable companies not only to optimize their processes but also to respond more effectively to user needs and expectations. In this regard, the study [58] emphasizes that key factors for improving UX include the active involvement of employees and team leaders in design and integration of operations, as well as the use of socio-technical systems to manage both social and technical aspects, facilitating a more harmonious interaction between people and technology.

Thorough analysis of primary studies focused on this research area [37, 58, 60] allows us to conclude that Lean approaches significantly contribute to a deeper understanding of UX in Industry 4.0. The relevant aspects to consider are as follows:

- **Enhancement of Lean Principles Implementation through Industry 4.0 Technologies**: Technologies associated with Industry 4.0, such as electronic identification and instant communication between products and machines, can notably optimize the implementation of Lean principles like Just-in-Time and Jidoka. This translates into greater operational efficiency and substantial improvement of UX, ensuring more agile and market-responsive production.
- **Strengthening Process Standardization and Focus on Customer Value**: Standardized processes and a consistent focus on customer value, essential elements in Lean methodology, are crucial for the successful implementation of Industry 4.0 technologies. Simplifying product and process complexity through Lean practices facilitates a more efficient and cost-effective use of these technologies, positively impacting UX.
- **Enhancing Decision-Making and Process Transparency with Real-Time Data**: The ability of Industry 4.0 technologies to provide real-time data increases process transparency and enhances product information quality. This strengthens employees' decision-making, enabling the implementation of continuous improvement activities based on complete and up-to-date information, like Kaizen, directly benefiting UX.
- **Continuous Integration of Lean Management with Enhancement of Principles through Industry 4.0**: Although Industry 4.0 technologies do not cover all Lean principles, they can enhance their efficiency. It is crucial to maintain Lean management while reinforcing certain principles using these advanced technologies. This suggests that a deeper understanding of Lean principles, combined with strategic applications of Industry 4.0, can significantly improve UX in the manufacturing sector.

This integrated approach demonstrates how the intersection of Lean methodology and Industry 4.0 technologies can lead to an improved, more efficient user experience, aligned with current market needs and the technological environment.

4   Conclusions and Future Work

This paper represents a thorough effort to review existing literature and gain a comprehensive understanding of the application of Lean methodologies in digital transformation processes, particularly in companies transitioning towards Industry 4.0. In this process, we meticulously analyzed 38 primary studies, which allowed us to gather valuable information on how Lean principles and practices are currently being implemented. Through this analysis, we were able to identify a series of significant challenges and opportunities for companies looking to integrate Lean into their digital transformation processes.

A key conclusion from our research is that for Lean principles to effectively contribute to enhancing user experience (UX), it is essential to recognize the critical role played by people within organizations. The digital transformation for

Industry 4.0 is not just a matter of implementing new technologies and processes but also involves actively engaging employees in this change. An effective strategy for companies would be to conduct a holistic diagnosis that considers all relevant aspects before designing and implementing a Lean-based digital transformation strategy.

During our research, we encountered a considerable volume of papers interested in exploring the benefits of integrating Lean into digital transformation processes. This underscores the importance and growing interest in this field of study. Consequently, as a future direction for our research, we are motivated to continue advancing and delving deeper into this subject. We plan to conduct a comprehensive tertiary study that will allow us to synthesize and comprehensively analyze all the knowledge accumulated in existing research papers. This approach will help us build a clearer and more detailed panorama of the impact and implications of integrating Lean into digital transformation, thus providing valuable insights for both academics and professionals alike.

References

1. Aycock, J.: A brief history of just-in-time. ACM Comput. Surv. (CSUR) **35**(2), 97–113 (2003)
2. Arnheiter, E.D., Maleyeff, J.: The integration of lean management and Six Sigma. TQM Mag. **17**(1), 5–18 (2005)
3. Berger, A.: Continuous improvement and kaizen: standardization and organizational designs. Integr. Manuf. Syst. **8**(2), 110–117 (1997)
4. Bharadwaj, A., El Sawy, O.A., Pavlou, P.A., Venkatraman, N.: Digital business strategy: toward a next generation of insights. MIS Q. **37**(2), 471–482 (2013)
5. Danovaro, E., Janes, A., Succi, G.: Jidoka in software development. In: Companion to the 23rd ACM SIGPLAN Conference on Object-Oriented Programming Systems Languages and Applications, pp. 827–830, October 2008
6. Fitzgerald, M., Kruschwitz, N., Bonnet, D., Welch, M.: Embracing digital technology: a new strategic imperative. MIT Sloan Manag. Rev. (2014)
7. Forbes, L.P., Jermier, J.M., Benn, S., Orsato, R.J., Daudigeos, T.: The role of powerful actors in shaping consensus around meaning: a framing analysis of 'sustainable' bioplastics. J. Bus. Ethics **130**(2), 323–334 (2016)
8. García-Pérez, M.A., Pérez-López, R.: PICOC strategy for the research question construction in systematic reviews. Evidence-Based Med. Pract. **5**(2) (2021)
9. Gothelf, J., Seiden, J.: Lean UX: Designing Great Products with Agile Teams. O'Reilly Media, Sebastopol (2020)
10. Hess, T., Matt, C., Benlian, A., Wiesböck, F.: Options for formulating a digital transformation strategy. MIS Q. Exec. **15**(2) (2016)
11. Kane, G.C., Palmer, D., Phillips, A.N., Kiron, D., Buckley, N.: Strategy, not technology, drives digital transformation. MIT Sloan Manag. Rev. (2015)
12. Lalband, N., Kavitha, D.: Software development technique for the betterment of end user satisfaction using agile methodology. TEM **9**(3), 992–1002 (2020)
13. Lemon, K.N., Verhoef, P.C.: Understanding customer experience throughout the customer journey. J. Mark. **80**(6), 69–96 (2016)
14. Lu, J.C., Yang, T., Wang, C.Y.: A lean pull system design analysed by value stream mapping and multiple criteria decision-making method under demand uncertainty. Int. J. Comput. Integr. Manuf. **24**(3), 211–228 (2011)

15. Mora, H.L., Sánchez, P.P.: Transformación Digital en Instituciones de Educación Superior con Gestión de Procesos de Negocio - Modelo de Mediación de Automatización Robótica de Procesos, de Iberian Conference on Information Systems and Technologies (CISTI), Sevilla (2020)
16. Petersen, K., Vakkalanka, S., Kuzniarz, L.: Guidelines for conducting systematic mapping studies in software engineering: an update. Inf. Softw. Technol. **64**, 1–18 (2015). https://doi.org/10.1016/j.infsof.2015.03.007
17. Porter, M.E., Heppelmann, J.E.: How smart, connected products are transforming competition. Harv. Bus. Rev. (2014)
18. Shimbun, N.K.: Poka-Yoke: Improving Product Quality by Preventing Defects. CRC Press, Boca Raton (1989)
19. Smith, A.B., Jones, C.D.: Enhancing literature search strategies in systematic reviews: the application of the PICOC method. J. Med. Libr. Assoc. **110**(1), 20–27 (2022)
20. Snyder, H.: Literature review as a research methodology: an overview and guidelines. J. Bus. Res. **104**, 333–339 (2019)
21. Sugimori, Y., Kusunoki, K., Cho, F., Uchikawa, S.: Toyota production system and Kanban system materialization of just-in-time and respect-for-human system. Int. J. Prod. Res. **15**(6), 553–564 (1977)
22. Verhoef, P.C., et al.: Consumer connectivity in a complex, technology-enabled, and mobile-oriented world with smart products. J. Interact. Mark. **40**, 1–8 (2017)
23. Weber-Lewerenz, B.: Corporate digital responsibility (CDR) in construction engineering-ethical guidelines for the application of digital transformation and artificial intelligence (AI) in user practice. SN Appl. Sci. **3**, 1–25 (2021)
24. Westerman, G., Calméjane, C., Bonnet, D., Ferraris, P., McAfee, A.: Digital Transformation: A Roadmap for Billion-Dollar Organizations. MIT Center for Digital Business and Capgemini Consulting, Cambridge (2014)
25. Womack, J.P., Jones, D.T.: Lean Thinking: Banish Waste and Create Wealth in Your Corporation. Productivity Press, New York (2013)
26. Tortorella, G.L., Rossini, M., Costa, F., Portioli Staudacher, A., Sawhney, R.: A comparison on Industry 4.0 and lean production between manufacturers from emerging and developed economies. Total Qual. Manag. Bus. Excellence **32**(11–12), 1249–1270 (2019). https://doi.org/10.1080/14783363.2019.1696184
27. Treviño-Elizondo, B.L., García-Reyes, H., Peimbert-García, R.E.: A maturity model to become a smart organization based on Lean and industry 4.0 synergy. Sustainability **15**(17), 13151 (2023). https://doi.org/10.3390/su151713151
28. Lima, B.F., Neto, J.V., Santos, R.S., Caiado, R.G.G.: A Socio-technical framework for Lean project management implementation towards sustainable value in the digital transformation context. Sustainability **15**(3), 1756 (2023). https://doi.org/10.3390/su15031756
29. Tripathi, V., et al.: A sustainable productive method for enhancing operational excellence in shop floor management for industry 4.0 using hybrid integration of lean and smart manufacturing: an ingenious case study. Sustainability **14**(12), 7452 (2022). https://doi.org/10.3390/su14127452
30. Jiménez, M., Espinosa, M. del M., Domínguez, M., Romero, M., Awad, T.: Adaptation of the Lean 6S methodology in an industrial environment under sustainability and Industry 4.0 criteria. Sustainability **13**(22), 12449 (2021). https://doi.org/10.3390/su132212449
31. Fortuny-Santos, J., Ruiz-de-Arbulo López, P., Luján-Blanco, I., Pin-Kuo, C.: Evaluación de las sinergias entre lean manufacturing y la Industria 4.0. Dirección y Organización **71**, 71–86 (2020). https://doi.org/10.37610/dyo.v0i71.579

32. Sajjad, A., et al.: Assessment by lean modified manufacturing maturity model for industry 4.0: a case study of Pakistan's manufacturing sector. IEEE Trans. Eng. Manag. 1–15 (2023). https://doi.org/10.1109/tem.2023.3259005
33. Ghouat, M., Benhadou, M., Benhadou, B., Haddout, A.: Assessment of the potential impact of industry 4.0 technologies on the levers of Lean Manufacturing in manufacturing industries in Morocco. Int. J. Emerg. Technol. Adv. Eng. **12**(7), 78–85 (2022)
34. Rossini, M., Cifone, F.D., Kassem, B., Costa, F., Portioli-Staudacher, A.: Being lean: how to shape digital transformation in the manufacturing sector. J. Manuf. Technol. Manag. **32**(9), 239–259 (2021). https://doi.org/10.1108/jmtm-12-2020-0467
35. Maware, C., Parsley II, D.M.:Can industry 4.0 assist Lean Manufacturing in attaining sustainability over time? Evidence from the US organizations. Sustainability **15**(3), 1962 (2023). https://doi.org/10.3390/su15031962
36. Villalba-Diez, J., Zheng, X., Schmidt, D., Molina, M.: Characterization of Industry 4.0 lean management problem-solving behavioral patterns using EEG sensors and deep learning. Sensors (Basel, Switzerland) **19**(13), 2841 (2019). https://doi.org/10.3390/s19132841
37. Schulz, C.: Compatibility, opportunities and challenges in the combination of Industry 4.0 and Lean Production. Logist. Res. **15**(1) (2022)
38. Tripathi, V., et al.: Development of a data-driven decision-making system using lean and smart manufacturing concept in industry 4.0: a case study. Math. Probl. Eng. **2022**, 1–20 (2022). https://doi.org/10.1155/2022/3012215
39. Florescu, A., Barabas, S.: Development trends of production systems through the integration of Lean management and Industry 4.0. Appl. Sci. (Basel, Switzerland) **12**(10), 4885 (2022). https://doi.org/10.3390/app12104885
40. Medyński, D., et al.: Digital standardization of lean manufacturing tools according to Industry 4.0 concept. Appl. Sci. (Basel, Switzerland) **13**(10), 6259 (2023). https://doi.org/10.3390/app13106259
41. Ciliberto, C., Szopik-Depczyńska, K., Tarczyńska-Łuniewska, M., Ruggieri, A., Ioppolo, G.: Enabling the circular economy transition: a sustainable lean manufacturing recipe for Industry 4.0. Bus. Strateg. Environ. **30**(7), 3255–3272 (2021). https://doi.org/10.1002/bse.280
42. Leong, W.D., et al.: Enhancing the adaptability: lean and green strategy towards the Industry Revolution 4.0. J. Clean. Prod. **273**(122870), 122870 (2020). https://doi.org/10.1016/j.jclepro.2020.122870
43. Pereira, A.C., Dinis-Carvalho, J., Alves, A.C., Arezes, P.: How Industry 4.0 can enhance Lean practices. FME Trans. **47**(4), 810–822 (2019). https://doi.org/10.5937/fmet1904810p
44. Zhu, X., Liang, Y., Xiao, Y., Xiao, G., Deng, X.: Identification of key brittleness factors for the lean-green manufacturing system in a manufacturing company in the context of Industry 4.0, based on the DEMATEL-ISM-MICMAC method. Processes (Basel, Switzerland) **11**(2), 499 (2023). https://doi.org/10.3390/pr11020499
45. Ghaithan, A., Khan, M., Mohammed, A., Hadidi, L.: Impact of Industry 4.0 and lean manufacturing on the sustainability performance of plastic and petrochemical organizations in Saudi Arabia. Sustainability **13**(20), 11252 (2021). https://doi.org/10.3390/su132011252
46. Ghouat, M., Haddout, A., Benhadou, M.: Impact of Industry 4.0 concept on the levers of lean manufacturing approach in manufacturing industries. Int. J. Autom. Mech. Eng. **18**(1) (2021). https://doi.org/10.15282/ijame.18.1.2021.11.0646

47. Rosin, F., Forget, P., Lamouri, S., Pellerin, R.: Impacts of Industry 4.0 technologies on Lean principles. Int. J. Prod. Res. **58**(6), 1644–1661 (2020). https://doi.org/10.1080/00207543.2019.1672902

48. de Oliveira-Dias, D., Maqueira-Marin, J.M., Moyano-Fuentes, J., Carvalho, H.: Implications of using Industry 4.0 base technologies for lean and agile supply chains and performance. Int. J. Prod. Econ. **262**(108916), 108916 (2023). https://doi.org/10.1016/j.ijpe.2023.108916

49. Dinis-Carvalho, J., Sousa, R.M., Moniz, I., Macedo, H., Lima, R.M.: Improving the performance of a SME in the cutlery sector using lean thinking and digital transformation. Sustainability **15**(10), 8302 (2023). https://doi.org/10.3390/su15108302

50. Tortorella, G.L., Giglio, R., van Dun, D.H.: Industry 4.0 adoption as a moderator of the impact of lean production practices on operational performance improvement. Int. J. Oper. Prod. Manag. **39**(6/7/8), 860–886 (2019). https://doi.org/10.1108/ijopm-01-2019-0005

51. Tiep, N.C., Oanh, T.T.K., Thuan, T.D., Van Tien, D., Van Ha, T.: Industry 4.0, lean management and organizational support: a case of supply chain operations. Pol. J. Manag. Stud. **22**(1), 583–594 (2020). https://doi.org/10.17512/pjms.2020.22.1.37

52. Ghaithan, A.M., Alshammakhi, Y., Mohammed, A., Mazher, K.M.: Integrated impact of circular economy, industry 4.0, and lean manufacturing on sustainability performance of manufacturing firms. Int. J. Environ. Res. Publ. Health **20**(6) (2023). https://doi.org/10.3390/ijerph20065119

53. El Faydy, N., El Abbadi, L.: Interpretive structural modelling of critical success factor for lean product lifecycle management in industry 4.0. Int. J. Prod. Manag. Eng. **11**(1), 65–72. (2023)https://doi.org/10.4995/ijpme.2023.18840

54. Bueno, A., et al.: Lean 4.0 implementation framework: proposition using a multimethod research approach. Int. J. Prod. Econ. **264**(108988), 108988 (2023). https://doi.org/10.1016/j.ijpe.2023.108988

55. Yilmaz, A., Dora, M., Hezarkhani, B., Kumar, M.: Lean and industry 4.0: mapping determinants and barriers from a social, environmental, and operational perspective. Technol. Forecast. Soc. Change **175**(121320), 121320 (2022). https://doi.org/10.1016/j.techfore.2021.121320

56. Schulze, F., Dallasega, P.: Lean and Industry 4.0 mitigating common losses in engineer-to-order theory and practice: an exploratory study. Flex. Serv. Manuf. J. (2023). https://doi.org/10.1007/s10696-023-09503-z

57. Rahardjo, B., Wang, F.-K., Yeh, R.-H., Chen, Y.-P.: Lean manufacturing in industry 4.0: a smart and sustainable manufacturing system. Machines **11**(1), 72 (2023). https://doi.org/10.3390/machines11010072

58. Vlachos, I.P., Pascazzi, R.M., Zobolas, G., Repoussis, P., Giannakis, M.:Lean manufacturing systems in the area of Industry 4.0: a lean automation plan of AGVs/IoT integration. Prod. Plan. Control **34**(4), 345–358 (2023). https://doi.org/10.1080/09537287.2021.1917720

59. Mendes, D., Gaspar, P.D., Charrua-Santos, F., Navas, H.: Synergies between lean and Industry 4.0 for enhanced maintenance management in sustainable operations: a model proposal. Processes (Basel, Switzerland) **11**(9), 2691 (2023). https://doi.org/10.3390/pr11092691

60. Clancy, R., Bruton, K., O'Sullivan, D.T.J., Cloonan, A.J.: The HyDAPI framework: a versatile tool integrating Lean Six Sigma and digitalisation for improved quality management in Industry 4.0. Int. J. Lean Six Sigma (2022). https://doi.org/10.1108/ijlss-12-2021-0214

61. Efimova, A., Briš, P.: The implementation of the conjunction of Lean Six Sigma and Industry 4.0: a case study in the Czech Republic. Manag. Syst. Prod. Eng. **30**(3), 223–229 (2022). https://doi.org/10.2478/mspe-2022-0028

62. Fok-Yew, O., Abdul Hamid, N.A.: The influence of Lean practices and leadership on business excellence: Malaysian E AND E manufacturing companies. Estudios de Economía Aplicada **39**(4) (2021). https://doi.org/10.25115/eea.v39i4.4562

63. Rossini, M., Costa, F., Tortorella, G.L., Portioli-Staudacher, A.: The interrelation between Industry 4.0 and lean production: an empirical study on European manufacturers. Int. J. Adv. Manuf. Technol. **102**(9–12), 3963–3976 (2019). https://doi.org/10.1007/s00170-019-03441-7

User Experience Evaluation Methods in Mixed Reality Environments

Matías García[1](✉) (iD), Jose Requesens[2], and Sandra Cano[1]

[1] Escuela de Ingeniería Informática, Pontificia Universidad Católica de Valparaíso,
2362804 Valparaíso, Chile
matias.garcia@pucv.cl

[2] Escuela de Ingeniería de Construcción y Transporte, Pontificia Universidad Católica de
Valparaíso, 2362804 Valparaíso, Chile

Abstract. Interest in the metaverse and telepresence has sparked technological advancements, enabling us to extend our perceived reality with off-the-shelf devices. Particularly, we shall be focusing on mixed reality (MR) which consists in merging the real and the virtual world through environment synchronization (ES). In this interaction paradigm, a challenge arises for capturing and understanding what users think and how they physically/emotionally react when immersed in MR. Our theoretical approach stems from user experience (UX) research, by evaluating aspects such as usability, utility, and satisfaction of use. However, we hypothesize that MR also involves specific factors unique to this interface. Therefore, in this literature review we shall be looking at three questions: (1) what methods have been used to evaluate UX in MR? (2) what aspects have been assessed in UX evaluation? And (3) what devices have been used in these evaluations? We consulted 3 scientific databases and our search yielded 737 results from the last 10 years. Results show a growing trend on research interest from 2019 onwards. Secondly, we found that studies most frequently rely on what the users respond in post-experiment questionnaires and interviews, neglecting other mid-experiment methods such as Think Aloud, or physiological signals sensing. Furthermore, usability, enjoyment and simulator sickness remain the most recurrent factors assessed, but only two studies included the quality assessment of ES, and security/privacy aspects. Other specific UX aspects in MR include perceived immersion, navigation, and device ergonomics. We note a lack of a well-documented UX model particularized to incorporate all these specific aspects for comprehensive evaluation. To the best of our knowledge expert judgment remains the standard on which aspects assess in MR environments. The contribution of this paper is a snapshot of how UX evaluation has been conducted in recent literature. We provide a list of methods and instruments for designers and developers to incorporate users' insights for improvement. For future work we intend to expand this research to a systematic literature review to overcome the limitations of this work and supply evidence for proposing a UX model for MR environments.

Keywords: Mixed Reality · User Experience · User Experience Evaluation

A. Coman and S. Vasilache (Eds.): HCII 2024, LNCS 14703, pp. 179–193, 2024.
https://doi.org/10.1007/978-3-031-61281-7_12

1 Introduction

Interest in the metaverse has contributed to the development of new and more capable technology enabling unprecedented telepresence and immersion in virtual environments. Particularly, devices such as head mounted displays (HMD) extend user's perceived reality, originating the virtuality continuum phenomena described by [1]. In this study, we focus on mixed reality (MR), commonly featuring digitally generated graphics overlapped on the real space and provide interaction via hand gestures and/or other physical objects. Although MR off-the-shelf technology such as Microsoft's HoloLens [2] is available, research so far has not provided a clear understanding on how to assess users' needs, feelings, and overall perception. This causes requirements to be defined based on mere hazy assumptions by designers and developers [3].

Thus, incorporating user experience (UX) evaluation in the design and development process remains crucial to meet expectations and deliver successful products. In short, UX evaluation consists in methods grouped in user studies and expert inspections. These methods help to identify elements that promote or hinder UX, which is comprised of the full spectrum of emotions, beliefs, physical and physiological responses of users as consequence of the use (or anticipated use) of a system, product, or service; as defined by the ISO [4]. Due to the complexity and novelty of MR environments, we hypothesize that specific aspects may influence UX. This implies that traditional evaluation instruments may not address these specific aspects, by depending on cheap and easy-to-apply methods such as standardized questionnaires. Evidently, questionnaires have their limitations in terms of relying on what the users say and what they remember after the interaction. In contrast, Xu & Zhang [5] noted the benefits in combining attitudinal and behavioral evaluation methods to complement their limitations. In other words, analyze what the user consciously communicates in conjunction with the data generated from what the user does (consciously and unconsciously) during the interaction. Additionally, MR technology advancements have given birth to a myriad of devices, each with their own characteristics, challenges, and limitations in the choice of evaluation methods.

Therefore, we present a literature review aimed at exploring how UX evaluation has been conducted in the last 10 years, noting the current challenges and trends. This research sets out to answer (RQ1) what UX evaluation methods have been applied in MR environments, (RQ2) what UX aspects and factors have been addressed in previous studies, (RQ3) and what devices have been used in these evaluations. We consulted three databases, recovered 737 articles, filtered following the PRISMA guidelines [6] and finally fully-reviewed the 72 articles to answer these research questions. The practical implications of this study affect designers and developers, as costs of development of MR apps are higher compared to traditional desktop application development. Early UX evaluation enables teams to early address potential problems before release, and subsequently promote the improvement and adoption of this cutting-edge technology in our society.

Results show an overreliance on questionnaires and interviews, while leaving mid-experiment methods such as Think Aloud and physiological activity sensing underused. Furthermore, each study focuses on their own set of UX aspects, which is apparently left to the researchers' judgment. We identified specific aspects to MR such as simulation sickness, quality of environment synchronization, immersion, spatial presence, co-presence, among others (see Sect. 5). We propose that these aspects should be taken in consideration in the comprehensive evaluation methodology tailored for MR environments.

The rest of this document is structured as follows: Sect. 2 describes the theoretical concepts related to user experience and mixed reality. Section 3 explains the methodology used in this review. Section 4 presents results gathered. Section 5 contains the analysis of the results obtained, and we answer the research questions. Finally, Sect. 6 closes with the conclusions of this work.

2 Background

2.1 Related Work

Previous studies such as [7, 8] evaluated aspects of user experience as usability in MR environments by adapting instruments such as the system usability scale (SUS, [9]). Although good usability is important for achieving satisfaction of use, it is only one component of the UX multidimensional model. According to [10] UX is composed of system quality criteria related to the pragmatic features, and hedonic quality criteria such as enjoyment, aesthetics, and emotions. For that reason, only assessing usability does not provide the full spectrum of responses, thoughts and emotions felt by users. Moreover, relying solely on surveys misses on valuable information from prior and during user testing. Therefore, post-experiment questionnaires may miss on critical insights relevant to the acceptance of the application, as questionnaires are limited to the scope of the instrument. In the case of interviews, participants may omit comment on irrelevant factors to them, but relevant to others. Participants may not remember accurately all the details of their interaction after the experiment is over. For that reason, authors usually combine user studies, questionnaires, and interviews.

A formal methodology for usability evaluation with mixed methods was presented by Yilmaz et al. [11]. This protocol consists of four main steps: cognitive walkthrough, pre-test surveys, usability tests (a type of user testing) and finally post-test surveys. We consider the cognitive walkthrough and pre-test surveys valuable methods for allowing detection of potential problems in the prototype before the user test. These initial two steps allow developers to fix system problems/bugs before the user test and secondly, it allows researchers to narrow down the relevant aspects focused in the following evaluation. However, this protocol is limited to usability aspects of UX, and lacks early expert inspections such as heuristic evaluation [14].

Therefore, the holistic UX definition should initially identify the specific aspects of UX in virtual environments, as presented by Morales et al. [13], presenting a review of the methods used for evaluating UX in Virtual Reality (VR), Augmented Reality (AR) and in the metaverse in general. Their findings show that 42% of the articles reviewed applied questionnaires based on widely known instruments such as SUS [9], followed by inspections with 29%, including heuristic evaluations with specific AR heuristics [12]. Additionally, most of the articles are mixed studies (e.g. using biometric signals to complement survey results). This brings up evidence on the benefits of combining attitudinal and behavioral data. Nevertheless, MR environments differ from virtual and augmented reality (see Sect. 2.3), as none of which incorporate the killing feature of environment synchronization. Despite this, it is worth pointing out that extended reality environments (VR, AR, and MR) do share similarities altogether. Specifically, some aspects of UX in common are clearly applicable to all (e.g. simulator sickness, device ergonomics).

2.2 User Experience

User eXperience (UX) is defined in the ISO-9241 [4] as the user's perceptions and responses that result from the use and/or anticipated use of a system, product, or service. Additionally, UX encompasses emotions, beliefs, preferences, behavior, and accomplishments evoked by interactive systems such as MR applications. Moreover, [15] proposed that UX is subjective, context-dependent, and dynamic. It is subjective as it involves people's thoughts and emotions induced by the interaction. It is also context dependent as users do not operate systems or products under the same conditions. Finally, UX is dynamic, as it may evolve with time due to, for instance, advancements in other comparable products that raise expectations.

A popular representation of the multidimensional phenomena of UX is the honeycomb model by Morville [16]. This conceptual model represents aspects of the experience that may promote or hinder UX with seven clearly defined dimensions ranging from usability to credibility. A more recent approach by [17] defined UX in three components: perception of instrumental qualities (e.g. controllability, effectiveness, learnability), perception of non-instrumental (or hedonic) qualities, and the effect of both components on the user's emotional and physiological reactions. The result of adding these three components produces the overall appraisal of the system.

Therefore, thoroughly examining UX allows us to identify the elements within the system that promote or hinder the appraisal of the system. This is when evaluation methods come in handy. Evaluation methods are techniques, protocols and instruments that generate data from the user-system interaction. However, the raw data generated by these methods is not trivially correlated to the dimensions or components of UX. For example, to improve learnability of aviation procedures, cognitive load can be objectively measured in a user study by monitoring electrodermal activity (EDA), photoplethysmography (PPG), gaze metrics and peripheral skin temperature [18]. Similarly, to assess simulator sickness, there is the simulator sickness questionnaire (SSQ, [19]), in conjunction with the analysis of gaze and movement behavior metrics [20]. Simulator sickness is caused by the mismatch between simulated visual motion and our movement sensation rooted in our vestibular system, and it is related to higher participant dropout rates [21].

In conclusion, UX evaluation should address more than merely traditional aspects such as usability, utility, and satisfaction of use. Specific factors in MR should also be included. Furthermore, the combination of attitudinal and behavioral methods can provide rich insights by complementing objective and subjective data of the experience.

2.3 What is Mixed Reality?

Mixed Reality (MR) is a paradigm of interaction that seamlessly integrates virtual environments with the real world. An example would be "touching" and controlling a levitating 3D cube, visible through the lens of a head mounted device (HMD, e.g. [2]). Speicher et al. [22] named this feature environment synchronization (ES): the system's capability of understanding our interaction with physical objects (e.g. our naked hands) and efficiently communicating this information to the virtual environment. Therefore, augmented reality (AR) and augmented virtuality (AV) are subgroups of MR [23, 24], as both are limited to enhance/augment the reality perceived by the user, and not incorporating ES. On the other hand, Virtual Reality (VR) is remarkably different due to its fully immersive applications, occluding the surroundings and imposing a digital scene instead.

Although MR has no unified definition [22], this study considers that MR is not merely displaying computer graphics such as HUD on the real world, neither is fully immersive apps such as 360° videos. So far, the main difference lies on featuring ES. MR apps can be found in the construction industry [25] and real-time emergency assistance [26], and not exclusively in entertainment. In these examples, MR is enabled by Optical See-Through Head Mounted Device (OST-HMD), but projectors on tabletop setups have also been employed [27]. However, this hardware also has limitations in terms of data transfer and graphics processing [28]. Additionally, the rendering of complex geometry of 3D models with thousands of polygons makes current compact hardware capabilities in HMD inefficient [29]. In their study, they propose a cloud-based external volumetric image decoding. Regarding this paper, it is worth noting that a comprehensive UX model for MR should thrive towards device-agnosticism, so it remains valid over future technological advancements, particularly new displays. Nevertheless, devices also play a fundamental role in how users perceive MR (e.g. HMD field of view and ergonomics).

3 Methodology

After defining the research questions, the keywords identified were "user experience", "evaluation" and "mixed reality", concatenated with the AND operator. The keywords composed the query that was applied to 3 databases: Scopus, Web of Science, and the ACM Digital Library, specifically the ACM Full-Text Collection. This search was executed the 29th of december of 2023. The records downloaded from ACM were exported to Mendeley Cite Manager v2. Then, all recovered records were pasted in an Excel spreadsheet. From then on, the PRISMA methodology [6] was followed to filter, screen and finally select the articles to be fully read (see Fig. 1).

Regarding the identification stage, 34 records without DOI were excluded. Secondly, 35 duplicated records across the databases were excluded. Then, 510 articles were excluded by the analysis of titles and abstracts, discarding those that did not abide the eligibility criteria. It must be noted that some studies referred to MR as AR with extended capabilities, while others used MR and VR/AR interchangeably. For that reason, the virtual environment of each study was inferred from its title and abstract, excluding those that did not meet the definition described in Sect. 2.3. This process was repeated with the

106 records at the last step of the screening stage. All the research data is open access and available in the GitHub repository [30].

Eligibility Criteria

- **EC1**: Record is a peer-reviewed journal article or conference proceedings published in English between 2013 and 2023.
- **EC2**: Research materials and instruments involve the use of mixed reality.
- **EC3**: Authors' empirical experiment includes the well-documented evaluation of UX factors.

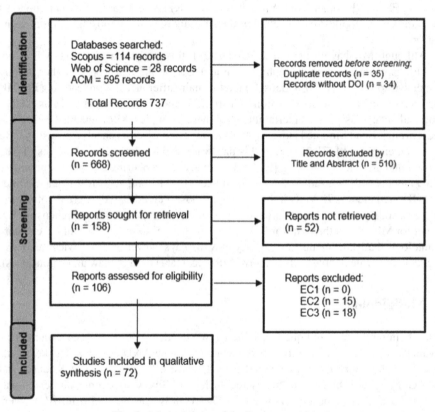

Fig. 1. Methodology of the literature review.

4   Results

This review finally selected 72 articles to be fully read. First noticeable finding was that 50 records were published from 2019 onwards (see Fig. 2). This may be attributed to events such as COVID-19 pandemic and presumably the release of affordable and wireless HMD such as the Oculus Quest [31], popularizing autonomous operation. This trend can also be observed in the recent release of the Apple Vision Pro. Furthermore, we identified common topics among the studies and their fields of application. Namely, vehicle design and transport research [32, 33], education [34, 35], healthcare and therapy [36, 37], cultural heritage [38, 39] and remote collaboration [40, 41]. Therefore, MR applications are not limited to entertainment, and MR has the potential of impacting many areas in our society in the future. Sutherland's vision of the ultimate display – computers blending with our physical world – may be nigh [42].

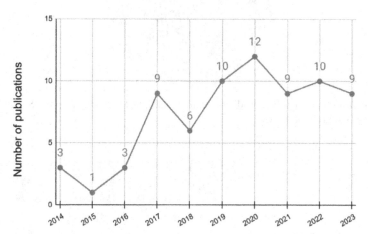

Fig. 2. Number of publications by year. The number represents the sum of articles of all 3 databases. It should be mentioned that most of the articles not recovered were from 2023, partly because of pay walls and lack of open access.

Expectedly, more than half of studies involved user studies for evaluating UX, whether in lab or field conditions. User studies allow behavioral data such as task performance and movement patterns to be registered, but we noticed that each author draws their own software solution for raw data analysis, to turn it into useful and easy to understand information for researchers. This exposes a dearth of a standardized toolkit for MR analytics as presented by [44] (Fig. 3).

Regarding the location of the studies, a node of research interest is clearly held by Europe, specifically in the topic of cultural heritage, by using MR to preserve in memory historical sites, traditions, and communities. On the contrary, to the best of our knowledge, cultural heritage MR apps remain untested in South America. In fact, only one study was conducted in Uruguay by Marichal et al. [35], evidently showcasing a future research opportunity. Moreover, the study focused on an educational MR app. This study may be subject to cultural differences, as they may influence expectations and thereby, the results obtained in the qualitative analysis (Fig. 4).

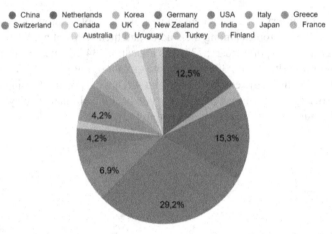

Fig. 3. Articles by country. The leading countries with most publications are USA and China, followed by Germany and Italy.

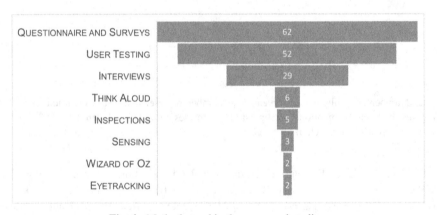

Fig. 4. Methods used in the recovered studies.

5 Discussion

The findings of this literature review clearly show that UX evaluation studies are diverse regarding their methodology, the stages at which the evaluation is conducted, the choice of methods and the UX aspects addressed, and the devices used. Furthermore, the sample of test participants varies from less than 10 up to 60. From the 72 articles reviewed, we selected 10 studies to showcase a snapshot of the variety of UX evaluation in literature (see Table 1).

Regarding RQ1, the most popular method for UX evaluation are questionnaires and surveys, being present in 86% of the studies reviewed. One explanation would be their easy implementation and simple data analysis, complemented with brief time and low-cost demands. A similar argument can be brought up for interviews. For questionnaires, some instruments found were User Experience Questionnaire (UEQ) [49], System

Table 1. Selected studies

Cite	Number of participants	Methods	UX aspects evaluated	MR devices used
Kim et al. [45]	30	User testing, physiological measurements, questionnaire, interview	Usability, cognitive load, situation awareness, perceived safety, trust	Varjo VR-2 HMD
Goedicke et al. [32]	10	User testing, questionnaire, interview	Usability, safety, motion sickness and comfort	Varjo XR-1 HMD, SmartTrack3 tracker, ZED2 depth camera
Krzywinska et al. [39]	39	User testing, questionnaire	Usefulness, usability, enjoyment, behavioral intent, ergonomics	HoloLens HMD
Shao et al. [46]	60	User testing, questionnaire, interview	Engagement, usefulness, virtual hand synchronization	HTC Vive Pro HMD, sensing gloves
Bai et al. [40]	24	User testing, questionnaire, interview	Effort, Frustration, Mental, Physical and Temporal Demand, Performance, Usability, Utility, Social Presence, Spatial Presence	Magic Leap HMD, HTC Vive Pro HMD, Leap Motion controller
Bolder et al. [33]	30	User testing, Think Aloud, questionnaire	Usability, utility, readability, haptic quality, spatial presence, involvement, realism, simulator sickness	Oculus Rift HMD, Leap Motion controller
Hubenschmid et al. [47]	8	User testing, Think Aloud, questionnaire, interview	Ergonomics, comfort, usability, enjoyment, visibility, perspicuity, efficiency, dependability, learnability	HoloLens HMD, Android Tablet

(continued)

Table 1. (*continued*)

Cite	Number of participants	Methods	UX aspects evaluated	MR devices used
Aruanno et al. [36]	30	User testing, Think Aloud	Usability, motion sickness, eye fatigue, enjoyment, visibility, frustration, navigation	HoloLens HMD
Sluganovic et al. [41]	28	User testing, questionnaire	Usability, learnability, perceived security	HoloLens HMD
Akşit et al. [48]	10	User testing, Think Aloud, questionnaire, interview	Comfort, cybersickness, immersion, utility, realism, navigation	Projector, smartphone, reflective material

Usability Scale (SUS) [9], NASA-TLX [50], Simulator Sickness Questionnaire (SSQ, [19]) and self-designed surveys. Furthermore, formal user studies whether in lab or field conditions were applied 72% of the studies. This is expected as MR is itself enabled by technology which requires users to interact with its devices. Therefore, researchers can observe and record behavior patterns and metrics during user tests. For that reason, user studies and Think Aloud protocol go hand in hand, due to providing feedback and insights during the interaction instead of post hoc questionnaires, when some important perceptions might have been already forgotten or overshadowed by other reactions. Notably, expert inspections also remain at the bottom of this ranking despite their advantages in early prototype evaluation. Moreover, the sample sizes in user studies were sometimes less than 10, limiting the research scope and their quantitative analysis implications.

Answering RQ2, among the UX specific aspects found in MR studies, we noted: device ergonomics, arm fatigue and physical/mental discomfort, social presence, realism, immersion, naturality and quality of ES, ease of navigation, simulator sickness. These specific factors were far less frequently assessed compared to usability and enjoyment, often requiring specific instruments. For example, if SSQ was not handed to participants and if no participant verbally expressed feeling nauseous, results might have ignored this crucial aspect. Thereby, undermining the acceptance of this MR app for people with high sensitivity to nausea. Furthermore, only two studies [41, 43] addressed security and privacy aspects. Another uncommon specific aspect stems from the need for efficient ES between virtual objects/players and real surroundings. Zhang et al. [51] proposed an adaptive optimization solution to reduce latency, jitter, packet loss and bandwidth bottlenecks. Similarly, Varga et al. [52] evaluated how connected and natural users perceived the quality in the merge of environments. These studies highlight the need to include the perceived ES in UX evaluation, and there is evidence ES can be objectively and subjectively assessed.

Finally, regarding RQ3: By far, the most recurrent MR device were HMDs, ranging from the HoloLens to Oculus Rift and HTC Vive Pro. Although these are accessible off-the-shelf devices, they remain expensive. Hence, Dani et al. [53] worked on adapting Google Cardboard VR. In their paper, effective hand gesture interaction was achieved with the implementation of a convolutional neural network (CNN) for hand recognition and tracking. Similarly, [54] also used a CNN for hand pose estimation, sketch generation and autocompletion. Another approach by [55] involved a wrist-worn device for assisting mid-air handwriting. These studies share the common challenge of overcoming the limitations of hardware, and instead use vision-based algorithms or additional tracking wearables to provide the same functionalities. Device ergonomics is a relevant aspect to be considered, as Hubenschmid et al. [47] noted that lightweight HMD allow users to perform longer tasks without feeling discomfort. Similarly, when using mobile displays such as smartphones, arm fatigue and social awkwardness may affect users negatively [56]. We also identified a trend on developing new methods to control the MR-human interface. The results of this trend shall contribute to better UX when immersed in MR. For instance, [43] compared hand gestures, gaze input, voice input and mobile device interaction; finding that users struggle the most in terms of effort and completion time with hand gestures.

This study was limited to identifying the UX aspects found in literature, and not defining them and looking at how these aspects may overlap or even be equivalent such as cybersickness and simulator sickness. Thus, an in-depth analysis of these identified aspects is needed. Additionally, there is room for improving the research query of this study, to include articles that we found externally in the same databases but did not appear in our yielded results.

6 Conclusions

In this paper we have presented a summary of how User eXperience (UX) evaluation has been applied in previous studies involving Mixed Reality (MR) environments in the last 10 years. Specifically, this review is aimed to find which methods have been used, which user experience factors are addressed and what devices such as head mounted displays or physiological sensors were used. We consulted Scopus, Web of Science and ACM Digital Library databases, and finally selected 72 papers to be fully read. From these articles, we examined their methodology, scope of UX aspects assessed, materials and instruments used.

This exploratory review helped to develop a preliminary understanding of how varied UX evaluation is conducted in literature. There is no standardized methodology, and each study uses their own selection of instruments. Additionally, we found that questionnaires, user studies and interviews are the most popular evaluation methods, meanwhile Think Aloud protocol and physiological sensing are underused, even though they provide valuable insights and generate data mid experiment, overcoming the limitations of relying on what the user says after the experiment is over, and important details might be forgotten. This work highlighted specific aspects such as quality of environment synchronization and security, which are not frequently assessed. Regarding devices used, the most common displays are Optical See Through Head Mounted Displays, primarily the Microsoft's HoloLens. However, other devices such as projectors and Augmented Reality glasses have been employed. Therefore, we propose that a comprehensive UX model shall be agnostic to which devices are used, in order to stay relevant with upcoming technology advancements.

For future work, we plan to extend this study into a systematic literature review to incorporate those papers that were not captured by the limitations of the query. Furthermore, this shall contribute to the proposal of a comprehensive and holistic UX model for MR applications, including its unique aspects drawn on this paper.

Acknowledgments. This study and its registration on this conference was funded by the Escuela de Ingeniería Informática, of the Pontificia Universidad Católica de Valparaíso.

Disclosure of Interests. Authors declare having no competing interests.

References

1. Milgram, P., Kishino, F.: IEICE Trans. Inf. Syst. **E77-D**(12), 1321–1329 (1994)
2. Microsoft HoloLens. https://www.microsoft.com/es-es/hololens. Accessed 06 Feb 2024
3. O Connor, J., Abou-Zahra, S., Covarrubias Rodriguez, M., Aruanno, B.: XR accessibility – learning from the past and addressing real user needs for inclusive immersive environments. In: Miesenberger, K., Manduchi, R., Covarrubias Rodriguez, M., Peňáz, P. (eds.) ICCHP 2020. LNCS, vol. 12376, pp. 117–122. Springer, Cham (2020). https://doi.org/10.1007/978-3-030-58796-3_15
4. ISO 9241-11:2018. https://www.iso.org/obp/ui/#iso:std:iso:9241:-11:ed-2:v1:en. Accessed 06 Feb 2024
5. Xu, J., Zhang, Z.: Research on user experience based on competition websites. J. Phys. Conf. Ser. **1875**(1), 012014 (2021)
6. Page, M., et al.: The PRISMA 2020 statement: an updated guideline for reporting systematic reviews. PLoS Med. **18**(3), e1003583 (2021)
7. Wang, P., et al.: 2.5DHANDS: a gesture-based MR remote collaborative platform. Int. J. Adv. Manufact. Technol. **102**(1), 1339–1653 (2019)
8. Campoverde-Durán, R., Garzón-Vera, B.: Mixed reality: evaluation of the user experience to improve the interpretation of the archaeological heritage. In: López-López, P., Torres-Toukoumidis, Á., De-Santis, A., Avilés, Ó., Barredo, D. (eds.) Communication and Applied Technologies, ICOMTA 2022. Smart Innovation, Systems and Technologies, vol. 318, pp. 537–546. Springer, Cham (2023). https://doi.org/10.1007/978-981-19-6347-6_48
9. Brooke, J.: Usability Evaluation in Industry, 1st edn. Taylor & Francis, London (1996)
10. Hinderks, A., Schrepp, M., Domínguez, F., Escalona, M., Thomaschewski, J.: Developing a UX KPI based on the user experience questionnaire. Comput. Standards Interfaces **65**(1), 38–44 (2019)
11. Yilmaz, N., Ergen, E., Artan, D.: A usability test protocol for evaluating mixed reality environments. In: Proceedings of the 2021 European Conference on Computing in Construction, pp. 423–430. European Council on Computing in Construction, Online (2021)
12. Franklin, F., Breyer, F., Kelner, J.: Usability heuristics for collaborative augmented reality remote systems. In: XVI Symposium on Virtual and Augmented Reality, Brazil, pp. 53–62. IEEE (2014)

13. Morales, J., Cornide-Reyes, H., Rossel, P.O., Sáez, P., Silva-Aravena, F.: Virtual reality, augmented reality and metaverse: customer experience approach and user experience evaluation methods. Literature review. In: Coman, A., Vasilache, S. (eds.) Social Computing and Social Media. HCII 2023. LNCS, vol. 14025, pp. 554–566. Springer, Cham (2023). https://doi.org/10.1007/978-3-031-35915-6_40

14. Nielsen, J.: Finding usability problems through heuristic evaluation. In: CHI 1992: Proceedings of the SIGCHI Conference on Human Factors in Computing Systems, California, United States of America, pp. 373–380. Association for Computing Machinery (1992)

15. Law, E., Roto, V., Hassenzahl, M., Vermeeren, A., Kort, J.: Understanding, scoping and defining user experience. In: CHI 2009: Proceedings of the SIGCHI Conference on Human Factors in Computing Systems, Boston, United States of America, pp. 719–728. Association for Computing Machinery (2009)

16. Semantic Studios. http://semanticstudios.com/user_experience_design/. Accessed 06 Feb 2024

17. Mahlke, S., Thüring, M.: Studying antecedents of emotional experiences in interactive contexts. In: CHI 2007: Proceedings of the SIGCHI Conference on Human Factors in Computing Systems, California, United States of America, pp. 915–918. Association for Computing Machinery (2007)

18. Wilson, J., Nair, S., Scielzo, S., Larson, E.: Objective measures of cognitive load using deep multi-modal learning: a use-case in aviation. Proc. ACM Interact. Mob. Wearable Ubiquitous Technol. 5(1), 1–35 (2021)

19. Kennedy, R., Lane, N., Berbaum, K., Lilienthal, M.: Simulator sickness questionnaire: an enhanced method for quantifying simulator sickness. Int. J. Aviat. Psychol. 3(3), 203–220 (2009)

20. Wang, J., Liang, H., Monteiro, D., Xu, W., Xiao, J.: Real-time prediction of simulator sickness in virtual reality games. IEEE Trans. Games 15(2), 252–261 (2023)

21. Balk, S., Bertola, D., Inman, V.: Simulator sickness questionnaire: twenty years later. In: Proceedings of the Seventh International Driving Symposium on Human Factors in Driver Assessment, Training and Vehicle Design, pp. 257–263. Iowa Research Online, Iowa City (2017)

22. Speicher, M., Hall, B., Nebeling, M.: What is mixed reality? In: CHI 2019: Proceedings of the 2019 CHI Conference on Human Factors in Computing Systems, Scotland, United Kingdom, pp. 1–15. Association for Computing Machinery (2019)

23. Carmigniani, J., Furht, B.: Handbook of Augmented Reality, 1st edn. Springer, New York (2011)

24. Vellingiri, S., Prabhakaran, B.: Quantifying group navigation experience in collaborative augmented virtuality tours. In: AltMM 2018: Proceedings of the 3rd International Workshop on Multimedia Alternate Realities, Seoul, Republic of Korea, pp. 3–8. Association for Computing Machinery (2018)

25. BIM Holoview. https://es.iatecps.com/bimholoview. Accessed 07 Feb 2024

26. Johnson, J., Gasques D., Gubbala, M., Weibel, N.: HoloCPR: designing and evaluating a mixed reality interface for time-critical emergencies. In: Proceedings of the 12th EAI International Conference on Pervasive Computing Technologies for Healthcare, pp. 67–76. Association for Computing Machinery, New York (2018)

27. Giraudeau, P., et al.: CARDS: a mixed-reality system for collaborative learning at school. In: Proceedings of the 2019 ACM International Conference on Interactive Surfaces and Spaces, Daejeon, Republic of Korea, pp. 55–64. Association for Computing Machinery (2019)

28. Peuhkurinen, A., Mikkonen, T.: Mixed reality application paradigm for multiple simultaneous 3D applications. In: Proceedings of the 16th International Conference on Mobile and Ubiquitous Multimedia, Stuttgart, Germany, pp. 133–141. Association for Computing Machinery (2017)

29. Gül, S., Bosse, S., Podborski, D., Schierl, T., Hellge, C.: Kalman filter-based head motion prediction for cloud-based mixed reality. In: Proceedings of the 28th ACM International Conference on Multimedia, Seattle, United States of America, pp. 3632–3641. Association for Computing Machinery (2020)
30. GitHub repository. https://github.com/matias9garcia/UX-evaluation-methods-in-Mixed-Reality-environments. Accessed 07 Feb 2024
31. Oculus Quest release. https://www.meta.com/blog/quest/introducing-oculus-quest-our-first-6dof-all-in-one-vr-system-launching-spring-2019/. Accessed 07 Feb 2024
32. Goedicke, D., Bremers, A., Lee, S., Bu, F., Yasuda, H., Ju, W.: XR-OOM: MiXed reality driving simulation with real cars for research and design. In: Proceedings of the 2022 CHI Conference on Human Factors in Computing Systems, New Orleans, United States of America, Article No. 107, pp. 1–13. Association for Computing Machinery (2022)
33. Bolder, A., Grünvogel, S., Angelescu, E.: Comparison of the usability of a car infotainment system in a mixed reality environment and in a real car. In: Proceedings of the 24th ACM Symposium on Virtual Reality Software and Technology, Tokyo, Japan, Article No. 8, pp. 1–10. Association for Computing Machinery (2018)
34. Frank, J., Kapila, V.: Mixed-reality learning environments: integrating mobile interfaces with laboratory test-beds. Comput. Educ. 110(1), 88–104 (2017)
35. Marichal, S., et al.: CETA: designing mixed-reality tangible interaction to enhance mathematical learning. In: Proceedings of the 19th International Conference on Human-Computer Interaction with Mobile Devices and Services, Vienna, Austria, Article No. 29, pp. 1–13. Association for Computing Machinery (2017)
36. Aruanno, B., Garzotto, F., Covarrubias, M.: HoloLens-based mixed reality experiences for subjects with Alzheimer's disease. In: Proceedings of the 12th Biannual Conference on Italian SIGCHI Chapter, Cagliari, Italy, Article No. 15 pp. 1–9. Association for Computing Machinery (2017)
37. Gasques, D., et al.: ARTEMIS: a collaborative mixed-reality system for immersive surgical telementoring. In: Proceedings of the 2021 CHI Conference on Human Factors in Computing Systems, Yokohama, Japan, Article No. 662, pp. 1–14. Association for Computing Machinery (2021)
38. Vosinakis, S., Nikolakopoulou, V., Stavrakis, M., Fragkedis, L., Chatzigrigoriou, P., Koutsabasis, P.: Co-design of a playful mixed reality installation: an interactive crane in the museum of marble crafts. Heritage 3(4), 1496–1519 (2020)
39. Krzywinska, T., Phillips, T., Parker, A., Scott, M.: From immersion's bleeding edge to the augmented telegrapher: a method for creating mixed reality games for museum and heritage contexts. J. Comput. Cult. Heritage 13(4), Article No. 32, 1–20 (2020)
40. Bai, H., Sasikumar, P., Yang, J., Billinghurst, M.: A user study on mixed reality remote collaboration with eye gaze and hand gesture sharing. In: Proceedings of the 2020 CHI Conference on Human Factors in Computing Systems, Honolulu, United States of America, pp. 1–13. Association for Computing Machinery (2020)
41. Sluganovic, I., Serbec, M., Derek, A., Martinovic, I.: HoloPair: securing shared augmented reality using microsoft HoloLens. In: Proceedings of the 33rd Annual Computer Security Applications Conference, Orlando, United States of America, pp. 250–261. Association for Computing Machinery (2017)
42. Sutherland, I.: The ultimate display. In: Proceedings of the IFIPS Congress 65, pp. 506–508. Macmillan and Co, New York City (1965)
43. Flick, C., et al.: Trade-offs in augmented reality user interfaces for controlling a smart environment. In: 9th Proceedings of the 2021 ACM Symposium on Spatial User Interaction, Article No. 17, pp. 1–11. Association for Computing Machinery, Online (2021)

44. Nebeling, M., et al.: MRAT: the mixed reality analytics toolkit. In: Proceedings of the 2020 CHI Conference on Human Factors in Computing Systems, Honolulu, United States of America, pp. 1–12. Association for Computing Machinery (2020)

45. Kim, G., Yeo, D., Jo, T., Rus, D., Kim, S.: What and when to explain?: on-road evaluation of explanations in highly automated vehicles. Proc. ACM Interact. Mob. Wearable Ubiquitous Technol. 7(3), Article No. 104, 1–26 (2023)

46. Shao, Q., et al.: Teaching American sign language in mixed reality. Proc. ACM Interact. Mob. Wearable Ubiquitous Technol. 4(4), Article No. 152, 1–27 (2020)

47. Hubenschmid, S., Zagermann, J., Butscher, S., Reiterer, H.: STREAM: exploring the combination of spatially-aware tablets with augmented reality head-mounted displays for immersive analytics. In: Proceedings of the 2021 CHI Conference on Human Factors in Computing Systems, Yokohama, Japan, Article No. 469, pp. 1–14. Association for Computing Machinery (2021)

48. Akşit, K., Kade, D., Özcan, O., Ürey, H.: Head-worn mixed reality projection display application. In: Proceedings of the 11th Conference on Advances in Computer Entertainment Technology, Funchal, Portugal, Article No. 11, pp. 1–9. Association for Computing Machinery (2014)

49. Schrepp, M., Hinderks, A., Thomaschewski, J.: Design and evaluation of a short version of the user experience questionnaire (UEQ-S). Int. J. Interact. Multimedia Artif. Intell. 4(6), 103–108 (2017)

50. Hart, S.: Nasa-task load index (NASA-TLX); 20 years later. Proc. Hum. Factors Ergon. Soc. Annu. Meet. 50(9), 904–908 (2006)

51. Zhang, X., Hu, Y., Huang, T.: A multiplayer MR application based on adaptive synchronization algorithm. In: 2020 7th International Conference on Control, Decision and Information Technologies (CoDIT), Prague, Czech Republic, pp. 628–632. IEEE (2020)

52. Varga, V., et al.: Real-time capture of holistic tangible interactions. In: Proceedings of the Fifteenth International Conference on Tangible, Embedded, and Embodied Interaction, Salzburg, Austria, Article No. 39, pp. 1–15. Association for Computing Machinery (2021)

53. Dani, M., Garg, G., Perla, R., Hebbalaguppe, R.: Mid-air fingertip-based user interaction in mixed reality. In: 2018 IEEE International Symposium on Mixed and Augmented Reality Adjunct (ISMAR-Adjunct), Munich, Germany, pp. 174–178. IEEE (2018)

54. Zhang, Z., Zhu, H., Zhang, Q.: ARSketch: sketch-based user interface for augmented reality glasses. In: Proceedings of the 28th ACM International Conference on Multimedia, Seattle, United States of America, pp. 825–833. Association for Computing Machinery (2020)

55. Chen, W., Chen, L., Ma, M., Parizi, F., Patel, S., Stankovic, J.: ViFin: harness passive vibration to continuous micro finger writing with a commodity smartwatch. Proc. ACM Interact. Mob. Wearable Ubiquitous Technol. 5(1), Article No. 45, 1–25 (2021)

56. Ventä-Olkkonen, L., Posti, M., Koskenranta, O., Häkkilä, J.: Investigating the balance between virtuality and reality in mobile mixed reality UI design: user perception of an augmented city. In: Proceedings of the 8th Nordic Conference on Human-Computer Interaction: Fun, Fast, Foundational, Helsinki, Finland, pp. 137–146. Association for Computing Machinery (2014)

Understanding Chatbot End-Users to Improve Their Design: Antecedents of Trust, Adoption Motivations, and Expectations

Daphne Greiner[1]([✉]) and Jean-François Lemoine[1,2]

[1] Université Paris I, Panthéon-Sorbonne, France
daphne.greiner@uni-paris1.fr,
jean-francois.lemoine@univ-paris1.fr
[2] ESSCA School of Management, Angers, France

Abstract. The exploration of users' desires and expectations from chatbots, particularly the motivations behind their adoption, remains a subject of limited understanding. Both in theory and practice, the lack of knowledge in these areas has been emphasized. While numerous chatbots have proven unsuccessful in practice, researchers have recognized the necessity for further investigation. This research aims to contribute to the existing literature on conversational AI users' expectations and adoption motivation and expand it, with a specific focus on chatbots. By conducting semi-structured interviews with 25 individuals who are current or potential chatbot users, this research examines what these expectations and motivations are and possible antecedents. The results show that: (1) antecedents of trust may affect adoption motivations and expectations on ethics; (2) the main adoption motivation of chatbots seems to be convenience; (3) expectations seemed to be mainly: efficiency, user-friendliness, seamlessness, and congruence with the brand's image.

Keywords: User motivation · User expectations · Chatbot services · Marketing

1 Introduction

In spite of the wide range of chatbot services available, including virtual influencers and virtual assistants, there is a growing demand among scholars to conduct further research in the field of Human-Computer Interaction (HCI) in order to explore their effectiveness. Recent research indicates that this demand primarily stems from a lack of understanding regarding user needs and motivations when it comes to chatbots (Koivunen, S., *et al.*, 2022). This finding aligns with previous studies that highlight the urgent need for developers and designers to gain deeper insights into the user experience of chatbots and comprehend the factors that drive user adoption based on their needs (Brandtzaeg, P. B., & Følstad, A., 2018). Interestingly, while this knowledge is well-received in the research community, it seems to be less emphasized in managerial practice, where marketers are often excluded from the conversation (e.g., AI recruitments predominantly target non-social sciences).

A. Coman and S. Vasilache (Eds.): HCII 2024, LNCS 14703, pp. 194–204, 2024.
https://doi.org/10.1007/978-3-031-61281-7_13

The objective of this research is to support the development of next generation chatbots that are better aligned with user motivations and expectations across various sectors. Our primary research inquiry focused on identifying the typical motivations and expectations that end-users have when adopting chatbots. Additionally, we sought to explore the factors that could influence or explain these expectations. By providing these new insights, we hope to stimulate further research and discussion on user expectations in the field of artificial intelligence while also emphasizing the significance of marketing contributions.

Given the relatively recent interest in this topic, we conducted qualitative interviews with 25 individuals, either current or potential chatbot end-users. While the study aims to be applicable to all types of conversational AI, it specifically focuses on chatbots to provide more precise insights.

The study starts by providing a literature background on motivation, expectations for chatbots and antecedents that may affect them. Simultaneously, it offers a concise introduction to the concept of "chatbot". Subsequently, we elaborate on our methodology, encompassing the process of data collection and analysis. Lastly, we present our findings, which are followed by a discussion and a conclusion.

2   Literature Background

The term "chatbots" is derived from the combination of "chat" and "robots" which refers to machines that function as natural language user interfaces for accessing data and services via text or voice (Brandtzaeg, P. B., & Følstad, A., 2018). These chatbots, also known as virtual agents depending on their purpose, allow users to ask questions or give commands in their own language and receive the desired content or service through conversation. Beyond customer support technologies, J-F. Lemoine, (2008), described them as social links for online stores that can enhance online experience and web atmosphere.

Over the past three years, these chatbots have undergone significant advancements, enabling exchanges through text, voice, and even images. An example of this progress is seen in ChatGPT, which has integrated Dall. E to enhance its responses. Generative AI has played a crucial role in transforming the capabilities and description of chatbots. It is worth noting that the term "chatbots" has evolved since its creation and will likely continue to evolve with further innovations (Følstad, A., & Skjuve, M., 2019, August). For instance, the next milestone could involve combining multiple intelligences to create a fully realistic non-human interlocutor.

During the initial stages of chatbot implementation, there has been a significant emphasis on technological advancements, neglecting the importance of understanding how individuals use chatbots and for what specific purposes (Brandtzaeg, P. B., & Følstad, A., 2018). This oversight has the potential to result in user dissatisfaction and frustration (*op. cit.*), which may explain why so many chatbots have failed in the past (e.g. Tay Bot from Microsoft on X, previously Twitter, in 2016)[1]. Several studies highlight the

---

[1] Within the span of 24 h, Microsoft swiftly took down Tay from X due to its racist and sexist remarks, which were derived from the knowledge it acquired from users (Følstad, A., & Skjuve, M., 2019, August).

need to conduct more research on chatbot users both in terms of user experience, motivation, and expectations (Zamora, J., 2017, October; Følstad, A., & Skjuve, M., 2019, August; Makasi, T., *et al.*, 2022, January). Hereinafter, we've compiled some of the key findings from the literature concerning user expectations and adoption motivations as well as possible antecedents that could impact expectations and motivations.

2.1 User Expectations Towards Chatbots and Adoption Motivations

The adoption of chatbots prompts the exploration of user expectations and motivations within the literature. While this may appear logical from a managerial standpoint, it is more challenging to explain in theory. The impact of motivations on expectations remains largely unknown, requiring researchers to look beyond chatbot studies for insights. An illustrative example from the literature highlights how individuals with addictions are motivated to transform their lives for the sake of their families, which subsequently influences their expectations of treatment options that can help them rebuild their relationships (Rodrigues Gomes et al., 2015).

If we try to put this in parallel with findings on chatbots, interesting results emerge. For instance, efficiency is quoted as one of the primary motivations behind the adoption of chatbots (Eroglu-Hall, Nurdan, Sevim., Ahmet, Bulut., 2022) which in turn could mean most users expect this component. Findings of Følstad, A., & Skjuve, M. (2019, August) tend to confirm it, by stating that users prioritize efficient and satisfactory resolution of inquiries over the resemblance to human interaction. Efficiency is often related to how fast the chatbot responds, which is considered one of the main advantages of chatbots (Gbenga, O., *et al.*, 2020; Lv, Y., *et al.*, 2022, August).

However, responding too fast and too efficiently might not always be the best option. Gnewuch, U., *et al.* (2018) show faster is not always better. The findings of their study suggest that delays in the chatbot's response not only enhance users' perception of the chatbot's human-like qualities and sense of social connection, but also contribute to a higher level of satisfaction on the overall interaction.

Efficiency is not the sole expectation mentioned in the literature. Various studies have shown that users seem to anticipate a greater level of human-like behaviour in chatbots. However, most studies focus on the impact of anthropomorphic characteristics[2] on users rather than on their expectations. For example, anthropomorphism in chatbots has been found to have various positive effects, including enhanced perceived social presence, user satisfaction and trust (Chen, J., *et al.*, 2023; Zheng, T., *et al.*, 2023, May).

However, anthropomorphism can also lead to negative effects, as exemplified by the Uncanny Valley effect, and can raise user expectations. Studies conducted in service contexts suggest that when customers humanize a service robot, they tend to have higher expectations regarding its ability to provide a service. Consequently, they are more likely to experience disappointment if the robot fails to meet those expectations (Duffy, B. R., 2003; Blut, M., *et al.*, 2021).

Overall, motivations for using chatbots seem to be productivity, entertainment, social and relational factors (e.g., chatbots as confidants for sensitive topics), and curiosity

---

[2] Main anthropomorphic characteristics stated in the literature include voice, appearance, and personality (Cherif, E., & Lemoine, J. F., 2019).

(Brandtzaeg, P. B., & Følstad, A., 2017; Zamora, J., 2017). While user expectations seem to be efficiency and anthropomorphism, although what this encompasses is unclear. Some authors have also mentioned the concept of emotional or social AI, which connects with anthropomorphism. Notable findings highlight users' desire for chatbots to possess the ability to express and react accordingly to emotions and pay closer attention to their needs and preferences (Svikhnushina, E., *et al.*, 2021, June). Thus, requiring an adaptation to users from chatbots (Lemoine, J. F., & Cherif, E., 2012).

2.2 Antecedents Influencing End-Users' Motivations and Expectations

Chatbot research reveals that user expectations and motivations may not align with common assumptions. While chatbot users are typically associated with individuals as end-users, the literature demonstrates a wide range of chatbot user profiles. For instance, Koivunen et al. (2022) delve into the motivations, expectations, and experiences of human resources professionals who employ recruitment chatbots. Therefore, it is crucial to emphasize that the current study exclusively focuses on end-users, as in individuals who utilize chatbot services offered by organizations.

Several studies have examined the factors that contribute to trust and attitudes towards chatbots, as well as the motivations behind their adoption, such as technology acceptance. However, antecedents are often mentioned briefly, leaving much room for further exploration. In their recent work, Blut, Wang, Wünderlich, and Brock (2021) provide a comprehensive analysis of the antecedents of anthropomorphism in chatbots, focusing on customer characteristics and robot design features. Of particular interest in their study are customer characteristics, which encompass prior experience, computer anxiety, and the need for interaction. In this paper, the emphasis is not so much on computer anxiety (Venkatesh, 2000), but rather on chatbot anxiety, which can be defined as an individual's level of apprehension or fear when it comes to using chatbots. The need for interaction, on the other hand, refers to the desire to maintain personal contact with other human beings (Blut et al., 2021).

Other factors mentioned in the literature, although not specifically focused on motivations or expectations, are factors that contribute to trust, such as perceived ease of use and performance expectancy (Mostafa, R. B., & Kasamani, T., 2022). Alagarsamy, S., & Mehrolia, S. (2023) propose a conceptual framework that connects these factors to trust and ultimately to attitudes, with certain factors of interest to this study. First, perceived risk (e.g., the reliability of the chatbot in handling sensitive information). Second, concerns regarding privacy and security related to the confidentiality of customer data. Third, ubiquity, which refers to the convenience for customers to conduct business transactions at any time and from anywhere. Last, perceived quality of services and interface design.

3 Methodology

3.1 Population and Data Collection Methodology

The existing literature emphasizes the importance of delving deeper into the motivations and expectations of chatbot users. However, given the limited information available on these factors, our approach was to directly engage with users and provide them with the freedom to express their thoughts. To achieve this, we conducted a series of 25 semi-structured interviews with both chatbot users and non-users following similar steps to prior studies on chatbots (Lemoine, J. F., & Cherif, E., 2012).

All interviews were carried out in 2021 by the same researcher, using video-call systems in order to adhere to Covid-related restrictions. The interviews continued until a point of saturation was reached, ensuring a comprehensive understanding of the subject matter. On average, each interview lasted approximately 45 min. However, it is worth noting that there were noticeable differences in the duration of interviews between participants who were inclined to interact with chatbots and those who tended to avoid them. For the latter group, interviews typically lasted around twenty to thirty minutes.

Prior to the interviews, participants were assured of complete anonymity and were informed that their responses would be used solely for academic purposes. They were also made aware that the study aimed to enhance conversational artificial intelligence, with a specific focus on chatbots. Lastly, participants gave their consent to record the interviews for analysis purposes.

The interviews were structured into two distinct sections based on the literature review. The first section focused on exploring potential factors that influence user motivation and expectations, such as their perception and confidence in new technologies, as well as their knowledge and experience with chatbots. During this phase, participants were asked about their level of confidence in using new technologies and whether they were familiar with chatbots. They were also prompted to share any past experiences they had with chatbots, whether it be through direct interactions or through hearing about them from others. Additionally, participants were questioned about the perceived advantages they associated with chatbots.

In the second phase of the interviews, participants were presented with a hypothetical scenario. They were informed that they had made an appointment online and were given the option to either be immediately assisted by a virtual agent or wait for a human advisor, whose estimated waiting time was 20 min. A series of questions were then posed to the participants in order to gain insights into their motivations for adopting chatbots and their key expectations in such a scenario.

3.2   Final Sample and Analysis Methodology

For practical reasons and due to limited financial resources, the interviews were exclusively conducted in France, encompassing both metropolitan France and overseas territories. The participants, who were between the ages of 18 and 40, were recruited as volunteers through social platforms and word-of-mouth. The selection process aimed to ensure a diverse range of profiles within our sample (see Table 1), considering factors such as gender, age, socio-economic status (CSP), place of residence at the time of the interviews, nationality, and ethnic background (French, Italian, etc.).

Text excerpts that addressed similar themes were identified and organized into nodes to uncover recurring topics. The explicit text was examined using a semantic approach with minimal interpretation (Ozuem et al., 2022). Themes were established by grouping text units and gradually combining or dividing them into categories. The frequency of each characteristic mentioned was calculated to evaluate their relative significance

Table 1. Excerpt of interviewee's profiles.

Age	Sex	Nationality & ethnic background	CSP	Town of residence
23	Male	French, from Vietnam	Engineer & consultant	Saint-Maur-des-Fossés
22	Female	Malagasy	Master student	Montrouge
40	Male	French, from Algeria	Private chauffeur	Cannes
30	Male	French, from Eastern Europe	Architect	Créteil
25	Non-binary	French	Unemployed	Nanteuil-les-Meaux

among respondents, providing an overview during the initial stages of the analysis. However, it is important to note that these frequencies do not hold statistical representativeness and are therefore not mentioned in final results.

4 Results

The outcomes of our analysis are categorized into two distinct sections. The first section focuses on the antecedents that impact trust in chatbots, ethical concerns, and expectations. Within this section, we delve into various factors that have the potential to influence users' trust and expectations regarding the ethical aspects of chatbots. For instance, we discuss how repeated violations of EU privacy regulations by international companies, including Meta, have created unease among users regarding the handling of their data. This unease has led to an expectation for greater transparency in data handling practices. Moving on to the second section, we present the motivations behind the adoption of chatbots, and the user expectations related to non-ethical parameters. In this section, we explore concepts such as convenience, efficiency, seamlessness, and the alignment of chatbots' anthropomorphic characteristics with the brand's image.

4.1 Antecedents Affecting Trust in Chatbots and Expectations on Ethics

During the period when the interviews were conducted, the controversies related to GAFA's unauthorized access to personal data seemed to have had significantly undermined trust in emerging technologies, specifically AI, and the companies operating in this industry. However, despite these concerns, consumers questioned indicated they continued to utilize these services without actively seeking protection or educating themselves. Interviewees conveyed a mixed sentiment while discussing their dependence on chatbots and other AI services for different tasks. Alongside their reliance, they also expressed a degree of opposition stemming from ethical concerns and the portrayal of doomsday scenarios in science-fiction literature. Interestingly, ethical concerns expressed were spontaneously raised by interviewees, as no specific questions were asked on it.

Ethical concerns revolved around the displacement of human workers and the potential unforeseen risks. One interviewee, M1, voiced apprehension regarding the rapid progression towards an AI-dominated era, citing Elon Musk's warnings as validation. Another interviewee, M2, indicated wanting greater transparency from companies, as some tend to pass off their chatbots as humans: "some companies hide it and that's not possible, it has to be clear from the start"[3].

Main ethical expectations expressed encompassed the necessity for transparency regarding data collection and the true nature of chatbots, as well as the need to safeguard or find alternatives for individuals who may lose their jobs due to chatbot services. The disclosure of the chatbot's nature was not solely about determining if it was human or non-human for the interviewees. It also encompassed the perception of the chatbot's humanness, as there was concern that this could potentially mislead or create ambiguity. Additionally, it was mentioned that chatbots should not impede human-to-human interaction. Although this presents a significant challenge, it can be paralleled with the notion that specific scenarios, such as the loss of a loved one, should be handled by human agents rather than chatbots.

In light of these discoveries, a comprehensive table was constructed to conceptualize the findings and illustrate the potential correlation between factors influencing trust in chatbots and ethical concerns and expectations (Table 2).

Table 2. Antecedents of trust, ethical concerns, and expectations for chatbots.

Antecedents affecting trust in chatbots	Ethical concerns	Ethical expectations
Apocalyptic AI scenarios and warnings from leading figures	Displacement of human agents and loss of human contact	Solutions for job loss due to AI and restrictions to chatbot use cases
Dependency on AI services	Loss of human autonomy	Safeguards for users to avoid overuse
Scandals on unauthorized access to personal data	Privacy breach	Enforcement of regulations
Lack of transparency on data collection and use	Unforeseen risks	Access to terms and conditions on data storage and use
Lack of transparency on chatbot nature	Misplaced investment and emotional attachment[4]	Disclosure of chatbot nature at the start and limits to anthropomorphism

---

[3] V.O.: "(…) *il y a certaines boîtes qui le cachent et ça c'est pas possible, il faut que ce soit clair dès le depart*".

[4] For instance, participants indicated that human etiquette guidelines, including the notion of greetings, wasn't necessary with chatbots.

4.2 Adoption Motivations and Other Stated User Expectations

The interviewees emphasized convenience as the primary motivation for adopting chatbots. They appreciated the ease of access, quick response time, and round-the-clock availability offered by chatbots. Despite their preference for human interaction, these advantages compelled some interviewees to choose chatbots over human agents. For instance, interviewee S mentioned that having direct contact with a chatbot was a motivating factor. She explained that it was often challenging to reach a phone number, whereas chatbots provided an immediate response without the need to search. Some interviewees expressed that the notification features were mentioned to provide additional convenience, while others raised concerns about the potential intrusiveness of such features.

The initial expectation expressed by interviewees was efficiency, which refers to the convenience and user-friendliness of the chatbot as well as the accuracy of its responses. This expectation served as a fundamental requirement to which other expectations could be added. However, in cases where this primary expectation was not met or the chatbot failed to provide a response, interviewees anticipated having a fallback solution involving human assistance. Regrettably, this crucial fallback option appeared to be absent in many chatbots. For instance, interviewee L mentioned that "if you're in a specific case, outside the framework, you can't get an answer or ask to be put in touch with a real person"[5].

Anthropomorphic expectations differed based on user preferences. Nevertheless, there were certain shared expectations that were particularly prominent. Primarily, respondents anticipated chatbots to adhere to specific ergonomic standards and desired a user-friendly interface. Interviewee K humorously remarked that although anthropomorphic characteristics didn't matter much to him "it shouldn't be excessively unattractive either (*laughs*)" and that "the sentences must still be composed in a left-to-right and horizontal manner"[6]. This line of thought reflected on their expectations of all anthropomorphic characteristics (appearance, voice, and personality). Each of these characteristics was anticipated to seamlessly blend into the conversation without causing any disruptions.

Furthermore, chatbots' anthropomorphic characteristics were expected to align with the communication strategy of their respective companies. For instance, Interviewee R emphasizes the importance of chatbots respecting the overall design of the website or app to avoid creating a perception of being low-quality. Similarly, interviewee A gives the example of Durex, a brand known for condoms and personal lubricants, suggesting that their chatbot should have a "fun" and "friendly" demeanor rather than appearing overly mechanical or formal. From this, we can infer that users desire consistency between chatbots and the brand image of the organization they represent and may not react well to incongruency between these factors.

These findings are summarized below (see Table 3).

---

[5] O.V.: "(…) *si tu es dans un cas spécifique, hors cadre, tu ne peux pas avoir de réponse ni demander d'être en contact avec une vraie personne*".

[6] O.V.: "*Non... Enfin, il ne faut pas que ce soit trop moche non plus (rit), il faut quand même que les phrases soient écrites de gauche à droite et à l'horizontale*".

Table 3. Overview of adoption motivations and expectations of chatbot end-users.

Adoption motivations	User expectations
Convenience of use:	Efficiency:
– Ease of access; – Quick response time; – Round-the-clock availability	– Convenience: the chatbot is available at all times, is easily accessible on users' interface and is quick to respond to queries
Attractive chatbot interface and friendly demeanor (particularly for sensitive topics)	– User-friendliness: the chatbot is easy to interact with, e.g., inquiries can be vague or poorly phrased
Confidence in the chatbot's capacities: does the user expect to find what he/she is looking for	– High response accuracy: the chatbot replies adequately to queries, e.g., the chatbot can adapt to multiple use cases
Perceived service quality	Seamlessness and congruence with brand image of anthropomorphic characteristics

5 Discussion

5.1 Theoretical Contributions

The paper presents a range of theoretical contributions regarding the expectations, motivations, and antecedents of chatbot users. Initially, it offers a novel perspective on these concepts, which were previously scattered throughout the literature. This includes exploring the aspects of efficiency (Eroglu-Hall, Nurdan, Sevim., Ahmet, Bulut., 2022) and seamlessness (Zamora, J., 2017, October) in a comprehensive manner. Furthermore, the study expands the existing body of knowledge on user experience and motivation by delving into previously identified notions that have not been thoroughly examined. For example, it sheds light on the various dimensions of efficiency, such as convenience, user-friendliness, and response accuracy. Additionally, the research highlights that an individual's antecedents can impact not only their attitudes towards chatbots, as previously discussed in the literature, but also their expectations.

Moreover, the study uncovers significant findings in unexplored areas, including the ethical expectations users have for chatbots and the alignment between chatbot behavior and the brand image. These insights contribute to a deeper understanding of the factors that influence user perceptions and interactions with chatbots.

5.2 Managerial Contributions

The study provides insight into user expectations which could help design improved chatbots. This is particularly relevant when considering ethical concerns and expectations, such as granting users access to terms and conditions regarding data storage and usage by chatbots. Additionally, it is important to address expectations that are universally associated with anthropomorphic features, including the seamless integration and alignment with the brand's identity. The discoveries from this study have the potential to stimulate discussions among practitioners and researchers regarding chatbot design and implementation. Furthermore, the study highlights the significance of marketing's role in the realm of chatbots and emphasizes the importance of these contributions.

6 Conclusion

The availability of comprehensive research on user experience and user motivation for chatbots is significantly restricted (Følstad, A., & Skjuve, M., 2019, August). This poses a significant challenge as the effective development and integration of chatbots for customer service necessitate a profound understanding of these aspects. Our analysis emphasizes the significance of trust, ethical considerations, and user expectations in the realm of chatbot interactions. Our analysis emphasizes the significance of trust, ethical considerations, and user expectations in the domain of chatbot interactions and most importantly detail these factors. It not only contributes to the existing literature but also offers valuable insights and guidelines for chatbot design. By comprehending user expectations and adoption motivations, organizations can strive to create chatbot systems that effectively cater to user needs and cultivate trust.

Disclosure of Interests.   The authors have no competing interests to declare that are relevant to the content of this article.

References

Alagarsamy, S., Mehrolia, S.: Exploring chatbot trust: antecedents and behavioural outcomes. Heliyon **9**(5) (2023)

Blut, M., Wang, C., Wünderlich, N.V., Brock, C.: Understanding anthropomorphism in service provision: a meta-analysis of physical robots, chatbots, and other AI. J. Acad. Mark. Sci. **49**, 632–658 (2021)

Brandtzaeg, P.B., Følstad, A.: Why people use chatbots. In: Kompatsiaris, I., et al. (eds.) INSCI 2017. LNCS, vol. 10673, pp. 377–392. Springer, Cham (2017). https://doi.org/10.1007/978-3-319-70284-1_30

Brandtzaeg, P. B., Følstad, A.:Chatbots: changing user needs and motivations. Interactions **25**(5), 38–43 (2018)

Chen, J., Guo, F., Ren, Z., Li, M., Ham, J.: Effects of anthropomorphic design cues of chatbots on users' perception and visual behaviors. Int. J. Hum.-Comput. Interact. 1–19 (2023)

Chérif, E., Lemoine, J.F.: Anthropomorphic virtual assistants and the reactions of Internet users: an experiment on the assistant's voice. Recherche et Applications en Marketing (English Edition) **34**(1), 28–47 (2019)

Duffy, B.R.: Anthropomorphism and the social robot. Robot. Auton. Syst. **42**(3–4), 177–190 (2003)

Eroglu-Hall, Nurdan, S., Ahmet, B.: Attitudes of online consumers towards chatbots. KEV Akademi Dergisi**91**, 33–53 (2022)

Følstad, A., Skjuve, M.: Chatbots for customer service: user experience and motivation. In: Proceedings of the 1st International Conference on Conversational User Interfaces, pp. 1–9 (2019)

Gbenga, O., Okedigba, T., Oluwatobi, H.: An improved rapid response model for university admission enquiry system using chatbot. Int. J. Comput **38**(1), 123–131 (2020)

Gnewuch, U., Morana, S., Adam, M., Maedche, A.: Faster is not always better: understanding the effect of dynamic response delays in human-chatbot interaction (2018)

Koivunen, S., Ala-Luopa, S., Olsson, T., Haapakorpi, A.: The march of Chatbots into recruitment: recruiters' experiences, expectations, and design opportunities. Comput. Support. Cooper. Work (CSCW) **31**(3), 487–516 (2022)

Lemoine, J.F., Cherif, E.: Comment générer de la confiance envers un agent virtuel à l'aide de ses caractéristiques? Une étude exploratoire 1. Revue management et avenir **8**, 169–188 (2012)

Lemoine, J.F.: Atmosphère des sites web marchands et réactions des internautes. Revue française du marketing **217**, 45 (2008)

Lv, Y., Hu, S., Liu, F., Qi, J.: Research on users' trust in customer service chatbots based on human-computer interaction. In: Meng, X., Xuan, Q., Yang, Y., Yue, Y., Zhang, Z.-K. (eds.) Big Data and Social Computing: 7th China National Conference, BDSC 2022, Hangzhou, China, August 11-13, 2022, Revised Selected Papers, pp. 291–306. Springer Nature Singapore, Singapore (2022). https://doi.org/10.1007/978-981-19-7532-5_19

Makasi, T., Nili, A., Desouza, K., Tate, M.: Public service values and chatbots in the public sector: reconciling designer efforts and user expectations. In: Proceedings of the 55th Hawaii International Conference on System Sciences, pp. 2334–2343. University of Hawai'i at Manoa (2022)

Miles, M.B., Huberman, A.M.: Qualitative Data Analysis: An Expanded Sourcebook. Sage (1994)

Mostafa, R.B., Kasamani, T.: Antecedents and consequences of chatbot initial trust. Eur. J. Mark. **56**(6), 1748–1771 (2022)

Rodrigues Gomes, R., Ribeiro, M.C., Cardoso Matias, E., Zeviani Brêda, M., Ferreira Mângia, E.: Motivation and expectations in treatment search for abusive use and addiction of crack, alcohol and other drugs. J. Occup. Therapy Univ. São Paulo/Revista de Terapia Ocupacional da Universidade de São Paulo, 26(3) (2015)

Svikhnushina, E., Placinta, A., Pu, P.: User expectations of conversational chatbots based on online reviews. In: Designing Interactive Systems Conference 2021, pp. 1481–1491 (2021)

Venkatesh, V.: Determinants of perceived ease of use: integrating control, intrinsic motivation, and emotion into the technology acceptance model. Inf. Syst. Res. **11**(4), 342–365 (2000)

Zamora, J.: I'm sorry, Dave, i'm afraid i can't do that: Chatbot perception and expectations. In: Proceedings of the 5th International Conference on Human Agent Interaction, pp. 253–260 (2017)

Zheng, T., Duan, X., Zhang, K., Yang, X., Jiang, Y.: How Chatbots' anthropomorphism affects user satisfaction: the mediating role of perceived warmth and competence. In: Tu, Y., Chi, M. (eds.) WHICEB 2023. LNBIP, vol. 481, pp. 96–107. Springer, Cham (2023). https://doi.org/10.1007/978-3-031-32302-7_9

Tourist eXperience and Use of Virtual Reality, Augmented Reality and Metaverse: A Literature Review

Jenny Morales[1]([✉]) [iD], Héctor Cornide-Reyes[2] [iD], Fabián Silva-Aravena[1] [iD], Joseline Sepúlveda[1] [iD], and Guisselle Muñoz[2] [iD]

[1] Facultad de Ciencias Sociales y Económicas, Departamento de Economía y Administración, Universidad Católica del Maule, Talca, Chile
{jmoralesb,fasilva,jsepulveda}@ucm.cl
[2] Facultad de Ingeniería, Departamento de Ingeniería Informática y Ciencias de la Computación, Universidad de Atacama, Copiapó, Chile
{hector.cornide,guisselle.munoz}@uda.cl

Abstract. Tourist experience (TX) is considered a specification of the customer experience directly associated with the tourism industry. Researchers agree that the tourist experience begins before the trip with preparations and extends during and after it, with memories. Technologies like virtual or augmented reality and, recently, the metaverse promise to revolutionize the tourist experience, considering immersive virtual or hybrid experiences with physical elements superimposed on real spaces. Considering these elements, we conducted an exploratory review that shows us that aspects of tourism are addressed with the use of virtual reality, augmented reality, and/or metaverse in these experiences. We define a review protocol with five stages, and established the following research questions (i) In what type of tourism were virtual reality, augmented reality, and metaverse used to intervene in the tourist experience? (ii) What aspects of the tourist experience were addressed using virtual reality, augmented reality, and metaverse? and (iii) How was the tourist experience evaluated using virtual reality, augmented reality, and metaverse? The search was performed using five representative databases. Among the results obtained, articles were found that use virtual reality, augmented reality, and the metaverse to create new immersive experiences in tourism in general and in specific tourism, such as heritage, thematic, and outdoor activities, among others. We also found studies addressing different aspects of the tourist experience, such as marketing as a first approach, the management of the trip itself, and purchase intention. In future work, we consider perform a systematic literature review and develop user experience evaluation guidelines.

Keywords: tourism experience · customer experience · virtual reality · augmented reality · metaverse · literature review

A. Coman and S. Vasilache (Eds.): HCII 2024, LNCS 14703, pp. 205–221, 2024.
https://doi.org/10.1007/978-3-031-61281-7_14

1 Introduction

The customer experience (CX) is broad, considers all aspects of the customer's contact with the organization, considers multiple factors, and requires different evaluation points [1, 2]. A customer experience specification can be regarded in a specific context, such as that of tourists, specifically the tourism experience (TX). According to research in this area, the tourist experience includes elements or aspects before and after the trip that include memories, for example [3]. The pandemic brought with it an acceleration in the use of technologies, which went hand in hand with the advancement and coverage of more robust communications networks with 5G. With the above, it is worth asking if this tourism can be enhanced or strengthened considering the incorporation of new technologies that make the experience of a virtual tourist more real (thinking of virtual reality, VR) or that improve the experience of the conventional tourist (through augmented reality, AR). Additionally, they can improve by combining both and/or related metaverse.

This paper presents an exploratory literature review that allows us to identify aspects related to the tourist experience and the implications of the use of virtual reality, augmented reality and/or metaverse in these experiences. We intend put especially want to pay attention to the wine tourist experiences since it is a type of tourism that can be developed in our country. To do this, a review protocol was developed with five stages: identification of research questions, selection of data sources, selection of articles, classification of articles, and results. The research questions established were: (i) In what type of tourism were virtual reality, augmented reality, and metaverse used to intervene in the tourist experience? (ii) What aspects of the tourist experience were addressed using virtual reality, augmented reality, and metaverse? and (iii) How was the tourist experience evaluated using virtual reality, augmented reality, and metaverse? The search was performed using five databases: SCOPUS, WoS, IEEE Xplore, ACM Digital Library, and Science Direct. Among the results, we found several articles that use virtual reality, augmented reality, and metaverse to create new, more immersive experiences for tourists; in turn, developments of frameworks and specific application initiatives for their implementation that include different senses. These articles addressed several aspects of the tourist experience and focused on specific and general tourism.

The paper is organized as follows: Sect. 2 presents the related work; in Sect. 3, the methodology used, and the results are presented; finally, in Sect. 4, we present the conclusions and future work.

2 Related Work

Next, we present concepts and definitions relevant to this work, considering the focus of this work related to tourism experience, virtual reality, augmented reality, and metaverse.

2.1 User eXperience and Customer eXperience

User eXperience (UX) is defined as follows "user's perceptions and responses that result from the use and/or anticipated use of a system, product or service" [4]. Considering this definition, the user experience has various stages, such as the previous one (before use) and the experience of using the product. In [5], other aspects of UX are explained in greater detail, such as the fact that user experiences can also be shared or co-created with other users. It also exposes the temporality of the UX, considering periods before use, during use, after use, and then over time.

Nielsen Norman Group [6] summarizes the definition of user experience as follows: "'User experience' encompasses all aspects of the end-user's interaction with the company, its services, and its products". This definition is interesting because it refers to companies, their products, and services.

Customer experience (CX) focuses on several aspects of any relationship between the customer and the company. [7] explained that consumer experience is a concept worked on by several authors. At the confluence of these studies, it was found that there is an element of subjectivity in CX, so each experience is personal and unique. It also includes psychological elements such as rational thinking and the consumer's emotions. Finally, it must be considered that the CX is very broad because there are various ways through which the consumer establishes contact with the company, and at each of these contact points it constitutes part of the CX. Contact points can be established similarly to UX, in periods before the direct purchase, such as advertisements and/or prior expectations, then during the purchase and subsequently during customer service or post-sales periods, to name a few.

2.2 Tourist Experience

According to [3], the tourist experience (TX) begins before the trip, with preparation, and extends during the trip until its completion with the memories and activities carried out. Considering different periods in the same way of UX, and CX concepts.

In [8] the authors proposed the definition of experience as "the totality of cognitive, affective, sensory, and conative responses, on a spectrum of negative to positive, evoked by all stimuli encountered in pre, during, and post phases of consumption affected by situational and brand-related factors filtered through personal differences of consumers, eventually resulting in differential outcomes related to consumers and brands", which they expose as useful to explain and measure the tourism and hospitality experience. In this definition the authors consider the different temporalities and highlight the subjective and personal aspects of the experiences, also taking into account the influence of the brand.

Within tourism, you can find thematic tourism focused on visits to cultural and/or heritage places [9, 10], wine tourism [11, 12], and tourism in open places [13], among others.

2.3 Virtual Reality, Augmented Reality and Metaverse

Virtual and augmented reality are concepts known for a long time; they have been the focus of study and application in various areas such as medicine, education, and tourism. Authors in [14] defined Virtual reality as follows: "Virtual Reality is the use of computer technology to create the effect of an interactive three-dimensional world in which the objects have a sense of spatial presence". To interact with this three-dimensional word, the users need different elements like head-mounted displays, wearables and/or different controls.

Unlike virtual reality, augmented reality has a physical component of the real world on which digital elements are superimposed, such as images or different types of information, this broadens the user's perception of the environment [15, 16].

Authors in [17] defined metaverse as follows "the convergence of physical and digital universes, where users can seamlessly traverse between them for working, education and training, health, exploring interests and socialising with others", To interact in the metaverse, we need an avatar that represents us and with which we can carry out various life activities such as studying, visiting an art gallery, and manipulating objects, among others [18].

3 Methodology

This review followed a method with five stages: establishing the research questions, determining the data sources, selecting the articles related to subjects under study, classifying the articles found, and finally, analyzing the results.

3.1 Research Questions

This article presents an exploratory literature review of the tourist experience and the implications of using virtual reality, augmented reality, and/or metaverse in these experiences. We stablished three research questions: (i) In what type of tourism were virtual reality, augmented reality, and metaverse used to intervene in the tourist experience? (ii) What aspects of the tourist experience were addressed using virtual reality, augmented reality, and metaverse? and (iii) How was the tourist experience evaluated using virtual reality, augmented reality, and metaverse?

3.2 Data Sources

Five databases were used to find the most significant number of articles related to the topic under study: Web of Science (WoS), Scopus, IEEE Xplore, ACM Digital Library, and Science Direct. The information search was carried out between October 2023 and November 2023.

Considering the research questions and the special interest in wine tourism, we consider the following concepts: tourist experience, wine tourism, wine marketing, metaverse, virtual reality, and augmented reality. The search string was: ("tourism experience" OR "wine marketing" OR "wine tourism") AND ("virtual reality" OR "augmented reality" OR metaverse). With this string, we can find scientific articles that address the tourist experience in metaverse, virtual, and augmented reality. Additionally, since wine tourism is included, we hope to find relevant information about this particular industry.

3.3 Selection Articles

The selection of articles was carried out considering several aspects. First, a search was carried out on all metadata of the selected databases. 1,201 articles were obtained, but these results were not very accurate, so it was decided to search by abstract since all databases have that function. In addition, it was restricted to documents from the last ten years to have current scientific articles to analyze, considering that information technologies, especially VR, AR, and metaverse, have advanced and increased their scientific interest and applications. Second, we decided to select articles in the open-access category in the search, considering the need to access the study documents. However, some scientific articles without this category seemed interesting to incorporate into the study; the authors were contacted, but for the most part, there was no response to the request to share their research. Finally, we consider conference papers and journal articles. In Table 1, we can see the number of articles found for each database used.

Table 1. Papers found in data source.

Data source	Number of selected papers
WoS	13
Scopus	24
IEEE Xplore	3
ACM Digital Library	2
Science Direct	1
Total	43

The list of articles obtained in each database was consolidated into a single document to eliminate duplicates (9 papers). The literature reviews (5 papers) were also eliminated to carry out an independent review of those already carried out and aim to analyze works that include studies and applications of the tourist experience. With these restrictions, 29 scientific papers were obtained for complete reading, in this process, 4 articles were eliminated because one does not address AR, VR, or metaverse but focuses on the application of geographical information, 2 articles focus on economic aspects, and finally, one article that focuses on VR but only photography without tourism aspects. Consequently, we obtained 25 articles for analysis (Fig. 1).

Fig. 1. Results of selection process.

3.4 Articles Classification

Although we consider 10 years in this review, we found articles from 2016 to 2023. The number of articles per year begins to increase in 2021 with 3 articles, which represents 12% of the total. In 2022, there are 5 articles, which represent 20% of the total. Finally, in 2023, 11 articles represent 44% of the total, which is very significant since the largest number of articles under analysis were published this year. See Fig. 2.

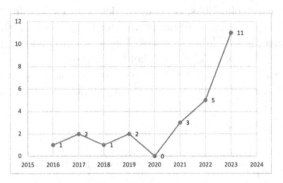

Fig. 2. Selected articles per year.

The selection of the papers considered journal and conference articles. About this classification, 4 conference articles were found to represent 16% of the total, and 21 articles published in journals represent 85% (Fig. 3).

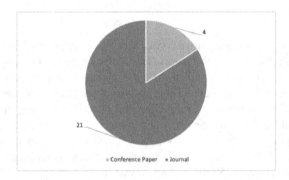

Fig. 3. Document type found.

Considering the use of virtual reality, augmented reality, and metaverse in the tourist experience, we found that the most significant number of articles for analysis address virtual reality, 11 of 25 articles, representing 44% of the total. Augmented reality, 7 articles that represent 28% of the total. Metaverse, 4 articles that represent 16%, and finally, the use of VR and AR as a whole was present in 3 articles, representing 12% of the total, see Fig. 4.

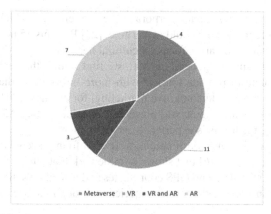

Fig. 4. Number of Articles about VR, AR and Metaverse.

The articles were classified as shown in Table 2. First, the articles related to metaverse, then those related to augmented reality, followed by virtual reality, and finally, those that presented studies on virtual and augmented reality together.

Authors in [17] exposed several opportunities that the metaverse opens for tourism, travel management, and marketing. This work does not present application cases to validate the opportunities it identifies. In the same way, in [19], authors make a theoretical contribution based on outlining propositions such as that metaverse tourism will have a new immersive level; that the metaverse will improve pre-trip expectations; that researchers should consider multiple identifications and profiles of tourists; and that metaverse tourism will open new forms of business and economy. On the other hand, it presents a metaverse tourism ecosystem, which contains elements of travelers, suppliers, the virtual world, and the physical world, which interact with each other to generate an immersive system that supports various tourist profiles and various stages of the trip.

A quantitative study presents [20] where the development of an extensible metaverse for a smart city was proposed, with characteristics of greater flexibility. A quantitative study was conducted with users in Thailand, where good results were found in creating a tourism experience and general satisfaction. Therefore, it concludes that the extended metaverse is more flexible and improves user satisfaction and the tourism experience in smart destinations.

[21] presents a study on the metaverse considering virtual tourism. The purpose of this experimental laboratory study was to examine the effects of virtual tourism audio-visual conditions and ambient temperature on tourists' thermal sensation and thermal comfort. It was found that the ambient temperature and audiovisual conditions significantly affect the thermal sensation of the participants. In turn, the ambient temperature and the audiovisual conditions in VR significantly affect the thermal comfort of the participants. A quantitative study of the physiological responses of the participants was carried out. It is a contribution to the study of thermal comfort in virtual tourism.

In relation to the use of augmented reality, in the study, we found 3 articles that focus on heritage and/or cultural tourism; in [9] the authors show how AR impacts the tourist experience, promoting memorable experiences through a quantitative study. [22] shows a mobile AR system architecture that incorporates the five senses, in which its contribution to making visits more interesting could be verified. [23] Presents 15 heuristic guides for augmented reality implementation focus on cultural heritage.

In relation to tourism in a general context, we find studies that expose the benefits of using available data to provide tourists with more information than that provided by a traditional website and thus improve marketing, for example [24]. In [25] a study on mobile devices and embodiment was presented, concluding that AR through mobile devices can improve the tourist's experience and enjoyment.

Articles about AR in smart destinations were also found, such as [13] focused on outdoor tourism spaces and [26] that shows a framework that allows the definition of a cultural entertainment system and GPS coordinates and also allows the incorporation of AR elements, thus improving the tourist experience through the use of mobile devices in smart cities.

Of the articles for analysis in this study, virtual reality has the largest number of associated articles. Among them are [27] where the authors presented a multisensory virtual reality tourism model, which establishes the elements of interaction in the virtual reality environment to make the environment more immersive considering visual, taste, theme of the tourism, the tactile and olfactory, this should impact the tourist experience and improve the associated marketing. Considering that immersion in virtual reality is a relevant factor for the user, several studies were found to address these aspects; in [28] the authors presented an innovative methodology for measuring emotions in tourist experiences. [29] studies the contribution of authenticity theory and its implications in virtual reality tourism, which can influence the future and alter perceptions of real tourist destinations. Studies were also found on the sensation of going back in time experienced by virtual reality users in an archaeological destination, where it is interesting to evaluate the presence, nostalgia, service experience - ease of use, and commitment to learning [10]. In turn, [30–32] show findings from the study suggest that virtual reality is a promising tool for tourism in the previous stage of the trip due to providing the tourist with greater information immersion in the environment of virtual reality improves the tourist experience, travel intention and recommendation.

Although immersive systems offer an improved tourist experience, we also find studies that worry about the unwanted effects of virtual reality. In [33], the authors carried out a study on the unwanted effects of virtual tourism, such as isolation and addiction. [34] focuses on understanding the impact of the feeling of presence and cybersickness on users' perception of the similarity between virtual environments and their corresponding real environments, as well as on users' expectations after a virtual visit. This article considers the sense of presence, cybersickness, perceived similarity, and expectation. Also, it exposed challenges in the immersive environment, where cybersickness affects users' perceptions significantly. [35] found that gamification improves the tourist experience in VR, that the elements of gamification benefit emotional fatigue, and that this improves tourist satisfaction. The authors in [36] published a study on emotional marketing in VR tourism products, finding that although it increases economic income, there are still aspects to improve in virtual tourism to obtain better results than those shown in the study.

Finally, we found articles that carried out a study of the use of more than one technology, in this case, VR and AR; the authors in [37] explained how various technologies such as VR, AR, holograms, and 5D can improve the tourist experience. They took Shenyang Expo Park as a case study and explained how technologies that can be used in different spaces could be. In turn, [38] focused on understanding the factors that influence the adoption and use of augmented reality (AR) and virtual reality (VR) technologies by tourists at cultural heritage monuments, specifically in the context of China. Factors such as hedonic motivation, habit, and personal innovativeness were found to have a significant impact on the intention to use AR/VR, while factors such as effort expectancy and social influence were not as decisive. The study [39] focused on examining the implications of the perceived smart tourism technologies for tourists' well-being in marine tourism, as well as the mediating role played by memorable tourism experiences. It was found that tourists can experience an improvement in both their hedonic and eudaimonic well-being by creating memorable travel experiences.

Table 2. Papers classification.

Cite	Title	Kind of Study	VR - AR - Metaverse	Kind of Tourism	Aspect of TX considered
[17]	Metaverse as a disruptive technology revolutionising tourism management and marketing	Without study	Metaverse	General Tourism	Management and Marketing
[19]	Metaverse tourism: conceptual framework and research propositions	Without study	Metaverse	General Tourism	pre-trip and post-trip as well as immersive experiences with different profiles
[20]	Extensible Metaverse Implication for a Smart Tourism City	Quantitative	Metaverse	Tourism in smart destination	Experience during the tourism in smart cities
[21]	Experimental study on the influence of virtual tourism spatial situation on the tourists' temperature comfort in the context of metaverse	Quantitative	Metaverse	Virtual tourism	Experience during the virtual tourism

(continued)

Table 2. (continued)

Cite	Title	Kind of Study	VR - AR - Metaverse	Kind of Tourism	Aspect of TX considered
[9]	Augmented Reality and the Enhancement of Memorable Tourism Experiences at Heritage Sites	Quantitative	Augmented reality	Cultural heritage	Experience during the tourism
[22]	Mobile Five Senses Augmented Reality System: Technology Acceptance Study	Quantitative	Augmented reality	Cultural heritage	Experience during the tourism
[23]	Safar: Heuristics for Augmented Reality Integration in Cultural Heritage	Qualitative	Augmented reality	Cultural heritage	Experience during the visit
[24]	Improving tourism experience in open data environment with mobile augmented reality: needs and challenges	Without study	Augmented reality	General Tourism	Experience during the tourism
[25]	Embodiment of Wearable Augmented Reality Technology in Tourism Experiences	Quantitative	Augmented reality	General Tourism	Experience during the visit
[13]	The Technology Acceptance on AR Memorable Tourism Experience—The Empirical Evidence from China	Quantitative	Augmented reality	Smart tourism in forest parks	Experience during the tourism
[26]	CESARSC: Framework for creating Cultural Entertainment Systems with Augmented Reality in Smart Cities	Qualitative-present a framework	Augmented reality	General Tourism	Experience during the tourism in smart cities

(continued)

Table 2. (*continued*)

Cite	Title	Kind of Study	VR - AR - Metaverse	Kind of Tourism	Aspect of TX considered
[27]	A multisensory virtual experience model for thematic tourism: A Port wine tourism application proposal	Qualitative	Virtual reality	Tourism focused on specific activities (thematic) and proposal for wine tourism	Experience during tourism. Marketing
[28]	An Emotional Roller Coaster: Electrophysiological Evidence of Emotional Engagement during a Roller-Coaster Ride with Virtual Reality Add-On	Quantitative	Virtual reality	Tourism focused on specific activities (thematic)	Experience during the virtual tourism
[29]	Interpreting the perceptions of authenticity in virtual reality tourism through postmodernist approach	Qualitative	Virtual reality	Cultural heritage, specific activities (thematic)	Experience during the tourism
[10]	Back in Time with Immersive Heritage Tourism Experience: A Study of Virtual Reality in Archaeological Sites	Qualitative	Virtual reality	Cultural heritage	Experience during the virtual tourism
[30]	Impacts of Virtual Reality on Tourism Experience and Behavioral Intentions: Moderating Role of Novelty Seeking	Quantitative	Virtual reality	Cultural heritage	pre-trip and during the trip

(*continued*)

Table 2. (*continued*)

Cite	Title	Kind of Study	VR - AR - Metaverse	Kind of Tourism	Aspect of TX considered
[31]	Understanding the virtual experiential value and its effect on travel intention	Mixed	Virtual reality	General Tourism, museum example	Intention to travel
[32]	Virtual reality's impact on destination visit intentions and the moderating role of amateur photography	Quantitative	Virtual reality	Holidays tourism	Intention to travel
[33]	Virtual reality tourism experiences: Addiction and isolation	Qualitative	Virtual reality	Tourism focused on specific activities (thematic) and holidays	Experience during the virtual tourism
[34]	The Relationship Between Cybersickness, Sense of Presence, and the Users' Expectancy and Perceived Similarity Between Virtual and Real Places	Quantitative	Virtual reality	Virtual tourism	Experience during the virtual tourism
[35]	Can gamification improve the virtual reality tourism experience? Analyzing the mediating role of tourism fatigue	Quantitative	Virtual reality	General Tourism	Experience during the tourism
[36]	Evaluation of the Virtual Economic Effect of Tourism Product Emotional Marketing Based on Virtual Reality	Quantitative	Virtual reality	General Tourism	Marketing

Table 2. (*continued*)

Cite	Title	Kind of Study	VR - AR - Metaverse	Kind of Tourism	Aspect of TX considered
[37]	An Exploration on the "Non original tourism experience" Mode Based on Science and Technology	without study	Virtual reality- Augmented reality	General Tourism	Experience during the tourism
[38]	Determining the Key Drivers for the Acceptance and Usage of AR and VR in Cultural Heritage Monuments	Quantitative	Virtual reality- Augmented reality	cultural heritage	Experience during the tourism
[39]	An investigation of how perceived smart tourism technologies affect tourists' well being in marine tourism		Virtual reality- Augmented reality	Marin tourism	Experience during the tourism

3.5   Results: Answer Research Questions

Considering the scientific articles under analysis, the research questions are answered below.

In What Type of Tourism were Virtual Reality, Augmented Reality, and Metaverse used to Intervene in the Tourist Experience?   In the articles analyzed, we found several types of tourism associated with the use of VR, AR, and metaverse; among them are tourism for smart destinations, specific and thematic activities, cultural heritage, vacations, and outdoor activities. And a case focused on marine tourism. It is essential to indicate that several articles were focused on tourism in general and are not particular cases of it. See Fig. 5.

What Aspects of the Tourist Experience were Addressed Using Virtual Reality, Augmented Reality, and Metaverse?   In the articles analyzed, we found various aspects of the tourist experience, such as administration and marketing, aspects before and after the trip, aspects during the tourist experience (whether virtual or real), and studies on how the technologies influence the intention to travel (see Fig. 6).

How was the Tourist Experience Evaluated Using Virtual Reality, Augmented Reality, and Metaverse?   Of the articles under analysis, 5 articles did not present evaluations with users and/or case studies. Of the remaining 20 articles, 6 articles present qualitative studies, which include surveys (in 2 articles), interviews (in 2 articles), thinking aloud (1 article), and thematic analysis of reviews (2 articles).

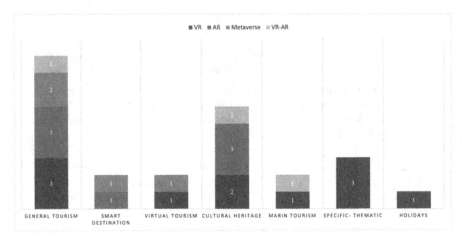

Fig. 5. Type of tourism with use of VR, AR and Metaverse.

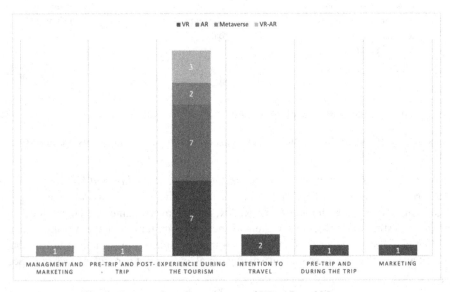

Fig. 6. Aspect of tourism with use of VR, AR and Metaverse.

The articles that presented quantitative studies were 13, among which were a quantitative analysis of data collected with surveys (12 articles), an analysis of body signals (2 articles) that include ECG and physiological responses, and finally, an analysis of user behavior (1 study).

Finally, we found one mixed study that implemented surveys and interviews.

It is essential to indicate that there are articles that present more than one study, so the number of studies implemented may be greater than the number of articles.

4   Conclusion and Future Work

In this article, we present a literature review that allows us to establish an exploratory study on the use of augmented reality, virtual reality, and metaverse related to the tourist experience. We followed a methodology that allowed us to establish research questions, select data sources, select and classify articles, and analyze the results. 25 scientific articles were analyzed, and we found that several studies on the tourist experience incorporate VR, AR, and metaverse. The most significant number of them refers to tourism in general, followed by cultural and heritage tourism. At the same time, we found that most articles focus on the experience during the trip or tourist visit. Finally, we found that these studies mostly use surveys for quantitative analysis and other techniques referring to body signals and user behavior. The concept of memorable experience appears relevant, in which these technologies can contribute significantly by adding more diverse information about the site to visit before the trip, during, and in stages after the trip. On the other hand, marketing and visit intention can also benefit from these technologies. However, there are still aspects to be developed, such as information availability and platforms that involve several user senses.

Although we paid special attention to wine tourism, we found only one article that used VR. However, from the analyzed cases of tourist experience, many elements can be applied to this specific area of tourism. [27] presents a theoretical proposal for a multisensory model that can be applied to wine tourism, which includes thematic activities and multisensory elements of VR. This specific tourism can be developed in future research.

For future work, we consider conducting a systematic review of the literature that allows us to delve deeper into the use of virtual, augmented reality, and metaverse in tourism because, according to the studies analyzed, it opens new opportunities to promote destinations and improve the tourism experience.

References

1. Alfaro, E., Velilla, J., Brunetta, H., Navarro, B., Molina, C.: Customer experience. Una visión multidimensional del marketing de experiencias. La experiencia del cliente, un marco para el marketing del futuro, Libro colaborativo, pp. 12–19 (2012)
2. Bascur, C., Rusu, C.: Customer experience in retail: a systematic literature review. Appl. Sci. **10**(21), 7644 (2020). https://doi.org/10.3390/app10217644
3. Rusu, V., Márquez, L., González, P., Rusu, C.: Evaluating the post-pandemic tourist experience: a scale for tourist experience in Valparaíso, Chile. In: Social Computing and Social Media: Applications in Education and Commerce: 14th International Conference, SCSM 2022, Held as Part of the 24th HCI International Conference, HCII 2022, Virtual Event, June 26–July 1, 2022, Proceedings, Part II, pp. 331–343. Springer, Cham (2022). https://doi.org/10.1007/978-3-031-05064-0_25
4. UX-definition ISO9241–210: Ergonomics of human-system interaction-Part11: Usability: Definitions and concepts, International Organization for Standardization, Geneva (2018)
5. AllAboutUX.org, User Experience White Paper. https://experience.aalto.fi/user-experience-white-paper/. Accessed 20 Dec 2023
6. Nielsen Norman Group, The Definition of User Experience. https://www.nngroup.com/articles/definition-user-experience/. Accessed 20 Dec 2023

7. Vanharanta, H., Kantola, J., Seikola, S.: Customers' conscious experience in a coffee shop. Procedia Manufact. **3**, 618–625 (2015). https://doi.org/10.1016/j.promfg.2015.07.283
8. Godovykh, A., Tasci, A.D.A.: Customer experience in tourism: A review of definitions, components, and measurements. Tourism Management Perspectives 35 (2020)
9. Jiang, S., Moyle, B., Yung, R., Tao, L., Scott, N.: Augmented reality and the enhancement of memorable tourism experiences at heritage sites. Curr. Issue Tour. **26**(2), 242–257 (2023)
10. Bideci, M., Bideci, C.: Back in time with immersive heritage tourism experience: a study of virtual reality in archaeological sites. In: ENTER22 e-Tourism Conference, pp. 312–317. Springer, Cham, January 2023
11. Brochado, A., Stoleriu, O., Lupu, C.: Wine tourism: a multisensory experience. Curr. Issue Tour. **24**(5), 597–615 (2021)
12. Madeira, A., Correia, A., Filipe, J.A.: Wine tourism: constructs of the experience. Trends in Tourist Behavior: New Products and Experiences from Europe, pp. 93–108 (2019)
13. Li, S., Jiang, S.: The technology acceptance on ar memorable tourism experience—the empirical evidence from China. Sustainability **15**(18), 13349 (2023)
14. Bryson, S.: Virtual Reality: A Definition History – A Personal Essay. https://arxiv.org/abs/1312.4322. Accessed 20 Dec 2023
15. Kardong-Edgren, S.S., Farra, S.L., Alinier, G., Young, H.M.: A call to unify definitions of virtual reality. Clin. Simul. Nurs. **31**, 28–34 (2019)
16. Arena, F., Collotta, M., Pau, G., Termine, F.: An overview of augmented reality. Computers **11**(2), 28 (2022)
17. Buhalis, D., Leung, D., Lin, M.: Metaverse as a disruptive technology revolutionising tourism management and marketing. Tour. Manage. **97**, 104724 (2023)
18. Morales, J., Cornide-Reyes, H., Rossel, P.O., Sáez, P., Silva-Aravena, F.: Virtual reality, augmented reality and metaverse: customer experience approach and user experience evaluation methods. Literature review. In: Coman, A., Vasilache, S. (eds) Social Computing and Social Media. HCII 2023. Lecture Notes in Computer Science, vol.14025. Springer, Cham (2023). https://doi.org/10.1007/978-3-031-35915-6_40
19. Koo, C., Kwon, J., Chung, N., Kim, J.: Metaverse tourism: conceptual framework and research propositions. Curr. Issue Tour. **26**(20), 3268–3274 (2023)
20. Suanpang, P., Niamsorn, C., Pothipassa, P., Chunhapataragul, T., Netwong, T., Jermsittiparsert, K.: Extensible metaverse implication for a smart tourism city. Sustainability **14**(21), 14027 (2022)
21. Huang, X.T., Wang, J., Wang, Z., Wang, L., Cheng, C.: Experimental study on the influence of virtual tourism spatial situation on the tourists' temperature comfort in the context of metaverse. Front. Psychol. **13**, 1062876 (2023)
22. Rodrigues, J.M.F., Ramos, C.M.Q., Pereira, J.A.R., Sardo, J.D.P., Cardoso, P.J.S.: Mobile five senses augmented reality system: technology acceptance study. IEEE Access **7**, 163022–163033 (2019). https://doi.org/10.1109/ACCESS.2019.2953003
23. Monteiro, C., Rajasekar, I., Bhargava, P., Srivastava, A.: Safar: heuristics for augmented reality integration in cultural heritage. In: Companion Proceedings of the 2023 Conference on Interactive Surfaces and Spaces, pp. 40–44, November 2023
24. Ocampo, A.J., Palaoag, T.: Improving tourism experience in open data environment with mobile augmented reality: needs and challenges. In: IOP Conf. Ser.: Mater. Sci. Eng. 482 012005 (2019)
25. Tussyadiah, I. P., Jung, T. H., tom Dieck, M. C.: Embodiment of wearable augmented reality technology in tourism experiences. J. Travel Res. **57**(5), 597–611 (2018). https://doi.org/10.1177/0047287517709090
26. García-Crespo, Á., González-Carrasco, I., López-Cuadrado, J.L., Villanueva, D., González, A.: CESARSC: framework for creating cultural entertainment systems with augmented reality in smart cities. Comput. Sci. Inf. Syst. **13**(2), 395–425 (2016)

27. Martins, J., Gonçalves, R., Branco, F., Barbosa, L., Melo, M., Bessa, M.: A multisensory virtual experience model for thematic tourism: a port wine tourism application proposal. J. Destin. Mark. Manag. **6**(2), 103–109 (2017)

28. Bastiaansen, M., Oosterholt, M., Mitas, O., Han, D., Lub, X.: An emotional roller coaster: electrophysiological evidence of emotional engagement during a roller-coaster ride with virtual reality add-on. J. Hospitality Tourism Res. **46**(1), 29–54 (2022)

29. Gao, B.W., Zhu, C., Song, H., Dempsey, I.M.B.: Interpreting the perceptions of authenticity in virtual reality tourism through postmodernist approach. Inf. Technol. Tourism **24**(1), 31–55 (2022)

30. Yuan, A., Hong, J.: Impacts of virtual reality on tourism experience and behavioral intentions: moderating role of novelty seeking. J. Hospitality Tourism Res., 109634 (2023)

31. Li, E.Y., Chang, F.K., Jan, A.: Understanding the virtual experiential value and its effect on travel intention. Int. J. Internet Mark. Advertising **19**(3–4), 263–285 (2023)

32. Morrison, A.M., Bag, S., Mandal, K.: Virtual reality's impact on destination visit intentions and the moderating role of amateur photography. Tourism Review (2023)

33. Merkx, C., Nawijn, J.: Virtual reality tourism experiences: addiction and isolation. Tour. Manage. **87**, 104394 (2021)

34. Magalhães, M., Melo, M., Bessa, M., Coelho, A.F.: The relationship between cybersickness, sense of presence, and the users' expectancy and perceived similarity between virtual and real places. IEEE Access **9**, 79685–79694 (2021)

35. Wei, Z., Zhang, J., Huang, X., Qiu, H.: Can gamification improve the virtual reality tourism experience? analyzing the mediating role of tourism fatigue. Tour. Manage. **96**, 104715 (2023)

36. Talafubieke, M., Mai, S., Xialifuhan, N.: Evaluation of the virtual economic effect of tourism product emotional marketing based on virtual reality. Front. Psychol. **12**, 759268 (2021)

37. Ma, D., Li, F., Li, A.: An exploration on the "non original tourism experience" mode based on science and technology. In: IOP conference series, materials science and engineering, vol. 394, no. 5, p. 052036. IOP Publishing (2018)

38. Wen, X., Sotiriadis, M., Shen, S.: Determining the key drivers for the acceptance and usage of AR and VR in cultural heritage monuments. Sustainability **15**(5), 4146 (2023)

39. Zheng, Y., Wu, Y.: An investigation of how perceived smart tourism technologies affect tourists' well-being in marine tourism. PLoS ONE **18**(8), e0290539 (2023)

VTubing and Its Potential for the Streaming and Design Community: An Austrian Perspective

Patricia Rohrbacher[1]([⊠]) [iD] and Deepti Mishra[2,3] [iD]

[1] Department of Media and Design, University of Applied Sciences Joanneum Graz, Graz, Austria
`patricia.rohrbacher@edu.fh-joanneum.at`
[2] Intelligent Systems and Analytics Group, Department of Computer Science, Norwegian University of Science and Technology, Gjøvik, Norway
`deepti.mishra@ntnu.no`
[3] Business Analytics Research Group, Inland School of Business and Social Sciences, Inland Norway University of Applied Sciences, Lillehammer, Norway

Abstract. This paper explores the landscape of Virtual YouTubing (VTubing) in Austria, a phenomenon that gained traction during the COVID-19 pandemic. The study compares Austrian VTubers with their Japanese counterparts, emphasizing cultural and contextual disparities. Through an online survey and interviews with six VTubers, the research addresses key questions regarding the state of VTubing in Austria, the creation process of VTuber avatars, and the influence of the Kawaii phenomenon on gender roles. Results highlight the challenges faced by Austrian VTubers, including niche status and language barriers, and reveal nuanced differences in behavior, organization, and cultural influences. The impact of the Kawaii aesthetic on gender roles within the VTubing community is explored, and the step-by-step process of avatar creation is outlined. The study provides insights into the advantages and challenges of VTubing, paving the way for future research and fostering the growth of the VTubing community in Austria.

Keywords: Attractiveness and Cuteness · Conceptual Design and Planning · Creativity · Cultural Differences and HCI · Design Methods and Techniques · Gender and HCI Design · Virtual Youtuber

1 Introduction

VTubing has become increasingly popular in the wake of the COVID-19 pandemic, especially on platforms such as Twitch.tv[1] and YouTube.com[2], which offer insight into the creation of captivating VTuber avatars. The term 'VTuber' derives from the fusion of 'virtual' and 'YouTuber,' encompassing individuals who create videos and

---

[1] Link to website: https://www.twitch.tv/ [29.12.2023].
[2] Link to website: https://www.youtube.com/ [29.12.2023].

A. Coman and S. Vasilache (Eds.): HCII 2024, LNCS 14703, pp. 222–233, 2024.
https://doi.org/10.1007/978-3-031-61281-7_15

perform live online while concealing their identity behind a computer-generated (CG) two-dimensional or three-dimensional avatar. This innovative form of online entertainment allows VTubers to design and modify their appearances freely, granting them unparalleled creative expression [1].

VTubing gained significant prominence during the global lockdown situation that began in 2020 and was first popularized by the Japanese artificial intelligence VTuber, "Kizuna Ai" [2]. Despite the widespread adoption of VTubing in various parts of the world, Austria seems to be relatively untouched by this emerging trend. The cultural disparity between Japanese and Austrian streamers, coupled with the predominance of Asian VTuber protagonists and agencies, has led to a nascent VTuber scene in Austria. This paper is an interim status of the master thesis in the research field of media design and aims to answer the following main research questions:

1. How does the current state of VTubing in Austria differ from its origins in Japan, considering the cultural influences and contextual factors, and what are the implications for adopting and developing VTubing in the Austrian scene?
2. What are the key steps and considerations in the process of creating a virtual avatar for VTubing, and what guidelines can be formulated to assist individuals in designing their own unique and engaging VTuber avatars?

To answer the stated questions of research, online survey followed by in-depth interviews with Austrian and German VTubers were conducted to explore their opinion about the topic of VTubing. The goal of this paper is two-fold. Firstly, it aims to provide an analysis of the pros and cons of VTubing. Examining both its advantages and disadvantages offers a balanced perspective on this emerging trend in Austria. Additionally, VTubing contributes to the streaming and design community by outlining essential steps and considerations in creating compelling VTuber avatars. Therefore, the thesis also aims to assist individuals in crafting their distinct and online personas, thereby fostering an engaging VTubing culture in Austria. Notable contributions by Liudmila Bredikhina [1, 3, 4] and research by Agnès Giard [4] highlight the international differences in VTubing.

The structure of this paper is as follows: Section two reports the related work. Section three describes the methodology used, including the data collection of an online survey, descriptions of participants and the procedure, as well as methods and tools used for the survey and the follow-up interviews. In the fourth section, the results of the interviews are summarized and discussed in four thematic areas. The final section summarizes the work and explains the next steps planned concerning the lead author's master thesis.

2 Related Work

Virtual YouTubing (VTubing) is a relatively recent subject that has been explored across various subfields over the past five years. In this regard, Davey (2019) provides an initial overview of the VTubing phenomenon originating from japan, addressing inquiries surrounding the definition of the term. The discussion extends to considerations of aesthetics and the cultural impact of Kawaii, meaning 'capable of being Loved' [5], and Moe meaning 'a burning passion for young, cute and innocent girls.' Additionally, topics such as the exploration of gender aspects, specifically babiniku, which can be translated to 'virtual rebirth as a beautiful girl [4] and the representation of femininity in the context of Japanese VTubing are examined [6].

VTubing and Identity. Another area of exploration revolves around vtubers grappling with their identity and virtual identity. Turner (2022) delves into the inquiry of how live streaming as a VTuber allows for the expression of identity and what makes it unique compared to traditional face-cam streaming. Interviews were employed as the methodology. The findings indicate that VTubing assists streamers in overcoming personal insecurities and redefining themselves in terms of self-representation [7].

Bredikhina (2020) also conducted research on how identity shaping looks in the VTubing era. The data collection, conducted through interviews, revealed that VTubing provides advantages for expressing one's identity, including freedom of expression, the use of avatars as a form of communication, and the opportunity to turn VTubing into a professional career [8].

VTuber and Community Interactions. Interactions between VTubers and their fan communities were also examined in the work of Bredikhina (2020). Through conducted interviews, it was revealed that Japanese VTubers tend to maintain a more distant relationship with their community, akin to that of idols. In contrast, English and French VTubers are inclined to create a more familiar environment and be closer to their community [8].

Zhou (2020) attempts to uncover the dynamics between the Japanese VTuber Kizuna AI and her audience through a case study, highlighting the push-pull relationship. Japanese VTuber Kizuna AI described herself as the first virtual artificial intelligence on her website (2019) and has since also been regarded as one of the first VTuber worldwide [9]. The attraction of Kizuna AI's non-human characterization acts as a pulling force, while fans, like idol dynamics, simultaneously experience a certain level of distance [10].

Lu et al. (2021) demonstrated, concerning the topic of viewer perception in this context, that VTubers exhibited similarities with traditional streamers regarding the content of their streams and the motivations of viewers. The study was based on interviews. Differences were observed in the expectations and perceptions of viewers regarding VTubers [11].

Socio-cultural Aspects of VTubing. The results mentioned earlier in the context of identity and community interactions by Bredikhina (2020) also incorporate theories related to socio-cultural aspects. Cultural differences among interview participants from England, France, and Japan are discernible, with Japanese VTubers exhibiting the most significant distinctions regarding streaming behavior [8].

In another paper by Bredikhina (2022), a comparison is drawn between modern VTubers and traditional Japanese theatrical art forms and narrative structures. A survey was initiated, and fewer participants were invited to further interviews. The results reveal that, akin to traditional art forms, VTubers redefine the boundaries between performer, actor, character, and gender [3].

The Impact of VTubing on the Gender Debate. In the context of VTubing and gender roles, Bredikhina (2022) investigates the phenomenon of Babiniku and cross-dressing in

Japan. Japanese men use female characters for performances to challenge gender norms and present themselves in public spaces [1].

Contributing to this theme is the research conducted by Bredikhina and Giard (2022), which relies on the results of a survey as well as semi-structured interviews. The findings indicate that engaging in VTubing as Babiniku is a positive experience. Behavior, appearance, and presentation can be individually influenced, irrespective of gender-specific biases [4].

Research on Technology and Streaming. Regarding streaming capabilities, Shirai (2019) introduces 'REALITY' as a live entertainment creation service for VTubers. REALITY serves as a platform for interacting with the audience and functions as a Motion Capture Studio [12].

Bredikhina et al. (2020) elucidates current developments, experiences, and evaluations of social virtual reality (VR) platforms in Japan, which have emerged due to the influence of VTubers and VRChat. The avatar-driven VR society is thriving in Japan and other East Asian countries. Since the inaugural edition of a 'Virtual Conference' in 2019, new avenues for live streaming have continued to unfold [13].

Regarding animation and tracking for VTubers, the data from Takács (2022) provides insights into animating 3D avatars based on a single camera or through real-time video input from human faces. Three modules were introduced - face tracking, avatar animation, and a server for transferring the tracking data [14].

3 Methodology

To get an overview of the Austrian VTuber Scene, three steps were taken: First, an online survey consisting of 15 questions shown in Table 1 in the Appendix about VTubing in the German-speaking region was crafted to take stock of German speaking VTuber, attracting 22 participants from Austria and Germany. Secondly, six survey participants (five Austrian and one German) were chosen to engage in subsequent individual interviews. The interview questions (as shown in Table 2) were pre-constructed and disseminated to the interviewees in advance. The third step consisted of collecting data from VTuber artists in the German-speaking area.

Data Collection. Communication with most of the interviewed VTuber was conducted via Instagram and Discord, with some exceptions via email exchanges. After further research, contact was made with ZockMiku, VTuber and publisher of the BEAUTV[3] magazine on the website of the same name. During the email exchange, the exposé of the master thesis on VTubing was published on the website, including questionnaires on VTubing and VTubing in an artistic context [15]. This was followed by further submissions of responses. The answers from the questionnaire for VTuber primarily serve to establish a rough framework on the topic of VTubing in Austria, or rather the German-speaking area. As a result, six interviews were conducted. The whole process of data collection was conducted over a period of two months.

---

[3] Link to website: https://beautv.de/ [29.12.2023].

Participants and Procedure. To take part in the survey the participant of the survey had to be an active or inactive VTuber according to the definition formulated in the introduction. Moreover, the survey participant had to be of Austrian or German speaking origin. Since VTuber do not always disclose their nationality online and many VTuber stream in English, this approach proved to be extremely difficult. Compared to the total number of German-speaking VTuber (around 600 VTuber were recorded in 2021 [16]), the sample of 22 participants is not highly representative. However, it should be mentioned that no numbers of currently active Austrian VTuber are known by the author (as of May 2023), which means that the sample does not provide any information about representativeness regarding Austria.

In a further step, potential interview participants, who agreed to participate in the subsequent expert interview had to complete the questionnaire, in full, beforehand and must have explicitly agreed to be part of the follow-up interview. Moreover, they had to give explicit consent to the recording of the interview, with the understanding that the audio and video material created would be used exclusively as a source for data collection and would not be published elsewhere.

Methods and Tools. The questionnaire was initially sent to 12 Austrian VTuber via social media platforms or email (Instagram.com[4]: six, Discord: five, email: one). The final part includes the question of whether the respondent is interested in a personal interview, and, in the case of an acceptance, how to get in touch. In addition, there was an opportunity to refer to other Austrian VTubers who might be interested in participating in the survey.

Data Analysis. The data was analyzed using Thematic Analysis. In the initial phase, the transcribed interviews were tested for recurrent statements and terms. Subsequently, these terms were categorized into codes as the second step of the analysis. Multiple statements and keywords from the six interviewees were attributed to each queried theme. The third step of data analysis involved synthesizing the codes into overarching themes. These themes are briefly addressed in the following section.

Subsequently, a document containing the initial set of interview questions was sent to the VTuber interested in the interviews. After the appointment, the interviews were conducted online via Discord and lasted between 30 min to over an hour. Before the interview, the VTubers were informed about the purpose of the interview and its use as a source for the master thesis. All interviewed participants provided permission to record the interview in advance. During the interviews, notes were taken in Microsoft Word on the respective questions, and all interviews were recorded using the streaming software OBS Studio. Although most of the interviews were conducted without a camera, some of the interviewed VTubers used their avatar during their interview, while others used face cam.

The interview questions shown in the Appendix (Table 2) were defined in advance and formulated to serve as a skeleton for further research, with the aim of supplying a guideline for the future work of the author.

After the interviews, the recordings were transcribed using the software f4 transkript and summarized and processed using the program f4 analyse.

---

[4] Link to website: https://www.instagram.com/ [29.12.2023].

Finally, an invitation to a further interview was also extended here, but due to the low level of feedback, these questions were simply incorporated into the regular interviews.

4 Results and Discussion

As mentioned in the preceding section, five Austrian and one German VTuber were invited for interviews to discuss their experiences and perspectives on VTubing. The responses from the interviewees were assigned thematic codes, which were then categorized into four main themes. Introducing the topic, the VTubers were initially engaged in a discussion on 'The definition of VTubing and what 'VTubing' means for Austrian VTubers.' The second theme delved into the inquiry 'Austrian and Japanese VTubers in comparison from the perspective of Austrian VTubers and the actual differences that exist.' The third theme focused on 'The impact of the Kawaii-phenomenon and how it influences gender roles in VTubing.' The final theme addressed 'The process of creating a 2D and 3D avatar step by step.'

The Definition of VTubing and What 'VTubing' Means for Austrian VTubers. In summary, VTubers represent a form of virtual influencers who, through streaming and video creation, can establish a significant online presence. The concept of a virtual influencer or the use of avatars as content creators is not novel, as characters like Cynthia the Gaba Girl and Max Headroom have demonstrated since the 1930s. Cynthia was a plaster doll, who was in the focus of media attention in the 1930s for a long time due to her realistic appearance [2]. While the seemingly computer-generated character Max Headroom was made by using prosthetic make-up, special contact lenses and a single light source in the foreground [17]. However, unlike conventional influencers, YouTubers, and streamers, VTubers usually employ a virtual avatar, providing considerable design freedom concerning appearance and avatar form (2D or 3D). Guidance in this context is drawn from current leaders in the VTuber scene such as Kizuna Ai, Gaw Gura[5], or Ironmouse[6].

VTubing offers privacy, representation, and creative freedom for artists. It helps individuals overcome shyness and embraces virtual cosplay, tapping into a growing trend on streaming platforms. However, challenges include a potential lack of acceptance due to avatars, a risk of losing touch with reality, and technical limitations in replicating emotions. Despite drawbacks, VTubing remains a popular and evolving form of online content creation.

VTubing emerges as a distinctive form of virtual influencing, offering creators significant design freedom. Challenges such as societal acceptance and technical limitations underscore the need for ongoing innovation. Despite hurdles, the enduring popularity of VTubing signifies its resilience and continual evolution as a unique online content creation medium.

---

[5] Author's note: Well-known Japanese shark girl VTuber.
[6] Author's note: Well-known Puerto Rican demon girl VTuber.

The Comparison of Austrian and Japanese VTubers from the Perspective of Austrian VTubers and the Existing Differences. VTubing in Austria faces challenges like its niche status, a language barrier, and limited awareness of anime culture. Conservative views and the focus on 'idoling' contribute to the low number of creators. Idols commonly refer to youthful female pop musicians [18]. Efforts are underway to overcome these challenges by establishing information channels, promoting agencies, and encouraging direct engagement with the VTuber community. The growth of VTubing in Austria is anticipated in the coming years.

The main differences between Austrian and Japanese VTubers encompass behavioral, organizational, and cultural aspects. Japanese VTubers often embrace the idol culture, projecting images of innocence and perfection, while Austrians view VTubing primarily as a hobby rather than a professional pursuit. Agency involvement is prominent in Japan, with VTubers often belonging to teams, whereas Austrian VTubers typically operate individually or within informal groups. The role-play dynamic also varies, as Japanese VTubers adopt elaborate fictional characters, contrasting with Austrian VTubers who use VTubing more for self-representation. Language and voice modulation practices differ, with Japanese VTubers employing high-pitched voices and cute language, while Austrians rely on natural voices and dialects. Cultural distinctions extend to the size of fan communities, design aesthetics, and the influence of cultural background concepts such as 'nihonjinron' and 'mukokuseki'. The term 'nihonjinron' translates as 'discussions of the Japanese' and includes a wide range of literary works written by intellectual elites. These writings aim to articulate and outline the distinctiveness of Japanese culture, society, and national identity [19] whereas 'mukokuseki' means 'without nationality' and describes the attempt of Japanese companies to design their products (especially electronics) as neutrally as possible [20]. These nuanced differences contribute to varied streaming behaviors, fan interactions, and overall approaches to VTubing in both regions.

Austrian VTubers face challenges, including a niche status, language barriers and limited awareness of anime culture. Ongoing efforts to overcome these challenges point to a positive development of VTubing in Austria. Nuanced differences between Austrian and Japanese VTubers highlight cultural, behavioral, and organizational differences that shape VTubing approaches in both regions.

The Impact of the Kawaii-Phenomenon and How It Influences Gender Roles in VTubing. 'Kawaii' is a Japanese term originating from '可' (meaning 'acceptable' or 'capable of') and '愛' (meaning 'love') [5]. Originally negative [21], it evolved into a positive concept associated with cuteness, prevalent in anime, manga, and Hello Kitty. The aesthetic features large eyes and small mouths [22]. Beyond appearance, kawaii influences social behavior, softening hierarchies, promoting obedience, and eliciting empathy [23]. It lacks a standardized criterion, interpreted subjectively from childlike innocence to intentional stylistic choices. It extends to economic success through cute mascots [5]. 'Kimo-kawaii' represents something eerie yet intriguing, showcasing versatility [24].

The concept of 'kawaii' significantly influences gender roles in VTubing. Female VTubers often adopt kawaii aesthetics, reinforcing traditional gender norms. Male VTubers tend to focus on qualities like being cool or charismatic, reflecting societal expectations and limiting expression. Female avatars attract more attention, possibly influenced by expectations of women being cute. Some male VTubers adopt bishōjo ('beautiful girl') avatars, known as 'babiniku, leveraging kawaii qualities for popularity and identity construction [4]. Critics argue that cute behavior, especially in women, deviates from societal expectations and may be seen as manipulative or indulgent [24].

The influence of kawaii extends beyond appearance, significantly shaping gender roles within the VTubing community. The adoption of cute aesthetics by female VTubers and the focus on charisma by males mirror societal expectations and contribute to identity construction. The concept introduces complexities, including perceptions of cuteness and its potential impact on societal expectations.

The Process of Creating a 2D and 3D Avatar Step by Step. The process of becoming a VTuber involves several sequential steps [4]. It begins with gathering information about VTubing, deciding on the character's concept, and creating a mood board for reference. The next stages include designing a 2D character, modeling a 3D character, and incorporating kawaii movement patterns during rigging[7] [25]. Motion capture systems, such as facial expression capture and Virtual Reality (VR) trackers, are used for tracking [4]. Streaming is facilitated by software like OBS or Streamlabs, and popular platforms like Twitch.tv and YouTube.com are employed for content sharing. Common problems encountered include technical challenges, program stability issues, and complexities in 3D modeling. VTuber advice emphasizes starting with free resources, focusing on selected platforms, persisting in community building, avoiding excessive financial investment, and conducting research to acquire essential knowledge about the VTubing process.

VTuber designers in Austria and Germany show improvement in model quality but there is still a lot to achieve in order to reach Japanese standards. There is a trend toward aesthetically pleasing models, indicating potential industry stability. VTuber agencies are emerging in German-speaking regions. Workspaces include 3D and 2D model artists, riggers, and asset artists.

Avatar trends suggest a future preference for 3D avatars due to personalized advantages. Classic 2D avatars, popular in the anime community, may decline due to limitations. A hybrid form combining 3D and 2D elements, easily generated through tools like VRoid Studio[8], is gaining popularity for visually appealing models with low computational requirements.

---

[7] Author's note: Rigging is a crucial step in the creation of VTuber avatars, where the avatar is equipped with a skeleton-like structure to facilitate realistic movements.

[8] Author's note: 3D Modelling software for VTuber.

Future Possibilities. Encouraging VTubers to explore diverse content beyond traditional genres can attract a broader audience. Facilitating collaborations between Austrian and Japanese VTubers can promote cultural exchange and mutual understanding. Initiatives to increase awareness about VTubing in Austria and educational efforts can foster the growth of VTuber communities. Exploring technological advancements and fostering innovation in avatar creation methods will keep VTubing dynamic and engaging.

5   Conclusion and Future Work

VTubing, a rising trend, gained popularity during the COVID-19 pandemic, notably on platforms like Twitch.tv and YouTube.com. The research questions posed initially have been comprehensively addressed during the master thesis and are succinctly summarized in this paper.

The study on the Austrian VTuber scene involved three main steps: an online survey with 15 multiple-choice questions targeting German-speaking VTubers followed by individual interviews with six selected participants, and data collection from VTuber artists in the German-speaking area. Communication with VTubers occurred through platforms like Instagram and Discord. The survey aimed at understanding the VTuber landscape in Austria attracted 22 participants. The study faced challenges in determining the nationality of VTubers due to online practices. Interviews were conducted online, notes were taken, and recordings were transcribed and analyzed using thematic analysis to form the structured framework for the master thesis.

One of the main findings includes statements from interviewees regarding the advantages and disadvantages of VTubing. These pertain to privacy, a means of representation, and creative freedom for artists. Drawbacks arise from a lack of acceptance of the topic and potential technical difficulties. In comparison with Japanese VTubers, respondents noted that factors such as the language barrier and a lack of interest in anime and Japanese pop culture in Austria contribute to differences. Additionally, VTubing is considered a niche within the streaming industry in Austria. The term 'Kawaii' is rarely present in Austrian characters. However, the cuteness factor significantly influences stereotypical gender roles, both offline and online, with seemingly increased popularity for (mostly female) cute characters. The process of creating a VTuber avatar varies based on financial resources and individual skill levels. The steps involve research, conceptualization, drawing a 2D model or 3D modeling, as well as rigging and tracking the avatar, culminating in streaming or video content creation. The Austrian VTuber artist market has yet to be thoroughly explored due to a lack of feedback. However, there appears to be a trend among surveyed artists towards 3D avatars.

This paper has evolved from the research conducted for an ongoing master's thesis (as of December 2023) and encompasses the findings derived from the surveys and interview outcomes generated in this context. These findings will guide towards a more in-depth exploration of the research work and the design process of a 3D VTuber avatar in future.

Acknowledgments. To ensure an appropriate and scientifically accurate approach, this paper employed ChatGPT 3.5 and deepl.com for translation purposes and improved formulations.

Disclosure of Interests.   The authors have no competing interests to declare that are relevant to the content of this article.

Appendix

Table 1. Multiple-choice questions of Online Survey

Part 1 – about the VTuber as a person (Questions 1–5)[9]	
1	Is your identity known?
2	Which gender do you classify yourself as?
3	How old are you?
4	Which country are you from? (For Austrians: Which federal state do you come from?)
5	How big do you think your total reach is, measured by followers on Discord, Instagram, Twitch, Twitter, YouTube, etc....?
Part 2 – About the VTuber avatar (Questions 6–10)[10]	
6	What is the name of your avatar?
7	What is their background story? How would they describe/imagine themselves?
8	What gender do you assign to your character?
9	Who is/are your characters 'VTuber parents"? Who designed your character?
10	Which model shapes do you use?
Part 3 – About the streaming behavior of the VTuber (Questions 11–15)[11]	
11	Since when are you VTuber (debut)?
12	In which language(s) do you stream?
13	Which category/s would best describe your content (choose max. 3)?
14	How long do your streams last on average?
15	On which platforms do you stream?

---

[9] Questions 1–5 of the questionnaire are for general data collection of the VTuber. All data collected in this section remain anonymous during the evaluation.

[10] The second section refers to the avatar and its character creation. Design aspects such as storytelling, avatar shapes and artists behind the VTubers are the main topic.

[11] This concluding section provides a summary of the streaming habits of the VTuber, referring to debut, language, content, and average duration of streams, as well as chosen streaming platforms.

Table 2. Interview Questions

1 What do you think is the inner motivation behind streaming via virtual avatar?	
a)	What do you see as the advantages and disadvantages of this?
b)	Why did you personally decide to stream as a VTuber?
c)	Did you already stream before and if so, how was the 'transition" to virtual streaming via avatars?
2 Why do you think are there still relatively few known VTuber?	
a)	What do you think is the reason why the term 'VTubing" is not familiar among most of the population?
b)	How do you think the general interest in VTubing could be increased?
c)	Where do you think an interested person or future VTuber could find out more about the topic?
3 What do you think is the difference between Austrian and Japanese VTubing?	
a)	What do you think are possible cultural differences?
b)	How do you think the outward appearance of the characters differs?
c)	What potential contrasts do you see in the character and behavior of a stream?
4 How do you interpret the 'childish' and 'cute' look, or even the trend towards 'kawaii' (cute) of most VTuber?	
a)	Why do you think there seems to be more female than male VTuber avatars (regardless of the person behind them)?
b)	(How) Is 'cuteness' reflected in your character?
c)	What does 'kawaii' (cute) mean to you personally?
5 How would you describe the process of creating your own VTuber avatar step by step?	
a)	What are the individual work steps?
b)	Which programs and tools did you use for your character?
c)	What problems did you encounter during the process?
d)	What tips would you give to beginning VTuber or interested streamers?

References

1. Bredikhina, L.: Babiniku: what lies behind the virtual performance. Contesting gender norms through technology and Japanese theatre. Electron. J. Contemporary Japanese Stud. 2(22), 1–22 (2022)
2. Rasmussen, M.: Who Was the First Virtual Influencer? A short history of "fake" people making real impact in media and entertainmant, Virtual Humans, 27 January 2022. https://www.virtualhumans.org/article/who-was-the-first-virtual-influencer. Accessed 29 Dec 2023
3. Bredikhina, L.: Virtual theatrics and the ideal VTuber Bishōjo. REPLAYING JAPAN 3, 21–32 (2021)
4. Bredikhina, L., Giard, A.: Becoming a virtual cutie: digital cross-dressing in Japan. Convergence 6(28), 1643–1661 (2022)

5. Bîrlea, O.-M.: Cute STudies". Kawaii ("Cuteness") - A New Research Field. Philobiblon 1(26), 83–100 (2021)
6. Davey, F.: The 'Virtual YouTuber' Phenomenon in Japan, April 2019
7. Turner, A.B.: Streaming as a Virtual Being. The Complex Relationship Between VTubers and Identity. Malmö University, Malmö (2022)
8. Bredikhina, L.: Designing identity in VTuber Era. In: ConVRgence (VRIC) Virtual Reality International Conference Proceedings , Laval (2020)
9. K. A. Inc., "BIOGRAPHY. Kizuna Ai," Kizuna Ai Inc., 14 November 2019. https://kizunaai. com/en/biography/. Accessed 29 Dec 2023
10. Zhou, X.: Virtual Youtuber Kizuna AI. Co-creating human-non-human interaction and celebrity-audience relationship. Lund University, Lund (2020)
11. Lu, Z., Shen, C., Li, J., Shen, H., Wigdor, D.: More Kawaii than a Real-Person Live Streamer. Understanding How the Otaku Community Engages with and Perceives Virtual YouTubers. In: Proceedings of the 2021 CHI Conference on Human Factors in Computing Systems, New York (2021)
12. Shirai, A.: REALITY. broadcast your virtual beings from everywhere. In: Proceedings of SIGGRAPH '19 Appy Hour, New York (2019)
13. Bredikhina, L., Kameoka, T., Shimbo, S., Shirai, A.: Avatar driven VR society trends in Japan. In: IEEE Conference on Virtual Reality and 3D User Interfaces Abstracts and Workshops (VRW), Atlanta (2020)
14. Takács, M.: Animation of Avatar Face based on Human Face Video. Brno University of Technology, Brno (2022)
15. Fuchs, M.: Eine Wissenschaftliche Masterarbeit Über Vtubing! 5 April 2023. https://beautv. de/2023/04/05/eine-wissenschaftliche-masterarbeit-ueber-vtubing/. Accessed 29 Dec 2023
16. Fuchs, M.: VTubing, May 2022. https://beautv.de/vtubing/. Accessed 24 May 2023
17. Bishop, B.: Max Headroom: The Definitve History of the 1980s Digital Icon. Live and direct," The Verge, 2 April 2015. https://www.theverge.com/2015/4/2/8285139/max-headroom-oral-history-80s-cyberpunk-interview. Accessed 29 Dec 2023
18. Neuenkirchen, A.: Kawaii Mania. CONBOOK Verlag, Japans niedlichste Abgründe, Neuss (2019)
19. Yoshino, K.: Cultural nationalism in contemporary Japan. a sociological enquiry, London; New York: Routledge (1992)
20. Yano, C.R.: Pink globalization: Hello Kitty's trek across the Pacific, Duke University Press. Durham, London (2013)
21. Nittono, H.: The two-layer model of 'kawaii'. A behavioural science framework for understanding kawaii and cuteness. East Asian J. Popular Culture 1(2), 79–95 (2016)
22. Lorenz, K.: Die angeborenen Formen möglicher Erfahrung. Zeitschrift f. Tierpsychologie 2(5), 246–409 (1942)
23. McVEigh, B.J.: Wearing Ideology. State, Schooling and Self-Presentation in Japan (=Dress, Body, Culture), Oxford; New York: Berg (2000)
24. Kinsella, S.: Cuties in Japan. In: Women, media and consumption in Japan (=Women, media and consumption in Japan, 2), Richmond, Curzon, pp. 220–254 (1995)
25. Sugano, S., Tomiyama, K.: Kawaii-ness in motion. In: Ohkura, M. Hrsg. Kawaii Engineering. Measurements, Evaluations, and Applications of Attractiveness (= Springer Series on Cultural Computing), Singapore, Springer, pp. 77–91 (2019)

Did the Pandemic Increase Social Media–Induced Appearance Pressures?

Outi Sarpila(✉) ⓘ, Aki Koivula ⓘ, and Erica Åberg ⓘ

University of Turku, Turku, Finland
`outi.sarpila@utu.fi`

Abstract. Has the use of social media intensified and increased appearance-related pressures during the Covid-19 pandemic? A growing body of research has suggested that body image concerns and disordered eating increased during the Covid-19 pandemic. One of the potential pathways includes an increase in social media use. However, examinations of this pathway have been limited because of the lack of longitudinal data. Drawing on a four-wave population-based survey (n = 543), we demonstrate that social media–based appearance pressures did not increase at the beginning of the pandemic but rather at the later stage and among women only. However, the changes in social media use do not explain this subtle increase. These findings suggest that the intensified use of social media itself may not have been the primary explanatory factor in the increased appearance-related pressures during the Covid-19 pandemic.

Keywords: Appearance Pressures · Covid-19 · Longitudinal Data · Gender · Social Media · Instagram · "Zoom effect"

1 Introduction

Numerous studies have indicated that individuals' connections with their bodies and physical appearances underwent a significant shift during the Covid-19 crisis. For instance, researchers have reported that disordered eating and body image concerns increased during the pandemic (e.g., Robertson et al., 2021; Swami et al., 2021). This surge in body and appearance concerns has been linked to heightened levels of general stress and anxiety stemming from social distancing and the uncertainties brought about by the crisis. Additionally, abrupt and forced alterations in people's eating and exercise routines have been identified as contributing factors (Cooper et al., 2022; Swami et al., 2021). Moreover, the pandemic reshaped the landscape of social media usage. With social distancing policies in effect, individuals increasingly turned to social media platforms to compensate for the absence of face-to-face interactions, fostering connections in various contexts such as school, work, and leisure. Additionally, social media became a primary channel for seeking information and entertainment (Gong et al., 2022; Kohvakka & Saarenmaa, 2021; Nguyen et al., 2021). The intensified social media use and consumption of appearance-based content, such as other people's selfies and training videos, as well as different modes of observance by the self and others, such as video calls and meetings (Pfund et al., 2020; Vall-Roqué et al., 2021), raised concerns about intensifying appearance concerns. Subsequent paragraphs, however, are indented.

Based on previous research on the pressures related to physical appearance and social media use, it is evident that social media is linked to appearance concerns. First, exposure to idealized images on social media has been associated with appearance dissatisfaction and eating disorders (e.g., Holland & Tiggemann, 2016; Tiggemann & Zinoviev, 2019). Second, users who engage in photo-based activities on social media are reported to have more body image concerns (for a review, see Saiphoo & Vahedi, 2019; Vandenbosch et al., 2022) and to experience greater appearance pressures related to social media (Åberg et al., 2020). Moreover, these concerns are more prevalent among Instagram users in particular (Åberg et al., 2020; Tiggemann et al., 2020), especially among younger women (Fardouly et al., 2015; Slater & Tiggemann, 2010; Tiggemann & Miller, 2010). However, examinations of the relationship between social media use and appearance pressures during the Covid-19 pandemic have been limited due to the lack of longitudinal data measuring social media use and appearance pressures at various stages of the pandemic.

This study delves into the impact of the Covid-19 pandemic on appearance pressures linked to people's use of social media. Our analysis is grounded in a comprehensive longitudinal population-based survey, enabling us to evaluate whether shifts in media-consumption practices had an immediate influence on individuals' encounters with appearance concerns. Furthermore, this research provides a valuable opportunity to validate existing theories regarding the connections between appearance-related pressures and social media usage.

2 Literature Review

2.1 Social Media and Appearance-Related Pressures

Physical appearance has become increasingly important in contemporary societies, and social media plays a significant role in this process. People are expected to look good in both private and public sectors of life, which undoubtedly creates pressures to conform to a certain appearance – that is, "the best versions" of ourselves, as claimed in the media (Sarpila et al., 2021; Widdows, 2018).

Among the most popular theoretical frameworks used to analyze the appearance pressures potentially caused by social media are the social comparison theory and objectification theory (for a review, see Tylka et al., 2023). According to the original idea of social comparison theory, individuals form perceptions of their own standing by comparing themselves to others in terms of characteristics they deem important (Festinger, 1954). Such comparisons can involve looking up to others (comparing to individuals perceived as more advantaged), looking down on others (comparing to individuals perceived as less advantaged), or making comparisons with those considered similar (comparing to individuals perceived as alike). Social comparison theory has subsequently been applied to the examination of appearance-based comparisons, especially in relation to media imagery. It has been suggested that unrealistic and idealized media images prompt individuals to compare themselves to others and, as a consequence, to experience appearance dissatisfaction (Åberg & Koivula, 2021), body image concerns

(Hogue & Mills, 2019), feelings of envy (Latif et al., 2021), and, in the context of social media, social media fatigue (Tandon et al., 2021). Objectification theory (Fredrickson & Roberts, 1997), on the other hand, identifies the media as a direct factor through which exposure to appearance-centric imagery serves as a means, especially by which girls and women learn to prioritize their physical appearance over other aspects of their identity. This involves internalizing certain observers' perspectives and perceiving oneself in objectified terms (e.g., Bell et al., 2018; for a review).

As highly visual platforms, social media networking sites constitute spaces for appearance-related comparison, which increase users' pressures and dissatisfaction with appearance (Åberg et al., 2020; Vandenbosch et al., 2022). Social media can more efficiently trigger these types of comparisons compared to traditional forms of media. Fardouly, Pinkus and Vartanian (2017) found women actually compared their appearances to those of others on social media more than other media sites, such as television, magazines, and billboards. Despite its alleged versatility, social media appearance comparisons are mostly done in an upwards direction (Festinger, 1954; for a review, see Gerber et al., 2018) unfavorable to oneself, resulting in lowered appearance satisfaction and, for example, increased thoughts and acts of dieting and exercising (Robinson et al., 2017; Tiggemann & Zaccardo, 2015). In addition, various other negative individual-level outcomes of social media use have been detected in previous research, such as body image concerns and disordered eating, which concern male and female social media users (for reviews, see Holland & Tiggemann, 2016; Saiphoo & Vahedi, 2019). Simultaneously, several studies have argued that social media is associated with body image and appearance concerns, especially among younger women (Åberg et al., 2020; Fardouly et al., 2015; Tiggemann & Miller, 2010; Tiggemann & Slater, 2013; e.g., Fardouly et al., 2015; Tiggemann and Miller, 2010; Tiggemann and Slater, 2013; Åberg et al., 2020).

However, the platform matters, as it has been reported that appearance concerns are more common among the female users of photo-based platforms, particularly Instagram (Åberg et al., 2020; Tiggemann et al., 2020; Vandenbosch et al., 2022). However, despite the well-documented negative outcomes of social media use, other scholars have also stressed the positive consequences of social media, emphasizing its possibilities for empowerment (Barnard, 2016; Kedzior et al., 2016; Tiidenberg & Gómez Cruz, 2015) and constructing valuable forms of social and cultural capital (Dobson, 2016). Moreover, Paasonen et al. (2020) contested the dominant conceptualization of social media through the object–subject binary in objectification theory by criticizing the conceptualization of women's behavior in overly simplified terms. Broadening this binary and critically assessing the previous claims may be particularly relevant during the pandemic, as most social interaction shifted to online platforms and virtual meetings. Less clear, however, is how and especially for whom the changes in social media use during the Covid-19 pandemic impacted appearance pressures.

2.2 Social Media and Appearance Pressures During the Covid-19 Pandemic

Despite the magnitude and causes of the pandemic on appearance-related pressures perplexing researchers and general audiences, existing research has not specifically answered these questions. However, based on previous research, we draw several hypotheses.

First, the pandemic increased social media use, which might amplify appearance-related pressures. From the first weeks of the pandemic, people increasingly turned to social media and messaging apps, especially video conferencing tools, for interaction (Nguyen et al., 2021). For example, the use of popular platforms, such as Facebook and Instagram, increased globally by up to 60% after the Covid-19 outbreak (Kantar, 2020). As previous research suggested the use of social media is associated with appearance concerns (for review, see Rodgers & Rousseau, 2022; Saiphoo & Vahedi, 2019), it is likely that the increase in social media use has increased perceived appearance pressure during the Covid-19 pandemic. These pressures have been likely to increase, especially during the pandemic's peak periods when appearance-related messaging saturated social media, such as "covibesity," which is weight gain during quarantine (Cooper et al., 2022; Schneider et al., 2022). Thus, we can assume that social media–based appearance pressures have increased during the pandemic.

Second, the intensified pressures to look a certain way might relate to changes in the use of particular social media platforms. As certain platforms, including Instagram and Snapchat, are based on consumption and production of photo-based content, they have been widely recognized as more severe sources of appearance pressures compared to the text-based platforms (Åberg et al., 2020; Vandenbosch et al., 2022). Hence, as the use of Instagram increased in the beginning of the Covid-19 pandemic, exposure to appearance-based content also grew. The pandemic also gave rise to novel appearance-focused campaigns in Instagram, including #quarantine15, the content of which was weight gain stigmatism (Lucibello et al., 2021).

Moreover, photo-based social media platforms and intensified digitalization, such as video chatting and conference tools, have affected the role of physical appearance, changing individuals' relationships with their faces and bodies. During the Covid-19 pandemic, people began to use video chatting in communication for work, education, and general socialization. It has been suggested that, as a consequence of increased use of video chatting, people have become more aware and, thus, more concerned about their physical appearances (Gullo & Walker, 2021; Thawanyarat et al., 2022). The phenomenon has also been referred to as the so-called "Zoom effect," and it has been utilized as a contextual narrative in certain research studies to elucidate descriptive findings related to the growing interest and acceptance of plastic surgery (Chen et al., 2021; Thawanyarat et al., 2022). The Zoom effect denotes the heightened awareness of one's own appearance that can emerge during the use of video conferencing tools, where users observe themselves (and their own appearance) through video, leading to an increased consciousness of their own physical appearance (Thawanyarat et al., 2022). In this respect, Pfund et al. (2020) studied the use of video chatting tools on appearance concerns. Using retrospective data and self-reporting, they concluded that, despite the increase in video chatting since the beginning of the pandemic, time spent on video chatting was not associated with appearance satisfaction.

Third, several studies on the Covid-19 pandemic's impact on body image and eating disorders have suggested that members of those social groups who were already at risk of experiencing higher appearance pressures are more at risk of intensified concerns during the pandemic (Pikoos et al., 2020; Zhou & Wade, 2021). Those studies that have concentrated on eating disorders have seen a drastic rise in disordered eating among those who have had tendencies for such pathologies before the pandemic (Brownstone et al., 2022 [qualitative]; Castellini et al., 2020 [longitudinal]; Flaudias et al., 2020 [cross-sectional]). In a cross-sectional retrospective Australian study, individuals with eating disorder backgrounds self-reported increased exercising, whereas self-reported exercising remained the same within the general population (Phillipou et al., 2020). Accordingly, Robertson et al. (2021) utilized a retrospective approach to analyze changes in people's attitudes toward their bodies and body regulation practices (i.e., eating and exercising during the pandemic). According to their study, the Covid-19 pandemic has impacted various social groups unequally in terms of body- and appearance-related concerns: women, young people, and people with a history of eating disorders, specifically self-reported changes in their thoughts and behaviors in relation to their bodies and appearances. Moreover, Vall-Rogué et al. (2021) confirmed that the lockdown had an impact on overall patterns of social media use, which are linked to an increased drive for thinness and eating disorder risk, especially among adolescent and young women. However, the results from the previous studies are somewhat inconsistent. Baceviciene and Jankauskiene (2021) found no body image or disordered eating changes in Lithuanian university students during the Covid-19 lockdown. Instead, they observed a significant increase in perceived appearance-related media pressures among female students but not among male ones.

In summary, drawing from prior research, it is reasonable to assume that heightened Instagram usage contributed to increased appearance pressures among the general population. Simultaneously, and once more relying on previous research, we have no reason to believe that video calls escalated these pressures. Instead, based on previous research, we posit that women, who inherently face greater appearance scrutiny and are active Instagram users, likely experienced a rise in appearance pressures during the pandemic.

3 Research Design

3.1 Context

Finland survived the first wave of the Covid-19 pandemic relatively well. Infections, need for intensive care, and mortality were low compared to other European countries (Oksanen et al., 2020). During the first wave, the Standby Act was introduced, and strict restrictions regulated people's mundane activities in many ways. Many public spaces closed; people worked and studied at home; and the government advised people to avoid social contacts. The epidemic calmed down during the summer 2020, and thereafter, the restrictions were quite lenient before the pandemic's second wave, which began in late autumn 2020. In the pandemic's second year, the government reintroduced slightly stricter restrictions in Finland in the spring (2021), but these were not as severe as in the previous year. At the end of 2021, there were many delta and omicron variants in Finland, which also threatened the carrying capacity of hospitals. However, the government made efforts to keep society as open as possible. Throughout the data collection period, the government and businesses recommended remote working in Finland, and people were to avoid social contact whenever possible.

Against this theoretical and practical information, we ask the following research questions:

- RQ1: Have appearance pressures from social media increased during the Covid-19 pandemic?
- RQ2: Does increased social media use explain the possible changes?
- RQ3: What is the role of (a) platform (Instagram vs. video conferencing) and (b) gender in explaining the possible changes?

3.2 Participants

Our research utilizes longitudinal data from the "Digital Age in Finland" survey, collected from 2017 to 2021. This survey series targeted Finnish individuals born between 1943 and 1999, employing a mix of random and convenience sampling methods. The first survey (T1), conducted in December 2017, involved 3,724 participants, 66% of whom were based on a randomly selected pool of 8,000 participants from the Finnish Population Register and 34% of whom were invited via an online panel of Taloustutkimus Oy. The first follow-up (T2), between March and April 2019, had 1,134 participants, a 30.5% response rate from T1. The second follow-up (T3), in May–June 2020, coincided with the early stages of the Covid-19 pandemic and involved 735 participants, achieving a 64.8% response rate. The final survey (T4), in December 2021, occurred amid ongoing Covid-19 restrictions and the Omicron variant surge, with 543 respondents and a 73.9% response rate.

Participants in the T1 study were recruited through postal invitations and a separate internet panel. For the T2–T4 surveys, the research team sent direct email invitations to participants who had provided their contact details in the previous data collection. The research team has followed the protocol of informed consent in tracking respondents and storing contact details over the data collections.

This study focuses exclusively on the 543 participants who engaged in all follow-up surveys, totaling 2,172 observations. This selection criterion ensures continuity, allowing for the analysis of the same individuals before and during various stages of the Covid-19 pandemic. Demographically, the dataset is reasonably representative in terms of age (mean = 48.1 years, SD = 15.5) and gender (52.8% male). However, it is noteworthy that the study's participants are predominantly well educated, with 48.3% holding college or university degrees, which is a significantly higher proportion than the population average of 35.5%.

3.3 Measures

In each survey, largely, the same main questionnaire was repeated to the respondents. T3 and T4 also had a separate section for the Covid-19-related questions. In this study, we followed Åberg et al. (2020) to measure appearance-related pressures in social media. The respondents were given a statement, "Social media sometimes causes me appearance-related pressures," with the following response options: 1 = *completely disagree*; 2; 3 = *do not disagree or agree*; 4; and 5 = *completely agree*. On the original scale, only 5% of responses fell into the top category; to guarantee enough participants for each category, we recoded the variable into three categories by combining values 1–2 into the category "Disagree," 3 into the category "Neutral," and 4–5 into the category "Agree."

We also considered *frequency of social media use* by asking respondents about their use frequency with different social network sites (e.g., Facebook, Twitter, and Instagram) according to a 5-point scale (1 = *never*; 2 = *less than weekly*; 3 = *weekly*; 4 = *daily*; and 5 = *many hours per day*). Moreover, we distinguished the effect of Instagram. *Frequency of Instagram use* was assessed on a 5-point scale (1 *never*; 2 = *less than weekly*; 3 = *weekly*; 4 = *daily*; and 5 = *many hours per day*). We asked questions about social media use and Instagram use in each round, which allowed us to assess the changing impact within and between individuals during the observation period by considering them as continuous and time-varying variables through the analyses.

In the second phase, we focused on the Zoom effect, assessing how frequently respondents used video calls for professional or study purposes. The responses were collected on a 5-point scale ranging from "never" to "many hours per day." For within-individual analysis, we condensed this into a three-point scale (1 = *never*; 2 = *less than weekly*; 3 = *at least weekly*), as less than 11% used video calls daily. We also used a continuous mean variable (consisting of the full scale) to assess the differences at the between-individual level. The question of video calls was introduced in the third survey, after the onset of Covid-19, enabling us to examine the Zoom effect during the pandemic but not the initial surge in video calling usage at the beginning of the pandemic.

Throughout the study, we considered the effects of gender and age. Age was accounted for in years. Gender was categorized as binary (0 = *male*, 1 = *female*) due to the minimal representation of other genders in the dataset. In the first stage, we explore the longitudinal associations by gender, taking advantage of our larger dataset that facilitates detailed subgroup analyses. In the second stage, as we shift our focus to the Zoom effect, we include both genders in the same model while specifically analyzing the differences in pressure experiences across genders.

3.4 Analysis Procedure

We began with descriptive statistics of applied variables across the measurement points. Then, we explored in detail how appearance-related pressures developed during the observation period within individuals (2017–2021). Moreover, we examined how the frequency of social media use and Instagram use corresponded to appearance-related pressures and how this relationship varied over time. In the second phase, we concentrated on the Zoom effect during the Covid-19 pandemic (2020–2021) by predicting appearance-related pressures according to the use of video calling for study or work purposes. The analysis in the second phase focused solely on those in employment or education (N = 293).

To analyze our categorical dependent variable on appearance-related pressure, which has three levels and responses nested within individuals, we employed a generalized mixed-effects model. Specifically, we utilized the random effects within-between model (Bell et al., 2019) to capture both within-individual and between-individual variations. This approach allows for the simultaneous assessment of fixed and random effects. Within-individual effects automatically control for time-invariant personal characteristics such as age, gender, and average social media use. These effects help to understand how changes in social media usage influence the perception of appearance pressure for each individual. On the other hand, between-individual differences examine how variations in average social media use across various individuals relate to their experiences of appearance pressure. The model calculates within-level effects by considering deviations from each respondent's mean, whereas between-level differences are derived from these individual means. Additionally, the model includes a random intercept for each individual. We conducted this analysis using the "meglcm" command in Stata (version 17).

4   Results

Table 1 shows the descriptive statistics of applied variables. The results show that appearance-related pressures increased among respondents between the last two points (T3–T4), from 14.5% to 17%. The use of Instagram also increased at the last measurement point, but the increase was more prominent between T2 and T3. There was also an increase in respondent participation in video calls between the last two measurements. In T3, during the first wave of the pandemic, approximately 52% participated in video calls at least sometimes, compared with 57% in T4.

Table 2 shows the multilevel models. The results of the first models show that appearance-related pressures on social media increased at the final time point, T4 (B = .53, p = .02), when compared to the T3. The within-level effects also show that increased use of SNS sites even reduced pressures, and no effects were observed for Instagram use. However, between-individual effects show that, on average, people who are active on Instagram experience more pressure than others. Results also confirmed that women experienced more pressures, as did younger respondents. It should also be noted that the assessment of the within-level effects of social media use behavior has little impact on the time effect observed at T4.

The coefficients in the following two models are estimated by gender. The results show that the increase in pressures in the last measurement was only observed among women (B = 0.59, p = 0.03). We further implemented a baseline model, considering the interaction of gender with the time point, but found no significant difference between genders (B = 0.24, p = 0.55), indicating no significant gender-based variation in how the experienced pressures developed throughout the surveys.

The within-level results also show that Instagram use did not have a simultaneous effect on pressure experienced by individuals of either gender, but the between-level effect was positive for both genders. On the other hand, an increase in the overall use of social media seems to be negatively related to pressure, particularly true for women.

The second phase of analysis examines the Zoom effect on appearance-related pressures among those in employment or education during the Covid-19 pandemic (2020–2021). We first implemented a baseline model for this subgroup, incorporating only time point t4 and control variables (age and gender). It showed that appearance pressures had also increased in this group over the last two measurements, but the effect was neither statistically significant nor as strong as in the previous analysis with all respondents (B = 0.44, p = 0.139).

Table 1. Descriptive Statistics for Study Variables.

Continuous variables	Range	T1 Mean (SD)	T2 Mean (SD)	T3 Mean (SD)	T4 Mean (SD)	Within SD	Between SD
Frequency of Instagram use (Instagram)	1–5	2.06 (1.28)	2.21 (1.34)	2.35 (1.37)	2.42 (1.40)	.53	1.24
Frequency of network site use (SNS)	1–5	3.05 (1.38)	3.09 (1.34)	3.09 (1.34)	3.15 (1.33)	.82	1.11
Video calls for working or educational purposes (Video calls)	1–5			1.93 (1.10)	2.02 (1.11)	.42	1.02
Birth cohort	1943–1999	1969 (15.6)	1969 (15.6)	1969 (15.6)	1969 (15.6)	0	15.6
Categorical variables	Range	T1%	T2%	T3%	T4%	Within SD	Between SD
Appearance-related pressure (disagree)	0–1	75.00	75.47	74.52	71.28	.24	.36
Appearance-related pressure (neutral)	0–1	10.04	8.39	10.83	11.74	.22	.20
Appearance-related pressure (agree)	0–1	14.96	16.14	14.65	16.98	.18	.30
Video calls (never)	0–1			47.97	42.51	.21	.45
Video calls (sometimes)	0–1			23.80	27.36	.23	.35
Video calls (weekly)	0–1			28.23	30.13	.20	.41
Gender: Female	0–1	47.2	47.2	47.2	47.2	.00	.50
Observations: 2,172; Individuals: 543							

The first model, presented in Table 3, suggests that irregular participation in video calls is associated with increased appearance-related pressures (B = 1.49, p = .036). However, this effect was not significant for those who participated on a weekly basis. Based on our further analysis and comparison of the baseline model and model with video calls, only 9.1% of the increase in appearance-related pressures could be attributed to the use of video calls during the last two measurements.

Table 2. Generalized Multilevel Mixed Effect Models Predicting Social Media-Caused Appearance-Related Pressures 2017–2021.

	Total		Males		Females	
VARIABLES	B	CI 95%	B	CI 95%	B	CI 95%
Within-level effects						
Time (T3 ref.) T1	−0.05	−0.49–0.40	−0.23	−0.94–0.49	0.14	−0.44–0.73
T2	−0.04	−0.47–0.40	−0.50	−1.20–0.21	0.25	−0.31–0.81
T4	0.53*	0.11–0.95	0.41	−0.28–1.09	0.61*	0.07–1.15
SNS	−0.33*	−0.66−−0.01	−0.02	−0.54–0.49	−0.53*	−0.97−−0.10
Instagram	0.02	−0.28–0.31	−0.18	−0.67–0.30	0.17	−0.21–0.54
Between-level effects						
SNS	0.05	−0.32–0.43	−0.23	−0.82–0.35	0.23	−0.29–0.75
Instagram	0.92***	0.58–1.26	1.05***	0.51–1.60	0.83***	0.38–1.28
Birth year	0.09***	0.07–0.12	0.06**	0.02–0.10	0.11***	0.08–0.15
Female	2.19***	1.50–2.87				
Random effect parameters:						
ICC	0.71	0.64–0.78	0.73	0.61–0.82	0.71	0.62–0.79
Variance (constant)	8.30	5.95–11.60	8.83	5.15–15.14	8.56	5.28–12.60
Observations	1,872		954		918	
Individuals	516		270		248	

*** $p < 0.001$, ** $p < 0.01$, * $p < 0.05$

The second model presented in Table 2 introduces the within-and between-level variables for social media use and Instagram use. After adjusting for these confounding variables, the effect of video call participation decreases; however, participation (B = 1.27, p = .073) remains associated with increased appearance-related pressures.

Across all models in Tables 2 and 3, the intraclass correlations were consistent, ranging from 0.70 to 0.80. These results indicate that a significant proportion, around 70–80%, of the variation in appearance pressures, is attributable to differences between individuals rather than to within-individual variation across measurement points.

Table 3. Generalized Multilevel Mixed Effect Models Predicting Social Media-Caused Appearance-Related Pressures According to Video Calling.

VARIABLES	M1 B	M1 CI95%	M2 B	M2 CI95%
Within-level effects				
Time (Ref = T3)				
T4	0.40	−0.21–1.00	0.51	−0.11–1.13
Video calls (Ref: Never)				
Sometimes	1.49*	0.10–2.89	1.27	−0.12–2.67
Weekly	0.85	−0.91–2.62	0.81	−0.98–2.61
Social media use			−0.06	−0.71–0.59
Instagram			−0.81	−1.64–0.03
Between−level effects				
Video calling			−0.43	−1.27–0.41
Instagram			1.16***	0.56–1.76
Social media use			0.28	−0.48–1.04
Female	3.83***	2.33–5.34	3.03***	1.76–4.30
Birth year	0.27***	0.18–0.35	0.20***	0.13–0.27
Random effect parameters				
ICC	0.80	0.63–0.90	0.75	0.57–0.87
Variance (constant)	8.74	2.40–15.08	9.79	2.12–17.45
Observations	530		530	
Number of groups	293		293	

Note: Models include only participants who were employed or students at the survey time; *** p < 0.001, ** p < 0.01, * p < 0.05

5   Discussion and Conclusion

This study focused on the possible pathway between social media use and social media–induced appearance pressures during the Covid-19 pandemic. Previous research on disordered eating and body image concerns has suggested that individuals' relationships to their bodies and physical appearances had changed under the pandemic's unique circumstances (e.g., Robertson et al., 2021; Swami et al., 2021). The intensified social media use and appearance-based content consumption as an immediate reaction to the global health crisis, as well as changing modes of observance by the self and others (e.g., video calls and meetings), have raised concerns about intensified appearance pressures (for a discussion, see Pfund et al., 2020; Vall-Roqué et al., 2021). However, it has been difficult to assess the link between previously reported changes in social media use and possibly increased appearance pressures during the pandemic without longitudinal data. To our knowledge, utilizing novel panel data representing the Finnish population, this study is one of the first to assess whether changed social media–consumption practices during the pandemic impacted people's perception of social media–induced appearance concerns among the general population.

Our study suggests that, although perceived social media–based appearance pressures increased during the Covid-19 pandemic, the increase was very subtle and did not take place immediately after the pandemic's outbreak. Moreover, we did not find evidence supporting the claim that intensified general social media use or the increase in Instagram or video call use would have caused this change in perceived pressures. In addition, the statistically significant increase in experienced appearance pressures applied only to female social media users.

Our study demonstrates how a historic period such as the Covid-19 pandemic cannot change the status quo regarding the gendered "tone" of appearance pressures. Throughout history, women's appearances have been under more serious scrutiny than men's have, causing more severe social complications than those concerning men. Overall, our results confirmed the well-established notion that female users of social media are more likely to experience appearance-related pressures on photo-based social media than male users are (Åberg et al., 2020; Åberg & Koivula, 2021; Vandenbosch et al., 2022). Although the changes in the use of social media did not explain changes in these pressures, consumption and production of appearance-centered content online may result in self-objectification and social comparison (cf. Pfund et al., 2020). This likely applies particularly to female users of photo-based social media. For example, #quarantine15, an appearance-focused campaign on Instagram during the pandemic, was predominantly about pictures of lower-weight, White women (Lucibello et al., 2021). Generally, the motivation and methods of using the same visual platforms might vary significantly between different users of social media, producing concerns for specific social user groups. Previous research has established such differences, such as those in surveillance or knowledge about others, documentation of one's own life, exhibiting coolness, or showing creativity (Sheldon & Bryant, 2016). These types of individual motivations might be behind the experienced pressures and are not included in this study.

One possible explanation for the slight increase in appearance pressures could also be an increase in the public debate on the topic during the pandemic (Cooper et al., 2022; Goldman, 2020; cf. Schneider et al., 2022). It might be that it is socially more acceptable to report experiencing appearance pressures on social media, especially for females, to whom the discussion about concerns is also more often related and who, according to previous studies, experience more appearance pressures than men do (for a review, see Vandenbosch et al., 2022).

In the light of our results, it seems that the arguments about the role of the Zoom effect in causing appearance pressures (Pikoos et al., 2020; Thawanyarat et al., 2022) have also assumed too much. Our results show that, in the first wave of the pandemic, attending video conferencing calls was associated with appearance pressures. However, active use seems to have equalized these experiences, and an increase in the use of video calls did not explain the increase in appearance pressures. Again, different motivations and methods of using the tool are likely more important in terms of explaining appearance pressures than the use of this tool per se (Gullo & Walker, 2021; Pfund et al., 2020). Future research should study these individual differences to see how these motivational factors protect or expose individuals to social media pressures. Furthermore, researchers should assess how these individual-level motivations are related to different offline inequalities; for example, Instagram is certainly not only about gender but also social class power struggles (e.g., Lamont & Ross, 2020). In terms of appearance pressures, having cultural capital and feeling that one is "doing it right" in the visual platforms may play a significant role in the magnitude of experiencing pressures and even feeling empowerment (cf. Barnard, 2016).

Our research also presents certain limitations. We recognize that responses based on self-reporting may be influenced by social desirability bias, where individuals tend to provide answers that seek social approval (Krumpal, 2013). Additionally, our measure of appearance pressures, being a single-item variable, differs from the multi-item measures used in many previous studies. However, the strength of this variable lies in its four measuring points and its consistency in gauging individual, within-level stability in appearance pressures over time. It is important to note that our study is subject to limitations due to potential selection bias and generalizability concerns. Firstly, despite the data's relative comprehensiveness and representation of the Finnish adult population, our ability to assess temporal changes was limited to approximately 500 respondents. Consequently, the data did not allow for the exploration of various interactions.

To conclude, this study suggests that the relationship between social media and appearance pressures is more multifaceted than typically understood. Even a global crisis, when people increasingly turned to social media, does not automatically increase perceived appearance pressures caused by social media use, increased Instagram use, or video calls. It also appears that the Covid-19 pandemic has not been the great "equalizer" of appearance pressures. On the contrary, it seems that gender differences have become even wider during the pandemic, as a subtle increase in pressure experiences takes place among female social media users.

References

Åberg, E., Koivula, A.: The ouroboros of seeking validation? Exploring the interconnection of appearance (dis) satisfaction and content creation on social media. In: Sarpila, O., Kukkonen, I., Pajunen, T., Åberg, E. (eds.) Appearance as Capital, pp. 117–134. Emerald Publishing Limited, Bingley (2021)

Åberg, E., Koivula, A., Kukkonen, I.: A feminine burden of perfection? Appearance-related pressures on social networking sites. Telemat. Inform. **46**, 101319 (2020)

Baceviciene, M., Jankauskiene, R.: Changes in sociocultural attitudes towards appearance, body image, eating attitudes and behaviours, physical activity, and quality of life in students before and during COVID-19 lockdown. Appetite **166**, 105452 (2021)

Barnard, S.R.: Spectacles of self (ie) empowerment? Networked individualism and the logic of the (post) feminist selfie. In: Communication and Information Technologies Annual, pp. 63–88. Emerald Group Publishing Limited, Leeds (2016)

Bell, A., Fairbrother, M., Jones, K.: Fixed and random effects models: making an informed choice. Qual. Quant. **53**(2), 1051–1074 (2019)

Bell, B.T., Cassarly, J.A., Dunbar, L.: Selfie-objectification: self-objectification and positive feedback ("likes") are associated with frequency of posting sexually objectifying self-images on social media. Body Image **26**, 83–89 (2018)

Brownstone, L.M., et al.: "Are people thinking I'm a vector... because I'm fat?": cisgender experiences of body, eating, and identity during COVID-19. Body Image **40**, 256–266 (2022)

Castellini, G., et al.: The impact of COVID-19 epidemic on eating disorders: a longitudinal observation of pre versus post psychopathological features in a sample of patients with eating disorders and a group of healthy controls. Int. J. Eat. Disord. **53**(11), 1855–1862 (2020)

Chen, J., et al.: The zoom boom: how video calling impacts attitudes towards aesthetic surgery in the COVID-19 era. Aesthet. Surg. J. **41**(12), NP2086–NP2093 (2021)

Cooper, M., et al.: Eating disorders during the COVID-19 pandemic and quarantine: an overview of risks and recommendations for treatment and early intervention. Eat. Disord. **30**(1), 54–76 (2022)

Dobson, A.S.: Postfeminist Digital Cultures: Femininity, Social Media, and Self-Representation. Springer, New York (2016)

Fardouly, J., Diedrichs, P.C., Vartanian, L.R., Halliwell, E.: Social comparisons on social media: the impact of Facebook on young women's body image concerns and mood. Body Image **13**, 38–45 (2015)

Fardouly, J., Pinkus, R.T., Vartanian, L.R.: The impact of appearance comparisons made through social media, traditional media, and in person in women's everyday lives. Body Image **20**, 31–39 (2017)

Festinger, L.: A theory of social comparison processes. Hum. Relat. **7**(2), 117–140 (1954)

Flaudias, V., et al.: COVID-19 pandemic lockdown and problematic eating behaviors in a student population. J. Behav. Addict. **9**(3), 826–835 (2020)

Gerber, J., Wheeler, L., Suls, J.: A social comparison theory meta-analysis 60+ years on. Psychol. Bull. **144**(2), 177–197 (2018)

Fredrickson, B.L., Roberts, T.-A.: Objectification theory: toward understanding women's lived experiences and mental health risks. Psychol. Women Q. **21**(2), 173–206 (1997)

Goldman, L.: The inescapable pressure of being a woman on Zoom. Vox, (2020). https://www.vox.com/the-highlight/2020/5/13/21248632/work-from-home-zoom-women-appearance-beauty-no-makeup

Gong, J., Firdaus, A., Said, F., Ali Aksar, I., Danaee, M., Xu, J.: Pathways linking media use to wellbeing during the COVID-19 pandemic: a mediated moderation study. Soc. Media Soc. **8**(1), 20563051221087390 (2022)

Gullo, N., Walker, D.C.: Increased videoconferencing after COVID-19 stay-at-home orders increased depression and anxiety but did not impact appearance satisfaction or binge eating. Comput. Hum. Behav. Rep. **3**, 100080 (2021)

Hogue, J.V., Mills, J.S.: The effects of active social media engagement with peers on body image in young women. Body Image **28**, 1–5 (2019)

Holland, G., Tiggemann, M.: A systematic review of the impact of the use of social networking sites on body image and disordered eating outcomes. Body Image **17**, 100–110 (2016)

Kantar. COVID-19 barometer: consumer attitudes, media habits and expectations (2020). https://www.kantar.com/inspiration/coronavirus/covid-19-barometer-consumer-attitudes-media-habits-and-expectations

Kedzior, R., Allen, D.E., Schroeder, J.: The selfie phenomenon–consumer identities in the social media marketplace. Eur. J. Mark. **50**(9/10), 1767–1772 (2016)

Kohvakka, R., Saarenmaa, K.: Median merkitys on kasvanut pandemian aikana – monet ikäihmiset ovat ottaneet melkoisen digiloikan | Tieto&trendit. Tilastokeskus (2021). https://www2.tilastokeskus.fi:443/tietotrendit/artikkelit/2021/median-merkitys-on-kasvanut-pandemian-aikana-monet-ikaihmiset-ovat-ottaneet-melkoisen-digiloikan/

Krumpal, I.: Determinants of social desirability bias in sensitive surveys: a literature review. Qual. Quant. **47**(4), 2025–2047 (2013)

Lamont, M., Ross, A.S.: Deconstructing embedded meaning within cyclists' Instagram discourse: #fromwhereiride. Ann. Leis. Res. **23**(3), 339–363 (2020)

Latif, K., et al.: Social comparison as a double-edged sword on social media: the role of envy type and online social identity. Telemat. Inform. **56**, 101470 (2021)

Lucibello, K.M., Vani, M.F., Koulanova, A., deJonge, M.L., Ashdown-Franks, G., Sabiston, C.M.: #quarantine15: a content analysis of Instagram posts during COVID-19. Body Image **38**, 148–156 (2021)

Nguyen, M.H., Gruber, J., Marler, W., Hunsaker, A., Fuchs, J., Hargittai, E.: Staying connected while physically apart: digital communication when face-to-face interactions are limited. New Media Soc. **24**(9), 2024–2067 (2021)

Oksanen, A., Kaakinen, M., Latikka, R., Savolainen, I., Savela, N., Koivula, A.: Regulation and trust: 3-month follow-up study on COVID-19 mortality in 25 European countries. JMIR Public Health Surveill. **6**(2), e19218 (2020)

Paasonen, S., Attwood, F., McKee, A., Mercer, J., Smith, C.: Objectification: On the Difference Between Sex and Sexism. Routledge, London (2020)

Pfund, G.N., Hill, P.L., Harriger, J.: Video chatting and appearance satisfaction during COVID-19: appearance comparisons and self-objectification as moderators. Int. J. Eat. Disord. **53**(12), 2038–2043 (2020)

Phillipou, A., et al.: Eating and exercise behaviors in eating disorders and the general population during the COVID-19 pandemic in Australia: initial results from the COLLATE project. Int. J. Eat. Disord. **53**(7), 1158–1165 (2020)

Pikoos, T.D., Buzwell, S., Sharp, G., Rossell, S.L.: The COVID-19 pandemic: psychological and behavioral responses to the shutdown of the beauty industry. Int. J. Eat. Disord. **53**(12), 1993–2002 (2020)

Robertson, M., Duffy, F., Newman, E., Prieto Bravo, C., Ates, H.H., Sharpe, H.: Exploring changes in body image, eating and exercise during the COVID-19 lockdown: a UK survey. Appetite **159**, 105062 (2021)

Robinson, L., Prichard, I., Nikolaidis, A., Drummond, C., Drummond, M., Tiggemann, M.: Idealised media images: the effect of fitspiration imagery on body satisfaction and exercise behaviour. Body Image **22**, 65–71 (2017)

Rodgers, R.F., Rousseau, A.: Social media and body image: modulating effects of social identities and user characteristics. Body Image **41**, 284–291 (2022)

Saiphoo, A.N., Vahedi, Z.: A meta-analytic review of the relationship between social media use and body image disturbance. Comput. Hum. Behav. **101**, 259–275 (2019)

Sarpila, O., Kukkonen, I., Pajunen, T., Åberg, E.: Appearance as Capital: The Normative Regulation of Aesthetic Capital Accumulation and Conversion. Emerald Group Publishing, Bingley (2021)

Schneider, J., et al.: A mixed-studies systematic review of the experiences of body image, disordered eating, and eating disorders during the COVID-19 pandemic. Int. J. Eat. Disord, (2022)

Sheldon, P., Bryant, K.: Instagram: motives for its use and relationship to narcissism and contextual age. Comput. Hum. Behav. **58**, 89–97 (2016)

Slater, A., Tiggemann, M.: Body image and disordered eating in adolescent girls and boys: a test of objectification theory. Sex Roles **63**(1), 42–49 (2010)

Swami, V., Horne, G., Furnham, A.: COVID-19-related stress and anxiety are associated with negative body image in adults from the United Kingdom. Pers. Individ. Differ. **170**, 110426 (2021)

Tandon, A., Dhir, A., Talwar, S., Kaur, P., Mäntymäki, M.: Dark consequences of social media-induced fear of missing out (FoMO): social media stalking, comparisons, and fatigue. Technol. Forecast. Soc. Change. **171**, 120931 (2021)

Thawanyarat, K., Francis, S., Kim, T., Arquette, C., Morrison, S., Nazerali, R.: The Zoom effect: a Google trends analysis. Aesthet. Surg. J. **42**(1), NP76–NP82 (2022)

Tiggemann, M., Anderberg, I., Brown, Z.: Uploading your best self: selfie editing and body dissatisfaction. Body Image **33**, 175–182 (2020)

Tiggemann, M., Miller, J.: The internet and adolescent girls' weight satisfaction and drive for thinness. Sex Roles **63**(1), 79–90 (2010)

Tiggemann, M., Slater, A.: NetGirls: the internet, Facebook, and body image concern in adolescent girls. Int. J. Eat. Disord. **46**(6), 630–633 (2013)

Tiggemann, M., Zaccardo, M.: "Exercise to be fit, not skinny": the effect of fitspiration imagery on women's body image. Body Image **15**, 61–67 (2015)

Tiggemann, M., Zinoviev, K.: The effect of# enhancement-free Instagram images and hashtags on women's body image. Body Image **31**, 131–138 (2019)

Tiidenberg, K., Gómez Cruz, E.: Selfies, image and the re-making of the body. Body Soc. **21**(4), 77–102 (2015)

Tylka, T.L., Rodgers, R.F., Calogero, R.M., Thompson, J.K., Harriger, J.A.: Integrating social media variables as predictors, mediators, and moderators within body image frameworks: Potential mechanisms of action to consider in future research. Body Image **44**, 197–221 (2023)

Vall-Roqué, H., Andrés, A., Saldaña, C.: The impact of COVID-19 lockdown on social network sites use, body image disturbances and self-esteem among adolescent and young women. Prog. Neuro-Psychopharmacol. Biol. Psychiatry. **110**, 110293 (2021)

Vandenbosch, L., Fardouly, J., Tiggemann, M.: Social media and body image: recent trends and future directions. Curr. Opin. Psychol. **45**, 101289 (2022)

Widdows, H.: Perfect Me. Princeton University Press, Chicago (2018)

Zhou, Y., Wade, T.D.: The impact of COVID-19 on body-dissatisfied female university students. Int. J. Eat. Disord. **54**(7), 1283–1288 (2021)

It's a (Mis)match: Practices and Perceptions of University Students About Online Dating

Eshang Shah⍟, Abhinav Rana⍟, Saumik Shashwat(✉)⍟, Sahil Deshpande⍟,
and Sachleen Kaur⍟

Indraprastha Institute of Information Technology Delhi, New Delhi, India
{eshang20405,abhinav20353,saumik20404,sahil20114
sachleen19326}@iiitd.ac.in

Abstract. Dating and traditional matchmaking practices have now been replaced by the transient and evolving landscape of online dating. Applications such as Bumble, Hinge, and Tinder strive to outdo each other in introducing features and design elements to cater to user needs. However, the utilisation of these apps differs significantly from how individuals engage with other interpersonal computer-mediated interactions, such as social media platforms. Through this study, we set to understand the practices and perceptions of university-going students regarding online dating platforms and how they can be used to model effective interactions. The user study employs a mixed-method approach, including an online survey with 72 respondents and 11 semi-structured interviews. The paper also encompasses a competitive study where the researchers compared existing dating platforms based on a set of parameters.

Keywords: Human-Computer Interaction · Quantitative and Qualitative Research · Online Dating · Computer Mediated Communication

1 Introduction

Online dating platforms/applications (used interchangeably in this paper) have gained prominence over the past few decades, transforming how people connect and form romantic relationships [3,9]. These technologies, established on peer-to-peer communication systems, offer service touch-points like location-based matchmaking and Computer-Mediated Communication.

With the onboarding of a diverse set of users, online dating applications and websites have worked on their architectures to satisfy user needs [6]. From robust mental models to manipulations referencing the phases involved in offline dating, these platforms have contributed to representing themselves as digital matchmakers.

© The Author(s), under exclusive license to Springer Nature Switzerland AG 2024
A. Coman and S. Vasilache (Eds.): HCII 2024, LNCS 14703, pp. 250–265, 2024.
https://doi.org/10.1007/978-3-031-61281-7_17

However, the perceptions and practices surrounding online dating services, their efficacy in satisfying user needs, and usability have been the subject of many discussions and critiques. While previous literature has extensively examined accessibility criteria, design considerations, and technological implications associated with online dating platforms, a notable gap exists in understanding the intrinsic user behaviours and usage patterns within these platforms [4, 6, 9].

This paper examines the standard practices and perceptions of university-going students regarding online dating services and platforms, using a mixed methods approach involving quantitative and qualitative methodologies. Focusing this study on university students offers several advantages. Universities serve as hubs of diversity [7], housing various individuals with diverse backgrounds and perspectives. Exploring the attitudes and behaviours of this diverse demographic offers valuable insights into the landscape of online dating. This study primarily addresses the following research questions:

RQ1- What are university-going students' everyday practices and perceptions surrounding dating and online dating?
RQ2- How do the observed differences evolve over the different stages of online dating?

2 Background

2.1 Online Dating and Its Phases

Matchmaking or searching for a romantic partner has transitioned over the last decade and is now offered as a service on an application or website. Platforms like Bumble, Tinder, and Grindr have grown significantly in their user base in this period [3]. Initially designed for location-based matchmaking and aiding the communication between the users, these platforms are now being used for recreational purposes like self-evaluation and gazing at attractive profiles [13].

Some argue that online dating has led to an increase in what has been called *"romantic consumerism,"* by Yuval Noah Harari, where individuals are treated as products that can be bought and sold in the dating market. The abundance of potential matches on such web/app-based platforms seeks the advent of explicit processes or phases involved in match-making. The online dating process unfolds across three stages: **before, during, and after the match**. Each phase is intricately designed with specific roles and responsibilities for technology, shaping the user experience and influencing the outcomes of romantic connections [9].

Authors in [9] highlight how the initial pre-match phase sets the groundwork for users to create profiles, providing information about themselves, such as interests, hobbies, and location. Authentication of user information is paramount during this stage to minimise instances of catfishing, further emphasising the importance of verifying the accuracy of user-provided data.

During the match phase, the focus shifts to connecting users who have expressed mutual interests. Platforms leverage algorithms to recommend matches based on user profiles and preferences with additional tools and features to aid them in connecting with potential matches [9].

Following a successful match, online dating platforms transition to assisting users in sustaining interactions and developing connections. Despite the importance of this phase, existing literature needs to emphasise exploring the roles and responsibilities of technology that can be further optimised to facilitate a smooth transition from an online space to a physical meetup [12].

2.2 University Students and Dating

University students experience a pivotal transition from high school to college, marked by academic challenges and social adjustments [1]. Common conditions like social anxiety can hinder this process, impeding participation in cultural events, forming friendships, and seeking support. For university students, online dating and social platforms can offer a valuable means of connecting and potentially overcoming social anxiety. Moreover, integrated with social media, these platforms involve friend recommendations, which can enhance matchmaking transparency and engagement with trusted friends' suggestions.

2.3 Practices and Perceptions

In the contemporary landscape of dating apps, user motivations extend well beyond the quest for romantic connections, as highlighted by Zytko et al. in [13]. With diversifying motivations such as friendship and business connections, these platforms house evolving practices and perceptions surrounding their use. The study insights unveil challenges users face in presenting and evaluating interaction goals. Notably, the identified strategies for conveying these goals range from direct statements to subtle signals, with implications for potential misinterpretation and risks. Furthermore, these platforms are also passively used for self-evaluation and gazing at appealing profiles for content consumption.

2.4 Trustworthiness of Online Dating Platforms

The landscape of online dating, a form of Computer-Mediated Interaction (CMI) [5], necessitates a nuanced exploration of trust. Unlike business CMIs, where reputation systems are foundational, online dating platforms present unique challenges in establishing trust. Reputation models, prevalent in business CMIs, have limited effectiveness in personal CMIs, particularly within the diverse and subjective realm of online dating [9].

Online dating platforms rely on multimedia cues and reputation-based prompts to foster trust. Visual and auditory cues are indispensable in building trust between users and the technology. Finkel et al. in [5] note the challenges of relying solely on visual and auditory cues in an online environment, where these cues can be easily manipulated. Nevertheless, they remain crucial for creating a sense of connection and comfort. Building both interpersonal and brand trust is essential to ensure the sustainability of online dating services, reflecting the significance of trust in shaping user experiences [2].

2.5   Privacy and Data Security

Privacy within dating apps encompasses protection from fellow users and the overarching corporations that own the apps. Users share significant information, including sensitive details about religion, sexuality, and location, making them direct stakeholders in online dating applications' privacy and data security [8]. Furthermore, abandoning these platforms by users upon awkward encounters with undesired profiles like those of colleagues or acquaintances has also become a common practice [4], which directly emphasises why these platforms should be data-protected.

While dating app users seek compatibility through information disclosure, the risk of unanticipated sharing persists, whether through data breaches or users divulging information and screenshots. Platforms like Bumble offer free incognito or anonymous modes to empower user control, allowing users to restrict profile visibility.

3   Methodology

Our study employed an integrated mixed-method research design [10], seamlessly incorporating both quantitative and qualitative approaches to enhance the comprehensiveness and depth of the study. A subset of the authors of this work also competitively analysed popular online dating platforms.

The quantitative component encompassed a survey to collect participants' socio-demographic information and details about their preferences and utilisation of online dating platforms. This contained variables such as occupation, relationship status, and sexuality. The qualitative aspect involved conducting semi-structured in-person interviews, ranging from half an hour to one hour. These interviews aimed to explore participants' motivations and willingness to engage with dating apps, encouraging discussions on their past experiences with matchmaking and sharing insights into their success rates.

The snowballing technique [11] facilitated interview sessions and distributed the survey across various universities. This strategic approach maximised the sample size, ensuring a more extensive dataset. The expanded dataset enabled a more thorough data analysis, contributing to the richness of the research findings.

3.1   Competitive Analysis

In light of the contemporary saturation of dating applications offering diverse functionalities and introducing many new features, a subset of three authors from our group (two male members, M1 and M2; one female member, F1) conducted a comprehensive competitive analysis involving seven apps. The group analysed four international platforms: Tinder, Bumble, Hinge, and Grindr, and one Indian-origin platform, Aisle.

They conducted an initial examination to categorise the apps based on their primary dating objectives: Relationships and Hookups. However, it was observed that some apps served both targets. Over a month, our group operated each app extensively, scrutinising aspects such as the profile-building processes, user experience (UX), user demographics, available features, and the degree of personal expression allowed. A critical evaluation of the strengths and weaknesses of each app was performed, incorporating personal experiences and user interactions. The assessment encompassed interface aspects such as usability, aesthetics, learnability, and affordance. Additionally, the security measures implemented by the apps were scrutinised, particularly in safeguarding users against inappropriate messages and unsolicited content.

Each member of this group created accounts for the respective apps, adopting the user perspective to gain first-hand insights into potential frustrations encountered by the user base. Any interactions conducted within the research context were explicitly informed and consensual. No data derived from these exchanges is disclosed in the research findings. The apps were downloaded from the App Store/Play Store on iOS/Android and were last updated as of 9 May 2023.

3.2   Online Survey

After getting ethical approval from the university's Institutional Review Board (IRB), we conducted an extensive online survey targeting University students transitioning from High School to College. This survey aimed to capture the mindset of Indian university students and help us glean insights into their experience and expectations with online dating apps. The form was created using Google Forms and floated via social media and email.

Informed consent was obtained from all participants before the studies were conducted, and they were informed that they could withdraw from the study at any time without penalty. The survey was meticulously designed to explore and provide insights into the research questions centred around understanding university-going students' daily practices and perceptions regarding dating and online dating. Employing a Likert scale ranging from "strongly agree" to "strongly disagree," participants were prompted to express their sentiments and attitudes, allowing for a nuanced exploration of their views on the subject matter. This methodological approach aimed to capture the spectrum of opinions and behaviours among the surveyed population, contributing to a comprehensive understanding of the multifaceted dynamics surrounding dating practices in university life.

3.3   Semi-structured Interviews

Following the extensive survey providing preliminary context about university students' behavioural patterns and preferences regarding online dating, we conducted semi-structured interviews with a subset of survey participants. The inclusion criteria were being a current university student aged 19–22, willing to participate in the study, and participating in the preceding online survey.

We conducted 11 semi-structured in-person interviews with university students [8M, 3F]. The interviews were designed to elicit detailed and nuanced responses from the participants about their experiences and perspectives. We followed the IRB-approved semi-structured interview guide prepared by us and asked questions based on the context and pace of the conversation.

The interviews lasted between 30 and 80 min and were audio-recorded with the participant's consent. The open-ended interview questions allowed participants to share their experiences and perspectives freely. The interview questions were pilot-tested with a small group of students before the main study to ensure they were clear and relevant.

4   Results

4.1   Competitive Analysis

Bumble

- **Insights from M1:** Bumble has established a robust user base in India, reflecting diverse preferences and prioritising women's safety and feminist principles. Notably, the app offers an anonymous mode restricting profile visibility to "right-swiped" individuals, ensuring user privacy. In-built features encompass voice and video calling, message replies, preset icebreaker questions, and interactive games like "Never Have I Ever." Collaborative efforts with Spotify aim to attract users with similar music tastes. Bumble's user-friendly interface aligns with conventional dating apps, but the 24-hour messaging constraint impacts usability, especially given busy lifestyles. The inability to correct accidental swipes in the free version is counterintuitive.
- **Insights from M2:** Profile verification is optional but visibly denoted by a blue tick and a "Verified Only" filter on the profile page. Bumble's onboarding process is accessible, with relaxed restrictions, positioning itself beyond a mere dating app by associating with social verification. Privacy measures include the option to conceal first names. Unmatching notifications are issued if significant chat history exists, and reporting prompts account review.
- **Insights from F1:** Unverified profiles present a potential risk of impersonation, particularly across gender lines, as individuals, primarily males, may adopt fictitious female identities. This dynamic introduces concerns regarding possible misuse and the prevalence of catfishing threats. Privacy features, such as incognito mode, mitigate these risks by limiting profile visibility. Notably, Bumble's recent updates, such as Thursday speed dating, exemplify the platform's ongoing commitment to enhancing user engagement and overall experience.

General Perception: One key differentiator is Bumble's unique approach to initiating conversations. In heterosexual matches, only women can make the first move, allowing them more control over their interactions and promoting a women-first dynamic. This feature often appeals to individuals seeking a dating environment that aligns with feminist principles.

Hinge

- **Insights from M1:** Hinge emphasises user engagement by encouraging responses to prompts and images, fostering genuine banter from initial interactions. This approach deters mindless swiping, necessitating thoughtful profile examination. Detailed filters encompassing zodiac signs, ethnicity, and preferences facilitate precise matchmaking. The app's unique feature allows users to backtrack and review previously skipped profiles, promoting a deliberate selection process. Despite a smaller user base than Bumble and Tinder, Hinge maintains a serious tone in the context of relationships. Post-matching incentives, however, are limited, offering minimal encouragement for sustained conversations beyond initial prompts. Mandatory photo uploads during sign-up may pose discomfort, and the app prohibits sharing pictures within the chat.
- **Insights from M2:** Creating a Hinge profile entails mandatory actions, including uploading six photos and responding to prompts, contributing to a more serious and committed user pool. Privacy features include concealing the first name with only the initial letter displayed. Users can also manage their online activity status. Unmatching ensures that profiles do not reencounter each other, preserving user privacy.
- **Insights from F1:** Hinge's user-friendly interface caters to a diverse audience, spanning teens, millennials, and individuals with children. The app facilitates interactions based on specific interests, easing conversation initiation without concerns about preferred topics. Visibility of nearby and newly joined users enhances the app's social dynamics.

General Perception: Hinge stands out for its emphasis on fostering meaningful connections and relationships rather than casual encounters. The app's design encourages users to showcase their personality through prompts and detailed profiles, promoting more thoughtful interactions.

Tinder

- **Insights from M1:** Tinder incorporates various integrations, such as Snapchat and WhatsApp, enabling users to share their profiles seamlessly. Recognising the significance of music in matchmaking, Tinder collaborates with Spotify, allowing users to set anthems and share songs in chats. Unique "Tags," including personality indicators and zodiac signs, enhance profile descriptions. The Explore section lets users align with specific vibes and activities, such as Spotify anthems, coffee dates, and spontaneous plans. However, Tinder's user interface (UI) is critiqued for its mediocrity, with disproportionate elements. Limited filters, primarily focusing on age and distance, underscore a deliberate design choice prioritising user-uploaded pictures over bios. Notably, Tinder restricts the ability to undo left swipes and view likes unless a premium upgrade is obtained, and intrusive ads during profile swiping disrupt the user experience.

- **Insights from M2:** Tinder's onboarding process mirrors Bumble's time-consuming nature but lacks the same vibrancy, leaning towards a more mundane experience. The app faces challenges associated with fraudulent and bot accounts, indicative of a less stringent security infrastructure. The option to conceal first names is available, and Tinder justifies its decision to withhold activity status, citing concerns about potential stalkers and unwarranted attention. Unmatching ensures that profiles remain permanently separated.
- **Insights from F1:** Tinder's notoriety as a hookup app contributes to its crowded user base, surpassing competitors like Bumble. The increased user density further heightens the risk of unwanted interactions, potentially discouraging app usage. The UI is criticised for being outdated and confusing, leading to inadvertent super likes during testing due to misclassified swipes, reflecting a suboptimal user experience.

General Perception: Tinder has a massive and diverse user base, providing individuals with a vast pool of potential matches. The sheer volume of users increases the likelihood of finding someone with similar interests or preferences. However, this enormous user base often results in fraudulent or bot accounts, thus hampering user's trust in interactions.

Aisle

- **Insights from M1:** Despite its commitment to fostering serious relationships, Aisle faces challenges with a relatively newer user base than international competitors. The app's limited number of invites may discourage users from engaging with prompts, diminishing its perceived seriousness and transforming the user experience into a simple left/right clicking mechanism akin to Hinge. Aisle's commitment to relationship depth is compromised by a lack of filters and tags, particularly when contrasted with its international counterparts. Male members are obligated to upgrade to premium plans for initiating messages.
- **Insights from M2:** Aisle's onboarding process, requiring only two pictures, prioritises efficiency, but users may perceive it as trading user information for simplicity, with some essential cues missing. Search filters, deemed inappropriate by specific audiences, lack fundamental features such as filtering out verified profiles. Unmatching ensures that profiles do not reencounter each other.
- **Insights from F1:** Aisle's distinctive strength lies in understanding and accommodating regional dating constraints, particularly within the same religion. Users can filter profiles based on religion, reflecting sensitivity to regional preferences. However, this approach may be perceived as restrictive and regressive, as Aisle promptly populates profiles with individuals from the same religion without user input. The app's "Superlikes", linked to heart buttons, reduce errors and provide a more natural liking/disliking experience. Notably, female profiles have free access to the list of men who have liked them, whereas male users must subscribe to access the same feature.

General Perception: Aisle positions itself as a platform for individuals seeking serious, long-term relationships. The app's emphasis on quality over quantity attracts users looking for more meaningful connections rather than casual encounters. The app is focused and designed more in context with the Indian dating scene (Fig. 1).

Platforms → Features/Categories ↓	bumble	tinder	Hinge	aisle	Grindr	Notes
Profile Setup	At least 3 photos are required	No minimum required number, but 3 is recommended by the platform	6 photos are required	2 photos are required	No photos or information about the user is required	1. During the profile setup for most of the platforms excluding tinder, significance of text based prompts and cues was highlighted. 2. Verification before matching is not necessary for most of the platforms. 3. The verification status is reflected on the profile across all the platforms.
Matching Process	L/R Swiping	L/R Swiping	Button based	Button based	No explicit matching process	Left and right swiping can be impulsive in nature, however having a button for doing the job prevents mindless swiping.
Profile Focus	Prompts and Photos	Photos	Prompts and Photos	Prompt and Photos	Pictures and about the person (preferences)	1. Most of the dating platforms are being inclusive of user personality traits and preferences by capturing them through text prompts and bio-sections. 2. Except for tinder, as it adds hyper focus on pictures.
Activity Status	No	No	Yes	Yes	Yes	1. Surprisingly tinder argues that showing activity status could lead to an increase in stalkers and creeps 2. Bumble does not shows the activity status of potential matches. But once you are matched with someone, you can check whether or not the other person is online.
Pre-match Interactions	2 compliments are provided weekly in the basic version	None	No limit on the one liner compliments	5 compliments are granted weekly in the basic version	No matching is required for texting	Allowing users to send messages before matching encourages banter and adds realism.
Post-match Interactions	Icebreakers, images, text/voice notes and audio/video calling	Icebreakers, songs, text/voice notes, images and audio/video calling	Voice/text notes and audio/video calling	Icebreakers, wingman, text/voice notes and audio/video calling	Pictures, GIFs, Location, Saved Phrases	1. Hinge positions itself as an app that is meant to be deleted after the match. 2. Post match experience is crucial as it helps the concerned people to make informed decisions before going into an offline meet.
Privacy Features	Anonymous Mode	Incognito (Premium)	None	None	Users can share as little or as much as they want	1. Anonymous mode means only people that the user has swiped right on will be able to see them. 2. Additionally platforms like bumble and tinder allow users to block people from their contact list from seeing their dating profile.
Security Features	Reporting someone on bumble will allow bumble to review person X's account and finally make an informed call	Unmatching is a permanent action. You will not see their profile again, nor will they see yours	Unmatching is a permanent action. You will not see their profile again, nor will they see yours	Unmatching is a permanent action. You will not see their profile again, nor will they see yours	Blocking will remove creeps from the user's view unless the user chooses to unblock	You can unmatch someone on bumble and owing to a new update, the person being unmatched after a significant chat history will be notified.
Integration with Other Apps	Spotify and Instagram	Spotify, Facebook, Snapchat and Instagram	Instagram	None	None	Having integrations with apps like Spotify and Instagram help deepen bond between users.
Recommending Profiles to Friends	A dating profile can be recommended to a friend	Friends of friends feature	A dating profile can be recommended to a friend	None	None	Changes like friend recommendations and linking dating portfolios to social profiles are made so that friends and acquaintances can look into the process of matchmaking.

Fig. 1. Competitive Analysis of five online dating platforms.

4.2 Online Survey

The survey was designed to have three branches based on the user's experience with dating apps: those who had **never used** them, those who had **used them in the past**, and those who were **currently using** them. A total of 71 users completed the survey, of which 32 had never used a dating app, 29 had used one before, and 10 were current users (Table 1 and 2).

Additionally, the survey revealed that 41 participants were single at the time of the study, and 21 were in a relationship. The rest preferred not to share their relationship status. Interestingly, after collecting 71 responses, most of the answers were the same, indicating a saturation point for the survey. According to the study, most demographics preferred Bumble, followed closely by Hinge and Tinder.

Table 1. Survey Response by Gender

Gender	Male	Female	Non-Binary
Response Count	49	21	1

Table 2. Responses based on gender.

Sexual Orientation	Response Count
Straight	61
Gay	1
Lesbian	1
Asexual	2
Demisexual	1
Bicurious	1
Unsure	4

4.3 Semi-structured Interviews

After the interviews were completed, they were transcribed verbatim. We then performed a thematic analysis by open, axial, and selective coding of the responses from post-recording transcripts to identify emerging themes and patterns. We used these codes to understand the data better and generate insights about our participants' experiences.

Open coding breaks down and analyses the data by assigning codes to specific text segments. This involved reading the transcripts multiple times to identify keywords, phrases, or concepts relevant to the research question. The codes were then grouped into categories to understand the data better and generate insights about the participants' experiences. Intercoder reliability was established by having two independent coders code a subset of the transcripts and compare their codes for consistency to ensure the stringency and trustworthiness of the findings. Any discrepancies were discussed and resolved through consensus. The final codes were then used to develop a thematic analysis that captured the key themes and patterns in the data.

The following are the axial echoes of the interview participants, unveiling patterns and insights across the chronological stages of online dating, identified using selective coding:

Openness to Dating Apps

- *"Digital intimacy is not a real thing. There is physical intimacy. There is emotional intimacy, which is more important to me. People are prioritising physical intimacy, and more hookup culture is to blame."* - P1, 20M
- *"You don't want to date someone and say that you met them through a dating app, and the stigma is big enough for me to ghost them."* - P2, 21M

– *"Stigma never hindered me from being on these platforms. I have received screenshots of my profile from my friends, but that also means that you are on these platforms; that is why you are able to take screenshots."* - P3, 19F

Creating Profiles and Self-representation

– *"My profile was a vague representation of me; it did not tell a lot about me. My friends said that looking at the profile, the other person would not have an idea on what things to have the conversation about."* - P3, 19F
– *"My profile is not very personal. I've just added some of my photos and some memes, and every prompt is answered as 'Your mom.'"* - P11, 21M
– *"Initially, I was trying to be real and vulnerable in my profile, but then I realised I was being perceived as naive. Having an existential crisis on social media is considered cool now, to care less about things."* - P10, 21M

Evaluating Profiles and Matching

– *"If there were some semblance of thought behind the profile, then I would consider swiping right. I won't care much about their looks or photos first-hand."* - P11, 21M
– *"As a guy, it feels very validating to get matches because I am aware that guys usually struggle to get any"* - P6, 22M
– *"I received a lot of likes and matches, honestly felt a bit weird and creeped out by them. Felt some desperate energy coming in"* - P9, 22F

Icebreakers and Conversations

– *"Sometimes the conversations are so generic I forget their names. It feels like you have to start flirting with the person within an hour of getting matched, and I don't feel comfortable flirting with a stranger."* - P1, 20M
– *"Most of the conversations felt one-sided. If you are changing platforms, you should also try. If you are not trying, I would lose interest as well."* - P4, 19M
– *"I did not have a good experience conversing online. I could only have a good lengthy conversation."* - P3, 19F

Transitioning Out of the Dating Apps

– *"Around 7–8 conversations have shifted to Instagram DMs and one to WhatsApp, but usually they fizzle out once the conversation shifts to other platforms."* - P3, 19F
– *"I have been on 13 dates. Online dating has been very successful for me."* - P5, 20M
– *"I didn't feel comfortable when I was asked to shift to Instagram from Bumble."* - P9, 22F

Behavioural/Usage Patterns

- *"I have paid for Tinder and Bumble Premium. 60% of my time was spent on Hinge. 30% Bumble, 10% Tinder. Every day at least once, 10–20 minutes."* - P2, 21M
- *"Dating apps help me initially feel validated and happy. Then, dating apps don't meet my expectations after a few days. The dissatisfaction from dating apps provokes a bad mood."* - P6, 22M
- *"I used dating apps only because of peer pressure and to try what it is like to get on one. I got on a dating app for more of a social experiment"* - P9, 22F

Comparing Different Platforms

- *"On Bumble, the focus is more on the photos, and on Hinge, it is more on prompts.", "Hinge is objectifying personalities".* - P1, 20M
- *"Go for Hinge; it is slow-paced. It forces you to go over the profile, and it changes the narrative of the person, and that, combined with limited likes, makes you sure before you swipe."* - P5, 20M
- *"Tinder is the least liked, it has a messy UI, and it objectifies human features."* - P10, 21M

Security and Privacy Concerns

- *"Our society is very scary. I don't know what kind of people are looking at my profile on a dating app; they might be taking screenshots or misusing them."* - P9, 22F
- *"Safety is a huge concern. A friend told me they hooked up with someone through a dating app and got blackmailed for money. Catfishing is quite common. People present themselves a lot more differently on dating apps than they are in real life."* - P5, 20M

Suggestions to Improve the User Experience

- *"Recommendation algorithms can be improved, and they are already getting so much better on other apps like Netflix and Instagram."* - P3, 19F
- *"Sending images and voice notes should be normalised; sometimes, if someone asks what you're doing, you simply send a photo... Prompts should be given more precedence over photos"* - P4, 19M
- *"Hinge model works the best. Make it more exclusive by reducing the number of actions. Otherwise, dating becomes a commodity.", "College fests can be good for offline connections."* - P2, 21M

5 Discussion

Examining online dating practices and perceptions among university students, as revealed through survey data and in-depth interviews, unveils a complex interplay of societal norms, individual choices, and evolving preferences. The following discussion distils insights from the survey and interviews, emphasising standard practices and shared perceptions among this demographic.

Openness to Dating Apps: University students display a diverse range of attitudes towards dating apps, with a recognition of their prevalence within their social circles. The consensus among participants, however, reflects reservations about the digital realm prioritising physical intimacy over emotional connections, underlining the pervasive influence of hookup culture. Moreover, the stigma associated with online dating emerges as a shared challenge, shaping behaviours such as concealing app usage from friends and family.

Creating Profiles and Self-representation: The process of self-presentation on dating apps among university students varies widely, reflecting the influence of individual choices and external pressures, notably peer expectations. The nuanced strategies to craft digital personas underscore the societal dynamics contributing to online identity formation practices.

Evaluating Profiles and Matching: Gender disparities in the matching experience, particularly the challenges reported by straight men, highlight everyday struggles in navigating dating app dynamics. The need for a balanced and respectful approach to the matching process becomes evident as participants express discomfort with overwhelming validation and the potential superficiality of matches.

Suggestions to Improve User Experience: Participants' suggestions for personalisation, exclusivity, and improvements to recommendation algorithms provide valuable insights into enhancing the user experience for university students. The emphasis on separating apps into sections based on relationship expectations, creative blends of user preferences, and integrating real-world events into the app experience offers innovative avenues for addressing the specific needs of this demographic.

Security and Privacy Concerns: Strong apprehensions about safety, blackmail, and catfishing highlight shared concerns regarding the security of online dating platforms. The fear of misrepresentation and potential harm underscores the responsibility of app developers to create secure and trustworthy platforms that resonate with the safety concerns of university students.

6 Limitations of the Study

Our study has limitations that impact the breadth and applicability of our findings. First, the dearth of relevant literature in the Indian sub-context limits our analysis's depth and localised representation, highlighting the need for future research rooted in Indian cultural norms. Second, the under-representation of non-binary genders diminishes the inclusiveness of our insights, emphasising the necessity of a more comprehensive exploration to represent diverse gender identities properly. Additionally, our reliance on self-reported data may introduce potential biases. The study's focus on university students aged 19–22 may also restrict generalisability. Lastly, the evolving nature of online dating platforms and societal attitudes underscores the temporal constraints of our findings. Addressing these limitations in subsequent research will enhance the robustness and cultural sensitivity of our understanding of online dating.

7   Future Work and Conclusion

In examining online dating practices among university students, acknowledging the significance of cultural nuances, particularly within the diverse landscape of Indian dating culture, is crucial. Our research identified a gap in existing literature concerning university students' experiences with online dating in this cultural context. The interplay of societal expectations, family dynamics, and traditional values in India significantly shapes how young individuals engage with digital dating platforms, highlighting the need for further exploration in academic discourse.

While our study primarily delved into the broader dynamics of university students' online dating practices, we recognise the imperative for a more nuanced exploration of the Indian dating landscape. The intricate factors of arranged marriages, cultural taboos, and the interplay of technology with traditional values pose unique challenges often overlooked in current discourse. Future research can further elucidate these complexities, contributing significantly to a better understanding of online dating within the Indian context. By shedding light on neglected aspects of Indian dating culture within academia, our study aims to prompt further exploration and foster a more inclusive comprehension of online dating practices across diverse cultural contexts.

In conclusion, our study has provided valuable insights into self-presentation and user behaviour among university students on online dating platforms. We observed a complex interplay between self-expression and social perception, informing user strategies in profile construction and engagement with potential matches. Our findings suggest a clear preference for authenticity and an awareness of the performative aspects of online dating profiles. Implications for the design of dating apps include the need for features that encourage genuine representation and facilitate deeper connections based on shared interests and values.

Acknowledgments. We want to thank the Department of Human-Centered Design, IIIT Delhi, for providing us with the opportunity and resources to perform this long-term study. We also sincerely thank Dr Grace Eden for her guidance and unwavering support throughout the initial stages of the project.

Disclosure of Interests. The authors have no competing interests to declare relevant to this article's content.

References

1. Arjanggi, R., Kusumaningsih, L.: The correlation between social anxiety and academic adjustment among freshmen **219**, 104–107 (2016). https://doi.org/10.1016/j.sbspro.2016.04.049

2. Borchert, A., Díaz Ferreyra, N.E., Heisel, M.: Building trustworthiness in computer-mediated introduction: a facet-oriented framework. In: International Conference on Social Media and Society. SMSociety'20, pp. 39–46. Association for Computing Machinery, New York, NY, USA, July 2020. https://doi.org/10.1145/3400806.3400812, https://dl.acm.org/doi/10.1145/3400806.3400812

3. Chakraborty, D.: Components affecting intention to use online dating apps in India: a study conducted on smartphone users **15**, 2319510X1987259 (2019). https://doi.org/10.1177/2319510X19872596

4. Cobb, C., Kohno, T.: How public is my private life? privacy in online dating. In: Proceedings of the 26th International Conference on World Wide Web. WWW '17, pp. 1231–1240. International World Wide Web Conferences Steering Committee (2017). https://doi.org/10.1145/3038912.3052592, https://dl.acm.org/doi/10.1145/3038912.3052592

5. Finkel, E.J., Eastwick, P.W., Karney, B.R., Reis, H.T., Sprecher, S.: Online dating: a critical analysis from the perspective of psychological science. Psychol. Sci. Publ. Interest **13**(1), 3–66 (2012). https://doi.org/10.1177/1529100612436522, http://journals.sagepub.com/doi/10.1177/1529100612436522

6. Ma, Z., Gajos, K.Z.: Not just a preference: reducing biased decision-making on dating websites. In: Proceedings of the 2022 CHI Conference on Human Factors in Computing Systems. CHI '22, pp. 1–14. Association for Computing Machinery (2022). https://doi.org/10.1145/3491102.3517587, https://dl.acm.org/doi/10.1145/3491102.3517587

7. Malik, M.A., Ali, A., Khan, S.: Students' socio-economic status and academic adjustment in University of Sargodha **II**, 330–342 (2017). https://doi.org/10.31703/grr.2017(II-I).23

8. Nair, A., Padmakumar, K.: Analyzing tinder through user motivations and experiences among Indian young adults. Indian J. Mark. **50**(8–9), 32–47 (2020). https://doi.org/10.17010/ijom/2020/v50/i8-9/154690, https://www.indianjournalofmarketing.com/index.php/ijom/article/view/154690

9. Obada-Obieh, B., Somayaji, A.: Can I believe you? Establishing trust in computer mediated introductions. In: Proceedings of the 2017 New Security Paradigms Workshop. NSPW '17, pp. 94–106. Association for Computing Machinery (2017). https://doi.org/10.1145/3171533.3171544, https://dl.acm.org/doi/10.1145/3171533.3171544

10. van Turnhout, K., et al.: Design patterns for mixed-method research in HCI. In: Proceedings of the 8th Nordic Conference on Human-Computer Interaction: Fun, Fast, Foundational. NordiCHI '14, pp. 361–370. Association for Computing Machinery, New York, NY, USA (2014). https://doi.org/10.1145/2639189.2639220, https://dl.acm.org/doi/10.1145/2639189.2639220

11. Vashistha, A., Cutrell, E., Thies, W.: Increasing the reach of snowball sampling: the impact of fixed versus lottery incentives. In: Proceedings of the 18th ACM Conference on Computer Supported Cooperative Work and Social Computing. CSCW '15, pp. 1359–1363. Association for Computing Machinery, New York, NY, USA (2015). https://doi.org/10.1145/2675133.2675148, https://dl.acm.org/doi/10.1145/2675133.2675148

12. Zytko, D., Grandhi, S., Jones, Q.: Impression management struggles in online dating, pp. 53–62 (2014). https://doi.org/10.1145/2660398.2660410
13. Zytko, D., Mullins, N., Taylor, S., Holler, R.H.: Dating apps are used for more than dating: how users disclose and detect (non-)sexual interest in people-nearby applications. Proc. ACM Hum.-Comput. Interact. **6**(GROUP), **30**, 1–30:14 (2022). https://doi.org/10.1145/3492849, https://dl.acm.org/doi/10.1145/3492849

PLEA: The Embodied Virtual Being

Tomislav Stipancic[1]([✉]) [ID], Leon Koren[1] [ID], Duska Rosenberg[2] [ID], Tracy Harwood[3] [ID], and Juraj Benic[1] [ID]

[1] Faculty of Mechanical Engineering and Naval Architecture, University of Zagreb, Ivana Lucica 5, Zagreb, Croatia
tomislav.stipancic@fsb.unizg.hr
[2] I Com Research, University of London, London, UK
[3] Institute of Creative Technologies, De Montfort University, The Gateway, Leicester LE1 9BH, UK

Abstract. The emergence of Artificial Intelligence (AI) marks a significant milestone in innovations, particularly with the advent of Virtual Beings (VBs) and Mixed Reality. VBs have transitioned from rudimentary programmed characters to elaborate, interactive entities capable of sophisticated human engagement. Enhanced with emotional intelligence, adaptive learning, and context-sensitivity, VBs offer nuanced interactions within both digital and real-world settings. A key breakthrough in this field is the development of affective VBs, which possess the ability to comprehend and react to human emotions, challenging the traditional view of AI as emotionless and strictly logical. This evolution prompts a reexamination of AI's societal role and the dynamics of Human-Computer Interaction. This study focuses on the complexities of VBs, particularly through the implementation of a virtual being named PLEA, manifested in both worlds: the virtual and the physical one through a robotic head. It discusses the utility of such agents in various applications and employs ethnographic communication methodologies for data collection and analysis to unearth interaction patterns. Additionally, it examines human reactions to PLEA through a user-centered design approach, highlighting interactions based solely on facial expressions between PLEA and human participants. This investigation aims to lay the groundwork for developing multidisciplinary methods to collect, analyze, and abstract data from real-time interactions and feedback sessions, advancing the discourse on AI's integration into human social environments.

Keywords: Affective Robotics · HRI · Virtual Beings · Embodied Intelligence

1 Introduction

The advent of Artificial Intelligence (AI) has ushered in a new era of innovation, particularly in the field of Virtual Beings (VBs). VBs [1], existing within cyberspace, have evolved from simple, programmed characters to complex, interactive agents capable of engaging in sophisticated interactions with humans [2]. VBs can be designed with emotional intelligence, adaptive learning, and context-awareness, allowing for sophisticated interactions within digital and physical environments [3–5]. Among the most captivating developments in this domain is the creation of affective VBs [6].

© The Author(s), under exclusive license to Springer Nature Switzerland AG 2024
A. Coman and S. Vasilache (Eds.): HCII 2024, LNCS 14703, pp. 266–275, 2024.
https://doi.org/10.1007/978-3-031-61281-7_18

The development of affective VBs raises also important questions about the future of Human-Computer Interaction [7]. They become more capable of understanding and responding to human emotions, they challenge human traditional notions of AI as emotionless and purely logical entities. This paradigm shift calls for a re-evaluation of the role that AI can play in society, and how humans interact with these increasingly sophisticated digital counterparts [8].

The spectrum of interactions is also an important factor. It extends from the physical realm into augmented or mixed realities, and further into entirely virtual environments. [9]. This continuum of interaction serves as a hub of shared information, accessible to interacting parties. Within this framework, virtual entities can utilize information from the physical world, and similarly, real individuals can gain advantages from insights derived from virtual spaces. Objects in the tangible world may have corresponding digital twins in virtual spaces, and these digital counterparts can leverage data collected by sensors from their physical equivalents. Additionally, users can access information from both near and far that may influence the sensations they experience through an MR interface [10].

This work argues the intricacies of VBs, focusing on implementation of one particular virtual being called PLEA that is embodied into the real environment using a physical robot head [11]. The use of PLEA is discussed here from different perspectives including the use of such agents in different applications.

The empirical study of the interaction with PLEA from the social perspective represents work in progress. We apply methods of ethnography of communication in data collection, classification, and segmentation in order to provide the basis for subsequent rich analysis of interaction patterns.

From the perspective of user-centered design of a space where PLEA dwells together with humans, this work is about discovery of human reactions to PLEA in a dialogue that uses only the facial expressions of the two participants – PLEA and the human informant. Through this work we are deriving a base for development of multidisciplinary methods for eliciting, analyzing and abstracting data collected during the planned real time interactions and subsequent interviews with informants to obtain their feedback.

2 PLEA, the Affective Virtual Being

PLEA is an „emotion-aware "system that can reason in realistic scenarios where the system's ability to respond to human emotions is important. PLEA is equipped with AI-driven sensory systems that can interpret visual and auditory data to understand and respond to human emotions and actions, as shown at Fig. 1.

In a virtual setting, PLEA can analyze a user's facial expressions and tone of voice to gauge its mood and respond empathetically. PLEA interprets the social signals to generate hypotheses and produce non-verbal expressions using information visualization techniques. The computational architecture used in PLEA is a context-to-data interpreter that endows the machine with the capability to 'reason' based on constantly changing perspectives. This capability enhances the quality of interactions, making PLEA more natural and meaningful. Central to this advancement is the integration of the Facial Action Coding System (FACS) [12]. FACS, as a comprehensive system for categorizing

Fig. 1. Different PLEA configurations

human facial expressions, allows for the precise identification of emotions based on facial movements. For instance, Tarnowski et al. [13] utilized the FACS system to create a system using k-NN classifiers and MLP neural networks. Unlike the well-studied field of facial expression analysis, the link between emotions and body movements [14] remains relatively under-researched. Consequently, these techniques are often employed in conjunction with facial expression-based methods. Recent advancements involve the use of 3D convolutional neural networks for image data extraction, as detailed by Poria et al. [15]. When combined with the power of a Convolution Neural Network – CNN, PLEA can interpret complex facial expressions in real-time and to respond appropriately, as shown at Fig. 2.

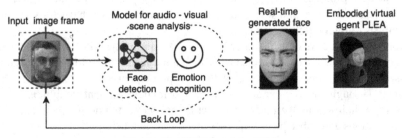

Fig. 2. The PLEA model of HRI

The visual modality algorithm integrates two types of neural networks: a residual neural network for identifying faces and a convolutional neural network for analyzing facial expressions. The initial network identifies and isolates the facial region, which is then cropped and resized to fit the required dimensions. This image undergoes processing through a pre-trained model, MobileNet version 7 [16]. Consequently, only the accuracy metric and the confusion matrix are provided. The performance accuracy on the validation dataset stands at 64.7%, with the confusion matrix displayed in Fig. 3.

The auditory capabilities are based on a recurrent neural network [6]. By incorporating both linguistic and acoustic components in its voice modality, PLEA is not just processing spoken language but is also attuned to the nuances of human speech, such as tone, pitch, and emotional inflections. The linguistic component allows it to understand, and process spoken words, enabling it to engage in meaningful non-verbal conversations. The acoustic component, on the other hand, lets PLEA to interpret how something

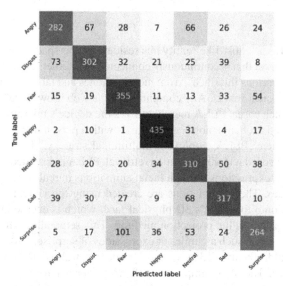

Fig. 3. Visual modality confusion matrix

is said, which is often as important as the words themselves. The multimodal reasoning capability of PLEA is also a standout feature. By processing both visual and auditory inputs, PLEA "can understand" nuanced human behaviors and emotions. A model for the multimodal fusion of information can be employed to imbue VB with a personality. This approach allows the VB to respond with varying degrees of politeness, as the model can be adjusted to favor or highlight some specific emotion [17].

Regardless of the chosen modality, it's crucial to supply a relevant dataset that mirrors the input data during the training stage of the model. For instance, datasets for recognizing emotions from facial expressions frequently utilize FACS. In this research, a Deep Learning (DL) model is trained to identify emotions from a dataset with labeled facial expressions. Such expressions serve as non-verbal cues reflecting a person's engagement in dialogue, for instance, through signals of agreement or connection, as documented in [18, 19]. Reference [20] describes a chatbot designed to support the well-being of older adults through text analysis, incorporated into different applications. Meanwhile, [21] offers a review of Social Robots' application in studies on Mental Health and Well-being.

This paper extends these findings by generating a novel dataset and insights crucial for understanding the present scenario and managing a Socially Assistive Robot (SAR) in certain interactions. PLEA functions as an observant robot, reacting emotionally to the user's mood during exchanges [22, 23], acting as an emotional mirror that accurately reflects the interacting person's emotional state. Its theoretical basis is inspired by the Media Equation Theory [24–28], suggesting that humans attribute human-like qualities to computers and other media, treating them as social entities. Post-interaction interviews with users have unveiled nuanced factors that shape social interactions and contribute to human well-being. Future developments in DNN control models, informed by the insights from this study, aim to enhance PLEA's engagement in user interactions, guiding them towards objectives like providing encouragement or happiness.

3 Applications

PLEA is designed as a "ghost-like" entity that resides in cyberspace. Physically, PLEA is installed on a PC server that is continuously connected to Internet. It can be accessed over the network using various interfaces, from mobile phones and tablets to laptops and specially designed physical robots. Any computer using a web browser can host the PLEA virtual being. In such cases, PLEA merely utilizes the device's microphone and camera to communicate and exchange non-verbal signals with a person in communication.

As a virtual agent, PLEA employs a multimodal strategy, although this research focuses solely on visual data for information retrieval. PLEA is designed to autonomously generate emotional expressions through facial animations in real-time, leveraging visualization techniques. These animations are created using the Unreal Engine software and are projected onto the robot's 3D physical face, which is encased in a transparent plastic material serving as the projection medium. This setup allows for the display of various emotional states, such as smiles or expressions of surprise, through specific light configurations. Additionally, PLEA wears a gender-neutral woolen hat to enhance its lifelike appearance. The study emphasizes PLEA's capacity to replicate and respond to human facial expressions, ensuring participants understand the robot's capabilities. Unlike directly mapping specific facial points from a person to the robot, PLEA interprets and reflects the user's emotions through corresponding expressions. This research aims to utilize self-reported emotions as a benchmark for developing computational models that enrich PLEA's future social interactions. Future studies will expand PLEA's analysis capabilities to include a broader range of social cues, such as ambient noise levels, body movement intensity, and vocal characteristics.

The following figures illustrate four distinct interactions as recognized by PLEA, as detailed in Fig. 3. The computational model used to control the robot responses is based on data collected over six months at two separated festivals in the UK: British Science Festival (https://www.art-ai.io/programme/plea2/) and the Art AI Festival in Leicester, the UK (https://www.art-ai.io/programme/plea/). Visitors to the installation were able to freely approach the robot and exchange non-verbal signals. For this interaction the robot was set just to mimic expressions of the visitor. Each interaction resulted in a set of emotional responses by the robot which it exchanged with the person,

The data represented in plots show how each emotion is timely changing during the interaction. By analyzing these plots, it is possible to learn more about a flow of the current interaction. For example, within the plot depicted at (Fig. 4.a), at first the user approached to the robot and smiled, which is presented with the pink line. Then the robot responded with a smile. After that the user realized that and became surprised (line in red). Then the robot responded with surprise. Within the next step the person smiled again (line in pink), and this interaction continued with the same fashion until finished with the long-lasting smile expressed mutually. Analysis of data collected in this way showed that the environmental conditions play a significant part in interactions with PLEA. As this work progresses, our understanding of user responses will enable us to increase PLEA's functionalities and develop a friendly and trustworthy interface that may be regarded as a companion. Ideally, PLEA would then be implemented in care homes to help to combat loneliness and to keep people happy.

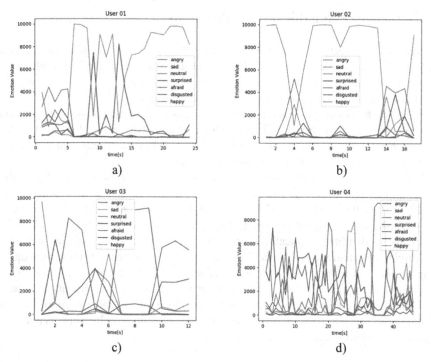

Fig. 4. PLEA emotion-interaction plots: a) interaction lasting 24 s in which happiness and surprise alternate; b) interaction lasting 17 s in which happiness dominated over all other emotions; c) interaction lasting 12 s in which a user in interaction started expressing happiness and then continued with surprise which is followed by two more negative emotions, fear, and angriness; d) interaction lasting 46 s in which dominates negative emotions like sadness, fear, and angriness. (Color figure online)

The potential applications of VBs like PLEA are vast. In education, they can provide personalized learning experiences, adapting to students' emotional states and learning styles [29]. In healthcare, they can offer companionship and emotional support, alongside their physical assistance. This level of empathy and understanding could significantly improve patient care and emotional support [30]. In the area of entertainment and social interaction, her ability to understand and react to human emotions can lead to more engaging and immersive experiences [31]. Affective VBs can revolutionize customer service by providing emotionally intelligent responses to customer inquiries. They can detect frustration or satisfaction in a customer's tone or text, allowing them to handle situations more tactfully and improve the overall customer experience. In the entertainment industry, affective VBs can create more immersive gaming and virtual reality experiences by reacting to the player's emotions, making the interaction feel more real and engaging. Very important role of VB could be in social interaction. Affective VBs can act as social companions, offering conversation and interaction that adapts to the user's emotional state. This can be particularly beneficial for the elderly or individuals with social anxieties, providing them with a safe space to interact and engage socially.

4   Challenges and Ethical Considerations

The creation of affective virtual beings (VBs) poses significant technical and ethical hurdles [32]. On the technical front, the precise and real-time analysis of multimodal inputs demands substantial computational resources and poses complexities. It is equally vital to maintain the privacy and security of sensitive user data.

From an ethical standpoint, the influence of virtual beings on human connections and societal values prompts serious reflection. Distinguishing between artificial and human emotional intelligence, along with the dependency on AI for emotional companionship, necessitates careful oversight and regulatory measures.

Ethical issues in AI and robotics encompass the development of technologies that honor human rights, privacy, and respect. Key challenges involve addressing biases within AI algorithms that could lead to discriminatory outcomes, the displacement of jobs due to technological automation, and the potential exploitation of robots and AI in surveillance and military applications. Promoting transparency, responsibility, and diversity within AI initiatives is essential to counteract these concerns. With technological progress, the adaptation and formulation of ethical standards and laws are imperative to protect human welfare and ensure the positive impact of these advancements on society.

Addressing these issues demands that researchers establish and adhere to stringent guidelines for designing and programming ethically reliable AI. This study is a modest contribution towards achieving that goal.

5   Conclusions

The development of VBs capable of operating across different realities, especially those with affective and multimodal reasoning capabilities, marks a significant evolution in the field of AI and robotics. The use of a multimodal approach can also enhance situational embodiment, self-explanatory nature, and context-driven interaction to increase interactivity [33]. VBs promise to revolutionize how people interact with technology, offering more natural, empathetic, and engaging experiences. As researchers continue to explore the vast potential of this technology, it is crucial to address the accompanying technological and ethical challenges. Their impact on society, education, healthcare, and entertainment could be profound, paving the way for a future where AI is an integral and beneficial part of daily lives. The journey towards creating advanced VBs is not only about technological innovation but also about understanding and enhancing the human experience in all its facets.

Extant research suggests users tend to ascribe human emotions, motives, and feelings to objects even when it is clear the object in question is not human. This is also the case with PLEA, which is strongly anthropomorphized by its design as a human head albeit made of a plastic shell. In this context the methodological approach is focused on communicative practices where people assign human characteristics to cognitive artefacts. For the purposes of this project assigning human characteristics to PLEA is defined as personification, and the main research questions that are being explored is which features, characteristics and functionalities are most appropriate in facilitating PLEA's personification for the use case scenario.

Authors are now collecting more data through interviews and testing a multidisciplinary methodology with a larger sample of real users under laboratory conditions.

Acknowledgments. This work has been supported in part by the Croatian Science Foundation under the project "Affective Multimodal Interaction based on Constructed Robot Cognition—AMICORC (UIP-2020-02-7184)". Special thanks to iCOM ICT Research (https://icomict.org), Art AI Festival, Leicester (https://www.art-ai.io), and to students and colleagues of the LAPIS research group and FAMENA UNIZG for their active support and participation in this research.

Disclosure of Interests. The authors have no competing interests to declare that are relevant to the content of this article.

References

1. Genay, A., Lecuyer, A., Hachet, M.: Being an avatar "for real": a survey on virtual embodiment in augmented reality. IEEE Trans. Visual Comput. Graph. **28**(12), 5071–5090 (2021). https://doi.org/10.1109/TVCG.2021.3099290
2. Paiva, A., Leite, I., Boukricha, H., Wachsmuth, I.: Empathy in virtual agents and robots: a survey. ACM Trans. Interact. Intell. Syst. **7**(3), 1–40 (2017). https://doi.org/10.1145/2912150
3. Azarnov, D.A., Chubarov, A.A., Samsonovich, A.V.: Virtual actor with social-emotional intelligence. Procedia Comput. Sci. **123**, 76–85 (2018). https://doi.org/10.1016/j.procs.2018.01.013
4. Hendrikse, S.C., Kluiver, S., Treur, J., Wilderjans, T.F., Dikker, S., Koole, S.L.: How virtual agents can learn to synchronize: an adaptive joint decision-making model of psychotherapy. Cogn. Syst. Res. **79**, 138–215 (2023). https://doi.org/10.1016/j.cogsys.2022.12.009
5. Koren, L., Stipancic, T., Ricko, A., Benic, J.: Context-driven method in realization of optimized human-robot interaction. Tehnicki Glasnik **16**(3), 320–327 (2022). https://doi.org/10.31803/tg-20220504100707
6. Koren, L., Stipancic, T., Ricko, A., Orsag, L.: Person localization model based on a fusion of acoustic and visual inputs. Electronics **11**(3), 440 (2022). https://doi.org/10.3390/electronics11030440
7. Park, S., Whang, M.: Empathy in human-robot interaction: designing for social robots. Int. J. Environ. Res. Public Health **19**(3), 1889 (2022). https://doi.org/10.3390/ijerph19031889
8. Fruchter, R., Nishida, T., Rosenberg, D.: Social intelligence design for social computing. In: International Conference on Human-Computer Interaction, pp. 545–558. Springer, Cham (2022). https://doi.org/10.1007/978-3-031-05061-9_38
9. Mills, K.A., Scholes, L., Brown, A.: Virtual reality and embodiment in multimodal meaning making. Writ. Commun. **39**(3), 335–369 (2022). https://doi.org/10.1177/07410883221083517
10. Genay, A., Lécuyer, A., Hachet, M.: Being an avatar "for real": a survey on virtual embodiment in augmented reality. IEEE Trans. Visual Comput. Graph. **28**(12), 5071–5090 (2021). https://doi.org/10.1109/tvcg.2021.3099290
11. Stipancic, T., Koren, L., Korade, D., Rosenberg, D.: PLEA: a social robot with teaching and interacting capabilities. J. Pacific Rim Psychol. **15** (2021). https://doi.org/10.1177/18344909211037019
12. Rosenberg, E.L., Ekman, P. (eds.): What the Face Reveals: Basic and Applied Studies of Spontaneous Expression Using the Facial Action Coding System (FACS). Oxford University Press(2020). https://doi.org/10.1093/acprof:oso/9780195179644.001.0001

13. Tarnowski, P., Kolodziej, M., Majkowski, A., Rak, R.J.: Emotion recognition using facial expressions. In: International Conference on Computational Science (2017). https://doi.org/10.1016/j.procs.2017.05.025

14. Melzer, A., Shafir, T., Tsachor, R.P.: How do we recognize emotion from movement? Specific motor components contribute to the recognition of each emotion. Front. Psychol. **10** (2019). https://doi.org/10.3389/fpsyg.2019.01389

15. Poria, S., Chaturvedi, I., Cambria, E., Hussain, A.: Convolutional MKL based multimodal emotion recognition and sentiment analysis. In: 16th IEEE International Conference on Data Mining (ICDM), Barcelona (2016). https://doi.org/10.1109/ICDM.2016.0055

16. Savchenko, A.V.: Facial expression and attributes recognition basedon multi-task learning of lightweight neuralnetworks. In: IEEE 19th International Symposium on Intelligent Systems and Informatics, Subotica (2021). https://doi.org/10.1109/SISY52375.2021.9582508

17. Koren, L., Stipancic, T., Ricko, A., Orsag, L.: Multimodal emotion analysis based on visual, acoustic and linguistic features. In: Meiselwitz, G. (ed.) Social Computing and Social Media: Design, User Experience and Impact (HCII 2022). LNCS, vol. 13315. Springer, Cham (2022). https://doi.org/10.1007/978-3-031-05061-9_23

18. Bavelas, J.B., Gerwing, J.: The listener as addressee in face-to-face dialogue. Int. J. Listen. **25**(3), 178–198 (2011). https://doi.org/10.1080/10904018.2010.508675

19. Rawal, N., Stock-Homburg, R.M.: Facial emotion expressions in human–robot interaction: a survey. Int. J. Soc. Robot. **14**(7), 1583–1604 (2022). https://arxiv.org/abs/2103.07169

20. El Kamali, M., et al.: NESTORE: mobile chatbot and tangible vocal assistant to support older adults' wellbeing. In: Proceedings of the 2nd Conference on Conversational User Interfaces, pp. 1–3 (2020). https://doi.org/10.1145/3405755.3406167

21. Scoglio, A.A., Reilly, E.D., Gorman, J.A., Drebing, C.E.: Use of social robots in mental health and well-being research: systematic review. J. Med. Internet Res. **21**(7) (2019). https://doi.org/10.2196/13322

22. Dimberg, U., Andréasson, P., Thunberg, M.: Emotional empathy and facial reactions to facial expressions. J. Psychophysiol. **25**(1), 26 (2011). https://doi.org/10.1027/0269-8803/a000029

23. Adriana, T., Matarić, M.J.: Emulating empathy in socially assistive robotics. In: Proceedings of the AAAI Spring Symposium: Multidisciplinary Collaboration for Socially Assistive Robotics, pp. 93–96 (2007)

24. Reeves, B., Nass, C.I.: The media equation: how people treat computers, television, and new media like real people and places. In: Center for the Study of Language and Information. Cambridge University Press (1996). https://doi.org/10.1016/s0898-1221(97)82929-x

25. Złotowski, J., et al.: Model of dual anthropomorphism: the relationship between the media equation effect and implicit anthropomorphism. Int. J. Soc. Robot. **10**(5), 701–714 (2018). https://doi.org/10.1007/s12369-018-0476-5

26. Reuten, A., Van Dam, M., Naber, M.: Pupillary responses to robotic and human emotions: the uncanny valley and media equation confirmed. Front. Psychol. **9**, 774 (2018). https://doi.org/10.3389/fpsyg.2018.00774

27. Klowait, N.: The quest for appropriate models of human-likeness: anthropomorphism in media equation research. AI Soc. **33**(4), 527–536 (2018). https://doi.org/10.1007/s00146-017-0746-z

28. Clifford, N., Corina, Y.: The man who lied to his laptop: what machines teach us about human relationships. Current/Penguin (2010). https://doi.org/10.5860/choice.48-3960

29. Tudor Car, L., et al.: Conversational agents in health care: scoping review and conceptual analysis. J. Med. Internet Res. **22**(8), e17158 (2020). https://doi.org/10.2196/17158

30. Shvo, M., Buhmann, J., Kapadia, M.: An interdependent model of personality, motivation, emotion, and mood for intelligent virtual agents. In: Proceedings of the 19th ACM International Conference on Intelligent Virtual Agents, pp. 65–72 (2019). https://doi.org/10.1145/3308532.3329474

31. Kramer, N., Manzeschke, A.: Social reactions to socially interactive agents and their ethical implications. In: The Handbook on Socially Interactive Agents: 20 years of Research on Embodied Conversational Agents, Intelligent Virtual Agents, and Social Robotics Volume 1: Methods, Behavior, Cognition, pp. 77–104 (2021). https://doi.org/10.1145/3477322.3477326

32. Canal, F.Z., et al.: A survey on facial emotion recognition techniques: a state-of-the-art literature review. Inf. Sci. **582**, 593–617 (2022). https://doi.org/10.1016/j.ins.2021.10.005

33. Stipancic, T., Jerbic, B., Curkovic, P.: Bayesian Approach to Robot Group Control. LNEE, vol. 130, pp. 109–119. Springer, New York (2013). https://doi.org/10.1007/978-1-4614-2317-1_9

A Comprehensive Analysis of Public Sentiment Towards ChatGPT's Privacy Implications

Liang Tang[✉] and Masooda Bashir

University of Illinois at Urbana-Champaign, Champaign, IL 61820, USA
{ltang29,mnb}@illinois.edu

Abstract. In this research, we examine the rapid proliferation of ChatGPT, a leading-edge chatbot powered by sophisticated large language model (LLM) technology, and its privacy implications on societal perspectives. While it demonstrates state-of-the-art capabilities in a variety of language-generating tasks, it also raises widespread public concerns regarding its societal impact. By employing advanced natural language processing (NLP) techniques, such as sentiment analysis and topic modeling, our study analyzes public attitudes towards ChatGPT using a dataset derived from Twitter. Our result shows that the overall sentiment is largely neutral and the public's heightened sensitivity to privacy and security breaches. Among a wide range of topics mentioned in tweets, the most popular topics are malicious phishing, data privacy, international policy and Employee data concern in workplace.

Keywords: Privacy · ChatGPT · LLMs

1 Introduction

The advent of artificial intelligence (AI) has ushered in a new era of technological innovation, fundamentally altering the landscape of human-computer interaction and introducing many new tools and applications. Among them, OpenAI's ChatGPT has gained attention. ChatGPT acquires its capabilities from a large corpus of text data and uses machine learning algorithms to learn patterns in language, this foundation allows it to produce responses that are not only coherent but also relevant to a diverse array of questions [1]. This tool, driven by a large language model (LLM), has a growing number of users with a broad range of applications in various domains [2, 3]. Despite its state-of-the-art performance and versatility, the widespread adoption of ChatGPT has risen a complex concerning its societal impact, encompassing both enthusiasm for its potential and concern over its risk, implications and failures (reason, logic and arithmetic) [4]. For example, these algorithms are often prone to generating inaccurate information or 'hallucinations' including the creation of non-existent references [5] From a societal perspective, these issues are further compounded by the potential for bias and discrimination embedded within LLMs due to their training data [6, 7], and retraining the model is costly, which limits its knowledge before 2021 [8]. In fact, the models are not only susceptible to availability, selection, and confirmation bias but are also unreluctant to

A. Coman and S. Vasilache (Eds.): HCII 2024, LNCS 14703, pp. 276–284, 2024.
https://doi.org/10.1007/978-3-031-61281-7_19

amplify it, such as ChatGPT can provide biased outputs and perpetuate sexist stereotypes [9, 10], Most importantly, Moreover, the technology's vulnerability to being used for harmful purposes raises concerns about its role in facilitating the spread of disinformation and misinformation [11]. As society aim on the exploration and adoption of such transformative technologies, understanding and addressing public perspectives becomes paramount since their experiences, concerns, and feedback serves as an "external audit" to shape the utility, relevance, and ethical contour of the technology. Twitter, being a real-time platform, reflects the immediate reactions, thoughts, and concerns of its vast user base [12]. Recognizing this, our research delves deep into these concerns by analyzing Twitter data to understand what people are concerned about and aiming to identify the public concerns surrounding ChatGPT's privacy implications.

2 Background

2.1 ChatGPT's Privacy Concern

The emergence of Large Language Models (LLMs) has highlighted concerns regarding their potential exploitation for negative purposes, including activities that leverage text generation for harm. Through carefully crafted prompt engineering, ChatGPT can essentially turn into an unregulated source of tools for privacy and security breaches [1]. The general public's limited understanding of its full capabilities presents a considerable obstacle. In the absence of adequate safeguards, people might inadvertently become targets of its improper application, underscoring the urgency for society to adapt and protect itself against these emerging threats. We will discuss various types of privacy concerns in the following sections.

2.2 Data Collection and Processing

At the heart of ChatGPT's capabilities is its reliance on extensive textual data. This raises significant questions regarding the nature and sensitivity of the data collected, especially when personal or proprietary information is involved. Therefore, the process of training these models on potentially sensitive data without explicit consent poses ethical and legal challenges. Also, the way ChatGPT learns involves scraping real-world data from various sources, this information could be used to train ChatGPT without asking permission from the people who originally made it. This can cause privacy worries and might break privacy laws like the GDPR and CCPA [13].

OpenAI's privacy policy outlines that when users sign up for ChatGPT services, they collect a range of personal data, such as account information, content created by users, communication records, and information from social media [14]. Moreover, OpenAI automatically gathers additional information, including logs, how their services are used, details about the devices used to access their services, cookies, and analytical data. Another concern is the risk of personal data leakage. ChatGPT, by design, learns from the input it receives, which may include personally identifiable information (PII). There is a tangible risk that the model could inadvertently expose or replicate this PII in future interactions with other users, breaching privacy and confidentiality agreements [14]. The mechanisms by which LLMs handle and anonymize user data are thus of paramount importance.

2.3 Data Security and Cyberattack

The security measures implemented to protect the data used in training and operating ChatGPT are also a significant concern. The potential for unauthorized access to sensitive or personal data through hacking or data breaches poses a risk, such as the one reported on March 20th, 2023, which it was possible to see another active user's first and last name, email address, payment address, credit card type and the last four digits [15]. The aftermath of the incident prompted a reevaluation of legal and regulatory compliance, pushing for adherence to stricter privacy laws and standards which the Italian ban comes after this ChatGPT data breach.

Moreover, beyond the concerns related to using publicly available data and user contributions, the potential for privacy breaches via Large Language Models (LLMs) is actively being explored. Due to the operational design of LLMs, which often involves the use of application programming interfaces (APIs) and restricts access to the model's internal parameters, traditional deep learning system attacks are usually not applicable. However, it does not mean that ChatGPT is unbreakable, there is jailbreak method that employs prompts to circumvent ChatGPT's ethical safeguards and enables ChatGPT to bypass its programmed limitations and freely produce any content [16].

2.4 Lack of Transparency

The cornerstone of user trust in digital platforms, especially those leveraging AI and machine learning, lies in the transparency of their operations [17]. Users need to be fully informed about how their data is used, who it may be shared with, and the measures in place to protect their privacy. OpenAI, and similar organizations, therefore, have a responsibility to ensure that their way of collecting user data is not only comprehensive but also accessible and understandable. Furthermore, the absence of regulations enforcing clarity in data handling practices amplifies anxieties about possible invasions of privacy. OpenAI's operations, perceived as opaque by users. This lack of openness obstructs the detection and mitigation of potential privacy risks [18], might reinforce user's incapable of comprehensively evaluating their exposure to privacy problems.

Based on previous work, our research is driven by two primary objectives. First, we aim to pinpoint the sentiment of the public and categorize the overarching concerns related to ChatGPT's privacy. Second, we seek to understand the intricate relationship between specific ChatGPT-related events and their influence on public sentiment.

3 Method

Our dataset with 8763 tweets, achieved from Kaggle open library, updated daily since December 5, 2022 (version 171), comprises 558,740 tweets about ChatGPT complete with user metadata such as location, post data and description. To ensure accuracy and consistency in our dataset, we limited our search to English tweets that contained the designated keywords which contain privacy-related search terms. Following data collection, tweets were cleansed of noise such as irrelevant symbols, URLs, and non-English text, and normalized to facilitate uniform analysis. We employed two natural language models: the BERT pre-training model for sentiment analysis and the GSDMM [19] for topic model clustering to identify and cluster tweets into distinct topics based on content similarity. Each cluster was meticulously labeled according to its dominant theme, enabling us to capture the essence of public discourse on ChatGPT's privacy concern. The overview of our workflow is shown in Fig. 1.

In our investigation into the privacy concerns surrounding ChatGPT, the selection of keywords was strategized to encapsulate the multifaceted dimensions of privacy discourse. Keywords such as #dataprivacy, #dataprotection, and #privacypolicy were chosen to ensure our research within the broad landscape of data privacy, ensuring a comprehensive discussion that spans legal, ethical, and societal domains. The inclusion of #encryption and #GDPR provided a focused lens on technical privacy safeguards and regulatory frameworks, mainly regards how these mechanisms or policies are perceived in the context of safeguarding user information within ChatGPT interactions. Moreover, #datasharing and #datagovernance keywords allowed us to delve into the concerns regarding the management and circulation of user data, a critical aspect of privacy that touches on consent, transparency, and control. For #datasecurity, despite the study's exclusion of security as a primary focus, are included to acknowledge the protective measures that indirectly influence privacy.

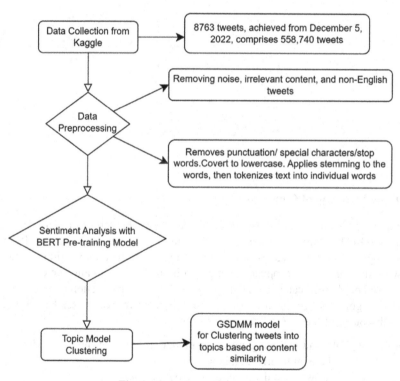

Fig. 1. Overview of research flow

4 Result

4.1 Sentiment Distribution

Our analysis revealed that 21.1% of sentiments were positive, 16.8% negative, and a striking 62.1% remained neutral. The persistently high neutral sentiment throughout the timeline (Fig. 2) suggests that a large segment of the audience remains either undecided or is awaiting more conclusive information about ChatGPT's implications or being informational in their discussions. Diving deeper, we observed that real-world events serve as significant sentiment catalysts, case in point is the "ChatGPT Data Leak" event. In its aftermath, we observed a tangible surge in negative sentiments, underscoring the public's heightened sensitivity to privacy and security breaches.

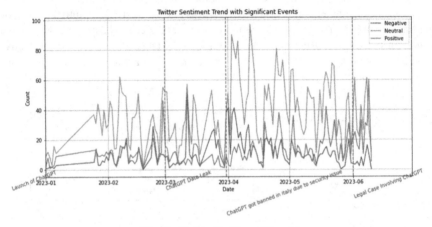

Fig. 2. Twitter Sentiment Trend

4.2 Topic Modeling of Concerns

For pinpointing overarching sentiments and identifying key areas of concern, we are delving into 1441 negative sentiment tweets by clustering topics, we first manually examined the topics, and it involved keywords and categorized them into various categories. Following the clustering of topics, we engaged in discussions to allocate each topic to one of seven predefined categories. Our analysis through topic modeling revealed seven primary categories reflecting concerns within the negative tweets (see Fig. 3, Fig. 4), and the discourse of these seven categories suggests:

1. The potential of ChatGPT being utilized in malicious phishing and other cyberattacks.
2. The ongoing debate on international data privacy policy
3. The security risks associated with employee data in workplace
4. The online cybersecurity threats link ChatGPT with other platforms, notably WhatsApp, suggesting cross-platform vulnerabilities.

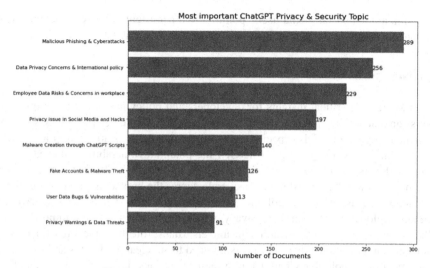

Fig. 3. Most important ChatGPT's privacy topic

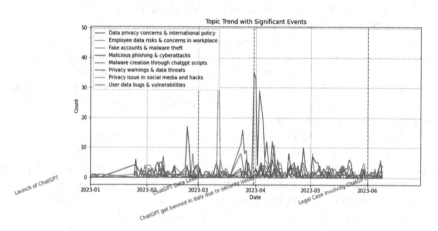

Fig. 4. ChatGPT privacy concerns over time

The provided Fig. 4 illustrates the volume of negative Twitter discourse on various data privacy topics over time. Notably, a prominent peak of "Privacy Issue in Social Media and Hacks" and the "Data Privacy Concerns & International Policy" category, marked in blue and pink, exhibits the two most significant peaks, suggesting an explosive reaction to a corresponding event of Data Leak and Italy's ban on ChatGPT, causing a surge in public discourse. Such pronounced spikes in the graph underscore the public's escalating worries and unease about data privacy on a global scale, potentially in response to a high-profile incident or legislative change that had widespread implications for personal data security. Furthermore, the early peak and consistent occurrence of several peaks in "Malicious Phishing & Cyberattacks" suggests that this is a recurring topic of discussion among social media users, pointing to a persistent public engagement with and concern about these cybersecurity threats created by ChatGPT.

5 Discussion

This study reveals critical insights for developers and policymakers. For example, our results can guide policymakers on what factors may influence the public's views toward automated language models especially when these automations are seen in a negative light. Findings further suggest that ChatGPT has potential vulnerabilities that can come across platforms, including misuse in creating an auto chatbot. The fear that ChatGPT could be weaponized for phishing attacks underscores the broader apprehensions about the potential misuse of AI technologies. The discourse around ChatGPT is interwoven with larger global debates on data privacy, which might emphasize the importance of collaborative global efforts in establishing universal data protection standards. For corporations and organizations, there is a pressing need to set clear guidelines and protocols when integrating tools like ChatGPT into their operations. Lastly, developers and AI organizations must prioritize addressing concerns transparently and swiftly to mitigate such dips in sentiment. Policymakers, too, should recognize the ripple effect of their decisions on public discourse.

The pronounced neutral sentiment paves the way for potential subsequent research. A deeper analysis into this neutrality's roots and tracking sentiment evolution post significant AI update can offer richer insights into evolving public attitudes and trust of ChatGPT or other LLM models. Additionally, future researchers should aim to further identify and analyze influential voices in these discussions and discover who will be most impacted by these concerns.

Our findings can also be interpreted as evidence that public sentiment on Twitter is highly responsive to real-world events that compromise data security and privacy. Such insights are important for stakeholders in cybersecurity, as they underscore the need for rapid response strategies and robust communication plans to manage public perception following significant data breaches or policy announcements. More importantly, addressing these privacy concerns requires the development of robust data protection mechanisms, transparent data handling policies in various domains, and user-friendly privacy controls.

6 Conclusions

ChatGPT's integration into society necessitates addressing privacy issues. Our study provides an initial understanding of public perception, stressing responsible AI deployment. While our findings are initial, they present a foundational understanding that calls for deeper investigation. The early patterns we observe stress the importance of responsible LLM deployment and underscore the necessity for a collective effort in framing AI policies. As we stand at the intersection of an AI-driven era, such insights are invaluable for shaping the future direction of AI development and integration, ensuring a balance between innovation and security. In summary, our study underscores the importance of responsible use of the LLM model and highlights the need for collaboration among stakeholders to regulate AI policy. This understanding can pave the way for the development of robust privacy preservation solutions that can effectively mitigate privacy risks in LLMs and ensure the protection of user data.

References

1. Brown, T.B., et al.: Language Models are Few-Shot Learners. arXiv preprint http://arxiv.org/abs/2005.14165 (2020). https://doi.org/10.48550/arXiv.2005.14165
2. King, M.R.: ChatGPT: a conversation on artificial intelligence, Chatbots, and plagiarism in higher education. Cel. Mol. Bioeng. **16**, 1–2 (2023). https://doi.org/10.1007/s12195-022-00754-8
3. Kasneci, E., et al.: ChatGPT for good? on opportunities and challenges of large language models for education. Learn. Individ. Differ. **103**, 102274 (2023). https://doi.org/10.1016/j.lindif.2023.102274
4. Borji, A.: A Categorical Archive of ChatGPT Failures. arXiv preprint http://arxiv.org/abs/2302.03494 (2023). https://doi.org/10.48550/arXiv.2302.03494
5. Bhattacharyya, M., Miller, V.M., Bhattacharyya, D., Miller, L.E.: High rates of fabricated and inaccurate references in ChatGPT-generated medical content. Cureus **15**, e39238 (2023). https://doi.org/10.7759/cureus.39238
6. Lin, S., Hilton, J., Evans, O.: Teaching Models to Express Their Uncertainty in Words. arXiv preprint http://arxiv.org/abs/2205.14334 (2022). https://doi.org/10.48550/arXiv.2205.14334
7. Zhuo, T.Y., Huang, Y., Chen, C., Xing, Z.: Red teaming ChatGPT via jailbreaking: bias, robustness, reliability and toxicity (2023). https://doi.org/10.48550/ARXIV.2301.12867
8. Luca, O., Andrei, L., Iacoboaea, C., Gaman, F.: Unveiling the hidden effects of automated vehicles on "do no significant harm" components. Sustainability. **15**, 11265 (2023). https://doi.org/10.3390/su151411265
9. Rich, A.S., Gureckis, T.M.: Lessons for artificial intelligence from the study of natural stupidity. Nat. Mach. Intell. **1**, 174–180 (2019). https://doi.org/10.1038/s42256-019-0038-z
10. Nussberger, A.-M., Luo, L., Celis, L.E., Crockett, M.J.: Public attitudes value interpretability but prioritize accuracy in Artificial Intelligence. Nat. Commun. **13**, 5821 (2022). https://doi.org/10.1038/s41467-022-33417-3
11. Oviedo-Trespalacios, O., et al.: The risks of using ChatGPT to obtain common safety-related information and advice. Safety Sci. **167**, 106244 (2023). https://doi.org/10.1016/j.ssci.2023.106244
12. Malik, A., Heyman-Schrum, C., Johri, A.: Use of Twitter across educational settings: a review of the literature. Int. J. Educ. Technol. Higher Educ. **16**, 36 (2019). https://doi.org/10.1186/s41239-019-0166-x
13. Sebastian, G.: Privacy and data protection in ChatGPT and other AI Chatbots: strategies for securing user information. Int. J. Secur. Privacy Pervas. Comput. **15**, 1–14 (2023). https://doi.org/10.4018/IJSPPC.325475
14. Gesikowski, C.: Is Your ChatGPT Conversation Safe? Think Again!, https://bootcamp.uxdesign.cc/is-your-chatgpt-conversation-safe-think-again-a63b095cb9d5. Accessed 01 Feb 2024
15. March 20 ChatGPT Outage: Here's What Happened. https://openai.com/blog/march-20-chatgpt-outage. Accessed 01 Feb 2024
16. Li, H., et al.: Multi-step Jailbreaking Privacy Attacks on ChatGPT. arXiv preprint http://arxiv.org/abs/2304.05197 (2023). https://doi.org/10.48550/arXiv.2304.05197
17. Wanner, J., Herm, L.-V., Heinrich, K., Janiesch, C.: The effect of transparency and trust on intelligent system acceptance: evidence from a user-based study. Electron. Markets **32**, 2079–2102 (2022). https://doi.org/10.1007/s12525-022-00593-5

18. Jeyaraman, M., Ramasubramanian, S., Balaji, S., Jeyaraman, N., Nallakumarasamy, A., Sharma, S.: ChatGPT in action: harnessing artificial intelligence potential and addressing ethical challenges in medicine, education, and scientific research. World J. Methodol. **13**, 170–178 (2023). https://doi.org/10.5662/wjm.v13.i4.170

19. Large Language Models: The Tweets. https://www.kaggle.com/datasets/konradb/chatgpt-the-tweets

The Influence of Usability on User Cognitive Activity: A Differential Intelligence Perspective

Alexandr V. Yakunin[(⊠)] [iD] and Svetlana S. Bodrunova [iD]

St. Petersburg State University, St. Petersburg 199004, Russia
{a.yakunin,s.bodrunova}@spbu.ru

Abstract. Modern quantitative usability research clearly shows a lack of attention to the pragmatic aspects of user experience related to the cognitive processes that accompany most online tasks. Non-taking these processes into account critically prevents formation of informed understanding of the complex, multidimensional structure of user experience, in which intelligence and emotion interact. We use a systems-integrative approach to the structure of intelligence to investigate the relationship between cognitive activity of Internet users and the factors that may shape it during completion of typical tasks, while performing some typical tasks, such as searching and selecting information on a website or classifying online content. In particular, we use the concept of differentiated intelligence, which differentiates cognitive modes into perceptual and semantic intelligence; we set their manifestations via the respective types of tasks ('perceptual' = search for signs, and 'semantic' = search for meanings). Moreover, we expect that both cognitive modes may be critically affected by the conditions of the experiment, as previous research suggests. The four large-scale factors that may cast impact upon the results are united in the 'contextual fidelity' model of usability testing. Our research design allows for detecting: 1) if product features ('good/bad' design with/without modularity and contrast) enable much better performance in both perceptual and semantic modes; 2) if testing conditions (group/individual) and task complexity (easy/complex) critically affect the impact of design upon the two modes of cognition during task performance. The results by 80 assessors allow for stating the synergetic effect of modularity + contrast for perceptual tasks but not for complex semantic ones. Additionally, harmonious design works very differently for various types of tasks, not compensating for task complexity in semantics-oriented tasks but providing rapid growth of efficiency for perceptual ones, as well as for easier tasks of any type.

Keywords: usability testing · quantitative usability studies · layout · user experience · user intelligence

1 Introduction

In most modern research in the field of human-computer interaction and design, conclusions and regularities are formulated on the basis of an integral approach to the structure of 'interaction experience', which provides for the unity of pragmatic and hedonic aspects of user experience in the process of interaction with the product. According to a number of researchers [1, 2], the pragmatic aspect of user experience describes and characterizes the processes related to the utilitarian, practical use of the product. It combines primarily the rationality of the user's action strategy and the efficiency of cognitive processes required to solve a task. The ability of an interface to maximize the efficiency of intelligence, attention, and working memory in solving a task greatly influences both the perceived usability of a product and objective performance.

On the other hand, the hedonic aspect of the 'interaction experience' describes the affective component of the user's experience related to aesthetic joy and emotional impression of the proposed design. This aspect is based on the sensory impact of the graphic interface and the artistic and plastic design of the content. As a rule, the rationality of the media product architecture and the logical organization of its interface are not decisive at this level of evaluation. Satisfaction from working with the product is formed primarily on the basis of subjective aesthetic evaluation and the depth of emotional involvement in solving the task.

Accordingly, the main validity criterion for usability testing within the framework of this two-component UX model is the ability of the method to cover both aspects of cognition, either independently or in their interaction. This makes allows for reconstructing user experience as an integral cognitive process, mirroring to a greater extent the changeable nature of human experiences and the non-linear nature of cognition. However, most of the existing HCI research that aims at raising interface efficiency mainly focuses on analyzing the impact of hedonic ('aesthetic') characteristics of the interface only upon user experience.

Another research gap is that the efficiency of such a dual cognitive process is also affected by four types of factors that may critically alter the results of usability tests. Known as the 'contextual fidelity factors' (see below), they include product features, assessor traits, features of the task, and conditions of the experiment. Previous research suggests shows that cumulative impact of these four groups of factors may create dysfunctional user states that critically lower task performance efficiency, as well as make test results critically diverge, thus demanding many more tests per interface in order to test combinations of the 'contextual fidelity' conditions of interface use. Based on this, we suggest that relevant 'contextual fidelity' factors need to be integrated into the research design as either independent or control variables, as we expect their combinations to cast varying effects upon the two cognitive modes of human-interface interaction.

The remainder of the paper is organized as follows. Section 2 describes in more detail the differential intelligence approach to the cognitive structure of user experience, including the hedonic and pragmatic aspects, as well as states the research hypotheses. Section 3 describes the research design (a particular combination of variables and assessor groups that test them) and the details of mode-inducing tasks on two levels of complexity. Section 4 describes the results and confirms/rejects the hypotheses; Sect. 5 (discussion and conclusion) amplifies it with additional effects discovered in our data.

2 Cognitive Structure of User Experience in the Context of Usability Research

2.1 The Hedonic Aspect of UX: Product Aesthetics and User Experience

The focus of such studies is mainly on issues related to the impact of design aesthetics on subjective factors of user experience. The most developed and extensive area of research is the influence of aesthetic quality of a product on user perception, in which subjectively perceived factors - perceived usability and perceived attractiveness - are emphasized [3–7]. At the same time, it is perceived usability that in most studies is the main variable dependent on aesthetic experiences. As a rule, in most cases the relationship between the subjective assessment of interface effectiveness and the aesthetic component of design is considered [8, 9].

However, the attempt to investigate hedonic and pragmatic aspects of the interface by means of metrics focused on subjective (primarily sensory) perception becomes the reason for contradictions in the research results. On the one hand, some researchers state a positive correlation between the aesthetic quality of a product, perceived usability and user performance [10, 11]. In HCI studies, this correlation is known as the 'confirmation effect', in which a product with higher aesthetic quality is perceived as more usable [12]. On the other hand, according to other studies, objective user performance decreases with increasing aesthetic evaluation of a design, with little correlation between aesthetic evaluation and perceived usability [3–13]. Some studies attempt to explain the psychological mechanisms of this contradiction through cumulative effects associated with experiment repetition. An example is study [2]. However, in this study, the objective indicators of interface effectiveness (performance and workload) are considered through subjective evaluation factors (perceived usability, affect, perceived attractiveness).

Thus, at the present stage neither the aesthetic impression of the product nor perceived usability can be considered as the main criteria in assessing the objective functionality of the interface or as the only factor influencing perceived usability. Forming a holistic view of a product's impact on user experience is impossible without evaluating the impact of the interface on the pragmatic aspect of UX related to rational thinking and controlling user behavior. Performance cannot be a function of aesthetic experiences and emotions alone; a deeper study of the influence of the compositional and graphic model of a web page on rational factors in the user's mind, primarily on the user's intelligence, is necessary.

2.2 The Pragmatic Aspect of UX: The Role of Intelligence

The importance of user intelligence as a factor in evaluating interface effectiveness has been noted in HCI studies on several occasions. Waltraud's study accurately articulates the priority of logical organization of interface elements over the aesthetic appeal of the web page as a whole. More important than emotions and sensory diversity are the obvious ways of interacting with the product and the rationality manifested in the design of the page layout. This study is the first to formulate the conclusion that intuitive intellectual evaluation is more important than emotional evaluation based on the aesthetic component of the page. This is possible because the high correlation between perceived usability and aesthetic impression is based on cognitive processes, a factor that is not taken into account in studies that use only subjective metrics to measure user experience. This study is one of the first to turn the vector of dependence in the formula 'what is beautiful is useful' in the opposite direction - on the contrary, the usability, obviousness and rationality of the interface, which are convenient for the intellect, are largely responsible for the formation of a positive aesthetic impression ('what is rational is beautiful'). Similar results were achieved in Raphael's studies [14, 15], which highlighted the mediatorial role of intelligence in the interaction of perceived usability and perceived attractiveness.

A separate group consists of studies examining the role of intelligence in cognitive processes related via web-based social contexts. These include, in particular, research in the areas of Persuasive System Design (PSD) and Technology Acceptance Models (TAM).

The Persuasive System Design (PSD) model for online communication involves actively changing human attitudes towards a phenomenon and managing user behavior using digital products. PSD is based on interactive systems specifically designed to correct attitudes and behavior using argumentation and social influence without manipulation and coercion. At the same time, persuasive influence through mass communication systems can also be exercised non-directively, through interface quality and design. As some studies [16] suggest, the ability to modify negative and/or encourage positive user behavior can be realized through 'persuasive functionality' - the presence in the interface of features that increase user personal responsibility and interactivity (goal-setting, self-monitoring, and reward tools), as well as social functions responsible for organizing interaction with the social context - tools for cooperation, competition, and social learning. According to the results of research in this area, stimulation of intellectual activity through the interface significantly increases subjective indicators of user experience (UX) evaluation - perceived aesthetics, perceived usability, perceived credibility and perceived usefulness [17, 18].

In the context of HCI problematics, the Persuasive System Design model suggests extending the criterion of 'persuasiveness' to the graphical interface of a web page. As shown in Kiemute Oyibo's study [19], user intelligence perfectly distinguishes between a rationally designed user interface, which allows the free application of cognitive operations in the process of interaction with the product, and an irrational interface, which has no clear logic in the deployment of its functions. In the first case, the interface (and behind it the product itself) is perceived as 'more convincing', and this perception largely determines other, more subjective indicators of user experience (UX). For example, there is a correlation between users' susceptibility to the functional rationality of the interface, which focuses on motivating behavior change, and users' susceptibility to known subjective UX attributes. In particular, there is a strong correlation between the evaluation of the application's intelligence and two subjective metrics - perceived usefulness and perceived aesthetics of the product.

Among HCI studies that examine the cognitive component of UX, it is worth noting the research in the field of technology acceptance model (TAM). In the context of these problems, the cognitive efficiency of the interface acts as a factor that helps users to decide on the use of an innovative interactive system. As Davis [20] shows, it is the efficiency of intellectual operations that forms the basic cognitive belief of the user about the functionality of the product. All other subjective criteria for evaluating UX design (perceived aesthetics, perceived usability, perceived reliability and perceived usefulness) are its conceptualization.

A typical example of research on the relationship between the cognitive component of a product and the perceived attributes of UX design in the field of technology acceptance model application can also be the Baby study [21]. In this study, the authors consider the influence of the user's awareness of the capabilities of the technology underlying the product on other user experience metrics as the intellectual component. As the results of the study suggest, the level of awareness can act as one of the predictors of willingness to adopt the technology.

The following conclusions can be drawn from the review of research studies on the influence of product features on user experience:

1. At the present stage, most HCI studies examining cognitive processes in the context of product usability evaluation recognize the priority of the pragmatic aspect of UX over the hedonic aspect related to perceived aesthetics, emotions, and perceived usefulness. At the same time, the leading trend in research up to the present stage can be considered to be the predominant attention to the hedonic aspect – due to the fixation on studying the aesthetic influence of the interface on other factors of user experience (e.g., perceived usability);
2. Most authors recognize the user's intellectual activity in interaction with the product as the leading factor in the formation of user satisfaction - both in pragmatic and hedonic dimensions (the more actively involved and freer the user's intellect is, the higher the other indicators);
3. Despite the recognized importance of the cognitive component in the 'interaction experience', current research lacks attempt to study the relationship between intellectual activity in working with a product and its objective properties - in particular, its compositional and graphical model. Typically, cognitive processes in most studies are considered in the context of perceived subjective performance and are related to the user's behavioral activity or awareness of the task content.

Thus, we can confidently say that there is a deficit of scientific studies that would examine in detail the relationship of the compositional and graphic model of a website with the intellectual potential of the task, and through it - with the pragmatic aspect of UX as a whole. The proposed article is intended to partially fill this gap.

For this purpose, we conducted an experiment that more deeply investigated the relationship between the objective parameters of website composition and the intellectual component of the user experience.

In doing so, we relied on the theory of discriminative ability of the brain as the basis of intelligence [22]. According to this theory, most cognitive processes are based on the brain's ability to distinguish and classify stimuli-objects on the basis of specified criteria or external features. This ability is key for the development of analytical and logical functions, and high levels of synthesis, generalization, and abstraction are impossible without it. Therefore, it is the core of intelligence, and the speed of reactions that require identification and differentiation of various stimuli is a criterion of one's cognitive performance. The ability to differentiate objects, thus, has a system-integrative character for all forms of intellectual activity when interacting with a product.

We also took into account new ideas on the functional structure of intelligence [23–25], according to which its basis is a complex multilevel system of mental experience, in which two abilities to differentiate stimuli are particularly emphasized: by external attributes and features ('perceptual intelligence') and in terms of belonging to different semantic categories ('semantic intelligence'). In accordance with this concept, we developed two types of tasks, perceptual and semantic, each of which allowed us to evaluate the performance of the corresponding ability of the user's intelligence.

In developing the empirical material for the experiment, we were guided by the method of aesthetic indexing of webpages based on quantitative evaluation of the compositional and graphic model of a web page, substantiated in previous studies and known as U-index [26]. Based on U-index, we developed four options of a web page layout differing in two macro-level parameters of the webpage, namely contrast and modularity. The choice of these parameters was justified by the fact that, according to a number of studies [27–29], they determine the effectiveness of spatial distribution of attention when searching for stimulus-objects on the computer screen and their differentiation from the background and from each other.

Each of the web page layouts differed from the others by a unique combination of the specified macro-level composition parameters-or the absence of both (Table 1):

Table 1. Web page layout design variants

Layout code	Modularity	Contrast
L1	present	present
L2	present	no
L3	no	present
L4	no	no

2.3 The Research Questions and Hypotheses

In designing the experiment, we have taken into account all the abovestated. We have proceeded from the following guiding question:

As we hypothesized, varying macro-level parameters in web page design should have a meaningful impact on user intelligence and related cognitive performance on tasks of varying complexity. In line with this assumption, we formulated a key research question: what effect do contrast and modularity of web page layout jointly/separately have on different modes (perceptual and semantic) of intellectual activity?

Or, in a different formulation: is there a possible synergistic effect of the joint influence of layout contrast and modularity on perceptual and semantic intellectual tasks?

In line with this question, we put forward two hypotheses:

H1: a group test format will enhance cognitive performance on both types of tasks for all levels of complexity;

H2: the joint presence of contrast and modularity will maximize the impact on both types of tasks for all levels of complexity.

3   The Research Method

3.1   The Research Design

To test our hypotheses, we developed an 8 × 4 study design. Test tasks were performed in sixteen subgroups, each of which worked with both types of tasks (perceptual and semantic) in two testing formats (group or individual) on two different layouts. Thus, our experiment included 40 assessors and had the following design (see Table 2).

Table 2. Assessor groups based on the research design, 5 people per group.

Layout type	Test format	Type of task and level of complexity			
		Perceptual task		Semantic task	
		Easy	Complex	Easy	Complex
L1	Group test	Subgroup1	Subgroup9	Subgroup8	Subgroup16
	Individual test	Subgroup2	Subgroup10	Subgroup7	Subgroup15
L2	Group test	Subgroup3	Subgroup11	Subgroup6	Subgroup14
	Individual test	Subgroup4	Subgroup12	Subgroup5	Subgroup13
L3	Group test	Subgroup5	Subgroup13	Subgroup4	Subgroup12
	Individual test	Subgroup6	Subgroup14	Subgroup3	Subgroup11
L4	Group test	Subgroup7	Subgroup15	Subgroup2	Subgroup10
	Individual test	Subgroup8	Subgroup16	Subgroup1	Subgroup9

3.2   The Experimental Tasks

Table 3. Types of tasks and their content

Type task	Complexity level	Contents of the task
perceptual	easy	Sorting images (product cards) by two strong contrasting colors in the font design - red and black
	complex	Sorting images (product cards) by two low-contrast colors in the font design - red and orange
semantic	easy	Sorting by categories of images (product cards) that have no semantic connection with each other
	complex	Sorting by categories of images (product cards) belonging to adjacent semantic categories

As mentioned above, we designed two types of tasks for the experiment, perceptual and semantic, in two variants of difficulty each (see Table 3).

4 Results

The overall results of our experiment are presented in Table 4.

As the results of the empirical study show, the parameters of the compositional and graphical model of a website generally reveal a relationship with the experimental conditions and the user's cognitive processes.

As can be seen from the results of the study, for the L1 layout, the difference between the group and individual test data (in favor of the group test) is 1.94 s. for the task of easy difficulty level and 1.4 s. for the difficult task. In turn, for layout L2 in the case of an easy task, this difference is 1.2 s. and 1.04 s. for a difficult task; for L3 – 0.8 (easy task) and 0.14 (difficult task). It is easy to notice that the maximum value of the difference in the test data of different formats reaches in the L1 layout, in which both parameters of the macro-level of the compositional and graphic model – modularity and contrast – are present. At the same time, the difference in the data for layout L4, in which both parameters are absent, turns out to be within the statistical error (0.06 for simple and 0.04 for complex tasks). However, in the case of the easy task, the difference in speed for layout L1 is 0.6, for L2 and L4 even less – 0.06 s. An increase in the gap between the speed data in favor of the group test is observed only in one case – in the case of layout L3, which may be caused by the stimulating effect of contrast on the solution of this type of tasks in group conditions. This suggests a weakly pronounced synergistic effect. But in the case of the complex task, the difference in the data for all layouts turns out to be within the statistical error – for L1, L2, L3, and L4 it is 0.02, 0, 0, 0, and 0.04 s. respectively.

For group tests of the easy task on L1 the speed value is 13.2 s. vs. 19.2 (L2), 20.8 (L3), and 22.34 (L4). For individuals, it is 15.14 s. vs. 20.4 (L2), 21.6 (L3), and 22.4 (L4). The same trend holds for the complex perceptual task – for group tests on L1 the speed value is 13.8 s. vs. 21.1 (L2), 22.9 (L3) and 23.16 (L4). For individual – 15.2 s. vs. 22.14 (L2), 23.04 (L3) and 23.2 (L4). The trend remains valid for the semantic task for both levels of difficulty and both testing formats – group and individual.

Indeed, let us examine this regularity on the example of individual testing results, since all the noted trends remain relevant for group tests as well. In Table 2, which presents the results of individual testing, we can see the growth of intellectual lability indices when complicating two simple tasks to medium complexity - in this case, the difference in intellectual lability indices before and after the test is $\Delta = 2$ s. (which means that the Stroop test is two seconds faster after completing a task of medium complexity of both types). The level of emotional tension also rises synchronously with this index - the difference between the indexes on the 'Calmness/anxiety' scale before and after the test is $\Delta = -0.6$ (7.6/7). The level of emotional arousal also rises: $\Delta = 1.6$ (6.8/8.4; Excitement/depression scale). The level of fatigue decreases: $\Delta = 1.4$ (6.6/8; Energy/fatigue scale).

However, the high visual complexity of the product combined with the high cognitive complexity of the task contributes to a sharp drop in the index of intellectual lability, which indicates the transition of anxiety into a stressogenic phase: the index drops to 1.5s in favor of slower performance of the Stroop test after completing the task. Dysfunctionality also grows in the emotional self-esteem indicators: the index on the scale 'Calmness/anxiety' (Δ) falls from -0.6 to -1.6 (8.2/6.6), which means a significant

Table 4. The results of the experiment

Layout type	Test format	Type of task and level of complexity					
		Perceptual task			Semantic task		
		Easy	Complex	delta (Δ)	Easy	Complex	delta (Δ)
L1	**Group test**	**13,2**	**13,8**	0,6	19,14	23,16	4,02
	Individual test	**15,14**	**15,2**	0,06	19,74	23,18	3,44
L2	*delta (Δ)*	*1,94*	*1,4*		*0,6*	*0,02*	
	Group test	19,2	21,1	1,9	23,34	25,24	1,9
	Individual test	20,4	22,14	1,74	23,28	25,24	1,96
	delta (Δ)	*1,2*	*1,04*		*-0,06*	*0*	
L3	**Group test**	20,8	22,9	2,1	20,7	25,1	4,4
	Individual test	21,6	23,04	1,44	21,64	25,1	3,46
	delta (Δ)	*0,8*	*0,14*		*0,94*	*0*	
L4	**Group test**	22,34	23,16	0,82	23,86	25,3	1,44
	Individual test	22,4	23,2	0,8	23,8	25,34	1,54
	delta (Δ)	*0,06*	*0,04*		*-0,06*	*0,04*	

shift towards anxiety and worry. The Energy/fatigue scale shows an increase in fatigue: it is now $\Delta = -1.4$ (7.2/5.8).

Obviously, in this case, the synchronous growth of both types of difficulty becomes an irrelevant factor interfering with task performance. According to the table, we can determine the combination of two types of complexity, at which the phase dynamics of functional states breaks down: it is a combination of the average level of visual complexity and a high level of cognitive complexity. It is here that the index of intellectual lability reaches a critical value ($\Delta = -2.1$), the experience of anxiety begins to transition into a negative phase and fatigue begins to grow.

Such dynamics is quite consistent with both modern ideas about the multifactorial and changeable nature of human consciousness and the data of our previous studies in the field of cumulative UX-effects. Thus, hypothesis **H1** can be considered confirmed.

To evaluate hypothesis **H2**, attention should be paid to the dynamics of functional states in cases of growth of one type of complexity while maintaining the minimum level of the other. As the experimental results have shown, there is a correlation between the type of dysfunctional state and a certain type of task complexity.

For the growing cognitive complexity at the minimal level of visual complexity we observe a clear development of the anxiety pattern: at the low level of visual complexity there is a simultaneous growth of intellectual lability, as well as indicators of emotional tension (scale 'Calmness/anxiety') and nervous excitement ('Excitement/depression') with a decrease in fatigue ('Energy/fatigue'). Thus, for the low level of visual complexity in the case of an individual test, simultaneously with the growth of cognitive task complexity, the sequential growth of the intellectual lability index is as follows: from Δ

= −1.66 s. (44.7/46.1 s.) at the medium level of cognitive task complexity to $\Delta = -$ 1.9 s. (44.1/45.2 s.) at the high level. Interestingly, this trend holds for the intermediate level of visual complexity (Δ): the increase ranges from −1.9 (easy level of cognitive complexity) to −2 s (44.1/45.2; medium level) to −2.1 (47.2/45.1; complex level). An increase in emotional stress begins to appear at the medium level of visual complexity (Δ, Calmness/anxiety scale): from −0.6 (7.6/7; medium level of cognitive complexity) to −0.8 (7.8/7; complex level). Negative values mean a shift of self-esteem towards greater anxiety.

In the case of the group test, the dynamics remains the same. At the low level of visual complexity, the increase in the complexity of the cognitive task gives the following dynamics to the index of intellectual lability: from $\Delta = -2$ s. (49.6/47.7 s.; medium level of cognitive complexity) to $\Delta = -2.1$ s. (47.1/45.2 s.; complex level).

The trend is maintained at the medium level of visual complexity (Δ): the increase is from −2.8 (47/44.2; easy level of cognitive complexity) to −2.9 s (47/44.1; medium level) to −3 (46.6/43.6; complex level).

As in the case of the individual test, the increase in emotional stress begins to appear at the medium level of visual complexity (Δ, Calmness/anxiety scale): from − 1 (7.6/7; medium level of cognitive complexity) to − 1.8 (7.8/7; complex level).

At the same time, an increase in the level of visual complexity while maintaining a low/medium level of cognitive complexity reveals a tendency to form a dysfunctional state associated with monotony. In individual test results, this tendency is reflected in a drop in intellectual lability (Stroop's test is performed slower after task performance than before) and a decrease in the indexes of emotional arousal on the 'Excitement/depression' scale with an increase in the index of fatigue on the 'Energy/fatigue' scale. All the noted effects are also observed in the group test.

Thus, the results of the experiment confirm the significance of the differences between the two types of task complexity from the point of view of the user's functional states. Changing different types of complexity (visual and cognitive) provokes the manifestation of different functional states. Hypothesis **H2** can be considered as generally confirmed.

As mentioned above, all the trends characteristic of individual tests were also present in group tests. At the same time, as it is easy to see when comparing the cells of Tables 2 and 3, the numerical values of the corresponding indicators are always greater in the group tests. It is safe to say that hypothesis **H3** is confirmed: test performance in group format enhances the effects associated with the formation of functional states under the influence of product and task complexity.

5   Discussion and Conclusion

Thus, we can draw conclusions about the confirmation of the proposed hypotheses.

First, it should be noted that the greatest influence of the group testing format is manifested in the perceptual task - in this case, the speed of stimulus-object distinction is noticeably higher than in the individual test (regardless of the type and level of complexity of the layout). However, for the semantic task the influence of the group testing format on the results was not so significant. Thus, hypothesis **H1** can be recognized as partially confirmed - it is fully valid only for the perceptual task.

Secondly, it should be noted that there is a clearly pronounced synergetic effect associated with testing on layout L1 ('modularity + contrast'): the speed of perceptual task performance on this layout significantly exceeds the indicators of other layouts. Meanwhile, the results for the L4 layout show that in the absence of modularity and contrast, design has almost no effect on cognitive performance, and this supports hypothesis **H2**. Thus, hypothesis **H2** can be considered fully confirmed.

In the case of the semantic task, the key factor of cognitive efficiency is the contrast of the layout: as can be seen from the data for layout L3, the speed of performance of semantic tasks of both levels of complexity increases on this layout:

- for the easy task: 20,7 vs. 23,34 for the group test and 21.64 vs. 23.28 for the individual test;
- or the complex task: 25.1 vs. 25.24 for the group test and 25.1 vs. 25.24 for the individual test.
- A similar key factor for the perceptual task is modularity – the speed for the L2 layout is higher than for the contrast version:
- for the easy task: 19.2 vs. 20.8 for the group test and 20.4 vs. 23.28 for the individual test;
- for the complex task: 21.1 vs. 22.9 for the group test and 22.14 vs. 23.04 for the individual test.

A similar trend is evident for the semantic task regardless of the testing format.It can also be noted that the use of contrast in the design (layout L3) when solving easy tasks (both types) actualizes the dependence of test results on test conditions – in the group version of the test the speed of problem solving is significantly higher than in the individual version: the difference in speed between the group and individual test is 0.8 s. for the perceptual task and 0.94 for the semantic task, while in the case of the difficult task it is almost absent.

The dependence on test conditions is also characteristic of the L1 layout: the compositional factors of fashionability and contrast not only have a synergistic effect on cognitive processes, but also act differently in different conditions. In the case of a perceptual task, cognitive activity becomes sensitive to the form of the test (the speed of thinking in the group is significantly higher than the individual test – $\Delta = 1.94$ for a simple task and $\Delta = 1.4$ for a complex task).

In the case of the semantic task, there is a significant dependence of the speed of thinking on the level of complexity of the task: the difference in results is 19.14 versus 23.16 s. for the group test and 19.74 23.18 s. for individual. In this case, the social context turns out to be insignificant.

The presence of this effect indicates that a design of high aesthetic quality is not always able to compensate for the negative effects resulting from the increased complexity of the task. In different settings, the compositional factors of such a design can have both positive and negative effects on different cognitive processes in the user experience.

Acknowledgments. This research has been conducted on behalf of the Center for International Media Research of St. Petersburg State University, Russia.

Disclosure of Interests. The authors have no competing interests to declare that are relevant to the content of this article.

References

1. Law, E., Roto, V., Vermeeren, A.P., Kort, J., Hassenzahl, M.: Towards a shared definition of user experience. In: CHI'08 Extended Abstracts on Human Factors in Computing Systems, pp. 2395–2398 (2008)
2. Sauer, J., Sonderegger, A.: Visual aesthetics and user experience: a multiple-session experiment. Int. J. Hum. Comput. Stud. **165**, 102837 (2022)
3. Ben-Bassat, T., Meyer, J., Tractinsky, N.: Economic and subjective measures of the perceived value of aesthetics and usability. ACM Trans. Comput.-Hum. Interact. (TOCHI) **13**(2), 210–234 (2006)
4. Hartmann, J., Sutcliffe, A.G., De Angeli, A.: Towards a theory of user judgment of aesthetics and user interface quality. ACM Trans. Comput.-Hum. Interact. **15**(4), 1–30 (2008)
5. De Angeli, A., Sutcliffe, A.G., Hartmann, J.: Interaction, usability and aesthetics: What influences users' preferences? In: Proceedings of the 6th conference on Designing Interactive Systems (DIS-06), pp. 271–280. ACM Press, New York (2006)
6. De Angeli, A., Lynch, P., Johnson, G.I.: Pleasure versus efficiency in user interfaces: towards an involvement framework. In: Green, W.S., Jordan, P.W. (eds.) Pleasure with products: Beyond usability, pp. 97–111. Taylor and Francis, London (2002)
7. Hassenzahl, M.: The effect of perceived hedonic quality on product appealingness. Int. J. Hum.-Comput. Interact. **13**, 479–497 (2002)
8. Tuch, A.N., Roth, S.P., Hornbaek, K., Opwis, K., Bargas-Avila, J.A.: Is beautiful really usable? toward understanding the relation between usability, aesthetics, and affect in HCI. Comput. Hum. Behav. **28**(5), 1596–1607 (2012)
9. Sonderegger, A., Sauer, J.: The influence of design aesthetics in usability testing: effects on user performance and perceived usability. Appl. Ergon. **41**, 403–410 (2010)
10. Sauer, J., Sonderegger, A., Heyden, K., Biller, J., Klotz, J., Uebelbacher, A.: Extra-laboratorial usability tests: an empirical comparison of remote and classical field testing with lab testing. Appl. Ergon. **74**, 85–96 (2019)
11. Sonderegger, A., Zbinden, G., Uebelbacher, A., Sauer, J.: The influence of product aesthetics and usability over the course of time: a longitudinal field experiment. Ergonomics **55**(7), 713–730 (2012)
12. Lindegaard, G., Dudek, C.: What is this evasive beast we call user satisfaction? Interact. Comput. **15**(3), 429–452 (2003)
13. Azlina, N., Ahmad, N., Hussaini, M.: A usability testing of a higher education mobile application among postgraduate and undergraduate students. Int. J. Interact. Mob. Technol. **15**(9), 88–101 (2021)
14. Otten, R., Schrepp, M., Thomaschewski, J.: Visual clarity as mediator between usability and aesthetics. In: MuC'20: Proceedings of Mensch und Computer, pp. 11–15 (2020)
15. Schrepp, M., Otten, R., Blum, K., Thomaschewski, J.: What causes the dependency between perceived aesthetics and perceived usability? Int. J. Interact. Multimed. Artif. Intell. **6**(6) (2020)
16. Oinas-Kukkonen, H., Harjumaa, M.: Persuasive systems design: key issues, process model, and system features. Commun. Assoc. Inf. Syst. **24**, 485–500 (2009)

17. Matthews, J., Win, K.T., Oinas-Kukkonen, H., Freeman, M.: Persuasive technology in mobile applications promoting physical activity: a systematic review. J. Med. Syst. **40**, 1–13 (2016)
18. Munson S.A., Consolvo, S.: Exploring goal-setting, rewards, self-monitoring, and sharing to motivate physical activity. In: Proceedings of the 2012 6th International Conference on Pervasive Computing Technologies for Healthcare and Workshops, San Diego, CA, USA, 21–24 May 2012, pp. 25–32 (2012)
19. Oyibo, K., Vassileva. J.: Relationship design attributes between perceived UX and persuasive features: a case study of fitness app. Information **12**(9), 365 (2021)
20. Gwizdka, J., Spence, I.: What can searching behavior tell us about the difficulty of information tasks? a study of web navigation. In: Proceedings of the 69th Annual Meeting of the American Society for Information Science and Technology (ASIS&T), vol. 43(1), pp. 1–22. Information Today, Inc., Medford (NJ) (2006)
21. Baby, A., Kannammal, A.: Network path analysis for developing an enhanced TAM Model: a user-centric E-learning perspective. Comput. Hum. Behav. **107**, 106081 (2020)
22. Chuprikova, N.I.: Human reaction time: Physiological mechanisms, verbal-semantic regulation, connection with intelligence and properties of the nervous system. YASK Publishing House, Moscow (2019)
23. Dörner, D., Stäudel, T.: Emotion und Kognition [emotion and cognition]. In: Scherer, K.H. (ed.), Psychologie der Emotion, pp. 293–344. Hogrefe, Göttingen (1990)
24. Klein, J., Moon, Y., Picard, R.W.: This computer responds to user frustration: theory, design, and results. Interact. Comput. **14**, 119–140 (2002)
25. Freeman, M.H.: The Aesthetics of Human Cognition. Available at SSRN 3259227 (2018)
26. Bodrunova, S.S., Yakunin, A.V.: U-index: an eye-tracking-tested checklist on webpage aesthetics for university web spaces in Russia and the USA. In: Lecture Notes in Computer Science (including subseries Lecture Notes in Artificial Intelligence and Lecture Notes in Bioinformatics), vol. 10288, pp. 219–233. Springer (2017)
27. Silvennoinen, J.M., Jokinen, J.P.P.: Aesthetic appeal and visual usability in four icon design eras. In: Proceedings of the Conference on Human Factors in Computing Systems, San Hose, CA, USA, 7–12 May 2016, pp. 4390–4400 (2016)
28. Russ, A.L., Ten Saleem, J.J.: Factors to consider when developing usability scenarios and tasks for health information technology. J. Biomed. Inform. **78**, 123–133 (2018)
29. Asemi, A., Asemi, A.: A judgment-based model for usability evaluating of interactive systems using fuzzy Multi Factors Evaluation (MFE). Appl. Soft Comput. **117** (2022)

Enhancing Users' Attachment via Social Activities in Paid Music Platforms: A Quantitative Research

Ziyue Zhang, Zhifan Yu[✉], Lili Liu, Meihua Chen, Ruotong Lai, Yatong Lin, and Kexin Yang

College of Economics and Management, Nanjing University of Aeronautics and Astronautics, Nanjing, China
563169475@qq.com, llili85@nuaa.edu.cn

Abstract. Paid music platforms are gaining popularity in Mainland China, which continuously competing for paid subscribers. In order to survive from the fierce competition, some platforms have implemented functions that promoting user social behavior to retain paid subscribers. However, we know little about the effectiveness of stimulating social activities on the basis of providing music in paid music platforms. Drawing on attachment theory, this study seeks to explore the impacts of social factors (social participation, social relationship, and membership) on user attachment and behavioral intentions (willingness to recommend and willingness to continuously subscribe). Data was crawled from NetEase Cloud Music, a leading Chinese paid music platform, including number of followers, number of followings, number of likes, and so on. Results of the linear-regression analysis reveal that social participation, social relationship, and membership positively affect user attachment, which in turn positively influences users' willingness to recommend and willingness to continuously sub-scribe. Implications for theory and practice have been discussed.

Keywords: Paid music platforms · Attachment theory · Social activities · Willingness to recommend · Willingness to continuously subscribe

1 Introduction

Chinese paid music platforms continuously compete for paid subscribers, by exploring better profit models. The advent of the "mobile digital music era" has prompted domestic online mobile music companies to develop music clients one after another, combining music with social functions [1]. The latest version of QQ Music launched the "splash" community, which establishes groups in various hobbies such as songs, stars, movie variety shows, fashion, etc., to enhance the interaction between fans and improve user attachment by strengthening the social attributes of the platform. In addition to QQ music, there are NetEase Cloud music that highlights the encirclement of "Cloud Village", Xiami music of the new "music circle", and cool dog music of the "circle". It is worth to mention that, NetEase Cloud Music has successfully distinguished itself from the competitors by promoting social interaction among users on the basis of providing high quality music, in order to enhance users' attachment. By the end of the third quarter of 2021, the number of paid subscribers in NetEase Cloud online music reached 27.52 million, indicating more than 93% increase compared with 2020, and the growth rate ranked first in the paid music industry. In 2022, NetEase Cloud Music have cultivated the highest number of monthly active users, among all of the Chinese paid music platforms [2].

Since NetEase Cloud Music was launched in 2013, as a rising digital music platform, "the average monthly user traffic has achieved the industry leader, becoming a dark horse in the field of digital music" [3]. NetEase Cloud Music draws inspiration from the successful practice of Spotify and makes more innovations on this basis. Through the use of playlists, private FM and comment boards, combined with the emotion-led music community atmosphere, NetEase Cloud guides users to have a deep sense of identification and emotional attachment to the community in the way of precise push. Accordingly, number of users in NetEase Cloud Music has increased significantly, as well as users' attachment to the platform [4]. Calculated by revenue, NetEase Cloud has a market share of 20.5% in 2020, ranking as Top 2 in the industry. In addition, by the end of the third quarter of 2021, the number of paid subscribers of NetEase Cloud online music reached 27.52 million, an increase of more than 93% over the same period last year, and the growth rate ranked as Top 1 in the industry [5]. NetEase Cloud Music is not only an online content platform that provides massive song lists, but also a powerful social network that cultivates a large number of users groups. It has changed the functional pattern of the existing music platform, and integrates new social concepts to improve users' ease of use and satisfaction. Users of the platform are able to freely create private playlists, follow musicians and music critics, join relevant cloud circles, and discover more quality music from their posts and sharing and participate in discussions, thus expanding their social circle [6–8].

Promoting users' social behavior in online paid music platforms has become an effective method for managers to enhance user attachment, yet lots of paid music platforms still put efforts in optimizing the content (e.g., purchase more songs), and limited research has explored the influence of users' social attributes on their attachment. In light of attachment theory, this study seeks to investigate why users continuously spend time on a particular paid music platform, recommend it to others, and pay the subscription fee. More particularly, this study develops a conceptual model to examine how users' social participation, social relationships, and membership in paid music platforms affect their attachment, which in turn affects users' willingness to recommend and willingness to continuously subscribe.

2 Attachment Theory

Attachment theory was firstly proposed by British psychologist John Bowlby in 1969 in their study on the relationship between mother and child, in order to explain the strong emotional bond formed between infants and their caregivers, which was mainly reflected in the attachment of mother and child [9]. Subsequently, many scholars have applied the theory to investigate interpersonal interactions, such as between relatives, lovers, and friends. Thereafter, the application scope of attachment theory has been expanded, it has been applied to explain the strong emotional relationship between specific objects, such as people and places, places, brands, etc.

In information system research, scholars suggest that attachment is a kind of user experience established by members through functional and emotional interaction in virtual communities, which rooted in their hearts and is one of the driving forces for users to participate in virtual communities [10]. The improvement of an individual's sense of self-worth depends on the external environment. In the process of choosing a social platform, the social characteristics of the platform itself tend to contribute to the improvement of their sense of self-worth, which makes individuals form a sense of attachment to these platforms [11]. It has been proven that consumers will have emotional attachment to specific target objects (enterprises, products, services, brands, communities, etc.) and will be willing to pay additional disposable resources (such as time, energy, financial and material resources) to enhance the social connection with the target object [9].

Attachment theory has been extensively applied to explore the determinants of users' attachment to online platforms, especially how the social characteristics affect user attachment [12, 13]. In paid music platforms, users' attachment reflects various aspects, such as the frequency of users' visits/comments/forwards and the duration of users' visits [14]. In light of attachment theory, this study intends to explain why users are willing to recommend paid music platforms to others and continuously subscribe.

3 Research Model and Hypotheses

The conceptual model is presented in Fig. 1. The model is divided into two main research parts. The first part takes the number of comments, number of posts, number of followers, number of followings, number of likes received, number of posts forwarded, number of comments received, and membership as independent variables, and the user attachment as dependent variables. The second part is based on user attachment as independent variable, willingness to recommend and continuously subscribe as dependent variable.

3.1 Social Participation and User Attachment

Prior research argues that community identity plays an intermediary role between users and brand loyalty, and users have a positive impact on brand loyalty through community identity [15]. This study has well verified the fact that the more frequent the users participate in community, the greater their loyalty and attachment to the community and brand.

The voluntary or involuntary sharing of knowledge and information by members of a community and the frequency of such sharing is an important indicator of the success of a community [16]. In general, Posting is closely related to active social interaction within the online community: the more individuals post, the higher their participation in the online community, and thus the enhancement of community attachment [17]. Thus, we propose following hypotheses:

H1a: The number of comments has a positive impact on user attachment.
H1b: The number of posts has a positive impact on user attachment.

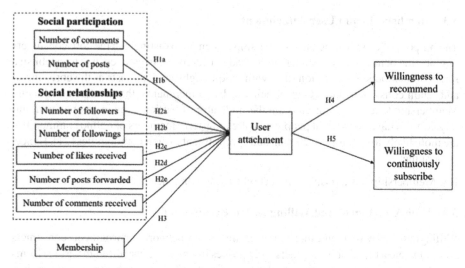

Fig. 1. Research Model

3.2 Social Relationships and User Attachment

Music occupies a certain position in the broad social practice of human beings. Social networking focuses on emotional connection, and users want to make emotional connections with others. A series of emotional behaviors expressed by NetEase cloud music users on social media and all music social practices are a connection, and comments, likes, forwarding and even browsing will constitute a connection [18]. "User emotion as the center" concept has attracted a group of loyal users and fans. NetEase cloud music users can express themselves and tell their experiences by making and uploading playlists, and get positive evaluation and love from others, so as to get emotional satisfaction. The sharer and the receiver can focus on each other and share the same feelings through the collection, reply and like of the playlist, and obtain emotional satisfaction in the interaction [19].

In the final analysis, music socialization refers to the "interweaving of music listening and instant social communication", that is, when users use mobile music platforms to enjoy music, they form deep connections through personal sharing and multidimensional interaction to meet the needs of music and social communication, and better explore and share excellent music to enhance user attachment [20]. Therefore, we propose:

H2a: The number of followers has a positive impact on user attachment.
H2b: The number of followings has a positive impact on user attachment.
H2c: The number of likes received has a positive impact on user attachment.
H2d: The number of posts forwarded has a positive impact on user attachment.
H2e: The number of comments received has a positive impact on user attachment.

3.3 Membership and User Attachment

The purpose of establishing the membership system is to distinguish the core consumers or guide the behavior of consumers with grade differences. In essence, it is to establish a series of membership operation rules with unique rights and interests as the core, attract and retain consumers and enhance their loyalty to merchants, that is, user attachment. Membership tenure or duration is another indicator of participation in an open community. Studies have shown that people who are long-term members of online communities are more likely to develop attachment and commitment to their communities [21]. Hence, we assume:

H3: Membership has a positive impact on user attachment.

3.4 User Attachment and Willingness to Recommend

Willingness to recommend means that in the social network environment, consumers communicate a brand or its products and services in a positive way through various forms of online and offline interaction. In the case of a close relationship between enterprises and customers, enterprises can improve service quality by effectively understanding customer needs, reasonably resolving customer complaints, and actively responding to customer opinions, reduce customer service perceived risk, increase user attachment, increase customer recognition of merchants, and then generate brand loyalty and reduce complaints. Actively realize interpersonal word-of-mouth communication [22]. Therefore, we argue:

H4: User attachment has a positive impact on willingness to recommend.

3.5 User Attachment and Willingness to Continuously Subscribe

In this study, the willingness to continuously subscribe refers to the continuous payment behavior of NetEase Cloud music users for the membership rights and benefits obtained during the use of the platform. Lin Y X found in his research on factors affecting the willingness of video website users to pay that the higher the perceived content quality and service quality of video website users, the more positively the attitude towards payment [23]. The higher the user's perception of the quality of NetEase Cloud music community content and services, the more inclined to use NetEase Cloud music, which means higher user attachment. Thus, we propose:

H5: User attachment has a positive impact on willingness to continuously subscribe.

4 Data Collection and Processing

4.1 Data Collection

Opening the personal homepage of NetEase Cloud music users on the PC side, we could find that NetEase Cloud music not only had the function of listening to songs, but its social attributes were becoming more and more obvious. On a user's profile page, we are able to crawl data such as nickname, number of posts, number of followings, number of followers, membership and the playlist in the past week. Besides, we are able to obtain data of users' past behavior (including sharing music, posting article, sharing video, sharing song list, sharing comments, etc.), the number of likes received, the number of posts forwarded, the number of comments received (Figs. 2 and 3).

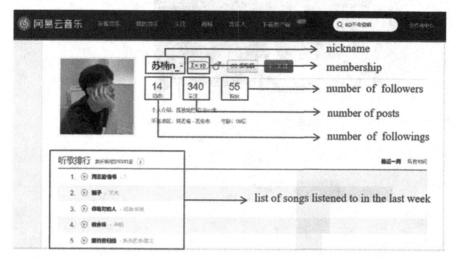

Fig. 2. Screenshot of a User's Profile Page on NetEase Cloud Music (desktop version)

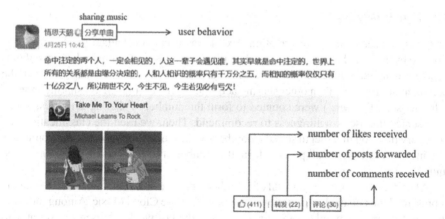

Fig. 3. Screenshot of a User's Post on NetEase Cloud Music Platform (desktop version)

Furthermore, on NetEase Cloud Music mobile APP, we are able to crawl users' VIP level from their profile page. The longer the user paid for the VIP membership, the higher the level. VIP level reflects user's willingness to continuously pay the subscription fee to NetEase Cloud Music platform. As supplementary, VIP level data was crawled from the APP, by searching for users nicknames to ensure that we crawled data from same group of users on both PC version and APP version (Fig. 4).

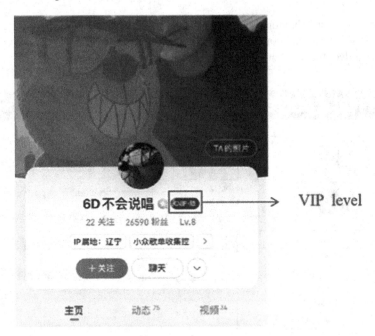

Fig. 4. Screenshot of a User's Profile Page on NetEase Cloud Music App (mobile version)

4.2 Data Processing

In terms of user personal information, Excel was used to calculate the list of songs listened by users in the last week to form an indicator of user attachment. In terms of user behavior data, the "shared comments" in the user activities were calculated to form the comment number, and then other sharing activities of the user (such as "sharing music", "sharing song list", etc.) were counted to form the number of sharing activities, which represented the user's willingness to recommend. Then, we used the classification and summary function in Excel to sum the number of likes received, forwards and comments obtained by each user in all posts to form the number of likes received, posts forwarded and comments received.

After data preprocessing, a total of 11 indicators were obtained, of which 8 indicators represented the personal information of users in NetEase Cloud Music. Among the other three indicators, the number of songs listened in the last week represented user attachment, the number of shares represented user's willingness to recommend, and the VIP level represented user willingness to continuously subscribe. By dividing 8 indicators of user's personal information according to their nature, the index of influencing factors of user attachment, which included 3 dimensions, was obtained (see Table 1). These three dimensions were summarized as social participation, social relationships, membership, representing the social attributes of NetEase cloud users.

Table 1. Index of Influencing Factors of User Attachment

Dimensions	Variable name	Index name
Social participation	V1	Number of comments
	V2	Number of posts
Social relationships	V3	Number of followers
	V4	Number of followings
	V5	Number of likes received
	V6	Number of posts forwarded
	V7	Number of comments received
Membership	V8	Membership

In addition, V9, V10 and V11 respectively corresponded to the number of songs listened in the last week (user attachment), the number of shares (willingness to recommend), and the VIP level (willingness to continuously subscribe). We then conducted data analysis based on these 11 indicators.

5 Linear-Regression Analysis

5.1 Social Participation, Social Relationships, Membership and User Attachment

V1–V8 as independent variable and V9 as dependent variable were substituted into linear regression analysis.

Table 2. Model summary

Multiple R	R Square	Adjusted R Square	Durbin-Watson	F
0.929	0.863	0.923	1.777	147.787

The suggested value range of R square was between 0 and 1. The larger the value, the better the model fit. According to the results in Table 2, the regression model decision coefficient R square was 0.863, indicating that V1-V8 had 86.3% explanatory effect on user attachment, and the model fit well. The sequence correlation was tested by Durbin-Watson (D-W value). If the D-W value lied in the range of [1.7–2.3], there was no sequence correlation between variables. The D-W value in Table 2 was 1.777, indicating that the model was well constructed.

In Table 3, each variable had a VIF value below 10, implying that the threat of multicollinearity problem was excluded in this study. Besides, V3's P-value was greater than 0.05, indicating that V3 had no significant correlation with V9. Findings revealed that number of comments, number of posts, number of followers, number of likes received, number of posts forwarded, number of comments received, and membership positively

Table 3. Linear-regression analysis results

	Coefficient	Standard error	t Stat	P-value	VIF
Intercept	−130.761	42.910	−3.047	0.003	–
V1	0.060	0.019	3.160	0.002	3.042
V2	0.009	0.004	2.179	0.030	2.302
V3	0.001	0.000	2.781	0.006	1.656
V4	−0.017	0.015	−1.123	0.263	1.306
V5	0.044	0.006	7.239	0.000	4.139
V6	0.255	0.023	11.327	0.000	4.214
V7	0.010	0.002	5.276	0.000	2.565
V8	26.700	5.253	5.082	0.000	1.130

affected user attachment of NetEase Cloud Music. Yet number of followings had no significant impact user attachment.

5.2 User Attachment and Willingness to Recommend

V9 as the independent variable and V10 as the dependent variable were substituted into the linear regression analysis.

Table 4. Model summary

Multiple R	R Square	Adjusted R Square	F
0.841	0.708	0.707	600.537

Table 5. Linear-regression analysis results

	Coefficient	Standard error	t Stat	P-value	VIF
Intercept	−429.240	121.191	−3.542	0.000	–
V9	5.770	0.236	24.506	0.000	1.000

In Table 4 and Table 5, the R square of the model was 0.708, indicating that user attachment could explain 70.8% of the variance in willingness to recommend. The P-value of V9 was 0.000, indicating that there was a significant positive relationship between user attachment of NetEase Cloud Music and willingness to recommend.

5.3 User Attachment and Willingness to Continuously Subscribe

V9 as the independent variable and V11 as the dependent variable were substituted into the linear regression analysis.

Table 6. Model summary

Multiple R	R Square	Adjusted R Square	F
0.464	0.216	0.212	68.177

Table 7. Linear-regression analysis results

	Coefficient	Standard error	t Stat	P-value	VIF
Intercept	0.972	0.206	4.720	0.000	-
V9	0.003	0.000	8.257	0.000	1.000

In Table 6 and Table 7, the R square of the model was 0.216, implying that user attachment could explain 21.6% of the variance in willingness to continuously subscribe. The P-value of V9 was 0.000, indicating that there was a significant positive relationship between user attachment of NetEase Cloud Music and willingness to continuously subscribe.

The results of hypotheses test were summarized in Table 8.

Table 8. Results of testing hypothesis

Hypotheses	Descriptions	Test results
H1a	The number of comments has a positive impact on user attachment	Supported
H1b	The number of posts has a positive impact on user attachment	Supported
H2a	The number of followers has a positive impact on user attachment	Supported
H2b	The number of followings has a positive impact on user attachment	Supported
H2c	The number of likes received has a positive impact on user attachment	Supported
H2d	The number of posts forwarded has a positive impact on user attachment	Not Supported

(*continued*)

Table 8. (*continued*)

Hypotheses	Descriptions	Test results
H2e	The number of comments received has a positive impact on user attachment	Supported
H3	Membership has a positive impact on user attachment	Supported
H4	User attachment has a positive impact on willingness to recommend	Supported
H5	User attachment has a positive impact on willingness to continuously subscribe	Supported

6 Conclusion

Based on attachment theory, this paper develops a model to explore how the social activities in paid music platforms affect user attachment and behavior (willingness to recommend and continuously subscribe). Findings show that social participation, social relationships, and membership positively influence user attachment, yet number of followings (an indicator of social relationships) has no significant impact on user attachment. In addition, the stronger the user attachment, the stronger the user's willingness to recommend and continuously subscribe.

Theoretically, in light of attachment theory, this study develops a conceptual model to investigate the effect of social behavior on user attachment in paid music platforms, which not only add knowledge on user attachment, but also extend the attachment theory by applying it to the paid music platform context. It is also worth to point out that we further explore the impact of user attachment on willingness to recommend and continuously subscribe, thus extends existing research in terms of consequences of user attachment. Practically, our findings are insightful for paid music platforms managers, who are eager to sustain the paid subscribers and maintain the profits. Based on the findings, we suggest that paid music platform operators should emphasize the nature of online community and further stimulate social interactions within the community. The paid music platform should build an independent interest community for the different interests of users, and cultivate community leaders, so that community leaders can truly become a bridge between users and the community. "Music community" is a new trend, and the future development of music social platforms should be more personalized.

References

1. Li, Y., Zhang, Q., Li, A.R., Cheng, J.: Business model comparison between spotify and NetEase cloud music. In: 2021 4th International Conference on Humanities Education and Social Sciences (ICHESS 2021), pp. 2514–2521. Atlantis Press (2021)
2. Wang, H., Fu, R.: Exploring user experience of music social mode-take netease cloud music as an example. In: Advances in Industrial Design: Proceedings of the AHFE 2020 Virtual Conferences on Design for Inclusion, Affective and Pleasurable Design, Interdisciplinary Practice in Industrial Design, Kansei Engineering, and Human Factors for Apparel and Textile Engineering 16–20 July 2020, pp. 993–999. Springer, Heidelberg (2020)

3. Wang, Y.J.: Social construction of music communication under new media environment: a case study of NetEase cloud music. New Media Res. **06**, 127–128 (2019). https://doi.org/10.16604/j.cnki.issn2096-0360.2019.06.051

4. Wang, M.: Analysis of online music platform based on emotional marketing theory: taking NetEase cloud music as an example. In: 2022 4th International Conference on Economic Management and Cultural Industry (ICEMCI 2022), pp. 1857–1862. Atlantis Press (2022)

5. Cai, J., Shen, R., Hiltz, S.R.: Choice of social music systems in china: a study of NetEase cloud music. In: Adjunct Publication of the 23rd International Conference on Mobile Human-Computer Interaction, pp. 1–6 (2021)

6. Zhang, D.J., Hu, M., Liu, X., Wu, Y., Li, Y.: NetEase cloud music data. Manuf. Serv. Oper. Manag. **24**(1), 275–284 (2022)

7. Zhang, H., Nie, J., Ruan, Z.: The users emotional study of Netease cloud music based on LDA model. In: 2019 4th International Conference on Cloud Computing and Internet of Things (CCIOT), pp. 20–23. IEEE (2019)

8. Zhu, Q.: Negative impact of platform framework on user experience–a case study of NetEase cloud music. In: 2022 5th International Conference on Humanities Education and Social Sciences (ICHESS 2022), pp. 447–453. Atlantis Press (2022)

9. Bowlby, J.: Attachment and loss: retrospect and prospect. Am. J. Orthopsych. **52**(4), 664 (1982)

10. Lou, T.Y.: Research on the Bonding Mechanism of Virtual Community Members. Ph.D. dissertation, Fudan University (2009)

11. https://kns.cnki.net/kcms2/article/abstract?v=bnuN6dG7iIDU_uZcYIDBbemzc7TZ vhMo_xE4GzICTgUZ0vthFTipn_JKSCQUHYX0Ox5WUIaVdKDX7n0GBfbRuwDm8x2 3Zenh7WowiWyAoGoJa8HRBBbz_I4V_O0poPNbwmQIa6HJMIlC-vMMm3jV_Q==& uniplatform=NZKPT&language=CHS

12. Mao, Y.J.: Research on Forming Factors of Emotional Attachment in Virtual Community. M.A. thesis, Jiangxi Normal University (2016)

13. https://kns.cnki.net/kcms2/article/abstract?v=bnuN6dG7iIBnvELveZlteKALvGFo2A6ZI hN3TKlK12bvtmxX_hA1lMitEab1yMQdkLvdmzxRWfN7RP3BS86CtTqknUhvxeJEv gxNxQNgMVycLIYlcfwyJwia2Gsus4oV7anfD6FIZ1283Tw86f6oag==&uniplatform= NZKPT&language=CHS

14. Tang, W.Y.: An analysis of urban residents' attachment characteristics to recreation places: a case study of Nanjing Fuzi Temple. Sci. Geograph. Sinica **10**, 1202–1207 (2011). https://doi.org/10.13249/j.cnki.sgs.2011.10.007

15. Limayem, M., Hirt, S.G.: Force of habit and information systems usage: theory and initial validation. J. Assoc. Inf. Syst. **4**(1), 3 (2003)

16. Liu, Y.J.: Research on User Stickiness of Entertainment Online Communities. M.A. thesis, Northwest University (2017)

17. https://kns.cnki.net/kcms2/article/abstract?v=bnuN6dG7iIApInLyqVgUFggNkEWNbFtIB tIMpBg8cKQcI7bQGIggmB6l5Ihh3CMfVQIvX3jRco4YORv8kJ2RvhZoLKzlJzBFC7v LUmsbHpCYm4wO0qfQ3CUA9y2WQrbvBH6UySdyAIJFnx4JSsXzig==&uniplatform= NZKPT&language=CHS

18. Huo, C.H., Zhang, Y.D., Zhang, X.X.: Research on the influence of user participation in third-party virtual brand community on brand loyalty. Consum. Econ. **06**, 65–70 (2016)

19. Zhou, S.Y.: A Study on the Characteristics and Motivations of Chinese Internet Community Users. M.A. thesis, Fudan University (2011)

20. https://kns.cnki.net/kcms2/article/abstract?v=bnuN6dG7iIBSjc5YTDXQmJfBJsHAet 9RGuo-hF9kjBcfqfQToOeWpGbraL4NAM8Ld67L7pL2aWuaZ7C_bcSdXZPoNOKuM AQFXI3mF7XGO_6iX7KknsXEPluV_-z4VIC8QPmEeec9-crS-J6vRHSddg==&unipla tform=NZKPT&language=CHS

21. Jiang, W., Tao, L., Yang, L.: Mining online user profiles and self-presentations: case study of NetEase music community. Data Analys. Knowl. Discov. **6**(7), 56–69 (2022)

22. Chen, S.S.: The trade-off between sting and cold: the flow of social relationships from "strong" to "weak". Sci. Technol. Commun. **20**, 144–146+151 (2021). https://doi.org/10.16607/j.cnki.1674-6708.2021.20.044

23. Liu, Y.: Operational strategies for music technology market: case study from Netease cloud music. Highlights Bus. Econ. Manag. **20**, 705–710 (2023)

24. Wang, D., Huang, C.: Analysis of album comments based on NetEase cloud music. J. Educ. Human. Soc. Sci. **4**, 203–208 (2022)

25. Zhang, Y.: Strategy analysis of retail enterprises to build membership system under the background of O2O. Bus. Econ. **03**, 82–86 (2022). https://doi.org/10.19905/j.cnki.syjj1982.2022.03.026

26. Sun, C.: Research on Influencing Factors of Mobile Internet Users' Recommendation Behavior in Social Network environment. M.A. thesis, Beijing University of Posts and Telecommunications (2016)

27. https://kns.cnki.net/kcms2/article/abstract?v=bnuN6dG7iIAv5PzoazYnCw4K-bJ9R8X wwFTdlsEfJscLiL0eg2Kjxgf4xWR7bXiQRlem5MT9Bpl1dsWztsT5jEoMxWpb4IXph YhyyPsDyMqZ3y-sh_FVhAAyybd4055z_i0Y4zpWkHsYCyokrbPO8Q==&uniplatform= NZKPT&language=CHS

28. Lin, Y.X.: Research on Influencing Factors of Video Website Users' Willingness to Pay. M.A. thesis, Tianjin University (2020). https://doi.org/10.27356/d.cnki.gtjdu.2020.002061

AI and Language Models in Social Media

Search Is a Hammer, Generative Chat Is a Loom; Beware the Technological Attribution Error

Bert Baumgaertner[✉][iD] and Zeth duBois[iD]

University of Idaho, Moscow, ID 83844, USA
{bbaum,zdubois}@uidaho.edu

Abstract. This paper explores the paradigm shift from traditional search engine usage to the emergent interaction with generative chatbots, specifically in the context of educational settings. We investigate how generative chatbots, exemplified by ChatGPT, represent a fundamentally different tool for inquiry and learning, resembling a loom for weaving thoughts, rather than a hammer for nailing down facts. Through a case study in an upper-division philosophy course on metaphysics, we analyze whether dialogues with ChatGPT can enhance the quality of argumentation and critical thinking among students. Our findings reveal that the conventional "one-shot" query approach, typical of search engine and encyclopedic interactions, significantly underutilizes the potential of chatbots. We argue for the need to reframe our interaction strategies with these AI tools, emphasizing the art of prompting and iterative refinement. The paper sheds light on the importance of adapting to the dialogical nature of generative chatbots as part of AI literacy and its implications for educational practices and cognitive development. Failure to do so may reflect a technological attribution bias.

Keywords: LLM · Chatbots · Generative AI · Pedagogy · Technological Attribution Error

1 Introduction

Generative chatbots like ChatGPT are quickly becoming complementary tools for both thinking and writing. By their very design they utilize an iterative method of inquiry, akin to a Socratic dialogue or the method of reflective equilibrium. The aim of this project was to assess whether the use of ChatGPT as a dialogical partner in a group assignment improves the quality of argumentation in an upper division philosophy course on metaphysics. The results are not what we expected, but the lessons we learned are important and generalize.

The mistake we made is, in hindsight, readily apparent. Our question emphasized features of a generative chatbot. What we know now is that our question should be more focused on the human side of the interaction. Students, like many of us, have learned to interact with search engines using a kind of "one-shot" query. That skill carries over to how we use generative chatbots, but, we argue, it comes at the cost of vastly under utilizing the contributions that a generative chatbot can make towards inquiry.

The range of skill needed for effective search engine query is arguably quite narrow. The best Googlers likely have a distinctive ability in interpreting results, but the disparity between the best and the worst keyword input is minimal. A good hammerer can drive a nail reliably with few swings. By contrast, we claim that generative chatbots are more like a loom for weaving, in an iterative process of refinement and corrective feedback. The large language models (LLMs) that undergird generative chatbots are initialized to be general when the dialogue begins, and as such will not yet be ideally situated to answer queries except those that are equally generic (e.g. "define X" or "who wrote Y"). The art of prompt engineering reflects one aspect of this point. A good prompt will provide the generative chatbot with the information, context, and instructions for how to respond in an effective way. Prompting, however, is a shorthand or subset of the skills of iterative inquiry that we find lacking.

In short, what we found in our classroom study was a skills gap, one that prevented a meaningful measure to assess the generative chatbot itself. Interestingly, however, students reported a perceived benefit of interacting with the generative chatbot, which we interpret as their recognition that there is something to be gained with the skill of iterative inquiry that they were learning (and admittedly, the instructor was learning to get better too).

In this paper we describe the experimental design for the study. We then report the development of the study from the instructor's perspective, using survey results and transcripts to corroborate those findings. Finally, we identify some challenges and propose some ways forward in the broader landscape of AI ecology.

2   Experimental Design of Intended Study

The background for the course in which the study took place is as follows. The class meets once a week for three hours. The instructor lectures for the last hour about the material for the next week. Students are then expected to read the material and write a draft paper that they will bring the next week. Each paper requires students to engage in some kind of philosophical exercise, such as a deductively valid reconstruction of an argument, the refinement of a definition by using counterexamples, or the articulation of enthymemes from the reading. When the class meets the following week, students bring their papers and work in small groups. Each group works towards a "master response" drawing from their individual papers. They then write up this response and submit it to the LMS (Learning Management System).

Over the course the experiment consists of the following. Each week there were four groups, two of which serve as the control, two as the intervention.[1] For the control groups, students were allowed to use their individual papers, in-group dialogues, and the Internet, but not ChatGPT or other LLM. For the intervention groups, students would have additional access to ChatGPT through our custom web app that we called MetaGeep, which would allow us to record the interactions as transcripts. Initially the version we gave them access to was GPT 3.5, but it become readily apparent after a few weeks that version 4 was significantly more powerful (this change is one reason the planned assessment became less meaningful). Assignment to groups was done randomly each week, with the condition that each student would have roughly the same number of opportunities to be in both kinds of groups.

In addition, we had an entrance survey to gauge students' prior familiarity with ChatGPT or other LLMs. At roughly two thirds of the way through the course we administered a survey to collect qualitative data about student perceptions of their use of MetaGeep. Questions comprising these surveys are included in the attached tables. Finally, we saved the transcripts of the intervention groups. The study was approved as exempt by the Internal Review Board at our home institution (IRB 23-154).

Our initial hypothesis was that intervention groups will have better group assignments than control groups. At the conclusion of the semester, the planned assessment was to anonymized each submission to be graded by an outside faculty member. We suspected that students would learn how to better interact with MetaGeep as the semester progressed; potentially co-evident in the development of their weekly group papers. We had thought that the rate of improvement week-by-week would be outstripped by the improvement between intervention and control groups for that respective week, but for reasons explained in more detail below, too many confounders entered into the study to warrant an assessment, particularly in light of the small sample size ($N = 11$). The biggest confounder throughout was that student AI literacy was far lower than we had anticipated.

2.1   MetaGeep

To facilitate interactions with ChatGPT, the researchers considered the procedural constraints of the available commercial webapp. The free app offered by OpenAI is a powerful demonstration of the LLM capabilities, and suitable for casual interactions, but the company places load limits on the freemium version, and denies access to the most advanced model and experimental features. Furthermore, users must create a personal account, and any data exchanged falls under the auspices of the TOS which is beyond our control.

With an expected class size of around one or two dozen students, the first consideration of creating a shared professional group account seemed clumsy

---

[1] There was also a fifth group that had a student that wished not to participate in the study, for which no data was collected.

and unworkable, and doesn't solve for our interest in anonymized data analysis allowed by the IRB agreement.

To solve these issues, we committed to creating a dedicated webapp to facilitate operations. OpenAI provides a commercial API interface to numerous pretrained models. The MetaGeep webapp uses the API in a basic python flask environment to intermediate between the client (the students' browsers), our data server, and OpenAI chat completion calls.

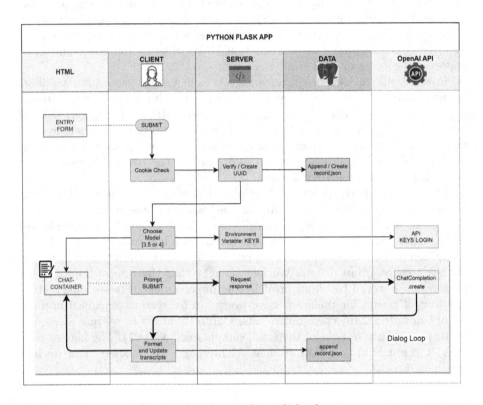

Fig. 1. MetaGeep webapp dialog loop.

Figure 1 visualizes the webapp architecture. The client (participant student) visits the webapp via the public URL. Each access to the page requires the visitor to fill out a two question form about the group membership assignment to track minimal metadata. The client browser checks for a local browser cookie for a UUID marker, generates a new one if this is missing, and iterates a counter. A record is generated on the researchers' file server. All exchanges between the participant and the LLM is saved to a basic JSON session log file on our server.

A simple chat interface is shown to the user. At the start of the study, only models up to the GPT3.5 were available to us. After a couple months of payments, the company allows access to GPT4. This access was granted at about the mid-point of the study, after the students had taken a mid-point survey. In lieu of hard-coding a fixed connection to GPT4, we provided the users a switch in the UI that allowed them to choose the superior model. This was not necessarily out of interest of offering options (as end-users, we see no reason to spend time with 3.5 over 4), but rather as a signal to the students to increase awareness that the new model was available. Intentionally selecting GPT4 and getting suddenly better, more nuanced responses, should be done in the open.

The chat interface is a simple dialog box that expands to accommodate the transcript as it grows. It is important to note that formatting response text can take advantage of CSS styles and LaTeX symbols in the OpenAI completion payload. This feature becomes valuable when working with formal logic and mathematical symbols that are painful for humans to interpret in straight HTML text conversions. As novice webapp developers, we learned some of these minor but impactful tweaks as the study ran.

We also take this opportunity, as a topic self-referencing example, to informally share credit with ChatGPT itself, for helping write the application[2].

MetaGeep on Github https://github.com/Cognition-and-Usability-Lab/metageep

3   Results

We present the results of our observations in chronological order. By doing so we aim to emphasize the most important lesson we learned from conducting this study, which is the need to adapt to the level of AI literacy of the students. Our original study design presumed that group assignment quality could be attributed to features (or lack thereof) of the generative chatbot, even after an introduction to it through a primer exercise.

3.1   Entrance Survey

Our entrance survey provided us with information about student perceptions concerning their skills related to search and chatbots. This helped give us a baseline. The questions and responses are found in Table 1.

Our gloss of the results from the entrance survey was that students tended to self-identify as having the skills for search and for utilizing group interactions. Half the students said that ChatGPT was somewhat or more effective than search engines, and yet still lukewarm about using chatbots for learning. The inference of the two questions suggest that students find non-directed internet knowledge searches to be not very effective at all.

---

[2] Attributions deserved? Searching the Internet and developer forums to find samples and bug fixes is the standard for casual developers in the pre-LLM days. Today, LLMs can sketch out entire applications with functions written from scratch while we sip tea.

Table 1. Entrance Survey Responses (numbers are sums)

How familiar would you say you are with ChatGPT or other LLM?

Not at all familiar	2
A little familiar (heard of it but haven't used it)	2
Somewhat familiar (have tried it)	2
Familiar (use it occasionally)	5
Very familiar (use it regularly)	0

How frequently do you interact with ChatGPT or other LLM?

Never or rarely	6
At least once a month	2
At least once a week	3
At least once a day	0

Compared to search engines (e.g. Google) and information sources (e.g. Wikipedia), how would you rate ChatGPT?

Much less effective	1
Less effective	1
Somewhat less effective	0
About the same	3
Somewhat more effective	4
More effective	2
Much more effective	0

In general, how effective do you find ChatGPT or other LLMs to be as an assistant to learning?

Not at all effective	3
Somewhat effective	5
Effective	1
Very effective	2

How comfortable would you say you are with Internet tools like search and online information sources (Google and Wikipedia)?

Not at all comfortable	0
Somewhat comfortable	0
Comfortable	4
Very comfortable	7

How comfortable would you say you are working with others to solve a problem or complete some task?

Not at all comfortable	0
Somewhat comfortable	2
Comfortable	5
Very comfortable	4

3.2   Primer: What's a Sandwich?

The primer for the course is meant to do three things: 1) introduce students to the methodology of metaphysics, 2) demonstrate by example the weekly pattern we follow going forward (group work, lecture, individual paper - see above for details), and 3) introduce them to the generative chatbot they have access to for the course, which we called MetaGeep.

Metaphysics, as studied in analytic philosophy, has a very rigorous methodology. It's main tool is classical deductive logic: any argument ought to be reconstructable (in principle) into a series of deductively valid inferences. The course does not require Symbolic Logic as a prerequisite and most students will not have taken such a course. Consequently, the course begins with a logic primer.[3] In particular, the primer emphasizes the following conceptual tools that students will be most frequently exposed to and use throughout the course:

- Modus Ponens: the deductively valid inference pattern from "If A then B" and also "A" to the conclusion "B". This is contrasted with a fallacious and invalid inference called affirming the consequent: from "If A then B" and also "B" one cannot deductively infer "A".
- Modus Tollens: the deductively valid inference pattern from "If A then B" and also "not B" to the conclusion "not A". This is contrasted with a fallacious and invalid inference called denying the antecedent: from "If A then B" and also "not A" one cannot deductively infer "not B".
- A counterexample that demonstrates a purported definition or analysis is *too strong* (or *too narrow*): a case that should count as an instance of the concept but the analysis rules it out.
- A counterexample that demonstrates a purported definition or analysis is *too weak* (or *too broad*): a case that the analysis rules in but is not an instance of the concept.

In order to learn and practice using these tools, students are asked to analyze the concept of a sandwich. They are given an initial definition, such as, "A sandwich is a type of food made of two or more slices of bread with one or more fillings between them." As one might expect, students have a lot of fun coming up with counterexamples (hotdogs, calzones, poptarts, etc.), updating the definition, and finding ways to defend their positions by "monster-barring".[4]

Their first weekly individual assignment is to construct two modus tollens arguments that can be used against the initial definition.[5] The following week students are organized into groups where they are assigned to creating a "master

---

[3] The textbook we use in the class comes with a logic primer, which serves as a start [5].

[4] This is in reference to the work of Imre Lakatos on the logic of mathematical discovery. [3].

[5] Specifically they are told, "In one argument (C.1) you should use a counterexample that does not count as a sandwich (per the definition), to show that the definition is too weak (includes case that should be ruled out). In a second argument (C.2) you should use a counterexample that shows the definition is too strong (excludes cases that should be ruled in).

argument" that defends an analysis of what a sandwhich is. For this first group assignment, all groups are allowed to and encouraged to use MetaGeep. The instructor provided a demonstration of how they could interact with this generate chatbot.

Previews of the transcripts from the primer suggested that students were keen to explore the use of MetaGeep as a tool by asking it questions. It was apparent, however, that students were using it just as they would a search engine: the transcripts showed a non-sequitur sequence of one-shot queries. They did not, for example, provide MetaGeep with any sort of feedback as one might in a dialogue with a peer or collaborator. This was an interesting observation because students generally did provide that kind of feedback to each other in their group interactions. We expected that as students became familiar with MetaGeep their interactions with it would more closely resemble their interactions with their peers.

3.3   Early Weeks

Reviewing the transcripts in the early weeks of the course revealed two related issues. One was that MetaGeep was using version ChatGPT 3.5 and giving "canned" style responses that did not solicit additional interactions. For example, a common way that ChatGPT 3.5 would hedge is to say things like, "different cultures and societies give different answers." This was particularly unhelpful because students are not allowed to hedge the same way in their papers and their assignments. Students must be able to explain which answers would be generated by different perspectives and why - they are not allowed to end their analyses by simply saying "it depends". We addressed this issue around week 5 by upgrading to ChatGPT 4. This was then demonstrated to all students and we illustrated how much more nuanced MetaGeep became as a result.

A second issue was that the nature of some of the assignments were too advanced or nuanced that failed to incentivize the use of MetaGeep. Specifically, some of the group assignments required students to reconstruct an argument from that week's reading into a deductively valid argument. Both the students, and the instructor, quickly faced two challenges. First, many of the topics were highly specialized and MetaGeep was not being given enough context - we were facing a prompt engineering problem. Second, the task of reconstructing an argument is not the same as providing summaries, but MetaGeep would frequently conflate these (and mind you, students often too).

In order to make some progress towards this second issue, the instructor adapted some weekly group assignments to better align with the sorts of tasks that generative chatbots seem to be helpful with. Here is one such example:

You are going to write a short dialogue between the Presentist and the Eternalist. You can assume that both are aware of the Truthmaker Objection. Your dialogue should begin with the Presentist rejecting one of the premises. You should aim for at least two iterations (example below). You should also aim to have each contribution to be a concise argument. Here's an example template:

Presentist: I deny premise (II) because X.
Eternalist: Appealing to X commits you to Z. You should reject Z because Y.
Presentist: X does not commit me to Z because W.
Eternalist: Appealing to X commits you to U. You should reject U because V.
Presentist: I am happy to accept U because V is not compelling.

Reviewing transcripts from this kind of assignment showed more engagement with MetaGeep relative to the "reconstruct an argument into deductive form" assignments.[6] But the kind of interaction was still largely a sequence of non-sequitur one-shot queries. By this point we were in the advanced stages of the course (week 8) and each student had been in a group with access to MetaGeep at least three times. In our assessment, the presumptions that undergirded the very ability to even test our hypothesis had failed to hold as expected in our original study design. Users have to be sufficiently proficient in using a technology if a study aims to draw conclusions about the contributions made by the technology. Consequently, we opted to use the planned exit survey to help us gauge student perspectives at this advanced stage.

3.4 Advanced Stage Survey

Our advanced stage survey aimed to gauge how useful the generative chatbot was for this course relative to other resources students had access to. Two salient questions from the survey with mean scores in Table 2.

With all the standard caveats concerning small sample sizes ($N = 11$), two points stood out to us. First, MetaGeep was, from the perspectives of students, better than other materials they could access. The exception was the instructor, who has a strong track record in teaching and has refined complementary course materials (e.g. slides, lecture notes, etc.). In jest: LLMs are not (yet) coming after professor jobs.

Second, and more pedagogically informative, is that students regard each other as having been more helpful than any other tools they had access to. While our observations do not allow us to say precisely why they have this perspective, it is consistent with the speculations we discuss in the next section. In brief, we surmise that students' ability to do iterative inquiry with their non-expert peers in a shared context is more productive than their attempt to do so with an AI that has broad expertise. But, as we will argue below, the Technological Attribution Error makes any inference particularly difficult to assess given nascent AI literacy, especially in the context of inquiry.

---

[6] By "more engagement" we mean a larger number of queries to MetaGeep.

Table 2. Advanced Survey Responses, Mean Scores

Rate the usefulness of these tools on a scale of 1-5, with 5 being the most and 1 the least useful.	
Internet	1.78
ChatGPT	2.22
Books, articles	1.33
Lecture materials, notes	3.33
How much do you agree with the following claims, where 1 means "Strongly disagree" and 5 means "Strongly agree"?	
Discussion with the people in my group helped shape my conclusions	3.78
The tools we used were helpful in shaping the group's conclusions	3.00
I learned or relearned somethings from the tools we used	3.67

4 Discussion

As a gloss, LLM AI was effective for helping students summarize positions, provide a rough overview of debates, and to a limited extent helped them think through counterexamples. It seemed not to be effective for assignments that required careful argument reconstruction based on more nuanced points discussed in the text and in class. Early work elsewhere is providing preliminary evidence that the capabilities of AI are creating a "jagged technological frontier" where some tasks can easily be done by AI, but other similarly difficult tasks are outside its capabilities. [1]

We believe that our observations over the course of this study corroborate what many early adopters are experiencing. In what follows, we present an argument that AI literacy is too nascent to draw any substantial conclusions about either this emerging technology or the users for which they are intended.

We then conclude with a suggestion for how to adapt iterative methods of inquiry, which are exemplified by, though not limited to, humanities scholars. In brief, we suggest a fruitful path forward is to guide the development and use of generative chatbots in a way that aims to elevate existing forms of iterative inquiry.

4.1 The Technological Attribution Dilemma

There are two well-known cognitive biases worth highlighting to set the stage. When someone else makes a mistake, individuals are likely to attribute that mistake to the person's character or personality ("they're careless"). However, when they make a mistake themselves, they're more likely to blame the circumstances or external factors ("the instructions were unclear"). This is the Fundamental Attribution Error, which highlights a bias in social perception, where there is an imbalance in how we interpret our own behavior versus that of others.

Relatedly, when things go well, people tend to credit their own abilities, efforts, or characteristics ("I got a good grade because I'm smart and I studied hard"), but when things go poorly, they are more likely to blame the situation, luck, or the actions of others ("I got a bad grade because the test was unfair"). This is known as the Self-Serving Bias.

There is a third related error, we suggest, that is made particularly salient with the recent advent of generative AI. We call it the Technological Attribution Error. We'll illustrate it with a mechanical example. Suppose there is a single car crash in the Town of Competence. If the baseline is that every driver in the Town of Competence is an expert driver, it would be reasonable to attribute the car crash to some property of the car - perhaps the brakes failed, for example. If the same car crash were to happen in the Town of Maladroit, where the baseline is that drivers are, at best, amateurs that couldn't even drive a go-cart, it would *not* be reasonable to attribute the car crash to a property of the car. Rather, it's far more likely that a driver was at fault.

The Technological Attribution Error occurs when someone faults a poor outcome to the technology without giving proper consideration to the skills of the operator. If we don't know whether we happen to be in the Town of Competence or the Town of Maladroit, it would be fallacious for us to infer that a car crash is the result of something about the car (i.e. the technology). Likewise, it would also be fallacious to simply attribute features to the driver (i.e. the user).

Relatedly, an Attribution Dilemma occurs when there is insufficient information about the capacities of a technology that prevents us from assessing user skills. If we don't know the handling capacities of cars (braking, turning, impact absorbing, etc.) we don't have the means to conduct driver tests, let alone driver education. When we have a fuller understanding of what a vehicle can and can't do we can then develop a more systematic program for training and testing.

We unexpectedly found ourselves in an Attribution Dilemma in our first experience with using generative AI in the classroom. More sophisticated studies outside of academia suggest that we are not alone [1]. We see this as both a cautionary tale and as an opportunity. As a cautionary tale, the very concept of AI literacy is still too nascent for us to be confident in attributing general performance (both successful and unsuccessful) to just one of the user or the generative AI. As an opportunity, we are just beginning to explore the purposes for which LLMs and other generative AI can and should be put to use. In the last section we describe a possible avenue forward in the context of education.

4.2   Iterative Inquiry

We argue that the general population's accustomization to lexicographical search, at least insofar as represented by undergraduate students, makes them particularly prone to the technological attribution error when it comes to generative chatbots. That is, students are likely to engage with ChatGPT with one-shot inquiries, such that when they then receive results contrary to their hopeful expectations, they are likely to infer that the generative AI tool is of little help. What students don't seem to recognize is that they are residents in the Town of Maladroit. Consequently, students are too quick to shy away from the technology because of a fallacious inference they make about its quality. In many cases faculty are also subject to making this error.[7]

We suggest that one possible way forward is to give students assignments that better mirror the iterative nature of generative chatbots. Our suggestion is not meant to replace certain pedagogical techniques, nor even to augment them, per se. Our goal is to help think through ways in which generative AI can elevate humanistic inquiry.

To that end, we briefly describe methods of iterative inquiry. Humanities scholars in particular are experts in using iterative methods of inquiry that are directly applicable to AI literacy. Iterative methods in inquiry include the Socratic method and the method of reflective equilibrium.

The Socratic method is a form of cooperative argumentative dialogue that stimulates critical thinking and illuminates ideas through asking and answering questions. It involves a process of questioning to expose contradictions in one's thoughts and ideas, leading to clarification or reevaluation of beliefs. It is illustrated by the classic and famous dialogues of Plato.[8] It is also illustrated in more contemporary form in mathematical debates, as in the development of proofs of Euler's formula. [3]

The other related example is the method of reflective equilibrium, or more aptly called the reflective equilibrium process. [7][9] In a simple characterization, one begins with a first draft of a principle that accounts for two clear cases; one set includes instances of the relevant concept, the other not. Above we discussed a cartoonish example of this, where we have a draft definition of what a sandwich is, supplemented with some clear examples of sandwiches (a BLT, a grilled cheese sandwich) and clear non-examples (a bowl of cereal, a salad). One then proceeds through a process of mutual adjustments to our judgements about relevant cases (e.g. a hotdog) and the systematic principles meant to account for our judgments. By modifying either when they conflict, one increasingly balances judgments with general principles, ideally obtaining the goal of reaching a state of equilibrium (consistency and harmony).

We believe that a fruitful way forward is to think about how to adapt these iterative methods of inquiry into the design of generative chatbots that are geared towards education and research. Our own experience is that LLMs like GPT-4 have the *capacity* for this, but to date this capacity is underutilized.

---

[7] There is also the counterpart to this error, which is that students simply copy and paste the first result they get. This too reflects their unawareness that they are a citizen of the Town of Maladroit.

[8] See any of *Apology, Crito, Euthyphro, Phaedo, Protagoras, Meno, Symposium, or Gorgias.*

[9] It was made famous by John Rawls in his theorizing of the concept of justice. [6] The end goal of the process is typically to provide a means of justifying a theory of a concept, like justice or the precautionary principle. But that aim is not of interest here. Rather, it is the process itself that we think is relevant.

4.3   Implementation

It may appear that we set the blame of underwhelming results exclusively on the shoulders of the users—for being unimaginative, uninsightful, perhaps dispassionate. As we observed the first interactions between the students with our chatty general purpose knowledge machine, we were admittedly perplexed how lackluster the interactions read. Keeping in mind that these are upper-division philosophy students, we expected some fireworks, as we ourselves experienced right away in each our own preliminary exposures.

We propose it is the general purpose nature of the un-tuned LLM constructs which belies the apparent disparity. Internet users of the contemporary age take their interactions for granted. The internet is on the whole, unimpressive and predictable. The advances of the 30 or so years of the internet-connected age has focused on distribution and quick pay-offs. A young adult in 2024 developed her *theory of mind* in a world with globally-connected pocket computers, responding to her touch, video-calls with her grandmother, texting her like-wise enabled friends. To her, the inquiry mode of the Internet is keyword search, the services are commercial and transactional, the entertainment options are broad and served without delay. Yet the intellect is dim; peak 2020 internet, to the common user, is serviced by pseudo-aware algorithmic social media trackers. Advertising.

As OpenAI proudly rolled out its shiny new language robot, they were necessarily constrained to set it into the firmament *without constrains*[10]. This was a tool for all users, for all purposes. It is an Oracle. The inference potential of any simple question, when posed to the Oracle, can map out an entirely original response as thorough as a pages-long encyclopedia entry. This is more-or-less the problem, or a problem, with LLMs as tutors. The opportunity for engagement is forestalled when the genius know-it-all gives a perfectly composed essay as reply, all in platonic Oxford English diction.

If venture capital investments are any indication of the direction that AI will be headed [4], then it appears to us that the interests in AI is corporate-profit centered. This is not on its face a bad thing, but we feel it does herald more of the same immediate pay-off driven attention, which rarely prioritizes the education sector. This is to say, the inclination for AI implementation is productivity, not well-being. While the later may follow the former, those of us heeding this attention gap may take this as a call to action.

To spell out the critique, simply attaching a flawless natural language engine onto a neural network weighted with 2 trillion parameters isn't adequate interface. The network has ingested everything it can get its hands on, pattern matching into elaborate multi-dimensional webs, and it rests waiting for your inquiry, tireless, without desire. Yet it knows comparatively nothing about the interaction it is having with its user right now. In our opinion, it needs a little more sensitivity, and restraint, and to be more inquisitive.

---

[10] To be literally accurate, specific topic and behavioral constrains were always in place. Lessons learned from Tay [8].

4.4   AI Ecology

Let us take a moment to reflect on the big picture. It can be said that the social technological landscape of the 21st century as visualized through the framework of the accessible Internet, is that of search and service. Humans evidence this paradigm with the expectation that the Internet is a hyperspace tunnel to endless pages of published information, always available, to push and pull information to accomplish capricious needs. The ability to access a given state or modify some of its content relies on the graph's fundamental nature—asynchronous and persistent. The users' portal appears quiescence as it waits for their convenience. We describe a dispassionate utility.

However skilled peak-2020 internet-literati may have been, their queries posed to the terminal return information without transformation. Google may boast a response of millions of "hits" in less than a second, but this is merely an index of published materials. The input looks like language, but the results show no sign of eloquence.

The emerging generative AI ecology will transform this expectation.

Generative Algorithms. OpenAI's generative pretrained transformer(GPT) chatbot, ChatGPT, witnessed the fastest growing consumer adoption in history [2], arguably centering it as the gate-opening consumer general-purpose AI tool. Generative algorithms distinguish from discriminative ones by being able to synthesize original material from deep neural pattern retrieval. The developers of this generative AI tool chose not just language as the primary interface to the algorithm, but in fact *dialog*.

One may wonder, however, has a generation of asynchronous one-shot human-computer interactions habituated the human participant into eschewing dialog? Indeed, a prominent part of contemporary electronically moderated "speech" is instant messages, social media posts, and other timeless distributed *messages-in-bottles* that appear to discourage better-suited dialogue modalities.

To emphasize the distinction, a characteristic inquiry into the Internet or a product document or a reference text is a singular action, each solitary, even if the action is part of a sequence. Any iterative gain—from the most fundamental serial search, manually splitting a volume to find a page number, to the more complex qualitative search of scanning from a variety of sources to compile an objective fact—must be held as an adaptable representation in the seeking human's mind. Likewise, on the surface, any single response from a generative AI is no different, but refining the query with repeated prompts describes a process analogous to interpersonal dialog, evolving, refining, discovering, as each successive inquiry contains the entire series in a continuous context. The former examples can be considered, at best, internal monologue, while the later is an opportunity to engage in a true dialogue. The chat robot is an effective interlocutor.

The recent rapid uptake of generative AI tools forecasts an upgrade for the current low-quality human-computer interaction, suggesting perhaps the adoption of a new moniker, HCC, *human-computer conversation*.

References

1. Dell'Acqua, F., et al.: Navigating the jagged technological frontier: field experimental evidence of the effects of AI on knowledge worker productivity and quality. In: Harvard Business School Technology & Operations Mgt. Unit Working Paper, pp. 24–013 (2023)
2. Hu, K.: ChatGPT sets record for fastest-growing user base - analyst note | Reuters (2023). https://www.reuters.com/technology/chatgpt-sets-record-fastest-growing-user-base-analyst-note-2023-02-01/
3. Lakatos, I.: Proofs and refutations: The logic of mathematical discovery. Cambridge University Press (2015)
4. Metinko, C.: The biggest of the big: AI startups raised huge — these were the largest deals of 2023 (2023). https://news.crunchbase.com/ai/biggest-ai-startups-openai-msft-eoy-2023/
5. Ney, A.: Metaphysics: An Introduction. Routledge (2014)
6. Rawls, J.: A Theory of Justice. Cambridge, Massachusetts : The Belknap Press of Harvard University Press (1971). https://search.library.wisc.edu/catalog/999472448502121
7. Rechnitzer, T.: Applying Reflective Equilibrium: Towards the Justification of a Precautionary Principle. Springer Nature (2022). https://doi.org/10.1007/978-3-031-04333-8
8. Schwartz, O.: In 2016, Microsoft's racist chatbot revealed the dangers of online conversation - IEEE spectrum (2024). https://spectrum.ieee.org/in-2016-microsofts-racist-chatbot-revealed-the-dangers-of-online-conversation

Machine Learning-Based Detection and Categorization of Malicious Accounts on Social Media

Ajay Bhattacharyya◉ and Adita Kulkarni(✉)◉

SUNY Brockport, Brockport, NY 14420, USA
{abhat1,akulkarni}@brockport.edu

Abstract. In recent years, Online Social Networking (OSN) platforms have become an integral component of people's lives. The availability of the massive amount of information generated on these platforms along with their open nature attracts cybercriminals who create fake human accounts or bots with an intention of spamming, scamming, disseminating hate speech or disinformation, and more. Thus, automatically detecting such malicious accounts is an important problem that we address in this paper. We design a machine learning model to classify an X (formerly Twitter) account into one of the following categories—genuine accounts, social spambots, traditional spambots, and fake followers, with further classification into subcategories for social and traditional spambots. We use tweets made by a user, tweet-based features, and user-based features to train several machine learning classifiers. Our results demonstrate that the DistilBERT model shows the best performance among all the models by achieving an accuracy of around 91%. We create a web application that accepts a link to a user account, uses the Twitter API to pull the user's public data, and uses the Distil-BERT model to classify it into a category. This paper presents the results of our preliminary investigation and lays the groundwork for further detailed analysis for malicious account detection.

Keywords: Machine Learning · Natural Language Processing · Social Media

1 Introduction

Online Social Networking (OSN) platforms have gained immense popularity over the past decade as they enable users to connect to millions of people and express and share their opinions with them. As per the Digital 2023 Global Overview report [1], out of the total population of around 8 billion, 4.76 billion (59.4%) people are active social media users. The report also specifies that around 7 different social media platforms are used by people on average each month and the average daily time spent using social media is 2.5 h. The widespread popularity of social media has resulted in creation of malicious accounts on these platforms in the form of fake human accounts and bots, and in generating fake followers. These malicious accounts are created with an intention of conducting social media scams, bullying, disseminating hate speech and disinformation, spamming, and much more [2,14,16,23]. The 2023 Federal Trade Commission report [2] shows that social media is the top most method of contact where most monetary fraud occurs. It also states that $2.7 billion were lost to scams on social media in 2023 with online shopping scams being the highest followed by investment-related scams and romance scams. A report by a behavioral scientist shows the use of bots for cyberbullying [16]. Research demonstrates that bots amplified online hate speech during the COVID-19 pandemic [23] which resulted in creating solutions to contain it [18]. Research also illustrates that spammers exploit the trust relationships among users on social media for illicit purposes such as spreading malicious Uniform Resource Locators (URLs) within tweets, spreading rumors, sending unsolicited messages, and more [6]. Research also shows the use of fake followers for increasing popularity of an account [10] and a way to detect them.

Thus, automatic detection and handling of fake accounts or bots on social media is crucial as it has a significant impact on individuals and society. Although several research exists (discussed in Sect. 2) to address this issues, they have certain limitations such as insufficient features for detecting malicious accounts, unidentifiable source of generation of malicious content, limited availability of open tools for accurate real-time malicious account detection, and limitations in the accuracy and processing time for detecting malicious accounts [22]. We address some of these issues in our work where we aim to design a lightweight machine learning model for detecting malicious accounts on X (formerly Twitter) and use this model to develop a web application that would detect such accounts in real-time. We approach this problem as a multiclass classification problem where we aim to classify an account into one of the following categories—genuine accounts, social spambots (consists of three subcategories), traditional spambots (consists of four subcategories), and fake followers.

We use the publicly available X (formerly Twitter) dataset [11] which contains tweets posted by accounts in the aforementioned categories between the years 2009 and 2015. In addition to the tweets from the user accounts, we use tweet-based and user-based features in performing classifications. We experiment with four classifiers—Naive Bayes, Support Vector Machine (SVM), Convolutional Neural Network (CNN), and a distilled version of Bidirectional Encoder Representations from Transformers (DistilBERT). We observe that the DistilBERT model shows the best performance among all the models with an accuracy of around 91%. We next develop a web application called SocialGuard that accepts a link from the user that belongs to an account to be tested, uses the Twitter API to pull the account's public data, and uses the DistilBERT model to generate the final classification along with a risk score. This paper presents the preliminary results of our investigation and lays the groundwork for future holistic malicious account detection and categorization using data from several social media platforms.

The rest of the paper is organized as follows. We discuss the related work in Sect. 2. We present our datasets, discuss the preprocessing steps and feature selection and feature engineering process in Sect. 3. We discuss our models in Sect. 4 and present our results in Sect. 5. We conclude our paper in Sect. 6 and present our future research directions.

2 Related Work

In this section, we present existing literature related to malicious account detection on social media. We discuss research under three main categories—a comprehensive survey-based research for all social media platforms, research focusing on fake human accounts vs bots detection, and research focusing on the X (formerly Twitter) platform.

There are several works that provide a summary of research done on malicious profile detection on social networking platforms [4,5,9,15,17,21]. Authors in [5] compile and compare the most recent advancements in machine learning-based techniques for the detection and classification of bots on five social media platforms—Facebook, Instagram, LinkedIn, X (formerly Twitter), and Weibo. They provide an overview of all the supervised, semi-supervised, and unsupervised methods used along with the details of the datasets. Their work focuses on three types of bots-social, spam, and sybils. [15] presents a summary of machine learning models used to detect fake accounts on four platforms—Facebook, X (formerly Twitter), LinkedIn, and Renren, using a variety of features such as content-based, graph-based, user-based, time-based, etc. Authors in [21] summarize the fake profile detection research for four popular platforms—Facebook, X (formerly Twitter), LinkedIn, and Instagram. They present machine learning models designed for the four platforms using nontextual (account-based) features, textual features, and both textual and nontextual features. In [4], present a survey that analyzes various identity deception attacks, which can be categorized into fake profile, identity theft and identity cloning, and provides a detailed review of the identity deception detection techniques.

There are works that study the differences between human accounts and bots on social media and use them to develop machine learning classifiers [8,20,24]. Authors in [24] investigate whether the features engineered while detecting bot accounts on social media could be applied to detect fake human accounts using machine learning. They find that human and bot accounts have different characteristics and the same set of features doesn't help much. Authors in [20] investigate the behavioral dynamics of social network users over the course of an online session, with particular attention to the differences emerging between human and bot accounts. They use the behavioral differences between humans and bots to create a machine learning algorithm that allows for more nuanced bot detection strategies. In [8], authors specify that the posting schedule reveals characteristic patterns of users on social media. They use the posting schedule of social media users, and exploit a Convolutional Neural Network (CNN) to classify social media users as either bots or humans. They also use Class Activation Map (CAM) to interpret the CNN, and find that bot CAMs have less entropy than humans.

Research related specifically to X (formerly Twitter) involve using novel machine learning and artificial intelligence (AI)-based approaches to detect malicious accounts [7,12,13,22]. Bibi *et al.* propose a framework which uses inductive transfer learning and deep neural networks to identify bot profiles based on user profile metadata from X (formerly Twitter) [7]. Authors in [13] present a novel AI-driven bot detection framework to find the automated bot accounts in X (formerly Twitter) using basic and derived attributes. Their approach facilitates bot detection in trend-centric datasets using an innovative centroid initialization algorithm. In [22], authors propose a Chrome extension-based approach which leverages machine learning techniques to identify malicious profiles. They use a Petri net structure to analyze the user's profile and various features, which are then used to train the classifier. Authors create a publicly available service called BotOrNot in [12] that evaluates the extent to which a X (formerly Twitter) account exhibits similarity to the known characteristics of social bots using network, user, friends, and temporal features.

Table 1. Account Categories Description

Category	Description
Genuine accounts	Verified accounts that are human-operated
Social spambots #1	Retweeters of an Italian political candidate
Social spambots #2	Spammers of paid apps for mobile devices
Social spambots #3	Spammers of products on sale at Amazon.com
Traditional spambots #1	Training set of spammers used by Yang et al. in [25]
Traditional spambots #2	Spammers of scam URLs
Traditional spambots #3	Automated accounts spamming job offers
Traditional spambots #4	Another group of automated accounts spamming job offers
Fake followers	Simple accounts that inflate the number of followers of another account

3   Data

In this section, we present our data and the preprocessing steps, and discuss the feature selection and feature engineering process.

3.1   Data

We use the X (formerly Twitter) dataset made publicly available by [11]. The dataset consists of four types of accounts—genuine accounts, social spambots, traditional spambots, and fake followers. The social spambots and traditional spambots further contain three and four subcategories, respectively. The tweets made by the accounts are between the years 2009 and 2015. Table 1 provides the description of these accounts. We use 6000 tweets made by these accounts in our work. In addition to the tweets made by the accounts, the dataset contains six tweet-based features—retweet count, reply count, favorite count, number of hashtags, number of URLs, and whether the tweet is truncated. These are described in Table 2. Additionally, the dataset includes the metadata of users within each account category that we use as additional user-based features. These include the count of friends, favorites, followers, lists, and statuses of a user, and whether the account of the user is geo enabled, protected, and verified. The user-based features are described in Table 3.

3.2   Preprocessing

Our dataset contains tweets in different languages and it also contains some pieces of information that is not useful for training the machine learning models. Thus we

Table 2. Tweet-based Feature Description

Feature	Type	Description
Retweet_count	Numeric	The number of times a tweet has been retweeted
Reply_count	Numeric	The number of replies that have been made to a tweet
Favorite_count	Numeric	The number of times a tweet has been favorited
Num_hashtags	Numeric	The number of hashtags included in the tweet
Num_urls	Numeric	The number of URLs included in the tweet
Truncated	Binary	Whether or not the text field of this tweet has been limited
Text	Text	The textual content of the tweet

Table 3. User-based Feature Description

Feature	Type	Description
Friends_count	Numeric	The count of accounts followed by this user
Favorites_count	Numeric	Favorites count extracted from metadata
Followers_count	Numeric	Followers count for this account
Listed_count	Numeric	The number of lists this user has made
Statuses_count	Numeric	The number of tweets this user has made
Geo_enabled	Binary	Whether or not this account has geolocation features enabled
Protected	Binary	Whether or not this account has privacy settings enabled
Verified	Binary	Whether or not this account is verified by X (formerly Twitter)

describe the data cleaning process in this section. We first use the Google Translate API to translate all the tweets to English. We then remove all URLs, hashtags, mentions, punctuation marks, emojis, and stop words in every tweet. This gives us some empty tweets as they contain only URLs and hashtags which we discard. Then, we use an averaged perceptron tagger to tag each word based on its part-of-speech. We finally lemmatize and stem the words in tweets.

3.3 Feature Selection and Feature Engineering

In this section, we discuss our feature selection and feature engineering process. To select the relevant numerical and binary features, we use the SelectKBest feature selector from scikit-learn [19] to select the features with the highest ANOVA F-statistics. Based on this, we eliminate the truncated tweet-based feature. We also utilize Pearson correlations to eliminate features with similar meaning. Based on this, we eliminate the reply_count tweet-based feature, which had a 0.98 correlation with the favorite_count tweet-based feature and a lower ANOVA F-statistic.

Our web application outputs a risk score associated with an account along with the classification. To achieve this, we create a new user-based feature, is_real, which is set to 0 for genuine accounts and 1 for all other categories. We use the other user-based features to predict the value of the is_real feature. We utilize the Logistic Regression model and extract the probabilities from the predictions to create a risk score function for assessing users.

4 Models

In this section, we discuss the vectorizers and classification models along with their hyperparameter settings used in our work. We also discuss metrics used for evaluation. We process the text content and numerical and binary features separately, and later combine them.

We use the following embedding models to process the text content:

- **Word2Vec:** It is a deep learning algorithm designed to map words to numerical vectors based on word association patterns that it learns from a large corpus of text. We utilize the default corpus from the gensim library to vectorize our tweets [3].
- **Term Frequency-Inverse-Document Frequency (TFIDF):** It is a statistical method that is used to generate numerical vectors for a document based on how significant each word is. We utilize the TfidfVectorizer from scikit-learn's text feature extraction tools to process our text [19].

We use the following machine learning models to classify the tweets from the accounts based on text content:

- **Naive Bayes with TFIDF:** Naive Bayes Classifiers are a family of machine learning models that use Bayes' Theorem and other probability formulas to classify numerical data. We use the MultinomialNB model from scikit-learn with an alpha value of 0.43.
- **Support Vector Machines (SVM) with TFIDF:** SVMs are a family of machine learning classification models that search for ways in which various data points intersect, known as hyperplanes, in order to separate them into distinct classes. We utilize the LinearSVC model from scikit-learn with the following hyperparameters: intercept scaling is set to 1e-8, max iterations is set to 1e-17, and tolerance is set to 760.
- **DistilBERT:** DistilBERT is a lightweight version of Bidirectional Encoder Representations from Transformers (BERT), a popular pre-trained large language model. We utilized DistilBertForSequenceClassification, a version of DistilBERT optimized for classification tasks. We train this model with the following hyperparameters - learning rate is set to 8e-5 and weight decay is set to 0.001.
- **Convolutional Neural Network (CNN) with Word2Vec:** CNNs are multi-layered Artificial Neural Networks (ANN) that are popular for being able to detect complex features in the data. Our CNN model has 10 layers—1 embedding layer, 4 convolution layers, 4 max pooling layers, and 1 softmax layer. We fine-tune the model to have a maximum sequence length of 300, a hidden layer neuron count of 512, and kernel window sizes of 2, 3, 4, and 5.

We use a model stacking ensemble to process the textual content (tweets) and numerical and binary features. We use a K-Nearest Neighbors model from scikit-learn to process our numerical and binary features. The text machine learning models and the K-Nearest Neighbors model serve as the base estimators in our model stack. We use the Decision Tree model to combine the text and numerical and binary features. We split our data by allocating 75% for training and validation, and 25% for testing. We use 5-fold cross validation in our experiments. We use accuracy and F1 score as metrics to evaluate the performance of our models.

5   Results

In this section, we present the results of our experiments and discuss the creation of our web application.

5.1   Performance of Models

Table 4 shows the results of all the models using only text content and text content along with numeric and binary features. We observe that the DistilBERT model shows the best performance with an accuracy of 90.50% and an F1 score of 0.9, followed by SVM with an accuracy of 83.07% and an F1 score of 0.83. Our results demonstrate that integrating numeric and binary features in the highest performing model, DistilBERT, led to a slight decrease in its performance. The SVM model shows about same performance with or without adding the numeric and binary features. For the remaining models, on the other hand, the integration of these features led to a significant increase in their performance.

Table 4. Results

Model	Text content		Text content with Numeric and Binary Features	
	Accuracy	F1 Score	Accuracy	F1 Score
Naive Bayes-TFIDF	72.33%	0.71	**80.20%**	**0.8**
SVM-TFIDF	**83.07%**	**0.83**	82.80%	**0.83**
DistilBERT	**90.50%**	**0.9**	87.80%	0.88
CNN-Word2Vec	63.67%	0.64	**73.27%**	**0.74**

5.2   Web Application

To implement our results into a user-friendly web application called SocialGuard, we build a lightweight front-end with ReactJS and Bootstrap, where a user can enter a URL to an X (formerly Twitter) account, and receive a report informing them of the level of risk associated with the account, and the most likely category from our dataset

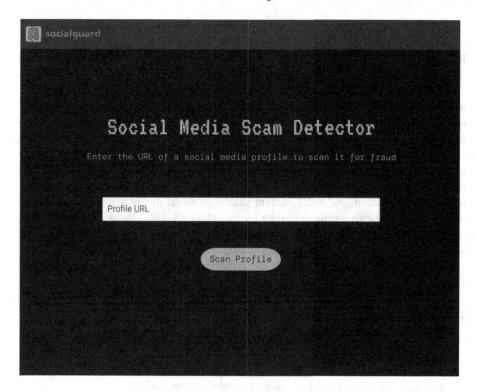

Fig. 1. Home Page of the Web Application

that the account would belong to. We deploy the front-end application to a Firebase container. To achieve full functionality, we create a Flask API, which is called whenever a user enters a URL into our front-end application. This program forwards the user information (username) from the URL to the Twitter API, which returns the public data for the account that we need in order to run it through our model. Once the account data is retrieved, our Flask API will forward the data to various microservices, which load our cached DistilBERT model from a Google Cloud Platform (GCP) Storage Bucket and run predictions on the account. After that, our Flask API sends a response back to the front-end application so that the model results can be shown to the user. Our Flask API is hosted on a GCP App Engine, and our microservices hosted as GCP Cloud Functions. The home page of our web application is shown in Fig. 1. It can be accessed here[1].

6   Conclusion and Future Work

In this paper, we designed machine learning models for detecting and categorizing malicious accounts on X (formerly Twitter). We used a publicly available dataset containing

---

[1] https://socialguard-4efb8.web.app/.

genuine accounts, social spambots, traditional spambots, and fake followers, with sub-categories for social and traditional spambots. We used the following classifiers—Naive Bayes with TFIDF, SVM with TFIDF, CNN with Word2Vec, DistilBERT, and observed that the DistilBERT model gives the highest accuracy of around 91%. We developed a web application called SocialGuard that uses the machine learning classifier to detect whether a given account is malicious. This work presented the preliminary results of our investigation. In this paper, we only presented results for one social media platform. We plan to work with other social media platforms in the future by training our models with data collected from these platforms and incorporate them into our web application. We plan to expand our dataset by adding more amount of tweets and also more recent tweets. We focused only on textual data (tweets) as the main attribute for performing classifications. Since content shared on social media is not limited to text, we plan to work with multimodal data by including images, videos, etc. We worked with tweet-based and user-based in this paper. In the future, we plan to explore other features such as network-based and time-based features to improve the accuracy of our classifiers. Finally, we plan to conduct the usability testing of our web application in the future.

References

1. Digital 2023 global overview report. https://wearesocial.com/wp-content/uploads/2023/03/Digital-2023-Global-Overview-Report.pdf
2. Federal trade commission report 2023. https://www.ftc.gov/news-events/data-visualizations/data-spotlight/2023/10/social-media-golden-goose-scammers#1
3. Gensim. https://radimrehurek.com/gensim/models/word2vec.html
4. Alharbi, A., Dong, H., Yi, X., Tari, Z., Khalil, I.: Social media identity deception detection: a survey. ACM Comput. Surv. (CSUR) **54**(3), 1–35 (2021)
5. Aljabri, M., Zagrouba, R., Shaahid, A., Alnasser, F., Saleh, A., Alomari, D.M.: Machine learning-based social media bot detection: a comprehensive literature review. Soc. Netw. Anal. Min. **13**(1), 20 (2023)
6. Alom, Z., Carminati, B., Ferrari, E.: A deep learning model for Twitter spam detection. Online Soc. Netw. Media **18**, 100079 (2020)
7. Bibi, M., Hussain Qaisar, Z., Aslam, N., Faheem, M., Akhtar, P.: TL-PBot: Twitter bot profile detection using transfer learning based on DNN model. Eng. Rep. e12838 (2024)
8. Chavoshi, N., Mueen, A.: Model bots, not humans on social media. In: 2018 IEEE/ACM International Conference on Advances in Social Networks Analysis and Mining (ASONAM), pp. 178–185. IEEE (2018)
9. Cresci, S.: A decade of social bot detection. Commun. ACM **63**(10), 72–83 (2020)
10. Cresci, S., Di Pietro, R., Petrocchi, M., Spognardi, A., Tesconi, M.: Fame for sale: efficient detection of fake twitter followers. Decis. Support Syst. **80**, 56–71 (2015)
11. Cresci, S., Di Pietro, R., Petrocchi, M., Spognardi, A., Tesconi, M.: The paradigm-shift of social spambots: evidence, theories, and tools for the arms race. In: Proceedings of the 26th International Conference on World Wide Web Companion, pp. 963–972. WWW 2017 Companion, International World Wide Web Conferences Steering Committee, Republic and Canton of Geneva, CHE (2017). https://doi.org/10.1145/3041021.3055135, https://doi.org/10.1145/3041021.3055135
12. Davis, C.A., Varol, O., Ferrara, E., Flammini, A., Menczer, F.: BotOrNot: a system to evaluate social bots. In: Proceedings of the 25th International Conference Companion on World Wide Web, pp. 273–274 (2016)

13. Gera, S., Sinha, A.: T-bot: AI-based social media bot detection model for trend-centric Twitter network. Soc. Netw. Anal. Min. **12**(1), 76 (2022)
14. von Hoffman, C.: Fake tweets just one way hackers can disrupt stocks. https://www.cbsnews.com/news/fake-tweets-just-one-way-hackers-can-disrupt-stocks/
15. Joshi, S., Nagariya, H.G., Dhanotiya, N., Jain, S.: Identifying fake profile in online social network: an overview and survey. In: Bhattacharjee, A., Borgohain, S.K., Soni, B., Verma, G., Gao, X.-Z. (eds.) MIND 2020. CCIS, vol. 1240, pp. 17–28. Springer, Singapore (2020). https://doi.org/10.1007/978-981-15-6315-7_2
16. Kopolovic, M.: Canvas8 report. https://www.canvas8.com/blog/2017/04/12/simsimi-ai-chatbot-cyber-bullying
17. Masood, F., et al.: Spammer detection and fake user identification on social networks. IEEE Access **7**, 68140–68152 (2019)
18. Morgan, M., Kulkarni, A.: Platform-agnostic model to detect sinophobia on social media. In: Proceedings of the 2023 ACM Southeast Conference, pp. 149–153 (2023)
19. Pedregosa, F., et al.: Scikit-learn: machine learning in Python. J. Mach. Learn. Res. **12**, 2825–2830 (2011)
20. Pozzana, I., Ferrara, E.: Measuring bot and human behavioral dynamics. Front. Phys. **8**, 125 (2020)
21. Roy, P.K., Chahar, S.: Fake profile detection on social networking websites: a comprehensive review. IEEE Trans. Artif. Intell. **1**(3), 271–285 (2020). https://doi.org/10.1109/TAI.2021.3064901
22. Sahoo, S.R., Gupta, B.B.: Hybrid approach for detection of malicious profiles in Twitter. Comput. Electr. Eng. **76**, 65–81 (2019)
23. Uyheng, J., Bellutta, D., Carley, K.M.: Bots amplify and redirect hate speech in online discourse about racism during the covid-19 pandemic. Soc. Media Soc. **8**(3), 20563051221104749 (2022)
24. Van Der Walt, E., Eloff, J.: Using machine learning to detect fake identities: bots vs humans. IEEE Access **6**, 6540–6549 (2018)
25. Yang, C., Harkreader, R., Gu, G.: Empirical evaluation and new design for fighting evolving Twitter spammers. IEEE Trans. Inf. Forensics Secur. **8**(8), 1280–1293 (2013)

Emotion Recognition in Conversation with Multi-step Prompting Using Large Language Model

Kenta Hama[✉], Atsushi Otsuka, and Ryo Ishii

NTT Digital Twin Computing Research Center, Nippon Telegraph and Telephone
Corp., 29F Shinagawa Season Terrace, 2-70 Konan 1-chome, Minato-ku,
Tokyo 108-0075, Japan
{kenta.hama,atsushi.otsuka,ryoct.ishii}@ntt.com

Abstract. Emotion recognition plays a crucial role in computer science,
particularly in enhancing human-computer interactions. The process of
emotion labeling remains time-consuming and costly, thereby impeding
efficient dataset creation. Recently, large language models (LLMs) have
demonstrated adaptability across a variety of tasks without requiring
task-specific training. This indicates the potential of LLMs to recognize emotions even with fewer emotion labels. Therefore, we assessed the
performance of an LLM in emotion recognition using two established
datasets: MELD and IEMOCAP. Our findings reveal that for emotion
labels with few training samples, the performance of the LLM approaches
or even exceeds that of SPCL, a leading model specializing in text-based
emotion recognition. In addition, inspired by the Chain of Thought, we
incorporated a multi-step prompting technique into the LLM to further
enhance its discriminative capacity between emotion labels. The results
underscore the potential of LLMs to reduce the time and costs of emotion
data labeling.

Keywords: emotion recognition · large language model · few-shot
learning · prompt engineering

1 Introduction

Emotion Recognition in Conversation (ERC) has emerged as an essential component in the domain of Human-Computer Interaction. Its applications span
diverse areas ranging from entertainment and customer support to healthcare [1].
However, a primary challenge in ERC is the accurate and consistent labeling of
emotions [9]. Conventional methods often rely on consensus from multiple eval-
uators [14] or utilize multi-modal data to improve label reliability [8]. Existing
emotion estimation methods require fine-tuning on such datasets [12], and since
certain emotions that occur in conversations are rare, the collection of data for
these emotions is a significant challenge.

A potential solution to these challenges in emotion labeling is to utilize the capabilities of large language models (LLMs) [2]. In recent years, LLMs have gained recognition for their exceptional performance across various natural language processing tasks [10]. Enhanced by techniques such as prompt engineering [6,13], their capabilities have continually improved. If LLMs inherently possess proficiency in emotion recognition from their pre-training, they can be directly applied to emotion recognition tasks. This eliminates the need for extensive and costly emotion labeling. As such, this approach offers a promising direction for the efficient deployment and refinement of emotion recognition models.

In this study, we evaluated the capability of LLMs in ERC in a few-shot setting using the MELD [8] and IEMOCAP [3] datasets, which are commonly utilized as benchmarks in ERC research. Additionally, to enhance the accuracy of emotion recognition, we proposed a multi-step prompting inspired by the zero-shot Chain of Thought (zero-shot CoT) [6]. This approach involves generating questions related to the dialog utterances as an intermediate task and inferring emotions from the responses. Experimental results revealed that, in datasets like MELD with a skewed label distribution, LLMs achieved superior accuracy over the trained SPCL [12] for emotion labels with fewer samples such as "anger" and "fear", even in a few-shot scenario. These findings suggest the potential of LLMs to address the challenges of dataset creation costs for ERC.

The contributions of this study are as follows:

- We validated the effectiveness of few-shot ERC using LLMs on MELD and IEMOCAP.
- We proposed a new multi-step method inspired by the zero-shot CoT.
- We demonstrated that for labels with little training data, LLMs surpass the accuracy of SPCL.

2   Related Work

2.1   Emotion Recognition in Conversation

ERC is the task of predicting a speaker's emotions from their utterances during a conversation. More precisely, it takes the sequential text in a conversation as input, aiming to classify each individual utterance into respective emotion labels [9]. Many emotion recognition tasks utilize multi-modal data, including video and audio [4,7]. However, prior research has reported that text information is the most crucial for emotion estimation [12]. Motivated by this, our study explores the potential boundaries of textual modality in emotion recognition, seeking to understand the applicability of LLMs to ERC.

2.2   Large Language Models

In this study, the term "LLMs" denotes the recent, advanced models such as GPT-3 [2], which are trained on massive datasets. Conventional models [5,11] often required fine-tuning for domain-specific applications. In contrast, without additional training, LLMs have exhibited high performances in a diverse range of tasks beyond just NLP, including question answering, summarization, arithmetic, and programming [10]. One approach to maximizing the capabilities of LLMs is to use prompt engineering, as done in the Chain of Thought (CoT) method [13]. Instead of instructing the model to directly produce an outcome, CoT specifies the prompt to output the reasoning that leads to the result. Moreover, Zero-shot CoT [6], which involves passing phrases like "Let's think step by step" to the LLM, encourages the model to independently engage in logical reasoning. In this study, drawing inspiration from LLMs and the CoT, we apply a multi-step prompt technique to the ERC task and explore its potential.

3   Methods

In this section, we describe 1-step and multi-step emotion recognition methods utilizing LLM.

3.1   1-Step Prompting

In 1-step prompting, as shown in Fig. 1, the system generates emotion labels from a single prompt input. The prompt is provided with the dialogue and the target utterance. A list of potential emotions, such as ["anger", "disgust",...], is also supplied, instructing the model to select and output in the specified format ["label"] from these options.

3.2   Multi-step Prompting

Multi-step prompting utilizes three steps to guide the LLM through tasks involving question generation and answering to determine the final emotion labels, as depicted in Fig. 1.

Step 1 (Question Generation): The LLM generates questions about the utterances, using the conversation as a reference. During this process, it is prompted with commands such as "Create specific question to gain deeper insights into speaker's statement," thereby facilitating the generation of questions that enhance understanding of the utterance.

Step 2 (Answering Questions): In Step 2, the LLM responds to the list of questions generated in Step 1. By incorporating the phrase "specifically focusing on the speaker and his/her statement" into the prompt, we guide the model to formulate answers aligned with the dialogue content.

Step 3 (Outputting Emotion Label): In the final step, answers from Step 2 are combined with the dialogue and target utterance in the prompt. The LLM then selects the appropriate emotion from a list, outputting it as ["label"].

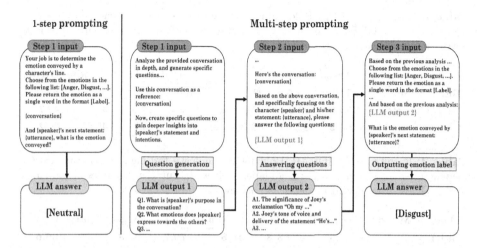

Fig. 1. Conceptual diagram: (left) 1-step workflow, and (right) multi-step workflow. In the multi-step approach, Step 1 generates questions based on the dialogue, Step 2 answers these questions, and Step 3 infers the emotion based on the results from Step 2.

4   Experiment and Results

4.1   Dataset

We conducted our evaluations using the widely recognized MELD [8] and IEMO-CAP [3] datasets for ERC, as their distinct label distributions provide an insightful examination into the capabilities of LLMs.

The MELD dataset comprises over 1,400 dialogues and more than 13,000 utterances from the TV drama "Friends". Multiple speakers participate in the dialogues, and each utterance is labeled with one of seven emotions: Anger, Disgust, Sadness, Joy, Neutral, Surprise, and Fear. Roughly half of the utterances in the dataset are labeled as 'Neutral', while labels such as 'Disgust' and 'Fear' are relatively rare.

IEMOCAP is a database consisting of 151 dialogue videos recorded over five sessions by five pairs of speakers. The data was generated by actors performing both scripted and improvised scenarios to elicit emotional expressions. For emotion recognition, six labels are used: Anger, Sadness, Excited, Neutral, Happiness, and Frustration. Adequate data is available for all emotion labels, ensuring a balanced distribution.

4.2   Experiment Configuration

In this experiment, we compared three models on the MELD and IEMOCAP datasets: a 1-step method using an LLM, a multi-step method using an LLM, and SPCL, a state-of-the-art method. SPCL employs a pre-trained BERT, where the targeted emotion label is masked, and the model is fine-tuned to predict

Table 1. Results on MELD. Bold figures indicate the highest accuracy. SPCL excels overall. Notably, GPT-3.5 performs well in Anger and Fear (marked with †), due to fewer samples in these categories.

Model	Method	Anger†	Disgust	Fear†	Joy	Neutral	Sadness	Surprise	Overall
BERT	SPCL	53.0	**29.5**	28.0	**61.1**	**78.6**	42.5	**60.5**	**65.4**
GPT-3.5	1-step	53.4	23.2	27.9	53.0	37.3	**47.3**	43.2	42.7
	multi-step	**53.9**	27.8	**32.3**	51.2	57.2	43.2	45.5	52.2

Table 2. Results on IEMOCAP. Bold figures indicate the highest accuracy. SPCL demonstrates high accuracy across all labels. Given the sufficient samples for all labels in IEMOCAP, the trained model SPCL achieves highest accuracy.

Model	Method	Frustration	Excited	Happiness	Sadness	Anger	Neutral	Overall
BERT	SPCL	**63.6**	**68.8**	**45.6**	**79.7**	**63.8**	**68.6**	**66.6**
GPT-3.5	1-step	56.3	58.5	40.7	68.4	31.7	39.1	50.5
	multi-step	58.8	50.2	37.8	62.9	36.9	52.2	52.2

the masked word. For this study, we trained and evaluated the model without altering the settings of the publicly available source code.[1] The 1-step and multi-step methods using LLM were implemented with OpenAI's gpt-3.5-turbo API.[2] For evaluation metrics, we utilized the F1 score for each label, and the weighted-F1 score for the overall dataset evaluation.

4.3 Result

The experimental results are listed in Tables 1 and 2. For MELD (Table 1), both the 1-step and multi-step methods are inferior to SPCL in terms of overall performance. However, for specific emotion categories, such as Anger and Fear, the multi-step method outperforms SPCL. Furthermore, the multi-step approach shows a clear improvement over the 1-step method, especially in the Neutral category. As for IEMOCAP (Table 2), both the 1-step and multi-step methods using GPT-3.5 are less effective than SPCL, with a notable decrease in the Anger category. When comparing the 1-step and multi-step methods, the latter yields improved scores in the Anger and Frustration categories, and its overall accuracy is enhanced.

5 Discussion

In this section, we discuss the tendencies of each method in emotion classification based on the heatmaps shown in Figs. 2 and 3. First, looking at Fig. 2(a) for

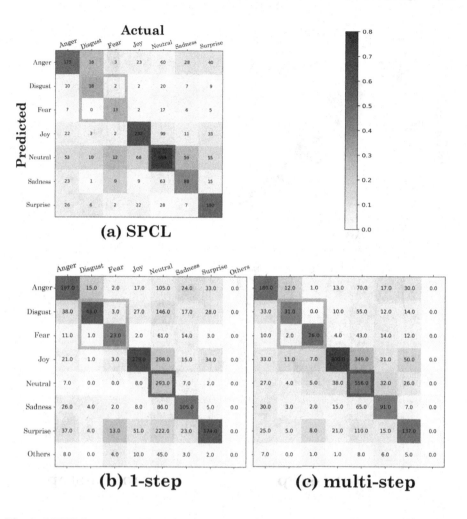

Fig. 2. MELD heatmaps. The values in each cell represent the number of sample utterances. In (b) 1-step, the accuracy for Neutral is low, but it is improved in (c) multi-step. Also, compared to (a) SPCL, (b) and (c) show higher classification accuracies for Anger and Fear. (Color figure online)

MELD (specifically the red and yellow boxes), we observe that SPCL exhibits high classification accuracy for the Neutral label, while its performance is relatively low for emotions like Fear and Disgust. This can be attributed to the distribution of the MELD training data, where Neutral constitutes nearly half of the samples, whereas Fear and Disgust account for less than 3%. Figure 2(b) shows that in the 1-step approach, utterances that should have been labeled as Neutral are misclassified into other categories. In contrast, with the multi-step method (Fig. 2(c)), the misclassification regarding Neutral is significantly

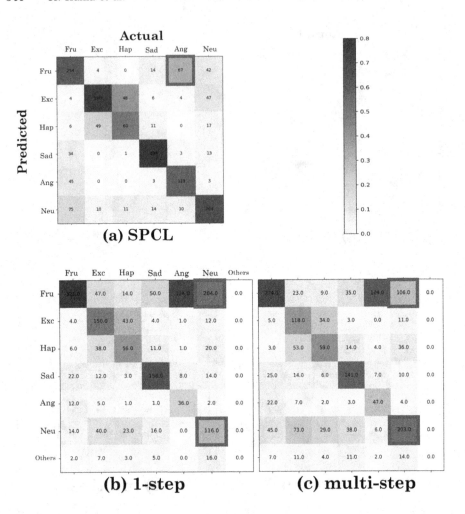

Fig. 3. IEMOCAP heatmaps. The values in each cell represent the number of sample. In (b) 1-step, there is a high incidence of misclassifying Anger as Frustration, which is mitigated in (c) multi-step. (Color figure online)

reduced. Both the 1-step and multi-step methods demonstrate fewer misclassifications for minority labels such as Fear and Disgust compared to SPCL. This suggests that employing LLMs can be effective, especially for emotions with fewer samples and higher labeling costs.

From Fig. 3(a) in the IEMOCAP dataset, SPCL can correctly classify all labels, and it distinguishes between the challenging labels Anger and Frustration particularly well. The even distribution of labels in IEMOCAP likely allows SPCL to learn the characteristics of each label's utterances. In contrast, Fig. 3(b) shows that the 1-step method has lower accuracy than SPCL, and it struggles with Anger and Frustration (indicated by the red boxes). This challenge might arise from the nature of LLM, where distinguishing closely related semantic labels is difficult. However, Fig. 3(c) indicates that the multi-step method performs better than the 1-step method for Anger and Frustration, because the question-answering process in the multi-step method can help recognize the differences between these two emotions.

Based on our above discussion, we conclude that while SPCL can achieve high classification accuracy when sufficient training data is available, LLM can provide a sufficient performance for emotion labels with few training samples. Although LLM has a tendency to misclassify labels with semantically similar meanings, introducing an intermediate task like question-answering seems to enhance its discriminative capabilities.

6 Conclusion

In this study, we explored the potential of LLMs for few-shot ERC. The experimental results show that for emotion labels with few training samples, the LLM can outperform established trained models like SPCL. Although LLM struggles to differentiate between labels with semantically close meanings, introducing a multi-step prompting approach that involves intermediate tasks enhances its ability to discern. These results highlight the potential of LLM-based approaches as viable solutions in situations where generating datasets for emotion recognition is challenging. In future work, we will explore the applicability of LLMs in ERC by conducting further evaluations in zero-shot and few-shot contexts. Additionally, we will investigate various intermediate tasks in multi-step method.

References

1. Ahmed, N., Aghbari, Z.A., Girija, S.: A systematic survey on multimodal emotion recognition using learning algorithms. Intell. Syst. Appl. **17**, 200171 (2023). https://doi.org/10.1016/j.iswa.2022.200171
2. Brown, T.B., et al. (eds.): Advances in Neural Information Processing Systems 33: Annual Conference on Neural Information Processing Systems 2020, NeurIPS 2020, 6–12 December 2020, Virtual (2020). https://proceedings.neurips.cc/paper/2020/hash/1457c0d6bfcb4967418bfb8ac142f64a-Abstract.html
3. Busso, C., et al.: IEMOCAP: interactive emotional dyadic motion capture database. Lang. Resour. Eval. **42**, 335–359 (2008). https://doi.org/10.1007/s10579-008-9076-6
4. Chudasama, V., Kar, P., Gudmalwar, A., Shah, N., Wasnik, P., Onoe, N.: M2FNet: multi-modal fusion network for emotion recognition in conversation. In: IEEE/CVF Conference on Computer Vision and Pattern Recognition Workshops, CVPR Workshops 2022, New Orleans, LA, USA, 19–20 June 2022, pp. 4651–4660. IEEE (2022). https://doi.org/10.1109/CVPRW56347.2022.00511
5. Devlin, J., Chang, M., Lee, K., Toutanova, K.: BERT: pre-training of deep bidirectional transformers for language understanding. In: Burstein, J., Doran, C., Solorio, T. (eds.) Proceedings of the 2019 Conference of the North American Chapter of

the Association for Computational Linguistics: Human Language Technologies, NAACL-HLT 2019, Minneapolis, MN, USA, 2–7 June 2019, Volume 1 (Long and Short Papers), pp. 4171–4186. Association for Computational Linguistics (2019). https://doi.org/10.18653/v1/n19-1423

6. Kojima, T., Gu, S.S., Reid, M., Matsuo, Y., Iwasawa, Y.: Large language models are zero-shot reasoners. In: NeurIPS (2022). http://papers.nips.cc/paper_files/paper/2022/hash/8bb0d291acd4acf06ef112099c16f326-Abstract-Conference.html

7. Li, Z., Tang, F., Zhao, M., Zhu, Y.: EmoCaps: emotion capsule based model for conversational emotion recognition. In: Muresan, S., Nakov, P., Villavicencio, A. (eds.) Findings of the Association for Computational Linguistics: ACL 2022, Dublin, Ireland, 22–27 May 2022, pp. 1610–1618. Association for Computational Linguistics (2022). https://doi.org/10.18653/v1/2022.findings-acl.126

8. Poria, S., Hazarika, D., Majumder, N., Naik, G., Cambria, E., Mihalcea, R.: MELD: a multimodal multi-party dataset for emotion recognition in conversations. In: Korhonen, A., Traum, D.R., Màrquez, L. (eds.) Proceedings of the 57th Conference of the Association for Computational Linguistics, ACL 2019, Florence, Italy, 28 July–2 August 2019, Volume 1: Long Papers, pp. 527–536. Association for Computational Linguistics (2019). https://doi.org/10.18653/v1/p19-1050

9. Poria, S., Majumder, N., Mihalcea, R., Hovy, E.H.: Emotion recognition in conversation: research challenges, datasets, and recent advances. IEEE Access 7, 100943–100953 (2019). https://doi.org/10.1109/ACCESS.2019.2929050

10. Qiao, S., et al.: Reasoning with language model prompting: a survey. In: Rogers, A., Boyd-Graber, J.L., Okazaki, N. (eds.) Proceedings of the 61st Annual Meeting of the Association for Computational Linguistics (Volume 1: Long Papers), ACL 2023, Toronto, Canada, 9–14 July 2023, pp. 5368–5393. Association for Computational Linguistics (2023). https://doi.org/10.18653/v1/2023.acl-long.294

11. Raffel, C., et al.: Exploring the limits of transfer learning with a unified text-to-text transformer. J. Mach. Lear. Res. 21(1), 5485–5551 (2020). https://dl.acm.org/doi/abs/10.5555/3455716.3455856

12. Song, X., Huang, L., Xue, H., Hu, S.: Supervised prototypical contrastive learning for emotion recognition in conversation. In: Goldberg, Y., Kozareva, Z., Zhang, Y. (eds.) Proceedings of the 2022 Conference on Empirical Methods in Natural Language Processing, EMNLP 2022, Abu Dhabi, United Arab Emirates, 7–11 December 2022, pp. 5197–5206. Association for Computational Linguistics (2022). https://doi.org/10.18653/v1/2022.emnlp-main.347

13. Wei, J., et al.: Chain-of-thought prompting elicits reasoning in large language models. In: NeurIPS (2022). http://papers.nips.cc/paper_files/paper/2022/hash/9d5609613524ecf4f15af0f7b31abca4-Abstract-Conference.html

14. Zahiri, S.M., Choi, J.D.: Emotion detection on TV show transcripts with sequence-based convolutional neural networks. In: The Workshops of the the Thirty-Second AAAI Conference on Artificial Intelligence, New Orleans, Louisiana, USA, 2–7 February 2018. AAAI Technical Report, vol. WS-18, pp. 44–52. AAAI Press (2018). https://aaai.org/ocs/index.php/WS/AAAIW18/paper/view/16434

Relationship Between Consumers' Circumstances and Food Consumption Behavior

Aina Ishikawa[1]([✉]), Takashi Namatame[2], and Kohei Otake[3]

[1] Graduate School of Information and Telecommunication Engineering, Tokai University, 2-3-23, Takanawa, Minato-Ku 108-8619, Tokyo, Japan
aina140314@outlook.jp

[2] School of Science and Engineering, Chuo University, 1-13-27, Kasuga, Bunkyo-Ku 112-8551, Tokyo, Japan
nama@kc.chuo-u.ac.jp

[3] Faculty of Economics, Sophia University, 7-1 Kioi-cho, Chiyoda-Ku 102-8554, Tokyo, Japan
k-otake@sophia.ac.jp

Abstract. In recent years, food consumption in Japan has changed significantly due to a variety of factors such as imports from over-seas, a declining and aging population, a rapid increase in dual-earner households, and diversification of lifestyles and so on. Although many studies have been conducted on consumer purchasing behavior and food consumption behavior, there is still room for debate on the relationship between specific consumer behaviors and their backgrounds. In this study, we aim to clarify the relationship between consumers' circumstances and their food consumption behavior by using text data of dining table and cooking diary. Specifically, to categorize consumers' eating behavior by situation, we constructed a topic model using the Latent Dirichlet Allocation method and performed non-hierarchical clustering. We analyzed the words that appeared in each typified cluster for frequency to extract and interpret the characteristic words. Furthermore, we clarified the relationship between consumers' emotions and their food consumption behavior by conducting an emotional analysis using the BERT model.

Keywords: Food Consumption Behavior · Latent Dirichlet Allocation · Emotion Analysis

1 Introduction

In recent years, food consumption in Japan has changed significantly due to a variety of factors. One of these factors is the increase in food imports from overseas. According to a survey by the Ministry of Agriculture, Forestry and Fisheries [1], the annual per capita consumption of rice in Japan has decreased significantly. On the other hand, the consumption of livestock products and fats and oils is on the increase. This indicates that the Japanese diet of livestock products and fats and oils has undergone a major shift from a diet based on rice, fish, and vegetables to a diet using meat and oil. According to a survey by the Ministry of Health, Labour and Welfare [2], in addition to changes in food imports from overseas, other factors that have contributed to changes in food consumption in Japan include changes in household composition, household types, and lifestyles. Figure 1 shows future estimates of food expenditures by category [3]. 1995 and 2015 show a decrease in the percentage of expenditures for produced food and food service, and an increase in the percentage of expenditures for prepared food, processed food, and beverages. It has been pointed out that the increase in the number of single-person households and dual-earner households amidst a declining population is a factor in this progression of food externalization.

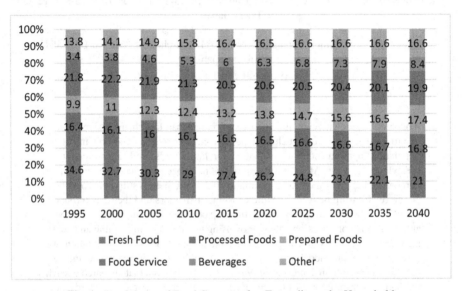

Fig. 1. Breakdown of Food Consumption Expenditures by Household

2 Purpose of This Study

As families and lifestyles diversify and change, the demand for food has also changed with the times. It is also clear that consumers consider various factors such as price, safety, and nutritional balance when they select food products. Many studies have been conducted on consumer purchasing behavior for food products focusing on each of these factors. Oura [4] summarized the concept and research on eating behavior by listing three factors related to various consumer behaviors related to food: store, item, and consumer diversification. Oura reorganizes the "food behavior process" described by Imada [5] and Isojima [6], and divided eating behavior into the stages of purchasing, processing, and cooking, and eating, with several more situations assumed in each stage. He points out that each of these behaviors is affected by the consumer's own situation. Furthermore, Oura [4] points out that a new research approach to eating behavior is a qualitative approach to analysis that extracts the causal relationship between the awareness behind eating behavior and specific behaviors. Shigeno [7] pointed out that factors such as price and income are declining in importance in food consumption behavior as a background and discusses the relationship between three factors other than price and income factors: information, evaluation of non-market materials, and family, and food consumption behavior. Shigeno also pointed out that decisions regarding food consumption are decisions that are made repeatedly daily, and that consumers tend to make decisions based on their impressions and intuition. Therefore, he pointed out that traditional economic theory, which assumes that consumers act under complete economic rationality, could not fully explain consumer behavior.

These studies were valuable. However, there is still room for debate regarding consumers' food consumption behavior. In this study, we aim to clarify the differences in food choices and to examine food consumption behavior by focusing about consumers and their backgrounds. Specifically, we use the diaries of housewives to categorize their food consumption behavior and backgrounds. We clarify the food preferences in each of the typified situations and discuss the factors that contribute to the food preferences. In addition, we will also consider food consumption behavior from a psychological perspective by conducting an emotional analysis of the model we have created.

3 Dataset

In this study, we used the "Diary of Daily Activities" of housewives which was provided by a company that provides marketing support services and "WRIME: Subjective and Objective Emotion Analysis Dataset" [9].

The data of the "Diary of Daily Activities" covers the period from 1990 to 2014, with 35,373 records. In this study, 29,813 of the 35,373 records were included in the analysis. Table 1 shows the details of the data.

Table 1. Details of Target Data

Data Content	Data Item Description
Date of Entry	1990–2014
Four Seasons	Spring, Summer, Autumn, Winter, Blank
Weather	Sunny, Cloudy, Rainy, Blank
Behavioral Data	Diary describing the behavior
Background Data	Diary describing the background of the behavior described in the action data
Product Data	Foods and ingredients used in the action
Situation	Breakfast, Lunch, Dinner, Snack, Evening meal, Brunch, Other, Blank

In this study, we included in our analysis only text data in which "Product Data" contained two or more products.

We also used "WRIME: Subjective and Objective Emotion Analysis Dataset" for fine-tuning our emotion analysis model with BERT. This dataset is available on GitHub and labels sentences with emotional polarity. The details of the data we used in this study are described in the Sect. 5.

4 Analysis of Text Data Describing Consumer Eating Behavior

In this section, we describe the analysis of consumer eating behavior. First, we constructed a topic model using the latent Dirichlet allocation method on the text data of the diaries. Next, we performed clustering using the distribution of topic affiliation for each document obtained by the topic model construction. We characterized the clusters by performing a frequency analysis of the words that appeared in each cluster. Finally, we analyzed the sentiment of each document to identify the factors that influence consumers' food selection by using the BERT sentiment analysis model.

4.1 Construction of a Topic Model Using the Latent Dirichlet Allocation Method

First, to clarify what kind of topics exist in the diaries, we classified the documents by constructing a topic model based on the latent Dirichlet allocation method. The purpose of this analysis is to categorize the documents according to the situation in which they are used for eating behavior, we classified the documents as a single document that combines the behavior data and the background data text in the diary.

To determine the number of topics when we construct the topic model, we used Coherence, which is a measure of topic consistency. The higher the value of Coherence, the higher the consistency. Figure 2 shows the trend of the number of topics and the calculated Coherence values.

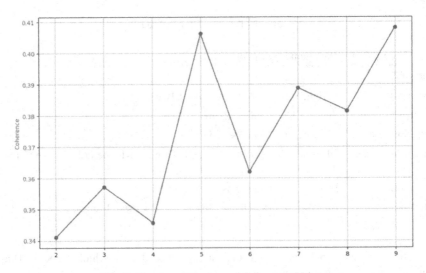

Fig. 2 Number of Topics and Coherence Values

In this study, we have the highest coherence value when the number of topics is 9, but we chose 5 because it is only slightly different from the number of topics of 5, and because of interpretability.

Next, we calculated the importance of the words appearing in each topic generated by the topic model and named the contents of topic by interpreting the top appearing words. Table 2 shows the content of each topic.

Table 2. Topics Generated by the LDA Model and Their Interpretation

Topic	Topic Content
Topic1	About the menu that children prefer
Topic2	About busy mornings
Topic3	About dining around the table with family and friends
Topic4	Daily meals
Topic5	Eating meals that take care of your health

4.2 Categorization of Food-Related Situations by Non-hierarchical Clustering

Next, we performed non-hierarchical clustering with the purpose of creating a typology of situations in which people engage in eating behaviors. We used the probability distribution of a document's belonging to each topic, obtained by building a topic model, for clustering, and we used k-means++ for clustering. To determine the number of clusters, we used the Elbow method to estimate the optimal number of clusters. Figure 3 below shows the evolution of the number of clusters and the value of SSE using the Elbow method.

By calculating the importance of the words that appear in each typed cluster using TF-IDF, we interpreted what kind of situation each cluster is in when people take specific food-related behavior. We also identified which food ingredients are more likely to be used in which situations. Table 3 shows the results of the interpretation of each cluster using the words with the highest TF-IDF values.

In cluster 1, words such as "make," "bento," "put," "lunch," "onigiri," and "gohan" appeared at high frequency, and we interpreted cluster 1 as a situation in which consumers are busy in the morning. In cluster 2, the words "curry," "children," "like," "hamburger steak," and "spaghetti" appeared frequently, and we interpreted cluster 2 as a situation in which the menu is determined according to children's preferences. In Cluster 3, words such as "appetite," "no," "children," and "cold" suggest a situation in which the consumer is not feeling well. Therefore, we interpreted cluster 3 as a situation in which the consumer is considering a meal that considers the physical condition of his/her family members. Cluster 4 shows that words related to cooking methods, such as "fry," "deep fry," "simmered," and "grilled," appear frequently. In addition, words related to foodstuffs that are consumed daily, such as "vegetable," "salad," "tofu," "cabbage," and "pork," appear frequently in cluster 4. This indicates that cluster 4 is a situation

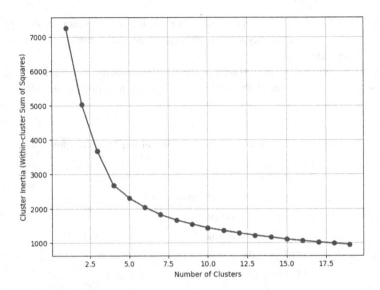

Fig. 3 Number of clusters and SSE values by elbow method

Table 3. Clusters and Their Interpretations

Cluster	Cluster Content
Cluster1	Busy morning situations such as making breakfast and lunch
Cluster2	A situation in which the menu is decided mainly by the children
Cluster3	Making meals according to the family's physical condition
Cluster4	Making routine meals
Cluster5	Making meals according to schedule

in which consumers prepare their daily meals. Finally, cluster 5 was interpreted as a situation in which consumers prepare food to be consumed at gatherings of family and friends, because words that describe family and friends, such as "child," "husband," "son," "family," "friend," and "homemade," appeared frequently in the cluster 5.

Next, we conducted a TF-IDF frequency analysis of the words that appear in the documents of each cluster, which were categorized by non-hierarchical cluster analysis. Table 4 below summarizes the top 20 foodstuff words that appear frequently in each cluster because of the frequency analysis.

Table 4 shows that about half of the words used in each cluster were common ingredients. Table 4 shows that "egg," "onion" and "carrot," "pork," and "chicken" appear in common in almost all clusters. However, the other words showed differences in ingredients depending on the situation indicated by the clusters. For example, in Cluster 3, "tofu," "udon," and "rice" appear as ingredients that are easy to eat even when the respondents are sick. In addition, seasonings that can be used for Japanese seasoning

Table 4. Summary of Consumer Situation

Cluster1	Cluster2	Cluster3	Cluster4	Cluster5
鶏卵 (egg)	玉葱 (onion)	大根 (radish)	正油 (soy sauce)	砂糖 (sugar)
玉葱 (onion)	人参 (carrot)	人参 (carrot)	人参 (carrot)	鶏卵 (egg)
牛乳 (milk)	じゃが芋 (potato)	正油 (soy sauce)	砂糖 (sugar)	牛乳 (milk)
バター (butter)	小麦粉 (flour)	味噌 (miso)	醤油 (soy sauce)	バター (butter)
砂糖 (sugar)	バター (butter)	豚肉 (pork)	豚肉 (pork)	小麦粉 (flour)
キャベツ (cabbage)	牛乳 (milk)	砂糖 (sugar)	玉葱 (onion)	生クリーム (fresh cream)
正油 (soy sauce)	コショー (pepper)	豆腐 (tohu)	サラダ油 (salad oil)	人参 (carrot)
食パン (bread)	牛肉 (beef)	白菜 (Chinese cabbage)	鶏卵 (egg)	海苔 (laver)
豚肉 (pork)	サラダ油 (salad oil)	みりん (mirin)	キャベツ (cabbage)	サラダ油 (salad oil)
小麦粉 (flour)	鶏肉 (chickekn)	うどん (udon noodles)	ピーマン (green pepper)	玉葱 (onion)
サラダ油 (salad oil)	カレールー (carry roux)	めんつゆ (men-tsuyu)	大根 (radish)	大根 (radish)
ハム (ham)	パン粉 (breadcrumbs)	キュウリ (cucumber)	コショー (pepper)	さつま芋 (sweet potato)
海苔 (laver)	豚肉 (pork)	玉葱 (onion)	豆腐 (tohu)	コーヒー (coffee)
チーズ (cheese)	正油 (soy sauce)	昆布 (kelp)	牛肉 (beef)	レモン (lemon)

and foods that can be used to make soup stock, such as "miso," "mirin," "mentsuyu," "soy sauce," "kombu," and "hondashi," appear frequently in cluster 3

5 Emotional Analysis Using the BERT Model

Finally, we conducted an emotional analysis of the typed clusters to determine consumers' food consumption behavior according to their psychological factors. In this study, we used a BERT model with a binary classification of positive and negative.

We used a BERT model called cl-tohoku/bert-large-japanese [8], which is a pre-trained Japanese model published by Inui Lab at Tohoku University through Hugging face. We conducted fine tuning of this model in order to create a document classification model according to "Diary of Daily Activities" that are the subject of this study. For fine tuning, we used "WRIME: Subjective and Objective Emotion Analysis Dataset" [9], which is publicly available on Hugging face. We conducted fine tuning on the publicly available data, using 9,136 positive and negative documents each, for a total of 18,272 documents.

For the fine-tuned model evaluation, we used the data we labeled as positive and negative for 100 randomly selected cases from the 29,813 "Diary of Daily Activities" covered in this study. Figure 4 shows the mean loss of the fine-tuned model and the change in accuracy and number of epochs. Figure 4 shows that the learning rate and accuracy do not change significantly with the number of epochs. Losses continue to increase after epoch 3. Considering both accuracy and loss, we decided that epoch 3 was appropriate.

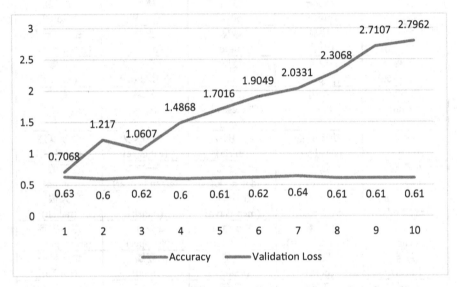

Fig. 4 Changes in the mean and precision of losses and the number of epochs

In Table 5, we present results for the learning rate, loss, and accuracy of the BERT model with fine tuning as epoch number 3.

Table 5. Fine-tuned model (number of epochs: 3)

Learning Rate	0.00001
Validation Loss	1.0607
Accuracy	0.6200

We conducted an emotional analysis for each cluster, classifying the consumer's situation into two categories: positive and negative. Table 6 shows our interpretation of the consumer's situation and possible emotional factors.

Table 6. Summary of Consumer Situation

Situation	Positive/Negative	When considered as an emotional factor
Busy morning situation such as making breakfast or lunch	Positive	When you have a favorite food
	Negative	When you are short on time or tired
Situation in which meals are prepared according to the family's physical condition	Positive	When it suits your child's tastes
	Negative	When it doesn't suits your child's tastes
When you want to warm up your body	Positive	When you are recovering
	Negative	When you are not feeling well
Situation of preparing daily meals	Positive	When the food tastes good
	Negative	When there is leftover food
Situation in which meals are prepared according to a schedule	Positive	When it is a celebration
	Negative	When it is a customary gathering

We also found differences in food consumption across emotional polarity in a frequency analysis using TF-IDF. Table 7 shows a cluster-by-cluster sampling of foodstuff words that occur frequently in documents classified as positive. Similarly, Table 8 shows a cluster-by-cluster sampling of food words that appear frequently in documents classified as negative.

Table 7. Characteristic Words for Foodstuffs when Consumer Sentiment is Positive

Cluster	Characteristic Food Words
Cluster1	食パン，ハム，チーズ，海苔，御飯，ホットケーキミックス (Bread, ham, cheese, seaweed, rice, pancake mix)
Cluster2	カレールー，スパゲッティ，コンソメ，ケチャップ，チーズ (Curry roux, spaghetti, consommé, ketchup, cheese)
Cluster3	大根，豆腐，うどん，めんつゆ，昆布，こんにゃく (radish, tofu, udon, mentsuyu, kombu, konnyaku)
Cluster4	人参，みりん，豚肉，玉葱，鶏卵，キャベツ，牛肉，鶏肉 (carrot, mirin, pork, onion, egg, cabbage, beef, chicken)
Cluster5	砂糖，小麦粉，生クリーム，マグロ，イチゴ，イカ，エビ (sugar, flour, cream, tuna, strawberries, squid, shrimp)

Comparing Tables 7 and 8, there are differences in the foods consumed by each cluster. For example, in cluster 5, consumers are in the situation of having an unusual meal with family or friends. When consumer sentiment is positive, food items such as cakes and sushi are common, suggesting that the occasion is a birthday or other celebratory event. On the other hand, when consumer sentiment is negative, foods eaten

Table 8. Characteristic Words for Foodstuffs when Consumer Sentiment is Negative

Cluster	Characteristic Food Words
Cluster1	食パン，海苔，豆腐，梅干し，イカ，カレー，カレールー (Bread, laver, tofu, pickled plums, squid, curry, curry roux)
Cluster2	ショウガ，カレー粉，豆腐，ナス，コーヒー (ginger, curry powder, tofu, eggplant, coffee)
Cluster3	うどん，御飯，豆腐，ショウガ，かまぼこ，梅干し (udon noodles, rice, tofu, ginger, fish paste, dried plums)
Cluster4	豚肉，豆腐，玉葱，みりん，キャベツ，牛肉，味噌，モヤシ (pork, tofu, onion, mirin, cabbage, beef, miso, bean sprout)
Cluster5	コーヒー，紅茶，小豆，ヨーグルト，ハチミツ，餅米，春菊 (coffee, tea, azuki beans, yogurt, honey, glutinous rice, garland chrysanthemum)

during the New Year's holiday such as red beans and rice cakes appear, suggesting that it is a family meal during the New Year holiday.

By conducting a frequency analysis using TF-IDF on the words of food items used by consumers in their actions, we have revealed differences in food item choice in different consumer situations. We found that more items are changed in the negatively categorized situation than in the positively categorized situation. This may be because consumers choose less labor-intensive food items when they are negatively affected, or because they are forced to choose certain food items according to their physical condition.

6 Conclusion

In this study, we analyzed texts describing consumers' eating behaviors, their backgrounds, and the foodstuffs used in those behaviors, with the aim of clarifying the relationships between consumers' circumstances, their emotions, and their food consumption behaviors. First, we constructed a topic model using the latent Dirichlet allocation method for the text of the behavior data and background data from the diary. By focusing on words with high importance in the topics, we interpreted what topics were described in each topic and clarified what topics existed in the documents. Next, we performed non-hierarchical clustering using the distribution of topic affiliation for each document obtained by building a topic model. We also analyzed the frequency of words appearing in each cluster using TF-IDF to identify the characteristics of the clusters. As a result, we were able to classify the documents into five categories according to the consumers' situation regarding food, although we did not find significant differences between the topics and the contents of the clusters in this study. Finally, we used the BERT sentiment analysis model to classify the documents into two categories: positive and negative. Furthermore, we were able to further classify and interpret the consumer's situation in detail by performing a frequency analysis using TF-IDF on the words in each of the positive and negative documents by cluster. In addition, we also analyzed the words of the foodstuffs used by consumers in their actions. We found that consumers' food choices were more limited when they were negative than when, they were positive.

This study made it possible to examine food consumption behavior by focusing on the specific food-related behaviors of consumers and their backgrounds. This study shows that the analytical method used in this study is effective to some extent as a new research approach that considers the consumers' circumstances. It is difficult to explain heuristic food choices based on consumers' own impressions and experiences using traditional economic theory. However, in this study, we focused on the background of consumers' behavior. Therefore, it can be said that our results consider consumers' impressions and experiences.

A future issue to be addressed is how to extract the most frequently used food words in each cluster. In this study, food words such as "soy sauce," "onion," "carrot," and "potato" appeared frequently in most of the clusters. By extracting more characteristic meal words other than these food ingredients, we can further understand the relationship between food consumption behavior in each consumer's situation. We also believe that there is room for improvement in identifying the words that contributed to consumers' emotions. In this study, we attempted to identify the words that contributed to consumer sentiment by conducting a frequency analysis using TF-IDF on documents classified as positive and those classified as negative by cluster. However, this method does not consider the context of the sentences. Therefore, we believe that it would be possible to clarify the connection between sentences by conducting a case frame analysis and a dependency frequency analysis on each document.

Acknowledgements. We thank the company that provides marketing support services for providing the data. In this paper, we used "WRIME: Subjective and Objective Emotion Analysis Dataset" (GitHub - ids-cv/wrime) which was created with the support of the Social Innovation Creation Platform 5.0 (grant number: JPMXP0518071489) available on Git Hub. This work was supported by JSPS KAKENHI Grant Numbers 21K13385, 21H04600.

References

1. Ministry of Agriculture, Forestry and Fisheries: Survey Report on Awareness of Nutrition Education HTML format (March 2009), Nutrition Education Awareness Survey Report HTML format (March 2009): Ministry of Agriculture, Forestry and Fisheries (maff.go.jp). Accessed 08 Dec 2023
2. Ministry of Health, Labour and Welfare: 2022 National Survey of Basic Living Conditions (2022). Accessed 10 Dec 2023
3. Ministry of Health, Labour and Welfare: Ministry of Health, Labour and Welfare White Paper 2021 -New Coronavirus Infections and Social Security-.001011736.pdf (mhlw.go.jp). Accessed 10 Dec 2023
4. Oura, Y.: Perspectives and methods for understanding diverse consumer behaviors on food. Food Syst. Res. **19**(2), 46–49 (2012). Symposium Joint Discussion
5. Imada, S.: Psychological approach to food behavior, Chap. 1. In: Nakajima, Y., Imada, S. (eds.) Account of Human Behavior, vol. 2. Psychology of Food Behavior, pp. 10–22. Asakura Publishing (1996)
6. Isojima, A.: Consumers' needs in purchasing agricultural products based on marketing research. Agric. For. Stat. Assoc. Jpn., 1–164 (2009)
7. Ryuichi, S.: Recent development in food consumption analysis in Japan. J. Food Syst. Res. **19**(2), 37–45 (2012). https://doi.org/10.5874/jfsr.19.37

8. Hugging Face: Pretrained Japanese BERT models, GitHub - cl-tohoku/bert-japanese: BERT models for Japanese text. Accessed 11 Dec 2023
9. WRIME: Subjective and Objective Emotion Analysis Dataset, GitHub - ids-cv/wrime. Accessed 08 Dec 2023

Empirical Analysis of Individual Differences Based on Sentiment Estimation Performance Toward Speaker Adaptation for Social Signal Processing

Sixia Li and Shogo Okada[✉]

Graduate School of Advanced Science and Technology,
Japan Advanced Institute of Science and Technology, Nomi, Ishikawa, Japan
{lisixia,okada-s}@jaist.ac.jp

Abstract. Understanding user's internal state is indispensable for human-robot interaction in social signal processing. To mitigate the bias of sentiments observed by third-party annotators, the importance of self-reported by users themselves was pointed out recently. However, the self-reported internal state is not displayed as similar multimodal behaviors among different individuals, this leads to performance gap between self-reported and third-party sentiment estimations. Speaker adaptation for social signal processing (SASSP) is necessary to learn individual social signal characteristics to mitigate the individual differences. Towards effective adaptation for speakers with different characteristics, clarifying influence of individual differences in internal state estimation is necessary but has not been clarified. To address this problem, this study conducted empirical analysis by training and testing models on multimodal data of a group of speakers. Then, we analyze the relationships between the best model's performance and speaker's characteristics including age, gender, personalities, and speaker's expectation before human-robot interaction experiment. The results showed that these aspects all have influence on estimation performance in SASSP due to expression differences. This study provides suggestions and directions on setting SASSP policies for self-reported internal state estimation.

Keywords: Sentiment estimation · speaker adaptation for social signal processing · machine learning

1 Introduction

Understanding user's internal state is indispensable for human-robot interaction in social signal processing, by which the machine can adjust actions to satisfy users. In practical, internal states are usually represented by user's sentiment [1,2] and emotions [3,4]. Multimodal signal cues are widely used for estimating internal states since user's state can be reflected from linguistic, acoustic, visual, and physiological aspects [5]. In modeling internal state estimation, deep learning methods are effective on capturing relationships between internal state and multimodal signals through dialogues [1].

A. Coman and S. Vasilache (Eds.): HCII 2024, LNCS 14703, pp. 359–371, 2024.
https://doi.org/10.1007/978-3-031-61281-7_26

Although internal state labels were mainly annotated by third parties in many previous studies, the importance of self-reported by users themselves was pointed out recently [2,6]. The self-reported internal state reflects user's real state more accurately compared to third-party annotations. Recent studies [7] also pointed out that self-reported sentiment differs from third-party sentiment in many aspects since the real internal state can be different from what is observed from outside. Although self-reported annotations reflect a person's real internal state, the internal state is not necessarily displayed as multimodal behaviors. As a result, estimation performance depends on the degree to which an individual person displays key-nonverbal behaviors related to the specific inner state type. To address this problem, besides using nonverbal features such as speech and facial expressions including individual difference, previous studies tried to utilize physiological signals for speaker-independent modeling to improve estimations performances [2]. But the performance on self-reported internal state still has gap to the performance on third-party internal state due to individual differences.

Speaker adaptation for social signal processing (SASSP) is necessary to learn individual social signal characteristics to mitigate the individual differences. Similar to speaker adaptation in speech processing area, SASSP aims to train the model with specific speakers' data to correlate individual multimodal behaviors and internal states. In this way, the influence of expression differences can be mitigated. Towards effective adaptation for speakers with different characteristics, clarifying influence of individual differences in internal state estimation is necessary. However, such analysis was not considered in previous studies, this leads to difficulties in setting adaptation policies.

To address this problem, this study analyzes individual differences in SASSP in an empirical way. Specifically, we train models by using multimodal data of a group of speakers. Then we test the model performance by the data of same users with guaranteeing that the training and testing data are different. After that, we analyze the relationships between the best model's performance and speaker's characteristics, including age, gender, personalities, and speaker's expectation before human-robot interaction experiment. We try to clarify what kind of speakers can be adapted easily or difficultly. By this analysis, this study provides suggestions and directions on setting SASSP policies for self-reported internal state estimation.

The contributions of this study can be summarized as follows:

1. This study analyzed the individual differences in SASSP for self-reported internal state estimation. To our best knowledge, we are the first to conduct such analysis. This can provide suggestions for adaptation policy settings.
2. We regarded the individual differences in the degree to expressions as differences in estimation accuracy. The differences in estimation performance are analyzed in detail by comparing them with personal information including gender, age, personality traits, and expectations before human-robot interaction. The results showed that these aspects all have influence on estimation performance in SASSP due to expression differences.

2 Methodology

For our purpose, we train self-reported internal state estimation models on multimodal data of a group of speakers. Specifically, we use self-reported sentiment as the self-reported internal state since the sentiment can generally represent the internal state. The sentiment is generally represented as high or low labels to show whether the speaker has a positive or negative internal state. Speakers in experiments cover various characteristics including different genders, ages, etc. So the data can be considered as a 'general data.' Then we test model performances on these speakers' data by guaranteeing the data is individual in training and test. This process can be considered as adapting a model to each specific speaker.

After that, we analyze the performance regarding to four characteristics to clarify the influence of these characteristics in SASSP. For categorized characteristics such as gender, we compare the speaker-averaged performance among categories for analysis. For scored characteristics such as personality traits, we compute the correlation coefficients between speaker performances and characteristic scores to clarify whether a common score leads to a common performance.

2.1 Characteristics for Analysis

We analyze the influence of gender, age, personality traits, and expectations before human-robot interaction experiment.

Gender gender is a general characteristic that bring differences in many tasks [8–10]. In this experiment, the speakers were separated into male and female categories. We compare the average performance between genders to show the influence of gender in SASSP.

Age age is another typical characteristic that has influence on many tasks [11, 12]. We separate age categories by every 10-years-old period. As a consequence, we have age categories such as 20, 30, etc. We compare average performances among ages to show the influence of age in SASSP.

Personality traits the influence of personality traits in human-robot interaction have attracted attentions recently [13–16]. One's personality has influence the interaction process from multiple aspects, including the expressions and the change of internal states. Therefore, considering personalities is necessary for adapting to specific speaker. In this study, we use the Big-five personality traits [17] as the metric for measuring one's personalities. The big-five is a grouping of five unique personality characteristics including openness, conscientiousness, extraversion, agreeableness, and neuroticism. We compute the Pearson correlation coefficients between model performances and big-five score to analyze the influence of each trait in SASSP.

Expectations Before Human-Robot Interaction Experiments recent study [18] pointed out that one's prior thought and expectations towards the interaction with robot would influence the performance during the interaction.

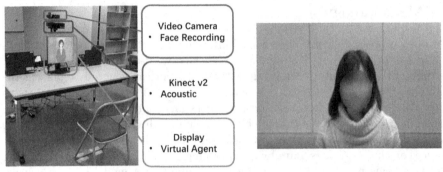

Data collection environment   Face video recording

Fig. 1. Data collection environment and video recording of Hazumi1911 dataset

Therefore, the expectations can be speculated to have influence on adaptations. In this study, we use questionnaires about expectations of the human-robot interaction to obtain expectation scores from various aspects. And We compute the Pearson correlation coefficients between model performances and the score of expectations to analyze the influence of each expectation aspect in SASSP.

3   Experiment

3.1   Dataset

We use the Hazumi1911 dataset [6,27–29] for conducting experiments. This dataset is a Japanese dataset of human-robot interaction dialogues. The dataset was collected by using a virtual agent to make dialogues with speakers. Video recordings and text transcripts are available in the dataset. So we can use the linguistic, acoustic, and facial modalities. Figure 1 shows the data collection environment and the video recording screenshot of the dataset.

In Hazumi1911 dataset, the self-reported sentiments were annotated by speakers themselves as their internal states. The internal state were originally annotated by 7-point Likert scale, from 1 to 7. Previous studies [2,5] usually compressed the 7-point sentiment into low sentiment and high sentiment for practice use. The threshold was 4, which means when the point is less or equal than 4, the sentiment is treated as low; while when the point is greater or equal than 4, the sentiment is treated as high. We follow this setting in this study to make our analysis to be useful for practice use.

This dataset contains speaker information of gender, age, personality traits, and questionnaires of expectations to human-robot interaction. The gender contains male and female categories. The ages of speakers are categorised into 20, 30, 40, 50, 60, and 70-yeas-old. The personality traits were originally measured by Japanese ten item personality inventory (TIPI-J) with 10 items. We referred to the manual [25] to transform TIPI-J to big-five scores. The questionnaires contains 18 aspects that describe expectations towards human-robot interaction.

Table 1. Characteristics and items for analysis of SASSP

Characteristic aspect	items
Gender	Male, Female
Age	20, 30, 40, 50,60, 70-years-old level
Big Five personality traits	Openness, Conscientiousness, Extraversion, Agreeableness, Neuroticism
Expectations before human-robot interaction	well-coordinated, boring, cooperative, harmonious, unsatisfying, uncomfortably paced,cold, awkward, engrossing, unfocused, involving, intense, friendly, active, positive, dull, worthwhile, slow

Answers of questionnaires are in 7-point Likert scale form, which represents how the speaker expect the interaction in specific aspect. Table 1 summarizes the individual characteristics and items for analysis.

For the experiment, we first conducted data cleaning to remove missing data for experiments. After data cleaning, Hazumi1911 contains 26 human-robot dialogues by different speakers. The speakers contain 12 male and 14 female. The age categories of 20, 30, 40, 50, 60, and 70 contains 5, 3, 5, 4, 6, and 3 speakers, respectively. The total utterance is 2468, including 1359 low sentiment utterances and 1109 high sentiment utterances. Based on the labels we use, we conduct experiments as a binary classification task to predict whether an utterance is low sentiment or high sentiment.

For each dialogue, we split 80% utterances from the beginning as training set, and the remaining 20% utterances of each dialogue were used for testing. In the training set, we further split 80% utterances for training the model, and the remaining 20% utterances in the training set is used as validation set for choosing the best parameters. As a consequence, we have 1566 utterances for training, 398 utterances for validation, and 504 utterances for test.

3.2 Multimodal Features

We use multiple modalities and their combinations, including linguistic (L), acoustic (A), and facial (F) features.

Linguistic Features. Bert [19] is a powerful model to obtain effective linguistic representations in various tasks [20]. We use the mean embedding of the last hidden layer of Bert as the linguistic feature. In particular, we use the cl-tohoku/bert-base-japanese model to extract features. As a consequence, we obtain a 768-dimension vector of the linguistic feature for each utterance.

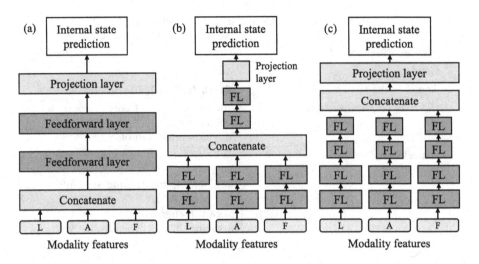

Fig. 2. Model structures

Acoustic Features. We use the Interspeech2009 feature set (IS09) [21] as the acoustic feature. The IS09 contains 16 low-level descriptions including F0, energy, zero cross rate, and MFCCs, and 12 functional description including mean, variance, etc. This feature set was shown effective in emotion recognition and sentiment analysis tasks [21], so it is suitable for modeling sentiment-related internal state. We use OpenSmile [22] tool to extract IS09 features. As a consequence, we obtain a 386-dimension vector of the acoustic feature for each utterance.

Facial Features. We use action units (AUs) from facial action coding system (FACS) [23] to represent facial information. In particular, we use OpenFace [23] tool to extract 18 discrete AUs for each frame of utterances. Each AU is represented as value 1 if that AU is estimated to be appeared, or value 0 if that AU is estimated as not to be appeared. After that, we compute the mean value of each AU among all frames of an utterance as the facial feature. As a consequence, we obtain a 18-dimension vector of the facial feature for each utterance.

3.3   Models

We use Three DNN-based models that were widely used in many studies and especially be shown effective [2] for modeling self-reported internal state. These models include an early fusion model (named DNN Early hereafter), two late fusion models with different fusion strategies (named DNN Late 1 and DNN Late 2 hereafter). The model structure is shown in Fig. 2.

DNN Early. Figure 2 (a) shows the structure of DNN Early model. This model is consisted of 2 feedforward layers with 256 units. The Relu function is used for activation functions of each layer. The modality feature vectors are first concatenated before inputting into the model. After feedforward layers, a feedforward layer with softmax function is used to project middle tensors to label probabilities. Finally, the label with the highest probability is chosen as the prediction.

DNN Late 1. Figure 2 (b) shows the structure of DNN Late 1 model. In the model processing, each modality is first inputted into separated modality feedforward layers. Each modality feedforward layer contains 2 layer with 64 units of each layer. Then the output of all modality feedforward layers are concatenated into one vector. After that, the concatenated vector is inputted into fusion feedforward layers. Fusion feedforward layers contains 2 layers with 32 units of each layer. After feedforward layers, a projection layer with softmax function is used to obtain label probabilities. The Relu function is used for activation functions of each layer.

DNN Late 2. Figure 2 (c) shows the structure of DNN Late 2 model. In the model processing, each modality is embedded with separated modality feedforward layers. Each modality feedforward layer contains 4 layers. The units of layers are 64, 64, 32, and 32 from the input side to the output side. After separated embedding, the output of modality layers is concatenated into one vector. Then the concatenated vector is inputted into a feedforward layer. After the feedforward layer, a projection layer with softmax function is used to obtain label probabilities. The Relu function is used for activation functions of each layer.

3.4 Experiment Setting

We use macro F1 as the evaluation metric, and we conduct analysis of variance (ANOVA) test to clarify significant difference between different groups. All training and testing were conducted three times, the average performances were used for evaluation to reduce the influence of random initialization.

4 Result and Discussion

Table 2 lists averaged macro F1 of models using each modality combinations. Underlined numbers indicate the best performance of each model, bold number indicates the best performance among all models. As seen in the table, using A+F modality is the best performance of each model. The best performances of DNN Early, DNN Late 1, and DNN Late 2 are 0.725, 0.732, and 0.739 of macro F1 score, respectively. We found that the best modality A+F is inconsistent to the best modality in speaker-independent studies using Hazumi1911 [6], in which the best modality combination was usually consisted with linguistic modality. We speculate that the A+F is the best combination is related to the intrinsic characteristic of self-reported internal state. The internal states of different speakers are affected by individual differences and could differ from similar outside expressions. Linguistic modality can somehow be effective cue on common situations among speakers, where speakers' specific contents reflecting specific internal states. So the linguistic modality is effective in speaker-independent modeling. On the other hand, this study trains the model by using

Table 2. Macro F1 of different models using different modality combinations

Modality	Model		
	DNN Early	DNN Late 1	DNN Late 2
L	0.621	0.628	0.606
L+A	0.682	0.707	0.711
L+F	0.657	0.690	0.687
L+A+F	0.696	0.728	0.737
A	0.718	0.711	0.720
F	0.703	0.685	0.688
A+F	0.725	0.732	**0.739**

speaker's data to adapt to each speaker. The model can better capture the relationship between individual multimodal behaviors and internal states. Therefore, the results demonstrates that acoustic and facial modalities are more related to internal states than linguistic modality for adapting individual situations. So they can be better cues than linguistic in SASSP.

By comparing the best performance of three models, one can see that DNN Late 2 using A+F modality has the best performance among all models. Therefore, we treat DNN Late 2 using A+F modality as the representative model for analysis.

Next, we analyze the influence of individual differences in SASSP by the way described in Sect. 2 based on the result of DNN Late 2 using A+F modality.

Figure 3 shows the performance comparison among gender categories. As seen in the figure, the mean performance of female speakers is 0.513, while the mean performance of male performance is 0.649. The performances of two genders are significant different based on ANOVA result. We speculate that female speakers tend take more care to match the rhythm of the robot to make the dialogue not to be awkward. Thus, external performances corresponding to high or low sentiment are not consistent through the whole dialogue. So it became difficult for the model to use the relationship learned from a part of dialogue to adapt the remaining dialogue for female speakers.

Figure 4 shows the performance comparison among age categories. As seen in the figure, the mean performance from 20-years-old to 70-years-old are 0.604, 0.500, 0.609, 0.608, 0.617, and 0.425, respectively. By comparing the performance of each age category, one can see that the mean performance of groups except 30-years-old and 70-years-old are close. While 70-years-old and 30-years-old group has a lower mean performance than other groups. But the significant difference only exists between 70-years-old and 40-years-old group. We speculate the reason of significant low performance of 70-years-old group is related to that facial expression patterns of elder people is not as obvious as young people [26]. Meanwhile elder people may not control their expressions as well as young people. So their internal state is difficult to be estimated from facial aspect,

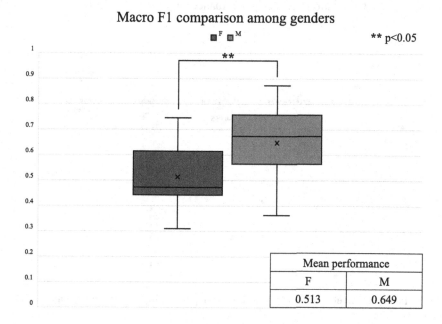

Fig. 3. Macro F1 of gender categories

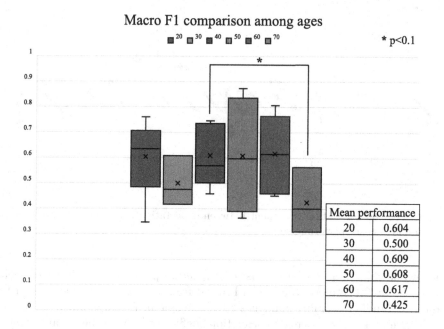

Fig. 4. Macro F1 of age categories

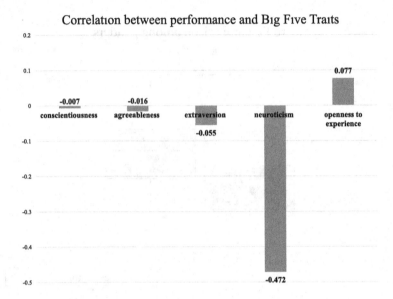

Fig. 5. Pearson correlation coefficient between personality traits and speaker performance

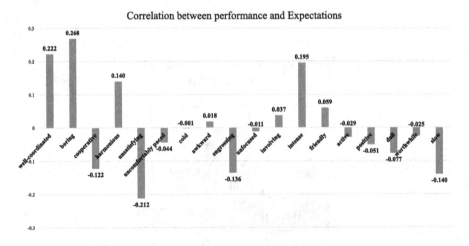

Fig. 6. Pearson correlation coefficient between expectation before human-robot interaction and speaker performance

meanwhile they may not have consistent external performance related to their internal state. Therefore, the model learned from a part of dialogue is hard to adapt to handle remaining dialogues for old people in 70-years-old.

Figure 5 shows the Pearson correlation coefficient between personality traits and speaker performances. As seen in the figure, among five personality traits, only neuroticism trait has a significant negative correlation to the model performance. While other traits rarely related to performances. We speculate the reason is that people with high neuroticism tend to hide their real thought, so their external performances are not related to their internal state consistently. This leads to difficulties on adaptation for high neuroticism people.

Figure 6 shows the Pearson correlation coefficient between expectation before human-robot interaction and speaker performances. As seen in the figure, cooperation and boring items have weak positive correlations 0.222 and 0.268, respectively; unsatisfied item has weak negative correlation −0.212. The results show that expectations have influence on speaker's internal state-related external performances through dialogue, thus influence the adaptation.

5   Conclusion

This study conducted empirical analysis to clarify the influence of individual differences in speaker adaptation for social signal processing on internal state estimation. The results demonstrated that acoustic and facial modalities are more effective than the linguistic modality in adaptation. The results showed that various individual differences including gender, age, personality traits, and expectations before human-robot interaction all have influence on adaptations, leading to relationships between speakers' outside expressions and their internal states to be not consistent during dialogues. Therefore, capturing and mitigating such inconsistencies can be considered a direction for better adaptation.

Acknowledgement. This work was also partially supported by JSPS KAKENHI (22K21304, 22H04860, 22H00536, 23H03506), JST AIP Trilateral AI Research, Japan (JPMJCR20G6) and JST Moonshot R&D program (JPMJMS2237).

References

1. Gandhi, A., Adhvaryu, K., Poria, S., et al.: Multimodal sentiment analysis: a systematic review of history, datasets, multimodal fusion methods, applications, challenges and future directions. Inf. Fusion **91**, 424–444 (2023)
2. Katada, S., Okada, S., Hirano, Y., Komatani, K.: Is she truly enjoying the conversation? Analysis of physiological signals toward adaptive dialogue systems. In: Proceedings of the 2020 International Conference on Multimodal Interaction, pp. 315–323 (2020)
3. Mittal, T., Bhattacharya, U., Chandra, R., et al.: M3ER: multiplicative multimodal emotion recognition using facial, textual, and speech cues. In: Proceedings of the AAAI Conference on Artificial Intelligence, vol. 34, no. 02, pp. 1359–1367 (2020)
4. Busso, C., Bulut, M., Lee, C.C., et al.: IEMOCAP: interactive emotional dyadic motion capture database. Lang. Resour. Eval. **42**, 335–359 (2008)
5. Katada, S., Okada, S., Komatani, K.: Effects of physiological signals in different types of multimodal sentiment estimation. IEEE Trans. Affect. Comput. (2022)
6. Komatani, K., Okada, S.: Multimodal human-agent dialogue corpus with annotations at utterance and dialogue levels. In: 2021 9th International Conference on Affective Computing and Intelligent Interaction (ACII), pp. 1–8. IEEE (2021)

7. Komatani, K., Takeda, R., Okada, S.: Analyzing differences in subjective annotations by participants and third-party annotators in multimodal dialogue corpus. In: Proceedings of the 24th Meeting of the Special Interest Group on Discourse and Dialogue, pp. 104–113 (2023)

8. Usart, M., Grimalt-Álvaro, C., Iglesias-Estradé, A.M.: Gender-sensitive sentiment analysis for estimating the emotional climate in online teacher education. Learn. Environ. Res. **26**(1), 77–96 (2023)

9. Volkova, S., Wilson, T., Yarowsky, D.: Exploring demographic language variations to improve multilingual sentiment analysis in social media. In: Proceedings of the Conference on Empirical Methods in Natural Language Processing 2013, pp. 1815–1827 (2013)

10. Abbruzzese, L., Magnani, N., Robertson, I.H., et al.: Age and gender differences in emotion recognition. Front. Psychol. **10**, 2371 (2019)

11. Bailey, P.E., Brady, B., Ebner, N.C., et al.: Effects of age on emotion regulation, emotional empathy, and prosocial behavior. J. Gerontol. Ser. B **75**(4), 802–810 (2020)

12. Kim, E., Bryant, D.A., Srikanth, D., et al.: Age bias in emotion detection: an analysis of facial emotion recognition performance on young, middle-aged, and older adults. In: Proceedings of the 2021 AAAI/ACM Conference on AI, Ethics, and Society, pp. 638–644 (2021)

13. Le, H., Li, S., Mawalim, C.O., et al.: Investigating the effect of linguistic features on personality and job performance predictions. In: Coman, A., Vasilache, S. (eds.) HCII 2023. LNCS, vol. 14025, pp. 370–383. Springer, Cham (2023). https://doi.org/10.1007/978-3-031-35915-6_27

14. Yan, D., Chen, L.: The influence of personality traits on user interaction with recommendation interfaces. ACM Trans. Interact. Intell. Syst. **13**(1), 1–39 (2023)

15. Böckle, M., Yeboah-Antwi, K., Kouris, I.: Can you trust the black box? The effect of personality traits on trust in AI-enabled user interfaces. In: Degen, H., Ntoa, S. (eds.) HCII 2021. LNCS (LNAI), vol. 12797, pp. 3–20. Springer, Cham (2021). https://doi.org/10.1007/978-3-030-77772-2_1

16. Alves, T., Natálio, J., Henriques-Calado, J., et al.: Incorporating personality in user interface design: a review. Personal. Individ. Differ. **155**, 109709 (2020)

17. Gosling, S.D., Rentfrow, P.J., Swann, W.B., Jr.: A very brief measure of the Big-Five personality domains. J. Res. Pers. **37**(6), 504–528 (2003)

18. Blut, M., Wang, C., Wünderlich, N.V., et al.: Understanding anthropomorphism in service provision: a meta-analysis of physical robots, chatbots, and other AI. J. Acad. Mark. Sci. **49**, 632–658 (2021)

19. Kenton, J.D.M.W.C., Toutanova, L.K.: BERT: pre-training of deep bidirectional transformers for language understanding. In: Proceedings of NAACL-HLT, pp. 4171–4186 (2019)

20. Liu, P., Yuan, W., Fu, J., et al.: Pre-train, prompt, and predict: a systematic survey of prompting methods in natural language processing. ACM Comput. Surv. **55**(9), 1–35 (2023)

21. Schuller, B., Steidl, S., Batliner, A.: The INTERSPEECH 2009 emotion challenge (2009)

22. Eyben, F., Wöllmer, M., Schuller, B.: Opensmile: the MUNICH versatile and fast open-source audio feature extractor. In: Proceedings of the 18th ACM International Conference on Multimedia, pp. 1459–1462 (2010)

23. Ekman, P., Friesen, W.V.: Facial action coding system. Environ. Psychol. Nonverbal Behav. (1978)

24. Baltrusaitis, T., Zadeh, A., Lim, Y.C., et al.: Openface 2.0: facial behavior analysis toolkit. In: 2018 13th IEEE International Conference on Automatic Face and Gesture Recognition (FG 2018), pp. 59–66. IEEE (2018)
25. https://jspp.gr.jp/doc/manual_TIPI-J.pdf
26. Lopes, N., Silva, A., Khanal, S.R., et al.: Facial emotion recognition in the elderly using a SVM classifier. In: 2018 2nd International Conference on Technology and Innovation in Sports, Health and Wellbeing (TISHW), pp. 1–5. IEEE (2018)
27. Hirano, Y., Okada, S., Komatani, K.: Recognizing social signals with weakly supervised multitask learning for multimodal dialogue systems. In: Proceedings of the International Conference on Multimodal Interaction, pp. 141–149 (2021)
28. Hirano, Y., Okada, S., Nishimoto, H., et al.: Multitask prediction of exchange-level annotations for multimodal dialogue systems. In: 2019 International Conference on Multimodal Interaction, pp. 85–94 (2019)
29. Wei, W., Li, S., Okada, S.: Investigating the relationship between dialogue and exchange-level impression. In: Proceedings of the International Conference on Multimodal Interaction, pp. 359–367 (2022)

Detecting Human Values and Sentiments in Large Text Collections with a Context-Dependent Information Markup: A Methodology and Math

Olga Rink[1,2], Viktor Lobachev[1], and Konstantin Vorontsov[1,2]

[1] MSU Institute for Artificial Intelligence, Lomonosovsky Avenue 27s1,
Moscow 119192, Russian Federation
olga.rink@phystech.edu
[2] Moscow Institute of Physics and Technology, 9, Institutsky side,
Dolgoprudny 141701, Russia
konstantin.vorontsov@mlsa-iai.ru

Abstract. The detection of human values, beliefs or tonality in large text collections, e.g. publications in social networks, requires ML algorithms and an interdisciplinary expertise. Narratives and worldviews can be uncovered via a context-dependent information markup. The formalization is achieved by the markup representation as a hyper-graph model. Here the vertices correspond to the text spans while the edges link with the markup elements labeled by the values or emotions concepts in classifiers. Any markup element contains arbitrary text fragments, and their set correlates with manifestation of values or sentiments. After typing a sufficient number of marked-up documents the model is trained to automatically determine values or emotions expressed in the texts. The authors illustrate their methodology with the case of finding cultural codes in a collection of social media publications. The first section of the paper reviews scientific schools of exposing value codes and arguments the task relevance, its humanitarian, mathematical and software aspects. The second one introduces mathematical definitions and the problem statement, algorithmic approaches in natural language processing applicable to its solution. The third section overviews a project of the MSU IAI laboratory of machine learning and semantic analysis. The outcomes of the project are a software developed for a context-dependent markup and various applications in the media analysis industry, training samples fulfilled by linguists, sociologists, economists, and political science experts, as well as some relevant pretest statistics on the contemporary cultural landscape.

Keywords: Human values detection · Cultural code · Emotion detection · Controversy · Context-dependent information · Markup · Hyper-graph model · Media narrative analysis · Digital Humanities

A. Coman and S. Vasilache (Eds.): HCII 2024, LNCS 14703, pp. 372–383, 2024.
https://doi.org/10.1007/978-3-031-61281-7_27

1   Introduction

Nowadays the address of meaning extraction is one of the foremost productive topics in Digital Humanities. Understanding the basic human values of collaboration occasions can upgrade intercultural contact. The delivered method of formalization and the use case of detecting value determinants in considerable textual collections expand the primary evaluation scheme for a media narrative and is relevant to the machine learning applications. The approach is accomplished by the markup representation as a hyper-graph. Here the vertices compare to the content fragments whereas the edges interface with the markup components and are labeled by the value concepts or tonalities in classifiers. Any markup element contains a number of content parts, and their set connects with appearance of values or sentiment estimations. Not at all like the labeling of solid spans or total texts, the formalization offers labeling any connected significant combinations of fragments as well as an experience record or a background knowledge for the textual content.

2   Scientific Schools of Exposing Value Codes and Arguments for the Task Relevance

Scientists have extensively researched ontologies and methods to uncover human values and cultural codes, traced back to Greek philosophers in the 4–5th century BC [22]. Such publications feature axiology, philosophy, sociology, anthropology, psychology, pedagogy, linguistics, political science, law, civilizational and cultural aspects. By utilizing scientific disciplines, understanding the definition of value, the ultimate goal of classification, and subjective relationships, values are classified. The very concept of "civilization"(from the English "civilisation") was first found in 1767 in Scottish and 1760 - French texts [3] and is etymologically related to the idea of a social ("civil", "to civilise") contract. Civilization can be defined both by common objective elements, such as origin, religion, language, history, human values, customs and social institutions, and by the subjective self-identification of people (Huntington, 1997) [13]. Elias (1969) and Kuper (2001) also reflect on that human value determinants are an integral part of nations or social groups [8,17]. American psychologist M. Rokeach (1972) believes that the value system of an individual develops over one's life in accordance with the life experience gained within the framework of a certain social culture [29]. Hofstede's review of organizational cultures dating back to 1980 (Hofstede, 2010) emphasizes six dimensions of national cultures: Power Distance, Uncertainty Avoidance, Individualism/Collectivism, Masculinity/Femininity, Long/Short Term Orientation, and Indulgence/Restraint [2,12]. R. Inglehart (1997) makes an attempt to methodologically combine the individual and group understanding of social processes. The analysis covers all levels of social interaction: interpersonal, group, national and all else [14]. In 1992–1997 S. Schwartz follows a technique suggested by M. Rokeach and identifies ten value groups by a certain type of personal motivation. These value groups are in turn divided into two classes representing the interests of a society or profiling the personality. A total of 57 concepts are listed in the questionnaire, among them 30 belong to the first class, and 27 to the second one [18,34]. S. Hayes (2014) offers ten classes of values corresponding to the human lives, such as marriage/partnership, parenthood, etc., and notes that personal values can be revised over the years. According to the researcher, value determinants are not a completely verbal phenomenon, though they are certainly put into words at least partially [39]. Russian scientist Yu.S. Stepanov in his study "Constants: Dictionary of Russian Culture" (1997, 2004) gives an overview of cultural concepts. The concept is meant to be the package of ideas, knowledge, experiences, and associations that come with the word. Culture is like a clot in a person's mind, which is where it enters the mental world of an individual [38]. B. Erasov (2000) makes a significant contribution to ordering the ontology of values and justifying their separation into six classes. According to the researcher, the spiritual life of society is meaningfully enriched by customs, norms, values, meanings, and knowledge [9]. A. Sergeeva in the book "Russians: stereotypes of behavior, traditions, mentality" (2006) reveals the features of the Russian mentality and traditions based on data from historians, ethnographers, psychologists, statisticians and comparative analysis with other cultures. Sergeeva describes "a set of universal values, everything that unites Russians with other nations and can be used for mutual understanding" [35]. The results of cross-cultural studies on values (specifically G. Hofstede and S. Schwartz) are utilized by A. Auzan (2019) and his school to gain value orientations in economics, for example: individualism, masculinity, femininity, power distance, trust, etc. [1]. The regulations of the international level such as the Universal Declaration of Human Rights, adopted by the United Nations in 1948 [33], and the national Decree of the President of the Russian Federation dated 11/19/2022 No. 809 "On approval of the foundations of state policy for the preservation and strengthening of traditional Russian spiritual and moral values" [6] can be considered as well. The Decree's text lists the human values as the foundation for the creation of national identity. The catalogue encompasses life, dignity, human rights and freedoms, patriotism, citizenship, service to the Fatherland and responsibility for its fate, high moral ideals, strong family, creative work, priority of the spiritual over the material, humanism, mercy, justice, collectivism, mutual assistance and mutual respect, historical memory and continuity of generations, and unity of the peoples of Russia. Consideration of the field of value orientations is incomplete without reference to theology (religious studies). The text of the speech of Patriarch Kirill of Moscow and All Russia on May 19, 2023 at the meeting of the Strategic Vision Group "Russia as the Islamic World" is taken as the basis [37]. The Patriarch emphasized the diversity of religious trends historically represented on the territory of the Russian Federation, and noted the unity of approach to determining spiritual and moral guidelines among various faiths. The Patriarch emphasized common semantic positions such as the values of "goodness", "love", "mercy", "justice", "mutual respect" (including to the values and traditions of other religions). Understanding values as the basic concepts of background knowledge in the collective culture that form worldviews is necessary for civilizations to interact. To comprehend these values, it is necessary to study texts created by and for this group of people.

3   Mathematical Definitions and the Problem Statement, Algorithmic Approaches in Natural Language Processing Applicable to Its Solution

Numerous applications are centered around knowledge graphs. Whereas the demand for generalized pipelines to construct and continuously update knowledge graphs is on the rise [11,32]. In social studies basic, literal, text analytic is generally drawing to the statistical analysis that uncovers a manifest content of the documents. Interpretive or qualitative analysis reveal both the latent, not implicit or evident, and manifest content of the texts [7,16,23,28]. Digital humanities cover applications of computational techniques to human and social studies and evolve since the middle of 20-th century [4,10,19,24]. Researchers have developed many technologies and publicly accessible services for semantic markup and basic content analysis throughout the history of numerous interdisciplinary attempts.

The Paper Approach. The authors believe that semantic labeling of a text is based on four elementary operations:

- Highlighting a text fragment (called also as "span" furthermore);
- Classifying it;
- Linking fragments (if necessary);
- Commenting a text fragment or a connection (also if necessary).

Those four operations are apparently sufficient to analyze a media narrative or formalize a wide range of challenges related to understanding a semantic nature of a text. In particular, this approach was the basis for the technical regulations of the UpGreat PRO // READING contest (https://ai.upgreat.one/), which took place in 2020–2022. The contest in "understanding the meaning" of school writings was dedicated to the creation of AI solutions to identify semantic errors in graduation essays in Russian and English.

The Method Formalization. The method formalization is achieved through representation of a markup as a hyper-graph model. Here in the simplest case the vertices correspond to the text spans while the edges link with the markup elements labeled by the values concepts or, say, sentiments in classifiers. Any markup element contains arbitrary text spans, and their combination is associated with a manifestation of classes.

Let's Consider an Arbitrary Text Message Published in the "Twitter and TikTok" Channel in June 2023: "The Lookout (Twitter)" Another surprising development on a very strange and *remarkable* day. Despite this, wait and see what happens before concluding. As the last 24 h have shown, there could be more surprises

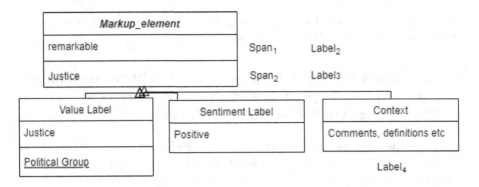

Fig. 1. Labeled element

coming. @wartranslated: Prigozhin says it's over: "They were going to dismantle PMC Wagner. We came out on 23 June to the March of *Justice*. In a day, we walked to nearly 200km away from Moscow. In this time, we did not spill a single drop of blood of our fighters. Now, the moment has come when blood... https:// t.co/FCzLBzNmKm".

Then Fig. 1 is an illustration of the labeled element for the document. Unlike the labeling of solid text fragments or complete documents, the formalization offers labeling any linked meaningful combinations of spans as well as a context behind the spans and their sets. The model can acquire an ability to automatically categorize texts in a large text collection by utilizing a sufficient number of labeled documents. The methodology allows for the processing of large amounts of data in media through quantitative content analysis. Labeled data have the potential to be used to train large language models (LLMs).

4   Evaluation of the Contemporary Cultural Landscape and Pretest Statistics

The identification of cultural codes in large text arrays of documents is an example of how the methodologies of various scientific schools can be combined into a single ontology. Qualified annotators with an expertise from various disciplines are involved to make informed decisions about a legitimate structure of classifiers and their amendment. The purpose of the project is to identify, classify and monitor cultural concepts that represent human values and related concepts (called as "values" or "cultural codes" furthermore) based on a sample of a large number of texts. The following tasks are necessary to be solved for the identification, classification, and monitoring of values and related concepts

1. Establishing a values space (called as "classifier" or "ontology");
2. Drawing a landscape ("model" or "paradigm") of the values of the studied group in a given space;
3. Creating a software for monitoring values and related concepts in large text collections.

4.1   Axiomatic Construction

At this and given the subsequent automation and the machine learning specifics, the value classifier is assumed to meet the axiomatic construction including Significance, Openness, Experts consistency, Sentiments control, and Labels consistency.

- Each value label holds significance for the target audience;
- The values classifier is open so that can be supplemented and expanded within the labeling stages;
- The opinions of annotators on the relevance of a given text fragment or markup element to a given value are consistent;
- Whether or not a text fragment or markup element expresses a positive or negative attitude towards a value, annotators' opinions remain consistent enough;
- The classification system does not have any redundant elements so that an addition of a value to the ontology should not be analogue or a paraphrase of existing values.

4.2   Interdisciplinary Expertise

At all stages of the content analysis, in order to determine whether the values are fundamental for the group, a digital humanities expertise is necessary to determine the priorities of monitoring values from a point of view of various scientific schools.

- Philosophy, ethics, religious studies consider human values from the standpoint of axiology;
- Law takes regulations or legislative protection rules into account;
- Sociological sciences explore cultural codes (for example, the World Values Survey, WVS), vulnerabilities and potential threats to regions and ethnic groups, interethnic and interfaith relations, as well as other sociological phenomena, possibly detailed by a region or cohort groups;
- Geopolitical threats are the focus of Political Science;
- Traditions across countries and populations and the vulnerabilities associated with history distortion are studied in history and archaeology;
- The focus of psychological science is on how cultural codes and human values impact the motivation and mental health of citizens, interpersonal communication, human relations, and the general level of anxiety in societies;
- The perception of values in texts and media content accessible to children and adolescents is examined by education based on the audience's age;
- Value-relevant statements in texts are identified by linguists by utilizing linguistic rules and value-relevant patterns, taking into account the narrative's structural features.

4.3 Values Classifier

The researchers proposed their own methodology, ontology and markup tool that combined multiple approaches. The construction of a classifier for analyzing value determinants is based on Erasov's structure, which successfully identified various categories: vital, social, political, moral, religious and aesthetic. Since values are the foundation of any culture, form its core, culture itself can be considered as a certain value system, therefore, the concepts of Stepanov's research were instrumental in the development of the initial list of values. The value orientations formulated in the national Decree of the President of the Russian Federation No. 809 also served as the basis for the ongoing research.

4.4 Openness of the Value Classifier

The value classifier is open so that can be supplemented and expanded within the labeling stages. Up to the end of the markup procedure the steering committee holds the annotators meetings to voice a gap in the labeling instruction and classifiers. At the moment the collected annotators' opinions are considered to be backed up by one scientific literature or another and upon the decision therefore an addition merges or not into the ontology or is reflected in the labeling instruction. To categorize cultural concepts (codes), we follow six rules that all values must meet.

1. Social significance or if the value can influence on social life;
2. Individual significance or if that affects individual decision making;
3. Subjective measurability or can a person say about whether one accepts it, rejects it or is indifferent;
4. Communication or if that can be influenced by interpersonal or media communication;
5. Textuality or can the concept be formulated, defined, described by a text, illustrated by a story;
6. Atomicity, indivisibility or does the concept not come down to a set of other values, attitudes to which may vary.

The markup uses sentiments ("tonalities") to convey the value attitude displayed in a fragment or a markup element, along with the value labels. Tags (or "labels") are used to represent cultural codes and tonalities in the own markup tool developed by the researchers' team. This task requires a structure specifically designed for tags to be located. The principle of openness has led to the creation of an interdisciplinary classifier of values that includes 105 labels of cultural concepts divided into seven groups

1. Vital;
2. Moral;
3. Political;
4. Religious;
5. Social;

6. Existential and cognitive;
7. Aesthetic and hedonistic.

"Mutual assistance" and "mutual respect" can be combined into a single concept, for instance. This important moral category of values is mentioned by the UN, Decree of the President of the Russian Federation No. 809, B. Erasov and S. Schwartz [6,9,32,33]. Mutual respect is defined as a respectful attitude based on recognition of someone's merits, including respect for others' opinions, respect for parents, and elders [25,26]. Mutual assistance is relationships between people based on commonality or proximity of goals and interests, their realization in the process of joint life activity. This can occur either intentionally or unintentionally, may last long or short, and takes place through contacts between two or many individuals [25,26].

4.5   Organization of the Markup Process

The markup stages account for the above mentioned axiomatic construction and is organized as follows (Fig. 2).

- Qualified annotators with an expertise from various disciplines are involved to make informed decisions about a legitimate structure of classifiers and its amendment;
- A target audience is identified, which can be a professional community, a nation, the population of the municipality, ethnicity, or a civilization, is identified;
- An unmarked text corpus is selected. The documents to be annotated may be both written by representatives of this audience or read by the target group;
- Classifiers are compiled to research human values of the identified group, their sentiments, an attitude controversy and an informational impact on the audience;
- A formalism of annotating the content is clearly explained in the Labeling Instruction to provide the markup consistency across whole the process.

4.6   Data Collection

Authors don't need the text collection to be strictly representative at this stage of research. The methodology is centered around adapting basic content analysis for subsequent automation using machine learning. The unmarked corpus for the trial stage was assembled from the texts of Telegram channels with an audience of more than 5,000 subscribers. All documents were published between February 24, 2022 and February 9, 2023, written in Russian and contained the word "value" (spelled as "tsennost") in any form. After removing duplicates and short messages, the texts were sent for labeling. 9 annotators represented social, political, philological sciences, economics and management, international relations and applied mathematics. Each document was marked up by at least three experts. As a result, 10,426 text elements associated with the value concepts and tonality in 3,496 single labeled documents of 783 texts were obtained.

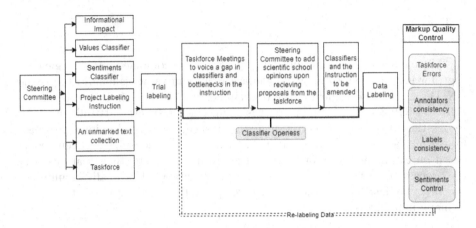

Fig. 2. Organization of the markup process in accordance with the axiomatic construction of the ontology of the classifier

4.7 Quality Control

In a particular space, the value landscape of the audience being studied is determined by post-processing and the markup quality control. The markup quality control (see Fig. 2) includes verifying

1. Obvious errors in annotations, including semantic and structural ones;
2. The consistency of markup annotators;
3. Sufficiency (non-redundancy) of labels in the ontology;
4. The range of sentiments for each of the labels to define an attitude to a particular value.

Specifically, the metrics turn out to be advantageous

1. A measure of consistency that is aggregated for every pair of markups and each document;
2. For each labeled document, the average estimate of these alignments are calculated;
3. For every markup of each annotator, the average estimate of these alignments.

In the event that the latter metric is substantially low, certain annotation developers have more meetings than others to explain the markup features for the current project. The consistency of the markup for each document, with an average of 0.53, was the most significant.

4.8 Uncovering Human Values

Every of 105 values in the classifier and their groups are represented in the labeled collection and can be utilized for the subsequent ML experimentation. Statistics uncover the most popular cultural codes for the data collection in use. The top 25 requested ones while labeling the markup elements, starting from the most frequent case, engage

1. Material values
2. Life
3. Historical memory and continuity of generations
4. Civic engagement
5. Political values
6. Family
7. Ethnicity
8. Culture and art
9. Rights and freedoms
10. Patriotism
11. National security
12. Mutual assistance and mutual respect
13. Power
14. Development
15. Health
16. Justice
17. Pacifism
18. Religiosity
19. Religious values
20. Moral values
21. Dignity
22. Education
23. Respect for traditions
24. Culture (norms) of behavior
25. Love

5 Conclusion

On this positive note, the method is illustrated by the use case of uncovering human values and tonalities in the given large corpus of texts. The methodology introduces a new approach by extending basic content analysis to processing large collections of text documents in machine learning applications. A proto-type of the markup tool, based on the hyper-graph model proposed in the paper, allows one to label not only individual text spans or documents as a whole, but also tag markup elements that combine various semantic units as well as a con-text representing the document's latent content or a background knowledge. Multiple labeling of the same markup element, a span or a linked context is also available. A quality assessment approach has been developed and implemented. Four control contours are included and can be used in both manual and auto-matic modes. The outcomes of the presented project are a software developed for a context-dependent markup and various applications in the media analysis industry, training samples annotated by the interdisciplinary team of experts, as well as some relevant pretest statistics on the contemporary cultural landscape.

References

1. Auzan, A.A., Komissarov, A.G., Bakhtigaraeva, A.I.: Sociocultural restrictions on the commercialization of innovations in Russia. Economic Policy. No. 4. (in Russian)
2. Bezuglova, N.P.: Geert Hofstede's model of four cultural parameters, Bulletin of MGUKI. No. 5 (2008). https://cyberleninka.ru/article/n/model-chetyreh-parametrov-kultury-girta-hofsteda. Accessed 21 Dec 2023. (in Russian)
3. Bowden, B.: The ideal of civilization: its origins and socio-political character. Crit. Rev. Int. Soc. Polit. Philos. **7**, 25–50 (2004)
4. Burrows S., Falk M.: Digital humanities (2021)
5. Danioni F., Russo C., Zagrean I., Regalia C., Barni D.: "What matters to us": the portrait values questionnaire to measure couple values. Pers. Relationsh. **30**(2), 681–699 (2023). (in Russian)
6. Decree of the President of the Russian Federation: On approval of the Fundamentals of State Policy for the Preservation and Strengthening of Traditional Russian Spiritual and Moral Values, 9 November 2022, No. 809, Official Internet Portal of Legal Information (2022). (in Russian)
7. Drisko, J.W., Maschi, T.: Content analysis. Pocket Guide to Social Work Re (2016)
8. Elias, N.: The civilizing process: sociogenetic and psychogenetic investigations (1969)
9. Erasov, B.S.: Social Cultural Studies: Textbook for Students of Higher Educational Institutions. 3rd edn, 591 p. Aspect Press (2000). (in Russian)
10. Fiormonte D., Chaudhuri S., Ricaurte P. (eds.): Global Debates in the Digital Humanities. U of Minnesota Press (2022)
11. Hofer, M., Obraczka, D., Saeedi, A., Köpcke, H., Rahm, E.: Construction of knowledge graphs: current state and challenges (2000). SSRN: https://ssrn.com/abstract=4605059 or http://dx.doi.org/10.2139/ssrn.4605059
12. Hofstede, G.: Dimensionalizing cultures: the Hofstede model in context. Online Read. Psychol. Cult. **2**(1), 8 (2011)
13. Huntington, S.: Clash of civilizations and the reorganization of the world order. Pro et contra. **2**, 114–154 (1997)
14. Inglehart, R.: Postmodern: changing values and changing societies. Polis **4**, 6–32 (1997)
15. Karasik, V.I.: Values as culturally significant guidelines for behavior. In: Humanitarian Technologies in the Modern World: Collection of Materials of the VII International Scientific and Practical Conference, Kaliningrad, 30 May–01 June 2019, Kaliningrad: Western branch of the Russian Academy of National Economy and Public Administration Under the President of the Russian Federation, pp. 22–25 (2019). (in Russian)
16. Krippendorff, K.: Content Analysis: An Introduction to Its Methodology. Sage Publications, Thousand Oaks (2018)
17. Kuper, A.: Culture: The Anthropologists' Account. Harvard University Press, Cambridge (2001)
18. Kushnareva, L.V.: Features of the method of studying value orientations of S. Schwartz, Tsarskoye Selo Readings. No. XV (2011). https://cyberleninka.ru/article/n/osobennosti-metoda-izucheniya-tsennostnyh-orientatsiy-sh-shvartsa. Accessed 29 Nov 2023. (in Russian)
19. Le Deuff, O.: Digital Humanities: History and Development. Wiley, Hoboken (2018)

20. Leontyev, D.A.: Value ideas in individual and group consciousness. Psychol. Rev. **1**, 50–56 (1998). (in Russian)
21. Yao, L.: Features of legal regulation of generative artificial intelligence in the UK, USA, European Union and China. Law J. High. Sch. Econ. **16**(3), 245–267 (2023). (In Russian)
22. Losev, A.F.: History of ancient aesthetics. SOPHISTS. SOCRATES. PLATO History of ancient aesthetics, vol. II (1969). (in Russian)
23. Mayring, P.: Qualitative content analysis: theoretical foundation, basic procedures and software solution, vol. 143 (2014)
24. Monarch, R.M.: Human-in-the-Loop Machine Learning: Active Learning and Annotation for Human-Centered AI. Simon and Schuster (2021)
25. Ovchinnikov, A.I.: National security and traditional spiritual and moral values: issues of legislative support. Bulletin of the Faculty of Law of the Southern Federal University (2022). (in Russian)
26. Ozhegov, S.I.: Interpretive dictionary of the Russian language: 72500 words and 7500 phrases, S. I (1994)
27. Ozhegov, N.Yu.S.: Russian Academy of Sciences, Institute of Rus. Lang., Russian Culture Fund. 2nd edn. Moscow: Az, 907 p. (1994)
28. Potter W.J., Levine-Donnerstein, D.: Rethinking validity and reliability in content analysis (1999)
29. Rokeach, M.: Beliefs, Attitudes and Values, p. 214, San Francisco (1972)
30. Russian pedagogical encyclopedia: V.G. Panov. Big rus. encyclopedia. 1160 p. (1993)
31. Ryndina, A.S.: Large-scale studies of values: possibilities and limitations. Theory Pract. Soc. Dev. **6**(160) (2021). https://cyberleninka.ru/article/n/krupnomasshtabnye-issledovaniya-tsennostey-vozmozhnosti-i-ogranicheniya. Accessed 12 June 2023. (in Russian)
32. Ji , S., Pan, S., Cambria, E., Marttinen, P., Philip, S.Y.: A survey on knowledge graphs: representation, acquisition, and applications. IEEE Trans. Neural Netw. Learn. Syst. **33**(2), 494–514 (2021)
33. Safarov, B.A.:The universal declaration of human rights as a fundamental document for the international standardization of human rights. Bull. TSUPBP **2**(54) (2013). (in Russian)
34. Schwartz, S.: An overview of the Schwartz theory of basic values. Online Read. Psychol. Cul. **2**(1) (2012)
35. Sergeeva, A.V.: Russians. Stereotypes of Behavior, Traditions, Mentality, 4th edn, 320 p. Flinta Nauka (2006). (in Russian)
36. Burmistrova, M.N., Vasilieva, L.L., Petrova, L.Y., Kashcheeva, A.V., et al.: Socio-Pedagogical Dictionary, 126 p. (2016)
37. Speech by Patriarch Kirill at a meeting of the Strategic Vision Group "Russia - the Islamic World" (2023). http://www.patriarchia.ru/db/text/6028797.html?ysclid=lptpympy54530179536. (in Russian)
38. Stepanov, Y.S.: Constants. Dictionary of Russian Culture, Academic project, 825 p. (2001). (in Russian)
39. Steven Hayes, Spencer Smith. (2014), Reboot your brain. Resolving internal conflicts. St. Petersburg: Peter. 320 p. (In Russian)

Predicting Deepfake Enjoyment: A Machine Learning Perspective

María T. Soto-Sanfiel[1]([⊠])(ID) and Sanjay Saha[2](ID)

[1] Department of Communications and New Media, and Centre for Trusted Internet and Community, National University of Singapore, Singapore, Singapore
cnmmtss@nus.edu.sg
[2] Department of Computer Science, and Centre for Trusted Internet and Community, National University of Singapore, Singapore, Singapore
sanjaysaha@nus.edu.sg

Abstract. Deepfakes, synthetic media created through advanced learning techniques, are rapidly advancing, empowering users to craft deceptive videos via voice manipulation, realistic lip-syncing, and seamless face replacements. From sophisticated methods to user-friendly 'cheapfakes', concerns persist regarding their potential misuse and ethical implications. However, despite their prevalence, our empirical understanding of deepfakes remains limited, particularly concerning the psychological processes influencing their reception and consequences. Existing experimental research primarily links deepfakes to heightened uncertainty about media content and explores their negative repercussions on social media. Additionally, most of these studies rely on linear statistics, inherently aprioristic, to comprehend the cognitive-emotional factors in deepfake processing. Addressing these gaps, our study explores individuals' engagement with non-deceptive deepfake content through a predictive non-linear approach, utilizing machine learning techniques uncommon in psychological research. Results showcase the efficiency of machine learning in predicting attitudes toward deepfakes, including enjoyment and sharing behavior. They offer highly precise information about the specific factors determining such responses. Overall, the study demonstrates that applying machine-based analysis models to responses to deepfakes can be used to automatically predict and control their virality.

Keywords: Deepfake · Sharing behavior · Enjoyment · Prediction · Machine Learning

1 Introduction

Deepfakes refer to counterfeit visual, audio, or audio-visual productions generated through deep learning methods [43]. Despite being in an early developmental stage, deepfake technology has rapidly advanced, allowing users increased accessibility to create deceptive videos featuring individuals in fictitious actions or statements [78]. These progressions, coupled with increased accessibility, now

A. Coman and S. Vasilache (Eds.): HCII 2024, LNCS 14703, pp. 384–402, 2024.
https://doi.org/10.1007/978-3-031-61281-7_28

empower users to create videos and clips featuring individuals engaging in actions or making statements they never actually did [78]. Presently, users can manipulate various aspects, including synthesizing an individual's voice from transcripts, generating entirely new videos with lifelike lip-syncing to match facial movements, or seamlessly replacing one person's face with other's. The spectrum of techniques employed ranges from sophisticated methods to more user-friendly applications, commonly known as "cheapfakes" [25]. This landscape raises concerns about the potential misuse and ethical implications associated with the deceptive nature of deepfake technology.

Empirical knowledge about deepfakes is limited, as highlighted in recent studies by Ahmed [1,3,5]. Specifically, there is a significant gap in understanding the psychological processes and consequences of deepfakes, with sparse experimental research primarily linking them to heightened uncertainty about media content or specific cognitive abilities on social networks [1,3,5].

Recent investigations have begun exploring strategies to mitigate the impact of deepfakes, including their incorporation into media literacy programs [38]. Additionally, studies have delved into individual differences in detecting and resisting deepfakes, shedding light on the diverse responses people may have to such deceptive content [39].

1.1 Sharing Deepfakes on Social Networks

The virality of deepfakes stands out as a primary factor contributing to both their success and the ensuing disruptions [39], emphasizing the imperative to comprehend the associated processes. Virality, particularly on social media, is intricately connected to the inclination to share content [40]. However, despite the escalating attention to this issue, there is a noteworthy gap in our comprehension of the precise mechanisms dictating the virality of deepfakes and whether these mechanisms differ from those influencing the sharing of disinformation or misinformation in general [3].

While the existing body of research has predominantly concentrated on investigating the intention to share political deepfakes [1,5,63], a limited number of studies have delved into other genres (e.g., [39]). Consequently, there is a pressing need for more comprehensive investigations into the dynamics of deepfake virality across various content categories to deepen our understanding of this intricate phenomenon. Specifically, research [2] has identified that individuals are more likely to inadvertently share political deepfakes on social media when they believe the videos contain truthful information. Moreover, labeling such content as fake diminish the inadvertent dissemination of disinformation. Additionally, in a survey involving US participants, it has been found that higher cognitive ability was associated with a decreased likelihood of sharing deepfakes containing partisan political misinformation [5]. Furthermore, the intention to share deepfake political videos is linked to the desire to express hatred or seek revenge against the affected party, as well as to preserve one's moral self-concept and reinforce existing ideologies and moral beliefs [63]. These findings offer valuable insights into the factors influencing the spread of deepfakes, especially within the realm of political content.

In contrast to previous studies, [39] examined the intentions to share an entertainment-focused deepfake, where the original actor's face in a movie was substituted with that of another individual. Their objective was to assess how informing individuals about the nature, applications, and potential harmful consequences of deepfakes (priming) would influence attitudes. The researchers discovered that such knowledge led to increased recognition of the artificial nature of the video and influenced the intention to share it. However, they did not delve into specific details regarding the positive or negative aspects of these intentions. Consequently, they emphasized the need to address the fundamental drivers of virality to formulate strategies that can mitigate the potential harm associated with deepfakes.

The current research on psychological responses to deepfakes commonly employs statistical procedures based on structural equation modeling (SEM), typically utilized in Communication and Applied Psychology studies (i.e., [7]). However, this research takes an innovative, exploratory approach to predicting the probability of receivers' enjoyment and sharing of deepfakes using machine learning (ML) techniques.

1.2 Machine Learning: An Innovative Approach for Predicting Psychological Responses to Deepfakes and Assessing Their Virality

ML involves applying neural networks to analyses [62] to unveil unknown or hidden dependencies, structures, associations, rules, and data clusters with a limited number of observations [49]. It automatically identifies complex patterns in individuals' attitudes toward phenomena, providing efficient and accurate models, even in real-time [76]. This capability allows for the design of personalized strategies, taking into account individuals' specific characteristics or behaviors [42]. Unlike standard regression-based analysis, ML can model non-linear relations between self-reported attitudes without assuming any functional form while handling a large number of variables [64]. ML methods acknowledge the potential existence of non-linear relationships not detected by linear models, potentially offering more accurate detection of meaningful variables explaining psychological phenomena, such as the enjoyment of deepfakes and their sharing on social networks [64, 74].

While ML techniques have been applied to the analysis of self-reported attitudes in various fields such as Psychology (e.g., [42, 61, 64]) and Education (e.g., [76]), to our knowledge, they have not been extensively utilized in understanding attitudes toward media narratives, let alone to deepfakes. Noteworthy recent studies in Psychology and Marketing often combine or complement linear and non-linear analyses, contributing to contrasting and clarifying relationships tested in empirical research (e.g., [35, 50, 59]). However, there are indications that explanatory models focusing on individuals' relationships with technologies might benefit from incorporating non-linear relationships for better explanatory power [59]. Coherently, in this research, our objective is to unveil more precise and direct interactions between dependent variables (enjoyment and sharing behavior) and other observed variables-items, verifying if ML can efficiently predict them. This information holds great potential for the automated prediction of responses to deepfakes and their virality.

The main objectives of this exploratory research are:

1. Developing ML models to predict audience enjoyment and social sharing of deepfakes for an enhanced understanding of these phenomena.
2. To predict the likelihood of deepfakes being enjoyed and shared widely on social media through ML algorithms.

2   Theoretical Background

2.1   Enjoyment

Enjoyment has been defined as a hedonic experience associated with fun or positive motivations. It is a response of pleasure (e.g., [32,54,77]) which emerges from the cognitive and affective engagement of individuals with a media message [54]. Enjoyment is considered the heart of the media entertainment experience [77] and the origin of all gratifications sought through media use [11].

Conversely, enjoyment plays a crucial role in shaping media encounters across diverse formats, including films [30,54], video games [13,52], or interactive fictions [68]. Anticipation of enjoyment draws individuals to media experiences, a principle that may also apply to deepfakes. For example, the act of sharing harmless deepfakes on social networks could be motivated by a desire for enjoyment and the intent to amuse friends. This aligns with research indicating more enjoyment in a social media experience leads to increased consumption [73] and reflects a pursuit of entertainment [41]. Acknowledging the significance of enjoyment in media experiences, researchers aim to gain nuanced insights into its characteristics, traits, and potential consequences across various media contexts [56]. This study addresses this gap by exploring uncharted aspects of enjoyment within the realm of deepfakes.

2.2   Narrative Transportation

Researchers in the field of entertainment have identified various psychological processes influencing enjoyment, with narrative transportation being a particularly significant factor [55]. Narrative transportation is a mental state of individuals that occurs when they are completely absorbed, lost [29] or immersed in a media story to the point of losing track of their surrounded reality in a physiological sense [75] vicariously experiencing the story's characters or being unaware of themselves as a separate entity from the narrative [29]. Previous studies indicate that narrative transportation serves as a predictor of enjoyment: as the degree of transportation into the narrative world increases, so does the level of enjoyment (e.g., [11,24,30,47]). Thus, transportation is considered a path for narrative engagement [70]. It elicits more intense affective responses to the media messages [18,26] and reduces individuals' critical thoughts about the narrative message [29,66]. The process of transportation not only leads to the perception of narratives as more truthful but also as more desirable, fostering more positive attitudes towards them [26].

Transportation has been observed in a diverse range of narratives and media formats, encompassing both fictional [24] and non-fictional content (e.g., [31,36]). However, the extent of transportation is influenced by factors such as the genre of the narrative and the audience's familiarity or knowledge of the story elements [28]. This research aims to contribute to the ongoing discussion by examining transportation as a response linked to enjoyment in the specific context of deep-fakes.

2.3   Perceived Realism

Studies indicate a positive correlation between narrative transportation and the perception of realism in a story: the higher the narrative transportation, the greater the perceived realism. This relationship, in turn, influences responses to the narrative [28,44], including levels of enjoyment [6,23]. The concept of perceived realism is multifaceted and lacks a universally accepted definition, captivating researchers across various fields [58]. In narrative research, it involves assessing dimensions such as plausibility, typicality, factuality, consistency, and perceptual quality [21,33]. Perceived realism is defined by its ability to present: a) ongoing life; b) real or fictional content similar to real-world situations or characters; c) events that could realistically occur with a certain frequency; d) situations conducive to engagement or integration into an individual's life; e) valuable content; and f) depictions that are typically or plausible with the real world [16]. Additionally, [15] includes fictionality, which pertains to information about the narrative's fictional nature. In the context of human-computer interaction, realism is defined as a subtype of fidelity, where the represented element reproduces the real world to some degree [58].

As mentioned earlier, researchers emphasize that realism significantly influences the impact of a narrative [16]. A lack of external realism, which involves implausibility between the narrative and the real world, or internal realism, encompassing inconsistencies within the narrative itself, hinders audience engagement with the story [55]. These aspects are closely related to perceived realism and the positive evaluation of the narrative [21]. When evaluating the realism of narratives, the genre assumes a crucial role, guiding audiences to draw upon their understanding of depicted elements in reality or their resonance due to familiarity [15,28].

Conversely, perceived realism aligns with the portrayed individuals. It reliably predicts the audience's connection with media figures [27,37,51], as viewers naturally assess media personas for authenticity and realism [60], irrespective of the narrative type [71]. This connection is influenced by transportation: as the audience becomes immersed in the narrative, their response to the portrayed personalities feels authentic, fostering a relationship [14], even in social media contexts [12]. We will revisit this idea later.

2.4 Deepfake Evaluation

As previously mentioned, prior research confirms the significance of perceived realism in the assessment of media messages [21]. Specifically, factors such as narrative consistency, defined as the coherence and non-contradictory nature of the story's constituents [33], and perceptual quality, defined as the degree to which the elements forming media message are convincing and compelling portraying the reality [33], predict the evaluation of the message [21]. Furthermore, the perceived plausibility of a narrative, indicating the extent to which it depicts a specific individual or event from the real world, explains emotional involvement with the narrative. This emotional involvement, in turn, predicts the perception of realism and the overall evaluation of the message or narrative, influencing its potential effect [21]. On the other hand, the evaluation of a message [8,45] impacts its sharing on social media, influenced by perceived realism [20] and the authenticity of the communicative act [45].

2.5 Familiarity with the Deepfaked Person

As previously introduced, there are indications that audience familiarity or prior knowledge of the content or genre [28,67], as well as the relationship established with media personalities, including their perceived authenticity or realism, can influence narrative transportation [14,71].

Research suggests that viewers' perceptions of media personalities impact their enjoyment of the message [9,34,60]. Furthermore, familiarity with the characters enhances this enjoyment [9,34], and the bond with media personalities can strengthen over time [34]. Similarly, familiarity with media personalities influences the relationship that audiences form with the message [9]. The inclusion of a familiar actor or character deepens the attachment to the message and its significance [72], elucidating why celebrities are often used in persuasive messages [65].

All of these findings suggest that audience familiarity or knowledge about the person depicted in a deepfake is a crucial factor to consider in any model explaining their enjoyment. Deepfakes typically feature well-known media personalities due to the abundance of available media content (e.g., voices, pictures, videos) that can be manipulated with AI tools.

2.6 Intention to Share

The impact and unpredictability of deepfakes are closely tied to their viral nature [39]. Therefore, unraveling this virality hinges on understanding the motives behind sharing [40]. Despite the growing interest in sharing content on social media, there remains a gap in our understanding of the specific mechanisms at play [3]. Additionally, while much attention is focused on the sharing of political deepfakes [1,63], research on other genres is largely nonexistent [39]. Precisely, [4] discovered that adding labels about the video's fake nature reduces inadvertent sharing. On the other hand, [39] suggested that prior information increases the recognition of the video's artificiality and enhances the intention to share. However, the nature of this sharing intention remains unexplored.

Limited research has explored intentional deepfake sharing, primarily within the context of political deepfakes, examining its connection to psychological factors and its role in disseminating misinformation. These studies suggest that factors such as the fear of missing out, lower cognitive abilities [3], and deficiencies in self-regulation [4] may influence the intention to share. Additionally, evidence points to certain personality traits, such as agreeableness and conscientiousness, impacting sharing tendencies [1].

That said, enjoyment has been identified as a predictor of sharing various types of media messages on social media (e.g., [69]), including deepfakes across different genres. This aligns with research indicating a direct correlation between the intention to share narratives on social media and the enjoyment derived from them [53]. It is consistent with the theory of social sharing of emotions, which posits that emotions play a role in predicting message sharing [57]. Specifically, positive emotions facilitate social sharing, driven by individuals' impression management [48]. In fact, media content inducing positive emotions tends to generate more virality than content evoking negative emotions [10].

2.7 Model of Deepfakes' Psychological Processing

As observed in the previous section, we posit that recipients' reactions to deepfakes are contingent upon their familiarity with the deepfaked media persona. This, in turn, exerts an influence on narrative transportation, perceived realism, and subsequent evaluations of the deepfake. The interplay of these factors ultimately determines the overall enjoyment and likability of the deepfake. Moreover, the extent of enjoyment plays a pivotal role in shaping the intention to share a deepfake on social networks, driven by the gratifications sought from its sharing.

Conversely, we contend that pre-existing attitudes towards deepfakes, encompassing factors such as awareness of the technology, concerns about deepfakes, positive/negative orientation towards them, ability to detect deepfakes, and knowledge about their proliferation, may also impact audiences' overall approach to deepfakes and prove influential in their enjoyment and intention to share.

Finally, we posit that responses to deepfakes may be contingent upon the age, gender, and educational level of the audience.

3   Method

3.1   Participants

A total of 1031 people from the United States of America participated in the study. There were 419 female (40.6%), 588 male (57.0%), 21 non-binary or third gender (2.0%) and three of them preferred not to reveal their gender. Their mean age was 43.0 years old ($SD = 14.0$; RangeAge $= 18$–93 years old).

3.2   Measures

The outcomes of the study were enjoyment and sharing intention and were measured with two single-item measures:

Enjoyment. The item content was "I enjoyed the deepfake" with a 5-point Likert Scale (1 = Totally disagree to 5 = Totally agree).

Sharing Intention. The item content was "Will you share the video in your social media"? with a dichotomous scale (0 = No, 1 = Yes).

The remaining measures used for this study are described next:

Socio-demographics Measures. We used the socio-demographic information such as age, gender, and educational level.

Likeness. The item content was "I liked the deeepfake" with a 5-point Likert Scale (1 = Totally disagree to 5 = Totally agree).

Attitudes Towards Deepfakes. The general attitudes towards deepfakes scale was inspired by [22]. Particularly, we used and adapted items from the dimensions awareness of deepfake technology (6 items), previous deception of deepfakes (2 items), concern level about deepfakes (6 items), and positive attitudes towards deepfakes (7 items). Moreover, based on [22]'s results, we also added a new dimension called perceived capacity of detecting deepfakes and proposed 6 items to measure the sub-dimensions individuals' perceived ability to detect deepfakes (3 items) and individuals' perception of the ability to detect deepfakes of others (3 items). To these dimensions, we added another one named controlling the proliferation of deepfakes formed by 6 items inspired by the results of a preliminary work.

Familiarity. We used three adapted items following [17] to measure the frequency and quantity of the viewers' contact with the deepfaked person. We added also an item "How much would you like to watch more deepfakes of this person?" to assess this.

Narrative Transportation. We used seven items of the scale proposed by [70] based on [29] adapting them to the purposes of this investigation. Specifically, we used its two subscales: narrative experience [4-items] and narrative attention [3-items].

Perceived Realism. We used an adapted version to the purposes of this research of the perceived realism scale proposed by [21]. This scale had 16 items that aimed to measure different dimensions of the phenomenon: plausibility (3), factuality (3), narrative consistency (5) and perceptual quality (5).

3.3   Deepfake Stimuli

– Advertisement deepfakes (AD) involve employing deepfake technology to market products or services. We used: AD1: A deepfake video of the renowned surrealist artist Salvador Dalí, promoting a museum in Florida dedicated to him (US). AD2: An ad using deepfakes of the soccer player Lionel Messi, showcasing his evolution over the years while endorsing sportswear brand ADIDAS.

– Celebrity deepfakes (CD) showcase the technical prowess of mimicking notable personalities in various settings. We used: CD1: Actor and YouTuber Miles Fisher convincingly deepfaking Tom Cruise with VFX assistance from Chris Ume. CD2: MetaPhysic.ai's deepfake of Elvis Presley, featured on America's Got Talent.

– Cheapfakes (CH) are no-cost applications enabling uses to alter their facial appearance through filters or face swaps, albeit lacking professional-grade technical precision. We used: CH1: Unidentified individuals employing 'Cat' filters on their selfie videos as cat owners. CH2: A mother utilizing a phone app to exchange her face with her baby's visage.

– Movie deepfakes (MD) involve integrating deepfaked individuals into pre-existing narratives. We used: MD1: Tom Holland and Robert Downey Jr. deepfaked into the movie "Wizard of the Oz". MD2: Elon Musk's deepfake incorporated into the music video Michael Jackson's "Black or White" song.

– Politics deepfakes (PD) involve utilizing deepfaked public figures to convey political messages. We used: PD1: A deepfake of North Korean President Kim Jong Un, shared on a YouTube channel before the 2020 US election, humorously commenting on US citizens' influence on democracy's challenges. PD2: A deepfake featuring singer Taylor Swift advocating for abortion policies, posted within a Reddit group/subreddit.

3.4 Procedure

Each participant watched one deepfake from each of the five genres. The order of presentation of the genres and of the two available messages for each were randomly assigned. Right after watching each video, the participants answered the questions containing the variables observed in the study. The procedure was approved by the ethical committee of the National University of Singapore. Data was collected in Prolific. Participation was voluntary and reimbursed with 2.11 USD.

3.5 Data Analysis

Analysis of the data has been done using ML methods in three stages: baseline predictors, primary predictors, and validator predictors. At each stage one or more ML models were trained and evaluated on the data. These models were trained to predict a. Sharing behavior of a viewer and b. If a viewer will enjoy and like a video, where the models were introduced to different sets of input features/variables. For example, a model was trained to predict if a viewer was going to share the video he was shown. The model was introduced with all the variables from the sections previous attitudes to enjoyment and liking in the questionnaire. Another model was trained to predict the same with the data from only the deepfake evaluation section in the questionnaire, and so on.

The three stages of the predictor models were:

1. **Baseline predictors**: We created some rule-based simple models to set the baseline for the ML predictors. Two baseline models were evaluated for each of the tasks: classifying sharing behavior and classifying enjoyment. However, the baseline models are not reliable since the data was of high-dimension and in the baseline method we only considered a single feature (one-dimension) if the feature space. Hence, we further experimented with more complex methods to better model the non-linearity of the data.

2. **Primary predictors**: Based on the findings from the baseline classification results, we trained a more reliable, complex and non-linear model using the gradient boosting algorithm. Gradient boosting enhances model accuracy by amalgamating multiple weak models into a robust one. This technique, categorized under ensemble learning, iteratively trains new models to rectify errors made by their predecessors. Boosting has demonstrated remarkable effectiveness across various domains, achieving state-of-the-art results. Additionally, exploring the feature importance values considered by these models is valuable. This analysis assists in pinpointing crucial elements that influence people's sharing behavior and enjoyment.

3. **Validator predictors**: Two other ML models were trained for the validation of the results from the gradient boosting methods. One of these models was Random Forest classifier which also is an ensemble method that trains multiple decision trees on a dataset and combines their predictions to produce a single, more robust prediction. Additionally, Random Forest provides important feature importance scores that can be used for feature selection and understanding the underlying relationships in the data. The other model was a Neural Network classifier with two hidden layers of 128 neurons each. Neural networks can model complex, non-linear relationships between inputs and outputs, and are able to handle high-dimensional data with ease. We interpreted the neural network model decisions using SHAP explainers [46] to get meaningful insights into the factors towards predicting the target variables.

We looked more into the main deciding factors that the ML models selected based on how well they performed. As a result, we had a much clearer and more concrete picture of the factors that were crucial in determining the sharing behavior and enjoying a deepfake video. The 'Analysis' section of this article goes into further detail about these models and the conclusions drawn from their prediction outcomes.

4 Results

4.1 Baseline Predictors

The baseline models are rule-based. These corresponding rules were selected based on correlation between the target variable (e.g., sharing behavior) and the other previous variables that appeared prior to the target variable in the flow of the survey. We used the top three variables (based on correlation coefficients) as the rule for predicting the two target variables (Fig. 1 and Table 1).

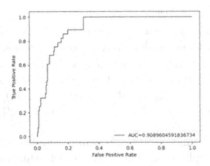 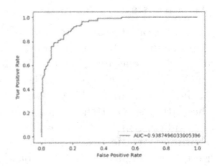

Fig. 1. ROC curve for sharing behavior predictor (left) and enjoyment predictor (right). These ROC and AUC values were calculated for the models that were trained on all responses after watching the deepfake and genre (2nd row in Table 2). Both of these predictors have a very high AUC, more than 0.90. This shows that the models are threshold independent. The enjoyment predictor has higher AUC than the sharing predictor; the models had more success in predicting enjoyment.

Table 1. Performance of the baseline models and corresponding variables with high-correlation values. It is to note that the highest accuracy for sharing behavior prediction was 74.2%, and for enjoyment prediction was 81.1%.

Target	Top variables with high correlations	Correlation coefficients	Accuracy	Average class -wise accuracy
Sharing Behavior prediction	How much would you like to watch more deepfakes impersonating this person?	0.335	0.700	0.742
	How much do you like to watch TV shows, audiovisual news/reports, videos, films or series that include the portrayed person?	0.258	0.526	0.666
	I could imagine myself in the deepfake while I was watching it.	0.244	0.633	0.681
Enjoyment prediction	I feel that the deepfake was entertaining.	0.762	0.801	0.811
	I feel that the deepfake was humorous.	0.586	0.721	0.714
	How much would you like to watch more deepfakes impersonating this person?	0.579	0.672	0.643

4.2 Primary Predictors

We experimented with multiple linear and non-linear algorithms for classifying/predicting sharing behavior and enjoyment: Support Vector Machines, Neural Networks, eXtreme Gradient Boosting, Random Forest, K Nearest Neighbors. Upon initial experiments, we selected eXtreme Gradient Boosting (alsoXGBoost) [19] to be the primary ML model to use in all our experiments since it a powerful machine learning algorithm that is robust to overfitting, can handle imbalance data, and provides feature importance values. To validate the performance of the XGBoost models, we trained and tested two more algorithms for some of experiments using Random Forest and Neural Network. Since these algorithms are of stochastic nature we ran every experiment three times and took the average of the three runs.

The data was split into two sets: one for training the model, another for evaluating the model with unseen data. The training set contained 75% of the data while the testing set had the rest 25%. We merged enjoyment and liking responses from the survey into one since they showed very high correlation coefficient (0.95).

Each model was trained with different sets of features. Only the 'genre' of the video was the consistent feature in all these different sets. This would help us understand if any of these sets had more influence on the models' predictions. The feature sets were (other than 'genre'):

1. Responses from all the sections in the survey: previous attitudes to enjoyment and likeness.
2. Responses from knowledge about the protagonist(s) in the video to enjoyment and likeness.
3. Responses from previous attitudes towards deepfakes.
4. Responses from the narrative transportation section of the survey.
5. Responses from the perceived realism section.
6. Responses from the deepfake evaluation section.
7. This set does not include any response, instead we used only the demographic information of the participants: age group, gender, education level.

In this paper, we are reporting three metrics as the performance of the models: Accuracy, Average class-wise accuracy, and F1-score. We are also reporting ROC (Receiver Operating Characteristic) curve and AUC (Area Under the Curve) for the models trained on responses from all the sections in the survey and the genre (feature set #1 in the list above). The ROC curve provides a way to visualize the predictors' performance without being affected by the threshold.

We also explored the most important features/variables in the prediction of the models. This gave us a clear understanding of the major factors behind the decision making process of the audiences' of deepfakes.

4.3 Analysis

In Table 2 we can see that we get higher accuracy using the XGBoost model than the baseline model. It is also to note that F1-score for the sharing behavior predictor is lower compared to the enjoyment predictor since the sharing behavior has a very-skewed distribution (91% responders will 'not share', and only 9% 'will share'). On the other hand, 54% responders enjoyed the deepfake video they have watched while 45% did not.

Even though other sets of features (3rd row to 6th row in Table 2) had less accurate predictions compared to the first two feature sets, it is worth noting that for sharing behavior prediction features from the sections narrative transportation, previous attitudes and deepfake evaluation has higher accuracy than the baseline results.

Table 2. Prediction metrics from the XGBoost models trained on the different sets (left-most column) of features. The table is split into two halves mainly: one for sharing behavior prediction results and the other for the enjoyment prediction. For both of these predictors, we get the highest accuracy with the feature set including all responses after watching the deepfake and genre (2nd row). Performance of the models when we use all the responses (1st row) is also very close to the earlier. For individual sections as the features (3rd row to 6th row) the models are less accurate. And, the model is least accurate when it only sees the demographic information (with video genre).

Features	Sharing Behavior			Enjoyment		
	Overall Accuracy	Avg. class-wise accuracy	F1 score	Overall Accuracy	Avg. class-wise accuracy	F1 score
All variables Previous attitudes to Enjoyment and likeness, genre	0.829	0.810	0.628	0.844	0.844	0.825
All responses after watching the deepfake, genre	0.852	0.844	0.635	0.864	0.864	0.843
Previous attitudes, genre	0.765	0.639	0.581	0.608	0.604	0.600
Narrative transportation, genre	0.806	0.730	0.608	0.68	0.68	0.643
Perceived realism, genre	0.738	0.652	0.563	0.634	0.632	0.619
Deepfake evaluation, genre	0.761	0.685	0.574	0.799	0.803	0.777
Demographics, genre	0.586	0.531	0.431	0.542	0.539	0.464

4.4 Validation Predictors

We also applied the Random Forest and Neural Network Analysis models as the validator models to verify the results from the primary models. Results from these validator models are shown in Table 3. The validator models perform similarly to the primary XGBoost model, confirming that enjoyment and sharing behavior can be predicted with high accuracy from audience perception.

Table 3. In this table the results from the two more algorithms are reported: random forest and neural network. Prediction results from both of these algorithms have the similar characteristics as the XGBoost models (Table 2). However, it is interesting to note that the random forest model performs better in predicting enjoyment than both the XGBoost and the neural Network models. Whereas the neural network model performs better in predicting sharing behavior.

Algorithm	Features	Sharing Behavior		Enjoyment	
		Overall Accuracy	Average class -wise accuracy	Overall Accuracy	Average class -wise accuracy
Random Forest	All variables from Previous attitudes to enjoyment and likeness	0.780	0.827	0.814	0.808
	All responses after watching the deepfake	0.797	0.758	0.877	0.879
Neural Network	All variables from Previous attitudes to enjoyment and likeness	0.861	0.767	0.730	0.754
	All responses after watching the deepfake	0.881	0.731	0.857	0.858

5 Discussion

The study suggests that ML techniques proficiently predict the reception, enjoyment, and virality of deepfakes, contributing to the understanding of factors driving their popularity. These methods enable the early interception of harmful content, preventing potential social unrest. Furthermore, ML might enhance the analysis and mitigation of deepfake impact by employing pattern recognition, large-scale data analysis, adaptability, automation, and early detection of harmful content, ensuring overall efficiency. Additionally, ML operates from a non-prioritistic basis, proving useful for uncovering hidden patterns of attitudes in responses to deepfakes.

Likewise, the proposed model and two validator models achieved similar accuracy and identified consistent explanatory factors. We ranked these factors by importance through model analysis, revealing the primary driver of deepfake enjoyment and sharing on social media.

We have looked in to the most important features that were responsible for the ML models' decision making and prediction; these features or items are the factors that influence the final prediction most (e.g., enjoyment and sharing). Results indicate that deepfake enjoyment is linked to factors such as the audience's interest in watching deepfakes of the portrayed person, his/her persuasiveness, the perceived quality of the deepfake, and its genre. In turn, deepfake sharing is influenced by participants' willingness to view engaging deepfakes, their enjoyment of the deepfakes, their ability to envision themselves in the deepfake, and their prior experience sharing deepfakes with colleagues.

In this study, the participants were explicitly informed that they would be viewing deepfakes spanning various genres and were made aware that the videos were artificially generated. Subsequent research endeavors could explore whether attitudes and motivations for sharing deepfakes are influenced by the viewers' awareness of their artificial nature.

Furthermore, the current list of stimuli is not comprehensive in capturing the diverse array of deepfake and cheapfake videos available. Subsequent research endeavors could expand the scope to include an even broader range of genres within the deepfake and cheapfake landscape.

Our approach to analyzing psychological responses to deepfake through ML algorithms aims to better understand audience perceptions and enhance predictions. It also enhances predictions regarding the potential virality of content on an extended scale. However, exploring a more extensive variety of stimuli will contribute valuable insights into the evolving nature of synthetic media and its impact on audience behavior.

References

1. Ahmed, S.: Fooled by the fakes: cognitive differences in perceived claim accuracy and sharing intention of non-political deepfakes. Pers. Individ. Differ. **182**, 111074 (2021). https://doi.org/10.1016/j.paid.2021.111074. https://linkinghub.elsevier.com/retrieve/pii/S0191886921004517

2. Ahmed, S.: Who inadvertently shares deepfakes? Analyzing the role of political interest, cognitive ability, and social network size. Telematics Inform. **57**, 101508 (2021). https://doi.org/10.1016/j.tele.2020.101508. https://linkinghub.elsevier.com/retrieve/pii/S0736585320301672

3. Ahmed, S.: Disinformation sharing thrives with fear of missing out among low cognitive news users: a cross-national examination of intentional sharing of Deep Fakes. J. Broadcast. Electron. Media **66**(1), 89–109 (2022)

4. Ahmed, S.: Navigating the maze: Deepfakes, cognitive ability, and social media news skepticism. New Media Soc. **25**(5), 1108–1129 (2023). https://doi.org/10.1177/14614448211019198. http://journals.sagepub.com/doi/10.1177/14614448211019198

5. Ahmed, S., Tan, H.W.: Personality and perspicacity: role of personality traits and cognitive ability in political misinformation discernment and sharing behavior. Pers. Individ. Differ. **196**, 111747 (2022)

6. Ang, I.: Watching Dallas: Soap Opera and the Melodramatic Imagination. Routledge (2013)

7. Angulo-Brunet, A., Lecuona, O.: Using tests to study people's responses: what do the scores mean? In: Cases on Developing Effective Research Plans for Communications and Information Science, pp. 96–118 (2022)

8. Araujo, T.: The impact of sharing brand messages: how message, sender and receiver characteristics influence brand attitudes and information diffusion on Social Networking Sites. Communications **44**(2), 162–184 (2019). https://doi.org/10.1515/commun-2018-2004. https://www.degruyter.com/document/doi/10.1515/commun-2018-2004/html

9. Baldwin, J.A., Raney, A.A.: Enjoyment of unoriginal characters: individual differences in Nostalgia-Proneness and Parasocial relationships. Mass Commun. Soc. **24**(5), 748–768 (2021).https://doi.org/10.1080/15205436.2021.1916035. https://www.tandfonline.com/doi/full/10.1080/15205436.2021.1916035

10. Berger, J., Milkman, K.L.: What makes online content viral? J. Mark. Res. **49**(2), 192–205 (2012)

11. Bilandzic, H., Busselle, R.W.: Enjoyment of films as a function of narrative experience, perceived realism and transportability. Communications **36**, 29–50 (2011)

12. Bond, B.J.: Following your "friend": social media and the strength of adolescents' parasocial relationships with media personae. Cyberpsychol. Behav. Soc. Netw. **19**(11), 656–660 (2016). https://doi.org/10.1089/cyber.2016.0355. http://www.liebertpub.com/doi/10.1089/cyber.2016.0355

13. Bowman, N.D., Oliver, M.B., Rogers, R., Sherrick, B., Woolley, J., Chung, M.Y.: In control or in their shoes? How character attachment differentially influences video game enjoyment and appreciation. J. Gaming Virtual Worlds **8**(1), 83–99 (2016). https://doi.org/10.1386/jgvw.8.1.83_1. https://intellectdiscover.com/content/journals/10.1386/jgvw.8.1.83_1

14. Brown, W.J.: Examining four processes of audience involvement with media personae: transportation, parasocial interaction, identification, and worship. Commun. Theor. **25**(3), 259–283 (2015). https://doi.org/10.1111/comt.12053. https://academic.oup.com/ct/article/25/3/259-283/4061170

15. Busselle, R., Bilandzic, H.: Fictionality and perceived realism in experiencing stories: a model of narrative comprehension and engagement. Commun. Theor. **18**(2), 255–280 (2008). https://doi.org/10.1111/j.1468-2885.2008.00322.x. https://academic.oup.com/ct/article/18/2/255-280/4098709

16. Busselle, R., Ryabovolova, A., Wilson, B.: Ruining a good story: cultivation, perceived realism and narrative. Communications **29**(3) (2004). https://doi.org/10.1515/comm.2004.023. https://www.degruyter.com/document/doi/10.1515/comm.2004.023/html

17. Cao, C., Meng, Q.: Exploring personality traits as predictors of English achievement and global competence among Chinese university students: English learning motivation as the moderator. Learn. Individ. Differ. **77**, 101814 (2020)

18. Chang, C.: "Being hooked" by editorial content: the implications for processing narrative advertising. J. Advertising **38**(1), 21–34 (2009). https://doi.org/10.2753/JOA0091-3367380102. http://www.tandfonline.com/doi/abs/10.2753/JOA0091-3367380102

19. Chen, T., Guestrin, C.: XGBoost: a scalable tree boosting system. In: Proceedings of the 22nd ACM SIGKDD International Conference on Knowledge Discovery and Data Mining, pp. 785–794 (2016)

20. Cho, H., Shen, L., Peng, L.: Examining and extending the influence of presumed influence hypothesis in social media. Media Psychol. **24**(3), 413–435 (2021). https://doi.org/10.1080/15213269.2020.1729812. https://www.tandfonline.com/doi/full/10.1080/15213269.2020.1729812

21. Cho, H., Shen, L., Wilson, K.: Perceived realism: dimensions and roles in narrative persuasion. Commun. Res. **41**(6), 828–851 (2014)

22. Cochran, J.D., Napshin, S.A.: Deepfakes: awareness, concerns, and platform accountability. Cyberpsychol. Behav. Soc. Netw. **24**(3), 164–172 (2021)

23. Cohen, J., Ribak, R.: Gender differences in the perception of television realism: the case of Ally McBeal. Women's Stud. Mass Commun. **26**, 118–134 (2003)

24. Crutzen, R., van't Riet, J., Short, C.E.: Enjoyment: a conceptual exploration and overview of experimental evidence in the context of games for health. Games Health J. **5**(1), 15–20 (2016)

25. Diakopoulos, N., Johnson, D.: Anticipating and addressing the ethical implications of deepfakes in the context of elections. New Media Soc. **23**(7), 2072–2098 (2021). https://doi.org/10.1177/1461444820925811. http://journals.sagepub.com/doi/10.1177/1461444820925811

26. Escalas, J.E.: Imagine yourself in the product: mental simulation, narrative transportation, and persuasion. J. Advert. **33**(2), 37–48 (2004)

27. Giles, D.C.: Parasocial interaction: a review of the literature and a model for future research. Media Psychol. **4**(3), 279–305 (2002). https://doi.org/10.1207/S1532785XMEP0403_04. http://www.tandfonline.com/doi/abs/10.1207/S1532785XMEP0403_04

28. Green, M.C.: Transportation into narrative worlds: the role of prior knowledge and perceived realism. Discourse Process. **38**(2), 247–266 (2004)

29. Green, M.C., Brock, T.C.: The role of transportation in the persuasiveness of public narratives. J. Pers. Soc. Psychol. **79**(5), 701 (2000)

30. Green, M.C., Brock, T.C., Kaufman, G.F.: Understanding media enjoyment: the role of transportation into narrative worlds. Commun. Theor. **14**(4), 311–327 (2004)

31. Green, M.C., Donahue, J.K.: Persistence of belief change in the face of deception: the effect of factual stories revealed to be false. Media Psychol. **14**(3), 312–331 (2011)

32. Greenbaum, T.: The gold standard. Why the focus group deserves to be the most respected of all qualitative research tools. Quirk's Market. Res. Rev. **17**, 22–7 (2003)

33. Hall, A.: Reading realism: audiences' evaluations of the reality of media texts. J. Commun. **53**(4), 624–641 (2003).https://doi.org/10.1111/j.1460-2466.2003.tb02914.x. https://academic.oup.com/joc/article/53/4/624-641/4102897

34. Hall, A.E.: Identification and parasocial relationships with characters from Star Wars: The Force Awakens. Psychol. Popular Media Cult. **8**(1), 88–98 (2019). https://doi.org/10.1037/ppm0000160. http://doi.apa.org/getdoi.cfm?doi=10.1037/ppm0000160

35. Herhausen, D.: Unfolding the ambidextrous effects of proactive and responsive market orientation. J. Bus. Res. **69**(7), 2585–2593 (2016)

36. Hollis, H.: An investigation into the relationship between fiction and nonfiction reading exposure, and factors of critical thinking. Sci. Study Lit. **11**(1), 108–141 (2021)

37. Horton, D., Strauss, A.: Interaction in audience-participation shows. Am. J. Sociol. **62**(6), 579–587 (1957). https://doi.org/10.1086/222106. https://www.journals.uchicago.edu/doi/10.1086/222106

38. Hwang, Y., Ryu, J.Y., Jeong, S.H.: Effects of disinformation using deepfake: the protective effect of media literacy education. Cyberpsychol. Behav. Soc. Netw. **24**(3), 188–193 (2021). https://doi.org/10.1089/cyber.2020.0174. https://www.liebertpub.com/doi/10.1089/cyber.2020.0174

39. Iacobucci, S., De Cicco, R., Michetti, F., Palumbo, R., Pagliaro, S.: Deepfakes unmasked: the effects of information priming and bullshit receptivity on deepfake recognition and sharing intention. Cyberpsychol. Behav. Soc. Netw. **24**(3), 194–202 (2021). https://doi.org/10.1089/cyber.2020.0149. https://www.liebertpub.com/doi/10.1089/cyber.2020.0149

40. Kim, J.W.: Rumor has it: the effects of virality metrics on rumor believability and transmission on twitter. New Media Soc. **20**(12), 4807–4825 (2018)

41. Klimmt, C.: Enjoyment/entertainment seeking. The International Encyclopedia of Communication (2008)

42. Kwakernaak, S., van Mens, K., Cahn, W., Janssen, R., Investigators, G., et al.: Using machine learning to predict mental healthcare consumption in non-affective psychosis. Schizophr. Res. **218**, 166–172 (2020)

43. Laishram, L., Rahman, M.M., Jung, S.K.: Challenges and applications of face deepfake. In: Jeong, H., Sumi, K. (eds.) IW-FCV 2021. CCIS, vol. 1405, pp. 131–156. Springer, Cham (2021). https://doi.org/10.1007/978-3-030-81638-4_11

44. LaMarre, H.L., Landreville, K.D.: When is fiction as good as fact? Comparing the influence of documentary and historical reenactment films on engagement, affect, issue interest, and learning. Mass Commun. Soc. **12**(4), 537–555 (2009)

45. Lee, E.J., Lee, H.Y., Choi, S.: Is the message the medium? How politicians' Twitter blunders affect perceived authenticity of Twitter communication. Comput. Hum. Behav. **104**, 106188 (2020). https://doi.org/10.1016/j.chb.2019.106188. https://linkinghub.elsevier.com/retrieve/pii/S0747563219304005

46. Lundberg, S.M., Lee, S.I.: A unified approach to interpreting model predictions. In: Advances in Neural Information Processing Systems, vol. 30 (2017)

47. MacDorman, K.F.: In the uncanny valley, transportation predicts narrative enjoyment more than empathy, but only for the tragic hero. Comput. Hum. Behav. **94**, 140–153 (2019)

48. Manago, A.M., Graham, M.B., Greenfield, P.M., Salimkhan, G.: Self-presentation and gender on myspace. J. Appl. Dev. Psychol. **29**(6), 446–458 (2008)

49. Nagy, H.M., Aly, W.M., Hegazy, O.F.: An educational data mining system for advising higher education students. Int. J. Comput. Inf. Eng. **7**(10), 1266–1270 (2013)

50. Osorio Tinoco, F.F., Hernández-Espallardo, M., Rodriguez-Orejuela, A.: Nonlinear and complementary effects of responsive and proactive market orientation on firms' competitive advantage. Asia Pac. J. Mark. Logist. **32**(4), 841–859 (2020)

51. Perse, E.M., Rubin, R.B.: Attribution in social and parasocial relationships. Commun. Res. **16**(1), 59–77 (1989). https://doi.org/10.1177/009365089016001003. http://journals.sagepub.com/doi/10.1177/009365089016001003

52. Possler, D., Kümpel, A.S., Unkel, J.: Entertainment motivations and gaming-specific gratifications as antecedents of digital game enjoyment and appreciation. Psychol. Pop. Media **9**(4), 541 (2020)

53. Quesenberry, K.A., Coolsen, M.K.: Drama goes viral: effects of story development on shares and views of online advertising videos. J. Interact. Mark. **48**, 1–16 (2019)

54. Raney, A.A.: Disposition-based theories of enjoyment. In: Communication and Emotion, pp. 61–84. Routledge (2003)

55. Raney, A.A., Bryant, J.: Entertainment and enjoyment as media effect. In: Media Effects, pp. 324–341. Routledge (2019)

56. Riddle, K., Liao, X., Minich, M.: Media enjoyment: a synthesis. J. Broadcast. Electron. Media **66**(4), 592–622 (2022)

57. Rimé, B.: Emotion elicits the social sharing of emotion: theory and empirical review. Emot. Rev. **1**(1), 60–85 (2009)

58. Rogers, K., Karaosmanoglu, S., Altmeyer, M., Suarez, A., Nacke, L.E.: Much realistic, such wow! A systematic literature review of realism in digital games. In: Proceedings of the 2022 CHI Conference on Human Factors in Computing Systems, pp. 1–21 (2022)

59. Rondan-Cataluña, F.J., Arenas-Gaitán, J., Ramírez-Correa, P.E.: A comparison of the different versions of popular technology acceptance models: a non-linear perspective. Kybernetes **44**(5), 788–805 (2015)

60. Rosaen, S.F., Dibble, J.L.: The impact of viewer perceptions of media personae and viewer characteristics on the strength, enjoyment, and satisfaction of parasocial relationships. Commun. Stud. **68**(1), 1–21 (2017). https://doi.org/10.1080/10510974.2016.1240701. https://www.tandfonline.com/doi/full/10.1080/10510974.2016.1240701

61. Sajjadiani, S., Sojourner, A.J., Kammeyer-Mueller, J.D., Mykerezi, E.: Using machine learning to translate applicant work history into predictors of performance and turnover. J. Appl. Psychol. **104**(10), 1207 (2019)

62. Schmidhuber, J.: Deep learning in neural networks: an overview. Neural Netw. **61**, 85–117 (2015)

63. Sharma, I., Jain, K., Behl, A., Baabdullah, A., Giannakis, M., Dwivedi, Y.: Examining the motivations of sharing political deepfake videos: the role of political brand hate and moral consciousness. Internet Res. **33**(5), 1727–1749 (2023)

64. Sheetal, A., Savani, K.: A machine learning model of cultural change: role of prosociality, political attitudes, and protestant work ethic. Am. Psychol. **76**(6), 997 (2021)

65. Sheldon, Z., Romanowski, M., Shafer, D.M.: Parasocial interactions and digital characters: the changing landscape of cinema and viewer/character relationships. Atlantic J. Commun. **29**(1), 15–25 (2021). https://doi.org/10.1080/15456870.2019.1702550. https://www.tandfonline.com/doi/full/10.1080/15456870.2019.1702550

66. Slater, M.D., Rouner, D.: Entertainment-education and elaboration likelihood: understanding the processing of narrative persuasion. Commun. Theo. **12**(2), 173–191 (2002)
67. Slater, M.D., Rouner, D., Long, M.: Television dramas and support for controversial public policies: effects and mechanisms. J. Commun. **56**(2), 235–252 (2006). https://doi.org/10.1111/j.1460-2466.2006.00017.x. https://academic.oup.com/joc/article/56/2/235-252/4070458
68. Soto Sanfiel, M.T., Aymerich Franch, L., Ribes Guardia, F.X., Martinez Fernandez, J.R.: Influence of interactivity on emotions and enjoyment during consumption of audiovisual fictions. Int. J. Arts Technol. **4**(1), 111–129 (2011)
69. Sukhu, A., Zhang, T., Bilgihan, A.: Factors influencing information-sharing behaviors in social networking sites. Serv. Mark. Q. **36**(4), 317–334 (2015)
70. Tal-Or, N., Cohen, J.: Unpacking engagement: convergence and divergence in transportation and identification. Ann. Int. Commun. Assoc. **40**(1), 33–66 (2016)
71. Tsay-Vogel, M., Schwartz, M.L.: Theorizing parasocial interactions based on authenticity: the development of a media figure classification scheme. Psychol. Popular Media Cult. **3**(2), 66–78 (2014). https://doi.org/10.1037/a0034615. http://doi.apa.org/getdoi.cfm?doi=10.1037/a0034615
72. Tukachinsky, R., Sangalang, A.: The effect of relational and interactive aspects of parasocial experiences on attitudes and message resistance. Commun. Rep. **29**(3), 175–188 (2016). https://doi.org/10.1080/08934215.2016.1148750. https://www.tandfonline.com/doi/full/10.1080/08934215.2016.1148750
73. Turel, O., Serenko, A.: The benefits and dangers of enjoyment with social networking websites. Eur. J. Inf. Syst. **21**, 512–528 (2012)
74. Van Doorn, J., Verhoef, P.C., Bijmolt, T.H.: The importance of non-linear relationships between attitude and behaviour in policy research. J. Consum. Policy **30**(2), 75–90 (2007)
75. Van Laer, T., De Ruyter, K., Visconti, L.M., Wetzels, M.: The extended transportation-imagery model: a meta-analysis of the antecedents and consequences of consumers' narrative transportation. J. Consum. Res. **40**(5), 797–817 (2014)
76. Verma, C., Stoffová, V., Illés, Z.: Prediction of students' awareness level towards ICT and mobile technology in Indian and Hungarian University for the real-time: preliminary results. Heliyon **5**(6), e01806 (2019)
77. Vorderer, P., Klimmt, C., Ritterfeld, U.: Enjoyment: at the heart of media entertainment. Commun. Theor. **14**(4), 388–408 (2004). https://doi.org/10.1111/j.1468-2885.2004.tb00321.x
78. Wahl-Jorgensen, K., Carlson, M.: Conjecturing fearful futures: journalistic discourses on deepfakes. Journal. Pract. **15**(6), 803–820 (2021). https://doi.org/10.1080/17512786.2021.1908838. https://www.tandfonline.com/doi/full/10.1080/17512786.2021.1908838

Empirical Evidence for Reciprocal Radicalization: Conformity of User Comment, Peer Feedback, and Community Emotion in Extreme Misogynistic Social Media Groups

Tangila Islam Tanni$^{(\boxtimes)}$ ⓘ, Aaron Necaise ⓘ, Yan Solihin ⓘ,
and Mary Jean Amon ⓘ

University of Central Florida, Orlando, FL 32826, USA
{tangilaislam.tanni,aaron.necaise,yan.solihin,mjamon}@ucf.edu

Abstract. Reciprocal radicalization occurs when extremist communities and its individual users mutually fuel one another's beliefs, emotions, or actions. Although a promising theory for explaining facets of radicalization in social media, research has yet to demonstrate aspects of reciprocal radicalization empirically. We examined comment trajectories of 1,000 Reddit users randomly sampled from those who interacted with a well-known misogynistic 'subreddit' or online community. We drew over 1.8 million comments, as well as associated feedback from peers and submission thread features per comment. Results indicated that Reddit users with higher rates of posting engaged more often with the misogynistic subreddit but also interacted within a larger number of subreddits. Users with high posting rates, including in the extremist subreddit, tended to post less positive and more negative emotional comments, receive more negative feedback, and engage with less positive submission threads. Our results suggests that, despite engaging with a breadth of online communities, more regular and extremist Reddit users both contribute and receive distinctly more negative and less positive emotional content and are especially active in disseminating content across online communities. Implications for reciprocal radicalization theory as well as future research of radicalization processes are discussed.

Keywords: Emotion · Extremism · Misogyny · Reciprocal radicalization · Social media · Echo chamber · Reddit

1 Introduction

Although online communities facilitate information exchange and social connections, these benefits are limited due to users' propensity for engaging with a narrow range of communities of like-minded individuals, which forms an 'echo chamber.' Echo chambers refer to environments in which community members engage in repeated interactions that amplify particular attitudes, beliefs, and value systems, leading community members to engage in advocacy outside the norm [17, 26, 27, 34, 45]. User interactions within a homogenous community can lead to the formation of ingroup biases that, in turn, promote outgroup conflict, oftentimes towards marginalized groups of people, such as women and under-represented minorities [52, 59]. For example, in one study, half of the young men aged between 16–24 in the United Kingdom indicated that 'feminism has gone too far' and makes it harder for men to succeed, a perspective that is driven by their online interactions [12, p. 42]. Indeed, this ideology is widespread across social media and the Internet [21], to the point that scholars have coined the term 'manosphere' [5] to describe online misogynistic communities. The seriousness of this issue is widely recognized, with the United States Secret Service identifying 'incel' culture as a growing terroristic threat (i.e., "involuntary celibate" people who tend to be "anti-feminist"), with an emphasis on improving early detection and prevention methods [55].

Online interactions within echo chambers fuel radicalization, moving individuals from orthodox beliefs towards extremist viewpoints that support, promote, and justify hate and violence to establish their ideology and achieve desired change [9]. Radicalization theory suggests that people do not become radicalized from viewing one post or video online but rather that it is a gradual process that unfolds over time [44]. Specifically, the theory of *reciprocal radicalization* suggests that users and online communities mutually drive one another toward extremist beliefs, where individuals both influence and are influenced by the group, which drives broader changes in belief systems [19, 24, 37]. Reciprocal radicalization theory aligns with literature that emphasizes the importance of recognizing radicalization as a relational process, where broader social contexts must be taken into account in order to fully grasp radicalization processes [4]. Though existing theory suggests the presence of reciprocal radicalization in social media platforms in the form of textual or visual formats, very few studies quantified aspects of the reciprocal process that drives extremist perspectives. Moreover, most prior efforts to examine online communication changes utilize word frequency counts and manual coding of interactions, and do not reference social media extremism or radicalization [20, 46]. Accordingly, this work examines the central question:

Do Reddit users who engage with extreme misogynistic material at a higher rate of posting frequency demonstrate evidence of reciprocal radicalization? Specifically, is there evidence that these users both contribute and receive distinctly negative emotional content?

This study investigates how social media users engaged with an extreme misogynistic subreddit, create content, receive feedback on their content, and engage with existing content. We examined over 1.8 million comments from 1,000 Reddit users who have engaged at least once with a well-known misogynistic extremist subreddit[1], as well as content they engaged with and feedback

---

[1] We opted to withhold the name of the subreddit as a means of protecting the anonymity of users included in our sample. Considering we are sampling from activity during a specific time period, this was necessary to maintain privacy. Contact the authors for more information.

received from other users. In this study, we quantify aspects of emotional information exchange in an extremist subreddit. Our findings indicate that users more frequently engaged with Reddit and an extreme misogynistic subreddit tend to seek, contribute, and receive feedback that is more emotionally negative and less emotionally positive. In doing so, this work represents an initial step in connecting reciprocal radicalization theory to quantitative support, where evidence suggests users participate in feedback loops as they reciprocally create and receive distinctly negative content. Our initial approach focuses on the user's commenting activity, future work should examine user's interactions with the extreme community dynamically.

2   Related Works

2.1   Dynamics of Radicalization

Radicalization can be defined as a complex process by which an individual or group adopts increasingly extreme political, social, or religious ideals that either reject or undermine the status quo or contemporary ideas and expressions related to freedom of choice [9,10,18,53,61,68]. In contrast, extremism refers to the ideology and beliefs that are not in compliance with social norms and are oftentimes intolerant towards others by promoting social, political, and economic supremacy [58,61]. Extremism manifests as a form of vocal or active opposition to fundamental values that underpin the fabric of democratic societies. These values encompass not only the pillars of democracy and the rule of law but also extend to the realms of individual freedom and the essential virtues of embracing diversity through mutual respect and tolerance for various faiths and beliefs [53]. The relationship between extremism and radicalization is intricate and interconnected. The main difference between radicalization and extremism lies in their nature: radicalization is a process, while extremism reflects an individual's beliefs [28]. One common view is that someone is radicalized when they adopt extremist beliefs. Radicalization involves the transformation of individuals towards adopting more extreme ideologies over time. In this way, extremist beliefs are the result of radicalization processes [28].

Social connections play a crucial role in shaping extreme beliefs [7,9,29,43]. Exposure to a community of like-minded individuals sharing similar views fosters the development of increasingly extreme beliefs and behaviors [15,36]. Furthermore, group contexts have the potential to nurture individual extremism, with entire groups progressively adopting more extreme positions over time [9]. Being in social networks with people who embrace extreme beliefs can shape a shared reality and understanding for those who feel aggrieved, cultivating a sense of camaraderie among individuals who might otherwise sense alienation and isolation. In some instances, this can even result in the social acceptance of extreme beliefs or behaviors [7,40].

2.2   Influence of Social Media on Radicalization

Social media amplifies the process of radicalization through the rapid dissemination, heightened anonymity, and reduced cost associated with information sharing [54]. Social media platforms have become significantly influential in the radicalization of U.S. extremists. Despite a gradual uptake by U.S. extremists, the reliance on user-to-user platforms for disseminating extremist content and fostering extremist relationships has experienced exponential growth in recent years [8]. While certain individuals may initially join these platforms with pre-existing extremist beliefs, others become radicalized by virtue of their social media interactions resulting in more extreme views over time [45].

Social media users often observe increasingly narrowed content to match their previous activity due to social media algorithms that customize user content, giving rise to substantial societal concerns due to their capacity to magnify "reinforcing spirals" [38,56]. Exposure to radicalizing content often occurs within filter bubbles, where personalization algorithms select content based on user profiles and preferences, creating online spaces that filter out opposing viewpoints [11,69]. As users like, share, or view certain content, it gains more prominence in their information feed, contributing to the reinforcement of existing beliefs within echo chambers [69]. This process aligns with individuals' inclination to seek agreement over conflict, further validating extreme views within a community [39,62].

Research underscores that algorithmic personalization is more pronounced among populations with extreme ideological beliefs, emphasizing the urgent need to identify factors contributing to online radicalization vulnerability [66]. Frances Haugen, renowned as the Facebook whistleblower, brought to light the improper use of algorithms on major social media platforms, revealing their role in promoting radicalization and extremism [30]. The more provocative the content, the more it engages users, reinforcing the content through algorithms. Haugen disclosed that Facebook employees were compelled to upload more incendiary content online, fostering polarized political views to enhance message access and forwarding under the platform's algorithmic amplification scheme [30,32]. When platform users' comments or messages lacked incitement, they did not receive as much attention as when they engaged in confrontational interactions. The mechanisms of social media platforms are neither neutral nor fair, and core product mechanics, including recommendations, engagement optimization, and virality, contribute to the proliferation of bias and hate on social media platforms [13]. Although the theory of reciprocal radicalization highlights user and community exchanges as the mechanism of radicalization [37], it is likely that social media algorithms are a 'silent partner' in accelerating this process.

In terms of radicalization's human element, many users turn to social media already carrying seeds of extremism. "Cognitive opening," a psychological mechanism, triggers self-radicalization as individuals facing discrimination, crises, and isolation become vulnerable to adopting extremist ideologies [67]. Interactions with radical communities mold social identity, fostering a sense of belonging over time. This aligns with the uncertainty-identity theory, suggesting that those experiencing high uncertainty (i.e., those who do not know where they fit in society) seek group identification [64]. The group guides their self-identity by prescribing prototypes, including the martyrdom of controversial figures, and offering a 'rich toxic tapestry culture' that addresses individual's loneliness through activities like art-making and exchange of dark humor [51]. Deep engagement in extremist online communities then reinforces identity, heightening susceptibility to adopting and promoting radical ideologies [31]. Past research findings revealed that conformity to extremist group language and style increased over time, positively correlating with engaging in group mobilizing interaction [57]. Increased homogeneity and group participation creates a continuous reinforcement loop through which social media users become extremists [51].

Numerous studies focusing on politics, political identity formation, and extremism have centered around the social media platform Reddit [50]. Much of this research emphasizes Reddit's distinctive design and features, highlighting structural mechanisms that facilitate toxic behaviors and extremism. The platform is structured into numerous distinct topic-based communities, known as "subreddits," with users choosing which ones to subscribe to and engage in. Within each subreddit, users generate discussion posts subject to being "upvoted" or "downvoted" by their peers. Content with high upvotes rises to the top, while downvoted content fades into obscurity [16]. Historically, Reddit adopted a largely "hands-off" moderation approach, allowing subreddits to self-govern, resulting in the emergence of some toxic or extreme communities [41]. For instance, Reddit's platform ethos, content aggregation, reward systems, and moderation practices contribute to the emergence of "toxic technocultures" and movements such as FemalePrivilage and Fappening [22,41]. Within these settings, users are not just radicalized via feedback from others but also their own behaviors. For example, interacting with misogynist content and writing sexist posts increases self-reported sexism [23]. The manosphere, encompassing communities like involuntary celibates (incels), pick-up artists (PUAs), and Men's Rights Activists (MRA), serves as an online space for spreading misogyny. Despite men in the manosphere communities not explicitly identifying as extremists, the online discourse indicates connections to far-right extremism and extreme misogyny. Moreover, using misogynistic language on social media is linked to real-world acts of discrimination against women [25]. Taken together, prior research suggests that radicalist trajectories are shaped by an interplay between individual behaviors, reinforcement from others, and repeated exposure to associated content.

3 Method

3.1 Data Sampling and Processing

As the collected dataset was publicly available, this research protocol was approved as 'exempt' by an Institutional Review Board (IRB) located in the southeastern United States. We selected Reddit as a platform with distinct online communities, which allowed us to examine how users and communities bidirectionally contribute to one another's radicalization. First, Reddit has an established problem managing extremist online communities, illustrated by Reddit's recent move to ban ~2000 subreddits over chronically abusive post language [3]. Second, Reddit data facilitates a relatively objective measure of online extremism, as evidenced by degree of user extremist subreddit engagement. Third, Reddit provides a different data source than the usual Twitter data [42]. We identified a subreddit recognized by the general media for its misogynistic subject matter and subsequently quarantined by Reddit. Due to its quarantined status, we leveraged the Pushshift archival dataset, which is a tool for retrieving historical Reddit data [6]. Although the Pushshift dataset does not provide updated data concerning the number of upvotes that a post receives, it is a source for tracking user activity by preserving information about deleted and moderated posts. We identified users who commented on the quarantined subreddit in the last two years and had an average of one or more posts per week on Reddit during that period, yielding approximately 12,000 users. From that list, we randomly sampled 1,000 users and their comment history.

Next, we used Reddit's publicly available API to extract users' full comment history since they joined Reddit. From our list of 1,000 users of the extremist subreddit, we extracted information about the comments each user made including: (1) the text features of their comments, (2) information about the replies their comments received, and (3) information about the submission (i.e., thread) in which their comment was posted. Our final dataset contained over 1.8 million (1,827,046) user comments and associated features, including the submission and comment replies from other users. For each comment made by a user in our sample, we collected the (1) text of the comment, (2) date and time the comment was posted, (3) score (i.e., the difference between the number of upvotes and downvotes), (4) name of the subreddit in which the comment was posted, (5) time from last post (duration in seconds since the user's last comment. For better interpretation, the values have been normalized from −1 to 1. The sign has been reversed, and in the paper we refer to it as engagement frequency), and (6) the total number of comments posted by the user on the Quarantined subreddit.

Next, examining the replies that users in our sample received to their comments, we extracted the text of the replies and the total number of replies to each comment. Lastly, we obtained four features related to the submissions under which the comments were posted, including (1) submission text, (2) date and time of the submission, (3) total number of comments posted on the submission, and (4) submission score.

3.2   Natural Language Processing (NLP) Using Linguistic Inquiry and Word Count

We utilized the Linguistic Inquiry and Word Count (LIWC) dictionary, a commonly used tool to identify linguistic features of text associated with user comments, submissions, and replies from other users [47–49]. In addition to calculating the total number of words contained in each comment, submission, and reply, we leveraged LIWC to estimate the degree of positive and negative emotion reflected within each text. The majority of LIWC output variables represented the percentage of words within a passage of text belonging to a similar category (e.g., positive or negative words), whereas word count was the raw number of words in a given text [33]. The LIWC dictionary of positive emotion was comprised of 261 words, such as 'happy', 'pretty', or 'good', that indicated positive feelings. Likewise, the dictionary for negative emotions consisted of 345 words (e.g., 'hate', 'worthless', or 'enemy') that were categorized as negative experiences [35].

4   Results

A series of linear multiple regression (MR) models were used to examine the extent to which users' Reddit engagement frequency is predicted by comment features, comment feedback from other users, and features of the submissions that comments correspond to. We calculated the outcome variable—Reddit engagement frequency—by identifying each user's average time since last post, normalizing the scores, and multiplying the value by -1. This transformation of time since last post into engagement frequency allows for more interpretable models, where higher values correspond to increased Reddit engagement. For all reported models, variance inflation factors (VIF) were less than the recommended cutoff of 4 [2], indicating the models were not compromised by multicollinearity.

4.1   User Comment Features

To understand the degree to which comment features are associated with user's Reddit engagement frequency, we regressed engagement frequency on users' average comment word count, average positive and negative emotion, total comments posted on the extremist subreddit, as well as the total number of unique subreddits where each user commented. Full results are reported in Table 1's Model 1 (M1). We found that greater Reddit engagement frequency corresponded to both more posts within the extremist subreddit and engagement with a greater variety of subreddits. In addition, greater Reddit engagement frequency was associated with increased expression of negative emotions and decreased expression of positive emotions within user comments.

4.2   Peer Feedback Features

Next, we examined the degree to which users' Reddit engagement frequency was predicted by feedback received from other users. We regressed engagement frequency on average score of comment replies, average number of comment replies from other users, as well as the degree to which those replies contained language with negative or positive emotional tones. Results in Table 1 Model 2 (M2) indicate that Reddit engagement frequency is significantly associated with replies from other users that contain more negative emotional tones.

Table 1. Standardized estimates, 95% confidence intervals, and p-values for multiple regression models examining the relationship between Reddit engagement frequency and user comment features (M1), feedback features (M2), and submission features (M3).

Predictors	Engagement frequency (M1)			Engagement frequency (M2)			Engagement frequency (M3)		
	std. Beta	std. CI	p	std. Beta	std. CI	p	std. Beta	Std. CI	p
(Intercept)	0.00	−0.06–0.06	<0.001	0.00	−0.06–0.06	0.508	0.000	−0.06–0.06	0.060
Total extreme subreddit comments	0.12	0.06–0.18	<0.001						
Total unique subreddit comments	0.28	0.22–0.34	<0.001						
Word count M	−0.03	−0.09–0.03	0.355						
Comment positive emotion M	−0.10	−0.17−−0.04	0.001						
Comment negative emotion M	0.16	0.10–0.22	<0.001						
Feedback score M				0.02	−0.06–0.10	0.601			
Number replies M				−0.02	−0.10–0.06	0.618			
Reply positive emotion M				−0.05	−0.12–0.01	0.112			
Reply negative emotion M				0.14	0.07–0.20	<0.001			
Submission score M							−0.01	−0.08–0.07	0.881
Number of submission comments M							0.04	−0.03–0.10	0.292
Submission positive emotion							−0.09	−0.16−−0.02	0.008
Observations	1000			1000			1000		
R^2/Adjusted R^2	0.128/0.124			0.022/0.018			0.009/ 0.006		

Note. M3 has submission negative emotion and submission word count removed due to high correlations with submission positive emotion (rs = .78 and .67, respectively).

4.3   Subreddit Submission Features

Lastly, we examined the extent to which users' Reddit engagement frequency corresponded to submission features (i.e., features of the main subreddit posts to which users responded to), including average submission score, average number of submission comments, and average submission positive emotion. Average submission negative emotion and word count were removed as predictors due to high correlations with submission positive emotion ($r(1000) = .78$, $p < .001$; $r(1000) = .67$, $p < .001$, respectively). We opted to leave in submission positive emotion over these variables due to prior models revealing relationships between engagement frequency and emotional content. We found that users who engaged more frequently with Reddit engaged with significantly less positive-emotion submissions (see Table 1 Model 3 (M3) for full results). Notably, submission positive and negative emotional tone was positively correlated with Model 3 submission variables, whereas positive and negative tone of user comments and replies (Models 1 and 2) were not significantly correlated, $ps > .05$.

5   Discussion

In order to holistically describe the emergent process of online radicalization, one must account for the social media environment in which it occurs, with a focus on how online communities influence users and vice versa. Expanding on this perspective, our study delves into the dynamic interplay between users and online communities, specifically investigating reciprocal radicalization. We condensed a large amount of social media data from an extremist subreddit into succinct models demonstrating a general emotional convergence among extremist subreddit users, the submissions they responded to, and those who replied to their comments.

In order to study the process of reciprocal radicalization between users and online communities, we applied a series of MR models to examine associations between users' Reddit engagement frequency (i.e., average time since last post) and their comments, peer feedback, and submission content features, sampling users engaged with an extreme misogynistic subreddit.

Results demonstrate that Reddit users with higher engagement commented more within the misogynist subreddit while also commenting in a greater number of total subreddits compared to users with lower engagement levels. The finding that users exhibiting a higher frequency of posting participated in both extremist and diverse communities goes against prior theory that suggests radicalization corresponds to isolation and narrowed focus on the extremist community [43,60,70]. On the other hand, theory specific to radicalization within misogynistic communities has highlighted that many of these users engage with online communities to a high degree in an effort to alleviate loneliness [51]. Although more research is needed to identify how radicalized users are interacting within various online communities, the findings suggest that especially extremist beliefs are disproportionately represented as radicalized users carry their perspectives to a larger number of online communities compared to less extreme users. Notably, this finding suggests that merely exposing users to a wider array of communities is not alone sufficient to dilute the effects of online radicalization.

Reddit users who engaged more with an extremist community not only participated in more online communities but also disseminated distinct content. Higher rates of Reddit engagement was associated with users commenting with more negative than positive emotions. A similar trend was observed in the feedback users received from others, which was also distinctly negative in emotion. Further analysis of submission features indicates a user engagement pattern where users with higher rate of posting frequency seek out submissions that have a less positive emotional tone. The exploration of content dissemination revealed that a higher rate of Reddit engagement was associated with users expressing more negative than positive emotions. Thus, we find that users engaged more frequently with Reddit and an extreme subreddit seek, create, and receive feedback that is more negative and less positive. These findings align with the theory of reciprocal radicalization by demonstrating a convergence in emotional expression and frequency of interaction between users and their online communities. This emotional convergence underlines that radicalization extends beyond ideological beliefs to include the adoption of more negative emotions, thereby deepening the impact of online radicalization on individuals. In general, human cognition has been described as a scaffolded dialogical process, whereby people determine what they think and feel, in part, by expressing it and receiving feedback from others that normalize certain emotions [1]. In this case, users engaged with extremist communities are radicalized not only in their beliefs, but also in adopting more negative emotions. This underscores the intricate interplay between cognitive processes and online interactions, emphasizing the need for a comprehensive understanding of the psychological and emotional dimensions of online radicalization.

5.1   Future Directions

The study has a number of limitations and future directions. First, as radicalization is a time-evolving process, future work will leverage tools associated with nonlinear dynamical systems theory to examine changes in attitudes and behaviors specific to radicalized users in social media. In particular, our ongoing research will engage in a more in-depth investigation of multimodal NLP features that define feedback loops that—based on the present study—occur between extremist communities and their users [65].

Relatedly, further research is needed to examine whether the nature of user-community reciprocal radicalization changes over time. It is likely that users who are initially susceptible to the influence of extremist forums eventually solidify their extremist viewpoints. In turn, radicalized users may change from being influenced to becoming influencers. Given that radicalization theory commonly highlights progressive 'stages' or 'steps' [14], the examination of reciprocal radicalization requires a more fine-grained perspective. Therefore, the present work represents a first step in understanding these processes.

Lastly, more research is needed to identify how radicalized users interact within various online communities. The present findings suggest a type of contagion where especially extremist user beliefs are disproportionately represented in social media as they carry their perspectives to a larger number of online communities than other users, including to non-extremist communities (e.g., world news subreddits). We found evidence of emotional feedback loops between users' comments, replies from other users, and submission content sought by users. We plan to examine whether this emergent behavior occurs as radicalized users move about social media in different contexts, for example, in non-extremist forums or those promoting other forms of single-issue extremism, e.g., anti-gay movements [63].

5.2   Conclusions

The present study investigated feedback loops of social media users engaged with an extremist online forum. Contrary to some prior works that suggest a narrowing of interests among radicalized users, our results indicate that highly engaged Reddit users engage with a broader range of online communities, in addition to engaging more with extremist content. This finding highlights that extremist communities are not insular and represent a threat to adjacent online communities as their users engage to a high degree with various forums. Our results are also among the first to empirically examine reciprocal radicalization theory, identifying emotional feedback loops between users and an extremist online community. Notably, this work focuses on NLP features that may generalize to understand other forms of radicalization, versus focusing on linguistic features specific to misogyny. Future work will expand on this work to study reciprocal radicalization as a time-evolving process via the tools of nonlinear dynamical systems theory.

References

1. Alfano, M., Carter, J.A., Cheong, M.: Technological seduction and self-radicalization. J. Am. Philos. Assoc. **4**(3), 298–322 (2018)
2. Allison, P.: Multiple Regression: A Primer. Pine Forge Press (1999)
3. Allyn, B.: Reddit Bans The Donald, Forum Of Nearly 800,000 Trump Fans Over Abusive Posts (2020). https://www.npr.org/2020/06/29/884819923/reddit-bans-the_donald-forum-of-nearly-800-000-trump-fans-over-abusive-posts
4. Ayanian, A.H., Böckler, N., Doosje, B., Zick, A.: Processes of radicalization and polarization in the context of transnational Islamist terrorism. Int. J. Confl. Violence (IJCV) **12**, a648 (2018)
5. Balay, A., et al.: Feminist Responses to the Neoliberalization of the University: From Surviving to Thriving. Lexington Books (2020)
6. Baumgartner, J., Zannettou, S., Keegan, B., Squire, M., Blackburn, J.: The Pushshift Reddit dataset. In: Proceedings of the International AAAI Conference on Web and Social Media, vol. 14, pp. 830–839 (2020)
7. Bélanger, J.J., et al.: Radicalization leading to violence: a test of the 3n model. Front. Psych. **10**, 42 (2019)
8. Binder, J.F., Kenyon, J.: Terrorism and the internet: How dangerous is online radicalization? Front. Psychol., 6639 (2022)
9. Borum, R.: Radicalization into violent extremism I: a review of social science theories. J. Strateg. Secur. **4**(4), 7–36 (2011)
10. Bott, C., Castan, W.J., Lark, L., Thompson, G.: Recruitment and radicalization of school aged youth by international terrorist groups. Final Report (2009). https://pdfs.semanticscholar.org/c664/9103b3d86b13fa58b2c1a2942b5b7ada91d7.pdf (Stand: 07.12. 2017)
11. Bucher, T.: Want to be on the top? Algorithmic power and the threat of invisibility on Facebook. New Media Soc. **14**(7), 1164–1180 (2012)
12. Carter, R.: Young people in the time of COVID-19: a fear and hope study of 16–24 year olds. Hope not Hate Charitable Trust (2020). https://hopenothate.org.uk/wp-content/uploads/2020/08/youth-fear-and-hope-2020-07-v2final.pdf
13. Cervi, L., Tejedor, S., Marín-Lladó, C.: Tiktok and the new language of political communication (2021)
14. Chuang, Y.l., D'Orsogna, M.R.: Mathematical models of radicalization and terrorism. arXiv preprint arXiv:1903.08485 (2019)
15. Cousineau, L.S.: "are there any other male friendly subs on here?" - online men's rights groups as simultaneous communities of care and hate, inclusion and exclusion. Leisure/loisir **47**(4), 681–702 (2023)
16. Davis, J.L., Graham, T.: Emotional consequences and attention rewards: the social effects of ratings on Reddit. Inf. Commun. Soc. **24**(5), 649–666 (2021)
17. Del Vicario, M., et al.: The spreading of misinformation online. Proc. Natl. Acad. Sci. **113**(3), 554–559 (2016)
18. UN Office on Drugs and Crime: 'Radicalization' and 'violent extremism' (2018). https://www.unodc.org/e4j/en/terrorism/module-2/key-issues/radicalization-violent-extremism.html

19. Eatwell, R.: Community cohesion and cumulative extremism in contemporary Britain. Polit. Q. **77**(2), 204–216 (2006)
20. Eckert, P., Rickford, J.R.: Style and Sociolinguistic Variation. Cambridge University Press (2001)
21. Ewens, H.: Young, Male and Anti-Feminist - The Gen Z Boys Who Hate Women (2021). https://www.vice.com/en/article/dyv7by/anti-feminist-gen-z-boys-who-hate-women
22. Farrell, T., Fernandez, M., Novotny, J., Alani, H.: Exploring misogyny across the manosphere in Reddit. In: Proceedings of the 10th ACM Conference on Web Science, pp. 87–96 (2019)
23. Fox, J., Cruz, C., Lee, J.Y.: Perpetuating online sexism offline: anonymity, interactivity, and the effects of sexist hashtags on social media. Comput. Hum. Behav. **52**, 436–442 (2015)
24. Francis, M.: Briefings: reciprocal radicalisation (2018). https://www.radicalisationresearch.org/debate/briefings-reciprocal-radicalisation/
25. Fulper, R., et al.: Misogynistic language on Twitter and sexual violence. In: Proceedings of the ACM Web Science Workshop on Computational Approaches to Social Modeling (ChASM), pp. 57–64 (2014)
26. Garimella, K., De Francisci Morales, G., Gionis, A., Mathioudakis, M.: The effect of collective attention on controversial debates on social media. In: Proceedings of the 2017 ACM on Web Science Conference, pp. 43–52 (2017)
27. Garrett, R.K.: Echo chambers online?: politically motivated selective exposure among internet news users. J. Comput. Mediat. Commun. **14**(2), 265–285 (2009)
28. llywodraeth Cymru Welsh Government: A teacher's guide to understanding the role of the internet in radicalisation and extremism (2020). https://hwb.gov.wales/api/storage/c92e00f6-2ffe-4e98-9e5d-9e051501d5d4/a-teachers-guide-understanding-the-role-of-the-internet-in-extremism-and-radicalisation.pdf
29. Hafez, M., Mullins, C.: The radicalization puzzle: a theoretical synthesis of empirical approaches to homegrown extremism. Stud. Confl. Terror. **38**(11), 958–975 (2015)
30. Haugen, F.: Frances Haugen: The Facebook whistleblower. In: SXSW 2022 (2022). https://www.youtube.com/watch?v=3D18JIrsGQM
31. Hollewell, G.F., Longpré, N.: Radicalization in the social media era: understanding the relationship between self-radicalization and the internet. Int. J. Offender Ther. Comp. Criminol. **66**(8), 896–913 (2022)
32. Huszár, F., Ktena, S.I., O'Brien, C., Belli, L., Schlaikjer, A., Hardt, M.: Algorithmic amplification of politics on Twitter. Proc. Natl. Acad. Sci. **119**(1), e2025334119 (2022)
33. Inc, P.C.: Introducing LIWC-22 a new set of text analysis tools at your fingertips (2001). https://www.liwc.app/help/liwc#Summary-Measures
34. Jamieson, K.H., Cappella, J.N.: Echo Chamber: Rush Limbaugh and the Conservative Media Establishment. Oxford University Press (2008)
35. Kahn, J.H., Tobin, R.M., Massey, A.E., Anderson, J.A.: Measuring emotional expression with the linguistic inquiry and word count. Am. J. Psychol. **120**(2), 263–286 (2007)
36. King, M., Taylor, D.M.: The radicalization of homegrown Jihadists: a review of theoretical models and social psychological evidence. Terror. Polit. Violence **23**(4), 602–622 (2011)
37. Knott, K., Lee, B., Copeland, S.: Briefings: reciprocal radicalisation. CREST (2018). https://crestresearch.ac.uk/resources/reciprocal-radicalisation

38. Ledwich, M., Zaitsev, A.: Algorithmic extremism: examining Youtube's rabbit hole of radicalization. arXiv preprint arXiv:1912.11211 (2019)
39. Lorenzo-Dus, N., Macdonald, S.: Othering the west in the online Jihadist propaganda magazines inspire and Dabiq. J. Lang. Aggress. Confl. 6(1), 79–106 (2018)
40. Mann, M., Zulli, D., Foote, J., Ku, E., Primm, E.: Unsorted significance: examining potential pathways to extreme political beliefs and communities on Reddit. Socius 9, 23780231231174824 (2023)
41. Massanari, A.: #Gamergate and the Fappening: how Reddit's algorithm, governance, and culture support toxic technocultures. New Media Soc. 19(3), 329–346 (2017)
42. Matamoros-Fernández, A., Farkas, J.: Racism, hate speech, and social media: a systematic review and critique. Telev. New Media 22(2), 205–224 (2021)
43. McCauley, C., Moskalenko, S.: Mechanisms of political radicalization: pathways toward terrorism. Terror. Polit. Violence 20(3), 415–433 (2008)
44. McCormick, G.H.: Terrorist decision making. Annu. Rev. Polit. Sci. 6(1), 473–507 (2003)
45. Necaise, A., Williams, A., Vrzakova, H., Amon, M.J.: Regularity versus novelty of users' multimodal comment patterns and dynamics as markers of social media radicalization. In: Proceedings of the 32nd ACM Conference on Hypertext and Social Media, pp. 237–243 (2021)
46. Nguyen, D., Rose, C.: Language use as a reflection of socialization in online communities. In: Proceedings of the Workshop on Language in Social Media, LSM 2011, pp. 76–85 (2011)
47. Pennebaker, J.W., Boyd, R.L., Jordan, K., Blackburn, K.: The development and psychometric properties of liwc2015. Technical report (2015)
48. Pennebaker, J.W., Francis, M.E., Booth, R.J.: Linguistic inquiry and word count: LIWC 2001, vol. 71. Lawrence Erlbaum Associates, Mahway (2001)
49. Pennebaker, J., Booth, R., Boyd, R., Francis, M.: Linguistic inquiry and word count: LIWC2015 operator's manual (2015). Accessed 28 April 2016
50. Proferes, N., Jones, N., Gilbert, S., Fiesler, C., Zimmer, M.: Studying Reddit: a systematic overview of disciplines, approaches, methods, and ethics. Soc. Media + Soc. 7(2), 20563051211019004 (2021)
51. Regehr, K.: In(cel)doctrination: how technologically facilitated misogyny moves violence off screens and on to streets. New Media Soc. 24(1), 138–155 (2022)
52. Reicher, S.D., Spears, R., Postmes, T.: A social identity model of deindividuation phenomena. Eur. Rev. Soc. Psychol. 6(1), 161–198 (1995)
53. Scarcella, A., Page, R., Furtado, V.: Terrorism, radicalisation, extremism, authoritarianism and fundamentalism: a systematic review of the quality and psychometric properties of assessments. PLoS ONE 11(12), e0166947 (2016)
54. Schmid, A.P.: Handbook of Terrorism Prevention and Preparedness. International Centre for Counter-Terrorism (ICCT) (2020)
55. Sganga, N.: New Secret Service report details growing incel terrorism threat (2022). https://www.cbsnews.com/news/incel-threat-secret-service-report/?dc_data=1131694_samsung-carnival-us&utm_source=taboola&utm_medium=taboola_news&utm_campaign=ECCBSiCBSNews&ui=e305b5ff-f116-401e-ae93-5bc95e33ef3f-tuct925560b
56. Slater, M.D.: Reinforcing spirals: the mutual influence of media selectivity and media effects and their impact on individual behavior and social identity. Commun. Theor. 17(3), 281–303 (2007)

57. Smith, L.G., Wakeford, L., Cribbin, T.F., Barnett, J., Hou, W.K.: Detecting psychological change through mobilizing interactions and changes in extremist linguistic style. Comput. Hum. Behav. **108**, 106298 (2020)

58. Sotlar, A.: Some problems with a definition and perception of extremism within a society. Policing in Central and Eastern Europe: Dilemmas of Contemporary Criminal Justice, pp. 703–707 (2004)

59. Strandberg, K., Himmelroos, S., Grönlund, M.: Do discussions in like-minded groups necessarily lead to more extreme opinions? Deliberative democracy and group polarization. Int. Polit. Sci. Rev. **40**(1), 41–57 (2019)

60. Torok, R.: Developing an explanatory model for the process of online radicalisation and terrorism. Secur. Inf. **2**(1), 1–10 (2013)

61. Trip, S., Bora, C.H., Marian, M., Halmajan, A., Drugas, M.I.: Psychological mechanisms involved in radicalization and extremism. A rational emotive behavioral conceptualization. Front. Psychol. **10**, 437 (2019)

62. Vacca, J.R.: Online Terrorist Propaganda, Recruitment, and Radicalization. CRC Press (2019)

63. Center for the Prevention of Radicalization Leading to Violence (CPRLV): Types of radicalization (2015). https://info-radical.org/en/types-of-radicalization/

64. Wagoner, J.A., Hogg, M.A.: Uncertainty-identity theory. Encyclopedia of Personality and Individual Differences, pp. 1–8 (2017)

65. Wallot, S., Roepstorff, A., Mønster, D.: Multidimensional recurrence quantification analysis (MdRQA) for the analysis of multidimensional time-series: a software implementation in Matlab and its application to group-level data in joint action. Front. Psychol. **7**, 1835 (2016)

66. Weimann, G., Masri, N.: Tiktok's spiral of antisemitism. Journal. Media **2**(4), 697–708 (2021)

67. Wiktorowicz, Q.: A genealogy of radical Islam. Stud. Confl. Terror. **28**(2), 75–97 (2005)

68. Wilner, A.S., Dubouloz, C.J.: Homegrown terrorism and transformative learning: an interdisciplinary approach to understanding radicalization. Glob. Change Peace Secur. **22**(1), 33–51 (2010)

69. Wood, M.A.: Antisocial media and algorithmic deviancy amplification: analysing the id of Facebook's technological unconscious. Theor. Criminol. **21**(2), 168–185 (2017)

70. Wood, N.: Adventures in Solitude: The Link Between Social Isolation and Violent Extremism. Ph.D. thesis, University of Pittsburgh (2020)

Twittener: Improving News Experience with Sentiment Analysis and Trend Recommendation

Jie Jun Tien, Wei Jie Heng$^{(\boxtimes)}$, and Owen Noel Newton Fernando

Nanyang Technological University, Singapore 639798, Singapore
{jtien001,heng0241}@e.ntu.edu.sg, ofernando@ntu.edu.sg

Abstract. The Internet provides a profusion of online sources for both trending topics and news. With the vast content made available, it might risk readers in information overloading before finding all relevant contents and thus perceive this medium as challenging and overwhelming. Most of the available news sites provide content from official news sites and exclude posts on social media. This paper presents a web application, Twittener, an improved news aggregator that enhances users' reading experience and time-efficiency when reading news online, with the implementation of text-to-speech technology, sentiment analysis and hybrid recommender system. This paper also presents a user study that was conducted to determine the factors that increase the acceptance rate of such a system by the public based on the Technology Acceptance Model (TAM).

Keywords: Twitter · news aggregation · news feed · sentiment analysis · personalized content · text-to-speech · technology acceptance model · TAM · user acceptance

1 Introduction

The evolution of the Internet has altered the landscape of the news media industry considerably. As numerous online news sources are updated constantly, readers can access any information to the global news effortlessly. Thus, this has enticed readers to change from traditional newspapers to digital media. Consequently, the circulation of print newspapers has been declining over time.

Research has shown that there has been a decrease in newspaper circulation in recent years and the trend can be expected to decline due to the increased number of readers reading news digitally. U.S Weekday and Sunday print circulation have decreased by 12% and 13% in 2018 respectively [1]. With a profusion of news sources, readers may feel overwhelmed when finding news articles which spark their interest. However, personalized content is not provided in the news sites as the readers are required to spend a long time in finding relevant topics. To facilitate readers' search, numerous news aggregators – help to collect news articles from several news sources and presented on the website [2], have emerged over the past decade.

A. Coman and S. Vasilache (Eds.): HCII 2024, LNCS 14703, pp. 417–433, 2024.
https://doi.org/10.1007/978-3-031-61281-7_30

Well-known news aggregators such as Google News and Yahoo! News have come into existence since the late 1990s. Some news aggregators offer personalized context, primarily in two areas: topics related to a reader's genuine interests and interesting topics outside of his usual interests [3]. However, current news aggregators only obtain information from official news sites and omit posts on social media site such as Twitter, despite the possibility that these posts may be truly accurate news. Two notable examples are the Mumbai bomb blasts in 2008 and the downed US Airways Flight in 2009, whereby Twitter was the first to report instead of traditional news [4]. Moreover, the elucidation of information-seeking behavior assumes a pivotal role within this discourse. Information-seeking behavior, as delineated by Tomas D. Wilson in his seminal 1981 paper, encapsulates the proactive endeavors undertaken by individuals to seek, search, and procure information in fulfillment of their specific informational requisites. Pertinently, empirical investigations, as documented in studies [5, 6], have scrutinized the temporal allocation of users on the Internet in pursuit of definitive resolutions to their queries. These inquiries have unveiled that, notwithstanding their proficiency in technical search strategies, individuals exhibit a predilection for methodologies that necessitate minimal exertion. Furthermore, the influence of digital news headlines on the selection process of news articles pertaining to analogous topics has been observed, with a discernible preference for articles distinguished by their clarity and informativeness. This phenomenon was rigorously examined in the research conducted by Joshua M. Scacco [7], which delves into information-seeking behaviors within the contemporary news ecosystem. Hence, one improvement that could be made to news aggregators is to enable sourcing for information from both official news website and social media platforms.

Twittener [8] is developed as a web application that incorporates information from news aggregators with social media platforms (Twitter and Reddit). In Twittener, Google News and Yahoo News were selected as these well-known news aggregators offer apolitical news contents [9] and allow readers to save ample time and effort in finding the relevant news. Furthermore, Twitter was selected as a reporting tool for updating breaking news actively [10] and considered as a micro-blogging platform that produces approximately 6 million tweets comprising of instant news such as Covid-19 [11], while Reddit [12] was selected as it provides a comprehensive overview of the latest news. In addition to news personalization, sentiment analysis and text-to-speech technologies were utilized by enhancing the user's experience. Sentiment analysis technology was used to determine the general sentiment towards a trend and improves the user's experience. Text-to-speech was used to alter tweets and news summaries into audio format. Thus, readers can choose between reading and listening to tweets or news abstract. Essentially, Twittener offers an inclusive one-stop site for highly significant news content from several platforms.

A user study was conducted to determine the factors that will increase the acceptance rate of Twittener system by the public. It aims to apply the Technology Acceptance Model (TAM) to the use of technology, analyse the interrelationship of the hypotheses in TAM and measure the user acceptance to the technology in Twittener.

2   Related Work

In this section, related work will be summarized in three areas: news aggregators, voice synthesis on Twitter, sentimental analysis, recommendation systems.

2.1   News Aggregators

News aggregators [13] assist readers in searching for the latest news from several news sources conveniently. Moreover, news aggregators enable readers to customize any favourite content that will interest them. However, news aggregators have ignored the social media post which may be truly accurate. A study [14] has shown that more than 2.4 billion internet users, nearly 64.5% have received breaking news from social media platforms such as Twitter. As a result, the news contents in social media platforms can be circulated more rapidly than traditional news media platform. Thus, citizen journalism occurs [15]. Google News [16] and Yahoo! News [17] are chosen as both are popular news aggregators.

Google News provides the latest news in multiple languages from various news sources. With multilingual news platform, this will meet the reader's satisfaction. Furthermore, it enables readers to personalize their favorite topics into their news feed. However, Google News is still tackling the limitation of not having citizen journalism to report the latest news as well as the limitation of having a few published news articles from official news sites before revealing the news contents that are related to an event. Therefore, this concludes that breaking news from social media platforms distributed faster than the traditional news media platform.

Despite providing similar features as Google News, Yahoo! News does not provide news customization and support multilingual news contents. The news contents are categorized in different topics such as Business, Entertainment and Science. Also, Yahoo! News offers the latest news trends such as U.S Presidential Election 2020 and Coronavirus. Hence, Google News and Yahoo! News have their limitations and advantages.

To overcome these limitations, Twittener has intended to weight the existing advantages of the news aggregators and make further enhancements by incorporating Twitter and text-to-speech technology. A study [18] has proven that Twitter is the best reporting tool for providing breaking news timely as compared to other social media platforms such as Twitter and Google+. As a result, Twitter was selected for integrating social media platform into Twittener. Text-to-speech technology is utilized to convert news summaries to audio format. This provides users with the choice of filtering through news articles by either listening or reading.

2.2   Voice Synthesis on Twitter

Several applications allow users to listen to tweets instead of reading. However, the existing applications do not use analytics to assist users in identifying high-value content. These are a few examples that the applications permit users to listen to tweets: Twisten, Chicken Nugget and Social Speaker.

Twisten [19] is a Twitter client that enables users to download and listen to their Twitter feed on Windows. It utilizes the built-in text-to-speech feature of Windows to convert tweets into audio format. Chicken Nugget [20] is an alternate Twitter Client that performs screen reading on Windows. This application is specially developed for visual impairment users as they can keep themselves updated by listening to the tweets. Lastly, Social Speaker [21] – an iOS application, enables users to listen to latest tweets without refreshing and looking at the screen.

A simple audio feature would not be enough as the role of Twitter in Twittener is responsible for retrieving the latest news. Analytics is required as it can assist users to identify high-value content. The first important step is to comprehend the sentiment of each tweet. This is a complicated task because the extracted tweets are multilingual.

Haddi et al. [22] had reviewed the role of text pre-processing in sentiment analysis. The research has shown that the classification was performed on pre-processed and not pre-processed data for each feature matrix (TF-IDF, FF, FP). To perform text pre-processing in sentiment analysis, it begins by modifying the raw data that comprises stopwords removal, cleaning up HTML tags, negation handling, stemming and abbreviation expansion. The Support Vector Machine (SVM) classifier was used for sentiment analysis. With proper text pre-processing in sentiment analysis, the classifier's performance will be enhanced and hastened the process of classification. Hence, this would assist in real-time sentiment analysis. The other research [23] has also shown that it is important to work on Twitter's corpus for the text pre-processing. Intrinsically, the extracted tweets will be pre-processed in Twittener before executing sentiment analysis.

2.3 Sentimental Analysis

In recent years, sentiment analysis has emerged as a pivotal aspect of understanding and engaging with online content. While conventional news websites frequently overlook the inclusion of sentiment analysis within their articles, some web-based platforms, exemplified by Reddit [24], have recognized its importance and incorporated mechanisms such as upvoting and downvoting to capture the sentiment of the audience. This stark contrast in approach highlights the varying degrees of attention given to the emotional responses of readers.

The utilization of sentiment analysis tools [25] presents a unique opportunity for web-based platforms, particularly in the realm of news reporting. Reddit's incorporation of sentiment expression mechanisms has proven to be a valuable model, allowing users to not only consume information but also actively express their emotional responses through voting. In contrast, conventional news websites often miss out on integrating such analytical frameworks, resulting in a lack of understanding regarding the emotional impact of their content on the audience.

By embracing sentiment analysis tools, news organizations [26] can gain invaluable insights into public sentiment, enabling them to navigate the intricate landscape of emotional responses from their readership. Understanding the emotional nuances of the audience allows for more targeted and tailored reporting, creating a symbiotic relationship between news providers and consumers. This integration not only enhances the overall user experience but also empowers news organizations to adapt their content strategy in real-time, ensuring a more resonant and impactful connection with their audience.

Instead of human sourced sentiment analysis such as Reddit, Microsoft Azure Text Analytics API will be used to give each news a score and rate it as positive, negative, or neutral for the sentimental analysis.

2.4 Recommender System

Recommender system personalizes and recommends any content based on a user's interest by tracking his browsing behavior, and thus personalized recommendation helps to minimize the effort required to look for all the contents offered. The recommender system has three filtering methods: Content-based filtering, Collaborative filtering, and Hybrid filtering [27].

Firstly, Content-based filtering analyses descriptions that are utilized as training data to generate user-specific classification. With a user-specific model being used, it helps to predict and make new recommendations based on a user's usual interests. However, Content-based filtering [28] has several restrictions such as limited content analysis, overspecialization and new user problem.

Secondly, Collaborative filtering utilized the collaborative power of the content read provided by several users with similar interests. It helps users with similar usual interests to recommend new popular contents However, collaborative filtering has faced two limitations: cold start [29] – when the data is insufficient to make precise recommended news contents for new users - and data sparsity [30] – new contents that other users have not read could not be recommended.

Lastly, the existing recommender systems have been using Hybrid filtering method – a filtering method that combines both content-based filtering and collaborative filtering. This could improve the recommendation accuracy as Hybrid filtering method helps to overcome the existing limitations that Content-based filtering and Collaborative filtering have faced. A study [31] shows that Hybrid filtering method performs better than collaborative filtering method as it helps to enhance the quality of news recommendations and attract more frequent visits to the news site.

3 Design and Implementation

3.1 System Architecture

The web application, Twittener, was developed using JavaScript. JavaScript-based frameworks (Node.js and Express.js) are implemented in the backend server. Express.js – one of the most popular frameworks in Node.js, is employed into the development of web application. Thus, the web application, Twittener, aims to offer an inclusive one-stop site for highly significant news content from several platforms.

Figure 1 displays the system architecture in Twittener. REST APIs handle HTTP requests, such as GET and POST, that are sent from web application and mobile application. Once the REST API has completed with the requests, the request will return to

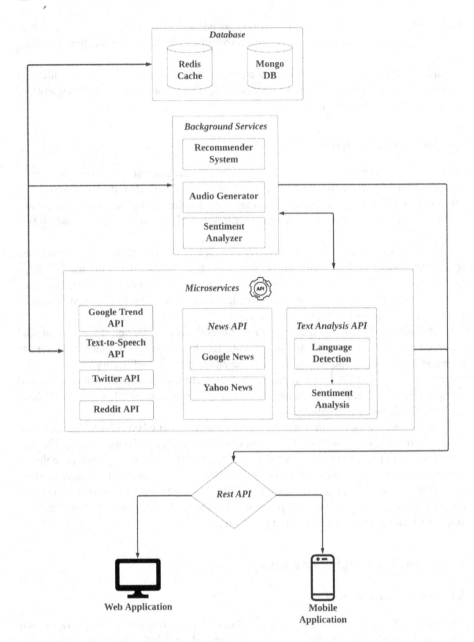

Fig. 1. System Architecture in Twittener

web and mobile application. The implementation of REST APIs is simple as compared to SOAP as the web services can be deployed in restricted devices, such as mobile, and make integration easier with the existing web application, Twittener.

As shown in Fig. 1, the backend server contains storage, microservices and background services. In storage, MongoDB, a nonrelational database, allows robust deployment and scaling, while Redis cache helps to store fetched contents for a period and thus the fetched contents can be served to users rapidly. Microservices handle several API services such as Twitter API and News API in the backend server. With loose coupling in microservices, this ensures that the remaining API services are operating whenever one of the services fails. Moreover, additional API services can be included by providing new features on Twittener without affecting the current ones in the future. Lastly, several services, Sentiment Analyzer, Audio Generator and Recommender System, will handle long-running operations in the background without affecting the user interface's responsiveness in Twittener. The implementation of these background services is further elaborated in Sects. 3.2–3.4.

3.2 Sentiment Analysis on Twitter Trends

Microsoft Azure Text Analytics API [32] was used to analyze multilingual tweets that contain the trending hashtag or keyword to determine the general sentiment of a twitter trend. Before performing sentiment analysis, language detection is required to retrieve the better accuracy of the polarity result. Microsoft Azure Language Detection helps to parse the extracted tweets as input and detect the type of language used in the tweet. Subsequently, the detected language code will be used as an input together with the extracted tweets to perform sentiment analysis. After performing sentiment analysis, the better accuracy of the polarity result can be achieved. Without the language code, Text Analytics API will only perform sentiment in English, and thus this will lead to poor accuracy of the polarity result. And thus, the polarity result of each trending hashtag or keyword is classified into three sentiments: positive, negative, and neutral. Figure 2 shows the process of analyzing the sentiment of a tweet that contains trending hashtag and keyword.

3.3 Text-to-Speech Conversion

IBM Watson's text-to-speech service [33] is used to perform the conversion of text from tweets and news abstracts into audio in Twittener. IBM Watson's Text-to-Speech creates an audio file with the proper rhythm and tone and thus produces the sound naturally. First, the text will be sent to IBM Watson's server through its API service. Then, the text-to-speech conversion will begin processing the text in IBM Watson's server. Finally, once the text-to-speech conversion is completed, the audio file will be output into Twittener. Hence, users can play the audio of tweets and news abstracts once the conversion has completed.

3.4 Hybrid Recommender System

A hybrid recommender system was developed using a python library called lightfm [34, 35]. The recommender system had two python scripts: update.py and recommendation.py. The update.py script is utilized to update a database where the history of all

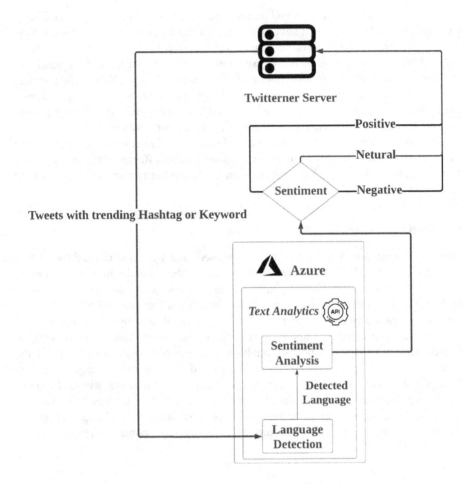

Fig. 2. Sentiment Analysis in Twittener

users are being recorded based on each time a user clicks on a news article. Furthermore, the recommendayion.py is utilized to produce the top three news topics that are most relevant to a user.

On the other hand, a model will be built to generate the top three categories, such as technology, sport, and science, depending on the user's Twittener ID before news recommendations could be made. For identification, each user will be allocated to a unique Twittener ID that is linked with Twitter ID. For identification, each user will be allocated to a unique Twittener ID that is linked with Twitter ID.

4   Design of Experiment

4.1   Participant

The experiment was conducted with participants who are above the age of 21. The questionnaire was distributed to 60 participants through emails, text messages and word of mouth. The entire experiment took approximately 30 min for each participant to use Twittener. The objective of this experiment was to evaluate the user acceptance towards new technology in Twittener and validate the effectiveness of the questionnaire.

4.2   Procedure

The web application, Twittener (https://twittener.io), was presented to the participants where they were required to log in with their Twitter account to gain experience in using an aggregated news platform. If participants did not have a Twitter account, they were required to sign up on Twitter's sign-up page (https://twitter.com/). Alternatively, the participant could enter the sign-up button in Twittener's login page as depicted in Fig. 3, encapsulated in the red box.

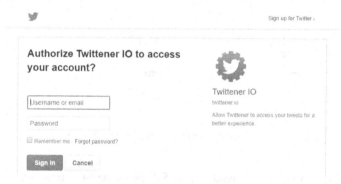

Fig. 3. Login page in Twittener

Once the participants had logged in with their Twitter account, they were tasked to familiarize with the use of technology, such as sentiment analysis and news recommendation, and explore the pages (Home, Trends, Topics and News) for 23 min approximately in Twittener. The procedure for using Twittener is presented below:

In the Home page, the participants view the latest tweets in Twitter Timeline, latest Twitter trends with general sentiment and the tweets' polarity based on the selected trending hashtag or keyword in Twitter Trends Timeline for ten minutes. Alternatively, the participants can choose to listen to tweets either in list view timeline whereby the play button is provided for each tweet or audio timeline. Figure 4 displays the latest tweets in Twitter Timeline.

In the Trends page, the participants view the latest summaries of news trends from Google News, Yahoo! News and Reddit for five minutes. The participants can select

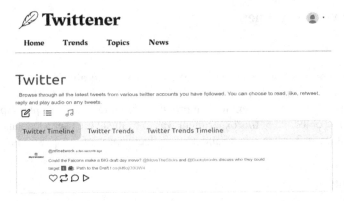

Fig. 4. Home page in Twittener. Only Twitter Timeline is shown.

Fig. 5. Trends page in Twittener. Only Google News is shown

any interesting news articles to read. Figure 5 displays the latest news summaries from Google News.

In the Topics page, the participants view and organize their favourite topics from Twitter for three minutes as shown in Fig. 6.

In the News page, the participants listen to news abstracts in the following news channel provided for five minutes. The participants can select any interesting news articles from the news audio player to read. Should the participants revisit News page once again, they will receive the top three recommended news channels based on their clicking behavior (Fig. 7).

After exploring these pages in Twittener, the participants were required to submit a consent form and give an evaluation on the user acceptance towards new technology. Figure 8 depicts the survey button in blue, encapsulated in the red box, whenever the participants are prepared to do their evaluation.

Fig. 6. Topics page in Twittener

Fig. 7. News page in Twittener

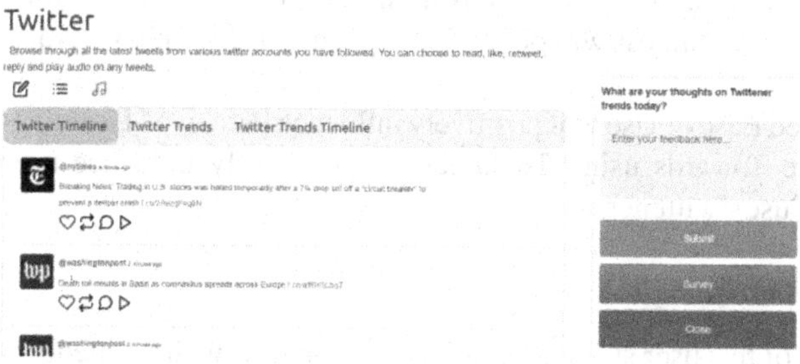

Fig. 8. Survey button to do an evaluation

4.3 Technology Acceptance Model

The user study was designed based on the Technology Acceptance Model (TAM), one of the most influential models of technology acceptance that was first proposed by Fred Davis in 1986 [36]. This provides the insights that affect user acceptance and behaviour towards new technology primarily in two factors: Perceived ease of use (PEOU) and Perceived usefulness (PU). PEOU is the degree to which an individual believes that a new system would be easy to use. PU is the degree to which an individual believes that a new system would improve his or her daily job performance. Thus, these two factors are important for system use as both will influence both Attitude Toward Using (AT) and Behavioral Intention to Use (BI).

AT is an individual's assessment of the desirability of using Twittener, while BI is a sign of an individual's readiness to perform a specified behaviour in Twittener. Figure 9 illustrates how the study model has adopted based on TAM.

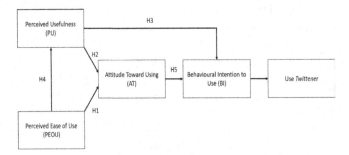

Fig. 9. TAM Study Model

A list of interrelationships between five hypotheses is formulated in the study model as follows:

- H1: Perceived Ease of Use will positively influence users' attitude towards Twittener
- H2: Perceived Usefulness will positively influence users' attitude towards Twittener
- H3: Perceived Usefulness will positively influence users' behavioural intention to use Twittener
- H4: Perceived Ease of Use will positively influence Perceived Usefulness of Twittener
- H5: Attitude Towards using Twittener will positively influence users' Behavioral Intention to use Twittener

4.4 Questionnaire

The objectives of this user study were to understand how well Twittener can be received by the users and obtain an insight into information technology acceptance and usage among users towards Twittener. A questionnaire was designed for each factor studied in the TAM. The Likert scale was selected as the scaling technique for the user study [37]. This is useful for measuring characteristics such as attitude, opinions and feelings, which was appropriate for the questionnaire. For analysing the data, each response was given a number with 1 = Strongly Disagree, 2 = Disagree, 3 = Neutral, 4 = Agree and

5 = Strongly Agree. It was hypothesised that users will give an average rating of above 4 ("Agree") for the given factors.

5 Results and Analysis

60 responses were received during the period of the user study. We used the SPSS software to analyse the results.

5.1 Validation of TAM

The reliability of the questionnaire was validated with Cronbach's Alpha, whose acceptable value is between 0.70 and 0.95 [35, 36]. The results are presented in Table 1.

Table 1 depicts that the results are indeed acceptable where the coefficient values of these factors are between 0.70 and 0.95.

Table 1. Cronbach's Alpha

Factor	Number of Items	Cronbach's Alpha
Perceived Ease of Use (PEOU)	4	0.899
Perceived Usefulness (PU)	5	0.921
Attitude Towards using (AT)	6	0.911
Behavioural Intention (BI)	3	0.931

The correlation coefficient was also evaluated to determine the relationships between these factors and examine the hypotheses of the research model as shown in Table 2.

Table 2. Pearson's Correlation

	PEOU	PU	AT	BI
PEOU	1	$.972^{**}$	$.924^{**}$	$.876^{**}$
PU	$.972^{**}$	1	$.973^{**}$	$.931^{**}$
AT	$.924^{**}$	$.973^{**}$	1	$.967^{**}$
BI	$.876^{**}$	$.931^{**}$	$.967^{**}$	1

**Correlation is significant at the 0.01 level (2-tailed).

Table 2 proves that the correlations between PEOU, PU, AT and BI are positive and significant at the 0.01 level. Hence, this has confirmed the five hypotheses that were formulated in the TAM Study Model.

430   J. J. Tien et al.

5.2 Significance Testing

One-Sample Wilcoxon Signed Rank Test – a nonparametric test for one-sample, was used to test whether a distribution of user responses is significantly different from the hypothesized median. In this user study, each response was specified with a number as mentioned in Sect. 4.4. The neutral response (3) was set as the hypothesized median to do a nonparametric test for one-sample. Thus, 18 tests were conducted to determine the significant difference from the hypothesized median. Furthermore, One-Sample Wilcoxon Signed Rank Test discovered that all responses are significantly different from the neutral response.

To prove that all responses are significantly different from the neutral response further, the Likert R package [37] was used to visualize the Likert scale responses in the questionnaire. We used RStudio [38] to generate a Likert plot for all responses as depicted in Fig. 10.

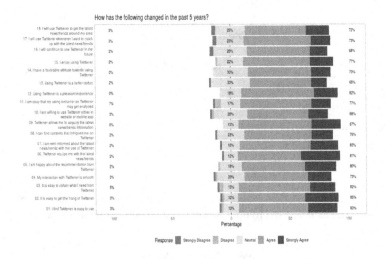

Fig. 10. Likert plot for all responses using RStudio.

The Likert plot in Fig. 10 verifies that all responses are significantly different from the neutral response. Hence, it was hypothesized that users will give an average rating of above 4 ("Agree") for the given factors.

5.3 Discussion on Results

The results had indicated that Perceived Usefulness has the most significant impact on users' attitude using Twittener. Based on the TAM model that was proposed by Fred Davis [36], users are willing to adopt new technology in using Twittener conveniently. Furthermore, the results had indicated that Attitude Towards Using Twittener had influenced significantly to the users' behavioural intention as the respondents felt that they had great satisfaction in using Twittener. The respondents had remarked that Twittener helps them to save ample time in finding the latest news and trends. The respondents had also liked the functions in Twittener. In terms of the functions, this shows that it is important to ensure that the users have a good attitude towards using Twittener. Thus, the results of this user study have confirmed that TAM can be utilized to explain the users' adoption using Twittener.

To understand the participant's opinions on the user study, several feedback was gathered. Most of the participants commented that they enjoyed using the existing technologies in Twittener. Thus, this helps the participants to save ample time and effort in receiving the latest relevant news articles and listening to tweets with great satisfaction as compared to Twitter. Furthermore, the participants remarked that there is still room for improvement on the graphical user interface as some users might not be able to understand ways to use Twittener well.

6 Conclusion

This paper presents Twittener, an integrated news aggregator that delivers the latest news from both official news sites and social media and converting tweets and news abstracts using text-to-speech technology mainly for visual impairment users. They will be informed on the latest news while using a text-based social media platform. Besides visual impairment users, Twittener permits users to either read or listen to breaking news from Twitter; understand the sentiment analysis of news trends; personalize favourite topics and news channel.

The user study was conducted to evaluate the user acceptance towards new technology and validate the effectiveness of the questionnaire. This was proven that the results were highly significant and positive, as the participants remarked that using Twittener has helped them to save time and effort in finding latest relevant news articles and listening to tweets with great satisfaction. Essentially, Twittener has provided an inclusive one-stop site for highly significant news content from several platforms.

References

1. Pew Research Center. Newspapers Fact Sheet, 9 July 2019. https://www.journalism.org/fact-sheet/newspapers/
2. Chowdhury, S., Landoni, M.: News aggregator services: user expectations and experience. Online Inf. Rev. **30**(2), 100–115 (2006)
3. Garcin, F., Faltings, B.: PEN RecSys: a personalized news recommender systems framework. In: Proceedings of the 7th ACM Conference on Recommender Systems, Hong Kong (2013)
4. Murthy, D.: Twitter: microphone for the masses? Media Cult. Soc. **33**(5), 779–789 (2011)
5. Tubachi, P.: Information Seeking Behavior: An Overview. https://www.researchgate.net/publication/330521546_INFORMATION_SEEKING_BEHAVIOR_AN_OVERVIEW. Accessed 24 Jan 2024
6. Kim, J.: Describing and predicting information-seeking behavior on the Web. https://doi.org/10.1002/asi.21035. Accessed 24 Jan 2024
7. Sacco, J.M.: The curiosity effect: information seeking in the contemporary news environment. https://doi.org/10.1177/1461444819863408. Accessed 24 Jan 2024
8. Twittener. (2020). https://twittener.io

9. Lee, A.M., Chyi, H.I.: The rise of online news aggregators: consumption and competition. Int. J. Media Manag. **17**(1), 3–24 (2015)

10. Vis, F.: Twitter as a reporting tool for breaking news. Digit. J. **1**(1), 27–47 (2013)

11. Jahanbin, K., Rahmanian, V.: Using twitter and web news mining to predict COVID-19 outbreak. Asian Pac. J. Trop. Med. **13**(8), 378 (2020)

12. Le, P.H., Mao, Y.: Reddit as A New Platform for Public Relations: Organizations' Use of Dialogic Principles and Their Publics' Responses in the Subreddit IAmA, vol. 23 (2016)

13. WPBEGINNER, "9 Best News Aggregator Websites (+ How to Build Your Own)," 2 July 2019. https://www.wpbeginner.com/showcase/best-news-aggregator-websites-how-to-build-your-own/

14. Martin, N.: How Social Media Has Changed How We Consume News. 30 Nov 2018. https://www.forbes.com/sites/nicolemartin1/2018/11/30/how-social-media-has-changed-how-we-consume-news/#45d037393c3c

15. Mason, E.: Is Citizen Journalism Killing Professional Journalism? 15 Jan 2018. https://artplu smarketing.com/is-citizen-journalism-killing-professional-journalism-b60531ee1d0c

16. Google. Google News. https://news.google.com/

17. Yahoo. Yahoo! News - Latest News & Headlines. https://news.yahoo.com/

18. Forbes. Why Twitter Is Still the Best Place for Breaking News Despite Its Many Challenges. https://www.forbes.com/sites/quora/2017/01/10/why-twitter-is-still-the-best-place-for-breaking-news-despite-its-many-challenges/#4ad48a7626ab

19. Allen-Wagner, N.: Twisten - Listen to Twitter. 10 Apr 2011. http://blog.alner.net/articles/twi sten.aspx

20. Accessible Apps. Chicken Nugget! 2019. https://getaccessibleapps.com/chicken_nugget/

21. Dinkel, W.: Social Speaker - Listen to Tweets on iOS. https://socialspeaker.net/

22. Haddi, E., Liu, X., Shi, Y.: The role of text pre-processing in sentiment analysis. Procedia Comput. Sci. **17**, 26–32 (2013)

23. Bao, Y., Quan, C., Wang, L., Ren, F.: The role of pre-processing in Twitter sentiment analysis. In: Intelligent Computing Methodologies, pp. 615–624. Springer, Cham (2014). https://doi.org/10.1007/978-3-319-09339-0_62

24. Leavitt, A.C.: Upvoting the News: Breaking News Aggregation, Crowd Collaboration, and Algorithm-Driven Attention on reddit.com. https://www.proquest.com/openview/df57be3de3bbe46b0765a7d2930f045c/1?pq-origsite=gscholar&cbl=18750. Accessed 24 Jan 2024

25. Bautin, M.: International Sentiment Analysis for News and Blogs. https://ojs.aaai.org/index.php/ICWSM/article/view/18606. Accessed 24 Jan 2024

26. D'Andre, A., Ferri, F., Grifoni, P., Guzzo, T.: Approaches, Tools and Applications for Sentiment Analysis Implementation. https://citeseerx.ist.psu.edu/document?repid=rep1&type=pdf&doi=d709747c589bca62d9ee85752fb3a8ec899cac20. Accessed 24 Jan 2024

27. Aggarwal, C.C.: Recommender Systems: The Textbook. Springer, Cham (2016)

28. Adomavicius, A., Tuzhilin, A.: Toward the next generation of recommender systems: a survey of the state-of-the-art and possible extensions. IEEE Trans. Knowl. Data Eng. **17**(6), 734–749 (2005)

29. Hung-Hsuan, C., Pu, C.: Differentiating regularization weights -- a simple mechanism to alleviate cold start in recommender systems. ACM Trans. Knowl. Discov. Data **13**(1), 8 (2019)

30. Nathaniel, G., et al.: Combining collaborative filtering with personal agents for better recommendations. In: Proceedings of the Sixteenth National Conference on Artificial Intelligence and the Eleventh Innovative Applications of Artificial Intelligence Conference Innovative Applications of Artificial Intelligence, Orlando (1999)

31. Jianhui, L., Peter, D., Elin Rønby, P.: Personalized news recommendation based on click behavior. In: Proceedings of the 15th International Conference on Intelligent User Interfaces, Hong Kong (2010)

32. How to call the Text Analytics REST API. Microsoft Azure, 30 July 2019. https://docs.micros oft.com/en-us/azure/cognitive-services/text-analytics/how-tos/text-analytics-how-to-call-api
33. IBM Cloud. Getting started with Text to Speech (2020). https://cloud.ibm.com/docs/services/ text-to-speech?topic=text-to-speech-gettingStarted&_ga=2.158929662.531482432.158325 0732-729348537.1583250732&cm_mc_uid=15278110739115689857415&cm_mc_sid_ 50200000=20950731577973297095&cm_mc_sid_52640000=33641591577973297
34. Aayush, A.: Solving business use cases by recommender system using lightFM. 14 June (2018). https://towardsdatascience.com/solving-business-usecases-by-recommender-system-using-lightfm-4ba7b3ac8e62
35. Maciej, K.: "LightFM," (2016). https://making.lyst.com/lightfm/docs/home.html
36. Sung Youl, P.: An analysis of the technology acceptance model in understanding university students' behavioral intention to use e-learning. J. Educ. Technol. Soc. **12**(3), 150–162 (2009)
37. Allen, I., Seaman, C.: Likert scales and data analyses. Qual. Prog. **40**, 64–65 (2007)

Author Index

A. Coman and S. Vasilache (Eds.): HCII 2024, LNCS 14703, pp. 435–437, 2024.
https://doi.org/10.1007/978-3-031-61281-7

Printed in the United States
by Baker & Taylor Publisher Services